D1202227

HOUGHTON MIFFLIN
SOCIAL STUDIES

★ UNITED STATES HISTORY ★

Visit **Education Place**®
www.eduplace.com/kids

HOUGHTON MIFFLIN   BOSTON

★AUTHORS★

Senior Author
Dr. Herman J. Viola
Curator Emeritus
Smithsonian Institution

Dr. Cheryl Jennings
Project Director
Florida Institute of
    Education
University of North
    Florida

Dr. Sarah Witham
Bednarz
Associate Professor,
    Geography
Texas A&M University

Dr. Mark C. Schug
Professor and Director
Center for Economic
    Education
University of Wisconsin,
    Milwaukee

Dr. Carlos E. Cortés
Professor Emeritus, History
University of California,
Riverside

Dr. Charles S. White
Associate Professor
School of Education
Boston University

Consulting Authors
Dr. Dolores Beltran
Assistant Professor
Curriculum Instruction
California State University, Los Angeles
(Support for English Language Learners)

Dr. MaryEllen Vogt
Co-Director
California State University Center
for the Advancement of Reading
(Reading in the Content Area)

The United States has honored the Louisiana Purchase and the Lewis and Clark expedition in a new nickel series. The first nickel of the series features a rendition of the Jefferson Peace Medal. Thomas Jefferson commissioned this medal for Lewis and Clark's historic trip, which began in 1804.

Louisiana Purchase/Peace Medal nickel circulating coin images courtesy United States Mint. Used with Permission.

HOUGHTON MIFFLIN
SOCIAL STUDIES

★ UNITED STATES HISTORY ★

 HOUGHTON MIFFLIN

BOSTON

Consultants

Philip J. Deloria
Associate Professor
Department of History
and Program in
American Studies
University of Michigan

Lucien Ellington
UC Professor of Education
and Asia Program
Co-Director
University of Tennessee,
Chattanooga

Thelma Wills Foote
Associate Professor
University of California

Stephen J. Fugita
Distinguished Professor
Psychology and Ethnic
Studies
Santa Clara University

Charles C. Haynes
Senior Scholar
First Amendment Center

Ted Hemmingway
Professor of History
The Florida Agricultural &
Mechanical University

Douglas Monroy
Professor of History
The Colorado College

Lynette K. Oshima
Assistant Professor
Department of Language,
Literacy and Sociocultural
Studies and Social Studies
Program Coordinator
University of New Mexico

Jeffrey Strickland
Assistant Professor, History
University of Texas Pan
American

Clifford E. Trafzer
Professor of History and
American Indian Studies
University of California

Teacher Reviewers

Skip Bayliss
Surfside Elementary
Satellite Beach, FL

Annette Bomba
Schenevus Central School
Schenevus, NY

Amy Clark
Gateway Elementary
Travelers Rest, SC

Melissa Cook
Machado Elementary
Lake Elsinore, CA

Kelli Dunn
Lindop School
Broadview, IL

Peggy Greene
Upson-Lee North
Elementary
Thomaston, GA

Elyce Kaplan
Kumeyaay Elementary
San Diego, CA

Julia McNeal
Webster Elementary
Dayton, OH

Theresa Powell
Harbor View School
Charleston, SC

Lesa Roberts
Hampton Cove Middle School
Huntsville, AL

Lynn Schew
Leila G. Davis Elementary
Clearwater, FL

Linda Whitford
Manning Oaks Elementary
Alpharetta, GA

Lisa Yingling
Round Hills Elementary
Williamsport, PA

Printed in the U.S.A.

ISBN: 0-618-42363-X

123456789-DW-13 12 11 10 09 08 07 06 05 04

Contents

Bringing the world to your classroom!

CHAPTER 9   Creating a Nation   294

References

Extend Lessons

Skill Lessons

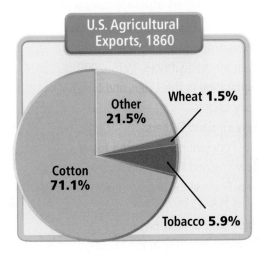

U.S. Agricultural Exports, 1860

Other 21.5%
Wheat 1.5%
Cotton 71.1%
Tobacco 5.9%

Visual Learning

Become skilled at reading visuals. Graphs, maps, and timelines help you put all the information together.

Maps

Charts and Graphs

About Your Textbook

① How It's Organized

Units The major sections of your book are units. Each starts with a big idea.

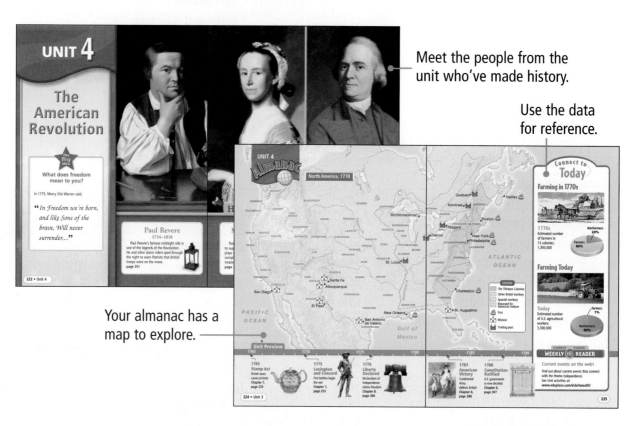

Meet the people from the unit who've made history.

Use the data for reference.

Your almanac has a map to explore.

Get ready for reading.

Chapters Units are divided into chapters, and each opens with a vocabulary preview.

Four important concepts get you started.

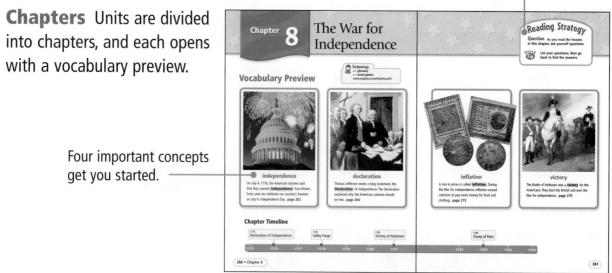

❷ Core and Extend

Lessons The lessons in your book have two parts: core and extend.

Core Lessons

Lessons bring the events of history to life and help you meet your state's standards.

Extend Lessons

Go deeper into an important topic.

Primary Sources

Core Lesson

Vocabulary strategies help with word meanings.

Before you read, use your prior knowledge.

Reading skills support your understanding of the text.

Practice summarizing the lesson.

Studying social studies means asking why ideas are important to remember.

After you read, pull it together!

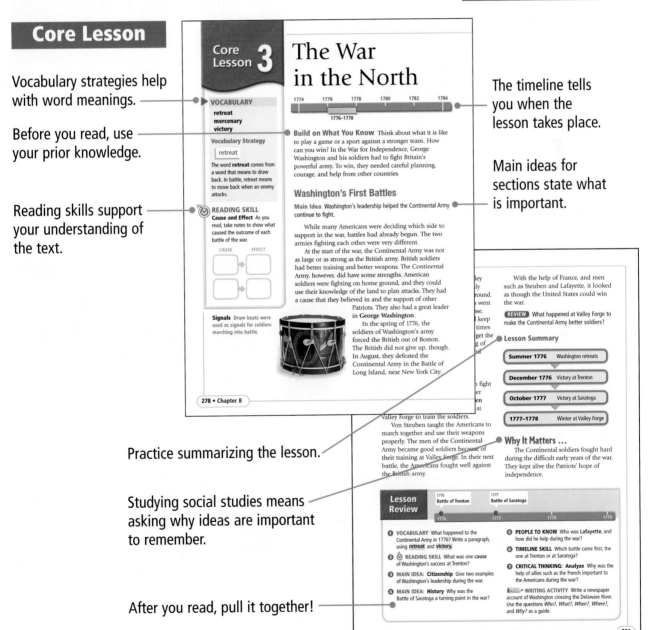

The timeline tells you when the lesson takes place.

Main ideas for sections state what is important.

Extend Lesson

Learn more about an important topic from each core lesson.

Dig in and extend your knowledge.

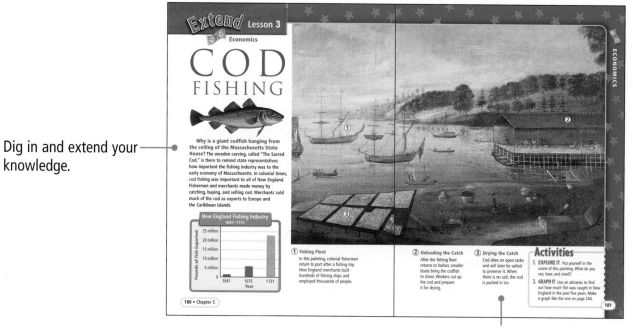

Look closely. Connect the past to the present.

Look for literature, readers' theater, geography, economics—and more.

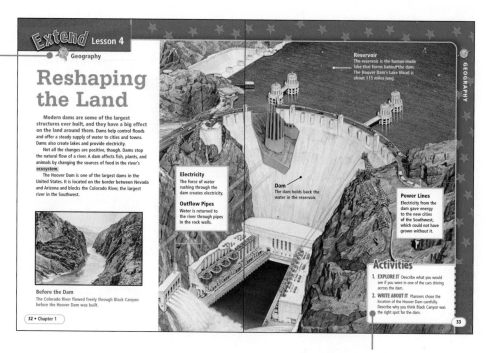

Write, talk, draw, and debate!

➌ Skills

Skill Building
Learn map, graph, and study skills, as well as citizenship skills for life.

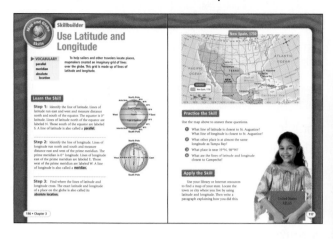

Each Skill lesson steps it out.

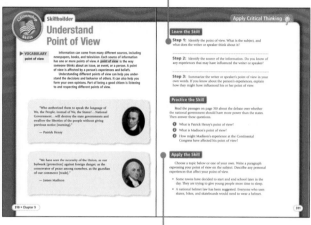

Practice and apply social studies skills.

➍ References

Citizenship Handbook
The back of your book includes sections you'll refer to again and again.

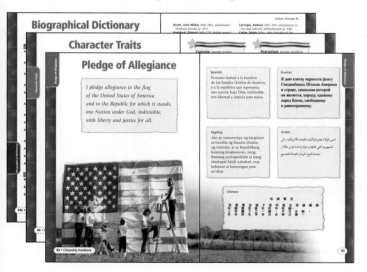

Resources
Look for atlas maps, a glossary of social studies terms, and an index.

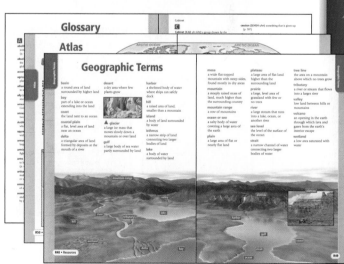

Reading Social Studies

Your book includes many features to help you be a successful reader. Here's what you will find:

VOCABULARY SUPPORT

Every chapter and lesson helps you with social studies terms. You'll build your vocabulary through strategies you're learning in language arts.

Preview
Get a jump start on four important words from the chapter.

Vocabulary Strategies
Focus on word roots, prefixes, suffixes, or compound words, for example.

Vocabulary Practice
Reuse words in the reviews, skills, and extends. Show that you know your vocabulary.

READING STRATEGIES

Look for the reading strategy and quick tip at the beginning of each chapter.

Predict and Infer
Before you read, think about what you'll learn.

Monitor and Clarify
Check your understanding. Could you explain what you just read to someone else?

Question
Stop and ask yourself a question. Did you understand what you read?

Summarize
After you read, think about the most important ideas of the lesson.

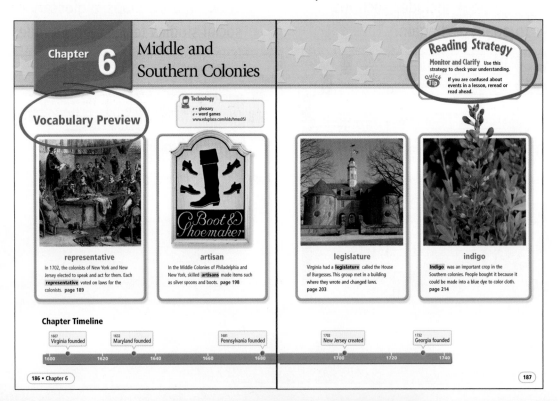

Chapter 6 — Middle and Southern Colonies

Technology
e • glossary
e • word games
www.eduplace.com/kids/hmss05/

Vocabulary Preview

representative
In 1702, the colonists of New York and New Jersey elected to speak and act for them. Each **representative** voted on laws for the colonists. page 189

artisan
In the Middle Colonies of Philadelphia and New York, skilled **artisans** made items such as silver spoons and boots. page 198

Boot & Shoemaker

Reading Strategy
Monitor and Clarify Use this strategy to check your understanding.
quick tip If you are confused about events in a lesson, reread or read ahead.

legislature
Virginia had a **legislature** called the House of Burgesses. This group met in a building where they wrote and changed laws. page 203

indigo
Indigo was an important crop in the Southern colonies. People bought it because it could be made into a blue dye to color cloth. page 214

Chapter Timeline

| 1607 Virginia founded | 1632 Maryland founded | 1681 Pennsylvania founded |
1600 — 1620 — 1640 — 1660 — 1680

| 1702 New Jersey created | 1732 Georgia founded |
1700 — 1720 — 1740

186 • Chapter 6

187

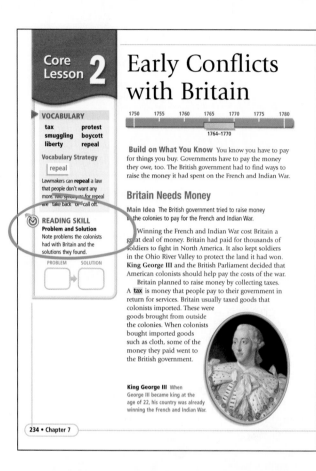

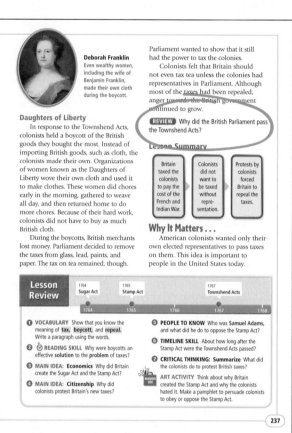

READING SKILLS

As you read, organize the information. These reading skills will help you:

Sequence

Cause and Effect

Compare and Contrast

Problem and Solution

Draw Conclusions

Predict Outcomes

Categorize (or) Classify

Main Idea and Details

COMPREHENSION SUPPORT

Build on What You Know
Check your prior knowledge. You may already know a lot!

Review Questions
Connect with the text. Did you understand what you just read?

Summaries
Look for three ways to summarize—a list, an organizer, or a paragraph.

Social Studies:
Why It Matters

Learning social studies will help you know how to get along better in your everyday life, and it will give you confidence when you make important choices in your future.

WHEN I
- decide where to live
- travel
- look for places on a map—

I'll use the geography information I've learned in social studies.

WHEN I
- choose a job
- make a budget
- decide which product to buy—

I'll use economic information.

TRAV

OOK STORE

UNIT 1

Our Land and First People

The Big Idea

What does the land around you look like?

" This land is your land, this land is my land. "

a song by Woody Guthrie

The United States in the World

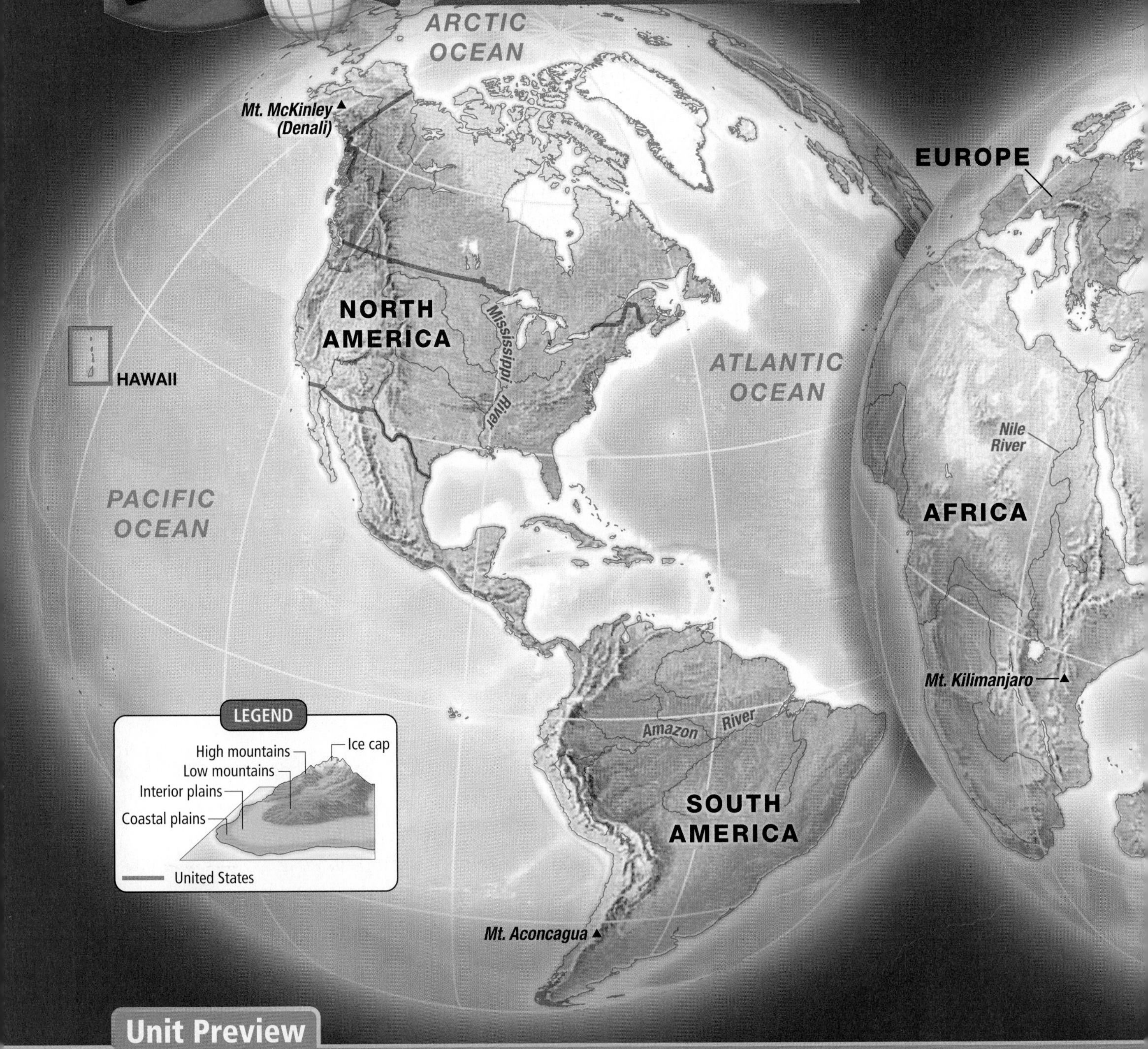

ARCTIC OCEAN

Mt. McKinley ▲
(Denali)

EUROPE

NORTH AMERICA

HAWAII

Mississippi River

ATLANTIC OCEAN

PACIFIC OCEAN

Nile River

AFRICA

Mt. Kilimanjaro ──▲

LEGEND

High mountains ── Ice cap
Low mountains
Interior plains
Coastal plains

──── United States

Amazon River

SOUTH AMERICA

Mt. Aconcagua ▲

Unit Preview

500   700   900   1100

500
Early Southwestern Civilization
Ancient Pueblo civilization begins
Chapter 2, page 42

1100–1600
Confederation Forms
Haudenosaunee League is founded
Chapter 2, page 70

1300
Aztecs Reign
Culture thrives in central Mexico
Chapter 2, page 43

Map Labels (Globe)

ARCTIC OCEAN

ASIA

Chang Jiang

Mt. Everest ▲

PACIFIC OCEAN

INDIAN OCEAN

AUSTRALIA

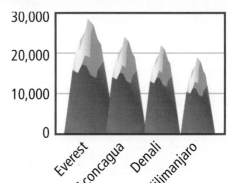

Connect to... The World

Mountains Around the World

Height (in feet)

30,000
20,000
10,000
0

Everest   Aconcagua   Denali   Kilimanjaro

Mountain

Rivers Around the World

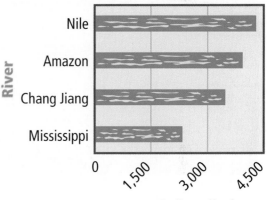

River

Nile
Amazon
Chang Jiang
Mississippi

0   1,500   3,000   4,500

Length (in miles)

Think about mountains and rivers near you. What is the highest mountain in your state? What is the longest river that runs through your state?

CURRENT EVENTS
WEEKLY (WR) READER

Current events on the web!

Find out about current events that connect with the content of this unit.
See Unit activities at:
www.eduplace.com/kids/hmss05/

Timeline

300   1500   1700

1350
Desert Life
Hopi are living in northeastern Arizona
Chapter 2, page 56

1600s
Plains Culture
Comanche begin riding and raising horses
Chapter 2, page 62

America's Land

Vocabulary Preview

Technology

e • **glossary**
e • **word games**
www.eduplace.com/kids/hmss05/

landform

The landscape of the United States takes many forms. Mountains are a type of **landform.**
page 8

conservation

When people save natural resources, they are working for **conservation.** Water is an important natural resource. **page 18**

Reading Strategy

Predict and Infer

As you read each lesson, use this strategy.

Quick Tip

Look at the pictures in a lesson to predict what it will be about. What will you read about?

specialization

Warm weather is a resource that Florida farmers use to grow oranges. Each region has certain resources that lead to **specialization.**
page 24

ecosystem

The soil, air, and plant and animal communities of a wetland area make up an **ecosystem.** Every part of this ecosystem needs the other parts. **page 31**

Land and Climate

Build on What You Know Is it easy to walk to your school or do you have to huff and puff to get up a hill? Take a look at the land near your school and where you live. It affects what you do every day.

A Varied Land

Main Idea The United States has many different landforms.

What would you call a land with sandy beaches, high mountains, wide-open plains, thick forests, and strong rivers? You might call it home. The United States, one of the three countries in North America, includes all these places.

In this book, you will learn about the people who have lived in the United States. As you read, you will see how important the land has been in their lives.

To understand the United States, we must learn geography. **Geography** is the study of the world and the people and things that live there. Geographers think about the Earth and the way people make it their home. They ask questions about where a place is, and what it is like. They also ask how the land affects people and how people affect the land. Their answers help us better understand our past, present, and future.

REVIEW What questions do geographers ask?

Coast Ranges

Sierra Nevada

Rocky Mountains

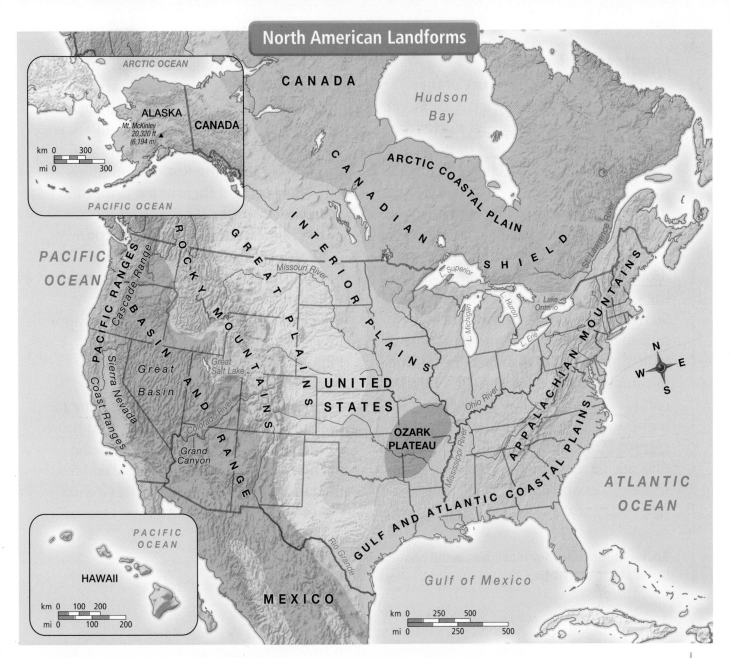

North American Landforms

ARCTIC OCEAN

ALASKA
CANADA
Mt. McKinley
20,320 ft
(6,194 m) ▲

km 0   300
mi 0   300

PACIFIC OCEAN

CANADA

Hudson
Bay

ARCTIC COASTAL PLAIN

CANADIAN   SHIELD

PACIFIC
OCEAN

PACIFIC RANGES

Cascade Range

ROCKY MOUNTAINS

GREAT PLAINS

INTERIOR PLAINS

Missouri River

L. Superior

St. Lawrence River

Sierra Nevada

Coast Ranges

BASIN AND RANGE

Great
Basin

Great
Salt Lake

L. Michigan

L. Huron

Lake
Ontario

L. Erie

APPALACHIAN MOUNTAINS

UNITED
STATES

Colorado River

Grand
Canyon

OZARK
PLATEAU

Ohio River

Mississippi River

N
W   E
S

ATLANTIC
OCEAN

GULF AND ATLANTIC COASTAL PLAINS

Rio Grande

MEXICO

Gulf of Mexico

PACIFIC
OCEAN

HAWAII

km 0   100   200
mi 0   100   200

km 0   250   500
mi 0   250   500

Landform Areas North America is covered with large areas of mountains and plains. The Rocky Mountains run from northern Canada through the United States and into Mexico. **SKILL** **Reading Maps** Which plains are along the Gulf of Mexico?

Great Lakes

Great Plains

Atlantic Coast

Appalachian Mountains

Landforms

Landforms give each part of the country its special character. A **landform** is a feature on the surface of the land, such as a mountain, valley, or plain. If you traveled across the United States from the Pacific to the Atlantic coast, you would see a variety of landforms.

Starting on the Pacific coast and moving east, you quickly climb up into mountains. These mountains are part of the Coast Ranges and the higher, rugged Sierra Nevada range. Beyond these mountains is the Basin and Range area, which includes bowl-shaped basins and mountain ranges. Plateaus (PLA tohz) are common in this area. A **plateau** is a high, steep-sided area rising above the surrounding land. Rivers flowing over the plateaus have worn away the rock in some places and carved out canyons.

Canyons are long, deep gaps cut into the earth. Rivers in Utah have carved the famous canyons at Bryce Canyon National Park and Zion National Park.

Moving east, you come to another mountain range, the Rocky Mountains. The "Rockies" get their name from their sharp, rocky peaks. They include some of the highest mountains in the country.

East of the Rockies you find wide, flat plains. The plains slope toward a broad valley in the middle of the country. At the center of this valley is the Mississippi River. Beyond the river, the Interior Plains rise again until they meet the Appalachian Mountains.

The Appalachians run from Maine to Alabama. They are older, lower, and more rounded than the Sierra Nevada range or the Rockies. East of the Appalachians, the land drops into the Atlantic Coastal Plain, which meets the Atlantic Ocean.

Rocky Mountains The mountains in this photograph are the Grand Tetons in Wyoming. They are part of the Rocky Mountains.

Climate

Main Idea The equator, landforms, and plants and trees affect a location's climate.

The climate in the United States is as varied as its landforms. **Climate** is the type of weather a place has over a long period of time. The climate of a place includes its temperature and the amount of precipitation it gets. Precipitation is rain, snow, sleet, and other moisture that falls to earth.

States in the southern half of the country usually have a warmer climate than northern states. One reason southern states are warmer is that they are closer to the equator. The **equator** is the imaginary line around the middle of the Earth. As the Earth moves around the sun, sunlight strikes it most directly at the equator. The more direct sunlight a place receives, the warmer it is.

Landforms, especially mountains, can affect climate, too. Lower places are warmed by the Earth's surface. As you climb higher into the mountains, you get farther from the Earth's surface and the air becomes cooler. Plants and trees also affect climate. Their leaves release water and create shade. By doing this, trees can make an area cooler.

REVIEW What is climate?

Lesson Summary

- The United States has many kinds of landforms, including mountains, canyons, and plateaus.
- Climate in the United States differs from place to place.
- Climate is affected by distance from the equator, landforms, and plants.

Why It Matters . . .

The land and climate of the United States affect every person in this country.

Lesson Review

1 VOCABULARY Choose the correct word to complete each sentence.

climate   plateau   equator

Florida has a warm _____.

A _____ is a high area that rises above the surrounding land.

2 READING SKILL Would you put the Sierra Nevada in the **category** of mountains or plains?

3 MAIN IDEA: Geography What are three landforms you might see if you took a trip across the United States?

4 MAIN IDEA: Geography Why are places closer to the equator warmer than places farther from the equator?

5 CRITICAL THINKING: Compare and Contrast Compare the Rocky Mountains with the Appalachian Mountains. How are they similar? How are they different?

HANDS ON **MAP ACTIVITY** Use library resources to find out about the geography of your state. Then make a map showing the state's major landforms.

TROUBLE
FROM THE
TROPICS

A hot sun over tropical waters can sometimes stir up trouble. When the sun beats down on the sea, the water warms and evaporates. The evaporated water forms clouds when it rises. In tropical seas where the sun is at its hottest, huge amounts of water evaporate. All that rising moisture can feed giant storms called hurricanes. Hurricanes are tropical storms with winds over 74 miles per hour.

During hurricane season, when tropical seas are warmest, weather forecasters are on the alert. They follow hurricanes as they form and move toward land. With strong winds and heavy rains, hurricanes are sometimes a dangerous part of the climate in North America.

The storm in the large picture formed over the Pacific Ocean. It is viewed from above, using satellite technology. You can see Mexico's Baja (BAH hah) Peninsula just above the storm and San Diego just above Baja.

Hurricanes often strike the East Coast. In 1992, Hurricane Andrew in Florida had winds up to 165 miles per hour.

San Diego

Activities

1. **DESCRIBE IT** In most parts of the country, weather changes from season to season. Which season is stormiest where you live, and what are those storms like?

2. **CREATE IT** If you knew a hurricane was coming, what would you do? Create a list of steps to prepare for a big storm.

Skillbuilder

Review Map Skills

Maps tell you many things about the world you live in. For example, the map on page 7 is a physical map. A physical map shows the location of physical features, such as landforms, bodies of water, or resources. The map on this page is a political map. A political map shows cities, states, and countries. Although different types of maps show different types of information, most maps share certain elements.

▶ **VOCABULARY**
physical map
political map

Map Title

Political Map of the United States

Map Legend

LEGEND
⊛ National capital
★ State capital
— National border
— State border

Inset Map

ARCTIC OCEAN
km 0   600
mi 0   600
PACIFIC OCEAN
CANADA
AK
Juneau

CANADA

The Great Lakes

Compass Rose

PACIFIC OCEAN

PACIFIC OCEAN
Honolulu ★
HI
km 0   300
mi 0   300

MEXICO

Gulf of Mexico

km 0   300   600
mi 0   300   600

Map Scale

ATLANTIC OCEAN

Learn the Skill

Step 1: Read the title and labels to find the subject of the map. Look at the area that is shown on the map. Check if there is an inset map. An inset map may show a close-up of an area or bring a distant area onto the map.

Step 2: Study the map legend. What symbols are used on the map?

LEGEND
⊛ National capital
★ State capital
── National border
── State border

Step 3: Check directions and distances. The compass rose shows the cardinal and intermediate directions. The map scale compares distance on a map to the distance in the real world.

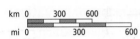

Practice the Skill

Use the map on page 12 to answer the following questions.

1. What is the distance between Santa Fe, New Mexico, and Phoenix, Arizona?

2. In what direction would you travel to go from Columbia, South Carolina, to Frankfort, Kentucky?

Apply the Skill

Use the maps on pages 7 and 12 to answer these questions.

1. Name three landforms in the United States.

2. Which of the two maps would you use to compare the size of different states?

3. Which mountains would you cross to travel from Denver, Colorado, to Salt Lake City, Utah? Use both maps.

Our Nation's Resources

VOCABULARY

capital resource
human resource
scarcity
opportunity cost
conservation

Vocabulary Strategy

conservation

A synonym for **conservation** is "saving." Conservation saves resources for the future.

READING SKILL

Draw Conclusions Use details from the lesson to decide whether protecting resources is important.

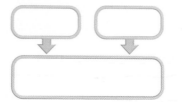

Build on What You Know You know that you need to eat food, wear clothes, and live in some sort of shelter. Do you know where all of these things come from? Almost everything we use starts with nature, but that is just the beginning.

Natural Resources

Main Idea Natural resources in the United States include renewable, nonrenewable, and flow resources.

Many of the things we use every day come from nature. The water you drink may come from rivers or lakes. The gasoline to run your school bus may have come from oil wells in Alaska. The bus itself began as iron ore that may have come from Minnesota.

Water, oil, and iron ore are natural resources, which are useful materials from nature. Nature also gives us air to breathe, and soil and sunshine for growing crops. Without natural resources, human beings would not be able to survive.

Corn Fields Natural resources such as soil, sun, and water are needed to raise corn and other crops.

Renewable Resources

One important natural resource is wood. People use wood to make paper, pencils, furniture, and hundreds of other products. Wood comes from trees, which are a renewable resource. Renewable resources are resources that can be replaced, or renewed.

In Georgia, for example, farmers grow trees just like other crops. When farmers cut down the trees after many years, they plant new ones in their place.

Fisheries are another renewable resource. A fishery is a place where many fish are caught. If people limit the number of fish they catch at one time, new fish will be able to hatch and grow.

Nonrenewable Resources

Some of the resources in nature are nonrenewable. Nonrenewable resources cannot be replaced once they are used up. Oil is one of the United States' nonrenewable resources. After oil is removed from the ground, no new oil will take its place.

Oil, iron ore, and copper are mineral resources. They are mined, or taken from the ground. Some mineral resources, such as oil and coal, give us energy to heat our homes, run our cars, and cook our food. Other mineral resources include metals, such as nickel, gold, and silver. All of these mineral resources are nonrenewable.

REVIEW What is the difference between renewable and nonrenewable resources?

Resources Across the Land Resources such as coal and oil are found underground. Other resources, such as forests, are above ground. **SKILL** **Reading Maps** Where are most of the country's forests found?

Natural Resources

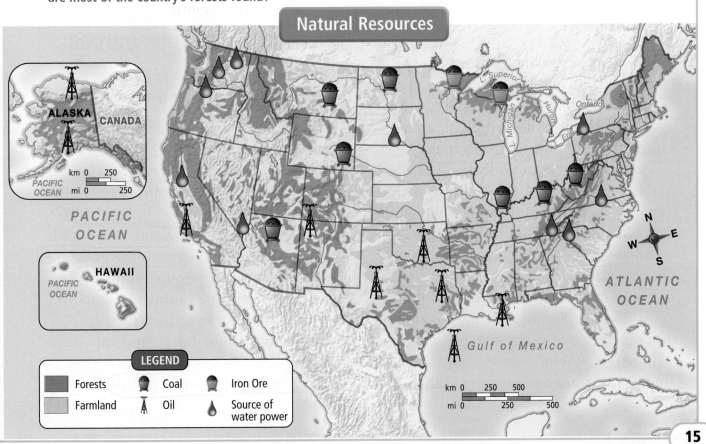

LEGEND

- Forests
- Farmland
- Coal
- Oil
- Iron Ore
- Source of water power

Producing Peanut Butter

1 Growing Peanuts The peanuts you eat are the seeds of peanut plants. The nuts grow in underground pods.

2 Harvesting Peanuts This farmer's knowledge and hard work move the process along.

Flow Resources

Flow resources are the third type of natural resource. Wind, sunlight, and water are flow resources. People use the energy of strong winds, sunlight, and running water to produce electricity.

Flow resources can only be used at a certain time or place. For example, people can use the power of the wind only while it is blowing. The wind turns the blades of a windmill, which changes that power into electricity. Special panels can turn sunlight into electricity, too, but only when the sun shines. Flow resources are not renewable or nonrenewable. People cannot use up wind, sun, or running water, and they cannot replace them, either.

Other Important Resources

Main Idea People use capital resources and human resources to produce goods and services.

Natural resources are important to us, but they are not enough. It takes many steps to turn these resources into products. For example, peanut butter starts out as peanuts growing on a farm. Natural resources such as soil, water, and sunshine are needed to grow the peanuts.

People depend on other kinds of resources to get the peanuts to a store or to turn them into a product, such as peanut butter. These other kinds of resources are not found in nature. They are created or supplied by people.

Capital Resource

④ **Finished Product** Natural, human, and capital resources go into every single product you eat, wear, and use, including this book.

③ **Supplies and Equipment** The machines that grind the peanuts and fill the jars are capital resources.

Capital Resources

People use capital resources to turn the peanuts into peanut butter. A **capital resource** is a tool, machine, or building people use to produce goods and services. To raise peanuts, farmers use tractors to plant and harvest the crop. The tractor is a capital resource. Later, factory workers roast the peanuts in ovens and use machines to grind the peanuts into peanut butter. The ovens and grinding machines are also capital resources.

The computer in your classroom or school library is a capital resource. The computer is a tool that helps students learn. Think of other capital resources found at your home or school.

Human Resources

All the natural resources and capital resources in the world would be useless without one other kind of resource: human resources. A **human resource** is a person and the skills and knowledge he or she brings to a job. The farmers who plant the peanuts, the people who invent the grinding machines, and the people who design the labels on the jars are all human resources. At every stage of making peanut butter or any other product, human resources make the process work. Your teacher and school principal are also good examples of human resources.

REVIEW What is the difference between capital resources and human resources?

17

Making Choices

Peanut butter is just one of many goods that a person might buy. Most people have a long list of things they want. However, there are not enough resources to provide all that people want. This problem is called scarcity. **Scarcity** means not having as much of something as people would like.

The problem of scarcity means that people have to make decisions about what they want most. For example, your teacher might want to buy a wall map and a video. The school may not have enough money to buy both. If your teacher chooses to buy the video, he or she gives up the opportunity to buy the map. The map is called an opportunity cost. An **opportunity cost** is the thing you give up when you decide to do or have something else. Every choice people make about how to spend their money or their time has an opportunity cost.

Conservation

Another choice that people make is how to use resources. People will always need natural resources. They have to find ways to make sure those resources are here for people in the future. One way to balance the needs of today with care for the future is to practice conservation. **Conservation** is the protection and wise use of natural resources.

There are many ways to conserve resources. Some people work to save soil from being washed or blown away. Others find ways to mine resources without harming the land.

The United States government supports conservation by creating national parks to protect plants and animals from human activities. Businesses can practice conservation by using containers that can be recycled, such as metal and cardboard.

Flow Resources Wind power can provide electricity while saving nonrenewable resources, such as coal. These windmills are in California.

People can practice conservation at home and in school, too. Everyone can use fewer resources by not wasting water, gas, or electricity. They can also make the resources they use last much longer.

Conserving Resources Through everyday actions, people can help conserve natural resources. Riding a bike instead of driving a car saves gas and oil.

When students write on both sides of a piece of paper instead of just one side, they use less paper. Everyone can also recycle paper, cans, and bottles, so that they can be used again. In all these ways, people help conserve natural resources for the future.

REVIEW Why do people practice conservation?

Lesson Summary

- Natural resources, human resources, and capital resources are used to provide goods and services.
- Because of scarcity, people make decisions about what they want most and what they can do without.
- Conservation is one important way to preserve natural resources and use them wisely.

Why It Matters . . .

Today and in the future, Americans will face many important decisions about how to use and protect natural resources.

Lesson Review

1 VOCABULARY Write a short paragraph about resources, using **scarcity** and **conservation.**

2 READING SKILL Why do nonrenewable resources need to be used wisely?

3 MAIN IDEA: Economics Why does scarcity force people to make choices?

4 MAIN IDEA: Geography What are two examples of each kind of resource: renewable, nonrenewable, and flow?

5 CRITICAL THINKING: Decision Making Describe the opportunity cost if you decide to check out a mystery book instead of a science video from the library.

6 CRITICAL THINKING: Synthesize What are some ways you could conserve resources such as paper and electricity in your classroom?

ART ACTIVITY Resources are necessary for businesses. Create a poster for a T-shirt company, showing the different types of resources the business uses to make its product.

The Race for SOLAR POWER

What fuel or power will the cars of the future run on? Most cars today run on gasoline. But gas-powered cars pollute the air and may add to overall warming of the Earth. Researchers want to find better, cleaner ways to power cars. Some think that solar power may replace gas as the energy source of the future.

To make solar power useful, solar technologies must be less expensive. Solar technology is better now than ever before, and scientists continue to look for new ways to improve it.

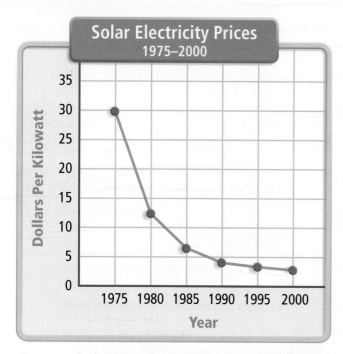

Solar Electricity Prices
1975–2000

Dollars Per Kilowatt
35
30
25
20
15
10
5
0

1975 1980 1985 1990 1995 2000
Year

How much did the price of solar electricity decrease between 1975 and 2000?

The Solar Challenge
Every year, teams of university students compete in solar-powered car races. Their discoveries may be useful in building future cars.

Power from the Sun

Solar-powered cars are covered with special panels that turn sunlight into electric energy. The electricity can either turn the car's wheels or be stored in the battery.

Activities

1. **TALK ABOUT IT** Look closely at the photo. Describe how the design of this car can help it collect energy from the sun.

2. **DRAW IT** Draw your own design for a solar-powered car that will make good use of the sun's rays.

Regions of the United States

Build on What You Know Imagine a pizza with different toppings on each slice. Each slice is different from the others, but together they make a whole. The United States can be divided into sections, too.

What Is a Region?

Main Idea Geographers divide the United States into many types of regions.

To learn more about the world around us, geographers divide it into regions. A **region** is an area that has one or more features in common. Those physical or human features make the region different from other regions.

One way to divide the United States into regions is to group together states that are close to each other. The feature the states have in common is their location. The United States can be divided into four regions this way: Northeast, South, Midwest, and West.

Deserts These regions are hot and dry. This desert is in Arizona.

These four regions have features that make each one special. For example, states in a region may share physical features, such as landforms. The Midwestern states have wide plains and few mountains. The West has many mountains.

The United States can be divided into political regions, such as states and counties. The country can be divided into climate regions, too. Look at the map on the next page to locate deserts and other climate regions.

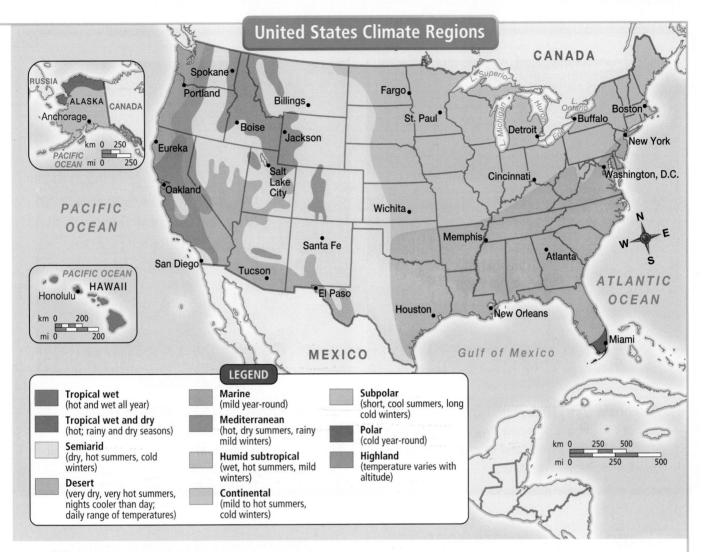

United States Climate Regions

LEGEND

Tropical wet
(hot and wet all year)

Tropical wet and dry
(hot; rainy and dry seasons)

Semiarid
(dry, hot summers, cold winters)

Desert
(very dry, very hot summers, nights cooler than day; daily range of temperatures)

Marine
(mild year-round)

Mediterranean
(hot, dry summers, rainy mild winters)

Humid subtropical
(wet, hot summers, mild winters)

Continental
(mild to hot summers, cold winters)

Subpolar
(short, cool summers, long cold winters)

Polar
(cold year-round)

Highland
(temperature varies with altitude)

SKILL **Reading Maps** Which cities on the map are in the marine climate region?

Regions and Human Activities

Regions can be defined by the activities people in the area share. For example, the United States can be divided into regions based on the kinds of work people do. The Dairy Belt region is good for dairy farming and produces a lot of milk. It includes parts of the Midwest and the Northeast. Other regions might be places where most people speak the same language or share the same customs.

People often have ideas about what regions are like, but those ideas can change over time. For example, people used to call the Great Plains the "Great American Desert." It looked too empty and dry to be good for farming.

When people developed better farming methods, the area blossomed with fields of crops. Today, it is called the "breadbasket" of the country, because so much food is grown there. The region produces much of the nation's wheat.

People's ideas about regions are also affected by their own experiences. If you have never been to the Great Plains you might guess that most people there are farmers. If you visit the region, you will see that people on the Great Plains have all kinds of jobs, and many live in cities.

REVIEW What are the different ways the United States can be divided into regions?

23

Wisconsin Dairy

Florida Citrus

Wisconsin Dairy Dairy farming is an important part of Wisconsin's economy. The state specializes in products such as milk and cheese, which are shipped to many other states.

Florida Citrus Because of its warm climate, Florida specializes in citrus fruit, such as oranges. Orange juice made from Florida oranges is sold all over the country.

Regions and Resources

Main Idea Each region uses its resources to focus on producing certain goods and services.

Another way to define a region is by its resources. Most regions have plenty of some resources and less of others. For example, the Appalachian Mountain region has many coal mines. The region lacks other resources, though, such as oil and deep soil.

Resources are important for the growth of a region's economy. An **economy** is the system people use to produce goods and services. These goods and services include the things people buy and sell and the work that people do for others. Through the economy, people get the food, clothing, shelter, and other things they need or want.

The resources of each region help people decide which crops to grow and which goods to produce for the economy. Farmers in the South use the resources of good soil and a warm climate to raise the cotton that is made into clothing, towels, and other goods. Cotton grows well in some places, such as the South, but not in others. In North and South Dakota, the climate and soil are good for producing large amounts of wheat, but not cotton.

When a region makes a lot of one product it is called specialization. **Specialization** happens when people make the goods they are best able to produce with the resources they have. By specializing, people can usually produce more goods and services at a lower cost and earn more money.

Specialization and Trade

When regions specialize in certain products, they do not produce all the goods and services that consumers may want. A **consumer** is someone who buys goods and services.

People and businesses in different regions trade with each other to make more goods available to consumers. **Trade** is the buying and selling of goods. For example, oil and natural gas from the Gulf of Mexico are sold beyond that region. People in the Gulf area use money from the oil and other products they sell to buy goods from other regions.

Countries such as the United States and Mexico also specialize in producing goods. They then trade with each other for products that their people want. For example, people in the United States buy oil from Mexico, which produces large amounts of oil.

The United States has many car makers. Mexicans, like people all over the world, buy American-designed cars. Businesses in countries around the world are connected through trading.

REVIEW Why do people in regions trade with each other?

Lesson Summary

Regions share physical or human features

Regions specialize

Regions trade

Why It Matters . . .

Specialization and trade increase the amount of goods and services people produce.

Lesson Review

1. **VOCABULARY** Write a short paragraph about where you live, using **region, specialization,** and **trade.**

2. **READING SKILL** If a region doesn't have resources that it needs, what is one **solution** to the **problem?**

3. **MAIN IDEA: Culture** Why did people's ideas about the Great Plains change?

4. **MAIN IDEA: Economics** How do the natural resources in a region affect which products people make?

5. **PLACES TO KNOW:** Where is the Dairy Belt region and what products is it known for?

6. **CRITICAL THINKING: Cause and Effect** What effect does trade have on consumers?

WRITING ACTIVITY Write a poem that describes the natural resources, climate, landforms, foods, customs, or other features that make your region of the United States different from the rest of the country.

Caretakers of the Earth

Today's geographers do much more than map the earth. They study how people interact with the land and the world around them. Using the latest computer technology, they can forecast earthquakes and track sea creatures across the ocean floor. They study regions with political troubles and help decide where boundaries should be drawn. Geographers today are problem solvers, helping to show how the physical world affects the lives of everyone.

Dawn Wright

An oceanographer is a geographer who studies the ocean. Dawn Wright knew that was what she wanted to do since she was a child in Hawaii, surrounded by the sea.

Wright is now a professor at Oregon State University. She uses computers to study underwater volcanoes and fissures, or cracks, along the sea floor. She is an expert in Geographic Information Systems (GIS), a computer program that can map the ocean floor in three dimensions. It can show how ocean temperatures affect sea creatures.

To future oceanographers, Wright says, "Get as much experience as you can on computers. That is a big part of oceanography today."

Mei-Po Kwan

Mei-Po Kwan likes being a geographer because she can travel and learn about different cultures. A professor at Ohio State University, Kwan uses new computer systems to learn about the behaviors of groups of people around the world. Kwan is interested in seeing whether women in different places have the same opportunities as men. She also studies how people in different nations use their resources. With this information she can find out whether they have enough medical care.

She says, "Geography provides us with training to see connections and understand the world better."

William Wood

As the geographer for the Department of State, William Wood works on issues that are on the front pages of newspapers around the world. Wood helps world leaders solve disagreements over land and water. He also works with countries recovering from war by showing them where to find resources, such as food and shelter.

Wood says, "Geography can help people better use natural resources, such as clean water and productive farmland, so that future generations in these countries can benefit."

Activities

1. **TALK ABOUT IT** Choose one geographer and tell what would be interesting about his or her work.

2. **WRITE ABOUT IT** Write about what a geographer might want to study in your community.

Technology Visit Education Place to read more biographies. www.eduplace.com/kids/hmss05/

People and the Land

Build on What You Know What makes the area where you live a good place for people? Maybe it is the geography. Geography always affects where people live and the work they do.

How Land Affects People

Main Idea The land and its resources affect where and how people live.

More than one million people live in San Diego, California. It is one of the largest cities in the United States. Why is San Diego so big? Geography is part of the reason. Like many large cities, San Diego has the resources and location that allow many people to live there.

San Diego is located on the Pacific coast. The city has a fine harbor, one of its most important resources. A harbor is a body of water where ships can load and unload goods. Shipping and trade have helped San Diego grow and are still important to the city's economy. Today, San Diego's economy provides many kinds of jobs for the people who live there.

San Diego, California Many business owners choose to start companies in San Diego because of its pleasant climate.

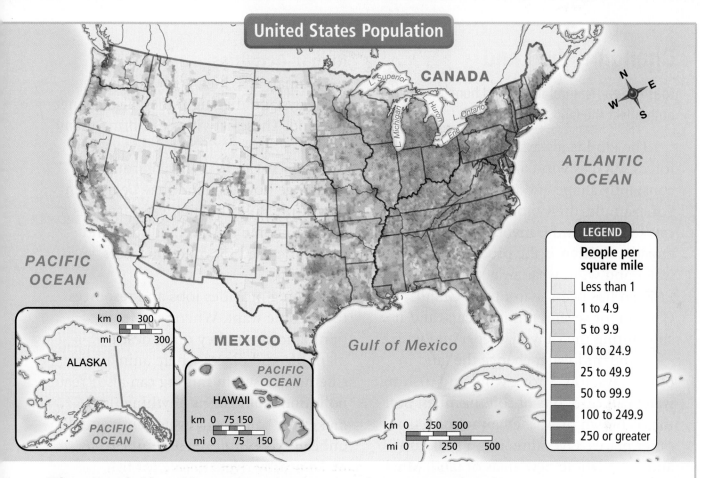

United States Population

CANADA

ATLANTIC OCEAN

PACIFIC OCEAN

MEXICO

Gulf of Mexico

ALASKA

HAWAII

PACIFIC OCEAN

km 0   300
mi 0   300

km 0 75 150
mi 0 75 150

km 0   250   500
mi 0   250   500

LEGEND

People per square mile

Less than 1
1 to 4.9
5 to 9.9
10 to 24.9
25 to 49.9
50 to 99.9
100 to 249.9
250 or greater

Where People Live This map shows that some areas have many people and other areas have very few. **SKILL** **Reading Maps** Do more people live in the eastern half or in the western half of the United States?

Where People Live

People often live near resources such as water, transportation routes, or jobs. Denver, Colorado, grew partly because gold and silver were discovered near there. Mining became a way for many people to earn a living. As the number of miners grew, so did the number of stores, restaurants, and other businesses that served the miners. Denver's population grew as its economy grew.

People settle in places where they are able to earn a living, but they also choose to settle in places they enjoy. Geography affects those choices, too. Many people live in Florida and Arizona because they like the environments there. The **environment** is the surroundings in which people, plants, and animals live.

A warm, sunny climate is part of the environment in the South and Southwest. These regions are the fastest growing in the United States. Millions of people have moved there from the Northeast, where winters can be long and cold.

Geography also affects the activities people do for fun. The mountains in Vermont make downhill skiing a popular winter activity and hiking a popular summer activity. People can't ski on snow in Florida, but many people like to waterski in that state's lakes and rivers.

REVIEW Why does San Diego's location attract businesses and people?

Changing the Land

Main Idea Natural forces and human activities both affect the land.

The land is always changing. Natural forces, such as wind and moving water, constantly shape and reshape the land. For example, the Colorado River has carved the Grand Canyon through erosion. **Erosion** is the process by which water and wind wear away the land. Erosion has been shaping the Grand Canyon for several million years, and it is still cutting the canyon deeper and wider.

Wind and water change the land in other ways, too. Strong wind and rushing water can carry bits of soil for miles. Soil that is blown or washed away collects in other places. Over time it can build up and form whole new areas of land. Much of Louisiana was formed from soil that was carried there by the Mississippi River.

Human Activities

Human activities, such as building highways and digging mines, also change the land. These activities can bring many benefits, but they often have costs too. Big projects can hurt the environment or change how the land may be used in the future. Building highways provides a way for people to travel, but the land cannot be used for other purposes, such as farming.

Mining provides jobs and resources that people want. When people dig mines, however, they often destroy plant life and places where animals live. Chemicals used in mining can also create pollution. **Pollution** is anything that makes the soil, air, or water dirty and unhealthy. Pollution from mines may make nearby rivers unsafe for fish, wildlife, and people.

Strip Mining Erosion from strip mining can carry pollution away from the site. An employee from a mining company (right) tests the quality of water in this lake to make sure it is safe for fish and wildlife.

Effects on the Environment

Humans sometimes make small changes to the environment that have big effects. The environment is made up of many ecosystems. An **ecosystem** is a community of plants and animals along with the surrounding soil, air, and water. Each part of an ecosystem affects the health of all the other parts. A lake is an ecosystem that contains water, plants, fish, and birds. If the water becomes polluted, the lake's plants and animals will suffer.

Human activity can affect an ecosystem in ways people never expected. Ships have accidentally carried plants and animals from one ecosystem to another. In their new ecosystems, these plants and animals sometimes spread quickly. This happened in the Great Lakes. The zebra mussel, a type of shellfish, came to the Great Lakes attached to ships. The mussels have spread throughout the Great Lakes and many of the country's rivers.

Zebra mussels can cause big problems. They form groups that clog pipes, and they eat the food that local fish depend on. Today, people are aware that what they do always has an effect on the environment.

REVIEW What is one example of how natural forces can change the land?

Lesson Summary

Landforms, natural resources, environment, and other features of the land affect where and how people live. People change the environment to meet their needs. Building highways and digging mines are two of the many ways humans have changed their environment. When people change the environment, the effects can be surprising.

Why It Matters . . .

People's lives are always connected to the land, so learning about the environment is important.

Lesson Review

1 VOCABULARY Write a sample e-mail to the editor of your local newspaper, using **environment** and **pollution.**

2 READING SKILL What is erosion's effect on the land?

3 MAIN IDEA: Economics Give an example from the lesson of how resources affect the work people do.

4 MAIN IDEA: Geography How does climate influence where people live?

5 CRITICAL THINKING: Draw Conclusions What is the relationship between the geography in your region and the activities people there do for fun?

6 CRITICAL THINKING: Cause and Effect What effect did the spread of zebra mussels have on the Great Lakes?

WRITING ACTIVITY Find out about an ecosystem near where you live. Prepare a short talk on the parts of that ecosystem and the impact people have on it.

Reshaping the Land

Modern dams are some of the largest structures ever built, and they have a big effect on the land around them. Dams help control floods and offer a steady supply of water to cities and towns. Dams also create lakes and provide electricity.

Not all the changes are positive, though. Dams stop the natural flow of a river. A dam affects fish, plants, and animals by changing the sources of food in the river's **ecosystem.**

The Hoover Dam is one of the largest dams in the United States. It is located on the border between Nevada and Arizona and blocks the Colorado River, the largest river in the Southwest.

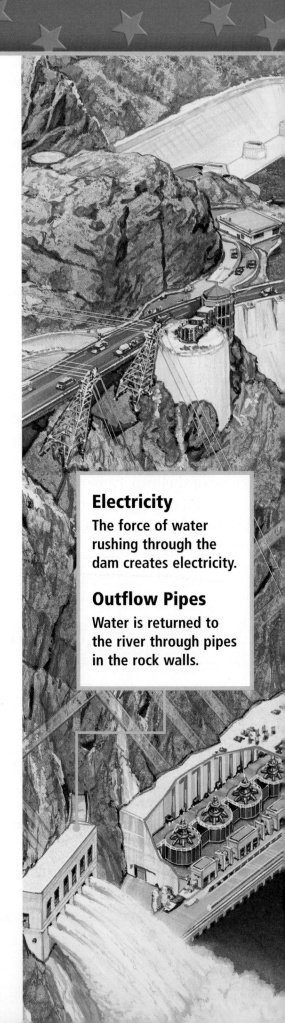

Electricity

The force of water rushing through the dam creates electricity.

Outflow Pipes

Water is returned to the river through pipes in the rock walls.

Before the Dam

The Colorado River flowed freely through Black Canyon before the Hoover Dam was built.

Reservoir

The reservoir is the human-made lake that forms behind the dam. The Hoover Dam's Lake Mead is about 115 miles long.

Dam

The dam holds back the water in the reservoir.

Power Lines

Electricity from the dam gave energy to the new cities of the Southwest, which could not have grown without it.

Activities

1. **EXPLORE IT** Describe what you would see if you were in one of the cars driving across the dam.

2. **WRITE ABOUT IT** Planners chose the location of the Hoover Dam carefully. Describe why you think Black Canyon was the right spot for the dam.

33

Review and Test Prep

Visual Summary

1.–3. 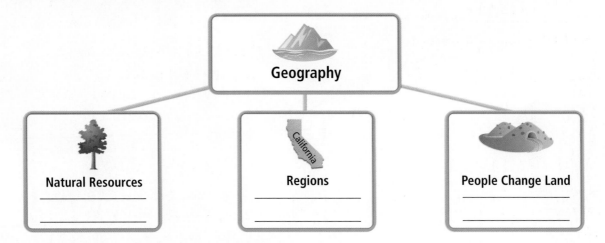 Describe what you learned about each item named below.

Geography

Natural Resources
_____
_____

Regions
_____
_____

People Change Land
_____
_____

Facts and Main Ideas

✓ **TEST PREP** Answer each question with information from the chapter.

4. **Geography** In what way does the equator affect the climate of a place?

5. **Citizenship** Name three ways people can conserve resources.

6. **Economics** How does specialization affect trade between regions?

7. **History** Why did the discovery of gold and silver help the city of Denver grow?

8. **Geography** Name two kinds of regions.

Vocabulary

✓ **TEST PREP** Choose the correct word from the list below to complete each sentence.

plateau, p. 8
scarcity, p. 18
consumer, p. 25
erosion, p. 30

9. Mountains wear down over time because of _____.

10. _____ exists when people cannot get everything they would like.

11. A _____ buys goods and services.

12. A _____ is a high, steep-sided area that rises above the surrounding land.

Apply Skills

 TEST PREP **Map Skill** Study the climate map below. Then use your map skills to answer each question.

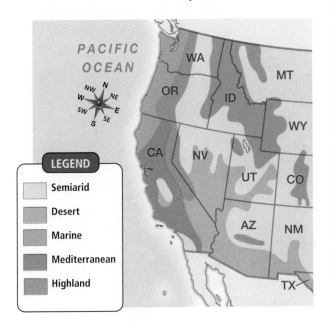

PACIFIC OCEAN

WA

MT

OR

ID

WY

CA

NV

UT

CO

AZ

NM

TX

LEGEND

Semiarid

Desert

Marine

Mediterranean

Highland

13. Which state shown here has the most climate regions?

   A. Nevada

   B. Oregon

   C. California

   D. Washington

14. In which direction would you travel to get from the marine climate region to the desert climate region?

   A. northeast

   B. southeast

   C. northwest

   D. southwest

Critical Thinking

 TEST PREP Write a short paragraph to answer each question.

15. **Classify** Place the resources named below in one of these categories: Renewable Resources, Nonrenewable Resources, or Flow Resources.

trees	oil	sunlight
wind	iron	coal

16. **Summarize** What geographic and economic features can influence where people choose to live?

Activities

Research Activity Use library or Internet resources to locate two states that have nicknames based on their landforms. Illustrate your discoveries with pictures or drawings.

Writing Activity If you had a choice, where in the United States would you live? Write a personal essay explaining your answer based on landforms, climate, and resources.

 Technology
Writing Process Tips
Get help with your essay at
www.eduplace.com/kids/hmss05/

Technology

e • **glossary**
e • **word games**
www.eduplace.com/kids/hmss05/

Vocabulary Preview

agriculture

Aztecs used a special type of farming, or **agriculture.** They grew their crops on floating islands. **page 40**

clan

People who are part of the same **clan** share a common ancestor. The Tlingit people organize themselves into clans. **page 48**

Chapter Timeline

about 1100
Earliest Ancient Pueblo stone buildings

about 1300
Aztecs rule Central Mexico

| 1100 | 1200 | 1300 | 1400 |

Reading Strategy

Question As you read, ask questions to check your understanding.

 Quick Tip Write down your questions. Go back to them once you finish reading.

irrigation

Farmers in the dry Southwest bring water from rivers and streams to their crops. This method of watering crops is **irrigation.** page 55

nomad

A **nomad** does not live in only one place. Nomads move when they need to find food or water. **page 61**

1700s
Comanche control large part of Great Plains

1500   1600   1700

Ancient Americans

| 30,000 years ago | 20,000 | 10,000 | Today |

27,000 years ago–500 years ago

VOCABULARY

glacier
migration
agriculture
civilization
pueblo

Vocabulary Strategy

migra**tion**

The word **migrate** means "to move." When the suffix **-ion** is added, the word becomes **migration**, or movement.

READING SKILL

Sequence As you read, use an organizer to put important events in order.

1	
2	
3	
4	

Build on What You Know We have built thousands of bridges in this country, but humans didn't build the earliest ones. The bridges formed naturally. Scientists think people first came to the Americas by walking across a land bridge that linked Asia and North America.

People Arrive in the Americas

Main Idea People began arriving in the Americas around 27,000 years ago.

Scientists are not sure how the first humans came to North America. They have more than one theory. A theory is an explanation or belief about how things happen or will happen. The most common theory is that hunters first came to the Americas by walking across a natural land bridge that linked Asia and North America. Another theory is that some people may have traveled by boat along the coast or across the oceans.

Glaciers Today, glaciers can still be found in the coldest parts of the world, such as Alaska (below) and Antarctica.

Beringia

Thousands of years ago, the Earth was much colder than it is today. This time in history is called the Ice Age because glaciers covered almost half of the world. A **glacier** is a huge, thick sheet of slowly moving ice.

During the Ice Age, much of the Earth's water was frozen in glaciers. In some areas, the ocean floor was no longer covered by water. At the Bering Strait, between Alaska and Asia, the ocean floor became grassland and formed a bridge that scientists call Beringia.

Beringia was a cool, wet land where many kinds of animals lived. Humans hunted the biggest animals. Over many years, hunters followed these animals from Asia across Beringia into North America. Movement like this, from one region to another, is called **migration.**

Scientists know that the migration over Beringia stopped about 10,000 years ago. Around that time, the Ice Age began to end. The glaciers slowly melted, filling the oceans with water. Water covered the land bridge between Asia and North America. It is still covered by water today.

The people who crossed into North America followed the migrating animal herds south. The hunters spread across North and South America. These ancient Americans are known as Paleo-Indians. Paleo (PAY lee oh) means past. They were the ancestors of modern American Indians. Ancestors are relatives who lived before you.

REVIEW According to scientists, how did people first come to North America?

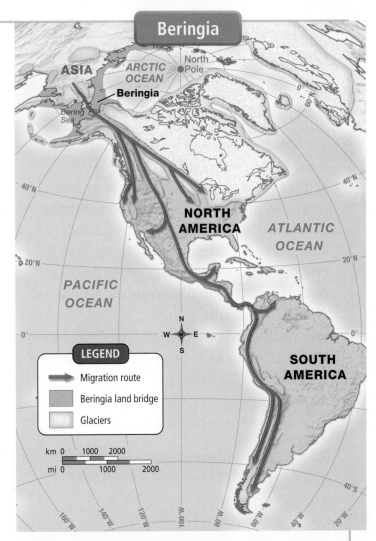

Land Bridge Over many years, Paleo-Indians crossed the Beringia land bridge and moved throughout the Americas.

SKILL **Reading Maps** How far south did Paleo-Indians migrate?

Woolly Mammoth This large animal was hunted by Paleo-Indians.

Civilizations Develop

Main Idea Farming led to villages, more people, and civilizations.

For thousands of years Paleo-Indians lived by hunting big animals. About 11,000 years ago, many of these animals began to die. Over time, people adapted by finding other ways of getting food. To adapt is to change a way of life to fit an environment. As the large animals died, people hunted smaller animals, fished, and gathered wild plants.

Around 9,000 years ago, some Paleo-Indians began to use agriculture to feed themselves. **Agriculture** is farming, or growing plants.

Scientists think that people in present-day Mexico were the first people in the Americas to practice agriculture. They gathered the seeds of useful wild plants and learned to grow them as crops. These crops included corn, beans, and squash.

Agriculture not only changed the food people ate, it changed the way they lived. It takes months to raise crops, so many Paleo-Indians began staying in one place to care for the plants. With a steady supply of food, more families could survive. Populations grew and people built villages and cities. These changes were all part of the growth of civilizations. A **civilization** is a group of people living together who have systems of government, religion, and culture.

Mississippian Village Mississippians made the tops of some of their mounds flat so they could build temples there.

The Mound Builders

The Adena (Uh DEE nuh), Hopewell, and Mississippians were among the earliest people to create large, complex villages in North America. These three civilizations are all called Mound Builders. They built giant mounds, or hills, out of the earth, which they often used to bury their dead. Both the Adena and the Hopewell buried jewelry, tools, and pottery inside their mounds. Some of these mounds still exist today. The town of Cahokia (Kah HOE kee uh) in Illinois is one of the most famous sites, with over 85 mounds.

The mound building civilizations began about 3,000 years ago and lasted for about 2,500 years. The Adena and Hopewell lived in what is now the Ohio River Valley.

The Adena made some of their mounds in the shape of animals or symbols. The Great Serpent Mound in Ohio is shaped like a snake.

The Mississippian civilization was similar to the Adena and Hopewell civilizations. It spread along the lower Mississippi Valley, over most of the South-east, and as far north as Wisconsin. Some experts believe that the Mississippians are the ancestors of Creek Indians.

REVIEW Where did the mound building civilizations live?

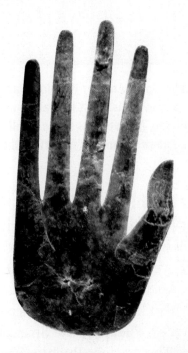

Hopewell Ornament
Holes in the palm may mean that a Hopewell person wore this hand symbol as a necklace.

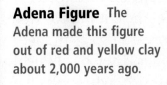

Adena Figure The Adena made this figure out of red and yellow clay about 2,000 years ago.

Cliff Palace Some Ancient Pueblo villages were built into canyon walls. The Cliff Palace in Mesa Verde, Colorado, (above) was like a small city. The Ancient Pueblo drew images (right) on their walls.

Ancient Pueblo Peoples

Another American Indian civilization lived in what is now the Southwest, from about the year 500 to about 1300. They were the Ancient Pueblo (PWEH bloh) peoples, also known as the Anasazi (Ahn uh SAH zee). **Pueblo** is the Spanish word for town. The Ancient Pueblo lived in large buildings with many rooms. The buildings looked like towns to the Spanish who arrived in North America many years later.

By constructing their houses out of stone, the Ancient Pueblo could group homes on top of one another. Around the year 1100, the Ancient Pueblo were building structures as large as modern apartment buildings. They built Pueblo Bonito in New Mexico, which was five stories high with hundreds of rooms.

The Ancient Pueblo also built underground rooms called kivas (KEE vahs). The kivas were used for religious ceremonies. Each village had a number of kivas. Pueblo Bonito had two huge kivas, where hundreds of people could gather.

Around 1300, the Ancient Pueblo left their villages. No one knows why. It is possible that lack of rain or wood and warfare with other people caused them to move. Many went south and settled along the Rio Grande and Little Colorado rivers. Today, the descendants of the Ancient Pueblo live in Arizona, New Mexico, and northern Mexico.

Aztec Coyote
Aztecs carved this coyote figure out of stone.

The Aztecs

The Aztec civilization ruled in Central Mexico for about 200 years, beginning around the year 1300. Their capital city was Tenochtitlán (teh NOHCH tee TLAN).

Tenochtitlán had hundreds of buildings, roads, and a population of 250,000 people. The Aztecs made their own calendar, and built large temples as part of their religion. Some temples had a playing court for a game that was like modern-day basketball.

At the time the Aztec civilization lived in Central Mexico, groups of American Indians had settled in almost every region of North America. These groups adapted to different environments and developed their own cultures.

REVIEW What were kivas?

Lesson Summary

- During the Ice Age, Asian hunters followed large animals across Beringia to North America.
- Around 9,000 years ago, people in the Americas began farming.
- Important early civilizations of the Americas included the Mound Builders, the Ancient Pueblo, and the Aztecs.

Why It Matters...

The history of the people of North America began with the American Indians. They practiced agriculture and built civilizations.

Lesson Review

3,000 years ago	About 1,500 years ago	About 700 years ago
Mound Builders civilizations	**Ancient Pueblo civilization grows**	**Aztecs rule in Central Mexico**

3,500 years ago 2,500 1,500 500 Today

① **VOCABULARY** Write an explanation of the Beringia land bridge using the words **glacier** and **migration.**

② **READING SKILL** Review your chart. Who were some of the earliest people to build large villages in North America?

③ **MAIN IDEA: History** Why do scientists think the migration over Beringia stopped 10,000 years ago?

④ **MAIN IDEA: Culture** In what ways did agriculture change life for Paleo-Indians?

⑤ **TIMELINE SKILL** Which civilization is older, the Ancient Pueblo or the Mound Builders?

⑥ **CRITICAL THINKING: Synthesize** Describe the ways the Aztec culture fits the definition of a civilization.

HANDS ON

ART ACTIVITY Find out more about the Great Serpent Mound by using library resources. Use clay to make a model of the mound or draw a picture of it.

Tenochtitlán

Caged geese honk, shopkeepers shout, cacao beans rattle out of sacks. These are some of the sounds the Aztecs heard 500 years ago in the busy markets of the city of Tenochtitlán. Aztec culture centered around Tenochtitlán, which was their capital city. The Aztecs ruled about 12 million people in the surrounding region.

The scene of Aztec life shown here comes from a mural called *The Great City of Tenochtitlán*, painted by Mexican artist Diego Rivera in 1945. He researched Aztec civilization so his painting would be accurate. This mural is now in Mexico City. Mexico City was built on the ruins of Tenochtitlán. Look closely at this portion of Rivera's mural. Find the details described below.

1 **Island City** The Aztecs built Tenochtitlán on an island in the middle of a lake. Their city included temples, palaces, paved roads, and a huge marketplace.

2 **Moctezuma** The ruler of the Aztecs is shown being carried through the streets of the city. Moctezuma holds a fan made of bird feathers. The feathers of tropical birds were a valuable trade item.

3 **Marketplace** Sellers brought rare goods such as jaguar skin and jade from distant lands to the marketplace.

4 **Corn** Rivera shows the different kinds of corn—red, blue, and yellow—the Aztecs grew and sold. They built artificial "floating gardens" on which they also grew onions, peppers, avocados, tomatoes, and other crops.

5 **Cacao Money** Aztecs used cacao beans as money. They also ground the beans into a powder to make chocolate.

Activities

1. **TALK ABOUT IT** What other things can you tell about the Aztec culture by looking at Diego Rivera's mural? Describe what you see.

2. **CONNECT IT** What should be shown in a mural of your city or town? Write a description of what an artist might show in such a mural and explain why.

Peoples of the Northwest

VOCABULARY

surplus
potlatch
clan

Vocabulary Strategy

surplus

To remember that **surplus** means an extra amount, think of the **plus** sign from arithmetic.

READING SKILL
Main Idea and Details
What details support the first main idea in the lesson?

Build on What You Know Can you think of a material that you use in different ways? Plastic is one such material. It can be made into a bag or part of a computer or a drinking cup. In a similar way, the Northwest Indians found many uses for wood.

The Pacific Northwest

Main Idea American Indians of the Northwest coast learned to make use of the natural resources around them.

The Pacific Northwest is a coastal area that stretches from Alaska to northern California. The region is bordered by mountains to the east and ocean to the west. The coastline has thousands of islands and bays. Thick forests cover much of the land.

Several American Indian groups lived in this region when Europeans first came to North America. Many still live there today.

Pacific Northwest Warm winds coming off the ocean keep the climate rainy and mild.

The People and the Land

American Indians who lived in the Northwest around the year 1500 hunted and gathered everything they needed from the land and waters near them. Salmon from the rivers was an important resource.

In spring and summer, thousands of these fish filled the streams. During these months, the Indians caught so much **surplus,** or extra, salmon that they dried and ate it all year. Dried salmon was part of everyone's diet, but it was not their only food. Northwest Indians also ate shellfish, whales, and seals. In the forests, they gathered berries and fern roots and hunted geese, deer, elks, and bears.

Wood was another important resource for the Northwest peoples. They carved cedar logs into canoes called dugouts. Dugouts were used to carry goods on trading trips along the seacoast and rivers. Some groups paddled out to sea in dugouts to hunt for whales.

The Northwest Indians built large houses using boards cut from cedar or spruce trees. They decorated the houses with carvings and paint.

Skilled craftspeople also used cedar logs to make totem poles. Totem poles are tall poles that are carved and painted with human and animal figures. Northwest peoples often used totem poles to mark the entrance to their houses. The figures on a totem pole told the history of the families who lived there.

Families held potlatches to celebrate important events, such as a marriage or the building of a house. A **potlatch** was a large feast that could last for several days.

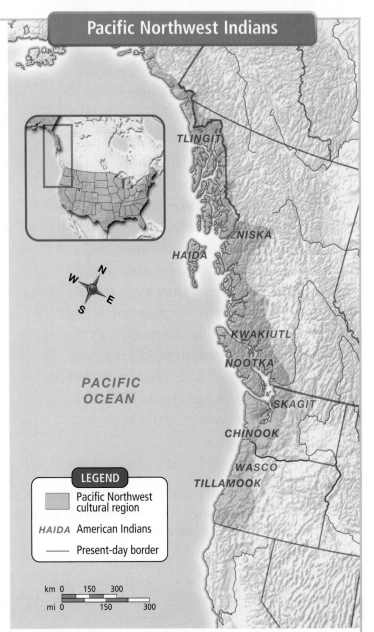

Pacific Northwest Indians

LEGEND
- Pacific Northwest cultural region
- *HAIDA* American Indians
- — Present-day border

TLINGIT
NISKA
HAIDA
KWAKIUTL
NOOTKA
SKAGIT
CHINOOK
WASCO
TILLAMOOK

PACIFIC OCEAN

km 0   150   300
mi 0   150   300

On the Coast The Pacific Northwest Indians settled in an area that was rich in natural resources.

SKILL **Reading Maps** Which American Indian group lived the farthest north in the Pacific Northwest region?

At a potlatch, the hosts served huge amounts of food and gave valuable gifts to the guests. At times, potlatches were like competitions. Families would try to give the largest and most expensive potlatch to show their wealth.

REVIEW Which two important resources helped the Northwest Indians live?

47

The Tlingit

Main Idea The Tlingit depended on the sea, rivers, and forests for their way of life.

The Tlingit (KLINK-it) were one of the largest American Indian groups in the Pacific Northwest. Their way of life was similar to that of other Northwest peoples. They built their villages near the coast or rivers to make hunting and trading easier. The Tlingit also found many uses for trees. They even made clothing from bark. Because the Tlingit did not farm or herd animals, they did not have cotton or wool. Instead, people used shredded cedar bark to make skirts, capes, and raincoats. They also made rain hats out of cedar bark and spruce roots.

Tlingit Clans

During the winter, the Tlingit wore fur and animal skins to keep warm and stayed indoors. They passed the time weaving, carving, painting, and sewing. People also gathered for dances, ceremonies, potlatches, and other feasts.

The Tlingit divided themselves into clans. A **clan** is a group of related families. The Tlingit had strict rules about how clans should treat one another. For example, a clan might pay a fine if one of its members insulted someone from another clan.

Several families from the same clan lived together. They put dividers in the houses so that each family had its own area. People gathered around a fire in the center of the house to cook and talk.

Trapping Salmon The Tlingit set up a wooden fence across the stream to stop the salmon. Fish that did not get speared were swept by the current into traps on either side.

The Tlingit Today

Today, about 17,000 Tlingit live in southeastern Alaska. Most live in cities, but some stay in villages. Many Tlingit have jobs fishing or working in the forests cutting wood. Others are business owners, teachers, doctors, and lawyers.

Tlingit Fishing Boat The Tlingit still fish the rivers and waters of the Alaskan coast.

The Tlingit carry on many cultural traditions. They have kept their dances, songs, and stories. Their clans are still strong, and people often wear clan or family symbols on their jewelry or clothes. The potlatch remains one of their most important traditions. It connects the modern Tlingit to their past.

REVIEW What role did clans have in Tlingit culture?

Lesson Summary

- Salmon and wood were two important resources for Northwest Indians.
- The potlatch is a giant feast given to celebrate important events.
- The Tlingit today have a modern way of life but keep many of their traditions.

Why It Matters ...

The Northwest Indians were the first to make use of the natural resources, such as wood, which are important to the Pacific Northwest today.

Lesson Review

1. **VOCABULARY** Choose the correct word to complete the sentence:

    potlatch   surplus   clan

    The Tlingit lived in large houses with members of their _____.

2. **READING SKILL** Which **details** explain how the Northwest Indians used salmon?

3. **MAIN IDEA: Economics** List three ways the Northwest Indians used wood.

4. **MAIN IDEA: Culture** What were totem poles used for and what did they look like?

5. **PLACES TO KNOW** In what state do many Tlingit live today?

6. **CRITICAL THINKING: Infer** How might the lives of Pacific Northwest Indians have been different if they had not had resources from the ocean?

WRITING ACTIVITY Use the information from this lesson to write a brief Table of Contents for the chapters of a nonfiction book on the Tlingit. Include chapters about their culture and the way they adapted to their environment.

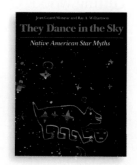

American Indians passed down what they learned about the world of nature through special stories called legends. Some stories gave human characteristics to objects in nature, such as stars and wind. The legend of Chinook Wind and Cold Wind was passed down from the Wasco people of the Northwest. The first paragraphs below tell about the wind along the Columbia River where the Wasco lived.

The grand Columbia River was a major passageway from the plateau region east of the Cascade Mountains to the Pacific Ocean, first for the Native Americans of the region and later for the white settlers who moved into the area. Living upriver of the long series of rapids and steep channels that cut through the Cascades, on a region of the river called the Dalles, the Wasco Indians and their neighbors on the north banks of the Columbia, the Wishram, established themselves as traders with the many visitors who passed their way each year. From the Plateau region came buffalo robes, dried roots, and camas bulbs. From the coast and along the Columbia came salmon, canoes, marine shells, and shell beads.

In the winter months, the wind brings with it the warmth of the Japanese current to the west, and it frees the snow-laden lower slopes of their winter burden. Because it comes from the direction of the Chinook tribe on the coast, the early traders called it the Chinook wind. The Cold Wind comes from the direction of Walla Walla to the east. The struggle between Cold Wind and Chinook Wind is a theme that appears in several Wasco stories.

As they looked up at the star pattern symbolizing the wrestling match during the nights when Cold Wind blew, the Wasco could take comfort that Chinook Wind would soon appear to overpower Cold Wind and unlock the ice-choked streams again. According to legend, this struggle began a long time ago when all stars were human beings.

Once there was an old grandfather who always caught many salmon in Big River. His grandson Chinook Wind was very proud of him. They always had plenty to eat and some to give away to more unfortunate fishermen's families. This began to change, however, when Chinook Wind left to visit relatives in a faraway camp. That was when Cold Wind decided he should take over.

Cold Wind wanted salmon too. But because he was lazy, he always came to Big River too late for good fishing. He would go down to the river to fish and see Chinook Wind's grandfather going home with plenty of salmon. Cold Wind usually caught nothing and this made him angry. He decided simply to take a salmon from Old Grandfather.

Of course, if he had been less impatient, he would not have had to steal the salmon. Old Grandfather was such a generous soul that he would gladly have given Cold Wind a share. But greedy people are seldom patient or courteous.

Every day, Cold Wind got up later and later. Every day he went down to fish too late to catch anything. Every day he stole a salmon from Old Grandfather. Oh, how bold he got!

One day, Chinook Wind returned from his journey. When he heard how Cold Wind had been taking salmon from Old Grandfather, he grew angry and decided to teach him a lesson.

Chinook Wind hid in Old Grandfather's tipi and waited patiently until he came home from fishing. That day Old Grandfather returned whistling merrily, for he had caught more fish than usual. Everyone in the village would feast that night.

As usual, Cold Wind came roaring up to the tipi demanding salmon. This time, however, Chinook Wind boldly stepped out. "You cannot take any more of my grandfather's salmon!" he exclaimed.

"You cannot stop me, you scrawny boy," said Cold Wind. "I will wrestle you for Old Grandfather's salmon."

All right," said Chinook Wind. "That is why I am come—to do whatever I have to do to protect the tribe and my grandfather."

And so the two wrestled. Chinook Wind fought hard and won the match. Because Chinook Wind won, Cold Wind can never again take salmon away from Old Grandfather. To this day, Chinook Wind is stronger than Cold Wind.

If you look closely at the sky, you can see Chinook Wind and his brothers in their canoe close to Old Grandfather's salmon. Cold Wind and his brothers are in a canoe far behind. Cold Wind can never get Old Grandfather's last salmon.

Activities

1. **THINK ABOUT IT** The story says "greedy people are seldom patient or courteous." Do you agree? Why or why not?

2. **WRITE ABOUT IT** What kind of weather is powerful where you live? Write a legend that explains why it is so powerful.

Peoples of the Southwest

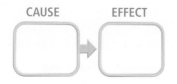
Build on What You Know Water is necessary for life. After all, two-thirds of the human body is made of water! In the Southwest, water is scarce. The American Indians who lived there learned to use water carefully.

The Southwest

Main Idea In different ways, the Southwest Indians solved the problem of having little water.

The Southwest is a region that includes all of present-day Arizona and New Mexico. It also stretches across sections of what are now Utah, Colorado, Nevada, Texas, southern California, and northern Mexico. Parts of the Rocky Mountains are in the Southwest.

A large part of the region is low, flat desert, but in places the desert rises to high plateaus. The land of the Southwest receives only a small amount of rain and is very dry. Most of the water in the area flows in rivers fed by melting snow in the mountains.

Canyons and Plateaus Thousands of years ago, rivers cut canyons through the high plateaus of the region.

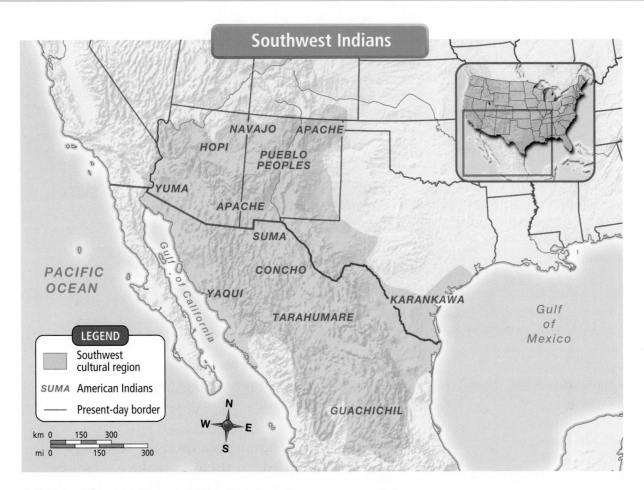

Southwest Indians

NAVAJO
APACHE
HOPI
PUEBLO PEOPLES
YUMA
APACHE
SUMA
PACIFIC OCEAN
CONCHO
YAQUI
KARANKAWA
Gulf of California
TARAHUMARE
Gulf of Mexico
GUACHICHIL

LEGEND
Southwest cultural region
SUMA American Indians
Present-day border

km 0   150   300
mi 0   150   300

N
W   E
S

A Dry Land The dry Southwest region spreads across parts of the United States and Mexico. **SKILL** **Reading Maps** The Hopi live in present-day Arizona. Which other Southwest Indians live in Arizona?

The People and the Land

Throughout history, the climate of the Southwest has influenced the way American Indians of the region lived. Much of the area was so dry that few trees grew there. To build their homes, Southwest Indians used sticks, stones, and a clay called adobe (uh DOH bee). They often built their homes on top of steep mesas to protect them from attack. Mesas are like small plateaus with steep sides and flat tops.

The climate of the Southwest affected life in another way. Many Southwest peoples were farmers. The lack of rain made agriculture difficult. They could never be sure that crops would survive.

Southwest Indians had to find ways to get water to their crops in order to have a successful harvest. Many used irrigation. **Irrigation** is a way of supplying water to crops with streams, ditches, or pipes. Some groups dug long, narrow ditches from the rivers to their fields. Water from the rivers flowed through the ditches to the crops.

Southwest Indians planted corn deep in the ground so that the roots of the plant could get moisture from the earth. They also planted crops in areas that flooded during the spring rains.

REVIEW Why was irrigation necessary for the Southwest Indians?

Hopi Pueblo The Hopi built their pueblos with many rooms and used ladders to connect the stories.

Image labels: Grinding Corn and Baking Bread, Making Pottery, Cooking, Weaving

The Hopi

Main Idea The Hopi found natural resources in a dry land.

The Hopi are among the oldest Indian groups in the Southwest. They began living in the northeastern part of present-day Arizona before 1350. They are one of several groups known as Pueblo Indians because of their large buildings. One of their villages is about a thousand years old.

Living in a Dry Land

The early Hopi used irrigation to grow beans, squash, and corn, their most important crop. Corn was the staple for the Hopi and part of every meal. A **staple** is a main crop that is used for food. The Hopi grew yellow, blue, red, white, and purple corn. They grew enough to last for the whole year and kept it in storage rooms in their pueblos.

Hopi people used the resources available to them to make containers to store their food and water. They dug clay and shaped it into large and small pots. The Hopi were some of the first people in the world to fire their pottery with coal. Firing pottery makes it strong and hard.

Religion was at the center of many Hopi customs. They believed that their creator had led them to the Southwest. The Hopi felt that they were meant to be caretakers of the land.

As caretakers, the Hopi tried to keep their land healthy. If the land was healthy, they would have good harvests and enough rainfall. For the Hopi, caretaking included prayer and a yearlong calendar of ceremonies. A **ceremony** is a special event at which people gather to express important beliefs. For example, at a ceremony called the Bean Dance, the Hopi danced and prayed for a good harvest.

Hopi Farmer
People still farm the Southwest. This Hopi farmer grows squash.

The Hopi Today

Modern-day Hopi still follow many of their cultural traditions. Most Hopi live in their villages in the Southwest and continue to take part in dances and ceremonies.

Many Hopi are skilled at making traditional pots, weavings, baskets, and silver jewelry. Others hold jobs in local companies, are teachers, or run their own businesses.

REVIEW What is the importance of the Bean Dance?

Lesson Summary

The Hopi and other American Indians built pueblos in the Southwest. They used irrigation and other methods to grow beans, squash, and corn in a dry climate. Hopi culture included religious ceremonies throughout the year. Many Hopi people today still take part in their cultural traditions.

Why It Matters ...

Lack of water is part of life in the Southwest, even today. The Southwest Indians showed how to adapt to this dry climate.

Lesson Review

❶ **VOCABULARY** Write a paragraph describing the way Southwest Indians used **irrigation.**

❷ **READING SKILL** What **effect** did the climate have on Hopi shelters?

❸ **MAIN IDEA: Technology** What were two methods the Southwest peoples used to water their crops?

❹ **MAIN IDEA: Culture** For what purpose did the Hopi make pots?

❺ **FACTS TO KNOW** What was the staple crop of the early Hopi Indians?

❻ **CRITICAL THINKING: Infer** Why did the Southwest Indians grow crops instead of relying on hunting and gathering?

SCIENCE ACTIVITY Southwest Indians had to think carefully about the water they used. Make a chart of the ways you use water in one week. Then, identify one or two ways you could use less water.

Keepers of Tradition

Many American Indians of the Southwest stay connected to their heritage. They want to keep alive the values and traditions of the past. Read about how a Laguna writer, a Navajo scientist, and a Hopi filmmaker share their traditions with others.

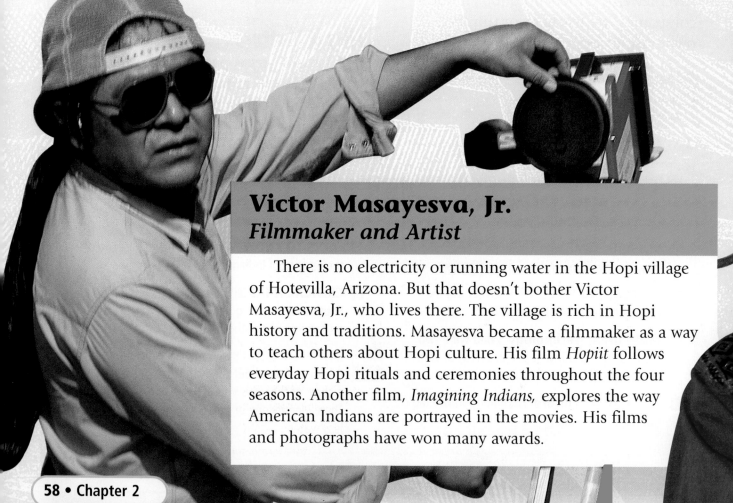

Victor Masayesva, Jr.
Filmmaker and Artist

There is no electricity or running water in the Hopi village of Hotevilla, Arizona. But that doesn't bother Victor Masayesva, Jr., who lives there. The village is rich in Hopi history and traditions. Masayesva became a filmmaker as a way to teach others about Hopi culture. His film *Hopiit* follows everyday Hopi rituals and ceremonies throughout the four seasons. Another film, *Imagining Indians,* explores the way American Indians are portrayed in the movies. His films and photographs have won many awards.

Fred Begay
Nuclear Physicist

Fred Begay believes that the Navajo traditions he learned as a boy helped prepare him for his career as a scientist. Begay's parents taught him Navajo prayers and songs that explain the origin of the natural world. As a young man, Begay trained to be a farmer, but after serving in the Army, he enrolled at the University of New Mexico and earned a degree in nuclear physics. Now he works at the Los Alamos National Laboratory and teaches science to middle school students on a Navajo reservation.

Leslie Marmon Silko
Writer

Author Leslie Marmon Silko was raised in the Laguna Pueblo in New Mexico. As a child, she spent many hours listening to her great-grandmother tell stories about the earth and sky. Silko planned to become a lawyer, but she felt an even stronger pull toward the Laguna tradition of storytelling. So she became a writer and teacher instead, publishing her first story in 1969. Silko says, "What I know is the Laguna. This place I am from is everything I am as a writer and a human being."

Activities

1. **TALK ABOUT IT** What questions would you like to ask each of these people about their traditions?

2. **SHOW IT** Research information about Southwest Indian traditions. Present the information in a bulletin board display.

 Technology Visit Education Place for more biographies. www.eduplace.com/kids/hmss05/

Peoples of the Plains

VOCABULARY

lodge
nomad
travois

Vocabulary Strategy

nomad

The word **nomad** comes from a word meaning "to wander in search of land." Nomads wandered the Great Plains in search of buffalo.

READING SKILL

Draw Conclusions Use details from the lesson to draw a conclusion about the importance of the buffalo to Plains Indians.

Conclusion

Build on What You Know When you see a large grassy field, do you think of it as empty? The Plains Indians lived on huge plains of grass that stretched for hundreds of miles in every direction. But those grasslands were far from empty.

The Great Plains

Main Idea American Indians lived as farmers and as migrating hunters on the Great Plains.

The Great Plains lie in the center of North America. The Plains stretch from the Mississippi River to the Rocky Mountains and from Texas into Canada. Much of the Plains used to be grassland. In the Eastern Plains, rainfall could cause the grasses to grow eight feet high. In the dry Western Plains, the grass was shorter. Although they might have seemed empty, the grasslands were a rich environment. American Indians have lived on the Plains for thousands of years. Over time they created two different ways of life from the two different environments where they lived.

The Great Plains Millions of buffalo used to roam over the Plains, eating the endless supply of grass.

Life on the Eastern Plains

Rainfall on the Eastern Plains made it possible for American Indians such as the Pawnee and the Omaha to farm successfully. They settled in villages near rivers and built earth lodges to live in. A **lodge** is a home that Plains Indians made using bark, earth, and grass. Lodges protected people from cold and stormy weather.

Each year, the Eastern Plains Indians spent spring and fall farming in their villages. Every summer and winter, they left their villages to hunt buffalo.

Life on the Western Plains

The dry land of the Western Plains made farming difficult. But the area had important resources, such as the buffalo. These huge woolly animals gave the Western Plains Indians everything they needed to live. Western Plains people ate buffalo meat. They carved the bones into tools and wove the hair into rope. They even turned the tail into a fly swatter! The buffalo skin had different uses. Plains people made it into covers for their shelters, blankets, clothing, drums, and shields. They decorated these everyday items with painted designs, porcupine quills, and other materials.

The Western Plains Indians were nomads who followed the buffalo herds. A **nomad** is a person who moves around and does not live in one place. These nomads used a travois (truh VOY) to carry their belongings. A **travois** was similar to a sled. It was made from two poles and usually pulled by a dog.

Plains Indians

BLACKFOOT OJIBWA
CROW MANDAN NAKOTA
LAKOTA DAKOTA
CHEYENNE
OMAHA IOWA
Great Salt Lake PAWNEE
KAW
KIOWA OSAGE
COMANCHE
TONKAWA
Gulf of Mexico
L. Superior
L. Michigan
Mississippi R.

LEGEND
- Plains cultural region
- *KAW* American Indians
- — Present-day border

N W E S

km 0 150 300
mi 0 150 300

Eastern and Western Plains In the vast area of the Plains, some American Indian groups controlled large sections of land.

Travois poles were also used to set up teepees. A teepee was a cone-shaped tent covered with buffalo skins. Teepees were easy to set up and take down.

Plains Indian groups could move between the Eastern and Western Plains. The Lakota, for example, used to farm the land along the Mississippi River on the Eastern Plains. Then they fought with another group, the Ojibwa (oh JEEB wah) and were forced to migrate to the Western Plains. There, they adapted to life in the west. They became nomads who used horses to hunt buffalo.

REVIEW In what ways were the lives of the Eastern and Western Plains Indians different?

Comanche Life This painting by artist George Catlin shows the Comanche scraping and stretching buffalo skins. **SKILL** **Reading Visuals** What kind of shelter did the Comanche live in?

The Comanche

Main Idea The Comanche Indians were skilled horse riders, hunters, and warriors.

Spanish explorers brought horses to North America in the 1500s. These animals changed the lives of the Plains Indians. By the mid-1700s, almost all the American Indians on the Great Plains had horses, which made it easier for the nomad groups to hunt and travel. Plains Indians valued horses so highly that wealth was measured by how many horses a person owned.

The Comanche (kuh MAN chee) Indians started riding and raising horses in the 1600s. They migrated from what is now Wyoming to the Great Plains. By the 1700s, they had spread across large parts of what are now Oklahoma and Texas, living as nomads. At times, the Comanche were at war with other American Indian groups.

The Comanche were fierce warriors on horseback. They could bend down and shoot an arrow from under a horse's chin, while riding at a full gallop.

The Comanche became one of the most powerful Plains groups, or nations. They owned more horses than any other American Indian nation and controlled a large area of the Plains. In the early 1800s, people called the Comanche "the lords of the Southern Plains" because of their wealth and strength.

Comanche Government

The Comanche had a system of government that fit their lives as nomads. They divided themselves into groups. Each group hunted and traveled freely. Members of the group chose leaders, called chiefs. They had different chiefs for war and for peace. At times, the chiefs of all the Comanche met to talk about and decide issues that affected the groups.

The Comanche Today

About 8,500 Comanche live in the United States today. Most of them live in Oklahoma, working as farmers or ranchers. Some work in the oil fields or cities of Oklahoma and Texas.

Though their way of life has changed greatly in the past 400 years, modern Comanche value their traditions.

Comanche Girl This Comanche girl is wearing traditional clothing at a pow-wow.

The Comanche still have their own government. Attending pow-wows, or dance gatherings, has been important in maintaining their culture.

REVIEW Why were horses important to Western Plains Indians?

Lesson Summary

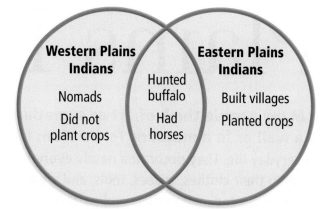

Western Plains Indians
Nomads
Did not plant crops

Hunted buffalo
Had horses

Eastern Plains Indians
Built villages
Planted crops

Why It Matters ...

Great Plains Indians, such as the Comanche, built some of the most powerful nations of all the American Indian groups.

Lesson Review

1. **VOCABULARY** Write a description of the life of the Western Plains Indians, using the words **travois** and **nomad.**

2. **READING SKILL** What did you **conclude** about the buffalo's importance? What details support it?

3. **MAIN IDEA: Geography** Why were the Eastern Plains Indians able to farm their land and live in villages?

4. **MAIN IDEA: Economics** Why was the horse so valuable to Western Plains Indians?

5. **CRITICAL THINKING: Summarize** What did the Comanche chiefs do as leaders?

6. **CRITICAL THINKING: Evaluate** Which animal was more important to the Western Plains Indians, the buffalo or the horse? Explain your answer.

HANDS ON

ART ACTIVITY Make a fact file on the life of Western Plains Indians. Illustrate their food, shelter, and way of traveling.

Art *of the* Plains Indians

Many people think of art as something that belongs on a wall or in a museum. For the Plains Indians, art was part of everyday life. They decorated nearly everything they made, including their clothes, tepees, tools, and weapons.

The Plains Indians' designs and patterns were inspired by the natural world—by plants, animals, the sky, and the land. These designs often had spiritual meaning for the Plains people, who expressed some of their most important ideas in their art.

Nakota Warrior's Shield
Plains Indian warriors rode into battle carrying shields made from thick buffalo hide. The shield was sturdy enough to protect a warrior from arrows or tomahawk blows.

Painted Designs
The owner of a shield believed its protection came from the painted designs, the eagle feathers, and blessings given the shield during a special ceremony.

Crow Warrior's Shirt

This shirt is made of buffalo skin. A shirt like this was usually sewn and decorated by a warrior's wife or mother. She might add locks of hair from family members, who believed that their prayers would protect the warrior.

Look Closely
Plains people decorated their clothing with tiny glass beads, which they sewed into patterns.

Activities

1. **DRAW IT** Make a picture of the images or symbols from the natural world you would want on your own shield.

2. **CONNECT IT** What kinds of special clothes do Americans wear today? When are these clothes worn? Write a short paper that answers these questions.

 Technology Visit Education Place for more primary sources. www.eduplace.com/kids/hmss05/

Skillbuilder
Summarize

► **VOCABULARY**

summary

A **summary** is a short description of the main points in a piece of writing. Knowing how to write a summary can help you to understand and remember the main ideas of what you read. The steps below will help you summarize this paragraph from Lesson 4.

> Western Plains people ate the buffalo meat. They made buffalo skin into tepee covers, blankets, clothing, drums, and shields. They carved the bones into tools and wove the hair into rope. They even turned the tail into a fly swatter!

Learn the Skill

Step 1: Identify the subject of the piece of writing. Write the subject in the top box of the diagram.

Step 2: Identify the main points of the piece of writing. Write each main point in a box.

Step 3: Use your own words to write a summary of the information. Combine the important ideas into one or two sentences.

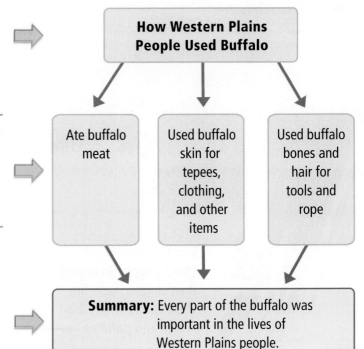

How Western Plains People Used Buffalo

- Ate buffalo meat
- Used buffalo skin for tepees, clothing, and other items
- Used buffalo bones and hair for tools and rope

Summary: Every part of the buffalo was important in the lives of Western Plains people.

Practice the Skill

Write a summary of the following paragraph. Make a diagram like the one on page 66 to help you identify the main points.

> The Lakota once lived along the Mississippi River. Fighting with the Ojibwa forced the Lakota to move west, onto the Great Plains. They met other American Indian nations already living there, such as the Cheyenne, Arapaho, and Crow. Later, settlers from the eastern United States arrived. Competition for land and resources increased. The Lakota felt they were being pushed off the land. They went to war against the settlers and other Plains Indians.

Apply the Skill

Read the four paragraphs on page 55 in Lesson 3 about how climate affected Southwest Indians. Fill out a diagram like the one on page 66. Then write a summary of the information.

Peoples of the East

VOCABULARY

longhouse
confederation
wampum
barter

Vocabulary Strategy

confederation

The prefix **con-** in **confederation** means "with." When groups join with one another, they form a confederation.

READING SKILL

Compare and Contrast
Note the ways that the Woodland Indians in the North and in the South were alike and different.

ALIKE	DIFFERENT

Build on What You Know When you team up with other people, you can do more than when you work alone. In this lesson, you will learn how five Eastern Woodland Indian nations decided to work together as a group.

The Eastern Woodlands

Main Idea Eastern Woodland Indians lived by farming, hunting, and gathering.

The eastern third of the United States is a large varied region. It has hills, mountains, plains, and valleys. Yet the whole area has one thing in common. It receives plenty of rain, enough to support a forest. This forest, known as the Eastern Woodlands, once stretched from the Atlantic Ocean to the Mississippi River, and from the Gulf of Mexico to the Great Lakes. Many different American Indian nations lived in these woodlands.

Eastern Woodlands The Woodlands are made up of different kinds of trees, such as cedar, oak, maple, pine, and birch.

The People and the Land

The natural resources of the Eastern Woodlands shaped the lives of the American Indians who lived there. The Woodland peoples hunted deer, bears, and rabbits for food. They also got food from the region's plants. In the north, they made syrup from the sap of maple trees. Near the Great Lakes, people gathered the wild rice that grew there. Unlike the Plains Indians, Woodland Indians did not rely on a single source of food, such as the buffalo, for their needs.

Farming and Building

Most Woodland Indians were farmers. They cleared fields in the forests by cutting down the larger trees and then burning the area. They planted crops between the tree stumps. Corn, beans, and squash were the staple for most groups and were known as "the three sisters."

Some Woodland Indians grew these three plants together. When the cornstalks grew, they supported the vines of the bean plants. The shade from the squash leaves kept the weeds from spreading.

Woodland Indians made different kinds of homes and clothing to fit the climate where they lived. In warm southern climates, people built houses without walls. These homes had just a roof for shade and protection from rain. People made light clothing, woven from grass and other materials, to wear in the hot weather.

Farther north, American Indians needed protection from the cold. They wore clothing made from deerskin.

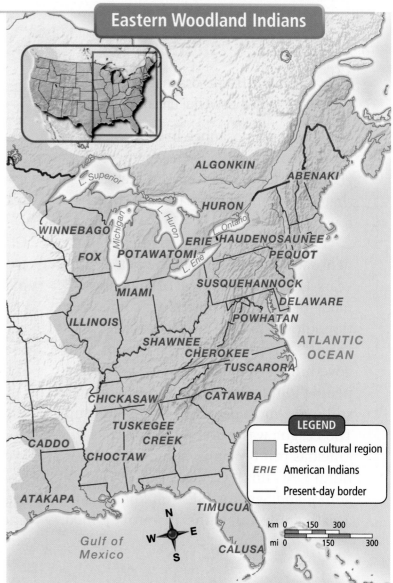

Eastern Woodland Indians

LEGEND

Eastern cultural region

ERIE American Indians

Present-day border

Land of Many Peoples The Great Lakes made traveling and trading easy for the Woodland Indians.

SKILL **Reading Maps** Which American Indians lived near the Great Lakes?

The Haudenosaunee (haw dah noh SAW nee), also known as the Iroquois (IHR uh kwoi), built longhouses for shelter. A **longhouse** was a large house made with wood poles and bark. Families lived in them and lit fires for cooking and warmth. These houses were so important to the Haudenosaunee that their name means "people of the longhouse."

REVIEW What were the three sisters?

The Haudenosaunee

Main Idea Five Haudenosaunee nations joined together to form a powerful union.

The Haudenosaunee lived in what is now New York State. There were several Haudenosaunee nations. Although they shared a common language, they often fought each other.

Fighting one another made the Haudenosaunee weak. Sometime between the years 1100 and 1600, five of the nations made peace. They joined in a confederation known as the Haudenosaunee League. A **confederation** is a type of government in which separate groups of people join together, but local leaders still make most decisions for their group. The League was a union of Mohawks, Oneidas (oh NY duhz), Onondagas (aw nuhn DAG uhz), Cayugas (ky YOO guhz), and Senecas (SEN uh kuhz). Later, a sixth group called the Tuscarora joined.

Hiawatha According to Haudenosaunee history, Hiawatha helped the five nations unite. The wampum belt (below) was made to celebrate the formation of the Haudenosaunee League.

Haudenosaunee Government

The League was governed by chiefs from each Haudenosaunee nation. The chiefs from each nation had a voice at League meetings. All five nations had to agree before the League would take any action. The chiefs talked together until they reached agreement.

The Haudenosaunee lived in clans. Clan mothers, who were the oldest women in the clan, played an important part in Haudenosaunee government. They chose the chiefs who led the nations. The clan mothers chose a chief for life, but they could replace him with someone else if he was not doing a good job.

Haudenosaunee Trading

The nations traded with other Woodland Indians. They sometimes used wampum to symbolize agreements. **Wampum** were pieces of carefully shaped and cut seashell. American Indians strung wampum like beads. The Haudenosaunee valued wampum highly and so did other Woodland Indians.

The Haudenosaunee bartered for goods. When people **barter,** they trade goods without using money. After Europeans arrived in the 1600s, the Haudenosaunee bartered fur for blankets and knives.

The Haudenosaunee Today

More than 50,000 Haudenosaunee live in North America. Some live in their homelands in New York and Canada. Many still follow their traditional customs and ceremonies.

More Haudenosaunee live in big cities and towns, however. They hold jobs in factory work, health care, and teaching. Mohawk ironworkers are famous for their skills in building skyscrapers. They helped build landmarks such as the Empire State Building and the Golden Gate Bridge.

REVIEW Why did the Haudenosaunee use wampum?

Lesson Summary

- The Eastern Woodlands was an area of forests and rich resources that spread across much of eastern North America.
- Most Eastern Woodland peoples used farming, hunting, and gathering to get food.
- The Mohawk, Oneida, Onondaga, Cayuga, and Seneca nations formed the Haudenosaunee League.
- The Haudenosaunee lived in longhouses and traded goods with other American Indian groups.

Why It Matters ...

The Haudenosaunee nations created a strong union when they stopped fighting each other and worked together.

Mohawk Ironworkers For more than 100 years, Mohawk ironworkers have built skyscrapers and bridges throughout the world.

Lesson Review

1 VOCABULARY Choose the correct words to complete the sentence.

    confederation   longhouses   wampum

The Haudenosaunee strung _____ to symbolize agreements, such as the formation of their

_____.

2 READING SKILL Contrast the differences in clothing for Woodland Indians in the North and in the South.

3 MAIN IDEA: History Why did Woodland Indians grow corn, beans, and squash together?

4 MAIN IDEA: Geography What did the Woodland Indians in the south do to adapt to a warm climate?

5 CRITICAL THINKING: Analyze What role did clan mothers play in Haudenosaunee government?

6 CRITICAL THINKING: Decision Making What were the effects of the Haudenosaunee groups' decision to form a confederation?

DRAMA ACTIVITY Prepare a skit in which two people barter food. What foods do they barter? Do they each end up getting what they want?

AMERICAN INDIAN SHELTERS

In a harsh climate, good shelter can mean survival. American Indians across the continent faced severe weather at times. Blizzards swept the Plains, hurricanes and rainstorms pounded the coasts, and long winters froze the Northeast.

In every region, American Indians built shelters for protection and comfort. Using local resources, they created homes that suited their needs and their environment.

Pacific Northwest

Type of Shelter
Large house

Materials Used
Boards cut from cedar trees

Unique Features
Totem poles were placed at entrances or used to support a roof. House heated by central open fireplaces.

Southwest

Type of Shelter
Pueblo

Materials Used
Stone and adobe bricks

Unique Features
Ladders connected several stories. Rooms heated by coal fires instead of wood.

Western Great Plains

Type of Shelter
Teepee

Materials Used
Buffalo skins and wooden poles

Unique Features
Easy to pack up and move. Flaps on teepee acted as vents to let out smoke or let in fresh air.

Northeastern Woodlands

Type of Shelter
Longhouse

Materials Used
Bark and wooden poles

Unique Features
Long enough to hold several families and keep several fires going.

Southeastern Woodlands

Type of Shelter
Roundhouse

Materials Used
Wooden poles covered with clay and bark

Unique Features
Used for dances and ceremonies. Sometimes used as shelter for the elderly.

Activities

1. **TALK ABOUT IT** In what ways were the shelters of American Indian groups the same? How were they different?

2. **RESEARCH IT** Research information about the shelters of a group of American Indians from the region where you live. Write and illustrate a one-page report.

Visual Summary

1–4. Write a description of how American Indians used the items pictured below: canoe, corn, buffalo skin, and longhouse.

Tlingit

_____
_____
_____
_____

Hopi

_____
_____
_____
_____

Comanche

_____
_____
_____
_____

Haudenosaunee

_____
_____
_____
_____

Facts and Main Ideas

✓ **TEST PREP** Answer each question with information from the chapter.

5. **Geography** What was Beringia, and where was it located?

6. **History** Name three ways the Hopi adapted to the dry climate of the Southwest.

7. **History** In what ways did horses change life for the Comanche?

8. **Economics** What is barter?

9. **Government** Who governed the Haudenosaunee League?

Vocabulary

✓ **TEST PREP** Choose the correct word to complete each sentence.

civilization, p. 40
staple, p. 56
lodge, p. 61
confederation, p. 70

10. The Haudenosaunee government was a _____.

11. Corn was a _____ for the Hopi and a part of every meal.

12. The Hopewell _____ was one of the first to create large villages in North America.

13. A Pawnee _____ was made of bark, earth, and grass.

| about 1100 Earliest Ancient Pueblo stone buildings | about 1300 Aztecs rule Central Mexico | 1700s Comanche control large part of Great Plains |

| 1100 | 1200 | 1300 | 1400 | 1500 | 1600 | 1700 |

TEST PREP

TEST PREP **Study Skill** Read the paragraph below. Then use what you have learned about summarizing to answer each question.

Totem poles are carved out of red cedar and painted in bright colors. They show images of human beings, birds, and animals. The images tell a story about the family or clan who had the pole made. Totem poles are sacred to Northwest Indian peoples because the poles represent a tie to their ancestors. Potlatches are held to celebrate the raising of a totem pole.

14. What is the subject of the paragraph?
   A. American Indian ancestors
   B. potlatches
   C. totem poles
   D. bird carvings

15. Which statement best summarizes the paragraph?
   A. Totem poles are important because they show images that tell family or clan stories.
   B. Being connected to ancestors is important to the Northwest Indian peoples.
   C. Totem poles are carved from red cedar.
   D. It takes a long time to carve the images on totem poles.

Critical Thinking

TEST PREP Write a short paragraph to answer each question.

16. **Cause and Effect** In what ways did agriculture change the lives of people in the Americas?

17. **Draw Conclusions** Were the Western Plains Indians or the Pacific Northwest Indians more dependent on one natural resource? Explain your answer.

Timeline

Use the Chapter Summary Timeline above to answer the question.

18. At what time did the Comanche control a large part of the Great Plains?

Activities

Speaking Activity Find an American Indian legend or folktale in your school or local library. Prepare a retelling of the story in your own words.

Writing Activity Write a description comparing a Mound Builder village with an Ancient Pueblo village.

Technology
Writing Process Tips
Get help with your description at
www.eduplace.com/kids/hmss05/

Vocabulary and Main Ideas

✔ **TEST PREP** Write a sentence to answer each question.

1. Why are **capital resources** and **human resources** important for producing goods and services?

2. In what way does **specialization** affect **trade?**

3. In what ways does **geography** influence where people live?

4. What is one theory about early **migration** to North America?

5. Why was a **surplus** of salmon important for the Northwest Indians' survival?

6. In what ways did the **climate** of the Southwest influence the way American Indians lived there?

Critical Thinking

✔ **TEST PREP** Write a short paragraph to answer each question.

7. **Infer** Silicon Valley and the Corn Belt are names for regions in the United States. What name would you give your region and why?

8. **Draw Conclusions** The Haudenosaunee made peace with each other and formed a confederation. Write a short paragraph giving a conclusion you might draw from their example.

Apply Skills

✔ **TEST PREP** Reading and Thinking Skill
Use the paragraph below to answer each question.

Agriculture changed the way people lived. The Paleo-Indians had to stay in one place to care for plants. Some people stopped migrating. With a steady supply of food, more families could survive. Populations grew. Over thousands of years, groups of Paleo-Indians farmed large areas and built villages and cities.

9. What is the subject of the paragraph?
   A. the migration of Paleo-Indians
   B. the villages and cities that Paleo-Indians built
   C. the way agriculture changed the lives of Paleo-Indians
   D. the methods Paleo-Indians used to raise crops

10. Which of the following statements best summarizes the paragraph?
    A. The Paleo-Indians ate different kinds of foods after they started farming.
    B. It took months to raise crops, so the Paleo-Indians did not migrate anymore.
    C. The population grew because farming provided a steady supply of food.
    D. Farming changed the way Paleo-Indians lived in many ways.

Unit Activity

Play a Place Card Game

- Choose a place in the United States that you have lived in, visited, or would like to visit.

- Write four fact cards about your place. Each card should identify the place and tell one fact about it.

- Mix up the cards. With a group of four, take turns picking a card from the pile.

- The first person to pick two cards about the same place wins.

At the Library

You may find these books at your library.

United States of America by Christine and David Petersen

This book gives an overview of United States geography, history, people, and culture.

The Wigwam and the Longhouse by Charlotte and David Yue

American Indian life in the East changed after European settlers arrived.

CURRENT EVENTS
WEEKLY READER

Connect to Today

Create a notebook about American Indians who are in the news today.

- Find articles about American Indians and issues affecting them today.

- Write or draw a short summary of each article.

- Place the articles and your summaries in a notebook for the class to share.

Technology

Get information about American Indians in the news from the Weekly Reader at **www.eduplace.com/kids/hmss05/**

Read About It

Look for these Social Studies Independent Books in your classroom.

UNIT 2

Exploration and Settlement

The Big Idea

Where would you like to explore?

"Gazing on such wonderful sights we did not know what to say."

A Spanish explorer, on arriving in the Aztec capital in 1519

Christopher Columbus
1451–1506

This explorer had a bold plan to sail west to Asia. Although he never reached his goal, his journeys to the Americas changed history for millions of people.
page 96

History Makers

Queen Isabella
1451–1504

Why did Queen Isabella take a chance on Columbus? She agreed to pay for his voyages because she thought they would bring power and wealth to Spain.

page 96

Moctezuma
1480?–1520

Moctezuma ruled the great Aztec empire in the 1500s. When Spanish explorers arrived in the Aztec capital, he welcomed them and treated them like honored guests.

page 105

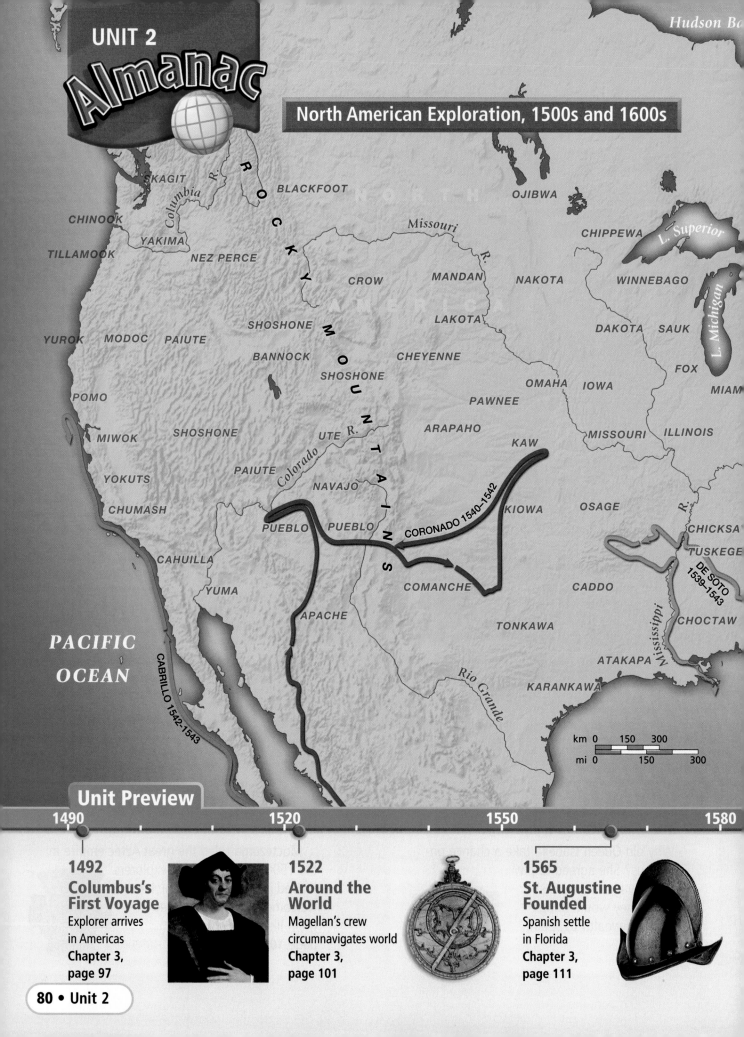

North American Exploration, 1500s and 1600s

Hudson Ba

SKAGIT
CHINOOK
TILLAMOOK
YAKIMA
BLACKFOOT
NEZ PERCE
Columbia R.
R O C K Y

N O R T H

Missouri

OJIBWA
CHIPPEWA
L. Superior

CROW
MANDAN
NAKOTA
WINNEBAGO
L. Michigan

A M E R I C A

YUROK
MODOC
PAIUTE
SHOSHONE
BANNOCK
SHOSHONE
LAKOTA
CHEYENNE
DAKOTA
SAUK
FOX
MIAM

POMO
MIWOK
SHOSHONE
UTE R.
ARAPAHO
PAWNEE
OMAHA
IOWA
MISSOURI
ILLINOIS

M O U N T A I N S

KAW
KIOWA
OSAGE
R.

YOKUTS
CHUMASH
PAIUTE
NAVAJO
PUEBLO
PUEBLO
Colorado
CORONADO 1540–1542
CHICKSA
TUSKEGE
DE SOTO
1539–1543

CAHUILLA
YUMA
APACHE
COMANCHE
CADDO
CHOCTAW

PACIFIC
OCEAN
CABRILLO 1542-1543
TONKAWA
ATAKAPA
KARANKAWA
Rio Grande
Mississippi

km 0   150   300
mi 0   150   300

1490   1520   1550   1580

1492
**Columbus's
First Voyage**
Explorer arrives
in Americas
**Chapter 3,
page 97**

1522
**Around the
World**
Magellan's crew
circumnavigates world
**Chapter 3,
page 101**

1565
**St. Augustine
Founded**
Spanish settle
in Florida
**Chapter 3,
page 111**

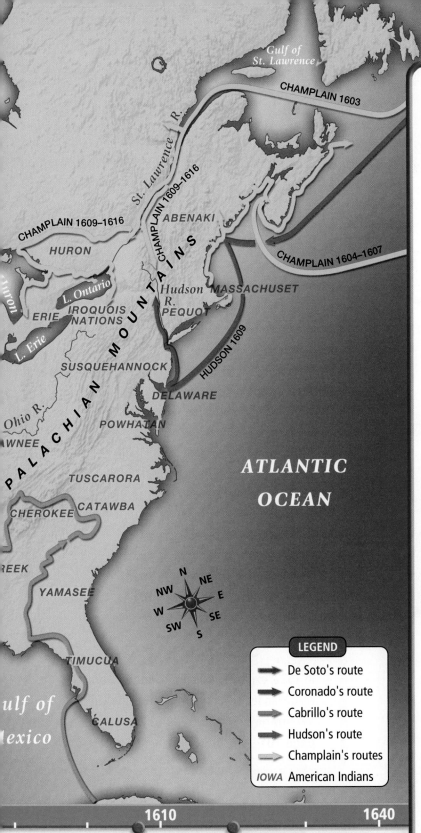

Gulf of
St. Lawrence

CHAMPLAIN 1603

St. Lawrence R.

CHAMPLAIN 1609–1616

CHAMPLAIN 1609–1616

ABENAKI

HURON

CHAMPLAIN 1604–1607

APPALACHIAN MOUNTAINS

L. Ontario

IROQUOIS
NATIONS

ERIE

L. Erie

Hudson
R.

MASSACHUSET

PEQUOT

SUSQUEHANNOCK

HUDSON 1609

DELAWARE

Ohio R.

POWHATAN

AWNEE

ATLANTIC
OCEAN

TUSCARORA

CATAWBA

CHEROKEE

REEK

N
NW NE
W E
SW SE
S

YAMASEE

TIMUCUA

ulf of
exico

CALUSA

LEGEND

De Soto's route
Coronado's route
Cabrillo's route
Hudson's route
Champlain's routes
IOWA American Indians

1610   1640

1607
**Jamestown
Founded**
First successful English
colony in Americas
**Chapter 4,
page 131**

1620
**Mayflower
Voyage**
Pilgrims land
at Plymouth
**Chapter 4,
page 137**

**Chapter 4,
page 131**

**Chapter 4,
page 137**

Connect to Today

Exploration in the 1500s

Explorer	Distance	Time
de Soto	3,000 mi.	3 yrs.
Coronado	2,500 mi.	2 yrs.

Exploration Today

Destination	Distance	Time
Moon	242,114 mi.	195 hrs.
Ocean Floor	4 mi.	3–4 hrs.

Why do explorers travel faster today?

CURRENT EVENTS
WEEKLY (WR) READER

Current events on the web!

Find out about current events that connect
with the Big Idea of this unit.
See Unit activities at:
www.eduplace.com/kids/hmss05/

Chapter **3** Age of Exploration

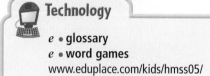

Technology

e • **glossary**
e • **word games**
www.eduplace.com/kids/hmss05/

Vocabulary Preview

navigation

In the 1400s, Europeans studied ways to improve **navigation.** They wanted to plan and control the direction in which they sailed on long voyages. **page 91**

circumnavigate

In 1522, explorers sailed around the world. Magellan led this first successful effort to **circumnavigate** the earth. **page 101**

Chapter Timeline

1271
Marco Polo goes to China

| 1270 | 1320 | 1370 | 1420 |

Reading Strategy

Monitor and Clarify Use this strategy to check your understanding of the events in this chapter.

Quick Tip If you are confused about events in a lesson, reread or read ahead.

expedition

Francisco Vazquez de Coronado led an **expedition** into present-day Arizona and New Mexico. He hoped to find wealth for Spain and for himself. **page 104**

colony

Spanish explorers took land in present-day Mexico for Spain. Settlers built towns and farmed in this **colony.**
page 112

1492		1540	
Columbus reaches West Indies		Coronado's explorations	

1470	1520	1570

World Travel and Trade

| 1200 | 1250 | 1300 | 1350 | 1400 | 1450 | 1500 |

1271–1465

Build on What You Know Have you ever traded one thing for something you wanted more? Hundreds of years ago, people made long journeys to trade the goods they had for other goods they wanted.

Trade with China

Main Idea Trade between Europe and Asia spread new ideas.

Before 1500, there were few connections between the Eastern and the Western hemispheres. Most Europeans, Africans, and Asians did not know that the Americas existed. The Vikings, a group of people from northern Europe, had sailed to what is now eastern Canada and started a settlement there. The settlement did not last, however, and other Europeans didn't follow them. Some historians believe that African or Asian sailors may have also traveled to the Americas, but if they did, few people learned of the journeys.

Marco Polo Travels to China

The travelers to distant places were often merchants. A **merchant** is someone who buys and sells goods to earn money. In 1271, three merchants from Venice, Italy, began a trading journey to China. One of them was **Marco Polo**. He was only about 17 years old when he left Italy with his father and uncle. The journey to China took three years.

Marco Polo stayed in China for 16 years. He worked for China's ruler, **Kublai Khan** (KOO bly KAHN). While traveling in China, Marco Polo saw many inventions, such as paper, printing, and gunpowder.

VOCABULARY

merchant
kingdom
caravan

Vocabulary Strategy

merchant

Trader is a synonym for **merchant**. To earn money, merchants trade goods that people want.

READING SKILL

Cause and Effect Note the effects that trade had on people in Europe, Asia, and Africa.

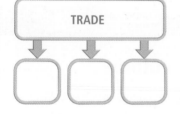

Traveling Merchants This illustration, made in the 1300s, shows Marco Polo and his family traveling by camel and horse on the Silk Road.

When Polo returned to Venice, he told about his travels in a book. His stories of China and the journey on the Silk Road fascinated Europeans. They became more interested in traveling to Asia.

The Silk Road was not one road, but several trade routes connecting China and Europe. Merchants traveled the routes to China to buy silk, spices, and other goods. The Chinese made silk, which is a very finely woven cloth. Wealthy Europeans were willing to pay high prices for silk. Merchants became rich by bringing goods from Asia to Europe on the Silk Road.

Chinese Sailors Explore

More than 100 years after Marco Polo visited China, the Chinese explored the world. The ruler of China wanted to impress other countries with China's power. He sent Admiral **Zheng He** (jung HUH) on a series of voyages. In 1405, Zheng He set sail with hundreds of ships and thousands of sailors. Some of the ships were longer than a football field.

Zheng He sailed throughout Southeast Asia and all the way to Africa's east coast. Zheng He traded goods, such as gold and silk, with the people he met. He once brought a giraffe from Africa back to China.

In 1434, a new ruler stopped Chinese exploration. He believed that China did not need to have contact with other countries. Zheng He's amazing voyages came to an end.

REVIEW What was the importance of the Silk Road?

Zheng He The Chinese explorer sits on one of his boats.

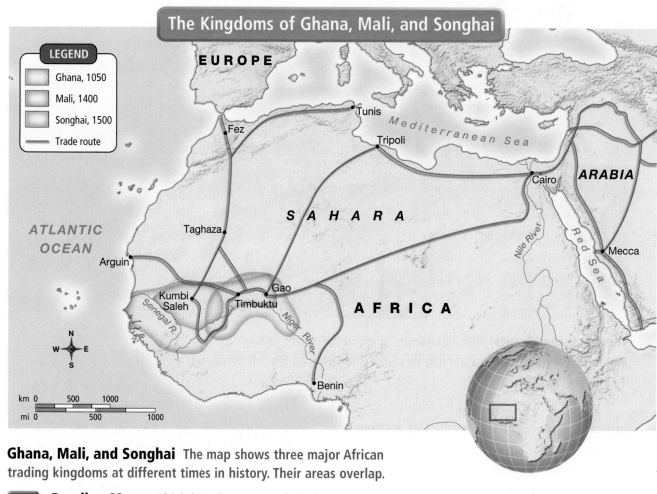

The Kingdoms of Ghana, Mali, and Songhai

LEGEND

Ghana, 1050
Mali, 1400
Songhai, 1500
Trade route

EUROPE

Mediterranean Sea

ARABIA

ATLANTIC OCEAN

SAHARA

AFRICA

Tunis
Fez
Tripoli
Cairo
Mecca
Taghaza
Arguin
Gao
Kumbi Saleh
Timbuktu
Benin

Senegal R.
Niger River
Nile River
Red Sea

N W E S

km 0 500 1000
mi 0 500 1000

Ghana, Mali, and Songhai The map shows three major African trading kingdoms at different times in history. Their areas overlap.

SKILL **Reading Maps** Which kingdom covered the largest area?

African Trading Kingdoms

Main Idea People in West Africa gained wealth and knowledge through trade.

Trade took place in Africa as well as in Europe and Asia. Several kingdoms in West Africa grew strong through trade. A **kingdom** is a place ruled by a king or queen.

The first West African trading kingdom was Ghana, which grew powerful in the 700s. Ghana was rich in gold, but did not have enough salt. Salt was used to keep food from spoiling. Merchants from Arabia brought salt to Ghana by crossing the Sahara, the largest desert in the world.

This desert crossing was dangerous. For safety, merchants traveled in large caravans, using camels to carry their goods and supplies. A **caravan** is a group of people and animals who travel together. After reaching Ghana, the Arab merchants traded their salt for gold.

Arab merchants taught people in Ghana about their religion, Islam. Many people in Ghana became Muslims, or followers of Islam.

In 1234, the nearby kingdom of Mali conquered Ghana. Mali's cities became new centers for trade. One of its largest and most important cities was Timbuktu (TIHM buhk TOO).

Mansa Musa

Mali's greatest king was the Muslim ruler, **Mansa Musa** (MAHN sah MOO sah). One person said that Mansa Musa was

> 66 the most powerful, the richest, the most fortunate, the most feared by his enemies, and the most able to do good to those around him. 99

In 1324, Mansa Musa traveled to Mecca, the most holy Muslim city in Arabia. He set up trade agreements with the cities he visited. When he returned to Mali, he brought scholars and artists from Arabia with him. They made Timbuktu a center for learning and art as well as trade.

Mali grew weaker after Mansa Musa's rule. A new kingdom called Songhai (SONG hy) took over much of Mali in 1468. For over one hundred years, Songhai continued the trade begun by the earlier kingdoms.

REVIEW What effect did trade with North Africa have on Ghana's culture?

Lesson Summary

Trade connected people in Europe, Asia, and Africa. Marco Polo, Zheng He, and Mansa Musa spread new ideas as well as goods. Their travels inspired others to explore even farther, seeking new trade routes and new knowledge.

Why It Matters . . .

Trade and travel brought the people of Asia, Europe, and Africa in contact with each other. Ideas and goods began to flow freely between them.

Mansa Musa
He brought hundreds of pounds of gold with him to Mecca to give away as gifts.

Lesson Review

1271 Marco Polo goes to China	1324 Mansa Musa visits Mecca	1405 Zheng He explores

1260 1290 1320 1350 1380 1410

❶ **VOCABULARY** choose the correct words to complete this sentence.

merchant   caravan   kingdom

A _____ traveled in a _____ for safety and protection.

❷ **READING SKILL** What **effect** did Mansa Musa's trip to Mecca have on Mali?

❸ **MAIN IDEA: Culture** What did Europeans learn from Marco Polo's trip to China?

❹ **MAIN IDEA: Economics** What did Ghana and Arabia trade with each other?

❺ **PEOPLE TO KNOW** Why do you think **Marco Polo** is remembered today?

❻ **TIMELINE SKILL** In what year did Mansa Musa visit Mecca?

❼ **CRITICAL THINKING: Synthesize** Explain how trade increased connections among Europe, Asia, and Africa.

✏️ **WRITING ACTIVITY** What were some of the reasons that people traded with each other in Marco Polo's time and Mansa Musa's time? Write two paragraphs explaining your answer.

Venice
Rome
EUROPE
Black Sea
Caspian Sea
Merv
Euphrates
Antioch
Mediterranean Sea
Tyre
Baghdad
Tigris R.
River
ASIA
AFRICA
ARABIA
Persian Gulf
Red Sea

LEGEND
— The Silk Road

N
W E
S

km 0   250   500
mi 0   250   500

Arabian Sea

The Silk Road

Eight hundred years ago, silk and spices from China traveled by caravan on the Silk Road. The Silk Road was a series of trade routes between Europe and Asia. Merchants traded goods, especially Chinese silks, in hopes of earning a profit. European traders often paid for silks with gold, because they had no goods the Chinese wanted.

The Silk Road was dangerous. It ran beside the hot, dry Taklamakan Desert and crossed high mountains. Merchants risked thirst, hunger, and attacks by bandits.

Kashi

TAKLAMAKAN
DESERT

Anxi

Huang He

Beijing

ASIA

Luoyang

CHINA

Indus River

Ganges River

HIMALAYAS

INDIA

Chang Jiang

Mekong River

South
China
Sea

Yo-Yo Ma and the Silk Road Project

Today, the Silk Road continues to inspire new discoveries. Yo-Yo Ma, a Chinese American cellist, directs the Silk Road Project. The project builds cultural understanding by performing the music that is still played along the Silk Road. He says, "We live in a world where we can no longer afford not to know our neighbors. The Silk Road Project is a musical way to get to know our neighbors."

Activities

1. **LOCATE IT** Look closely at the map. Trace a route from Beijing to Antioch. Find the distance in miles and kilometers between the two cities.

2. **WRITE IT** Write a dialogue between two merchants who have just arrived in Rome. Have them describe where they traveled on the Silk Road.

New Ideas in Europe

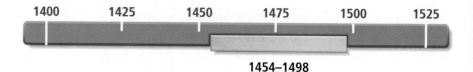

| 1400 | 1425 | 1450 | 1475 | 1500 | 1525 |

1454–1498

Build on What You Know Are there any recent inventions that are important in your life? How do you use them? Europeans in the 1400s used new inventions to find sea routes to Asia.

The Renaissance

Main Idea New learning spread through Europe, leading to better tools for sailors and explorers.

Important changes took place in Europe during the 1300s and 1400s. This period of time was called the Renaissance (REN nuh sahnce), which means rebirth. The Renaissance was a rebirth in learning and knowledge. Europeans took new interest in the writing, art, science, and ideas of the ancient Greeks and Romans. They also learned from people in Africa and Asia.

During the Renaissance, technology in Europe changed. **Technology** is the use of scientific knowledge and tools to do things better and more rapidly. The printing press was an example of new technology. Developed in 1454 by **Johannes Gutenberg,** the printing press made it possible to print many copies of a page of type quickly. Before the printing press, people had to copy books by hand. The printing press allowed books and ideas to spread across Europe.

Printing Press Books were printed by pressing one page at a time.

VOCABULARY

technology
navigation
astrolabe
profit
slavery

Vocabulary Strategy

navigation

To remember **navigation,** think of the word "navy." A navy uses navigation to know where to sail.

READING SKILL
Problem and Solution
Portuguese explorers faced a problem in trying to get to Asia. Find their solution.

PROBLEM	SOLUTION

Sea Exploration New technologies helped European explorers travel farther than ever before. Find the sailor who is using an astrolabe.

New Knowledge for Sailors

New technology also helped European exploration by making navigation easier and more accurate. **Navigation** is the science of planning and controlling the direction of a ship.

Europeans learned about a navigation tool called the astrolabe from North Africans. An **astrolabe** is a tool that measures the height of the sun or a star above the horizon. Using an astrolabe, sailors could tell how far north or south of home they were.

European sailors learned about the compass from the Chinese. A compass is an instrument with a magnetic needle that always points to the north.

Chinese sailors did not have to depend on the sun or the stars to tell them which direction they were traveling. They could use a compass to check whether they were heading north, south, east, or west.

Another Chinese invention that helped European sailors was gunpowder. Sailors used gunpowder in weapons such as guns and cannons. Cannons defended their ships. Guns gave sailors confidence that they could protect themselves if they were attacked or in danger on land.

REVIEW What did new technology do to make exploration easier?

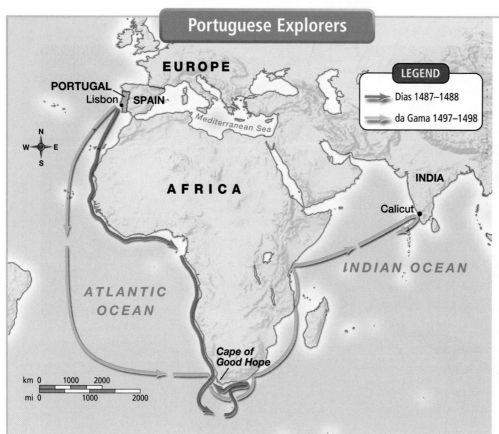

EUROPE

PORTUGAL
Lisbon SPAIN

Mediterranean Sea

AFRICA

INDIA

Calicut

INDIAN OCEAN

ATLANTIC
OCEAN

*Cape of
Good Hope*

km 0   1000   2000
mi 0   1000   2000

N
W   E
S

LEGEND
Dias 1487–1488
da Gama 1497–1498

A New Route to Asia
Vasco da Gama (above)
used the knowledge
gained by Bartolomeu Dias.

SKILL **Reading Maps**
Which explorer sailed the
farthest?

A Sea Route to Asia

Main Idea Portuguese explorers were the
first Europeans to find a sea route to Asia.

Merchants believed that they would
make more money if they found a sea
route to Asia. In Asia, merchants bought
spices such as pepper, and earned a profit
by selling them for a higher price in
Europe. A **profit** is the money a business
has left over after all of its expenses have
been paid.

A sea route to Asia was thousands of
miles longer than the Silk Road, but the
sea trip would be faster. The country that
found a sea route to Asia could trade more
goods than countries that used the slow-
moving caravans of the Silk Road.

Portugal was the first European
country to find a sea route to Asia.
Portugal is a small European country.

Portugal's location and coastline
made it a good starting place for sailors.
The Portuguese thought they could reach
Asia by sailing around the southern tip of
Africa. From there, they hoped to sail up
Africa's east coast and find a route to
India and China.

Prince Henry of Portugal created a
school for navigation. He brought
shipbuilders, mapmakers, and sea captains
to Sagres (SAH grehsh), Portugal. They
shared their knowledge of navigation and
sailing. People at Sagres improved sailing
technology by creating the caravel. This
small, light ship had triangular sails.
Caravels were good for exploring. They
could sail into the wind, unlike other
European ships. Because he encouraged
exploration, Prince Henry became known
as "the Navigator," even though he didn't
go on any voyages.

Dias and da Gama

Portuguese sailors' early voyages went south along Africa's west coast. In 1448, Portugal set up a trading post in West Africa. Portuguese traders forced Africans there into slavery and sold them in Europe. **Slavery** is a cruel system in which people are bought and sold and made to work without pay. Slavery had existed before the Portuguese arrived, but the Portuguese increased the number of enslaved people brought to Europe.

In 1487, **Bartolomeu Dias** (bart OH lo MEH oo DEE ahs) was exploring the coast of West Africa when a fierce storm blew his ships off course. When the storm ended, Dias realized he had actually sailed around the southern tip of Africa. The Portuguese named the tip of Africa the Cape of Good Hope. Dias proved that it was possible to sail around Africa and reach its east coast. From Africa's east coast, ships could then sail east to India.

Vasco da Gama led the first Portuguese voyage to reach India. In 1497, his fleet reached the Indian port of Calicut. Other Portuguese sailors soon followed da Gama's route to India and used it for spice trading.

REVIEW Why was sailing around the Cape of Good Hope important?

Lesson Summary

During the Renaissance, Europeans used new navigation tools. This technology helped them find faster ways to trade goods with Asia. Portuguese sailors, such as Vasco da Gama, sailed around Africa to reach Asia.

Why It Matters . . .

The search for a sea route to Asia led to important discoveries in navigation and geography.

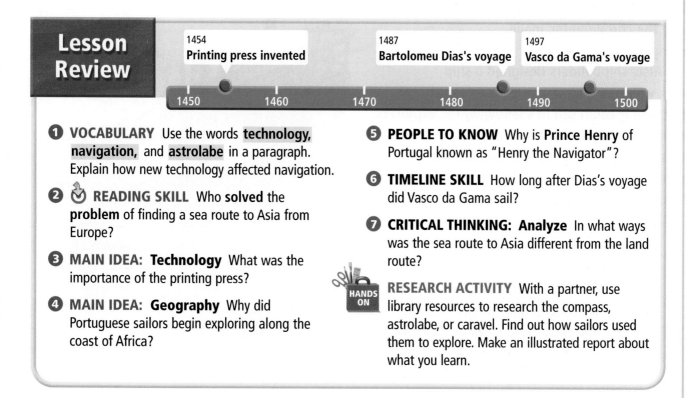

Lesson Review

1454	1487	1497
Printing press invented	**Bartolomeu Dias's voyage**	**Vasco da Gama's voyage**

1450   1460   1470   1480   1490   1500

❶ **VOCABULARY** Use the words **technology, navigation,** and **astrolabe** in a paragraph. Explain how new technology affected navigation.

❷ **READING SKILL** Who **solved** the **problem** of finding a sea route to Asia from Europe?

❸ **MAIN IDEA: Technology** What was the importance of the printing press?

❹ **MAIN IDEA: Geography** Why did Portuguese sailors begin exploring along the coast of Africa?

❺ **PEOPLE TO KNOW** Why is **Prince Henry** of Portugal known as "Henry the Navigator"?

❻ **TIMELINE SKILL** How long after Dias's voyage did Vasco da Gama sail?

❼ **CRITICAL THINKING: Analyze** In what ways was the sea route to Asia different from the land route?

RESEARCH ACTIVITY With a partner, use library resources to research the compass, astrolabe, or caravel. Find out how sailors used them to explore. Make an illustrated report about what you learn.

HANDS ON

Tools for Discovery

In 1420, the oceans of the world were a mystery to most Europeans. Sailors told stories of monsters and boiling seas. Portuguese explorers soon showed that those stories were false. They used new inventions and new ship designs and traveled farther than before.

Ship captains sailed with the latest maps and with new navigations tools, including the compass and astrolabe. Later inventions, such as the sextant and the chronometer, made navigation even better.

Also, shipbuilders designed a ship that was small, light, and easy to control. Because it could sail in shallow water, explorers could travel near coastlines and up rivers. Improvements also made it possible for explorers to sail over long distances. This ship, the *Santa Maria*, could cross the Atlantic Ocean.

Crew

Most of the space on a ship was used for equipment and supplies. In good weather, the crew could sleep on the deck, but if the weather was bad they slept in the storage rooms.

TECHNOLOGY

Sails
The sails hanging straight down helped this ship move quickly. The sail in the back hung at an angle, helping the ship sail against the wind.

Astrolabe
The astrolabe was an Arab invention. It measured the angle of the sun or a star above the horizon. Sailors could use this information to find out how far north or south they were.

Compass
European sailors used this ancient Chinese invention to find their direction. Its magnetic needle always points north.

maris stella

Activities

1. **TALK ABOUT IT** Voyages of exploration often lasted longer than a year. Sailors had to plan very carefully. What would you bring if you were going to be at sea for a year?

2. **PRESENT IT** Tools for navigation were important for explorers. Choose one of these tools, such as the astrolabe or the compass. Prepare a short presentation on how the tool was invented and how it works.

95

Europeans Arrive in the Americas

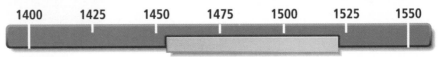

1400	1425	1450	1475	1500	1525	1550

1451–1522

Build on What You Know Many people today like spicy food. In the 1400s, European countries had very few spices. Europeans traveled far to bring spices and other riches back to Europe from distant lands.

Christopher Columbus

Main Idea Christopher Columbus sailed to the islands of the West Indies trying to reach Asia.

Christopher Columbus was born in 1451 near Genoa, in Italy. Columbus studied navigation and believed he could reach Asia by a new route. He wanted to sail west across the Atlantic Ocean, instead of south around Africa. He did not know that North and South America were between Europe and Asia.

In 1486, Columbus asked **King Ferdinand** and **Queen Isabella** of Spain to pay for a westward voyage to Asia. Ferdinand and Isabella didn't have money for exploration at that time. They were fighting to take back southern Spain from North African Muslims, who had ruled the region for 700 years. Spain's attempt to push the Muslims out was called the Spanish Reconquista (reh con KEY sta).

Christopher Columbus This explorer wanted to find a new route to India.

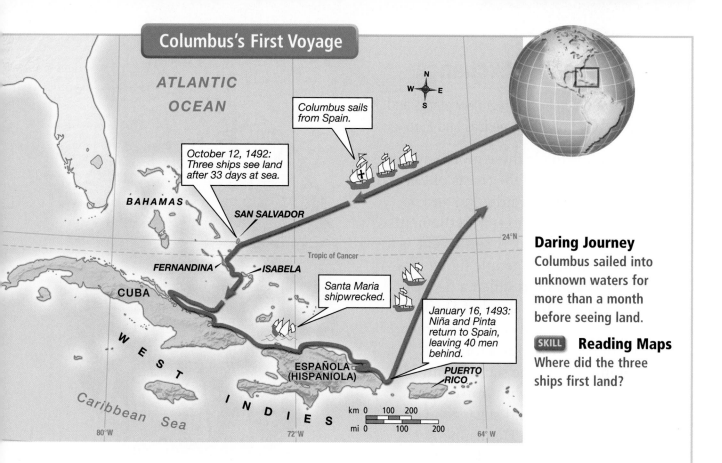

Columbus's First Voyage

ATLANTIC OCEAN

Columbus sails from Spain.

October 12, 1492: Three ships see land after 33 days at sea.

BAHAMAS

SAN SALVADOR

FERNANDINA

ISABELA

Tropic of Cancer

CUBA

Santa Maria shipwrecked.

January 16, 1493: Niña and Pinta return to Spain, leaving 40 men behind.

W E S T   I N D I E S

ESPAÑOLA (HISPANIOLA)

PUERTO RICO

Caribbean Sea

24°N

80°W   72°W   64°W

km 0   100   200
mi 0   100   200

Daring Journey
Columbus sailed into unknown waters for more than a month before seeing land.

SKILL **Reading Maps**
Where did the three ships first land?

Columbus Sails West

Six years later, in 1492, Columbus again asked Ferdinand and Isabella for money. This time they agreed. Spain had won the Reconquista and needed to pay for it. Ferdinand and Isabella hoped to make money from the gold and spices they believed Columbus would find in Asia. They also wanted to teach others about their religion, Roman Catholicism.

Columbus set sail from Palos, Spain, on August 3, 1492. He carried enough supplies for a year. Close to 90 men traveled in three ships named the Niña, the Pinta, and the Santa María. The sailors did not know how long the trip would take or where they would land. Shortly after midnight on October 12, 1492, a sailor aboard the Pinta saw land.

The ships had arrived at an island in the Caribbean Sea that Columbus named San Salvador. This island is part of the present-day Bahamas, east of Mexico.

Columbus mistakenly believed he had reached land off the coast of Asia, near India. He named the islands the West Indies and the people living on them Indians.

The sailors on this expedition were the first Europeans to meet people of the Caribbean. These people called themselves the Taíno (TY noh), which means "good." The Taíno were peaceful and fought only to defend their villages from attacks. More than 600,000 Taíno lived in the Caribbean at the time of Columbus's visit.

After meeting the Taíno and trading with them, Columbus sailed on with his crew. They visited two other large islands, Cuba and Hispaniola, before returning home.

REVIEW Why did Ferdinand and Isabella finally agree to give Columbus money for his voyage in 1492?

The Columbian Exchange

Main Idea Columbus carried new plants and animals to and from the Americas and Europe.

Columbus made three more voyages to the Caribbean and the coasts of Central and South America. Ferdinand and Isabella wanted him to start settlements and to search for gold. A **settlement** is a small community of people living in a new place. Columbus sailed a fleet of 17 ships back to the island of Hispaniola. He also explored and claimed more islands in the West Indies for Spain.

Columbus and the settlers with him brought ships filled with horses, cows, pigs, wheat, barley, and sugar cane plants to the Western Hemisphere. These animals and plants did not live in the Americas before Columbus brought them there. Some European crops were able to grow in places where local crops could not.

The arrival of Europeans in the West Indies had many harmful effects. Europeans cut down rain forests on Caribbean islands and built sugar plantations. Many American plants and animals were destroyed. The Europeans also brought diseases that the Taíno had never had before. Many Taíno died from epidemics. An **epidemic** is an outbreak of disease that spreads quickly and affects many people. Within 50 years of Columbus's arrival, almost no Taíno people were left.

Columbus returned to Spain with plants no one in Europe had seen. These included maize (corn), peanuts, potatoes, tomatoes, cacao (chocolate), and certain peppers, beans, and squashes.

Columbus Lands This woodcut from the 1500s shows Columbus meeting the Taíno people in the Caribbean.

This movement of plants, animals, and people between the Eastern and Western Hemispheres is known as the Columbian Exchange.

The Columbian Exchange benefited people all over the world. Potatoes from the Americas became an important food for most Europeans. Corn became an important crop in Africa. Sweet potatoes were grown as far away as China. Today, tomatoes, peanuts, and American beans and peppers are grown in many lands.

REVIEW How did the Columbian Exchange change the diet of Europeans?

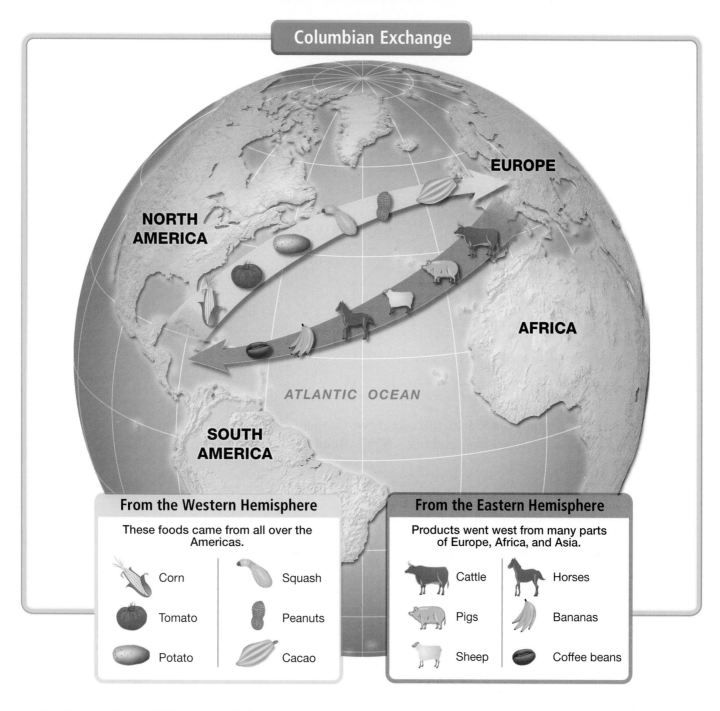

Columbian Exchange

EUROPE

NORTH AMERICA

AFRICA

ATLANTIC OCEAN

SOUTH AMERICA

From the Western Hemisphere

These foods came from all over the Americas.

Corn		Squash
Tomato		Peanuts
Potato		Cacao

From the Eastern Hemisphere

Products went west from many parts of Europe, Africa, and Asia.

Cattle		Horses
Pigs		Bananas
Sheep		Coffee beans

Mustangs These wild horses, called mustangs, were brought to the Americas by Spanish explorers.

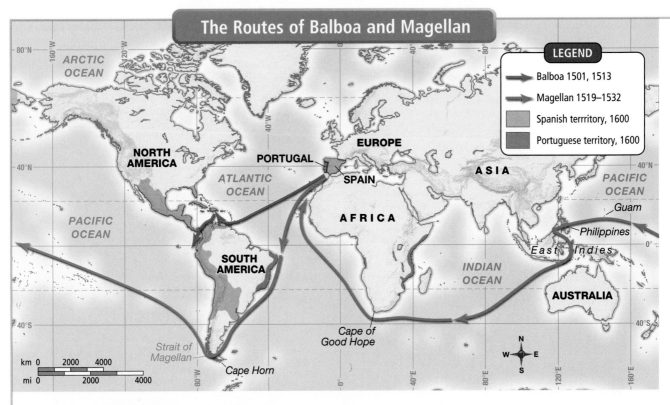

The Routes of Balboa and Magellan

ARCTIC OCEAN

NORTH AMERICA

ATLANTIC OCEAN

PACIFIC OCEAN

EUROPE

PORTUGAL

SPAIN

ASIA

PACIFIC OCEAN

AFRICA

SOUTH AMERICA

INDIAN OCEAN

Guam

Philippines

East Indies

AUSTRALIA

Cape of Good Hope

Strait of Magellan

Cape Horn

LEGEND

Balboa 1501, 1513

Magellan 1519–1532

Spanish terrritory, 1600

Portuguese territory, 1600

km 0   2000   4000
mi 0   2000   4000

N W E S

Magellan Sails Around the World This map shows the route of Magellan and his crew during the first round-the-world trip. **SKILL** **Reading Maps** How long did Magellan's voyage take?

Exploration Continues

Main Idea Explorers continued to sail to the Americas to search for new routes to Asia.

Word of Columbus's voyage spread throughout Europe. European rulers soon sent their own explorers to the Americas.

Pedro Alvarez Cabral (ka BRAHL) explored eastern South America in 1500 and claimed it for Portugal. An Italian named **Amerigo Vespucci** (vehs POO chee) made several voyages to South America and the Caribbean. A Spanish explorer, **Vasco Núñez de Balboa**, (VAS coh NOON yez deh bal BOH ah) sailed to present-day Panama in Central America. In 1513, he crossed the mountains and jungles of Panama and reached the Pacific Ocean.

Magellan

Ferdinand Magellan was a Portuguese soldier and sailor who sailed for Spain. Magellan had a daring idea. He believed that he could sail west, go around South America, cross the Pacific Ocean, and end up back in Spain.

Magellan left Spain in September 1519, with five ships and about 250 men. They crossed the Atlantic Ocean and arrived on the coast of present-day Brazil, where the crew waited for winter to pass. Magellan then sailed south down the east coast of South America. In November 1520, his ships entered the Pacific Ocean. He named it Pacific, which means "peaceful," because it looked so calm. Magellan and his crew had no idea how large the Pacific was.

Ferdinand Magellan
His voyage proved people could sail around the world.

Sailing west, Magellan and his crew did not see land for more than three months. Many sailors died of disease and starvation along the way. When they reached the Philippine Islands off the coast of Asia, Magellan was killed in a battle with people on the islands.

Only one ship of the original five survived the trip. It arrived back in Spain in September 1522. It was loaded with valuable spices. Of the 250 men who began the journey, about 18 remained. Magellan's crew became the first explorers to circumnavigate the world.

To **circumnavigate** is to sail completely around something. Although Magellan did not survive the voyage, he proved that Columbus's theory about sailing west to Asia was correct.

REVIEW Who named the Pacific Ocean and why?

Lesson Summary

> Columbus first landed in the Caribbean in 1492.

> Other explorers, including Vespucci and Balboa, traveled to the Americas.

> Magellan's crew was the first to circumnavigate the world.

Why It Matters...

The search for a route to Asia gave Europeans new knowledge of the world's size and geography.

Lesson Review

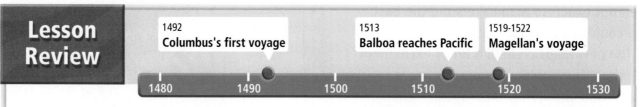

1492
Columbus's first voyage

1513
Balboa reaches Pacific

1519-1522
Magellan's voyage

1480   1490   1500   1510   1520   1530

❶ **VOCABULARY** Use the words **settlement** and **epidemic** in a paragraph about the Columbian Exchange.

❷ **READING SKILL** What qualities do you think the explorers probably had in common?

❸ **MAIN IDEA: Geography** What kinds of food went from the Americas to Europe?

❹ **MAIN IDEA: History** What was Magellan's goal? Did he succeed? Why or why not?

❺ **PEOPLE TO KNOW** Who was **Christopher Columbus**, and what did he think was the best way to sail to Asia?

❻ **TIMELINE SKILL** In what year did the first European see the Pacific Ocean?

❼ **CRITICAL THINKING: Evaluate** What were the effects of Columbus's journeys in Europe and the Americas?

➤ **WRITING ACTIVITY** Using what you have learned in this lesson, write an entry for a ship's log, or diary, summarizing Magellan's journey.

Mapping New Lands

European explorers faced an interesting problem: There were no maps to show the new land they had seen. In the 1500s, new maps had to be created to show people's expanding understanding of the world.

Early world maps look very different from today's maps. Whole continents are missing because Europeans didn't know about them yet. The land and oceans are the wrong size or oddly shaped. The locations and distances recorded by explorers on their voyages were often not exact, so mapmakers did the best they could with the information they had.

The new maps created a lot of excitement in Europe. They sparked interest in more exploration and changed Europeans' picture of the world.

New View of the World

In 1507, Martin Waldseemüller (VAHLT zay mool uhr) published the first map to use the word "America." It was also the first map to show North and South America as continents separate from Asia.

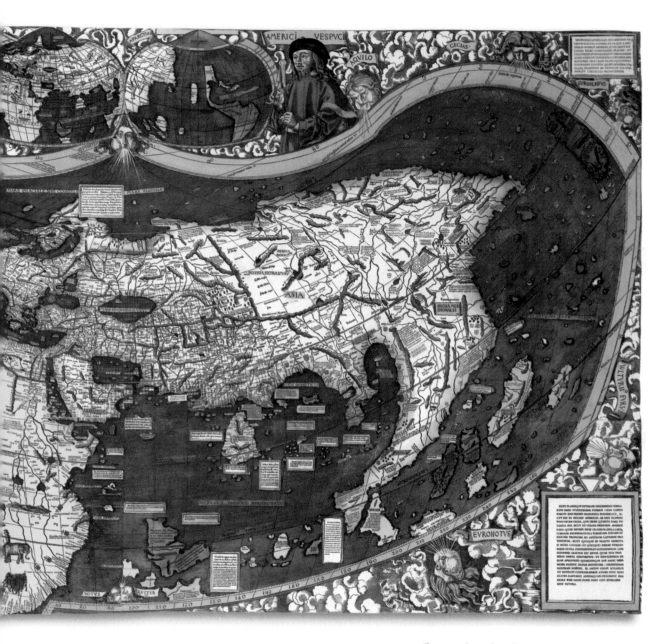

Amerigo Vespucci (1454–1512)

Vespucci is shown above on the border of the map. He realized that he and Columbus had not reached Asia but a continent unknown to Europeans. The land was named America, after Amerigo's first name.

Activities

1. **CONNECT TO TODAY** Compare this map with a modern world map. What parts of the old map do you recognize? What parts of the world are hard to recognize? Discuss the reasons for the differences.

2. **MAP IT** Make a map of your school playground or classroom. Discuss how to measure distances. Use your measurements to draw a map on graph paper.

Conquest of the Americas

VOCABULARY

expedition
conquistador
empire

Vocabulary Strategy

expedition

The word **expedition** begins with the prefix **ex-**, meaning "out." An expedition goes out to explore.

READING SKILL

Compare and Contrast
Contrast what Spanish explorers were looking for with what they found.

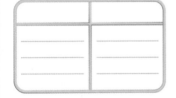

Build on What You Know Many books and movies today tell stories about people traveling to other worlds. In 1519, when the Spanish and the Aztecs first met, it was like a meeting of people from two different worlds.

Cortés Conquers the Aztecs

Main Idea Spanish soldiers conquered the Aztecs in present-day Mexico.

The travels of **Columbus** and **Balboa** were exciting news in Europe. Sending ships and soldiers across an ocean was expensive, but Spain's rulers believed the explorers would bring back gold.

One of these explorers was **Hernán Cortés** (er NAN kohr TEHS). In 1519, Cortés led an expedition to Mexico. An **expedition** is a journey to achieve a goal. Cortés' ships carried horses, weapons, and an army of 600 conquistadors (kohn KEY stah doors). **Conquistador** is Spanish for conqueror. The conquistadors were eager to find wealth and fame for themselves and their families.

Cortés had heard stories about the Aztec Indians in present-day Mexico. The Aztecs had built an empire by conquering other Indian nations. An **empire** is many nations or territories ruled by a single group or leader.

Aztec Sun Stone
The Aztec civilization had its own calendar. This carved stone is 13 feet across.

Cortés and Moctezuma A Spanish artist in the 1500s made this drawing of Cortés and Moctezuma at the gates of Tenochtitlán.

After landing in Mexico, Cortés met people who were enemies of the Aztec empire. Cortés convinced them to come with him to defeat the Aztecs. An Indian woman named **Malinche** (Mah LEEN chay) joined Cortés. She helped him to communicate with the Aztecs and gave advice about how to conquer them.

When the conquistadors arrived at the Aztec capital Tenochtitlán (tay nohch tee TLAHN), they were amazed by its size and beauty. One conquistador wrote,

66 Indeed, some of our soldiers asked whether it was not all a dream. 99

Tenochtitlán was twice as big as any European city and was built in the middle of a large lake. Long causeways, or land bridges, stretched across the lake to the city.

At first, the Aztec ruler **Moctezuma** welcomed Cortés, but the conquistador's greed for gold soon angered the Aztecs.

The Aztecs attacked the Spanish and drove them from Tenochtitlán. Cortés went to neighboring Indian nations that had been conquered by the Aztecs and persuaded them to join his army.

Contact with the Spanish had infected the Aztec army with disease. When Cortés returned to Tenochtitlán, he used guns, horses, and steel armor to defeat the weakened Aztec army. Cortés soon controlled the entire Aztec empire. By 1535, Spain had claimed all of Mexico and renamed it New Spain.

After Cortés, other conquistadors explored Central and South America to find more gold and treasures. In the 1530s, a conquistador named **Francisco Pizarro** defeated the powerful Inca empire in South America.

REVIEW Why did people inside the Aztec empire help Cortés defeat the Aztecs?

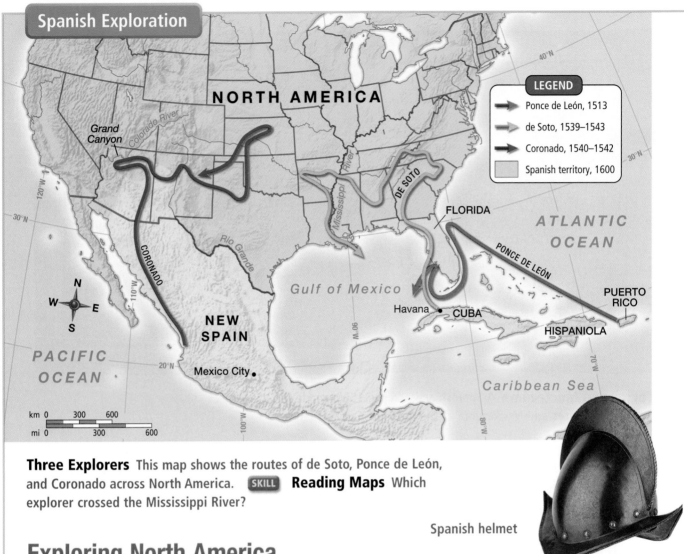

NORTH AMERICA

LEGEND

→ Ponce de León, 1513
→ de Soto, 1539–1543
→ Coronado, 1540–1542
▢ Spanish territory, 1600

Grand Canyon

Colorado River

FLORIDA

ATLANTIC OCEAN

CORONADO

DE SOTO

PONCE DE LEÓN

Rio Grande

Mississippi River

N W E S

Gulf of Mexico

Havana • CUBA

PUERTO RICO

HISPANIOLA

NEW SPAIN

Mexico City •

PACIFIC OCEAN

Caribbean Sea

km 0   300   600
mi 0   300   600

Three Explorers This map shows the routes of de Soto, Ponce de León, and Coronado across North America. **SKILL** **Reading Maps** Which explorer crossed the Mississippi River?

Spanish helmet

Exploring North America

Main Idea Spanish explorers went to the southern parts of the present-day United States looking for gold.

Conquistadors also explored North America in their search for gold. The first conquistador to reach the land that is now the United States was **Juan Ponce de León** (pon seh deh leh OHN). In 1513, he led an expedition to present-day Florida. Ponce de León claimed Florida for Spain. He was looking for a "fountain of youth" that legend said could make old people young again. A legend is a story handed down from earlier times.

In 1539, Spain sent a conquistador named **Hernando de Soto** to conquer and settle Florida and the lands beyond.

De Soto went to present-day Georgia. From there, he traveled thousands of miles through the American Southeast. De Soto was the first European explorer to reach the Mississippi River.

Along the way, De Soto found many American Indians but no riches. The conquistadors fought and enslaved American Indians they met. Many Spanish died in battles as well. De Soto died in 1542, without starting any settlements in North America.

In 1540, a conquistador named **Francisco Vásquez de Coronado** led an expedition into North America. Coronado was looking for cities of gold that he had heard about in legends.

The Grand Canyon Coronado's soldiers were the first Europeans to see the Grand Canyon in Arizona.

Cities of Gold

American Indians had told two earlier explorers named **Álvar Núñez Cabeza de Vaca** (AHL vah rehs NOON yez ca BEH sa deh VAH ca) and **Estevanico** (es STEH vahn EE KO) of rich cities to the north. Coronado and other explorers thought these cities might be the cities of gold. During the search for them, Coronado's soldiers traveled over 3,500 miles.

Spanish conquistadors faced many obstacles, including long distances, bad weather, and starvation as they explored the continent. They also learned much about the geography and peoples of North America.

REVIEW What did the Spanish hope to find in the lands north of Mexico?

Lesson Summary
- The Aztecs ruled a large empire in present-day Mexico. Hernán Cortés conquered the Aztecs in 1521.
- Spanish conquistadors explored much of the southern United States.

Why It Matters . . .

What the Spanish learned about the American Southwest helped future explorers for hundreds of years.

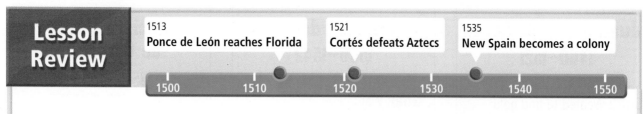

Lesson Review

1513 Ponce de León reaches Florida	1521 Cortés defeats Aztecs	1535 New Spain becomes a colony

1500   1510   1520   1530   1540   1550

① VOCABULARY Write a paragraph about Hernán Cortez using **conquistador** and **expedition.**

② READING SKILL What did the explorers find that was **different** from what they were looking for?

③ MAIN IDEA: History Why was Cortés able to defeat the powerful Aztec Empire?

④ MAIN IDEA: Geography What areas of the present-day United States did Coronado and De Soto explore?

⑤ PEOPLE TO KNOW Who was **Moctezuma**?

⑥ TIMELINE SKILL How long after Cortés conquered the Aztecs did New Spain become a colony?

⑦ CRITICAL THINKING: Fact and Opinion Write one fact about the Spanish conquest of the Americas. Then write an opinion about that fact.

ECONOMICS ACTIVITY Choose an explorer in the lesson. Think about his goals and the risks he took. Make a list of the risks.

SPANISH EXPLORERS

What were explorers looking for? What drove them to take great risks? Spanish explorers came to North America looking for treasures and for places they had heard stories about. They hoped their discoveries would make them rich and famous.

None of the expeditions of the Spanish explorers was easy. They didn't always find what they were looking for.

Juan Ponce de León
1460–1521

Goal: Wanted to find gold and a legendary "fountain of youth."

Explorations: Was the first European to set foot in Florida in 1513. Explored the Florida coast.

Interesting fact: Named Florida after the Spanish words for Easter, "Pascua de Florida" (Feast of Flowers), because it was the Easter season when he landed there.

Hernando de Soto
1500–1542

Goal: Wanted wealth and power.

Explorations: Led a large army through the American Southeast, from present-day Florida to Arkansas. Planned to conquer and colonize the region.

Interesting fact: He and his all-volunteer army were the first Europeans to see the Mississippi River.

Francisco Vásquez de Coronado
1510–1554

Goal: Wanted to find gold.

Explorations: An adventurer, Coronado assembled a large expedition and traveled throughout the Great Plains and the Southeast. He hoped to find some legendary cities of gold.

Interesting fact: Some of his men were the first Europeans to be in California, to see the Grand Canyon, and to live among the Pueblo Indians.

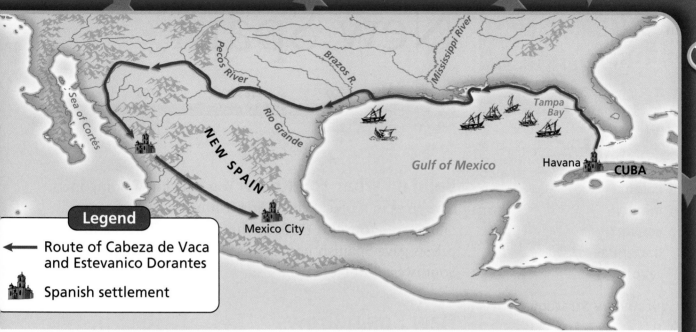

Legend

← Route of Cabeza de Vaca and Estevanico Dorantes

🏛 Spanish settlement

Cabeza de Vaca and Estevanico Dorantes spent eight years traveling on the route shown above.

Alvar Nuñez Cabeza de Vaca
1490–1557

Goal: Wanted travel and adventures.

Explorations: Was shipwrecked by a hurricane near present-day Texas. He and three other members of the expedition survived. They traveled across the Southwest, eventually reaching Mexico City.

Interesting fact: Published an account of his experiences, urging better treatment of American Indians.

Estevanico Dorantes
1500–1528

Goal: Wanted travel and adventures.

Explorations: Sold into slavery in Spain, he traveled as a servant to one of the officers on the same voyage as Cabeza de Vaca. He was one of only four survivors of the shipwreck.

Interesting fact: Was part of the first overland expedition to explore the American Southwest.

Activities

1. **THINK ABOUT IT** What were these Spanish explorers looking for? What did they find?

2. **REPORT IT** Write a letter to the king of Spain from the point of view of one of these explorers. Describe what you have found on your expedition, or what you hope to find.

New Spain

1550   1600   1650   1700   1750

1565–1692

VOCABULARY

colony
mission
convert
hacienda
revolt

Vocabulary Strategy

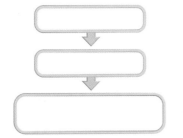

convert

The verb **convert** comes from a word meaning "to turn around." Someone who converts turns around, or changes, to a new religion.

READING SKILL

Draw Conclusions Note details that will help you draw a conclusion about life in New Spain for American Indians.

Build on What You Know You may know someone who lives in a place with a Spanish name, such as San Francisco. From the 1500s to the 1700s, explorers and priests gave Spanish names to settlements throughout the Southwest and Florida.

New Spain Grows

Main Idea The Spanish increased the size of New Spain and spread their rule in North America.

By 1535, the Spanish government controlled the former Aztec empire in Mexico. They made it a colony called New Spain. A **colony** is an area of land ruled by another country. In New Spain, Spanish settlers started towns and farmed the land. They built mines wherever they found valuable minerals, such as gold or silver. The colony of New Spain grew larger as government officials, settlers, soldiers, and priests arrived.

Spain's rulers sent priests with the explorers to spread Christianity. Over the next 200 years, Spanish explorers and priests traveled farther north and started settlements called missions. A **mission** was a religious community where priests taught Christianity.

Juana Inés de la Cruz
She was a well-known poet in Mexico City, the capital of New Spain.

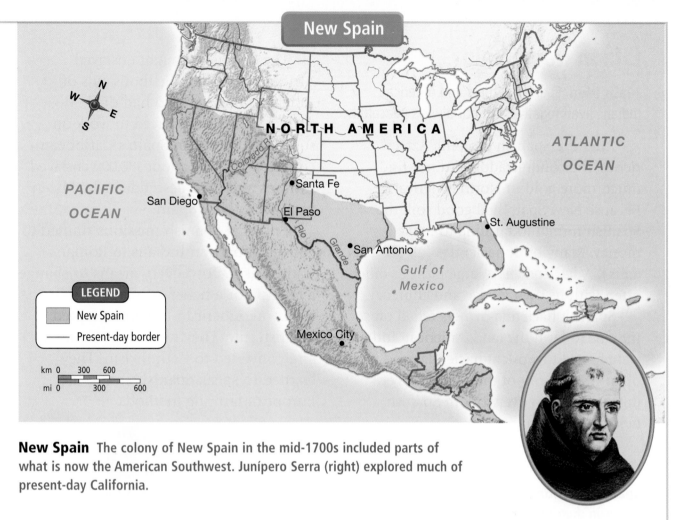

New Spain The colony of New Spain in the mid-1700s included parts of what is now the American Southwest. Junípero Serra (right) explored much of present-day California.

New Settlements

Spain was not the only nation trying to claim North American lands. The English, French, Dutch, and later the Russians, were also exploring North America. The Spanish hoped to prevent other countries from claiming land. They built forts called presidios to protect Spanish claims and guard themselves against attack.

In 1565, **Pedro Menéndez de Aviles** (AH vee lehs) started the settlement of St. Augustine in Florida. St. Augustine is the oldest city in the United States built by Europeans. The conquistador went north up the Gulf coast and started settlements all the way into present-day Georgia. Spanish settlers in Georgia tried to convert the Guale (WAH li) Indians to Roman Catholicism. The settlers forced them to work building roads and growing crops.

The Spanish also built settlements in what is now the southwestern United States. In 1598, the conquistador **Juan de Oñate** (ohn YAH teh) led settlers, soldiers, and priests to present-day New Mexico. In 1610, the city of Santa Fe became the capital of that part of New Spain.

Later, Spanish soldiers and priests also settled and explored present-day Texas and California. In 1769, a priest named **Junípero Serra** (hoo NEE peh roh SEH ra) led an expedition up the coast of California. After helping to build the settlement of San Diego, Serra continued north, building more presidios and missions along the way.

REVIEW Why did the Spanish build presidios in New Spain?

Life in New Spain

Main Idea Spanish settlers and American Indians lived together, but not always peacefully.

After the Spanish took the Aztecs' riches, the conquistadors did not find much more gold in North America. Because New Spain had good soil, the Spanish turned to farming to make money. Many built haciendas (ah see YEN dahs). A **hacienda** is a large farm or ranch, often with its own village and church.

Spanish hacienda owners relied on Indians to farm the land. American Indians were forced to work at haciendas and were often cheated out of their pay. Many of them died from overwork in Spanish fields and mines.

The Spanish brought enslaved Africans to replace the thousands of American Indians who had died. Most of these Africans were forced to work on sugar plantations in Spain's Caribbean colonies. By 1650, about 130,000 enslaved Africans and their descendants had been brought to New Spain.

Priests at Spanish missions wanted to convert American Indians to Roman Catholicism. To **convert** means to change a religion or a belief.

Some American Indians accepted Spanish rule. They moved to missions and converted to Catholicism. They learned to speak Spanish and to use European farming methods.

Spanish Missions This photo shows a mission in Carmel, California. The main church building is on the left. The bell at right is from a mission in Pala, California.

A Spanish priest named **Bartolomé de las Casas** wanted to protect all American Indians. He spoke out against their mistreatment in the Spanish colonies. He convinced the Spanish king to make laws to help protect them. Most settlers, however, ignored these laws and continued to mistreat them.

American Indians who did not live at missions continued to practice their own traditions and religions. In 1680, a Pueblo Indian leader named **Popé** (poh PEH) led a revolt against the Spanish in New Mexico. A **revolt** is a violent uprising against a ruler. The Pueblo kept the Spanish out of New Mexico until 1692, when the Spanish returned and conquered them again.

REVIEW What did some American Indians learn when they moved to Spanish missions?

Lesson Summary

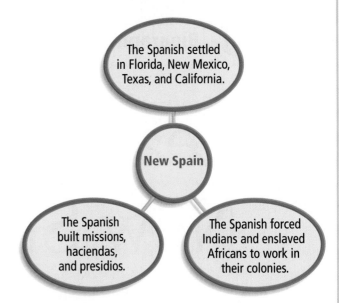

The Spanish settled in Florida, New Mexico, Texas, and California.

New Spain

The Spanish built missions, haciendas, and presidios.

The Spanish forced Indians and enslaved Africans to work in their colonies.

Why It Matters . . .

The growth of New Spain spread Spanish language and customs in the southern United States.

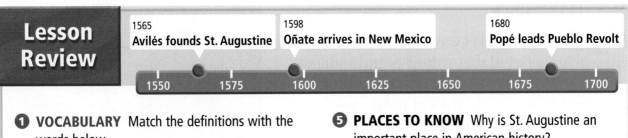

Lesson Review

1565	1598	1680
Avilés founds St. Augustine	Oñate arrives in New Mexico	Popé leads Pueblo Revolt

1550   1575   1600   1625   1650   1675   1700

❶ **VOCABULARY** Match the definitions with the words below.

    mission   **hacienda**   **revolt**

a. a Spanish farm **b.** a place where religion was taught **c.** an uprising

❷ **READING SKILL** In what ways did life change for American Indians who lived at missions?

❸ **MAIN IDEA History** Why did the Spanish build haciendas?

❹ **MAIN IDEA Culture** What was the main goal of the Spanish missions?

❺ **PLACES TO KNOW** Why is St. Augustine an important place in American history?

❻ **TIMELINE SKILL** How long after Oñate arrived in New Mexico did the Pueblo Revolt occur?

❼ **CRITICAL THINKING: Analyze** How was Menéndez de Aviles's exploration of Florida and Georgia similar to Serra's exploration of California?

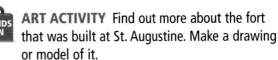

ART ACTIVITY Find out more about the fort that was built at St. Augustine. Make a drawing or model of it.

Leadership in New Spain

Leaders in New Spain were not always conquistadors. Religious leaders also played an important role in the way Spanish colonists and Indians lived together. Here are three who left a lasting mark on the history of New Spain.

BARTOLOMÉ DE LAS CASAS
(1474–1566)

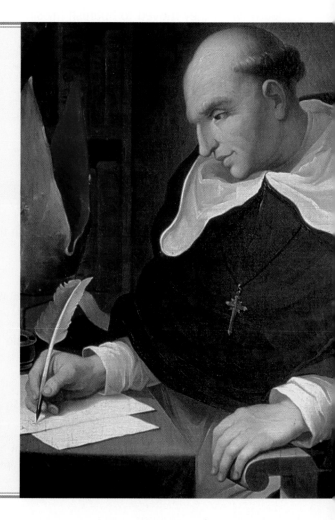

Bartolomé de las Casas was a priest who believed that colonists and Indians should live as equals. He devoted his life to improving the lives of Indian workers. In 1542, he wrote a book to tell people about the brutal treatment of Indians. He persuaded the king of Spain to issue laws that protected their rights. Although the laws were not fully enforced, de las Casas's ideas influenced the views of many Europeans.

Las Casas's most famous book, *A Brief Report on the Destruction of the Indies*, was read by people all over Europe.

JUNÍPERO SERRA
(1713–1784)

Junípero Serra was a priest and tireless explorer who helped found 21 missions along the coast of California. He believed he was serving his God by converting thousands of Indians to the Christian faith. However, many Indians suffered at the missions. They were overworked and some starved or died of diseases. Their work included building churches, canals, and mills for the Spanish.

Junípero Serra's statue stands in San Francisco's Golden Gate Park.

POPÉ
(1630–1690)

Popé was a religious leader of the Pueblo Indians. He thought the time had come to drive out the Spanish colonists who had been forcing the Pueblo to give up their religious beliefs. Popé planned a revolt against the Spanish and persuaded others to join him. In 1680, his followers burned churches and attacked haciendas and missions. After the Spanish fled to Mexico, Popé ordered the destruction of all Spanish buildings and artifacts. The Pueblo people's revolt was the most successful Indian uprising in the history of New Spain.

Activities

1. **TALK ABOUT IT** Why do you think the laws protecting Indians were not enforced?

2. **WRITE ABOUT IT** Choose one of the three religious leaders. Describe what you think were that leader's most important accomplishments.

Skillbuilder

Use Latitude and Longitude

▶ **VOCABULARY**

parallel

meridian

absolute
location

To help sailors and other travelers locate places, mapmakers created an imaginary grid of lines over the globe. This grid is made up of lines of latitude and longitude.

Learn the Skill

Step 1: Identify the line of latitude. Lines of latitude run east and west and measure distance north and south of the equator. The equator is 0° latitude. Lines of latitude north of the equator are labeled N. Those south of the equator are labeled S. A line of latitude is also called a **parallel.**

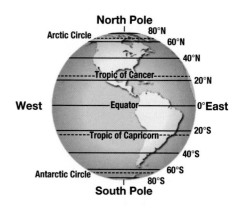

Step 2: Identify the line of longitude. Lines of longitude run north and south and measure distance east and west of the prime meridian. The prime meridian is 0° longitude. Lines of longitude east of the prime meridian are labeled E. Those west of the prime meridian are labeled W. A line of longitude is also called a **meridian.**

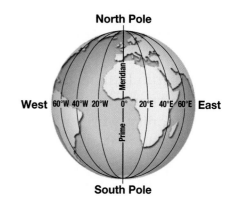

Step 3: Find where the lines of latitude and longitude cross. The exact latitude and longitude of a place on the globe is also called its **absolute location.**

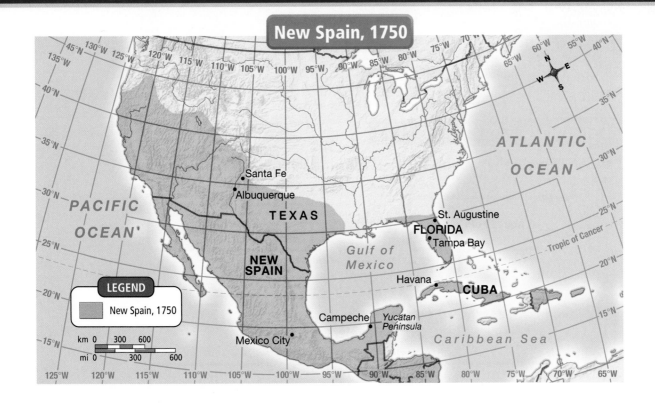

New Spain, 1750

Practice the Skill

Use the map above to answer these questions.

1. What line of latitude is closest to St. Augustine? What line of longitude is closest to St. Augustine?

2. What other place is at almost the same longitude as Tampa Bay?

3. What place is near 19°N, 98°W?

4. What are the lines of latitude and longitude closest to Campeche?

Apply the Skill

Use your library or Internet resources to find a map of your state. Locate the town or city where you live by using latitude and longitude. Then write a paragraph explaining how you did this.

Review and Test Prep

Visual Summary

1.–4. Describe what you learned about each person named below.

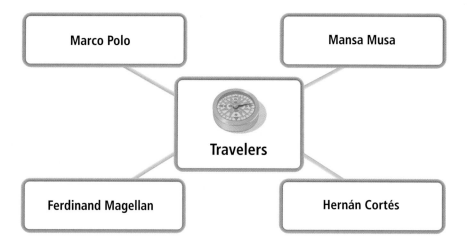

| Marco Polo | Mansa Musa |

Travelers

| Ferdinand Magellan | Hernán Cortés |

Facts and Main Ideas

TEST PREP Answer each question with information from the chapter.

5. Economics What was the Silk Road?

6. History What were two inventions that improved navigation?

7. Geography How was Christopher Columbus's route to Asia different from those of earlier explorers?

8. History Who were the Aztecs and why did Hernán Cortés want to conquer them?

9. History Why did priests travel to New Spain and what did they do there?

Vocabulary

TEST PREP Choose the correct word from the list below to complete each sentence.

merchant, p. 85
slavery, p. 92
circumnavigate, p. 101
colony, p. 112

10. The _____ of New Spain was started in present-day Mexico.

11. Marco Polo was a _____ who traveled to China to find spices and silk.

12. Members of Ferdinand Magellan's crew were the first people to _____ the world.

13. Many Portuguese traders forced Africans into _____ and sold them in Europe.

1271
Marco Polo goes to China

1492
Columbus reaches West Indies

1540
Coronado's explorations

1270   1320   1370   1420   1470   1520   1570

Apply Skills

✔ **TEST PREP** **Map Skill** Study the map of explorers in Florida. Then use what you have learned about latitude and longitude to answer each question.

LEGEND

Ponce de Leon, 1513

de Soto, 1539–1543

ATLANTIC OCEAN

28°N
Gulf of Mexico

FLORIDA

26°N

Tropic of Cancer

24°N

Havana

CUBA

22°N

km 0   100   200
mi 0   100   200

96°W   84°W   82°W   80°W   20°N   78°W   76°W

22°N

14. Which explorer or explorers started voyages at about 23°N, 83°W?

  A. Juan Ponce de León

  B. Juan Ponce de León and Hernando de Soto

  C. Hernando de Soto

  D. Francisco Vásquez de Coronado

15. What was the most northern line of latitude that Ponce de León reached?

  A. about 30°S.

  B. about 87°W

  C. about 30°N

  D. about 87°E

Critical Thinking

✔ **TEST PREP** Write a short paragraph to answer each question.

16. **Cause and Effect** What were four lasting effects of the Columbian Exchange?

17. **Fact and Opinion** Bartolomé de las Casas wanted to convince the king of Spain to protect American Indians. Write one fact and one opinion that he might have included in his argument.

Timeline

Use the Chapter Summary Timeline above to answer the question.

18. In what year did Europeans first arrive in the Americas?

Activities

HANDS ON

Art Activity The Spanish built different kinds of buildings in New Spain. Find pictures of a presidio, a mission, or a hacienda, and make your own drawing of it.

Writing Activity Write a personal essay telling what you think of Marco Polo's adventures. Include information about his journey to China on the Silk Road and the things he saw in China.

Technology
Writing Process Tips
Get help with your essay at
www.eduplace.com/kids/hmss05/

European Settlements

Technology

e • glossary
e • word games
www.eduplace.com/kids/hmss05/

Vocabulary Preview

armada

King Philip of Spain sent an **armada** to fight against England. This large fleet of ships sailed in 1588.
page 125

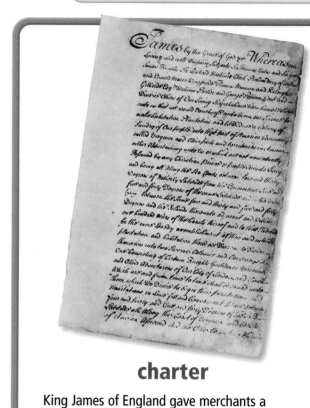

charter

King James of England gave merchants a **charter.** This document gave them permission to start a settlement, which they named Jamestown. **page 131**

Chapter Timeline

1497
John Cabot's explorations

1607
Jamestown founded

1490   1530   1570   1610

Reading Strategy

Summarize Use this strategy to focus on important ideas.

Review the main ideas. Then look for important details that support the main idea.

compact

The Pilgrims wrote a **compact** before they started their settlement. The Mayflower Compact was an agreement about the laws that would govern them. **page 137**

tolerance

Settlers in New Netherland practiced **tolerance.** People with different ideas and beliefs came to live in the colony. **page 145**

1620
Plymouth founded

1682
La Salle claims Louisiana territory

1650

1690

A Northwest Passage

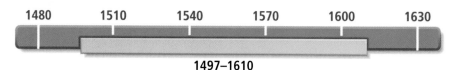

1480	1510	1540	1570	1600	1630

1497–1610

Build on What You Know Have you ever taken a shortcut? In the 1500s and 1600s, European explorers wanted a shortcut to Asia. They looked for a water route through North America.

Searching for a Passage to Asia

Main Idea In the 1500s and 1600s, explorers looked for a water route through North America to Asia.

Christopher Columbus first landed in the Americas while looking for a route to Asia. Over the next 125 years, European explorers looked for a sea route to Asia that would be faster than sailing around South America. Europeans wanted to bring back silk and spices from Asia.

Leaving England John Cabot prepares to sail across the Atlantic Ocean in 1497, five years after Columbus's first voyage.

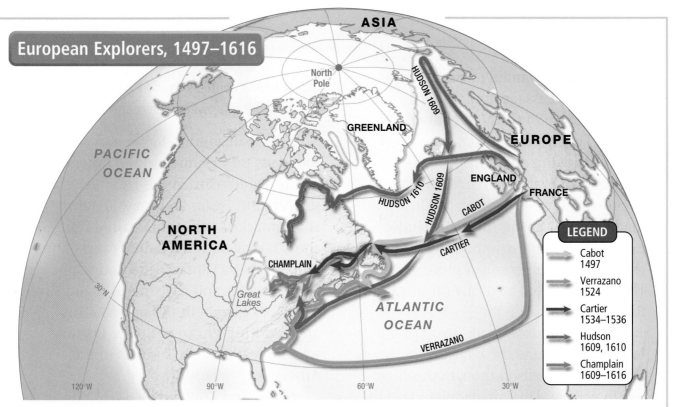

European Exploration Europeans explored the northeast coast of North America as they searched for a westward passage to Asia. **SKILL** **Reading Maps** Which explorer sailed the farthest south?

John Cabot

John Cabot, an Italian explorer, thought he could reach Asia by sailing across the Atlantic Ocean. The king of England agreed to pay for his voyage. Cabot left England in 1497. After a month at sea, he reached present-day Canada, which he thought was Asia. He explored the land and waters, but he found no people, silks, or spices. Cabot did find a rich fishing area off the coast of Canada. After he returned to England and told about what he had found, European fishing boats began sailing to these waters.

Once people knew that the land Cabot had found was not part of Asia, explorers continued their search for a water passage through the North American continent. The sea route that explorers looked for became known as the Northwest Passage.

France Explores North America

In 1524, France sent an Italian sea captain, **Giovanni da Verrazano** (VEHR uh ZAH noh), to look for a Northwest Passage. Verrazano explored much of the east coast of North America, including the area where New York City is now.

About 10 years later, **Jacques Cartier** (kahr TYAY) continued France's search for a water route to Asia. He sailed far up the St. Lawrence River in Canada.

In 1608, **Samuel de Champlain** (sham PLAYN) founded a fur-trading post on the St. Lawrence River. He called it Quebec (kwih BEHK), from the Indian word kebec, which means "the place where the river narrows." Quebec was the first permanent French settlement in North America.

REVIEW What did John Cabot find during his exploration of Canada?

Henry Hudson

The Dutch wanted to search for a Northwest Passage, too. The Dutch are the people of the Netherlands. In 1609, a Dutch trading company hired **Henry Hudson**, an English captain. Hudson sailed up the Hudson River in present-day New York. The Dutch made land claims in the areas Hudson explored. A **claim** is something declared as one's own, especially a piece of land. The Dutch started a colony on this land the following year.

In 1610, Hudson made a voyage for England. He found the bay now known as Hudson Bay. Hudson thought this huge bay in present-day Canada might lead to the Pacific Ocean, but it did not. England later claimed the land around Hudson Bay.

Neither Henry Hudson nor any other explorer ever found a Northwest Passage. Instead, they found more forests, fish, and wildlife than they had seen in Europe.

Spain and England

Main Idea Conflicts over treasure and religion led to fighting between Spain and England.

The Spanish found gold and silver in the lands they claimed in the Americas. Spanish ships carried this treasure across the Atlantic. Again and again, English ships attacked and stole treasure from ships sailing back to Spain. **Francis Drake**, an English sea captain, attacked many Spanish ships and gave the gold and silver to **Queen Elizabeth** of England. This angered **King Philip** of Spain. England was a threat to Spain's power in the Americas.

Spain and England also had conflicts about religion. Spain was a Roman Catholic country. England broke away from the Catholic Church and formed its own church during the Protestant Reformation.

England Fights Spain English ships led by Drake battle the Spanish Armada off the southern coast of England.

The Spanish Armada

King Philip was part of a movement called the Counter Reformation that tried to spread the Catholic religion. He wanted England to be a Catholic nation again. He also wanted to stop English attacks on his ships.

Philip built an armada of 130 warships. An **armada** is the Spanish word for a large fleet of ships. In 1588, the Spanish Armada sailed to England to attack.

England was prepared for Spain's invasion. An **invasion** is an attack by an armed force to conquer another country. When the Spanish Armada appeared off the coast of England, Francis Drake led the English into battle.

The English fleet chased the Spanish ships away from the coastline and sank many of them. The rest of the Armada returned to Spain. On the way, some ships were wrecked in bad weather.

After the defeat of the Spanish Armada, England used its new power to claim more land in the Americas.

REVIEW Why did the king of Spain attack England?

Lesson Summary

- Explorers searched for a Northwest Passage to Asia in the 1500s and 1600s.
- England, France, and the Netherlands made land claims in North America as they searched for a Northwest Passage.
- England and Spain went to war over religion and English attacks on Spanish ships.

Why It Matters ...

Spain was no longer the only European power exploring North America. England, France, and the Netherlands began to claim land on the eastern part of the continent during the 1500s and 1600s.

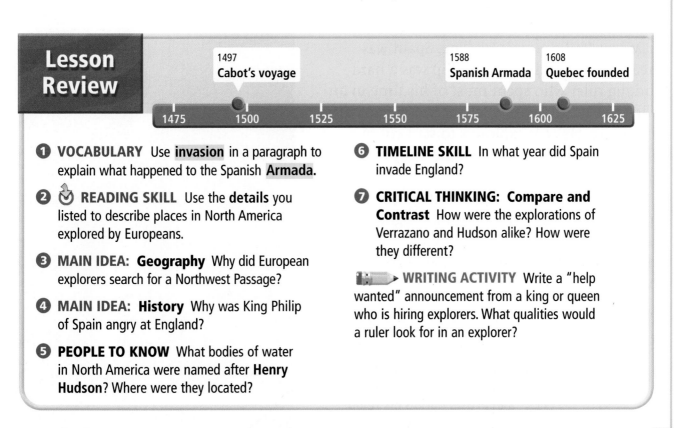

Lesson Review

Timeline:
1497 Cabot's voyage
1588 Spanish Armada
1608 Quebec founded
1475 — 1500 — 1525 — 1550 — 1575 — 1600 — 1625

❶ **VOCABULARY** Use **invasion** in a paragraph to explain what happened to the Spanish **Armada**.

❷ **READING SKILL** Use the **details** you listed to describe places in North America explored by Europeans.

❸ **MAIN IDEA: Geography** Why did European explorers search for a Northwest Passage?

❹ **MAIN IDEA: History** Why was King Philip of Spain angry at England?

❺ **PEOPLE TO KNOW** What bodies of water in North America were named after **Henry Hudson**? Where were they located?

❻ **TIMELINE SKILL** In what year did Spain invade England?

❼ **CRITICAL THINKING: Compare and Contrast** How were the explorations of Verrazano and Hudson alike? How were they different?

➤ **WRITING ACTIVITY** Write a "help wanted" announcement from a king or queen who is hiring explorers. What qualities would a ruler look for in an explorer?

Rulers of Land and Sea

In the 1500s, Elizabeth of England and Philip of Spain were the most powerful leaders in the world. Both wanted to rule the world's oceans and build colonies in the Americas. Yet they had different ways of ruling.

King Philip II
1527–1598

When Philip II became king, Spain was already a powerful nation. Philip was a hard-working ruler who spent most of his time in an office in Madrid, writing letters and managing his empire. He sent explorers to start colonies in the Americas and enlarged the army and the navy.

Philip was deeply religious, and wanted to strengthen Roman Catholicism throughout Europe and the Americas. He tried to conquer England and other countries. Spain was still a great power when Philip died in 1598.

A lover of books and paintings, Philip supported Spanish writers and artists during his reign.

Queen Elizabeth I
1533–1603

Here Elizabeth appears with her hand on a globe to show that England is a world power.

When Elizabeth Tudor became Queen of England in 1558, England was not as strong as Spain. Elizabeth reorganized the government so that it would run better. She surrounded herself with trustworthy advisors, and attended nearly every one of their meetings. She often appeared in public, making speeches and shaking hands with as many people as she could.

Elizabeth sent explorers on costly expeditions to find new trade routes. She built up the English navy, but was careful about money. By the end of her reign, England was one of the world's most powerful nations.

Activities

1. **THINK ABOUT IT** In what ways did Queen Elizabeth show her sense of **responsibility** for England and its people?

2. **MAP IT** How large was the Spanish Empire at the end of King Philip's reign? Find out. Color in the Spanish Empire on a world map.

 Technology Visit Education Place for more biographies. www.eduplace.com/kids/hmss05/

Skillbuilder

Use Parallel Timelines

► **VOCABULARY**

parallel timelines

A timeline shows events in the order that they happened. **Parallel timelines** are two or more timelines grouped together. They show events happening in different places during the same period of time. Comparing timelines can help you see connections between events.

Learn the Skill

Step 1: Find the subject of each timeline.

Step 2: Identify the time period between the first and last dates. Look at how each timeline is divided. Some timelines are divided into single years. Others are divided into decades, which are periods of 10 years, or centuries, which are periods of 100 years.

Step 3: Study the timelines to see how events might be related. Events that happen in one place may affect events in another place.

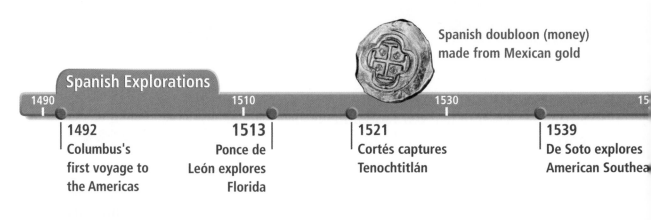

Spanish doubloon (money) made from Mexican gold

Spanish Explorations

| 1490 | 1510 | | 1530 | 15 |

1492 Columbus's first voyage to the Americas

1513 Ponce de León explores Florida

1521 Cortés captures Tenochtitlán

1539 De Soto explores American Southea

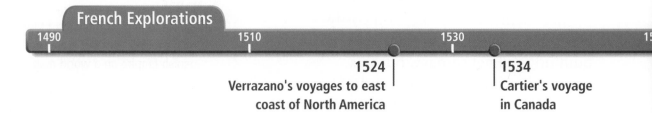

French Explorations

| 1490 | 1510 | | 1530 | 15 |

1524 Verrazano's voyages to east coast of North America

1534 Cartier's voyage in Canada

Practice the Skill

Answer the following questions using the parallel timelines below.

1 Which country sent more explorers to the Americas?

2 Which explorers came to the Americas during the decade of the 1520s?

3 How long after Columbus's voyage did France send an explorer to the Americas? Why might France have sent him at that time?

Apply the Skill

Create your own parallel timelines. Use a calendar to list the events taking place in your life this week. Then draw and label two timelines. Mark each day, starting with Sunday and ending with Saturday. Place the events at home on one timeline, and the events at school on the other. Then compare the timelines to see how they may be related.

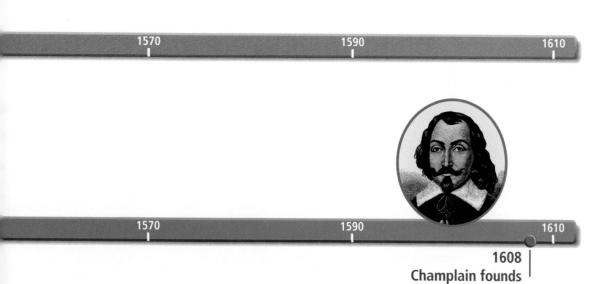

| 1570 | 1590 | 1610 |

| 1570 | 1590 | 1610 |

1608
Champlain founds
Quebec

Roanoke and Jamestown

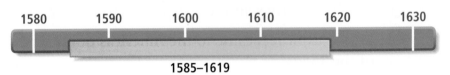

| 1580 | 1590 | 1600 | 1610 | 1620 | 1630 |

1585–1619

VOCABULARY

charter
invest
stock
cash crop
indentured servant

Vocabulary Strategy

cash **crop**

A **cash** crop is raised so that farmers can sell it for money, or cash.

READING SKILL

Draw Conclusions Use facts and details from the lesson to draw a conclusion about why Roanoke failed and Jamestown succeeded.

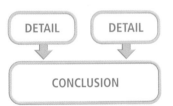

Build on What You Know Think of a time when you had to change your plans. When English colonists traveled to North America, they planned to look for treasure. They had to change their plans after they arrived.

The Lost Colony

Main Idea The first English settlements in North America failed.

England's rulers and merchants wanted a colony in North America. They hoped to find gold and silver, just as the Spanish had in their colonies. In 1585, about 100 English men settled on Roanoke Island, off the coast of present-day North Carolina. The colonists barely survived. They could not grow crops in the sandy soil. Most of them went back to England.

In 1587, the English tried again to settle Roanoke. **John White** was the leader of the colony. Shortly after landing in America, White returned to England for supplies. When he returned nearly three years later, the colonists had disappeared. White thought they had gone to live with nearby American Indians, but he never found them. The "Lost Colony" of Roanoke is still a mystery today.

The Lost Colony John White found a mysterious message when he returned to Roanoke. The Croatoan were American Indians who lived nearby.

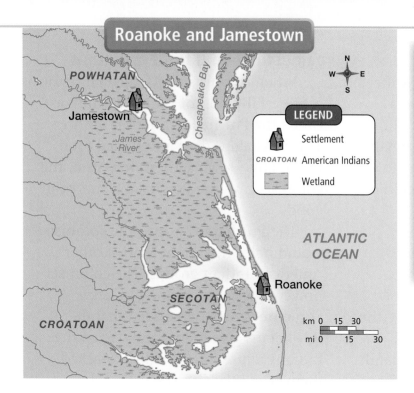

Roanoke and Jamestown

POWHATAN

Jamestown

James River

Chesapeake Bay

LEGEND

Settlement

CROATOAN American Indians

Wetland

ATLANTIC OCEAN

Roanoke

SECOTAN

CROATOAN

km 0 15 30
mi 0 15 30

English Settlements Roanoke and Jamestown were about 140 miles from each other. The photograph above shows the way land in Jamestown probably looked when settlers arrived.

The Jamestown Colony

Main Idea Jamestown was the first successful English settlement in America.

In 1606, English merchants started the Virginia Company of London. Their goal was to build a settlement in North America. The king of England gave the Virginia Company a charter to start their settlement. A **charter** is a document giving permission to a person or group to do something.

The owners of the Virginia Company needed money to buy ships and supplies. They raised money by asking people to invest in their company. To **invest** means to put money into something to try to earn more money. If colonists found treasure, people who invested in the company would earn money.

People invested in the Virginia Company by buying stocks. A **stock** is a piece of ownership in a company. The amount of money an investor earns or loses depends on how much stock the investor owns and the value of the stock.

In 1607, about 100 men and boys traveled to present-day Virginia. The settlers built a fort on the banks of a river. They named their colony Jamestown after **King James I.**

The land in Jamestown was damp and swampy. The water wasn't good for drinking, and insects carried diseases. Most of the settlers were gentlemen who had never worked hard. They did not know how to farm. Instead, they searched for gold. The settlers ran out of food, and within a few months, almost half of them had died from hunger and disease.

Then **John Smith** took command of Jamestown. He ordered people to plant crops. He said:

66 He who does not work, will not eat. 99

Life in Jamestown was still hard. Smith went back to England in 1609. During the following winter, known as the "starving time," most of the colonists died.

REVIEW Why did the Jamestown colonists run out of food?

Jamestown Succeeds

In 1612, a settler named **John Rolfe** learned from local American Indians that tobacco grew well in Virginia's hot, humid weather. Many people in England smoked tobacco. They were willing to pay a high price for the crop, which did not grow well in England.

Jamestown merchants grew and sold thousands of pounds of tobacco to England. Tobacco was a cash crop. A **cash crop** is a crop that people grow and sell to earn money. Tobacco gave the colony enough income to buy much-needed food and supplies from England.

In 1619, the first women and Africans arrived in Jamestown. The first Africans were probably indentured servants. An **indentured servant** was someone who agreed to work for a number of years in exchange for the cost of a voyage to North America. Later, enslaved Africans were forced to work in Jamestown.

Jamestown and the Powhatans

When colonists first settled Jamestown, a powerful group of American Indians called the Powhatans lived in the area. The Powhatans gave and traded food to the Jamestown settlers. In return, the colonists gave the Powhatans European goods.

The Powhatans hoped the colonists would help them fight against other American Indian groups. The colonists, however, were not willing to help. Sometimes they demanded that the Powhatans give them food. When the Indians refused, the English attacked them. The Powhatans saw that the English were trying to take over their land, and they fought back. The two sides made peace after John Rolfe married a Powhatan woman, **Pocahontas**, in 1614. Pocahontas was a daughter of the Powhatans' leader.

The Powhatans This Indian nation lived in domed houses. The chief of the Powhatans wore this deerskin cloak (right). SKILL **Primary Source** Look at the figures on the cloak. What do you think they represent?

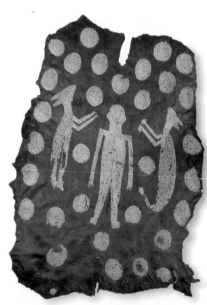

Peace did not last, however. The English tried to take more land. The Powhatans fought back until 1646, when the English killed many of them. The English then took control of most of the land around Jamestown.

REVIEW Why did colonists in Jamestown fight the Powhatans?

Pocahontas After Pocahontas married colonist John Rolfe, she went to England where her portrait was painted.

Lesson Summary

The Roanoake settlers disappeared mysteriously.

In 1607, Jamestown was founded in the colony of Virginia.

After John Rolfe began growing tobacco, the Jamestown settlement grew.

The Powhatan and the English colonists fought over land for decades.

Why It Matters ...

Jamestown was the first successful English settlement in North America. The Jamestown settlers led the way for other English settlements in North America.

Lesson Review

| 1585 First Roanoke colony | 1607 Jamestown founded | 1619 Africans arrive in Jamestown |

1580 — 1590 — 1600 — 1610 — 1620

❶ **VOCABULARY** Use the words **charter, invest,** and **stock** in a paragraph explaining how Jamestown began.

❷ **READING SKILL** Which fact or detail best explains why Roanoke failed? How did you **draw** this **conclusion**?

❸ **MAIN IDEA: History** Why did England's rulers and merchants want to start a colony in North America?

❹ **MAIN IDEA: Geography** How did the land in Jamestown affect the settlers?

❺ **CRITICAL THINKING: Decision Making** What might have been the opportunity cost for someone who went to Jamestown as an indentured servant? Remember that an opportunity cost is the thing you give up when you decide to do or have something else.

❻ **TIMELINE SKILL** Which colony was settled first, Jamestown or Roanoke?

HANDS ON

INTERVIEW ACTIVITY What questions might a reporter have asked John Smith about the Jamestown colony? Interview a partner who can answer as John Smith might have.

Jamestown · 1607

The welfare of the settlers in the Jamestown colony depended on the environment. Settlers chose a place that they thought had many geographic advantages. It lay sixty miles up the James River, out of sight of Spanish ships on the Chesapeake Bay. Forests provided lumber for buildings. Winters were not as harsh as in more northern locations.

The geography of the Jamestown settlement had major drawbacks. The area had wetlands full of mosquitos. The soil was not good for growing food crops, and the drinking water was unhealthy. However, tobacco could grow there, and it became an important cash crop.

THE PORTRAICTURE OF CAPTAYNE IOHN SMITH / ADMIRALL OF NEW ENGLAND

On the River
Jamestown's location on the river meant that settlers could travel by ship to the Chesapeake Bay and back to England.

Forest Resources
Settlers used tall upright logs to build walls called palisades. The fort had only three sides, making it easier to defend.

John Smith
Smith saw that the Powhatans did not drink the river water. He ordered settlers to dig wells for clean water.

Climate and Soil
The growing season was long and humid. Tobacco plants grew well in these conditions.

Activities

1. **EXPLORE IT** Step into the picture and imagine walking through the settlement or through the fields near the wetlands. Describe the environment around you.

2. **WRITE ABOUT IT** Write a first-person narrative that tells what Jamestown was like for one settler. Include the role of natural resources in his or her daily life.

135

New England Settlements

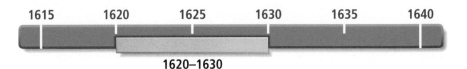

1615	1620	1625	1630	1635	1640

1620–1630

VOCABULARY

pilgrim
compact
cape

Vocabulary Strategy

compact

The prefix **com-** means together. People make a **compact,** or agreement, together with others.

READING SKILL

Cause and Effect As you read, list causes that led to the Pilgrims' and Puritans' settlements in North America.

CAUSE		EFFECT

Build on What You Know You know that religion is important to many people. It can affect the choices they make and what they think is right or wrong. Religion was very important to many of the first English settlers in North America.

The Plymouth Colony

Main Idea The Pilgrims came to America for religious freedom.

By law, everyone in England was supposed to belong to the Church of England. Some people, however, were not happy with that church. They had different beliefs. These people decided to break away, or separate, from the Church of England and set up their own churches. They became known as Separatists.

One small group of Separatists went to the Netherlands in the early 1600s to find religious freedom. These Separatists called themselves Pilgrims. A **pilgrim** is a person who makes a long journey for religious reasons.

The Mayflower This ship is an exact model of the original *Mayflower* that the Pilgrims sailed on in 1620.

Pilgrims Sail to North America

The Pilgrims could practice their religious beliefs in the Netherlands, but they wanted to live apart from people of other beliefs. The Pilgrims were also bothered that their children were learning Dutch customs. They decided to build a new religious community in North America. The Virginia Company of London agreed to let the Pilgrims start a settlement in the colony of Virginia.

In 1620, about 100 men, women, and children set sail across the Atlantic Ocean in the English ship *Mayflower.* Fierce storms pushed the ship off course, however. Instead of landing in Virginia, the *Mayflower* anchored off the coast of present-day Massachusetts.

Because the Pilgrims landed in Massachusetts, they would not be governed by the Virginia Company. The passengers created their own plan for government.

The Pilgrims called their plan the Mayflower Compact. A **compact** is an agreement. In this compact, the passengers agreed to make laws for the "general good" of the colony, and to obey them.

The Pilgrims landed briefly at the tip of Cape Cod. A **cape** is a strip of land that stretches into a body of water. They chose a site on the other side of Cape Cod Bay to build a settlement. The colony was named Plymouth after a town in England.

The Plymouth settlers had a hard time at first. They had arrived in November when it was too late to plant crops. They did not have enough food. During this first harsh winter, about half of the Pilgrims died.

REVIEW Why did the Pilgrims leave the Netherlands for North America?

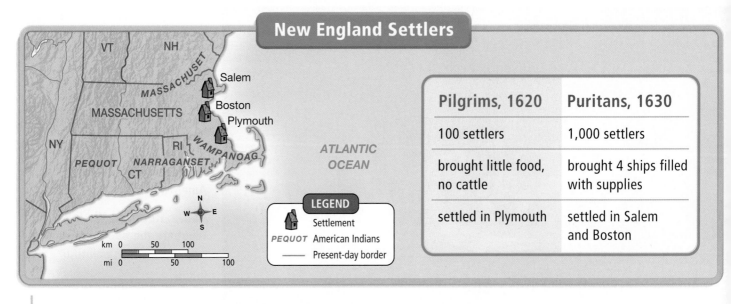

New England Settlers

Pilgrims, 1620	Puritans, 1630
100 settlers	1,000 settlers
brought little food, no cattle	brought 4 ships filled with supplies
settled in Plymouth	settled in Salem and Boston

LEGEND
🏠 Settlement
PEQUOT American Indians
— Present-day border

Pilgrims and Puritans This map shows settlements founded by the Pilgrims and the Puritans. **SKILL** **Reading Charts** How many Puritans first settled in New England?

Pilgrims Give Thanks

The following spring, an American Indian named **Squanto** (SKWAHN toh) visited the Pilgrims. Squanto had been to Europe and spoke English. He introduced the Pilgrims to **Massasoit** (MAS uh SOYT), the leader of the nearby Wampanoag (WAHM puh NOH ag). **William Bradford,** the governor of Plymouth, and Massasoit agreed to live in peace.

Squanto taught the Pilgrims how to plant crops such as maize (corn), pumpkins, and beans. He guided the Pilgrims in hunting and fishing. By the fall of 1621, the colony had become more successful. The Pilgrims had plenty of food, and new settlers and supplies had recently arrived from England.

The Pilgrims held a feast to thank their God for their first harvest. About 50 Pilgrims and 90 Wampanoags celebrated together for three days. People in the United States remember this feast during Thanksgiving, a national holiday celebrated every November.

Massachusetts Bay Colony

Main Idea English Puritans settled the Massachusetts Bay Colony.

The Puritans were another religious group who disagreed with the Church of England. Puritans, however, did not want to separate from the church. They wanted to make themselves and their church pure, or free from fault.

The Puritans decided to start a colony in North America. Unlike the colonists in Jamestown, the Puritans did not come to America to earn money. Like the Pilgrims, they wanted to create a community based on their religious beliefs.

John Winthrop, a lawyer, was the first governor of the new colony. He told his followers,

❝ We shall be as a city upon a hill. The eyes of all people are upon us. ❞

He meant that they should set a good example for others to follow. Puritans believed that if they lived by their religious beliefs, their community would succeed.

The Colony Grows

The Puritans were better prepared to settle in North America than the Pilgrims had been 10 years earlier. They had a large group of people with many different skills. The Puritans set sail in March, allowing enough time to plant crops once they came to America.

Winthrop and his followers arrived in the town of Salem, north of Plymouth, in June 1630. They soon moved a few miles south where they began building their colony in present-day Boston. They named their settlement the Massachusetts Bay Colony after the Massachuset Indians. The colony was so successful that many more Puritans left England to move there.

John Winthrop

By the 1640s, as many as 20,000 English Puritans had moved to what is now the northeastern part of the United States. This region became known as New England because so many people from England lived there.

REVIEW How did Squanto help the Plymouth colony succeed?

Lesson Summary

The Pilgrims sailed to North America to find religious freedom in 1620. They wrote the Mayflower Compact, the first written plan for government in North America. Ten years later, the Puritans, led by John Winthrop, settled the successful Massachusetts Bay Colony.

Why It Matters ...

The Massachusetts Bay Colony brought large numbers of English people to what would become the United States.

Lesson Review

1620
Pilgrims land at Plymouth

1630
Winthrop arrives in Salem

1615   1620   1625   1630

❶ **VOCABULARY** Match each word with its meaning:

cape   compact   pilgrim

(a) an agreement; (b) a person who makes a long journey for religious reasons; (c) a strip of land stretching into the water

❷ **READING SKILL** What **caused** the Puritans to move to North America?

❸ **MAIN IDEA: Citizenship** What was the purpose of the Mayflower Compact?

❹ **MAIN IDEA: History** Why were the Puritans better prepared for settlement than the Pilgrims?

❺ **TIMELINE SKILL** When did the Puritans land in Salem?

❻ **CRITICAL THINKING: Infer** What might have happened to the Pilgrims if Squanto had not helped them?

ART ACTIVITY Think about the way the feast shared between the settlers and the Indians was celebrated in 1621 and the way Thanksgiving is celebrated today. Draw a picture that compares the two celebrations.

This New Land

by G. Clifton Wisler

After living in Leyden, in the Netherlands, Richard Woodley, 12, and his family have sailed on the Mayflower to a new life in the settlement of Plymouth. Richard, his sister Mary, and brothers Thom and Edward have survived a brutal winter that took their mother's life. Spring has brought help from American Indian neighbors. The author, G. Clifton Wisler, tells this story from Richard Woodley's point of view.

❀

Our great benefactor during this time was the Patuxet Indian, Squanto. Samoset, our earlier visitor, had returned to his home to the north, but Squanto had adopted our village as his own. Indeed, he had been born on this very ground and knew the wood and fields. He devoted himself to becoming our tutor in all matters of importance.

Our first lesson was in the catching of eels. In the Netherlands, they were most expensive, and I had never tasted one. Eels abounded in the muddy bottom of the brook. We had attempted to catch them earlier, but they did not bite our hooks.

Squanto brought us to the brook each morning. We would remove our boots and stockings and wade into the waters. With our feet we searched the mud for eels. It was strange at first, waiting for the unearthly sensation of the ropelike creatures. Once we located an eel, we would plunge our hands into the shallow stream and capture it. Often we would also fall into the brook, splashing and laughing as the water enveloped us. For a moment we were children, and I thank Squanto as much for the joy we shared as for eels caught.

In such a manner Edward and I caught three eels in a single morn. Mary cooked them in Mother's great iron kettle, adding such seasoning as she had. The meat proved fat and sweet.

A boy in the role of a Pilgrim
at Plimoth Plantation

When berries appeared on the forest plants, Squanto taught us
which ones should be taken. Some could be eaten. Others provided
remedies for common ailments. We also dug certain roots near the
brook and gathered wild onions and turnips in the wood.

The women recognized familiar simples and herbs among the
plants. Mary removed some to her garden and placed them beside
the rows planted with seeds Mother had brought from Leyden.
Others were ground into powders to be added to our food or kept
ready for illnesses.

We made salt from the sea. Great buckets of seawater were
collected. As these dried in the sun or were boiled upon a fire, layers
of salt collected, which was of much use in the drying of fish.

While we rejoiced of the plentiful food and renewed warmth which visited us, the new season brought another anguish. I was in the wood with Edward when he suddenly became pale as death. I took his hand to lead him homeward, but we had not reached the brook before his breathing became heavy.

"Richard?" he gasped.

I thought for a moment that he would join Mother, but although his breathing was much labored, and he shivered as with a winter chill, I was able to help him to the fields. There Master Winslow took Edward in his arms and carried him to our dwelling.

We were fearful of a new plague, but Mary would hear nonesuch. She located two dried leaves of rosemary and rolled them in her fingers. She next drew the leaves close to Edward's nose. As he inhaled, his breathing eased, and his face grew bright.

As the trees regained their leaves, we began our preparations for the planting. Already the fields had been made ready for what wheat and barley we had seed to plant. A few acres of peas were to be set out. From Squanto we learned it was yet early to plant the corn.

In late March Master Carver was reelected our governor. Much work was carried out in the village, and Father planned a cottage to replace the small hut we now inhabited. Great barrels were brought ashore from Mayflower to be filled with fresh water for the ship's voyage back to England.

I found my heart growing heavy as the final preparations were made for Mayflower's departure. I had come to look upon the ship as both my friend and protector, as our home for so long a time. On the eve of her sailing, I found myself walking with Master Clarke on the beach.

"You will be asea once again on the morrow," I said, staring out past the horizon, imagining it was possible to see the distant coast of England.

"Aye, by sundown we will be out to sea," he said.

"It is a long way to Southampton."

" 'Tis but another ocean to cross. To a sailor, it is as green a pasture as yon field."

"You can't plant seed in an ocean," I told him.

"Aye, but a sailor's no planter. He is a reaper at times, for he harvests fish from the sea. Nay, more often he's a wanderer with no home port, cast upon a wind."

"I fear it would be a life I would grow weary of."

"There is a weariness, Richard Woodley, but there is a joy of discoveries, fair harbors, and new lands."

"Like this one?"

"Aye."

"Have you ever found a place you wished to make your home?"

"I have a home: the sea."

"And a family?"

"Aye, my mates. Upon occasion I acquire others."

"Boys who listen to tales?"

"Aye, and those who steer a ship or caulk a boat."

I found myself smiling, and I wish my tongue had been able to give him my thanks.

"Ye would have made a fine sailor," he told me. "But I see the heart of a farmer. Ye wish to grow things."

"Perhaps I shall grow myself," I said, hoping to lighten the mood.

"I never knew a boy to stand so tall," Master Clarke said. "If the winds were to blow me to the Americas years hence, I would find you a great man, Lord of the Manor or the like."

"There's a greater likelihood I'll be a poor farmer, but you will be welcome to share my table."

"Men who weather the storm are bound by it," he said, setting his great rough hand upon my head. I bid ye a fair harvest and a better winter."

"May you find the winds fair to England," I replied. Reluctantly I watched him walk to the ship's boat.

A reconstruction of the original Mayflower

Activities

1. **THINK ABOUT IT** What events and people in this story are real? Which are not real, but were made up by the author? How can you tell the difference?

2. **CHART IT** Make a chart that lists the foods mentioned in the story. Describe how the foods were gathered or prepared. Add pictures to illustrate your chart.

Dutch and French Colonies

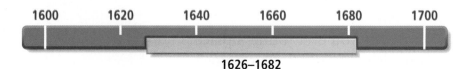

| 1600 | 1620 | 1640 | 1660 | 1680 | 1700 |

1626–1682

Build on What You Know Have you ever traded books or toys? People usually trade when they want something that someone else has. In the 1600s, American Indians and European settlers traded with each other.

New Netherland

Main Idea The Dutch settled in what is now the northeastern United States.

Remember that in the 1500s and 1600s, European explorers claimed land in North America. Henry Hudson made land claims for the Netherlands on one of his voyages. The Dutch called this land New Netherland.

The first settlements in New Netherland were fur-trading posts. In 1626, the governor of New Netherland, **Peter Minuit** (MIHN yoo IHT), bought Manhattan Island in present-day New York from the Manhates Indians. He started a settlement there called New Amsterdam, the capital of New Netherland. Minuit also set up a colony for Sweden on the Delaware River. New Sweden lasted for 17 years before it was taken over by New Netherland in 1655.

Peter Minuit He was the first leader of New Netherland.

VOCABULARY

diversity
tolerance
missionary

Vocabulary Strategy

mission**ary**

Look for the word **mission** in **missionary**. Missionaries have a mission, or goal, to teach others about their religion.

READING SKILL
Compare and Contrast
As you read, make a list of similarities and differences between the Dutch and French settlements.

ALIKE	DIFFERENT

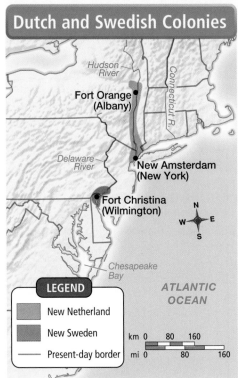

Dutch and Swedish Colonies

Dutch and Swedish Settlements Located at the mouth of the Hudson River, New Amsterdam (above) had one of the best harbors in North America. The map shows the location of the Dutch and Swedish colonies in 1650.

Settlers in New Netherland

The Dutch West India Company was an important trading company in the Netherlands. The owners of the company controlled the New Netherland settlements. The company brought some families to North America to farm, but few people from the Netherlands wanted to move across the Atlantic.

The company looked for settlers from other countries. They welcomed all people, no matter what country they came from or what religion they practiced. New settlers added to the diversity of New Netherland. **Diversity** is the variety of people in a group. In New Amsterdam alone, 18 languages were spoken. The population included German, English, Swedish, French, and free and enslaved African settlers.

New York

In 1647, **Peter Stuyvesant** (STY vih suhnt) became governor of New Netherland. Stuyvesant was a harsh man. He made laws that angered colonists. Unlike most settlers in New Netherland, he did not practice tolerance. **Tolerance** is respecting beliefs that are different from one's own. Stuyvesant did not want settlers with different religious beliefs in the colony.

In 1664, English ships sailed into the harbor at New Amsterdam to attack. The settlers of New Amsterdam were so unhappy with Stuyvesant that they refused to fight the English. The Dutch colony of New Netherland became an English colony. The English renamed New Amsterdam to honor the Duke of York. They called it New York.

REVIEW Why was Stuyvesant an unpopular governor?

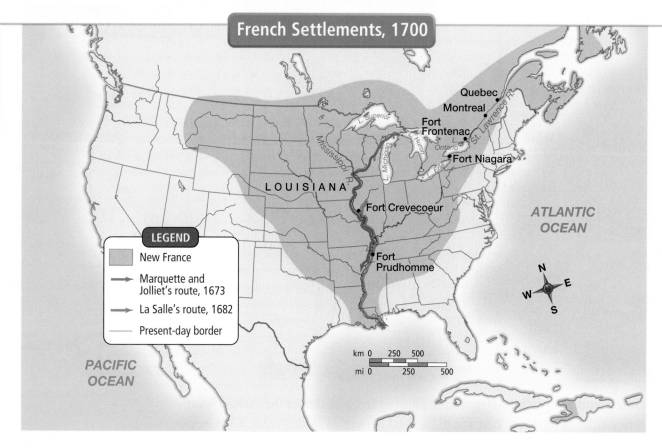

French Settlements, 1700

LEGEND
- New France
- → Marquette and Jolliet's route, 1673
- → La Salle's route, 1682
- — Present-day border

Quebec
Montreal
Fort Frontenac
Fort Niagara
Fort Crevecoeur
Fort Prudhomme
LOUISIANA
ATLANTIC OCEAN
PACIFIC OCEAN
L. Superior
L. Michigan
L. Huron
L. Ontario
L. Erie
Mississippi R.
St. Lawrence R.

km 0 250 500
mi 0 250 500

New France After 1682, France's land claims covered a large part of North America. **SKILL** **Reading Maps** Which river did Marquette, Jolliet, and La Salle explore?

New France

Main Idea France claimed much of North America in the 1600s, but few settlers lived there.

In the early 1600s, the French claimed land in present-day Canada. This land was called New France. Few settlers lived there. Its cold climate made farming difficult. Most settlers were young men who worked in the fur and fishing trades. They lived near the fur-trading post of Quebec.

Missionaries moved to New France as well. A **missionary** is a person who teaches his or her religion to others who have different beliefs. Missionaries from France taught people of present-day Canada about Catholicism. They built missions through-out New France.

The Fur Trade

Animals with thick fur, including beaver, fox, and otter, lived in the forests of North America. French merchants made money selling these furs in Europe.

Fur traders traveled throughout New France to trade with Indians. People of Indian nations gave the furs from animals they had trapped to the French. In exchange, the French traded goods such as beads, tools, pots, knives, and cloth.

The French formed a partnership with the Huron and Algonquin, who lived near Quebec. The Huron and Algonquin were at war with the powerful Iroquois, a group of five American Indian nations. French fur traders, led by **Samuel de Champlain,** fought with the Huron and Algonquin against their enemies.

Traveling by Canoe Marquette and Jolliet on the Mississippi River.

Exploring the Mississippi

Jacques Marquette (mahr KEHT) was a missionary in New France. In 1673, he traveled by canoe down the Mississippi River to set up missions. **Louis Jolliet** (JOH lee EHT), an explorer, joined him. Jolliet thought the Mississippi might lead to the Pacific Ocean.

Robert La Salle (luh SAL) also explored the region in 1682. He claimed the Mississippi River and all the land around it for France. La Salle named this vast area Louisiana after **King Louis XIV**.

REVIEW How did the traders of New France get fur to sell to Europeans?

Lesson Summary

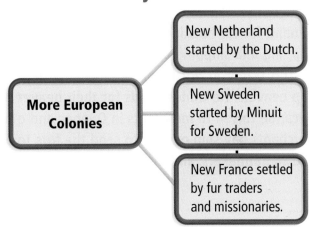

More European Colonies

New Netherland started by the Dutch.

New Sweden started by Minuit for Sweden.

New France settled by fur traders and missionaries.

Why It Matters ...

New Netherland and New France included land that would one day become part of the United States.

Lesson Review

1626 New Amsterdam founded	1664 New Amsterdam attacked	1673 Marquette and Jolliet's journey

1620 — 1640 — 1660 — 1680 — 1700

❶ **VOCABULARY** Write a short paragraph about New Netherland, using the word **tolerance.**

❷ **READING SKILL** What do you think was the most important **difference** between New Amsterdam and New France?

❸ **MAIN IDEA: Citizenship** What made the population of New Netherland diverse?

❹ **MAIN IDEA: History** Why did so few settlers live in New France?

❺ **PEOPLE TO KNOW** What reasons did **Jacques Marquette** and **Louis Jolliet** have for exploring the Mississippi River?

❻ **TIMELINE SKILL** Did New Amsterdam last for more than or less than 50 years?

❼ **CRITICAL THINKING: Evaluate** How did the partnership between the French and the Huron and Algonquin help the French? How did it help the Huron and Algonquin?

HANDS ON

MAP ACTIVITY Draw a rough map of the Mississippi River. Where does it begin and end? What states does it pass through? Label this information on your map.

French Fur Trading

A lone fur trader travels remote lands of northern New France. Though he is far from Europe, he is part of world trade in the 1600s. The demand for fur hats in Europe has resulted in an active business for the trapping and shipping of beaver pelts and other furs.

This trader in North America meets with Huron and Ottawa people who trap beavers. He trades goods for their beaver pelts. Then he carries the pelts by canoe to sell to merchants in Quebec and other trading posts. French merchants pay ship owners to send the furs to Europe. In Europe, the furs are sold to hatmakers, and their fur hats are sold to buyers.

Deerskin Clothes
Traders wore deerskin clothes as did the Huron and Ottawa. These clothes were strong and did not wear out.

Canoes
Traders could not travel on swift rivers without canoes. They used canoes like those the Huron and Ottawa built.

Why Did They Trade?

New France

American Indians in New France wanted European goods, especially iron goods. Iron kettles could be placed directly over a fire for cooking, and iron blades were strong enough to chop and carve wood.

Europe

Merchants earned money by selling furs to European hatmakers. Hatmakers prepared the pelts for different styles of hats which were warm, waterproof, and long-lasting. The beaver hat below is soft like felt.

Furs and Supplies

A canoe could carry about 40 pelts. Traders also needed to carry trade goods, which were heavy, to supply the American Indians.

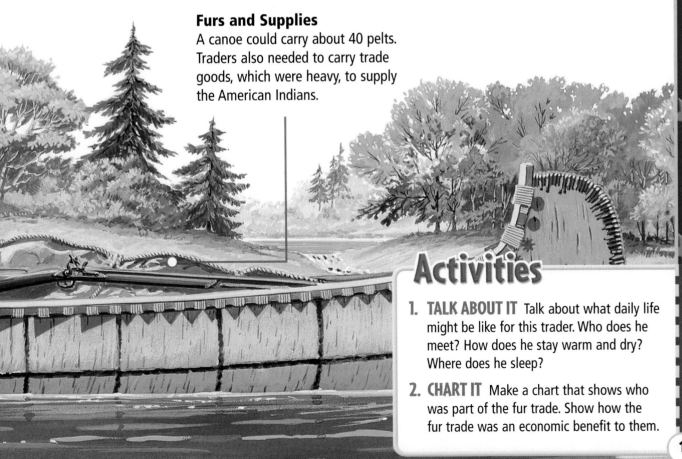

Activities

1. **TALK ABOUT IT** Talk about what daily life might be like for this trader. Who does he meet? How does he stay warm and dry? Where does he sleep?

2. **CHART IT** Make a chart that shows who was part of the fur trade. Show how the fur trade was an economic benefit to them.

Review and Test Prep

Visual Summary

1–3. ▮▭▶ Write a description of each colony named below.

Europeans in North America

Jamestown	New France	New Netherland
_____	_____	_____
_____	_____	_____
_____	_____	_____

Facts and Main Ideas

✓ TEST PREP Answer each question with information from the chapter.

4. **Geography** Why did explorers look for a Northwest Passage?

5. **Economics** How did the Virginia Company raise money to buy ships and supplies to start a settlement in North America?

6. **History** What difficulties did settlers in Plymouth and Jamestown have in common?

7. **Government** What was the Mayflower Compact?

8. **History** Why was it easy for England to take control of New Amsterdam?

Vocabulary

✓ TEST PREP Choose the correct word from the list below to complete each sentence.

armada, p. 125
charter, p. 131
tolerance, p. 145

9. A person who has respect for others' beliefs shows _____.

10. King Philip of Spain built an _____ to fight the English.

11. The King of England gave the Virginia Company a _____ to start a settlement.

English Colonies

| 1580 | 1590 | 1600 | 1610 | 1620 | 1630 | 1640 |

1585
Roanoke founded

1607
Jamestown founded

1620
Plymouth founded

1630
Massachusetts Bay Colony founded

French and Dutch Colonies

| 1580 | 1590 | 1600 | 1610 | 1620 | 1630 | 1640 |

1608
Quebec founded

1626
New Amsterdam founded

Apply Skills

☑ **TEST PREP** **Chart and Graph Skill** Use the parallel timelines above to answer each question.

12. Which colony was founded first?
    A. Jamestown
    B. Quebec
    C. Roanoke
    D. Plymouth

13. Which colony was settled just one year after Jamestown?
    A. Plymouth
    B. Roanoke
    C. New Amsterdam
    D. Quebec

14. How many colonies were founded in the 1620s?
    A. 0
    B. 2
    C. 4
    D. 6

Critical Thinking

☑ **TEST PREP** Write a short paragraph to answer each question.

15. **Compare and Contrast** How were the Pilgrims and the Puritans alike? How were they different?

16. **Classify** What three categories of information would you use for a report on the Jamestown colony?

Activities

Debate Activity Research one of the theories about why the Roanoke colonists disappeared. Prepare notes for a class debate on the lost colony.

Writing Activity Write a one-page short story about the celebration of the Pilgrims' first harvest. Write from the point of view of the Wampanoag Indians who were there.

Technology
Writing Process Tips
Get help with your story at
www.eduplace.com/kids/hmss05/

Vocabulary and Main Ideas

✓ **TEST PREP** Write a sentence to answer each question.

1. Why did Arab merchants travel by **caravan** across the desert?

2. What are three examples of **technology** used by sailors in the 1400s?

3. What was the reaction of the **conquistadors** when they arrived at Tenochtitlán? Why?

4. Why did the Dutch make land **claims** in present-day New York State?

5. Why did people **invest** in the Virginia Company?

6. Why would a **missionary** move to New France?

Critical Thinking

✓ **TEST PREP** Write a short paragraph to answer each question.

7. **Cause and Effect** How did European exploration affect the land and people of the Americas?

8. **Compare and Contrast** Write a short paragraph about the settlers of New Spain, New England, New France, and New Netherland. What did they have in common? What differences did they have?

Apply Skills

✓ **TEST PREP** Map Skill Use the map of Balboa's journey to answer each question about latitude and longitude.

9. What lines of latitude and longitude are closest to Spain?

   A. 20°N, 0°

   B. 40°S, 0°

   C. 40°N, 40°W

   D. 40°N, 0°

10. At about what line of longitude did Balboa first enter the Pacific Ocean?

   A. 0°

   B. 20°W

   C. 40°W

   D. 80°W

Unit Activity

Create Explorer Postcards

- Choose any place in North America that you would like to have explored.
- Research information about the geography and early people of the place you chose.
- Create one or more postcards an explorer might have sent home.
- One side of your postcard might be an illustration of the place. The other side might be a written message about it.

Your Majesty, I have discovered an amazing canyon!

At the Library

Check your school library for these books.

Hard Labor: The First African-Americans, 1619 by P. C. McKissack and F. L. McKissack Jr.

In 1619, twenty Africans came to Virginia as indentured servants, ready to begin life anew.

Sir Walter Raleigh and the Quest for El Dorado by Marc Aronson

This biography tells about successes and failures of Sir Walter Raleigh.

Connect to Today

Create a class book about exploration today.

- Find articles that tell about the exploration of new frontiers, such as the ocean and space.
- Write a summary of each article. Draw a picture or map to illustrate each summary.
- Gather your illustrated summaries into a class book.

 Technology

Get information for the class book from the Weekly Reader at **www.eduplace.com/kids/hmss05/**

Read About It

Look for these Social Studies Independent Books in your classroom.

Pocahontas by Carl W.

On Board the *Santa Maria* by Becky Cheston

Fur Traders of NEW FRANCE by Lisa Roore

UNIT 3

The English Colonies

The Big Idea

Why do people move to new places?

" I found a new world and new manners, at which my heart rose. "

Anne Bradstreet, colonial poet

Anne Hutchinson
1591–1643

This religious leader moved from England to Boston. She was not afraid to speak out about her beliefs. The things she said made Puritan leaders angry, but she did not back down.
page 167

History Makers

William Penn
1644–1718

William Penn created the first planned city in the colonies. He called it Philadelphia, "the city of brotherly love." He wanted people in the colony of Pennsylvania to live in peace. **page 189**

James Oglethorpe
1696–1785

This wealthy Englishman wanted to help people who owed money or were very poor. He started the colony of Georgia to give them a new beginning in North America. **page 204**

SKAGIT

BLACKFOOT

CHINOOK

Columbia R.

YAKIMA

OJIBWA

TILLAMOOK

NEZ PERCE

CHIPPEWA

Lake Superior

CROW

MANDAN

NAKOTA

WINNEBAGO

DAKOTA

SHOSHONE

LAKOTA

Missouri R.

Lake Michigan

SAUK

YUROK

MODOC

PAIUTE

BANNOCK

CHEYENNE

OMAHA

FOX

MIA

POMO

SHOSHONE

PAWNEE

IOWA

MIWOK

SHOSHONE

UTE R.

ARAPAHO

MISSOURI

ILLINOIS

PAIUTE

Colorado

KAW

YOKUTS

PUEBLO

OSAGE

CHICKSA

CHUMASH

PUEBLO

NAVAJO

KIOWA

R.

Mississippi

TUSKEG

Santa Fe

Albuquerque

CADDO

CAHUILLA

COMANCHE

CHOCTAW

YUMA

El Paso

APACHE

ATAKAPA

PACIFIC
OCEAN

Rio Grande

TONKAWA

New Orleans

KARANKAWA

Gulf of
Mexico

Unit Preview

1600   1625   1650   1675

1619
Legislature Established

Virginia House of Burgesses founded
Chapter 6, page 203

1664
New York Founded

English take control of New Netherland
Chapter 6, page 188

1675
King Philip's War

Wampanoag and colonists fight over territory
Chapter 5, page 169

Quebec

ABENAKI

Montreal

HURON

Lake
Ontario

MASSACHUSET

ERIE

IROQUOIS
NATIONS

Boston

PEQUOT

AWATOMI

Detroit

Lake Erie

SUSQUEHANNOCK

New York

Philadelphia

WNEE

DELAWARE

POWHATAN

Ohio R.

N
NW   NE
W   E
SW   SE
S

TUSCARORA

EROKEE

CATAWBA

ATLANTIC
OCEAN

EK

Charleston

YAMASEE

LEGEND

English

New France

New Spain

Disputed territory

English

Spanish mission

French trading post

PEQUOT American Indians

St. Augustine

TIMUCUA

CALUSA

0   150   300

0   150   300

---

700   1725   1750

681

**ennsylvania
ounded**

nn promotes
eedom and
lerance
**hapter 6,
ge 189**

1730
**Great
Awakening**

Religion spreads
throughout
colonies
**Chapter 5,
page 178**

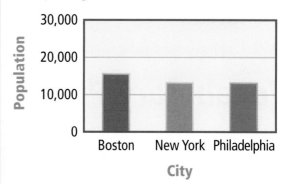

Connect to Today

City Populations, 1740s

In the 1740s, Boston, New York, and
Philadelphia were the three largest cities
in the English colonies.

City Populations Today

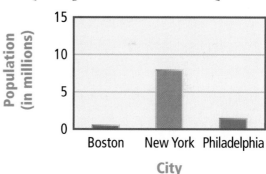

The population of
New York City today
is nearly 600 times
larger than it was
in 1740.

CURRENT   EVENTS

WEEKLY (WR) READER

Current events on the web!

Find out about current events that connect
with the Big Idea of this unit.
See activities at:
www.eduplace.com/kids/hmss05/

Technology

e • **glossary**
e • **word games**
www.eduplace.com/kids/hmss05/

Vocabulary Preview

growing season

The New England **growing season** is short because winters are long and cold. New England farmers of the 1600s could grow only enough to feed their families. **page 161**

town meeting

In Massachusetts Bay, almost every community made decisions in a **town meeting.** The townspeople met in a large meetinghouse. **page 166**

Chapter Timeline

1636
Rhode Island and Hartford founded

1647
Massachusetts school law passed

1630 1640 1650

Reading Strategy

Predict and Infer Use this strategy before you read.

Look at the titles and pictures. What can you tell about the people and events in the lesson?

dissenter

Some colonists did not agree with the laws of their leaders. One **dissenter** was Roger Williams, who started his own settlement.
page 167

industry

Many New England colonists made a living from the sea. Some fished. Others worked in the shipbuilding **industry.**
page 174

1675
King Philip's War begins

60   1670   1680

Geography of the Colonies

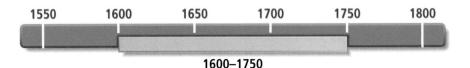

1550   1600   1650   1700   1750   1800

1600–1750

Build on What You Know What is the geography like where you live? Are you close to mountains or is the land flat for miles around? Think about where you live and how it affects the way you live.

The Thirteen Colonies

Main Idea The geography and climate of the thirteen colonies affected how colonists lived and worked.

During the 1600s and 1700s, many English settlers moved to North America. People believed that they had a better chance to make a living in North America or to find freedoms that they didn't have at home. These settlers established thirteen English colonies.

The colonies were located along the Atlantic Ocean, with New France to the north and New Spain to the south. The Appalachian Mountains formed a natural boundary to the west.

The geography and climate of the thirteen colonies separated them into three different regions: New England, the Middle Colonies, and the Southern Colonies.

New England Coast
Rocky coasts are common in New England.

New England

New England's geography was shaped by glaciers. During the Ice Age, thick sheets of ice covered much of North America. As the glaciers moved slowly across New England, they carried rocks trapped in the ice. The ice and rocks cut deep valleys through the mountains. They scraped up New England's rich soil and pushed it south, leaving a thin, rocky layer of dirt.

Farming was difficult in New England. Most of the land was filled with rocks or was too sandy to farm. The region's many forests and rugged mountains made it hard to find good farmland.

The climate also affected New England farming. Summers were warm, but winters were long and bitterly cold. The growing season was short. The **growing season** is the time of year when it is warm enough for plants to grow. In New England, the growing season lasted only from late May to early October. Most farmers could grow just enough food for their families, with a little left over to sell.

Farming in New England was hard, but the area had many natural resources. Colonists used these resources to make a living. They took wood from the thick forests to make buildings and ships. They caught fish and whales from the Atlantic Ocean to use for food and other products.

REVIEW Why was farming difficult for New England colonists?

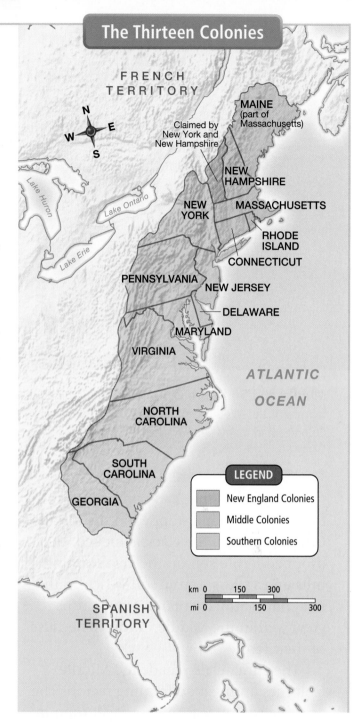

The Thirteen Colonies

LEGEND

- New England Colonies
- Middle Colonies
- Southern Colonies

km 0   150   300
mi 0   150   300

Three Regions This map divides the colonies into three regions. Each region has its own geography and climate. **SKILL** **Reading Maps** Which were the New England Colonies?

Farmland

Tidewater

Middle and Southern Colonies Gentle, rolling hills were a common feature of the Middle Colonies (left). The tidewater of the Southern Colonies had many rivers (right).

The Middle Colonies

The glaciers that had scooped up soil from New England stopped in the Middle Colonies. When the glaciers melted, they dropped fertile soil on the area's rolling hills and valleys. Fertile soil is rich in the material that helps plants grow. Crops grew well in the Middle Colonies because of their fertile soil.

The climate also made the Middle Colonies a very good farming region. The growing season was much longer than in New England. The Middle Colonies had many sunny days and plenty of rain.

The Middle Colonies' wide rivers, such as the Delaware and the Hudson, were ideal for transportation. Farmers used riverboats to sell their crops in nearby towns and to bring supplies to their farms. The woods near these farms were full of wildlife. Colonists hunted and trapped animals such as deer and beaver.

The Southern Colonies

The geography of the Southern Colonies was very different from that of the other colonies. The southern coast is a watery world of rivers, bays, and wetlands. This area is called the tidewater. In the **tidewater,** the water in rivers and streams rises and falls every day with the ocean's tides.

The climate and soil of the tidewater were excellent for farming. Many southern colonists grew cash crops. The weather was warm for much of the year, and crops could grow for seven or eight months. Soil in the tidewater was rich and fertile, and the area received plenty of rain.

Colonists used the waterways in the tidewater to ship crops to markets in other towns and countries. The tidewater ended at the fall line, about 150 miles inland. At the **fall line,** rivers from higher land flow to lower lands and often form waterfalls.

The fall line followed the eastern edge of the Appalachian Mountains, from the Southern Colonies to New England. The higher land on the other side of the fall line was known as the **backcountry.** The backcountry was "in back of" the area where most colonists settled. The land in the backcountry was steep and covered with forests. Farms there were small, and colonists hunted and fished for much of their food.

REVIEW Why was farming in the Middle and Southern colonies better than in New England?

Lesson Summary

The thirteen English colonies in North America formed three unique regions. New England had poor soil and a cold climate, but plenty of forests and fish. The Middle Colonies had fertile soil, a warmer climate, and rivers for transportation. The Southern Colonies had an even warmer climate and many waterways in the tidewater.

Why It Matters …

For the thirteen colonies to grow, colonists had to learn how to adapt to the geography and climate of each of these three regions.

Fall Line Waterfalls are common along the area where the backcountry and the tidewater meet.

Lesson Review

1 VOCABULARY Complete the following sentence, using two of the words listed below.

   fall line   tidewater   backcountry

   The _____ was the higher land on the western side of the _____.

2 READING SKILL Write a short paragraph that **compares** and **contrasts** the growing season and soil in each region.

3 MAIN IDEA: Geography Why was the tidewater good for growing crops?

4 MAIN IDEA: Economics In what ways did the geography and climate of the Southern Colonies affect how colonists made a living?

5 PLACES TO KNOW What natural resources did colonists have in New England?

6 CRITICAL THINKING: Draw Conclusions Why would colonists want to settle near rivers and other waterways? Use facts and details to support your answer.

7 CRITICAL THINKING: Analyze Climate is one way to divide places into regions. What are some other ways?

 ART ACTIVITY Use library resources to learn more about how glaciers changed New England's geography. Draw a picture to show what you learned.

THE APPALACHIANS

The Appalachian Mountains aren't the tallest mountains in the world, but they are some of the oldest, and they show it. For over 400 million years, wind, rain, and snow have worn them down. In the north, Ice Age glaciers ground and scraped them. This endless erosion created the rounded mountains and hills people know today.

Though the Appalachian Mountains are not very high, they were hard to cross in early colonial times. Settlers who tried to use rivers were usually stopped by waterfalls, rushing waters, and deep gorges.

Another challenge to travelers was the Appalachians' forests. The forests were so hard to pass through that few settlers lived west of the fall line at the edge of the Appalachians.

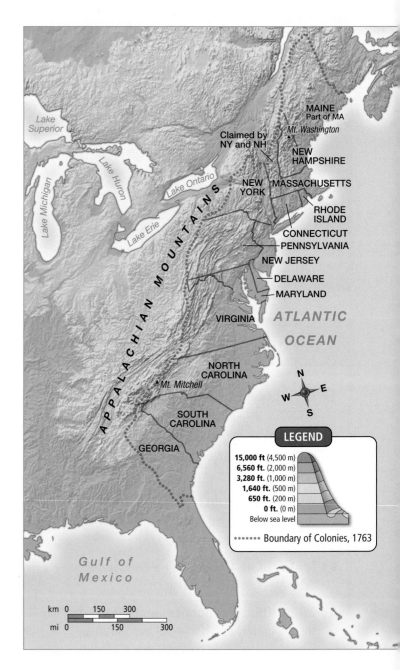

LEGEND
15,000 ft (4,500 m)
6,560 ft. (2,000 m)
3,280 ft. (1,000 m)
1,640 ft. (500 m)
650 ft. (200 m)
0 ft. (0 m)
Below sea level
•••••• Boundary of Colonies, 1763

km 0   150   300
mi 0   150   300

The Appalachian Mountains stretch 1,600 miles. In most places, the Appalachians are nearly 100 miles wide.

Ridges and Valleys Some areas of the Appalachians are rugged and steep. A narrow ridge can be seen in this photograph, running along the top of the mountains.

Activities

1. **TALK ABOUT IT** What challenges did people face crossing the Appalachians in the 1600s?

2. **CHART IT** Use an atlas to find the five highest mountains in the Appalachians. Make a chart giving the name, location, and altitude of each peak.

New England

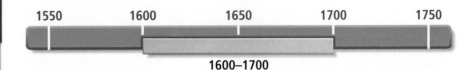

1550   1600   1650   1700   1750

1600–1700

VOCABULARY

town meeting
self-government
dissenter
banish

Vocabulary Strategy

dissent**er**

Dissent means to disagree. The suffix **-er** changes the meaning to a person who disagrees.

READING SKILL

Main Idea and Details
As you read, note details that support the second main idea in this lesson.

Build on What You Know Have you ever wanted to set a good example for others? Puritan colonists did. They believed that they should set a good example for other people by following laws based on the Bible.

Massachusetts

Main Idea Religion was at the center of Puritan government and community life.

The Puritans were English colonists who settled in New England in the 1600s. These settlers wanted to form communities where they could follow the rules of the Bible and serve their God.

Puritan religion shaped the government of the Massachusetts Bay Colony. Usually, only male church members could vote or serve in town government. Town leaders made laws to control how people worshipped. One law required all people to attend church services.

On Sundays, the town gathered at the meeting-house for church. The meetinghouse was the most important building in a Puritan community and was often built in the middle of town.

Community members came to the meetinghouse at least once a year for a town meeting. A **town meeting** was a gathering where colonists held elections and voted on the laws for their towns.

Puritan Meetinghouse This meetinghouse still stands in Hingham, Massachusetts.

Dissenters Roger Williams (above) receives advice from Narragansett Indians in Rhode Island. Both Williams and Anne Hutchinson (right) challenged Puritan teachings.

In Massachusetts Bay, everyone could attend a town meeting, but only men who owned property could vote. Even so, Puritans still had more self-government than people in most other European colonies. When people make laws for themselves, they have **self-government.**

The Puritans had some experience with self-government in England. The law-making body in England was called Parliament. Some members of Parliament were elected by the people.

Rhode Island

Some colonists thought that Puritan leaders should not tell them what to believe or how to act. These colonists were called dissenters. A **dissenter** is a person who does not agree with the beliefs of his or her leaders.

Roger Williams was a dissenter who wanted more religious freedom. Puritan leaders, however, believed that everyone had to follow the same religious laws.

Williams believed that the government should not make laws about religion. Because of his views, Puritan leaders, banished him from Massachusetts. To **banish** means to force someone to leave.

In 1636, Williams founded a new colony that became known as Rhode Island. There, people could worship freely. Williams also kept the government separate from the church. This was an important event in the history of religious freedom in North America.

Another Puritan who challenged church leaders was **Anne Hutchinson.** Hutchinson criticized Puritan ministers. She also held meetings in her home where men and women talked about religion. Puritan leaders did not like this. They said her beliefs went against Puritan teachings and that women should not teach men about religion. Like Roger Williams, Hutchinson was banished and moved to Rhode Island.

REVIEW In what ways were Roger Williams and Anne Hutchinson alike?

Connecticut, New Hampshire, Maine

A minister named **Thomas Hooker** also did not like some of the rules made by Puritan leaders. He wanted to form a new community where all men could vote, even if they were not church members.

In 1636, Hooker led about 100 colonists west to the Connecticut River. There they founded the town of Hartford. Colonists looking for good farmland started other towns in the area. These towns joined Hartford to create the colony of Connecticut. Other colonists from Massachusetts Bay moved north and settled the area that became New Hampshire and Maine.

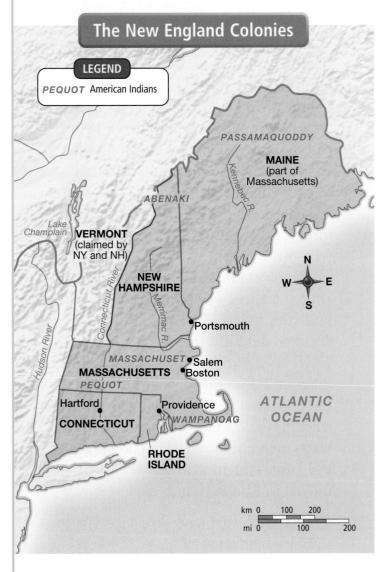

The New England Colonies

LEGEND

PEQUOT American Indians

PASSAMAQUODDY

MAINE
(part of
Massachusetts)

Kennebec R.

ABENAKI

Lake
Champlain **VERMONT**
(claimed by
NY and NH)

Connecticut River

**NEW
HAMPSHIRE**

Merrimac R.

●Portsmouth

Hudson River

N
W   E
S

MASSACHUSET ●Salem
MASSACHUSETTS ●Boston
PEQUOT

Hartford● ●Providence
CONNECTICUT *WAMPANOAG*

**ATLANTIC
OCEAN**

**RHODE
ISLAND**

km 0   100   200
mi 0   100   200

Conflicts over Land

Main Idea Puritans and American Indians fought over land in New England.

The New England colonies were founded on lands where American Indians lived. Indians and colonists disagreed about who owned the land. American Indians believed that land was for everyone to use and that no one could truly own it. They thought that when they sold land to colonists they were only agreeing to share it. Colonists, however, expected the Indians to move from the land once they sold it. These different views of ownership often led to conflict.

In the 1630s, a war broke out between colonists and the Pequot (PEE kwawt) Indians. This struggle over land became known as the Pequot War, and ended when the colonists killed most of the Pequots. The few surviving Pequots were enslaved or fled.

After the Pequot War, more colonists moved onto American Indian lands in New England. **Metacomet** (MEHT uh kah meht) was a leader of the Wampanoag (wahm pah NOH ahg) nation. He wanted to avoid war, but he believed that his people had to fight to stay on their lands.

New England Settlement here began in Massachusetts. From there, colonies started new communities elsewhere in New England.

SKILL **Reading Maps** Where in New England did the Pequots live?

Metacomet The Leader of the Wampanoags feared that the growth of English settlements would destroy his people's way of life.

In 1675, Metacomet, who was known to colonists as King Philip, attacked Massachusetts villages. Fierce fighting spread across New England in a series of battles called King Philip's War. The colonists had more soldiers and better weapons than Metacomet's small army.

In 1676, Metacomet was defeated. After the war, colonists killed and enslaved some of the defeated Indians. They forced many others to leave. Few American Indians remained in southeastern New England after the war.

REVIEW What caused the Pequot War?

Lesson Summary

- Religion was an important part of the government in the Massachusetts Bay Colony.

- Some people disagreed with Puritan leaders and left Massachusetts Bay to form new colonies.

- The settlement of New England led to war with American Indians.

Why It Matters ...

Self-government and the actions of dissenters led to freedom of thought and religion in parts of New England.

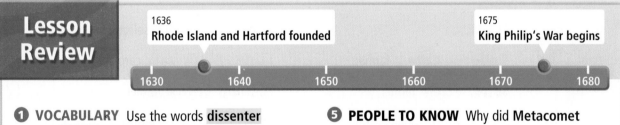

Lesson Review

1636
Rhode Island and Hartford founded

1675
King Philip's War begins

1630   1640   1650   1660   1670   1680

❶ **VOCABULARY** Use the words **dissenter** and **banish** in a paragraph describing people who disagreed with Puritan leaders.

❷ **READING SKILL** Use the **details** from your chart to answer this question: What did the English and American Indians disagree about who owned the land?

❸ **MAIN IDEA: Government** Who was allowed to vote in Massachusetts Bay?

❹ **MAIN IDEA: History** Why did some Massachusetts Bay colonists form new colonies?

❺ **PEOPLE TO KNOW** Why did **Metacomet** lead his people to war against the colonists?

❻ **TIMELINE SKILL** Did King Philip's War take place before or after Hartford was founded?

❼ **CRITICAL THINKING: Decision Making** What were the short-term and long-term effects of Puritan leaders' decision to banish Roger Williams from Massachusetts Bay?

WRITING ACTIVITY Write a letter that Anne Hutchinson might have written to Roger Williams discussing their disagreements with Puritan leaders.

Extend Lesson 2

Readers' Theater

Town Meeting

APRIL 5, 1749

The New England town of Linton has a problem to resolve. Colonists from the southern part of Linton want to form their own town, so they are meeting to try to reach an agreement. Today, many New England towns still hold town meetings. Listen to what the residents of Linton have to say to one another.

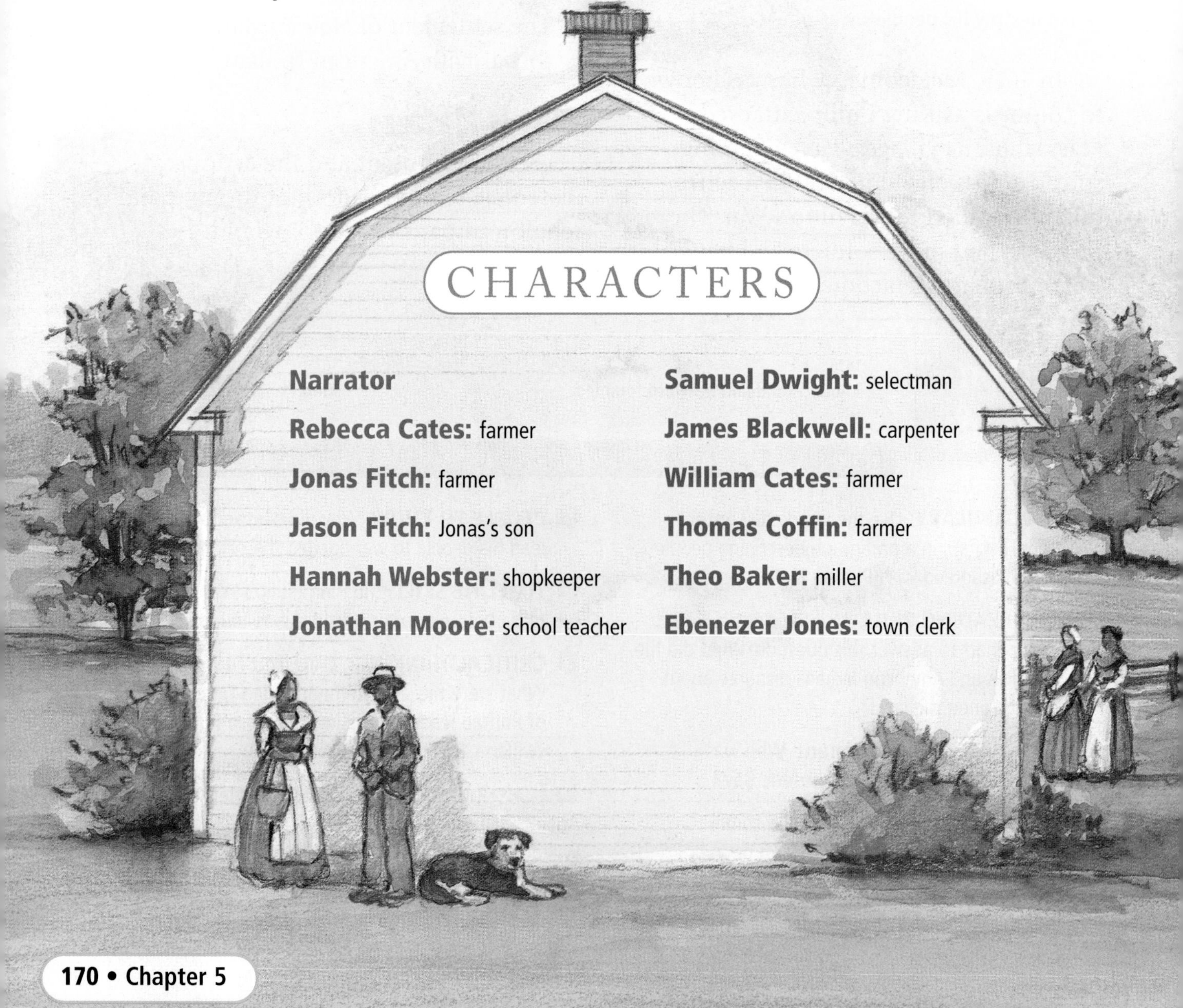

CHARACTERS

Narrator

Rebecca Cates: farmer

Jonas Fitch: farmer

Jason Fitch: Jonas's son

Hannah Webster: shopkeeper

Jonathan Moore: school teacher

Samuel Dwight: selectman

James Blackwell: carpenter

William Cates: farmer

Thomas Coffin: farmer

Theo Baker: miller

Ebenezer Jones: town clerk

Narrator: People are arriving for today's town meeting in Linton. Some families have walked for miles to get here.

Rebecca Cates: You see? This is why we need our own town! Just getting here in the spring is exhausting—never mind making the trip during the winter!

Jonas Fitch: Spring's bad enough. The mud was almost up to my knees in places. I had to carry Jason on my shoulders, didn't I, son?

Jason Fitch: Yes, sir. Nearly took us all day to get here.

Hannah Webster: I know you have hardships. But I hate to think of so many families leaving us. Shopkeepers will lose customers. What will we do if you don't come into town?

Rebecca Cates: I wish no disrespect, Hannah, but Linton has changed. Our families no longer live close together as we once did.

Jonathan Moore: True. And if we had our own school south of the river, it would be better for our children— and I wouldn't have to spend four hours a day walking back and forth to teach them.

Hannah Webster

Farmer Jonas Fitch

171

Narrator: The people have taken their seats inside the meetinghouse. Let's go in and listen. I see that Selectman Dwight has given Tom Coffin permission to speak.

Tom Coffin: I represent the families south of the Fox River. We want to split off from Linton and build our own meetinghouse and school. We need our own town now.

Samuel Dwight: How many families are you speaking for, Tom?

Tom Coffin: Eighty-two.

Samuel Dwight: That would be a heavy loss.

James Blackwell: A heavy loss to the town treasury! If taxpayers leave, we won't have enough money to keep the town going.

William Cates: May I speak, please?

Samuel Dwight: Yes, Mr. Cates.

William Cates: Why should we support a town we can't even reach easily? Remember how deep the snow was last winter?

Jason Fitch: It was over my head!

Theo Baker: We could hold a town meeting in the summer. Special meetings could be held near you.

Samuel Dwight

Tom Coffin

Theo Baker

William Cates: Summer is a bad time for farmers to leave their plows.

Rebecca Cates: It wouldn't matter where you hold the meeting. Just getting to town is hard. We are too far from you!

Samuel Dwight: Does anyone else wish to speak about that?

Theo Baker: Maybe we need to build a better road.

James Blackwell: Hold on there. The town does not have enough money for a new road. Perhaps in a year or so we could patch up the old one.

Samuel Dwight: Jonas Fitch, it's your turn to speak.

Jonas Fitch: For years, this meeting has been full of arguments about where money should go. You who live in the center of town are not farmers like us. Our problems are different from yours. I say it's time for us to part.

Theo Baker: Jonas, it makes me sad to say this, but I believe I must agree.

Narrator: All have had a chance to give their opinions, but only white men who are church members may vote. In many towns they must be property owners, as well. After the vote, the town clerk reads the decision aloud.

Ebenezer Jones: It is so decided in Linton Town Meeting on April 5, in the year of 1749: that part of the town of Linton which lies north of the Fox River shall remain Linton, and that part which lies south of the river shall be built into a town by the name of South Linton.

Rebecca Cates

Activities

1. **THINK ABOUT IT** In what ways did the townspeople show **civic virtue** in their discussion?

2. **DEBATE IT** With partners, decide on an issue to discuss and resolve in a class town meeting. Write reasons for and against the issue. Then hold a town meeting in your classroom.

VOCABULARY

industry
export
import
Middle Passage
slave trade

Vocabulary Strategy

| import; export |

To remember the difference between **import** and **export,** think of into and exit. Imports come into a country. Exports exit, or leave, a country.

READING SKILL
Problem and Solution
What problem did colonists face in trying to earn a living by farming? Look for their solutions.

PROBLEM	SOLUTION

Life in New England

1550   1600   1650   1700   1750   1800

1600–1750

Build on What You Know Have you ever helped an adult do chores around your home? Children in New England spent much of their time doing hard work to help their families.

Using the Sea

Main Idea New England colonists made a living by using resources from the land and the sea.

Most people in New England were farmers. They worked on small plots of land growing crops such as wheat, oats, and peas. Farmers usually grew just enough to feed their families. Because farming in New England was difficult, some colonists looked for other ways to earn a living.

The geography of New England made it a good place to make a living from the sea. The rocky coast had many good harbors, and thick forests provided wood to build ships. Boston soon became a center for New England's growing shipbuilding industry. An **industry** is all the businesses that make one kind of product or provide one kind of service.

Shipbuilding Workers used oak trees to build the bodies of ships. Pine trees were used for ships' masts, the tall pole where sails are attached.

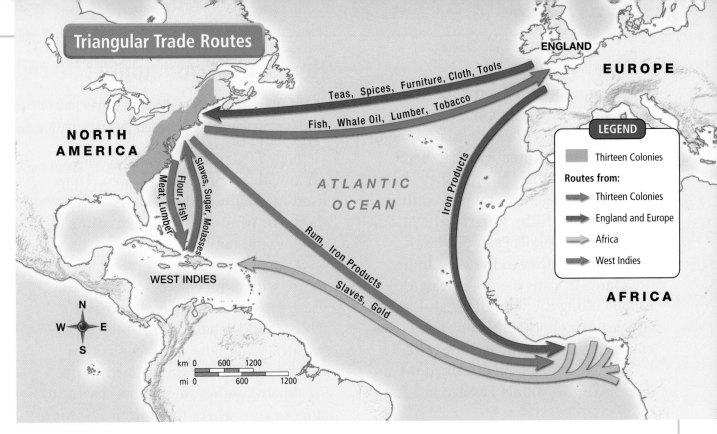

Triangular Trade Routes

Teas, Spices, Furniture, Cloth, Tools

Fish, Whale Oil, Lumber, Tobacco

ENGLAND

EUROPE

NORTH AMERICA

ATLANTIC OCEAN

Slaves, Sugar, Molasses

Flour, Fish

Meat, Lumber

Iron Products

Rum, Iron Products

Slaves, Gold

WEST INDIES

AFRICA

LEGEND

Thirteen Colonies

Routes from:

Thirteen Colonies

England and Europe

Africa

West Indies

km 0 600 1200
mi 0 600 1200

Triangular Trade This trade network exchanged imports and exports among three continents. **SKILL Reading Maps** What types of goods were traded from colonies in North America to countries in Europe?

Fishing and Whaling

The ocean waters off the New England coast were full of fish. Many people made their living by catching and selling fish, and the fishing industry grew quickly. New Englanders caught 600,000 pounds of fish in 1641. By 1675, their catch was ten times as much—six million pounds!

The most common fish was cod, which became a key part of New England's economy. Merchants sold much of the cod as exports to Europe and the West Indies. An **export** is a product sent to another country and sold.

Sailors from New England also hunted whales. Colonists used whales to make products such as oil for lamps. By the 1700s, whaling was one of the most important industries in New England.

Triangular Trade

The products of New England were often traded to other places. New England merchants shipped fish and lumber to Europe, Africa, and the West Indies. They traded these goods for imports to bring back to the colonies. An **import** is a product brought into one country from another. Ships from Europe carried imports, such as tea and spices, to sell in the colonies.

The shipping routes between North America, Europe, and Africa formed an imaginary triangle across the Atlantic. These trade routes became known as the triangular trade. Many of New England's merchants and traders became rich from this trade.

REVIEW What was triangular trade?

Slavery

Some traders in the triangular trade made money by selling human beings. In Africa, traders bought enslaved men, women, and children who had been captured from their homes. They chained the Africans together and packed them into crowded, filthy ships for the Middle Passage. The **Middle Passage** was the voyage from Africa to the West Indies.

Many Africans died of disease or hunger along the way. **Olaudah Equiano,** (OL uh dah eh kwee AH noh) who was enslaved as a boy, survived the Middle Passage. Years later, he described the horrors of the Middle Passage in a book:

> **I became so sick and low that I was not able to eat, nor had I the least desire to taste anything. I now wished for . . . death.**

Olaudah Equiano

In North America, the Africans who survived the ocean voyage were sold to colonists who forced them to work. During the 1600s and 1700s, hundreds of thousands of Africans were brought to the colonies in the slave trade. The **slave trade** was the business of buying and selling human beings.

Home and Community Life

Main Idea New England colonists had to work hard for the things they needed for everyday life.

New England families were large, often with six or seven children. They lived in small wooden houses with few rooms or windows. Most light came from candles and lamps.

Many homes had just one main room, with a huge fireplace. A cooking fire was kept burning at all times. A table stood in the middle of the room for meals. At night, families slept on mattresses near the fire to keep warm. Wealthier families might have a second story or loft, where there would be more room for sleeping.

Work in the Home

A colonial home was more than just a building where a family ate and slept. It was also a workshop. Almost everything a family needed had to be grown or made by hand at home.

Men and boys spent most of their time working in the fields. They planted crops such as wheat and corn in the spring and harvested them in the fall. They built and repaired buildings and tools and took care of the family's animals.

Colonial women and girls were just as busy. They spent much of their time preparing and preserving food for the family. Women and girls made household items such as clothing, soap, and candles. During planting and harvest seasons, they also helped in the fields.

REVIEW How did boys and girls help their families?

Colonial home Children were expected to help around the house. Below, a busy colonial family is gathered in their one-room home.

Daily Chores

Boys	Girls
Bring in wood for fireplace	Weave cloth for clothing
Care for farm animals	Preserve fruit and vegetables
Gather wild berries and vegetables	Cook food
Help plow fields and plant crops	Make soap and candles
Help build and repair buildings	Help with planting and harvesting

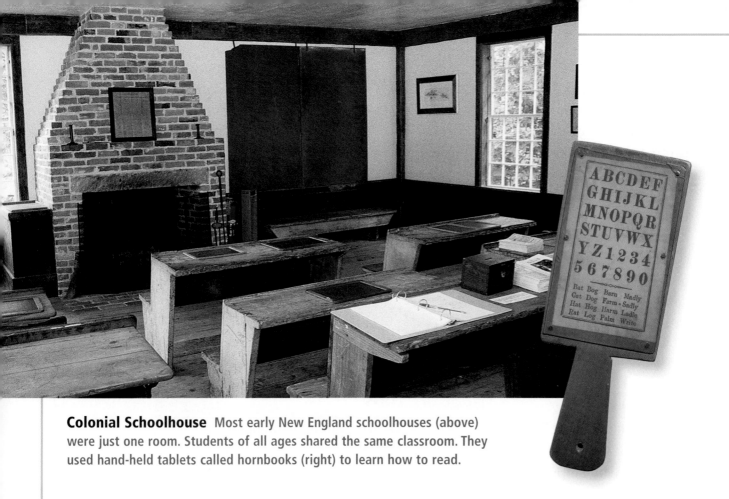

Colonial Schoolhouse Most early New England schoolhouses (above) were just one room. Students of all ages shared the same classroom. They used hand-held tablets called hornbooks (right) to learn how to read.

Education and Recreation

Puritans wanted everyone to be able to read the Bible. Some parents taught their children how to read and write at home, but many New England towns had schools.

In 1647, Massachusetts passed a law that said any town with 50 or more families had to build a school to teach reading and writing. Older boys could go on to study at colleges such as Harvard College in Massachusetts. Harvard was founded in 1636, and was the first college in the thirteen colonies.

Although New England colonists worked hard, they made time for play. Sports such as horseracing and bowling were common. People also played an early version of baseball called town ball. In winter, colonists went ice skating or sledding down hills.

The Great Awakening

Religion was a central part of New England life, but by the early 1700s, the church had become less powerful. Many colonists did not share the strong religious beliefs of their parents. Fewer people belonged to local churches.

This changed in the 1730s, when young, exciting ministers began speaking throughout the English colonies. The two most famous were **Jonathan Edwards** of Massachusetts and **George Whitefield** of England. These and other ministers traveled around New England urging people to renew their faith.

Both ministers gave inspiring sermons and many New England colonists began to make religion a more important part of their lives. This renewed interest in religion became known as the Great Awakening because people felt as if they were waking up with new faith.

George Whitefield The minister's fiery sermons inspired colonists to return to religion.

During the Great Awakening, new churches with new ideas developed throughout the colonies. Many people joined these new Protestant groups. Some of these churches accepted women, African Americans, and American Indians.

As the Great Awakening spread, people all over the colonies began to question their religious leaders and place more trust in their own beliefs.

REVIEW Why did many New England colonists return to religion in the 1730s?

Lesson Summary

- Most people in New England worked on family farms.
- Some New England colonists used the nearby ocean for fishing, shipbuilding, and trade.
- Thousands of Africans were enslaved and brought to the colonies.
- In the Great Awakening, exciting ministers inspired colonists to become more religious.

Why It Matters...

The triangular trade made the New England economy strong. The growth of the slave trade, however, would later lead to a war between American states.

Lesson Review

① VOCABULARY Use **industry** and **export** in a short paragraph describing the economy of New England.

② READING SKILL Write a paragraph about how New England colonists **solved** the **problem** of poor farming conditions.

③ MAIN IDEA: Economics What kinds of products did the colonies import from England in the triangular trade?

④ MAIN IDEA: History What was the Middle Passage?

⑤ EVENTS TO KNOW What was the Great Awakening?

⑥ CRITICAL THINKING: Compare and Contrast How were the chores New England girls did different from the chores New England boys did? How were they similar?

⑦ CRITICAL THINKING: Cause and Effect What effect did triangular trade have on Africans?

WRITING ACTIVITY Write a diary entry describing a day in the life of a New England girl or boy. Use what you have learned in the lesson to write in your entry.

Economics

COD FISHING

Why is a giant codfish hanging from the ceiling of the Massachusetts State House? The wooden carving, called "The Sacred Cod," is there to remind state representatives how important the fishing industry was to the early economy of Massachusetts. In colonial times, cod fishing was important to all of New England. Fishermen and merchants made money by catching, buying, and selling cod. Merchants sold much of the cod as exports to Europe and the Caribbean islands.

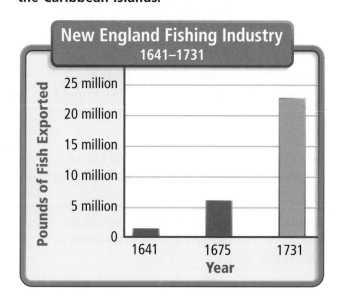

New England Fishing Industry 1641–1731

Pounds of Fish Exported — by Year: 1641, 1675, 1731
(values: 25 million, 20 million, 15 million, 10 million, 5 million, 0)

① Fishing Fleet

In this painting, colonial fishermen return to port after a fishing trip. New England merchants built hundreds of fishing ships and employed thousands of people.

② **Unloading the Catch**

After the fishing fleet returns to harbor, smaller boats bring the codfish to shore. Workers cut up the cod and prepare it for drying.

③ **Drying the Catch**

Cod dries on open racks and will later be salted to preserve it. When there is no salt, the cod is packed in ice.

Activities

1. **EXPLORE IT** Put yourself in the scene of this painting. What do you see, hear, and smell?

2. **GRAPH IT** Use an almanac to find out how much fish was caught in New England in the past five years. Make a graph like the one on page 244.

181

Graph and Chart Skills

Skillbuilder

Make a Line Graph

► **VOCABULARY**

data

line graph

Sometimes information, especially data, is easier to understand when it is presented as a graph or a chart. Data are facts or numbers. A line graph shows changes in data over time. Read the steps below to learn how to make a line graph.

Learn the Skill

Step 1: Collect the data you will use. You can arrange the data in a table, such as the one here.

Step 2: Draw and label the axes of your line graph.

Step 3: Create a grid for your line graph. Divide the axes into equal segments and label each grid line with a number.

Step 4: Draw dots on the graph to show the data. For each year, draw a dot where the grid line for that year and the correct value meet. You may have to estimate where to draw a dot.

Step 5: Draw a line to connect the dots.

Step 6: Give the line graph a title.

Year	Value of New England Exports to England (in British pounds)
1728	64,700
1729	52,500
1730	54,700
1731	49,000
1732	64,100
1733	62,000

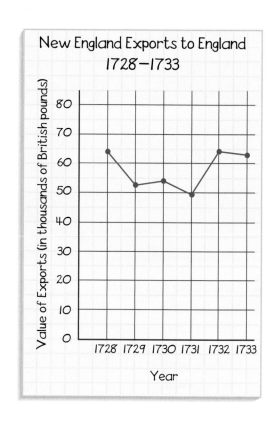

Practice the Skill

Make a line graph using the data below. Show how the number of ships built in New England changed between 1700 and 1706. Label the horizontal axis *Year* and the vertical axis *Number of Ships Built*.

Year	Number of Ships
1700	68
1701	47
1702	48
1703	43
1704	63
1705	75
1706	77

Apply the Skill

Collect data that shows change over a period of time. For example, you might collect data showing the change in your height over several years. Or you could research the change in temperature outside every day for a week. Arrange the data in a table, and then show it on a line graph.

Visual Summary

1–4. 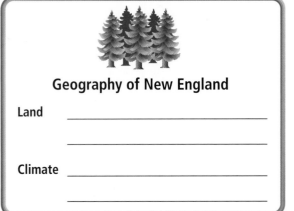 Write a description of each item named below.

Geography of New England

Land _____

_____

Climate _____

_____

Work in New England

Farming _____

_____

The Sea _____

_____

Facts and Main Ideas

TEST PREP Answer each question with information from the chapter.

5. **Geography** Why were the Southern colonies better for growing crops than the New England colonies?

6. **Government** Why did Puritan leaders banish Roger Williams and Anne Hutchinson from the Massachusetts Bay Colony?

7. **Citizenship** What did Thomas Hooker give people in Connecticut the right to do?

8. **History** What changes did the Great Awakening bring?

9. **Economics** Why were the Atlantic trade routes called the Triangular Trade?

Vocabulary

TEST PREP Choose the correct word to complete each sentence.

fall line, p. 162
town meeting, p. 166
dissenter, p. 167
export, p. 175

10. Roger Williams was a _____ who wanted more religious freedom.

11. Cod was an important _____ for the New England colonies.

12. Colonists voted on laws at a _____.

13. Rivers flowing from higher to lower ground form waterfalls at the _____.

CHAPTER SUMMARY TIMELINE

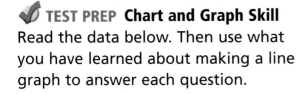

1636
Rhode Island founded

1647
Massachusetts school law passed

1675
King Philip's War begins

1630   1640   1650   1660   1670   1680

Apply Skills

✔️ TEST PREP **Chart and Graph Skill**
Read the data below. Then use what you have learned about making a line graph to answer each question.

Year	Population of Massachusetts
1650	14,000
1660	20,000
1670	30,000
1680	40,000
1690	50,000
1700	56,000

14. If you were making a line graph using the data above, what would you label the horizontal axis?

   A. Year
   B. 1650
   C. Massachusetts
   D. 1700

15. If you were making a line graph using the data above, what number would you place at the top of the vertical axis?

   A. 14,000
   B. 40,000
   C. 50,000
   D. 60,000

Critical Thinking

✔️ TEST PREP Write a short paragraph to answer each question.

16. **Summarize** Explain why colonists and American Indians fought over land.

17. **Cause and Effect** Why did the Massachusetts Bay Colony create a law that required communities to build schools?

Timeline

Use the Chapter Summary Timeline above to answer the question.

18. In what year did King Philip's War begin?

Activities

HANDS ON **Citizenship Activity** The Puritans in New England made laws for their communities. Create a list of rules for your classroom community. Explain the reasons behind each rule.

 Writing Activity Think about life on a New England farm in the 1600s. Use what you learned to write a description of what one day might have been like for someone your age.

 Technology
Writing Process Tips
Get help with your description at
www.eduplace.com/kids/hmss05/

Technology

e • **glossary**
e • **word games**
www.eduplace.com/kids/hmss05/

Vocabulary Preview

representative

In 1702, the colonists of New York and New Jersey elected to speak and act for them. Each **representative** voted on laws for the colonists. **page 189**

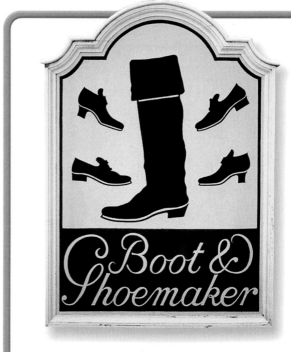

artisan

In the Middle Colonies of Philadelphia and New York, skilled **artisans** made items such as silver spoons and boots. **page 198**

Chapter Timeline

1607
Virginia founded

1632
Maryland founded

1681
Pennsylvania founded

| 1600 | 1620 | 1640 | 1660 | 1680 |

Reading Strategy

Monitor and Clarify Use this strategy to check your understanding.

quick Tip   If you are confused about events in a lesson, reread or read ahead.

legislature

Virginia had a **legislature** called the House of Burgesses. This group met in a building where they wrote and changed laws.
page 203

indigo

Indigo was an important crop in the Southern colonies. People bought it because it could be made into a blue dye to color cloth.
page 214

1702
New Jersey created

1732
Georgia founded

1700   1720   1740

The Middle Colonies

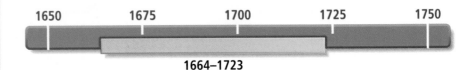

1650   1675   1700   1725   1750

1664–1723

Build on What You Know You know that people can own houses, businesses, or land. In the 1600s, a few wealthy people owned entire colonies.

New York and New Jersey

Main Idea The colonies of New York and New Jersey belonged to English landowners.

English settlement of the Middle Colonies began in 1664, when England captured the Dutch colony of New Netherland. The King of England gave this colony to his brother **James, the Duke of York**. James became the colony's proprietor. A **proprietor** was a person who owned and controlled all the land in a colony.

As proprietor of New Netherland, James could do what he liked with the land. He kept part of the large colony and changed its name to New York. He gave the rest to two friends, **John Berkeley** and **George Carteret.** Berkeley and Carteret divided their land into two colonies and named them East Jersey and West Jersey. In 1702, the colonies joined to form New Jersey.

New Amsterdam
After England captured New Amsterdam, it was renamed New York City. Many colonists there dressed and built in the Dutch style.

The proprietors of New York and New Jersey all wanted to make money from their colonies. They decided to divide the fertile land into smaller pieces and sell or rent the pieces to colonists to farm.

Because proprietors lived in England, it was difficult for them to control their faraway property. Their solution was to pick governors in the colonies to rule them. Each governor chose a small group of people called a council to help make important decisions.

The proprietors also allowed colonists to elect representatives to an assembly. A representative is someone who is chosen to speak and act for others. The assembly helped the governor and council make laws, but it did not have much power. Even so, the assembly was an important step toward self-government.

Pennsylvania and Delaware

Main Idea William Penn founded Pennsylvania as a place where people could worship freely.

The colony of Pennsylvania was the idea of **William Penn.** In England, Penn was a member of a religious group called the Society of Friends, or Quakers. Quakers believed that all Christians should be free to worship in their own way. Penn and many Quakers were put in jail for their beliefs. Some were even killed. In England, everyone was supposed to belong to the Church of England.

Penn hoped to start a colony where all Christians could live together in peace. In North America, he thought, there might be a place "for such a holy experiment."

In 1681, Penn's wish came true. King Charles II had owed money to Penn's family. The king repaid Penn by giving him a large piece of land in the Middle Colonies. The region was called Pennsylvania, which means "Penn's woods." The Duke of York later gave Penn even more land. For a time this land was part of Pennsylvania, but later it became the colony of Delaware.

REVIEW How did colonists in New York and New Jersey take part in government?

The Middle Colonies

LEGEND

DELAWARE American Indians

km 0   50   100
mi 0   50   100

The Middle Colonies The Middle Colonies had good ports and lots of rich, rolling farmland.

SKILL **Reading Maps** Along which river was Philadelphia built?

189

In Pennsylvania, Penn created laws that allowed colonists to voice their opinions and worship freely. Penn also let colonists elect representatives to an assembly, as colonists did in New York and New Jersey. The Pennsylvania Assembly, however, had more power. It could approve or reject laws that the governor and his council suggested.

Penn treated American Indians with respect. He tried to understand their culture and wanted colonists to live with them as equals. Penn made fair treaties with the Delaware, or Lenni Lenape (LEN ee LEN uh pee) Indians when he bought land from them. A **treaty** is an official agreement between nations or groups. Penn's fairness helped Pennsylvania's colonists and Indians live together peacefully for many years.

Philadelphia

William Penn did more than give Pennsylvania colonists a representative government. He also planned the colony's first large city, Philadelphia.

For the location of Philadelphia, Penn chose a site where the Delaware and Schuykill (SKOO kill) rivers meet. Ships bringing goods from other colonies and from Europe could land in the excellent harbor formed by these rivers. Penn designed wide, straight roads that made it easy to travel throughout the city. During the 1700s, Philadelphia became a center of trade. Soon it was the largest city in all the colonies.

Benjamin Franklin was Philadelphia's most famous citizen. He moved from Boston to Philadelphia in 1723. There, Franklin bought his own printing press.

Philadelphia William Penn (left) was the proprietor of Pennsylvania. He founded the city of Philadelphia shown below.

Franklin published a newspaper and a popular book of stories, jokes, and sayings called *Poor Richard's Almanack*. One of his well-known sayings is,

> 66 **Early to bed and early to rise, makes a man healthy, wealthy, and wise.** 99

Franklin had many other interests, too. He helped start Philadelphia's first public library, fire company, and hospital. He was also a talented scientist and inventor. In a famous experiment, he flew a kite in a lightning storm to show that lightning was a form of electricity. He invented a wood stove, a clock, and many other useful things. Franklin became famous for his many achievements.

REVIEW How did the government of Pennsylvania differ from those of New York and New Jersey?

Benjamin Franklin
He founded the Union Fire Company in 1736 to make Philadelphia a safer city.

Lesson Summary

- Proprietors owned the Middle Colonies.
- William Penn founded Pennsylvania as a place where colonists had religious freedom.
- Philadelphia became the biggest city in the British colonies, and Benjamin Franklin was its most famous citizen.

Why It Matters . . .

Today people still enjoy the religious freedoms that were practiced in Pennsylvania.

Lesson Review

1664 England takes New Netherland	1702 New Jersey formed	1723 Franklin moves to Philadelphia

1650 — 1675 — 1700 — 1725 — 1750

❶ **VOCABULARY** Choose the correct words to complete each sentence.

   treaty   representative   proprietor

   William Penn was the _____ of Pennsylvania. He made a _____ with the Lenni Lenape.

❷ **READING SKILL** Using your notes, write a paragraph telling how proprietors **solved** the **problem** of governing their faraway colonies.

❸ **MAIN IDEA: History** What events led to the founding of New York as an English colony?

❹ **MAIN IDEA: Citizenship** Why did William Penn start the colony of Pennsylvania?

❺ **PEOPLE TO KNOW** Who was **Benjamin Franklin,** and what were three things that he did for Philadelphia?

❻ **TIMELINE SKILL** Did New Jersey become a colony before or after England took control of New Netherland?

❼ **CRITICAL THINKING: Draw Conclusions** The name Philadelphia comes from a Greek word that means "brotherly love." Use information from the lesson to tell why Penn might have chosen that name.

HANDS ON

ART ACTIVITY Create a pamphlet to encourage people to move to Pennsylvania in the 1700s. Include drawings, maps, and persuasive reasons for moving.

Benjamin Franklin: Inventor

Thunder rumbles overhead. A bolt of lightning brightens the night sky. Thanks to lightning rods, invented by Benjamin Franklin, the lightning will probably not damage any buildings.

Today, Ben Franklin is remembered for the important role he played in the struggle for independence. But did you know that he was also a famous scientist and inventor?

Franklin's inventions helped to improve people's lives. Five of them are shown here. Which ones are still used today?

Battery
Franklin's experiments with electricity led to the creation of the first battery. It could store electricity for later use.

Odometer
This machine measured how far people traveled by counting the revolutions of wagon wheels. It led to the modern car odometer.

Bifocals

Some people need glasses to see both up close and far away. Franklin combined both types of glasses into a single pair called bifocals.

Lightning Rod

A metal lightning rod is attached to the roof of a building. When lightning hits, the electricity flows safely through a wire to the ground.

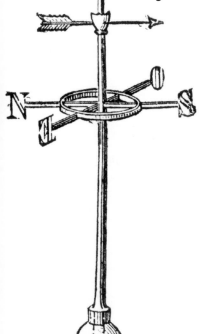

Pennsylvanian Fireplace

Franklin created an iron box with air chambers inside to spread heat more evenly.

Activities

1. **TALK ABOUT IT** Which of Benjamin Franklin's inventions do you think is the most useful? Why?

2. **REPORT IT** If you could interview Benjamin Franklin, what would you ask him about his inventions? Write your questions and his answers in the form of a radio or television interview.

Skillbuilder

Make a Decision

Europeans had to think about many things before deciding to move to the Middle Colonies. They had to choose from several possible actions and consider the costs and benefits of each. A cost is a loss or sacrifice. A benefit is a gain or advantage. The steps below will help you understand one way to make a decision.

Learn the Skill

Step 1: Identify the decision to be made. Think about why it has to be made.

Step 2: Gather information. What do you need to know to make the decision? Can research or other people help you to decide?

Step 3: Think of the options that you have.

Step 4: Consider the costs and benefits of each option.

Step 5: Choose an option. Which one has the most benefits and the fewest costs? Important decisions may include some uncertainty about which option to choose.

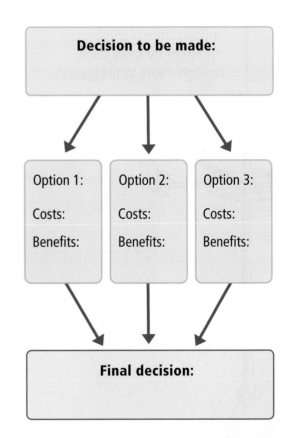

Decision to be made:

Option 1:	Option 2:	Option 3:
Costs:	Costs:	Costs:
Benefits:	Benefits:	Benefits:

Final decision:

Practice the Skill

What decisions do you think people had to make when coming to the Middle Colonies? Consider each person described below. Decide whether each one should leave Europe and move to the colony of Pennsylvania. Use a chart like the one on page 194 as you think about the costs and benefits of each person's options.

1 Quaker woman from England who is not allowed to practice her religious beliefs

2 Young German man who knows how to farm but has no land

3 Wealthy English man who will inherit a lot of land in a few years

Apply the Skill

Choose a current issue that people must make a decision about. You might choose a topic about the environment, your town's use of money, or some other important issue. Fill out a chart like the one on the page 194. Write a paragraph explaining your decision and how you made it.

Should our town raise taxes to build a new library?

Option 1: Don't raise taxes

Option 2: Raise taxes

Costs:

Costs:

Benefits:

Benefits:

Life in the Middle Colonies

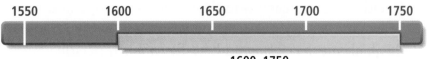

1550   1600   1650   1700   1750

1600–1750

VOCABULARY

free market economy
free enterprise
artisan
laborer
apprentice

Vocabulary Strategy

apprentice

An **apprentice** learns a skill from an expert. Apprentice comes from a word that means "to understand."

READING SKILL

Cause and Effect Take notes on what **caused** many people to come to the Middle Colonies.

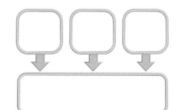

Build on What You Know If you and your family were moving to a new place, wouldn't you want to be accepted? In the 1600s, the Middle Colonies welcomed people of many different religions and countries.

A Mix of People

Main Idea People from many cultures and religions lived in the Middle Colonies.

The people of the Middle Colonies came from many lands. Colonists were German, Dutch, Scots-Irish, Scandinavian, and English. Some were enslaved Africans. Many colonists were Quakers or members of other Protestant churches. Others were Jews and Catholics.

Quaker Meetinghouse Quakers worshipped in meetinghouses. This New Jersey meetinghouse was built in 1683.

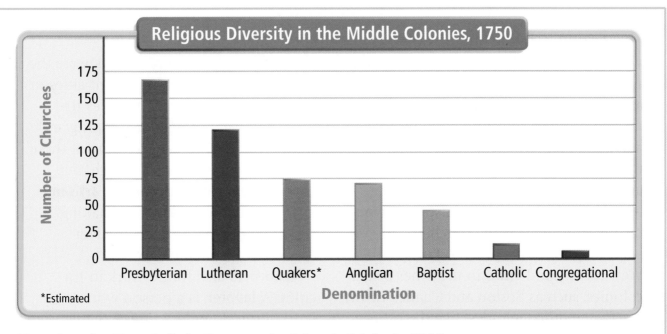

Religious Diversity in the Middle Colonies, 1750

Number of Churches (y-axis: 0, 25, 50, 75, 100, 125, 150, 175)

Denominations (x-axis): Presbyterian, Lutheran, Quakers*, Anglican, Baptist, Catholic, Congregational

*Estimated

Many People, Many Beliefs The range of religious beliefs in the Middle Colonies was more diverse than those of New England and the Southern Colonies.

SKILL **Reading Charts** Which religious groups had about the same number of churches?

The Middle Colonies had a diverse population because their proprietors believed in religious tolerance. Tolerance is respecting beliefs and practices that are different from one's own. **William Penn** supported tolerance. He believed that people of all religions should live together in peace. Other proprietors simply wanted colonists to buy or rent their land for farming. These proprietors did not care about colonists' religious beliefs as long as the colonists could pay for the land.

Religious tolerance and inexpensive land attracted people from many parts of Europe. Some came to escape punishment for their religious beliefs. Others came to farm their own land. All came to find a better way of life.

Newcomers to the Middle Colonies usually arrived at the ports of New York or Philadelphia. A few colonists stayed in the cities to find work, but most moved to the countryside to live and work on farms.

Making a Living

Main Idea Most people in the Middle Colonies farmed to earn a living, but cities were important centers of trade.

The climate and soil of the Middle Colonies were excellent for farming. Both men and women spent long hours working in the fields and in the home. As in New England, children helped out as soon as they were old enough. Boys helped plant and harvest crops. Girls cooked, sewed, and did housework. Children also cared for the family's animals and garden.

Farmers raised livestock such as cattle and pigs. They grew vegetables, fruits, and other crops in the fertile soil. Farmers grew many different grains, such as wheat, corn, and barley. In fact, they grew so much grain used to make bread that the Middle Colonies became known as the "breadbasket" of the thirteen colonies.

REVIEW Why did proprietors allow religious tolerance?

Agriculture in the Middle Colonies was so good that farmers usually grew enough to feed their families and still have a surplus. A surplus is more than what is needed. Farmers sold surplus goods to earn a living. Most farmers used the long, wide rivers of the Middle Colonies to ship grain and livestock to sell in Philadelphia or New York. Some colonists also sold wood or furs from their land. Merchants then sold the goods as exports to Europe, the West Indies, and cities in the other British colonies, such as Boston and Charles Town.

The Middle Colonies, like the other English colonies, had a free market economy. In a **free market economy,** the people, not the government, decide what will be produced. The Middle Colonies had a free market economy partly because the colonies' proprietors did not tell colonists what to do. Colonists were free to make the decisions they believed would earn them the most money. The economic system in which people may start any business that they believe will succeed is called **free enterprise.** Enterprise is another word for business.

City Life

Philadelphia and New York were the two largest and most important cities in the Middle Colonies. Both cities had ports and were centers of shipping and trade. The free market economy of these successful cities attracted merchants, shopkeepers, and artisans. An **artisan** is a person who is skilled at making something by hand, such as silver spoons or wooden chairs.

Laborers also found work in the cities. A **laborer** is a person who does hard physical work. Some of the laborers in the Middle Colonies were enslaved Africans. They worked in laundries, as house servants, or on the docks loading and unloading ships.

Hard at Work This boy at Colonial Williamsburg (right) shows visitors that children performed many chores on farms like the Pennsylvannia farm in the painting below.

Colonial Shops Signs like these hung outside artisan workshops. The pictures show what artisans made or repaired, such as furniture and clothing.

Many young people who lived in towns and cities became apprentices. An **apprentice** is someone who studies with a master to learn a skill or business. As a child, an apprentice often lived in the master's house. Apprentices usually worked with their masters for four to seven years. Boy apprentices learned skills such as shoemaking, printing, and bookmaking. Girl apprentices learned how to spin thread and weave cloth. By watching and helping, apprentices gained the skills they needed to enter the business as adults.

Most children in the Middle Colonies learned how to read and write, but many colonists believed that it was most important for children to learn useful work skills. Parents expected their children to learn a business or run the family farm instead of going to college.

REVIEW Why did colonial children become apprentices?

Lesson Summary

The Middle Colonies were a place where people from many different countries could live together and earn a good living. Most colonists were farmers, but New York and Philadelphia were busy centers of shipping and trade. Children learned skills by helping on farms, at home, or as apprentices.

Why It Matters . . .

The diversity of the people in the Middle Colonies would help shape the kind of country the United States would later become.

· Lesson Review

① **VOCABULARY** Write a short paragraph about children's lives in the Middle Colonies, using **artisan** and **apprentice.**

② **READING SKILL** What **caused** people with different religious beliefs to come to the Middle Colonies?

③ **MAIN IDEA: History** Why were the Middle Colonies known as the breadbasket?

④ **MAIN IDEA: Economics** How did most people in the Middle Colonies earn a living?

⑤ **PLACES TO KNOW** Why were Philadelphia and New York important cities?

⑥ **CRITICAL THINKING: Infer** How can a city's religious tolerance affect the growth and daily life of that city?

⑦ **CRITICAL THINKING: Evaluate** Do you think free enterprise was good for the Middle Colonies? Explain why or why not.

DRAMA ACTIVITY Create a dialogue between a 12-year-old colonist and his or her parents about becoming an apprentice. Use what you have learned in this lesson about an apprentice's work.

COLONIAL APPRENTICE

October 17, 1730

Today, 14-year-old Jacob Fielding will learn how to place type into the printing press at the print shop where he lives and works as an apprentice. He is excited and wants to do a good job so he can move up to the level of journeyman. One day he may even become a master at his own print shop. Until then, he will have to pay attention and work hard.

① Master
The master teaches the apprentice his trade, or work. Apprentices live and eat their meals with their masters.

② Apprentice
Apprentices live with their masters for as long as seven years. At first, a printer's apprentice does the messiest jobs, such as inking the press. Over time, an apprentice will learn to set type, or letters, which must be done skillfully.

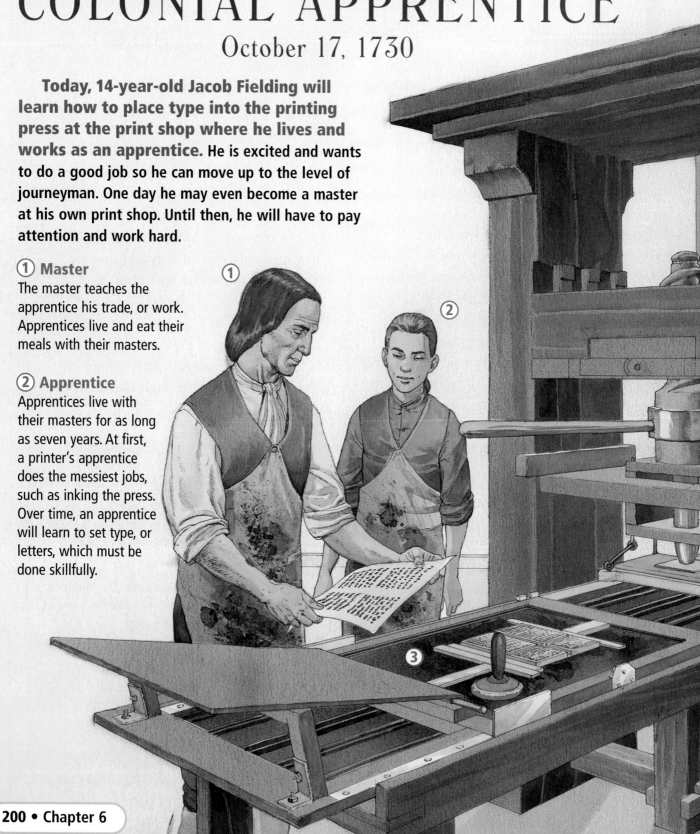

③ Setting the Type

Small, metal blocks of letters must be set in rows for each line on a printed page. All of the rows are held together in a wooden frame. The type is kept in the type case shown below.

④ Printing Press

The type is inked and paper is placed on it. The printer presses the paper onto the inked type to print a page. Colonial print shops printed newspapers, periodicals, pamphlets, and books.

⑤ Journeyman

After an apprentice learns his trade, he becomes a paid journeyman. Larger print shops had several experienced journeymen to work the presses. Often, a journeyman's wife would assist him.

Activities

1. **THINK ABOUT IT** If you were growing up in the colonies, what trade would you choose to learn? Why?

2. **WRITE ABOUT IT** Write a journal entry that Jacob Fielding might have written describing what he is learning about the printing trade.

The Southern Colonies

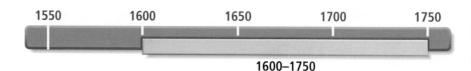

1550   1600   1650   1700   1750

1600–1750

VOCABULARY

plantation
legislature
refuge
debtor

Vocabulary Strategy

| plant**ation**

Think of the word **plant** to remember the meaning of **plantation.** A plantation is a very large farm on which crops are planted and grown.

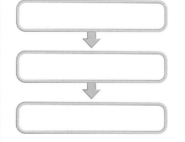

READING SKILL

Sequence As you read, list the main events in the order in which they occur.

Build on What You Know You go into a movie theater, but all the good seats are taken! In the Southern Colonies, the first settlers claimed the best farmland near the ocean. Later colonists had to settle farther inland.

Virginia

Main Idea Virginia was the largest and wealthiest English colony and had the first elected government.

In 1607, Virginia became the first permanent English colony in North America. The first colonists came to Virginia to search for gold. When they realized that there was no gold there, many started plantations on the rich soil of the tidewater. A **plantation** is a large farm on which crops are raised by workers who live on the farm.

In the Southern Colonies, most plantation workers were indentured servants or enslaved Africans. Many plantation owners, or planters, became wealthy by growing and selling cash crops such as tobacco and rice.

As large plantations filled the tidewater, new colonists had to settle in the backcountry, farther from the ocean. To get more farmland, colonists often moved to areas where the Powhatan Indians lived. The Powhatans did not want colonists to take over this land, and they fought back. Many colonists and Indians were killed in these conflicts.

Governing the Colony

As Virginia grew, colonists wanted to have a voice in the laws of the colony. In 1619, colonists created the first elected legislature in the colonies. A **legislature** is a group of people with the power to make and change laws. The legislature was called the House of Burgesses (BUR jihs iz) because the representatives in Virginia's legislature were known as burgesses. Colonists elected the burgesses, but only planters and other white men who owned property were allowed to vote or be elected.

Nearly all of the members of the House of Burgesses were members of the Church of England, or the Anglican (ANG gli kun) Church. In 1632, the House of Burgesses made the Anglican Church the official church of Virginia. Puritans, Quakers, and others who were not Anglican had to leave the colony.

New Colonies in the South

Main Idea England founded four more colonies in the South during the 1600s and early 1700s.

Between 1632 and 1732, English colonists settled four more southern colonies. The colonies of Maryland, North Carolina, South Carolina, and Georgia were all created for different reasons.

Maryland

The colony of Maryland began in 1632, when **King Charles I** of England gave land in North America to **Cecilius Calvert.** Calvert, also known as **Lord Baltimore,** was a Catholic. Like Puritans and Quakers, Catholics in England were often punished for their religious beliefs. Calvert hoped to make Maryland a refuge for Catholics. A **refuge** is a safe place. In 1649, the Maryland government passed the Toleration Act. The Toleration Act was the first law in North America to promise that all Christians could worship freely.

REVIEW Who were burgesses?

House of Burgesses The Virginia legislature first met in 1619. The burgesses later moved to this site (left).

The Carolinas

During the late 1600s, England, France, and Spain all claimed land that was south of Virginia. The new English king, **Charles II,** wanted to start another colony on this land. He hoped that a settlement would help keep France and Spain out of the area. In 1663, Charles II formed a new colony south of Virginia called Carolina.

Colonists first settled the southern part of Carolina. The southern area had good farmland and many excellent harbors. Planters built rice plantations in the tidewater. The city of Charles Town, later called Charleston, grew large and wealthy. The northern part of Carolina had few harbors and was not as good for farming. It grew more slowly than the south. In 1729, Carolina became two colonies, North Carolina and South Carolina.

Georgia

In 1732, England's King **George III** started another colony to keep the Spanish and French away from South Carolina. He gave this land to **James Oglethorpe,** an English lawmaker and army officer. The new colony was named Georgia to honor King George.

Oglethorpe wanted Georgia to be a place for poor people and debtors (DEHT ers). A **debtor** is a person who owes money. In England, debtors who could not pay the money they owed were put in prison. Oglethorpe thought it would be better to let debtors start new lives in Georgia. He offered them a free trip to Georgia and small farms of their own.

In 1733, Oglethorpe led the first group of settlers to Georgia. Soon, Oglethorpe developed friendly relations with nearby America Indians. He traded with Choctaws, Cherokees, and Creeks.

Oglethorpe made strict rules for his colony. Georgian colonists could not drink alcohol. They also could not own slaves or elect their own legislature.

The Southern Colonies

The Southern Colonies The region's fertile land and many waterways allowed most Southern colonists to make their living by farming.

SKILL Reading Maps Which places were named after people mentioned in this lesson?

Some colonists did not like these rules, and later many of the rules were changed. Slaves were brought to work on plantations as soon as slavery was allowed. Georgia quickly became a wealthy plantation colony like South Carolina.

REVIEW What were differences between North Carolina and South Carolina?

James Oglethorpe Under the leadership of this proprietor, the economy of Georgia succeeded.

Lesson Summary

Colony	Reason founded
Virginia	To find gold
Maryland	As a refuge for Catholics
Carolina	To help England control southeastern North America
Georgia	To help debtors and other poor people

Why It Matters ...

Establishing the Southern Colonies gave England control of the North American east coast, from New France in the north to Spanish Florida in the south.

Lesson Review

| 1619 House of Burgesses formed | 1729 Carolinas created | 1732 Georgia founded |

1600   1630   1660   1690   1720   1750   1780

1 **VOCABULARY** Choose the correct words to fill in the blanks.

refuge plantation legislature debtor

To be a member of the Virginia _____, a person had to own a _____ or other piece of land.

2 **READING SKILL** In what **order** were the Southern Colonies founded?

3 **MAIN IDEA: Government** What was the House of Burgesses?

4 **MAIN IDEA: History** Why was Maryland founded?

5 **PEOPLE TO KNOW** Who was **James Oglethorpe,** and why did he found Georgia?

6 **TIMELINE SKILL** How many years after the House of Burgesses was formed was Georgia founded?

7 **CRITICAL THINKING: Decision Making** If you were a debtor in England in the 1700s, what could have been the costs and benefits of moving to Georgia?

WRITING ACTIVITY Learn more about the Powhatan Indians. Then write a short speech from a Powhatan Indian's point of view. Explain how he or she might feel about the conflicts with colonists over land.

Ann's Story: 1747

by Joan Lowery Nixon

Fire! On the morning of January 30, 1747, the residents of Williamsburg, Virginia, find their Capitol building in flames. Now a new town might have to serve as the colonial capital. Ann McKenzie, the nine-year-old daughter of a doctor, is worried that her family might have to move. She wonders what her future will be like.

That evening, after supper, Ann sat with her parents in the parlor and knitted on a stocking. She listened quietly as they talked about the Capitol fire and the effect it might have on Williamsburg. But as Dr. McKenzie spoke of problems involved in moving his practice and his apothecary, Ann forgot herself.

"Papa, we can't go to the Pamunkey River. There aren't even any houses built yet! We can't live in a hut with snakes!"

Her father's eyes widened in surprise. "Ann, I don't know where you got a strange idea like that," he said. "We will not live in a hut. And there will be no snakes allowed in our house."

"But Matthew said …"

Mrs. McKenzie sighed and rolled her eyes. "We should have known. Matthew Davenport again. He seems to enjoy disturbing the younger children with wild tales." She kept her eyes on the small stocking she was knitting for William as she said, "I'm afraid the Davenport boys are not disciplined as carefully as they should be. Remember a number of years ago, when Matthew's older brother, Bedford, was reprimanded by the burgesses for writing indecent inscriptions on one of their chairs?"

"Really? What did he write?" Ann asked.

"I'm sure no one remembers now," Dr. McKenzie answered quickly. He smiled and added, "Trust me, Ann. I will do my best to take good care of you, your mother, and William for the rest of my life. Matthew was only jesting with you."

"It's not amusing," Ann grumbled. "And neither is Matthew."

"Pray don't think harshly of Matthew," Dr. McKenzie said. "He's a fine young man. He has shown an interest in my work, and it has been my pleasure to encourage him."

Before Ann could respond, Mrs. McKenzie leaned over to examine her knitting. "Dear," she said, "you dropped a stitch in this last row."

Ann groaned. "Will you tell me to pull them out and do them over?"

"It's all a part of learning," Mrs. McKenzie told her gently. "Someday you'll be grateful that you can knit well."

Ann let the stocking drop to the floor. "What good does it do to make neat stitches? Can't someone else make the stockings while I learn what I want to learn?"

"Exactly what is it that you want to learn?" her mother asked.

Even Ann's father looked up from his armchair in surprise.

"I want to learn Latin, and after that, Greek," she said. "The knowledge of Latin seems necessary to the study of medicine. I want to learn everything I'll need to know so that I can read all the books in Papa's library."

Mrs. McKenzie's expression showed that she had no patience with such a foolish wish. "Ann, you've learned to read well, and you find great pleasure in books, but the books in your father's library are beyond your abilities. They couldn't possibly interest you."

"But they do, Mama," Ann insisted. "Sometimes I take down one of Papa's medical books and read parts of it—the parts I can understand. I hope someday to know the meanings of all the words so that I can read entire books."

Mrs. McKenzie sighed. "Some of those books are not appropriate for you, daughter. There are many more useful things for you to learn. As you grow older, I hope there will be lessons for you in dancing and possibly the flute or harpsichord. And I'll continue to teach you how to manage a household."

"I'll study whatever you wish, Mama, but I still hope to study Latin and mathematics, too," Ann said.

She saw her mother give a knowing look to her father.

"Your father has greatly indulged you in taking you beyond the fundamental rules of arithmetic, in teaching you mathematics," Mrs. McKenzie told her. "But all you need is enough knowledge of arithmetic to keep your household accounts. Forget this ridiculous desire to become a doctor."

Ann took a deep breath. "Mama, Papa came to the colonies from Scotland. He once told me it was because he was searching for opportunity. Should it surprise you that I am looking for opportunity, too? Here in Virginia I should have the opportunity to study the practice of medicine."

Dr. McKenzie sighed. "It's not that simple, daughter," he said. "A woman doctor would not be accepted. We must follow custom."

"But—"

"You're an eager student, but I'm afraid the study of Latin is suitable only to young gentlemen. I'd suggest you might try harder to please your mother with the neatness of your knitting."

Ann bent down to pick up her stocking. The lump in her throat hurt. No one— not even her parents or her best friends— understood. How could she ever convince them that her life's work was to care for others?

Activities

1. **TALK ABOUT IT** Which events and people in this story are real? Which ones were made up by the author? Explain how you can tell the difference.

2. **WRITE ABOUT IT** Do you think Ann should "follow custom," as her father says, or search for her opportunity? Write a paragraph explaining your ideas.

Life in the South

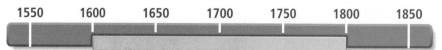

| 1550 | 1600 | 1650 | 1700 | 1750 | 1800 | 1850 |

1600–1800

VOCABULARY

indigo
overseer
spiritual

Vocabulary Strategy

overseer

The small two words in the compound word **overseer** show its meaning. An overseer watches over workers.

READING SKILL
Compare and Contrast
Note the similarities and differences between plantations and backcountry farms.

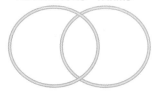
PLANTATIONS   FARMS

Build on What You Know Have you ever grown a plant from a seed or bulb? If you have, you know that plants need fertile soil, warm weather, and plenty of water. The Southern Colonies had all of these things.

Southern Agriculture

Main Idea Cash crops grew very well in the Southern Colonies.

The long growing season and warm, damp climate of the Southern Colonies made the region perfect for growing tobacco and rice. Many southern planters became very wealthy exporting these cash crops to other colonies and countries. Planters found, however, that tobacco and rice needed much more work and care than other crops. Planters used indentured servants and enslaved Africans to do this hard labor.

In Virginia and Maryland, the main cash crop was tobacco. Colonists grew tobacco on small farms as well as on large plantations. North Carolina had many small tobacco farms, but its greatest resource was its pine forests. Colonists took the sticky sap from pine trees and made it into a thick liquid called pitch. Pitch was used to seal the boards of ships and keep out water.

Tobacco Virginia farmers harvest tobacco leaves in the early 1600s.

Cash Crops

Tobacco

Southern tobacco was exported all over the world.

Rice

Rice needs a steamy, hot climate to grow well.

Indigo

Without indigo, blue jeans wouldn't have their special color.

South Carolina and Georgia had two main cash crops. One was rice, which flourished in the hot, wet tidewater region. Planters learned methods for growing rice from enslaved African workers. They brought their knowledge of rice growing from West Africa, where rice was an important food.

The other major cash crop in South Carolina and Georgia was indigo. **Indigo** is a plant that can be made into a dark blue dye. This dye is used to color clothing. Indigo was very difficult to grow, and planters had little success with it. Then 17-year-old **Eliza Lucas Pinckney** began to experiment with different kinds of indigo on her father's plantation.

In 1744, she developed a type of indigo that was much easier to grow. This indigo was so successful that colonists in South Carolina soon sold more than 100,000 pounds of indigo each year.

Charles Town

The Southern Colonies had many farms and plantations but fewer towns and cities than New England or the Middle Colonies. By the mid-1700s, however, several ports in the South had grown into large cities. Charles Town, South Carolina, which became known as Charleston in 1783, was the biggest southern city. It was a busy center of trade and the capital of South Carolina.

In Charles Town, traders and planters bought, sold, and exported thousands of pounds of tobacco, rice, and indigo. Ships brought goods from Europe and the West Indies to sell in the colonies.

Charles Town had a diverse population. Its people were English, Scots-Irish, French, and West Indian. Free and enslaved Africans lived in the city as well.

REVIEW Why was Charles Town an important city?

Plantations and Small Farms

Main Idea Southern plantations were large and needed many workers, but most southern colonists lived on small family farms.

The huge plantations in the South were more like small villages than farms. At the center of a plantation, often near a river or stream, was the planter's house. The planter's house was surrounded by horse stables, workshops, gardens, fields, and workers' houses.

Many laborers were needed to keep a big plantation running. Plantation workers were usually enslaved Africans. Most spent long hours working in the plantation's fields. Other workers took care of the gardens or animals. Cooks and maids worked in the planter's house.

The South was known for its large plantations, but small farms were much more common. Most southern colonists lived on small family farms in the backcountry, away from the tidewater. Backcountry colonists farmed with the help of family members and perhaps one or two servants or slaves. They grew their own food and sometimes small amounts of a cash crop, such as tobacco.

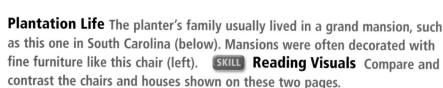

Plantation Life The planter's family usually lived in a grand mansion, such as this one in South Carolina (below). Mansions were often decorated with fine furniture like this chair (left). **SKILL** **Reading Visuals** Compare and contrast the chairs and houses shown on these two pages.

Backcountry Life Simple wooden cabins (right) were home to most farming families who lived west of the tidewater. Most of their belongings, such as this chair (above), were either made by hand or traded from others.

Family Life

The children of wealthy planters lived fairly easy lives. Most were educated at home. Their parents hired teachers to instruct the children in reading, writing, dancing, and music. Boys spent their free time outdoors, learning how to ride horses and hunt. Girls learned how to sew and sing. As children got older, fathers taught boys how to run the plantation. Girls learned how to manage a large household with many servants.

Life was very different on backcountry farms. Backcountry farmers often lived far from schools and towns. Children learned how to read and write only if their parents could teach them. Backcountry children started helping around the house and farm at an early age. This was how they learned skills such as plowing, hunting, sewing, and cooking.

Southern Slavery

Main Idea Slavery was cruel, but enslaved people developed a culture that helped them survive.

The importance of slavery in the Southern Colonies changed over time. In the early 1600s, indentured servants did much of the hard work on plantations. As the number of plantations grew, however, southern planters began to use enslaved Africans as laborers.

More and more enslaved Africans were brought to North America during the 1600s and 1700s. By 1750, greater numbers of enslaved Africans lived in all thirteen colonies, but most slaves lived in the Southern Colonies.

REVIEW How did the children of planters and the children of backcountry farmers learn how to read and write?

Life Under Slavery

Enslaved Africans were not treated as human beings. They were bought and sold as property. Under slavery, husbands and wives were often separated from each other, and families were torn apart.

On a plantation, slaves usually worked as laborers in the fields or as house servants. Even young children were forced to work. Field work was exhausting. Workers labored from morning to night in the heat and the cold, nearly every day of the year. Overseers sometimes whipped and punished workers to keep them working hard. An **overseer** is a person who watches and directs the work of other people. Enslaved people had to work so hard and had such poor food, clothing, and shelter that many died at an early age.

Planters used punishments and harsh laws to keep enslaved workers from resisting or running away. Many had to wear heavy iron chains. They could not leave the plantation without permission. They could be beaten or even killed by planters and overseers. Some slaves fought back by running away. Most resisted by working as slowly as they could without being punished.

African American Culture

To survive their harsh lives, enslaved Africans formed close ties with each other. They created a community that was like a large family. Enslaved Africans helped each other to survive the hardships of slavery.

Another source of strength was religion. Many enslaved people began to practice Christianity and looked to the Bible and its stories for inspiration. They combined Christian beliefs and musical traditions from Africa to create powerful spirituals. A **spiritual** is an African American religious folk song.

Over time, enslaved people created a new culture that blended African and American customs and religions. They remembered their past by telling stories about their homelands in Africa. They made up work songs to help the time pass while working in the fields. They invented and played music on the banjo, a musical instrument based on African ones. In South Carolina, enslaved Africans created a new language, Gullah, out of African languages and English.

REVIEW What did slaves do to survive the hardships of slavery?

Slave Cabins This painting shows slave cabins on a South Carolina plantation. Slave houses were small and cramped.

African Culture Enslaved Africans dance and make music in this painting called *The Old Plantation* (above). The banjo (right) became a popluar instrument in American folk music.

Lesson Summary

The Southern Colonies had an agricultural economy. Most colonists lived on small family farms, but some owned large plantations that produced cash crops such as tobacco and rice. Many slaves worked on plantations. Slavery was a cruel system. Enslaved Africans developed a culture that helped them survive.

Why It Matters . . .

Slavery would become a major source of conflict in the United States more than a hundred years later.

Lesson Review

1 VOCABULARY Write a short paragraph telling why **indigo** was important in the South.

2 READING SKILL What were some **differences** between plantations and backcountry farms?

3 MAIN IDEA: Economics What were the main cash crops in the Southern Colonies?

4 MAIN IDEA: Culture What new customs became part of the culture of enslaved Africans?

5 PEOPLE TO KNOW How did **Eliza Pinckney** affect the economy of the South?

6 CRITICAL THINKING: Infer Why did large plantations develop in the Southern Colonies?

7 CRITICAL THINKING: Compare and Contrast Compare and contrast the lives of children on plantations and on small farms.

WRITING ACTIVITY Do research and write a report about the many ways African American culture has affected American culture.

SLAVERY'S PAST

How did enslaved people live day by day? Narratives and clues dug up from historical sites are helping to answer this question.

In the 1700s, most slaves worked in the rice fields of South Carolina and the tobacco plantations of Virginia and Maryland. Researchers digging near Williamsburg, the colonial capital of Virginia, have found important information about the food that enslaved people ate, items they owned, and how they may have used the little free time they had.

Thousands of handmade objects and things bought in stores give clues to the past. Personal items such as hand-woven baskets, pencils, slates, and reading glasses show how people tried hard to keep part of their lives free from the burden of slavery.

Slave Quarters These cabins near Williamsburg, Virginia, have been restored to the way they looked in the 1700s.

② Possessions

Reading History's Clues

Dr. Theresa Singleton is a professor of archaeology at Syracuse University. She has a special interest in the lives of slaves. "To me," Singleton says, "the most important discoveries have been usable objects made from broken and discarded materials, such as fish-hooks from nails." Such findings prove that the people were not just victims, Singleton explains:

" *They were thinkers and doers who improved their situations as best they could despite the odds against them.* "

— Dr. Theresa Singleton

① **Inside the Cabins**
Fireplaces were made of clay and wood. As many as nine adults may have slept in one cabin on mattresses filled with corn husks.

② **Possessions**
Furniture was simple: barrels, old tables, and chairs. This pewter plate may have been purchased through extra labor.

Activities

1. **TALK ABOUT IT** What questions would you like to ask Dr. Singleton about her discoveries?

2. **WRITE ABOUT IT** Why is it difficult for historians to find information about the daily lives of enslaved people? Write a one-page paper that answers this question.

Review and Test Prep

Visual Summary

1–3. Complete the chart below with descriptions of each colony.

Colony	Founder	Reason for Settlement
Pennsylvania		
Maryland		
Georgia		

Facts and Main Ideas

TEST PREP Answer each question with information from the chapter.

4. **History** What events led to the founding of New York and New Jersey?

5. **History** Why did the Middle Colonies have such a diverse population?

6. **Citizenship** Who could vote and be elected to Virginia's House of Burgesses?

7. **Government** What was the Toleration Act in Maryland?

8. **History** Describe one thing that enslaved Africans did to survive life under slavery.

Vocabulary

TEST PREP Choose the correct word from the list below to complete each sentence.

representative, p. 189
free market economy, p. 198
legislature, p. 203

9. People in the Virginia _____ had the power to make and change laws.

10. Colonists were able to decide what crops and goods they wanted to produce in a _____.

11. A _____ was chosen by the colonists to speak and act for them in the House of Burgesses.

CHAPTER SUMMARY TIMELINE

1607	1632	1681	1702	1732
Virginia founded	Maryland founded	Pennsylvania founded	New Jersey created	Georgia founded

1600   1620   1640   1660   1680   1700   1720   1740

Apply Skills

✓ **TEST PREP** **Citizenship Skill** Read the paragraph below. Then use what you have learned about making a decision to answer each question.

> In the 1600s, many Catholics in Britain were punished for their religious beliefs. John is a young Catholic man living in England. He is thinking about moving to the new colony of Maryland.

12. John needs to learn more about life in Maryland. Which of the following people could best help him make a decision?

   A. someone who heard about Maryland

   B. someone who visited Maryland

   C. someone who lived in Georgia

   D. a Catholic who lived in Germany

13. For John, what would be a benefit of moving to Maryland?

   A. There would be no slavery in Maryland.

   B. It would be very expensive to get to Maryland.

   C. He could be a member of the House of Burgesses in Virginia.

   D. Colonists in Maryland believe in religious tolerance.

Critical Thinking

✓ **TEST PREP** Write a short paragraph to answer each question.

14. **Compare and Contrast** How was the Pennsylvania Assembly similar to and different from the New York and New Jersey assemblies?

15. **Summarize** What were the different ways people made a living in the Middle and Southern Colonies?

Timeline

Use the Chapter Summary Timeline above to answer the question.

16. Which of the colonies listed on the timeline were founded in the 1700s?

Activities

 Map Activity Make a map of crops grown in the Middle and Southern Colonies. Use library resources and information from the chapter.

 Writing Activity Write a short story about an apprentice. Describe his or her trade and life in the Middle Colonies.

 Technology
Writing Process Tips
Get help with your story at
www.eduplace.com/kids/hmss05/

Vocabulary and Main Ideas

✓ **TEST PREP** Write a sentence to answer each question.

1. Why is a region's **growing season** important to farmers who live there?

2. What was one way in which New England colonists took part in **self-government?**

3. Why did some proprietors of the Middle Colonies allow colonists to elect **representatives** to assemblies?

4. In what ways did colonists in the Middle Colonies participate in a **free market economy?**

5. What cash crops were grown most commonly on southern **plantations?**

6. Why did some colonial children become **apprentices?**

Critical Thinking

✓ **TEST PREP** Apply what you have learned about critical thinking to answer each question.

7. **Generalize** How can the geography and climate of a region affect how people earn a living there?

8. **Fact and Opinion** Write one fact and one opinion about life in each of the following regions: New England, the Middle Colonies, and the Southern Colonies.

Apply Skills

✓ **TEST PREP** Chart and Graph Skill Use the unfinished line graph below and what you know about making a line graph to answer each question.

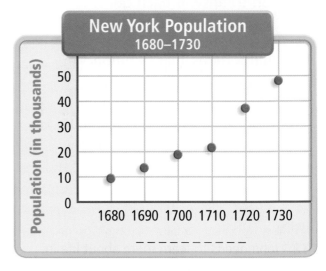

New York Population
1680–1730

9. Which is the best label for the horizontal axis of this line graph?

   A. Number of People

   B. Time

   C. Year

   D. Population Growth

10. What should you do after you draw dots to show the data on the line graph?

   A. Connect the dots with a line.

   B. Draw a bar from the bottom of the graph to where the dot is.

   C. Choose a color for the dot.

   D. Connect each dot to the correct year.

Interview Different Colonists

- With three classmates, interview three people who have moved to different colonies.

- Ask which colony each person moved to and why he or she chose that colony.

- Ask the colonists how life in the colonies has differed from their expectations.

- Act out the interview for your class.

At the Library

You may find these books at your school or public library.

The Voyage of Patience Goodspeed by Heather V. Frederick

After their mother dies, Patience and her brother sail with their father aboard his Nantucket whaler.

Giants in the Land by Diana Applebaum

Colonial New England's forests of giant white pine trees were cleared to build British war ships.

Connect to Today

Create a bulletin board about people moving to new places.

- Find articles about people moving to new places.

- Write a summary of each article, explaining why people are moving. Draw a picture or map to show where or how they are traveling.

- Display your summaries and pictures on a bulletin board in your classroom.

Technology

Get information for your bulletin board from the Weekly Reader at **www.eduplace.com/kids/hmss05/**

Read About It

Look for these Social Studies Independent Books in your classroom.

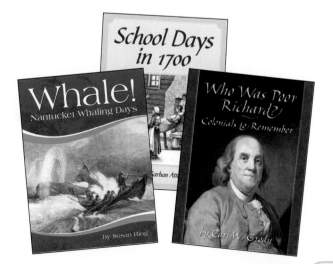

The American Revolution

The
Big
Idea

What does freedom mean to you?

In 1775, Mercy Otis Warren said,

> ❝ *In Freedom we're born, and like Sons of the brave, Will never surrender,...* ❞

Paul Revere
1734–1818

Paul Revere's famous midnight ride is one of the legends of the Revolution. He and other alarm riders sped through the night to warn Patriots that British troops were on the move.
page 251

History Makers

Mercy Otis Warren
1728–1814

This playwright used her skills as a writer to support the cause of freedom. Her plays made fun of British leaders and complained about how the British treated the colonies.

page 250

Samuel Adams
1722–1803

What weapon did this famous Patriot use against the British? His sharp mind. Adams got Patriots together and secretly planned the Boston Tea Party, which enraged the British.

page 235

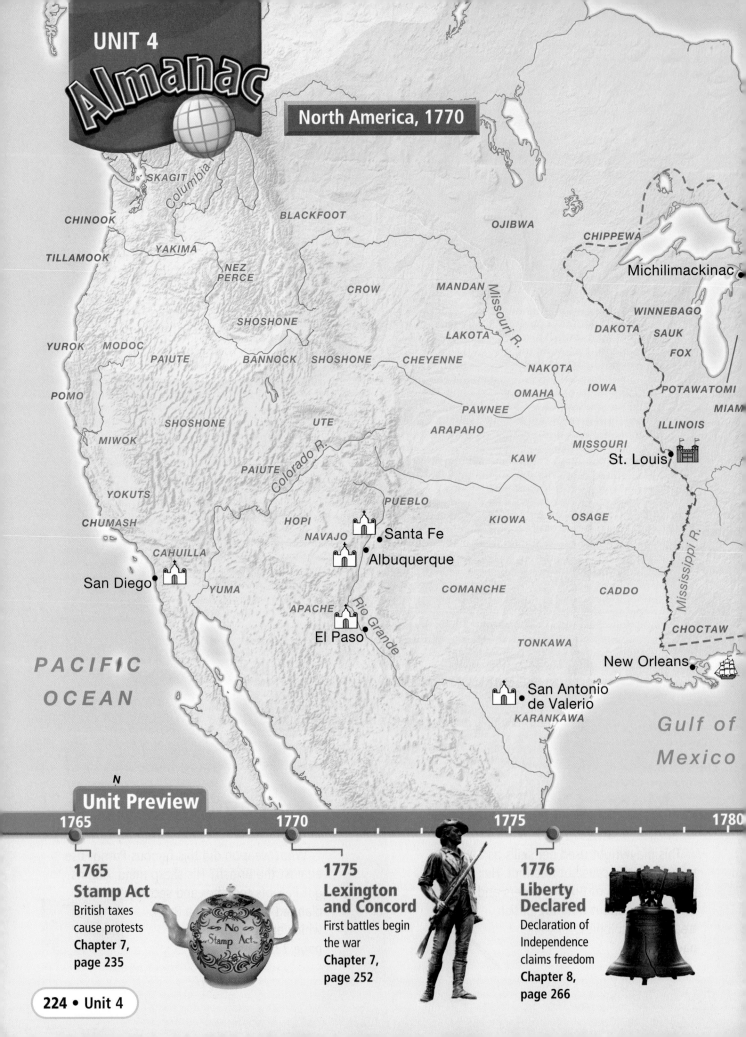

Almanac

North America, 1770

SKAGIT
Columbia
CHINOOK
BLACKFOOT
OJIBWA
CHIPPEWA
TILLAMOOK
YAKIMA
Michilimackinac
NEZ PERCE
CROW
MANDAN
Missouri R.
WINNEBAGO
SHOSHONE
LAKOTA
DAKOTA
SAUK
YUROK
MODOC
PAIUTE
BANNOCK
SHOSHONE
CHEYENNE
NAKOTA
FOX
POMO
OMAHA
IOWA
POTAWATOMI
PAWNEE
MIAM
SHOSHONE
UTE
ARAPAHO
MISSOURI
ILLINOIS
MIWOK
KAW
St. Louis
PAIUTE
Colorado R.
YOKUTS
PUEBLO
KIOWA
OSAGE
CHUMASH
HOPI
Santa Fe
CAHUILLA
NAVAJO
Albuquerque
Mississippi R.
San Diego
YUMA
COMANCHE
CADDO
APACHE
Rio Grande
CHOCTAW
El Paso
TONKAWA
PACIFIC
New Orleans
OCEAN
San Antonio de Valerio
KARANKAWA
Gulf of
Mexico

N

Unit Preview

1765 — 1770 — 1775 — 1780

1765
Stamp Act
British taxes cause protests
Chapter 7, page 235

No Stamp Act.

1775
Lexington and Concord
First battles begin the war
Chapter 7, page 252

1776
Liberty Declared
Declaration of Independence claims freedom
Chapter 8, page 266

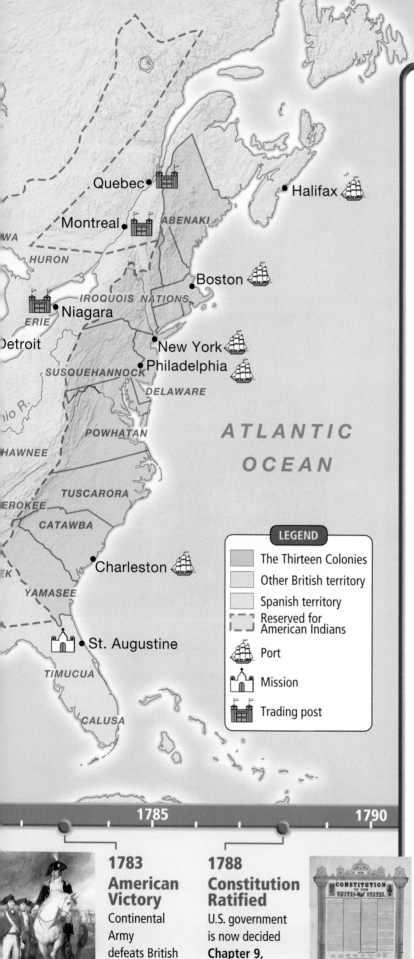

Quebec

Halifax

Montreal

ABENAKI

HURON

IROQUOIS NATIONS

Niagara

ERIE

Detroit

Boston

New York

Philadelphia

SUSQUEHANNOCK

DELAWARE

POWHATAN

ATLANTIC
OCEAN

SHAWNEE

TUSCARORA

EROKEE

CATAWBA

Charleston

YAMASEE

St. Augustine

TIMUCUA

CALUSA

LEGEND

	The Thirteen Colonies
	Other British territory
	Spanish territory
	Reserved for American Indians
	Port
	Mission
	Trading post

Connect to Today

Farming in 1770s

1770s
Estimated number of farmers in 13 colonies: 1,350,000

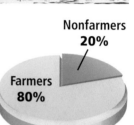

Nonfarmers
20%

Farmers
80%

Farming Today

Today
Estimated number of U.S. agricultural workers: 3,300,000

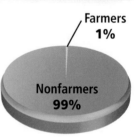

Farmers
1%

Nonfarmers
99%

CURRENT EVENTS

WEEKLY (WR) READER

Current events on the web!

Find out about current events that connect with the Big Idea of this unit.
See Unit activities at:
www.eduplace.com/kids/hmss05/

1785

1790

1783
American Victory
Continental Army defeats British **Chapter 8, page 288**

1788
Constitution Ratified
U.S. government is now decided **Chapter 9, page 307**

CONSTITUTION
OF THE
UNITED STATES.

Causes of the Revolution

Technology

e • **glossary**
e • **word games**
www.eduplace.com/kids/hmss05/

Vocabulary Preview

congress

In 1757, representatives from the colonies met in a **congress** at Albany to discuss how to fight France. The members of a congress gather to discuss important issues. **page 229**

boycott

Colonists refused to buy or use British goods. Protesters who joined the **boycott** of British tea dumped crates of it into Boston Harbor. **page 236**

Chapter Timeline

1754 Albany Congress		1763 Proclamation of 1763	1765 Stamp Act

1750   1755   1760   1765

Reading Strategy

Summarize Use this strategy to better understand information in the text.

A summary includes only the most important information. Use main ideas to help you.

commander

George Washington was in charge of all the colonial soldiers. He was the **commander** of the Continental Army.
page 254

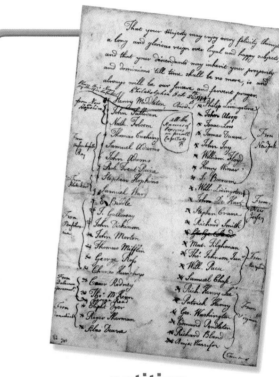

petition

Congress sent the Olive Branch Petition to King George. This **petition** asked for peace.
page 254

1774	1775
First Continental Congress	Battle of Bunker Hill

1770   1775   1780

The French and Indian War

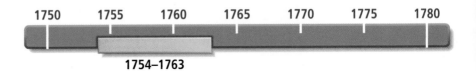

1750   1755   1760   1765   1770   1775   1780

1754–1763

VOCABULARY

ally
congress
rebellion
proclamation

Vocabulary Strategy

congress

A **congress** is a meeting of representatives. The word part **con-** means together. At a congress, representatives gather together.

READING SKILL

Sequence Note the events of the French and Indian War in order.

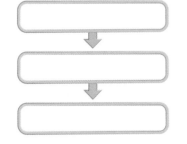

Build on What You Know Do you often work as part of a group? Sometimes you can get more done that way. When Britain and its colonies went to war with France, some people felt that the colonies would be stronger if they worked together.

War Between France and Britain

Main Idea Great Britain and France fought for control of eastern North America.

Britain and France both had colonies in North America. (In the 1700s, Britain became another name for England.) The two countries had been enemies for hundreds of years and had fought many wars. In the 1750s, they went to war again. This time, they fought over the Ohio River Valley.

The Ohio River Valley is the land around the Ohio River. This river flows 1,000 miles from the Appalachian Mountains to the Mississippi River. Many American Indians lived in the valley. They traded furs with the French in exchange for guns and other goods. The French wanted to have this trade all to themselves. They built forts to keep out the British.

British colonists wanted to trade furs and farm the land around the Ohio River. In 1754, the governor of Virginia ordered a young officer named **George Washington** to lead an army into the valley. A larger French army met them and defeated Washington's soldiers. After this defeat, the British government sent a stronger army to North America, and Britain went to war against France.

Choosing Sides

The war that began in the Ohio River Valley was called the French and Indian War. It spread through eastern North America. Britain and its colonists fought against France and its American Indian allies. An **ally** is a person or group that joins with another to work toward a goal.

Most American Indian nations were allies of the French. They included the Delaware, Ottawa, and Shawnee. France was their trading partner. To the French, trade was more important than settlement. Unlike the British, the French did not send many settlers to North America.

Some American Indian nations, such as the Mohawk, were allies of the British. The Mohawk had traded with the British for many years and had formed close ties.

Albany Plan Benjamin Franklin used this cartoon to tell colonists that working together was the only way to defeat the French.

SKILL **Reading Visuals** What do the initials stand for in the cartoon?

Benjamin Franklin's Albany Plan

In 1754, representatives from the colonies held a meeting to discuss how to fight France. Because they met in Albany, New York, the meeting was called the Albany Congress. A **congress** is a group of representatives who meet to discuss a subject. Representatives to a congress often vote on important issues.

Benjamin Franklin was at the Albany Congress. He had a plan to unite the colonies, known as the Albany Plan of Union. Franklin believed the colonies could fight better if they worked together. In his plan, each colony would keep its own government. The colonies would also have an overall government to solve problems that affected them all, such as wars. The colonies did not accept the plan. They were not ready to join together under one government.

REVIEW What was the Albany Plan?

George Washington The French and Indian War was his first experience in battle. This picture shows him at the capture of a French fort.

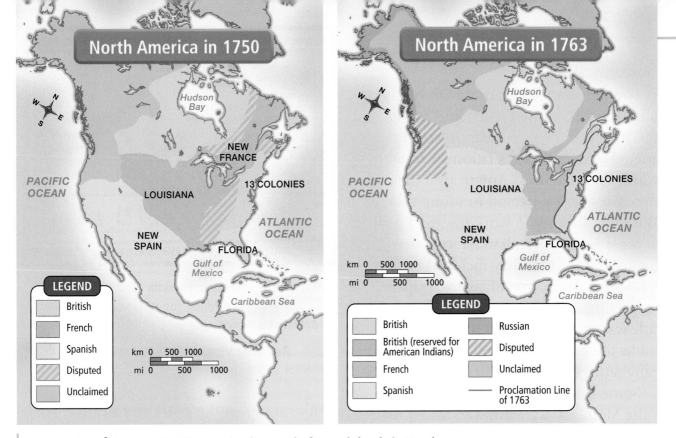

North America in 1750

Hudson Bay
NEW FRANCE
PACIFIC OCEAN
LOUISIANA
13 COLONIES
ATLANTIC OCEAN
NEW SPAIN
FLORIDA
Gulf of Mexico
Caribbean Sea

LEGEND
British
French
Spanish
Disputed
Unclaimed

km 0 500 1000
mi 0 500 1000

North America in 1763

Hudson Bay
PACIFIC OCEAN
LOUISIANA
13 COLONIES
ATLANTIC OCEAN
NEW SPAIN
FLORIDA
Gulf of Mexico
Caribbean Sea

km 0 500 1000
mi 0 500 1000

LEGEND
British
British (reserved for American Indians)
French
Spanish
Russian
Disputed
Unclaimed
—— Proclamation Line of 1763

New Lands By 1763, Britain gained control of French lands in North America. **SKILL** **Reading Maps** Describe how the map of North America changed between 1750 and 1763.

Victory for Britain

Main Idea Britain gained new land in the French and Indian War, but it also had new problems.

Britain was losing the French and Indian War until 1757, when **William Pitt** became the leader of Britain's Parliament, or government. Pitt was determined to win the war. He sent many ships and soldiers to North America, where they helped capture French forts. In 1759, a British army defeated the French near Quebec, which was a center of French power in Canada. The next year, Britain captured Montreal, another French city.

By 1763, France was ready to make peace with Britain. The two countries signed an agreement called the Treaty of Paris. As the map above shows, the treaty gave Britain control of Canada and most of the land east of the Mississippi River.

Troubles After the War

After the Treaty of Paris, British soldiers stayed in the Ohio River Valley. The American Indians who lived there wanted the British to leave. **Pontiac** (PAHN tee ak), an Ottawa chief, led American Indians in a war against the British, which was known as Pontiac's Rebellion. A **rebellion** is a fight against a government. Pontiac's warriors attacked British forts around the Great Lakes. Britain quickly defeated Pontiac's army. The rebellion lasted less than a year.

To prevent any more fighting with American Indians, Britain made a **proclamation,** or an official public statement. The Proclamation of 1763, as it was called, said that colonists could not settle west of the Appalachian Mountains. Britain recognized the Indian nations' rights to their land.

Many colonists were upset by the Proclamation of 1763. Now that the French were gone, colonists wanted to farm and settle in the Ohio River Valley. Colonists were also tired of British soldiers living among them. They no longer wanted the soldiers for protection.

As disagreements grew, colonists were willing to speak out. During the Great Awakening, 20 years before, colonists had challenged some of their church leaders.

The colonists disagreed with them about religious ideas. After 1763, colonists began working together to oppose the decisions of their government as well.

REVIEW Why were colonists upset with Britain after the French and Indian War?

Lesson Summary

Britain won control of the Ohio River Valley in the French and Indian War. Afterward, Pontiac's Rebellion caused Britain to make the Proclamation of 1763 to stop colonists from settling west of the Appalachian Mountains.

Why It Matters...

After the French and Indian War, colonists began to disagree with Britain's rule of the colonies.

Pontiac This Ottawa chief was determined to drive out the British. But without French support, he could not win.

Lesson Review

1754	1758	1763
French and Indian War	Battle of Quebec	Pontiac's Rebellion

1753 1755 1757 1759 1761 1763 1765

1. **VOCABULARY** Choose the correct word to complete each sentence.

   ally   congress   proclamation

   In Albany, the colonies held a _____ to discuss how to fight France.

   The Mohawk nation was an _____ of Britain.

2. **READING SKILL** Look at the **sequence** of events of the French and Indian War. What events were most important for Britain's success?

3. **MAIN IDEA: Economics** Why did British colonists want to control the Ohio River Valley?

4. **MAIN IDEA: Geography** Where did the Proclamation of 1763 divide British territory?

5. **PEOPLE TO KNOW** What role did **George Washington** play in the French and Indian War?

6. **TIMELINE SKILL** Which happened first, the Battle of Quebec or Pontiac's Rebellion?

7. **CRITICAL THINKING: Cause and Effect** What problems did Pontiac's Rebellion cause?

SPEAKING ACTIVITY Think about the advantages and disadvantages of the colonies joining together. Prepare a short speech to argue for or against the Albany Plan of Union.

George Washington
1732–1799

George Washington didn't know much about war. In 1755, he had been an army officer for only a year. He was 23 years old and hadn't had much success. Now he and British soldiers, led by General Braddock, were heading toward Fort Duquesne (doo KAYN), located on the Ohio River. General Braddock planned to seize the fort from the French.

Suddenly, shots rang out. A surprise attack! French soldiers and their American Indian allies had been waiting for the British. A tough battle followed. Washington helped lead injured soldiers to safety. After the battle, he found that his jacket was marked by bullet holes.

Three years later, Washington joined another British army. This time, the British soldiers weren't beaten, and they captured Fort Duquesne. Washington had learned from his experiences, and his bravery made him a hero in Virginia. Years later, he would apply his experience to a great challenge. He would lead an army against the British and create a new nation.

Major Achievements

1754–1763 Fights in French and Indian War

1775 Leads colonial army against British

1783 Wins Revolutionary War

1789 Elected
United States
President

Activities

1. **TALK ABOUT IT** How did Washington show **courage** during the French and Indian War?

2. **RESEARCH IT** Find out more about Washington's early career. Then write a journal account of one day in the life of young George Washington.

 Technology Read other biographies of people in this unit.
www.eduplace.com/kids/hmss05/

233

Early Conflicts with Britain

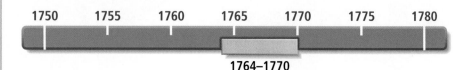

1750   1755   1760   1765   1770   1775   1780

1764–1770

Build on What You Know You know you have to pay for things you buy. Governments have to pay the money they owe, too. The British government had to find ways to raise the money it had spent on the French and Indian War.

Britain Needs Money

Main Idea The British government tried to raise money in the colonies to pay for the French and Indian War.

Winning the French and Indian War cost Britain a great deal of money. Britain had paid for thousands of soldiers to fight in North America. It also kept soldiers in the Ohio River Valley to protect the land it had won. **King George III** and the British Parliament decided that American colonists should help pay the costs of the war.

Britain planned to raise money by collecting taxes. A **tax** is money that people pay to their government in return for services. Britain usually taxed goods that colonists imported. These were goods brought from outside the colonies. When colonists bought imported goods such as cloth, some of the money they paid went to the British government.

King George III When George III became king at the age of 22, his country was already winning the French and Indian War.

Tax Stamps The Stamp Act put a tax on almost everything that was printed. To buy newspapers, calendars, and even playing cards, colonists had to pay for a tax stamp.

New Taxes

In 1764, Britain created a new tax with a law called the Sugar Act. This act taxed not only sugar, but many other imported goods such as coffee and cloth. Some merchants avoided paying the tax by **smuggling,** which means to import goods illegally. Merchants secretly brought the goods into the colonies so British officials could not tax them. In 1765, Parliament created another tax called the Stamp Act. This act taxed anything printed on paper.

Colonists were upset by the new taxes, because they could not take part in passing tax laws. Many believed that their local elected representatives, not Parliament, should pass tax laws for the colonies. American colonists had no representatives in the British Parliament, but did have representatives in their local governments.

Patrick Henry, a member of Virginia's House of Burgesses, made an angry speech against the Stamp Act. He said Britain was using its power unfairly. People all over the colonies heard about his speech, and many agreed with him.

Protests Colonists held protests to show how much they hated the Stamp Act.

Across the colonies, groups formed and called themselves the Sons of Liberty. **Liberty** means freedom from being controlled by another government.

Samuel Adams was an important leader of the Sons of Liberty in Boston. Adams and the Sons of Liberty organized protests against the Stamp Act. A **protest** is an event at which people complain about an issue.

Sometimes the Sons of Liberty and other groups used violence to resist the Stamp Act. Colonists wrecked the homes of a few British officials and beat up tax collectors.

REVIEW What was the goal of Samuel Adams and other Sons of Liberty?

Conflict Over Taxes

Main Idea Britain canceled the Stamp Act but then tried to pass new taxes.

In October 1765, nine colonies sent representatives to a meeting in New York City called the Stamp Act Congress. This congress decided that only the colonial governments could tax the colonists.

Merchants in large port cities such as New York and Philadelphia agreed to hold a boycott of British goods. In a **boycott,** a group of people refuses to buy, sell, or use certain goods. Colonists stopped buying British cloth and other goods. The boycott was a way of hurting British trade. The merchants hoped that the boycott would force the British government to cancel the Stamp Act.

The boycotts and protests worked. Parliament agreed to repeal the Stamp Act in 1766. To **repeal** a law means to cancel it.

The Townshend Acts

Although the British government repealed the Stamp Act, it still needed money. In 1767, Parliament created new taxes to pay for the services of British governors and soldiers in the colonies.

The new taxes, called the Townshend Acts, put a tax on the tea, glass, lead, paints, and paper that the colonies imported. Colonists were just as angry about the Townshend Acts as they had been about the Stamp Act.

Colonists in Boston threatened to use violence against British tax officials. After an angry mob injured several people, the British government sent soldiers to protect its tax officials. Many people in Boston did not want British soldiers in their city.

Colonial Imports from Britain
1764–1768

Value of Imports (in British Pounds) / Years

Boycott Colonial merchants in port cities refused to buy or sell goods brought from Britain by ship.

SKILL **Reading Graphs** Pounds are British money. How much did the value of imports decrease between 1764 and 1766?

Deborah Franklin
Even wealthy women, including the wife of Benjamin Franklin, made their own cloth during the boycott.

Daughters of Liberty

In response to the Townshend Acts, colonists held a boycott of the British goods they bought the most. Instead of importing British goods, such as cloth, the colonists made their own. Organizations of women known as the Daughters of Liberty wove their own cloth and used it to make clothes. These women did chores early in the morning, gathered to weave all day, and then returned home to do more chores. Because of their hard work, colonists did not have to buy as much British cloth.

During the boycotts, British merchants lost money. Parliament decided to remove the taxes from glass, lead, paints, and paper. The tax on tea remained, though.

Parliament wanted to show that it still had the power to tax the colonies.

Colonists felt that Britain should not even tax tea unless the colonies had representatives in Parliament. Although most of the taxes had been repealed, anger towards the British government continued to grow.

REVIEW Why did the British Parliament pass the Townshend Acts?

Lesson Summary

| Britain taxed the colonists to pay the cost of the French and Indian War. | → | Colonists did not want to be taxed without repre-sentation. | → | Protests by colonists forced Britain to repeal the taxes. |

Why It Matters . . .

American colonists wanted only their own elected representatives to pass taxes on them. This idea is important to people in the United States today.

Lesson Review

1764 **Sugar Act**   1765 **Stamp Act**   1767 **Townshend Acts**

1764   1765   1766   1767   1768

1 **VOCABULARY** Show that you know the meaning of **tax, boycott,** and **repeal.** Write a paragraph using the words.

2 **READING SKILL** Why were boycotts an effective **solution** to the **problem** of taxes?

3 **MAIN IDEA: Economics** Why did Britain create the Sugar Act and the Stamp Act?

4 **MAIN IDEA: Citizenship** Why did colonists protest Britain's new taxes?

5 **PEOPLE TO KNOW** Who was **Samuel Adams,** and what did he do to oppose the Stamp Act?

6 **TIMELINE SKILL** About how long after the Stamp Act were the Townshend Acts passed?

7 **CRITICAL THINKING: Summarize** What did the colonists do to protest British taxes?

HANDS ON

ART ACTIVITY Think about why Britain created the Stamp Act and why the colonists hated it. Make a pamphlet to persuade colonists to obey or oppose the Stamp Act.

Taxes in the Colonies

It is two in the afternoon on September 12, 1769. Anna and Tom Hart run an inn near New York City. They are working together on a letter to the British governor of New York. They want to tell him that they oppose the Townshend Acts. These new taxes have made some important items more expensive for them. The Harts are upset because they had no voice in creating the taxes. Colonists have no representatives in Parliament, so they cannot take part in decisions that affect them.

Paint
Better-quality paint comes from Britain, but the tax on it makes the price higher. To avoid the tax, the Harts painted this furniture and the walls with paints made in the colonies.

Tea
Like many other colonists, the Harts love British tea. Now, they refuse to drink it because of the British tax on it. This is Dutch tea, smuggled in from the Caribbean.

Glass
When Tom and Anna need to replace a broken windowpane, they find that the Townshend Acts make glass more expensive.

Paper
The Harts need lots of paper to keep track of their business, but there is a tax on paper from Britain.

Activities

1. **DRAW IT** Connect the Harts' experience to life today. Show a way that Americans can complain peacefully to the government.

2. **DEBATE IT** Many colonists felt that Britain's taxes were unfair, but the British felt that taxes were necessary. Hold a debate on the point of view of the colonists and of the British.

Conflicts Grow

1750   1755   1760   1765   1770   1775   1780

1770–1774

Build on What You Know Today, you can find out what is happening in the world from radio, television, newspapers, or the Internet. In colonial America, however, it was harder to learn about the news. Colonial leaders decided they needed better ways to share news.

Trouble in Boston

Main Idea Events in Boston created more trouble between the colonists and the British government.

Remember that Britain had sent soldiers to protect its officials in Boston. The people of Boston did not want British soldiers in their city. Frustrated colonists often fought with the soldiers.

On March 5, 1770, a fight began when a crowd of people in Boston argued with a British soldier. The crowd yelled insults and threw snowballs. More soldiers arrived, and suddenly one of them fired a shot. Then several other soldiers fired their guns. Five colonists were killed. One of them was **Crispus Attucks,** an African American sailor who is remembered today as a hero. Afterward, angry colonists called the fight a massacre. A **massacre** is the killing of many people.

Crispus Attucks One of the five men killed during the Boston Massacre was Crispus Attucks. He was a sailor who had escaped from slavery.

The BLOODY MASSACRE perpetrated in King—1—Street BOSTON on March 5th 1770 by a party of the 29th REGT

Unhappy Boston! see thy Sons deplore,
Thy hallow'd Walks besmear'd with guiltless Gore.
While faithless P—n and his savage Bands,
With murd'rous Rancour stretch their bloody Hands;
Like fierce Barbarians grinning o'er their Prey,
Approve the Carnage, and enjoy the Day.

If scalding drops from Rage from Anguish Wrung,
If speechless Sorrows lab'ring for a Tongue.
Or if a weeping World can ought appease
The plaintive Ghosts of Victims such as these;
The Patriot's copious Tears for each are shed,
A glorious Tribute which embalms the Dead.

But know, Fate summons to that awful Goal.
Where Justice strips the Murd'rer of his Soul:
Should venal C—ts the scandal of the Land,
Snatch the relentless Villain from her Hand.
Keen Execrations on this Plate inscrib'd,
Shall reach a Judge who never can be brib'd.

Engrav'd Printed & Sold by PAUL REVERE BOSTON

The Boston Massacre
Paul Revere made this image of the Boston Massacre.

SKILL **Primary Sources**
How close is this picture to the truth?

❶ Title
Revere's title begins with the words "The Bloody Massacre."

❷ Soldiers
British soldiers are shown taking aim and firing as a group.

❸ Colonists
Colonists are not shown attacking the soldiers. They do not look like an angry crowd.

Colonists Take Action

Paul Revere, a Son of Liberty and a Boston silversmith, created a picture of the Boston Massacre. It showed British soldiers shooting at colonists who are peaceful, not angry. The Sons of Liberty used the picture to convince colonists that British soldiers were dangerous.

The soldiers at the Boston Massacre were put on trial. **John Adams,** an important Boston lawyer, defended the soldiers at their trial. He wanted to show Britain that colonial courts were fair. Adams tried to prove that the soldiers had been protecting themselves from the crowd. Six soldiers were found innocent, and two were lightly punished.

At the time of the Boston Massacre, news traveled slowly. **Samuel Adams** wanted more colonists to know what was happening around the colonies. In 1772, Adams and other colonial leaders in Boston set up Committees of Correspondence to share news with the other colonies. **Correspondence** is written communication.

Soon every colony had Committees of Correspondence. They sent each other letters about what the British were doing and what actions colonists could take.

REVIEW What was the importance of the Committees of Correspondence?

Boston Tea Party
A crowd of colonists watched as Sons of Liberty, dressed up to look like Mohawk Indians, emptied 342 chests of tea into Boston Harbor.

The Boston Tea Party

Main Idea Colonists worked together to oppose British taxes and laws.

In 1773, Parliament passed the Tea Act. This law allowed the East India Company of Britain to sell tea in America at a very low price. For years, merchants had avoided paying taxes by smuggling tea into the colonies from other countries. The Tea Act made taxed tea even cheaper than smuggled tea.

If colonists bought the inexpensive tea, they would be paying a British tax at the same time. They did not believe that Parliament should tax them without their agreement. They also did not want only one company to control the tea trade.

Boston merchants would not sell the East India Tea. It sat unloaded on the ships in Boston Harbor. British officials refused to allow the tea to go back to Britain. Colonists decided to get rid of the unwanted tea.

On the night of December 16, 1773, several dozen Sons of Liberty boarded the ships illegally. They threw the tea into the harbor. This event is known as the Boston Tea Party.

The Boston Tea Party shocked the British. Parliament, led by Lord **Frederick North,** passed laws called the Coercive Acts to punish colonists in Massachusetts. To coerce means to force. The colonists called these laws the Intolerable Acts. Intolerable means unbearable.

The laws stopped trade between Boston and Britain, ended most town meetings, and gave Britain more control over the colony's government. British soldiers returned to Boston. Bostonians had to quarter the soldiers. To **quarter** people is to give them food and shelter.

Committees of Correspondence spread news of the Intolerable Acts. People throughout the colonies were furious with Britain. They felt the laws were too harsh.

The First Continental Congress

Colonists agreed to hold a meeting to discuss the Intolerable Acts. They sent delegates to meet in Philadelphia. A **delegate** is someone chosen to speak and act for others. On September 5, 1774, delegates from every colony except Georgia met. The meeting became known as the First Continental Congress.

The congress wrote a letter to the British government and the American colonists. The letter said that colonists should have the same freedoms as other British citizens. It asked **King George III** and Parliament to stop taxing colonists without their agreement and to repeal the Intolerable Acts.

The delegates decided to meet again in May if the king refused their demands. In the meantime, the colonists stopped trade with Britain. They began to train for battle in case war with Britain broke out.

The king made plans to send more soldiers to Boston. He declared that the colonists had begun a rebellion.

REVIEW Why did the First Continental Congress meet?

Lesson Summary

- British soldiers killed several colonists in the Boston Massacre.

- Committees of Correspondence helped different colonies stay in touch.

- In 1773, colonists dumped tea into Boston Harbor to protest the Tea Act.

- Britain passed the Intolerable Acts in response to the Boston Tea Party.

Why It Matters . . .

Disagreement over taxes increased conflict between colonists and the British government.

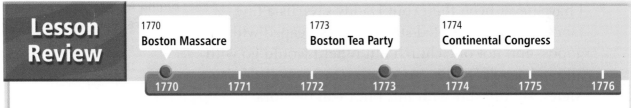

Lesson Review

| 1770 Boston Massacre | 1773 Boston Tea Party | 1774 Continental Congress |

1770 — 1771 — 1772 — 1773 — 1774 — 1775 — 1776

❶ **VOCABULARY** Show that you know what the words **delegate** and **correspondence** mean. Use the words in a paragraph about the First Continental Congress.

❷ **READING SKILL** Review the **prediction** you made as you read. What was the actual **outcome**?

❸ **MAIN IDEA: Economics** What is one reason some colonists did not like the Tea Act?

❹ **MAIN IDEA: History** What was one important effect of the Tea Act on the colonists?

❺ **PEOPLE TO KNOW** Why did **John Adams** defend in court the British soldiers involved in the Boston Massacre?

❻ **TIMELINE SKILL** How many years after the Boston Massacre did the First Continental Congress meet?

❼ **CRITICAL THINKING: Synthesize** Paul Revere's drawing of the Boston Massacre is on page 241. Describe what a British drawing of the event might have looked like.

WRITING ACTIVITY The First Continental Congress tried to persuade King George III to repeal the Intolerable Acts. Write a letter to King George III that the delegates might have written, explaining why he should repeal the Intolerable Acts.

Emma's Journal

by Marissa Moss

When ten-year-old Emma Millar is sent to Boston to help her Aunt Harmony, she decides to write and illustrate a journal. The year is 1774, and British troops have blockaded Boston Harbor.

July 18, 1774

The house is hush and still. I should be asleep, like everyone else, but I am too excited, so I have taken my journal to the windowsill and write by the light of the full moon. Tomorrow I leave our farm in Menetomy and go to Boston, such a big, bustling city. I have never been there, but Daddy says 'tis a fine, fancy city, with cobbled streets, stores heaped with rich goods, and not one church but nine! I would go with all my heart if Daddy, Mamma, or even my little sister, Mercy, should stay with me, but I will be alone. Except, of course, for Aunt Harmony — 'tis for her sake I go. She has no serving girl since the British blockaded Boston. (This past winter Americans dumped British tea into the harbor to protest the new tea tax. Daddy called it a "tea party," but with the blockade as punishment, no one feels festive now.)

Emma Millar – 10 years old

The Boston "Tea Party"

All of Aunt's boarders but one, Thankful Bliss, have left as well, fearful of the British troops that have taken over the city. I should think I should be fearful, too, but Daddy says we are good subjects of the King and have no cause to fret, especially not 10-year-old girls.

The city is as lively and fashionable as Daddy said. People dressed in London styles stroll the clean streets, and vendors hawk pies, eggs, and butter despite the blockade.

July 23, 1774

I woke in a strange room in a strange house to the sounds of fife and drum as the regulars drilled on the common. How I long for birdsong and the peaceful chirping of crickets! I miss the fresh country air and my dear Mamma and Daddy, Mercy, and my brothers, John, Paul, and Duncan. I feel out of place in this big, strange city, and out of sorts in this house.

I got this engraving from Mr. Revere when I took a spoon to his shop to be repaired. Boston, once full of merchantships, is now empty except for British warships.

July 28, 1774

Dr. Joseph Warren came to tea today. Aunt is very proud of her tea service as 'twas made by Paul Revere, a fine silversmith, and, like Dr. Warren, a noted Son of Liberty. I call it tea, but we drink coffee or chocolate — Aunt is a staunch Whig and boycotts all British goods.

Dr. Warren is a fine, handsome gentleman, elegantly dressed and wearing a brown tie wig (which I much prefer to powdered hair — how it makes me sneeze!). Aunt dotes on him, but Thankful distrusts him as she is a fierce Tory while he thinks the colonies should govern themselves without England's interference. Thankful says the patriots are "low rabble" who want mob rule, but Dr. Warren is no ruffian. He is charming and interesting. Talking with him I feel I understand the world better. (And elsewhere it seems such a muddle. Are we British or American? What does it mean to be a Whig or a Tory? Dr. Warren says we can support the King but must first stand up for ourselves.)

Dr. Warren

Hairstyles of the illustrious and wealthy

rolled hair

tied back

brown hair for every day

ringlets

gray for business

September 15, 1774

I have found a friend in Amos, our neighbor. He fishes in the harbor (but the regulars allow it only so long as he sells most of his catch to them). He is so cheery and full of news, I relish his visits. It has been near 3 months since I left home and I miss my family terribly, so I asked Amos if he could take me for a short visit. (Aunt said 'twas fine with her.)

But when we came to the city gates, the sentries refused to let us pass without a permit. Off we went to military headquarters to procure the needed document, but all I procured was a stiff back from sitting on a hard bench, waiting, waiting, waiting. Finally Major Small deigned to see me and I begged to leave to see my family. He did not even glance my way but said, "No."

After waiting so long, I could not leave it at that. "But why, sir?" I protested. "I am a mere child. What danger can I be to His Majesty's army?"

"I said no," he repeated, and this time he did look at me, glaring, "because you are saucy and do not know your place. Is it the air you breathe that makes you colonists so impertinent? Even a young maid dares to sass an officer? Out with you — you have wasted enough of my time!"

I dared not murmur a word. I ran out, crying. Would I never see Mamma and Daddy again? Was Boston a city or a prison?

Amos said 'twas our timing that was bad — the regulars just seized some fieldpieces from the militia in Cambridge and in response guns were stolen from the British battery in Boston (right under the sentries' noses!). The officers now suspect everyone of preparing for an armed rebellion. Will arms really be taken up?

The soldiers are called lobsterbacks because of their red uniforms.

Activities

1. **THINK ABOUT IT** What things does Emma find strange about living in Boston?

2. **WRITE IT** After Emma meets Major Small, she wonders if Boston is a city or a prison. Write a letter from Emma to a Boston newspaper that expresses her feelings about the British occupation.

Identify Causes and Effects

▶ **VOCABULARY**

cause

effect

Historians want to know what happened in the past. They also want to know why it happened. They look for the causes and effects of events. A **cause** is an event or action that makes something else happen. An **effect** is another event or action that is a result of the cause.

Some events have more than one cause. Some have more than one effect.

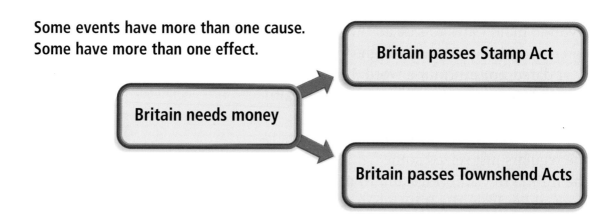

Many times, an effect can cause another event or action.

Learn the Skill

Step 1: Look for clue words that signal causes and effects. Words such as *because*, *since*, *led to*, and *the reason why* signal causes. Words such as *so*, *therefore*, *after this*, and *as a result* signal effects.

Step 2: Identify the cause of an event. Check to see if there is more than one cause.

Step 3: Identify the effect. Check to see if there is more than one effect. Think about whether any of the effects then become causes.

Practice the Skill

Reread pages 242-243 of Lesson 3. Copy and fill out a diagram like the one below. Then answer the following questions.

Intolerable Acts

① What was one cause of the Intolerable Acts?

② What was one effect of the Intolerable Acts?

③ Explain in a few sentences how you identified the causes and effects.

Apply the Skill

Organize the major events on pages 228-231 of Lesson 1. Place the Proclamation of 1763 at the center of the chart. Then fill in the causes and effects. Make sure you have at least one cause and one effect.

War Begins

| 1750 | 1755 | 1760 | 1765 | 1770 | 1775 | 1780 |

1775–1776

VOCABULARY

Patriot
militia
minutemen
commander
petition

Vocabulary Strategy

A **militia** is an army of ordinary people. It comes from the same word as military.

READING SKILL

Cause and Effect Note causes of the war between Britain and the colonies.

⬜ ⬜
⬇ ⬇

War with Britain

Build on What You Know When Britain and France could not agree on control of the Ohio River Valley, they went to war. What do you think happened when Britain and the colonists disagreed and could not get along anymore?

Moving Toward War

Main Idea Conflict between the colonists and Britain led to the Battles of Lexington and Concord.

In 1775, many colonists felt that the Intolerable Acts were too harsh. There were more than 3,000 British soldiers in Boston. The British navy blocked Boston Harbor to keep ships from entering or leaving Boston.

Patriots spoke out against the British government. Colonists who opposed British rule called themselves Patriots. **Mercy Otis Warren** was a Patriot writer. She wrote plays criticizing British officials in Boston. In Virginia, **Patrick Henry,** another Patriot, said that he was eager for a war with Britain. Many colonists shared his views.

Throughout the colonies, militias prepared for war. A militia is a group of ordinary people who train for battle. Most of the men in the militia were farmers.

Militia The men in militias did not have much training, but they were willing to fight to defend their homes.

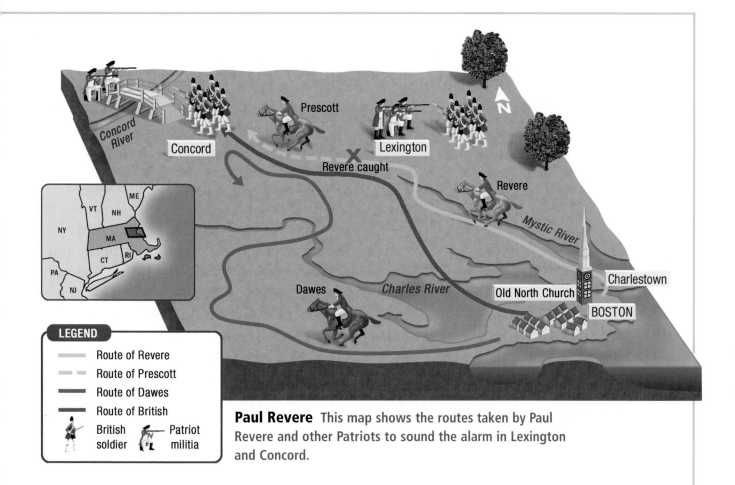

LEGEND

Route of Revere
Route of Prescott
Route of Dawes
Route of British
British soldier
Patriot militia

Paul Revere This map shows the routes taken by Paul Revere and other Patriots to sound the alarm in Lexington and Concord.

Paul Revere's Ride

British leaders were worried about the militias. General **Thomas Gage,** the new British governor of Massachusetts, had orders to stop any possible rebellion. He learned that Patriots were storing gunpowder and cannons in Concord, about 20 miles from Boston. Gage decided to send soldiers to destroy the supplies. The soldiers would march at night to take the Patriots by surprise.

General Gage could not keep his plan secret. Patriots in Boston soon knew what was planned. They used lanterns in the tower of Boston's Old North Church to warn Patriots outside the city that British soldiers were coming. Two Patriots also rode out to warn the militia. One rider was **Paul Revere,** the silversmith. The other was **William Dawes.**

On the night of April 18, 1775, an army of 700 British soldiers set off for Concord. Revere and Dawes galloped ahead, alerting sleeping minutemen along the way. **Minutemen** were militia with special training. They had to be ready for battle at a minute's notice.

Racing through the night, Revere told the minutemen, "The Regulars are coming out!" Regulars was a word for British soldiers. Other riders, such as **Samuel Prescott,** helped Revere and Dawes spread the alarm.

British soldiers captured Revere in Lexington, but Dawes and Prescott escaped. Prescott rode on to Concord. The soldiers later released Revere.

REVIEW Why did General Gage send British soldiers to Concord?

The First Battles

Main Idea Colonists and British soldiers fought two battles in Massachusetts.

The British soldiers reached Lexington just before sunrise on April 19. A small group of minutemen were waiting there. A British officer told the minutemen to leave. As the minutemen turned to go, someone fired a shot. No one knows whether the shot came from a British soldier or a colonist. Both sides began shooting. When they stopped, eight colonists were dead and nine were wounded. Only one British soldier had been hurt. The British marched on to Concord.

As the British searched Concord for hidden weapons, more minutemen gathered nearby. Fighting soon started.

The minutemen forced the British to turn back toward Boston. Many years later, the poet **Ralph Waldo Emerson** called this event

> 66 **the shot heard 'round the world.** 99

The British soldiers were in a dangerous situation on the way back. Patriots from the towns between Concord and Boston, as well as towns farther north and south, were ready. As the British marched back to Boston, colonists shot at them from behind trees and stone walls. More than 250 British soldiers were wounded or killed before the British reached Boston.

News of the Battles of Lexington and Concord spread quickly. More and more militias arrived in Boston. Soon thousands of armed colonists surrounded the city. The British in Boston were trapped.

April 19, 1775
Battles of Lexington and Concord

1 A.M. Paul Revere and others warn the minutemen that British soldiers are marching to Concord.

5 A.M. Minutemen clash with the British at Lexington. The minutemen are forced to flee. The drum on the left was used by the minutemen at Lexington.

Bunker Hill

After the Patriot militia surrounded Boston, they had time to plan. Militia leaders decided to build a fort on Bunker Hill, across the Charles River from Boston. From there, they could fire cannons at the British soldiers in Boston.

When the militia reached Bunker Hill, they chose to build their fort on Breed's Hill instead. It was closer to Boston. They worked through the night of June 16, building a fort with dirt walls six feet high. The next morning, the surprised British attacked the fort.

More than 2,000 British soldiers began to march up Breed's Hill. **William Prescott**, a Patriot leader, told the militia,

> 66 **Don't fire until you see the whites of their eyes.** 99

When the British were close enough, the militia in the fort began shooting. Many soldiers fell, and the British were forced back. Minutes later, the British attacked again and were turned back. The third time the British attacked, the Patriots ran out of gunpowder. The British finally captured the fort, but more than half of their soldiers were hurt or killed.

The battle was called the Battle of Bunker Hill, although it was fought on Breed's Hill. The British won, but the Patriots had proved that they could fight well. One British general said that winning another battle like it "would have ruined us." They could not afford to lose so many soldiers.

REVIEW Why was the Battle of Bunker Hill important for the colonists?

8 A.M. Colonists and British soldiers begin shooting at each other at the Old North Bridge in Concord. The British turn back after several of their soldiers are killed.

NOON The British begin to march back to Boston. During their long march, thousands of minutemen shoot at them from behind trees and stone walls. The British soldiers finally reach safety in Charlestown at 7 P.M.

A Colonial Army

Main Idea The Second Continental Congress prepared for a war against Britain.

Remember that the First Continental Congress had sent a list of demands to the British government. When Britain refused to meet their demands, the colonial delegates gathered again in Philadelphia in the spring of 1775. This meeting became known as the Second Continental Congress.

The delegates knew that they might soon be at war with Britain. They needed more than an untrained militia to win a war against the British. They needed an army. The militia only fought for a few months at a time. Soldiers in an army fight until a war is over.

Congress decided to create a new army called the Continental Army. The members of the Continental Army would be trained soldiers, like the British.

Congress looked for a commander for the new Continental Army. A **commander** is the officer in charge of an army. In June of 1775, they chose **George Washington.** Washington had fought in the French and Indian War. People knew he was a brave and skilled soldier. Washington rode to Boston to organize the Continental Army.

The Olive Branch Petition

Many delegates to the Second Continental Congress did not want war with Britain. They only wanted to be treated fairly. Congress made one more try at peace with Britain. In July of 1775, the delegates sent **King George III** the Olive Branch Petition. A **petition** is a written request from a number of people. The olive branch is a symbol of peace. The petition asked the king to help end the conflict. King George did not even read the Olive Branch Petition. Instead, he sent more soldiers to the colonies.

Washington in Command
Washington became commander of the Continental Army in 1775. He used the writing case below while he was leading the army.

Ticonderoga This important fort was captured from the British by Patriot militia in 1775. Its cannons were hauled to Boston to help the Continental Army.

For the next nine months, the British army stayed in Boston. Washington spent that time turning the colonial militia into a real army. He also sent a trusted officer, Colonel **Henry Knox,** to Fort Ticonderoga in New York. Americans had captured the fort and its cannons earlier that year.

Knox and his soldiers dragged the cannons to Boston. When the cannons arrived, the British decided to leave Boston. On March 17, 1776, they sailed out of Boston Harbor. Forcing the British to leave Boston was a success for the Patriots, but the war was just beginning.

REVIEW What was the Olive Branch Petition?

Lesson Summary

British soldiers and colonists fought at Lexington and Concord, and again on Breed's Hill. The Second Continental Congress made George Washington commander of the new Continental Army. Congress also sent King George III the Olive Branch Petition in an attempt to make peace, but he ignored it.

Why It Matters . . .

Battles in Massachusetts were the beginning of the war to free colonists from British rule.

Lesson Review

APRIL 1775
Battles of Lexington and Concord

JUNE 1775
Battle of Bunker Hill

1775   1776

1. **VOCABULARY** Write a news report about the Battles of Lexington and Concord using the words **Patriot, minutemen,** and **militia.**

2. **READING SKILL** Why were the Battles of Lexington and Concord a **cause** of war with Britain?

3. **MAIN IDEA: History** What prepared the militia for the arrival of the British soldiers at Lexington?

4. **MAIN IDEA: Government** Why did the Second Continental Congress send the Olive Branch Petition to King George III?

5. **PEOPLE TO KNOW** What did **Paul Revere** do to help the Patriot cause?

6. **TIMELINE SKILL** When did the battles of Lexington and Concord happen?

7. **CRITICAL THINKING: Compare and Contrast** In what ways are a militia and an army alike? In what ways are they different?

WRITING ACTIVITY The Battles of Lexington and Concord were the first fights between colonists and British soldiers. Write a description what happened on April 19 from the point of view of a minuteman or a British soldier.

Battle of Bunker Hill

"Don't fire until you see the whites of their eyes!"
A Patriot officer is said to have given this famous order as 2,000 British soldiers marched closer and closer up the hill. It was June 17, 1775. The Battle of Bunker Hill in Charlestown was the first major clash between large numbers of British soldiers and Patriot militia. The geography of Charlestown forced the British attackers to march uphill. Why did this make a difference?

2

5

1

Breed's Hill

4

Bunker Hill

Events of June 17th, 1775

1 Patriot militia built a fort on Breed's Hill to fire on British ships and soldiers in Boston. They first planned to build their fort on Bunker Hill, but it was too far from Boston.

2 Cannons on British ships could not destroy the Patriots' fort.

3 The British in Boston fired red-hot cannonballs and set Charlestown on fire.

4 Three times, British soldiers marched slowly uphill toward the fort. Hot, tired, weighed down by 125 pounds of gear, the British soldiers were easy targets for Patriot gunfire.

5 To save ammunition, the Patriots waited to shoot until the British soldiers were almost on top of them. The British only captured the fort when the Patriots ran out of bullets.

Activities

1. EXPLORE IT Step into the picture and tell what you think the Patriot fort looked like to British soldiers on their march.

2. WRITE YOUR OWN Write directions for a Patriot battle plan at Breed's Hill. Explain what your fort's position would be. Use compass directions.

Visual Summary

1–4. ✏️ Write a description of each event named below.

French and Indian War, 1755	Townshend Act, 1767	Boston Tea Party, 1774	Lexington and Concord, 1775
			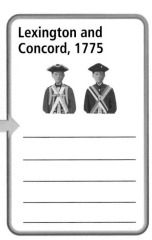
_____	_____	_____	_____
_____	_____	_____	_____
_____	_____	_____	_____
_____	_____	_____	_____
_____	_____	_____	_____

Facts and Main Ideas

✅ **TEST PREP** Answer each question with information from the chapter.

5. **Geography** What was the purpose of the Proclamation of 1763?

6. **Economics** What was the Stamp Act?

7. **Economics** Why did the British government need to tax the colonists?

8. **Government** Why were colonists angry about British taxes?

9. **History** Who was Paul Revere?

10. **History** Why did the Second Continental Congress decide to form a colonial army?

Vocabulary

✅ **TEST PREP** Choose the correct word from the list below to complete each sentence.

ally, p. 229
liberty, p. 235
petition, p. 254

11. Colonists opposed to the Stamp Act became members of the Sons of _____.

12. The Mohawk nation was an _____ of the British, not the French.

13. Colonists at the Second Continental Congress sent one final _____ to King George III.

1754	1763	1765	1774	1775
Albany Congress	Proclamation of 1763	Stamp Act	First Continental Congress	Battle of Bunker Hill

1750   1755   1760   1765   1770   1775   1780

Apply Skill

✓ **TEST PREP** **Reading and Thinking Skill** Use the organizer below and what you have learned about causes and effects to answer each question.

> The British went to find military supplies in Concord.

> The Battles of Lexington and Concord were fought.

> The Continental Army was formed.

> The British were forced out of Boston.

14. What was a cause of the Battles of Lexington and Concord?

   A. Committees of Correspondence formed.

   B. The British went to find military supplies in Concord.

   C. The British were forced out of Boston.

   D. The Continental Army was formed.

15. What was a result of the Battles of Lexington and Concord?

   A. Committees of Correspondence formed.

   B. The British went to find military supplies in Concord.

   C. British troops were sent to Boston.

   D. The Continental Army was formed.

Critical Thinking

✓ **TEST PREP** Write a short paragraph to answer each question.

16. **Infer** Why do you think King George III did not accept the Olive Branch Petition?

17. **Compare and Contrast** List ways in which the First and Second Continental Congresses were alike and different.

Timeline

Use the Chapter Summary Timeline above to answer the question.

18. How long after the Albany Congress did the First Continental Congress meet?

Activities

Art Activity Create a poster that would encourage colonists to join the Sons or Daughters of Liberty. Describe the group and why new members are needed.

Writing Activity Colonists learned about events through the Committees of Correspondence. Write a short story about a committee member informing others about Paul Revere's ride.

Technology
Writing Process Tips
Get help with your short story at
www.eduplace.com/kids/hmss05/

Chapter 8

The War for Independence

Technology
e • **glossary**
e • **word games**
www.eduplace.com/kids/hmss05/

Vocabulary Preview

independence

On July 4, 1776, the American colonies said that they wanted **independence** from Britain. Every year we celebrate our country's freedom on July 4, Independence Day. **page 262**

declaration

Thomas Jefferson wrote a long statement, the **Declaration** of Independence. The Declaration explained why the American colonies should be free. **page 264**

Chapter Timeline

1776
Declaration of Independence

1778
Valley Forge

1781
Victory at Yorktown

1775   1776   1777   1778   1779   1780   1781

Reading Strategy

Question As you read the lessons in this chapter, ask yourself questions.

Quick Tip List your questions, then go back to find the answers.

inflation

A rise in prices is called **inflation.** During the War for Independence, inflation caused colonists to pay more money for food and clothing. **page 273**

victory

The Battle of Yorktown was a **victory** for the Americans. They beat the British and won the War for Independence. **page 279**

1783
Treaty of Paris

1782   1783   1784   1785

Declaring Independence

VOCABULARY

independence
declaration
rights
treason

Vocabulary Strategy

> inde**pend**ence

Look for the word
depend in **independence.**
Independence means not
depending on others.

READING SKILL
Predict Outcomes
As you read, predict the
outcome of the arguments
over independence.

> PREDICTION
>
> OUTCOME

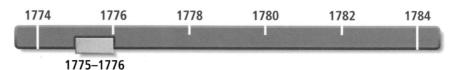

1774   1776   1778   1780   1782   1784

1775–1776

Build on What You Know You may have a birth
certificate at home. This paper tells when you were born.
In a way, our country has a birth certificate. It's called the
Declaration of Independence. The Declaration marks the
beginning of the United States.

The Steps to Independence

Main Idea *Common Sense* and debates in Congress changed
people's minds about being ruled by Britain.

After the battles of 1775, the American colonies and
Britain were at war. However, not all colonists felt this
was right. Many still thought of **King George III** as their
ruler. They did not want a war with Britain. Other
colonists were Patriots. They wanted independence.
Independence means freedom from being ruled by
someone else. Some Patriots felt that independence was
worth fighting for. **Patrick Henry**, a Patriot from Virginia,
said in a thrilling speech to a group of Virginia delegates,

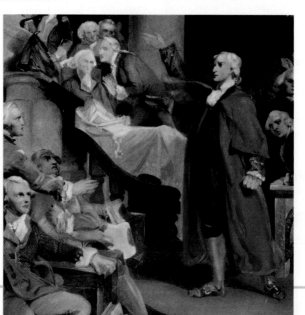

**❝ Give me liberty
or give me death! ❞**

Another Patriot,
Thomas Paine, used the
written word to argue for
independence.

Patrick Henry Bold, persuasive
speeches by Patrick Henry moved
colonists toward independence.

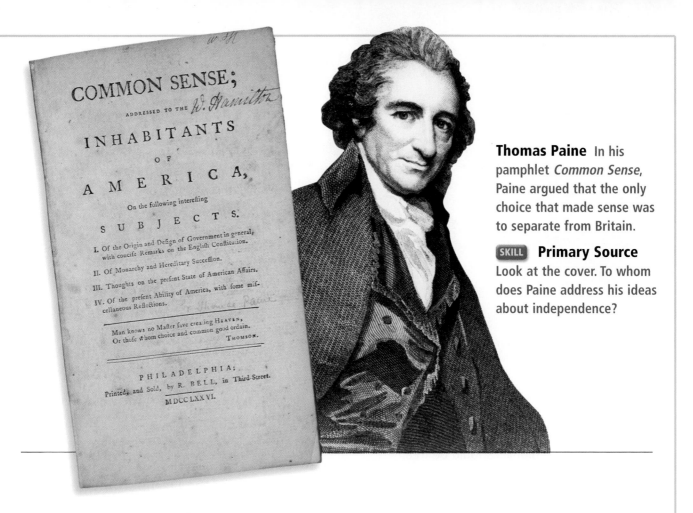

Thomas Paine In his pamphlet *Common Sense*, Paine argued that the only choice that made sense was to separate from Britain.

SKILL **Primary Source** Look at the cover. To whom does Paine address his ideas about independence?

Thomas Paine's *Common Sense*

Thomas Paine wrote a pamphlet called *Common Sense* in January 1776. *Common Sense* pushed for independence. The pamphlet was brief, inexpensive, and easy to understand. Paine wrote that King George treated the colonies unfairly. He claimed that the only way to stop this was to become independent from Britain.

Colonists bought over 100,000 copies of *Common Sense* within a few months. **George Washington** said, "I find *Common Sense* is working a powerful change in the minds of many."

Thomas Paine put into writing what many of the boldest Patriots were already saying. He wrote that colonists had nothing to gain and much to lose by staying tied to an unjust king.

Debate in Congress

Delegates to the Second Continental Congress had read *Common Sense*. Many agreed that independence from Britain was necessary, but they also knew it was risky. Britain was a powerful country. King George III was already gathering soldiers to attack the colonies. Could the colonies stand up to Britain? Some delegates also worried that not enough colonists wanted independence. However, support for independence was growing all across the colonies.

John Adams argued strongly for independence. More and more of the delegates agreed with his point of view. At last, on June 7, 1776, a Virginia delegate named **Richard Henry Lee** asked Congress to officially declare independence.

REVIEW What were Thomas Paine's arguments for independence?

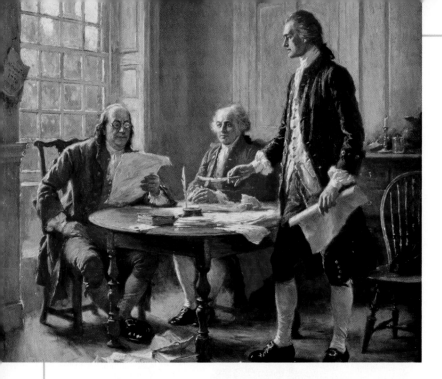

Writing the Declaration
It took Thomas Jefferson two weeks to write the Declaration. When he finished his draft, four other delegates helped edit it. Shown here are Benjamin Franklin (left), John Adams (center), and Jefferson, who is standing.

Declaration of Independence

Main Idea The Declaration of Independence explains why the colonies should be free.

Congress asked **Thomas Jefferson** and four others to write a declaration of independence. A **declaration** is a statement that declares, or announces, an idea. Congress needed a document to declare why the colonies had to become independent of Britain. In the Declaration of Independence, Jefferson wrote what many Americans believed about their rights. **Rights** are freedoms that are protected by a government's laws. Jefferson argued that all people are born with rights that no one can take away. He wrote that people have the right to live, the right to be free, and the right to seek happiness.

❝ We hold these truths to be self-evident, that all men are created equal, that they are endowed by their Creator with certain unalienable Rights, that among these are Life, Liberty, and the Pursuit of Happiness . . . ❞

Jefferson argued that a government should protect these rights. If it does not, then the people have the right to start a new government.

The ideas in the Declaration were not new. Jefferson used ideas that **John Locke** and other English thinkers had written about. Locke had said that governments should serve their people.

Jefferson listed many ways that Britain did not serve the colonists. For instance, King George had tried to take away rights. He had forced taxes on the colonists and sent soldiers to control them. Jefferson showed that the colonists had many reasons to separate from the king. They had the right to create their own government.

Mary Katherine Goddard
Congress hired Mary Katherine Goddard, a printer, to print an official copy of the Declaration.

Parts of the Declaration

You can read the full text of the Declaration on pages 581 and 582 of this book. The Declaration begins by promising to explain why the colonies must break away from Britain (see **1**). The next section explains that people have rights that cannot be taken away. It says that "all men are created equal"(see **2**). The longest section is a list of complaints against the king (see **3**).

The last section argues that the colonies have to be free to protect the colonists' rights. It declares that the colonies are independent (see **4**).

At the bottom of the document, delegates to Congress signed their names (see **5**). **John Hancock,** president of Congress, signed his name in large letters.

REVIEW According to the Declaration, why did the colonies have the right to their own government?

Connect to Today
Notice the date of the Declaration. What do you do every year to celebrate that day?

Signers of the Declaration Thomas Jefferson (1) presents the document to John Hancock (2) and the Continental Congress. Find John Adams (3) and Benjamin Franklin (4).

Importance of the Declaration

Main Idea The Declaration sets forth basic ideas of freedom and equality.

On July 4, 1776, the Second Continental Congress voted to accept the Declaration. The delegates knew that signing the Declaration was dangerous. Britain would call it treason. **Treason** is the crime of fighting against one's own government. Anyone who signed the Declaration could be charged with treason and hanged. Yet delegates signed.

The Declaration was read aloud to excited crowds across the new nation. People tore down pictures and statues of King George. They celebrated by ringing bells and firing cannons. The Declaration of Independence marked the moment when Americans chose to rule themselves.

Equality Then and Now

The Declaration is important today because it states that the people of the United States believe in equal rights for all. Today we know that Jefferson's words, "all men are created equal," include everyone: women as well as men, every race, every group, every ability. Is that what the words meant when the Declaration was written? Probably not.

In 1776, all Americans could not exercise the same rights. Only white men who owned property could vote. Many believed this was unfair. **Abigail Adams** wanted Congress to recognize the equal rights of women. She wrote to her husband, John Adams,

> 66 . . . in the new Code of Laws . . . Remember the Ladies . . . 99

It took many years, but women, African Americans, American Indians, and other groups have gained equal rights. In later lessons, you'll read about important laws that guarantee these rights. The Declaration has inspired people, past and present, to work for liberty and equal rights.

REVIEW Why is the Declaration so important to Americans?

Lesson Summary

- The colonies decided to declare their independence from Britain.
- Congress asked Thomas Jefferson to write the Declaration of Independence.
- The Declaration states that everyone has certain rights that no government can take away.

Why It Matters ...

The ideas in the Declaration of Independence have meaning today. The rights of freedom and equality that Jefferson wrote about are important American values and principles.

Martin Luther King Jr. In the 1960s, Martin Luther King Jr. was a great leader in the struggle for African Americans' equal rights. He and his wife, Coretta Scott King, led many marches to protest unjust treatment.

Lesson Review

January 1776
Common Sense printed

July 4, 1776
Declaration of Independence signed

1776   1777

❶ **VOCABULARY** Write a paragraph explaining why Americans needed **independence** to protect their **rights.** Use these words in your paragraph.

❷ **READING SKILL** Look at your **prediction.** Does it agree with what actually happened?

❸ **MAIN IDEA: History** How did *Common Sense* help lead to independence?

❹ **MAIN IDEA: Citizenship** Why did delegates need courage to sign the Declaration?

❺ **PEOPLE TO KNOW** Who was **Patrick Henry,** and what did he believe about independence?

❻ **TIMELINE SKILL** How many months before the signing of the Declaration was *Common Sense* printed?

❼ **CRITICAL THINKING: Compare and Contrast** How are *Common Sense* and the Declaration of Independence alike? How are they different?

SPEAKING ACTIVITY Would you have taken the risk of signing the Declaration? Prepare a short speech to explain your answer.

Thomas Jefferson

1743–1826

Thomas Jefferson is deep in thought. He must find the right words. Congress has chosen Jefferson to tell the king why the American colonies no longer belong to Britain. These are dangerous words, and they could cost Jefferson his life. Yet he loves his country and is writing the words that will create a new nation.

He dips his quill pen into the inkwell and rewrites a sentence in his draft. At this amazing moment in his life, he applies to his writing what he has learned and what he cares so much about.

All his life, Jefferson wanted to know the why and how of everything. He played the violin, studied the stars, invented things, and designed buildings.

He had read about government, history, and science as a young man. In his draft of the Declaration, he used ideas he had learned. The result was one of the most important documents in history.

Major Achievements

1768
Designs Monticello, a U.S. landmark

1776
Writes the Declaration

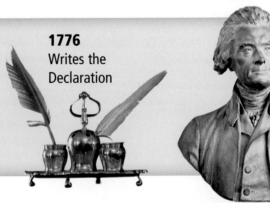

1801
Elected U.S. President

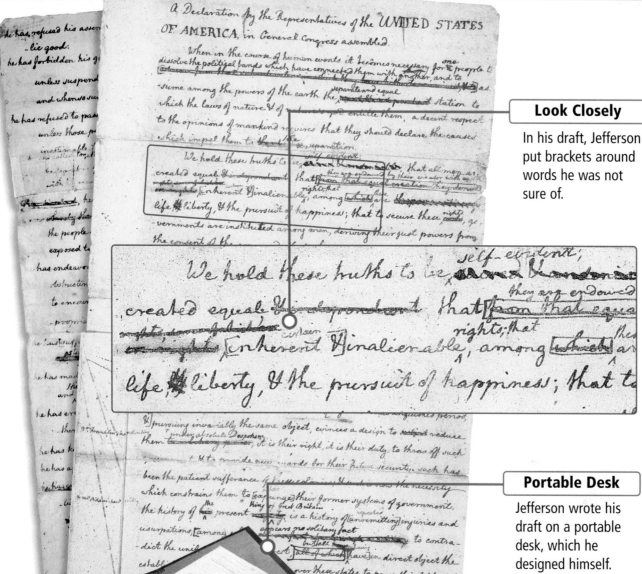

Look Closely

In his draft, Jefferson put brackets around words he was not sure of.

Portable Desk

Jefferson wrote his draft on a portable desk, which he designed himself.

1803
Doubles size of United States with the Louisiana Purchase

1804
Sends Lewis and Clark to explore the West

LOUISIANA PURCHASE

Activities

1. **TALK ABOUT IT** How might Jefferson's patriotism have helped him write an important document like the Declaration of Independence?

2. **WRITE ABOUT IT** What happens on June 28, 1776, when delegates in Congress hear the Declaration draft for the first time? Write a one-page story in the present tense.

 Technology Visit Education Place at www.eduplace.com/kids/hmss05/ for more biographies of people in this unit.

269

Life During the War

1774   1776   1778   1780   1782   1784

1775–1783

Build on What You Know Have you had to make a difficult decision? During the American Revolution, people had to make the hard decision whether to fight against Britain. How would a war affect their day-to-day lives?

Taking Sides

Main Idea Americans made difficult choices about whether to support Britain or the United States, or not to take sides at all.

On July 4, 1776, the Second Continental Congress declared independence. Not all Americans agreed that this was the right thing to do. Many felt that Britain should rule the colonies. Others believed that America should be independent. As the Revolutionary War began, people had to decide whether to support Britain, America, or neither side.

Almost half of all Americans were Patriots. Remember that a Patriot was someone who wanted independence for the colonies. About one-fifth of Americans were Loyalists. A **Loyalist** was someone who was still loyal to the king. Many Loyalists disagreed with how **King George III** governed the colonies, but they still wanted America to be part of Britain. The rest of Americans were neutral. To be **neutral** means not to take sides.

Loyalists in America

Loyalists had different reasons for supporting Britain. Most Americans who worked for the British government were Loyalists because they would lose their jobs if the Patriots won the war. Many wealthy merchants feared that war would hurt their businesses, so they supported Britain. Other Loyalists simply believed that the British cause was right.

Some enslaved African Americans became Loyalists. They were offered freedom if they helped the British. A few fought in the British army. Others built forts or drove carts.

More American Indians agreed to help the British than to help the Patriots. The Cherokee hoped that the British would win the war and stop settlers from taking land. Mohawk leader **Joseph Brant** also urged his people to side with the British. Most American Indians stayed neutral during the war. Two Iroquois nations, the Oneida (oh NYE duh) and the Tuscarora (tus kuh ROAR uh), fought for the Patriots.

James Armistead A Patriot hero, Armistead spied on the British army. He provided information that helped Patriots win an important battle.

Patriots

Patriots found many ways to support the cause of independence. Some joined the Continental Army and fought the British. Patriots who did not fight gave support in other ways. **Haym Salomon** (HI em SAHL uh mun), a banker from Philadelphia, helped the United States get loans. He also lent his own money.

Many African Americans were Patriots. Some enslaved African Americans were offered freedom if they became Patriot soldiers. **Peter Salem**, a Patriot hero of the Battle of Bunker Hill, was one of them. Free African Americans also became soldiers. About 5,000 African Americans fought in the Continental Army, and another 2,500 served in the navy.

REVIEW Why did enslaved African Americans fight on both sides in the war?

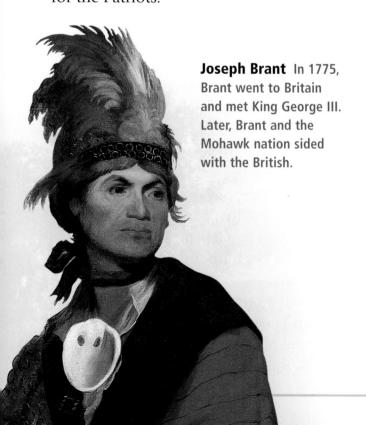

Joseph Brant In 1775, Brant went to Britain and met King George III. Later, Brant and the Mohawk nation sided with the British.

Women Patriots Mary Ludwig Hays (above) took over her husband's cannon after he was hurt. Deborah Sampson (right) disguised herself as a man and fought as a soldier in the Continental Army. She was wounded twice.

Women and the War

Some women Patriots worked as spies and messengers. A few women, such as **Deborah Sampson,** dressed in men's clothes and joined the Continental Army. Others spread the message of freedom in letters, plays, and poems. African American poet **Phillis Wheatley** wrote a poem for **George Washington,** praising him and the cause of freedom.

Phillis Wheatley
Her poems praised Washington and were popular in the colonies.

Many women, including General Washington's wife, followed their husbands who were in the army. Each winter during the eight years of the war, **Martha Washington** stayed at the general's camp. She did all she could to help the soldiers.

Some women cooked at camp or brought water to soldiers on the battle-field. They were nicknamed Molly Pitcher because of the pitchers of water they carried. A few of these women fought when their husbands were hurt or killed. One Molly Pitcher, **Mary Ludwig Hays,** was honored by General Washington for fighting in her husband's place after he was injured.

Another famous Patriot was **Nancy Morgan Hart** of Georgia. She once had to defend her home against a group of Loyalist fighters.

The Challenges of War

Main Idea Life was hard for many Americans during the war.

The War for Independence created many problems for Americans. When the British and American armies met in battle, people who lived nearby had to leave their homes. Both armies destroyed houses and robbed farms. Everyone was affected, whether a Patriot, a Loyalist, or neutral.

During the war, the prices of food, clothing, and supplies increased. Inflation caused hardship in the colonies. A rise in the prices of goods is called **inflation.** Higher prices made it difficult for people to buy the goods they needed.

Money Congress printed money called Continentals.

Some merchants and farmers would not sell their goods. They waited for prices to go even higher so that they could sell their goods for more money. Holding back goods lowered supplies of necessary items, which hurt people and made it difficult to feed and supply the army. Congress made it illegal to hold on to goods.

Life was hard because of the problems caused by war, but many Americans still wanted independence.

REVIEW Why was inflation a problem for Americans?

Lesson Summary

Americans were divided about which side to support during the American Revolution. Patriots found many ways to support the cause of independence. Whatever their choice, for most Americans, the war brought many hardships.

Why It Matters ...

Patriots believed strongly in their cause. They were determined not to give up the fight against British rule.

Lesson Review

❶ **VOCABULARY** Use the words **Loyalist** and **neutral** in a paragraph about taking sides during the war.

❷ **READING SKILL** **Compare** and **contrast** the different views of African Americans toward the war.

❸ **MAIN IDEA: History** What is one reason some American Indians helped the British?

❹ **MAIN IDEA: Economics** In what way did prices change during the Revolutionary War?

❺ **PEOPLE TO KNOW** What did **Phillis Wheatley** become known for during the war?

❻ **CRITICAL THINKING: Decision Making** For colonists in 1776, what were the costs and benefits of deciding to support the Patriots' fight for independence?

HANDS ON

ART ACTIVITY Create a poster to persuade people to side with the Patriots or the Loyalists, or to remain neutral. Think about the persuasive words and pictures you can use.

Patriot or Loyalist

Why were there so many different points of view? People from Georgia to New Hampshire talked and argued about the Revolution. The question of war was important to their lives. Listen to what these characters say.

Characters

Narrator

Samantha Jones (Patriot)

Max Stark (neutral)

Matthew Lynn (Loyalist)

James Morton (Patriot)

Joseph Tall Deer (Loyalist)

Mary Smith (Patriot)

Ann Bates (Patriot)

Reverend David Whittle (Loyalist)

Sarah Whittle (Patriot)

Paul Salem (Loyalist)

Lucy Thatcher (Patriot)

Meet Samantha Jones
She was a printer. How could she help the Patriot cause?

Narrator: Samantha Jones, you are a printer. Max Stark, you are a farmer who has come here from Germany. I'm told that the two of you don't agree about the war.

Samantha Jones (Patriot): I like what Tom Paine wrote in *Common Sense*. He understands that people who work very hard are tired of being pushed around by King George. We want our own government so we can make our own laws.

Max Stark (neutral): I don't feel that way, Samantha. I moved to this country to make a better life for my family, not to make war. You may want more freedom, but I just want peace.

Matthew Lynn (Loyalist): Let me say something! There's another side to this.

Narrator: Matthew Lynn. You collect taxes in the community. What is your view?

Matthew Lynn: I don't understand why the Patriots are complaining. Britain protects the colonies, doesn't it? That protection costs a lot of money. I think it's only fair that the colonists pay taxes for it. Besides, I'd lose my job if the Patriots won.

James Morton (Patriot): The taxes aren't fair, Matthew!

Narrator: James Morton? You are a tea merchant, correct?

James Morton: I'm sorry I interrupted. I get very upset.

Narrator: We can all talk politely. Tell us. What isn't fair?

James Morton: When the British taxed the tea I bought from them, many of my customers refused to buy it. The British hurt my business. That's why I turned against them.

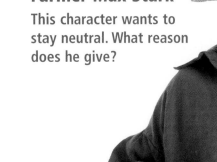

Farmer Max Stark
This character wants to stay neutral. What reason does he give?

Narrator: Each of you has a good reason for your opinion. There are many others here who have something to say. Joseph Tall Deer, you are of the Mohawk people. And Mary Smith, you are Oneida. Both of you are Iroquois. The Iroquois Nations have tried to stay neutral and united, but the war divides them. Do the Oneida support the Patriot cause?

Mary Smith (Patriot): We didn't take sides at first. Then a missionary came to live with us. He talked about reasons to fight the British. We had many discussions. I believe he is right.

Joseph Tall Deer (Loyalist): The British have been good to us, so we're on their side. The king told our leader, Joseph Brant, that no one will take away the land we live on. The colonists just want the land for themselves. We don't trust them.

Narrator: Ann Bates, what do you think?

Ann Bates (Patriot): We Quakers are against the whole idea of war. Some of us are determined to stay neutral, but I believe in the Patriot cause. Although I can't fight, I can do other things to support the Patriots. For example, I can refuse to buy British goods.

Opposing Views

All over the colonies, Americans shared their views. These people are dressed as characters. Who is a Patriot, a Loyalist, or neutral?

Sarah Whittle

Reverend David Whittle

Reverend David Whittle (Loyalist): I do not have Ann Bates's problem. I belong to Britain's official church. The king is the head of it. I believe I have a duty to be loyal to my church and my king.

Sarah Whittle (Patriot): Excuse me, please. I am Reverend Whittle's wife. I respectfully disagree with my husband. I feel the king does not take good care of us. Britain's laws and taxes are too harsh. Also, I like the idea of freedom. Maybe women will have more freedom in a country that says it believes in liberty and equal rights.

Narrator: The wish for personal freedom is very important to many. Lucy Thatcher, you are a free African American. Paul Salem, you are an enslaved African American. Both of you want freedom for all, yet you support different sides in the war. Please explain.

Lucy Thatcher (Patriot): We have to support the Patriots. Their Declaration of Independence says we are all born equal and have the right to be free. Maybe they will end slavery if they win.

Paul Salem (Loyalist): You are free already, but I am not. The Declaration doesn't say anything about ending slavery. I support the British. They have promised freedom if we fight for them.

Narrator: Did everyone have a chance to speak?

Everyone: Yes.

Narrator: Good! Thank you for sharing your views. Now, if you'll excuse me, I must say good-bye.

Lucy Thatcher (Patriot): Wait a minute, please! We all must live together, but we disagree. What do we do now?

Ann Bates (Patriot): Maybe we can agree to disagree. I respect that you have opinions and beliefs, just as I do.

Reverend David Whittle (Loyalist): Shall we respect each other's right to have an opinion?

Everyone: Yes! Thank you! Good-bye!

Lucy Thatcher

Ann Bates

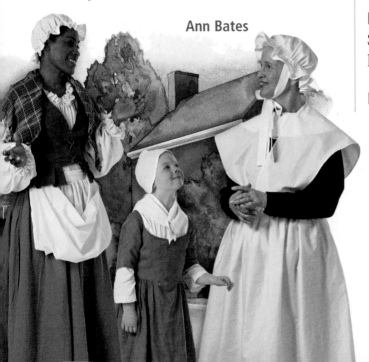

Activities

1. **THINK ABOUT IT** How did the characters show good citizenship in the Readers' Theater?

2. **WRITE ABOUT IT** Write a part for one more character. Your character should explain why he or she is a Patriot, a Loyalist, or neutral.

The War in the North

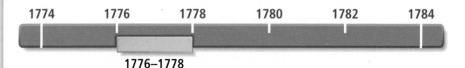

1774   1776   1778   1780   1782   1784

1776–1778

VOCABULARY

retreat
mercenary
victory

Vocabulary Strategy

retreat

The word **retreat** comes from a word that means to draw back. In battle, retreat means to move back when an enemy attacks.

READING SKILL

Cause and Effect As you read, take notes to show what caused the outcome of each battle of the war.

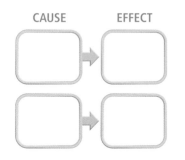

CAUSE   EFFECT

Signals Drum beats were used as signals for soldiers marching into battle.

Build on What You Know Think about what it is like to play a game or a sport against a stronger team. How can you win? In the War for Independence, George Washington and his soldiers had to fight Britain's powerful army. To win, they needed careful planning, courage, and help from other countries.

Washington's First Battles

Main Idea Washington's leadership helped the Continental Army continue to fight.

While many Americans were deciding which side to support in the war, battles had already begun. The two armies fighting each other were very different.

At the start of the war, the Continental Army was not as large or as strong as the British army. British soldiers had better training and better weapons. The Continental Army, however, did have some strengths. American soldiers were fighting on home ground, and they could use their knowledge of the land to plan attacks. They had a cause that they believed in and the support of other Patriots. They also had a great leader in **George Washington**.

In the spring of 1776, the soldiers of Washington's army forced the British out of Boston. The British did not give up, though. In August, they defeated the Continental Army in the Battle of Long Island, near New York City.

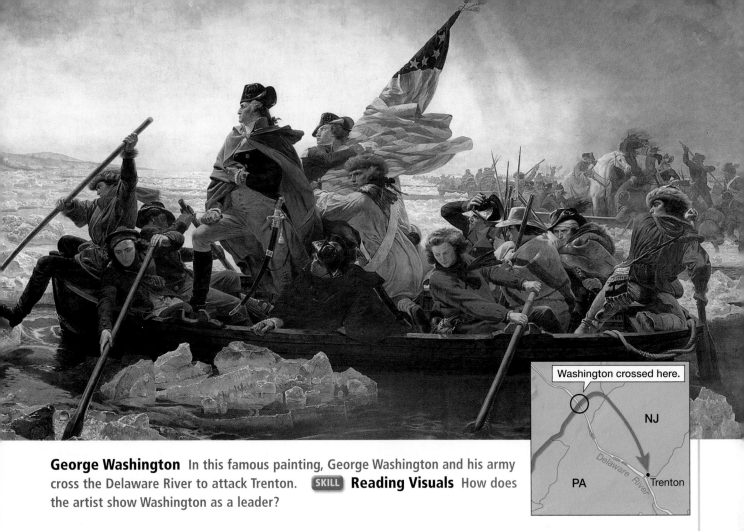

Washington crossed here.

NJ

Delaware River

PA   Trenton

George Washington In this famous painting, George Washington and his army cross the Delaware River to attack Trenton. SKILL **Reading Visuals** How does the artist show Washington as a leader?

Washington's army had to retreat. **Retreat** means to move away from the enemy. As his army retreated, Washington needed spies to keep track of the British. Captain **Nathan Hale** of Connecticut volunteered. Hale was sent to spy behind enemy lines, but he was captured and hanged. His last words are now famous:

> 66 **I only regret that I have but one life to lose for my country.** 99

Washington's army marched through New Jersey and into Pennsylvania. General Washington was worried. He only had about 3,000 soldiers left. Yet the British could not destroy the Continental Army. As long as Washington could keep his army together, he could prevent the British from winning the war.

Victory at Trenton

Washington wanted to win a battle so that his soldiers would not give up. He planned a surprise attack on an enemy camp in Trenton, New Jersey. The soldiers in Trenton were German mercenaries. A **mercenary** is a soldier who is paid to fight for a foreign country.

On the night of December 25, 1776, Washington and his soldiers rowed across the icy Delaware River to New Jersey. Just after dawn they attacked Trenton. The mercenaries were still sleepy after celebrating Christmas the night before. Washington's army caught them by surprise and took almost 1,000 prisoners. Patriots were overjoyed at the victory. A **victory** is the defeat of an enemy.

REVIEW Why did Washington decide to attack Trenton?

A Turning Point

Main Idea After the Battle of Saratoga, France joined the war against Britain.

In June 1777, the British began a new attack from Canada. General **John Burgoyne** (bur GOIN) led an army south toward Albany, New York. An army of Americans prepared to stop the British near Saratoga, New York. A Polish engineer named **Thaddeus Kosciuszko** (kahs ee US koh) helped them. He set up a long wall of earth and logs on a hill so that the Americans could fight from behind it.

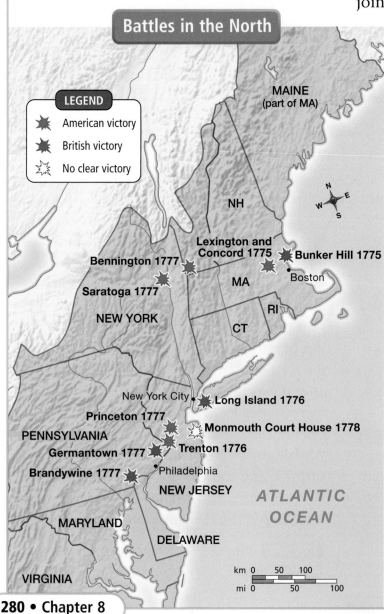

Battles in the North

LEGEND

American victory

British victory

No clear victory

MAINE (part of MA)

NH

Lexington and Concord 1775

Bunker Hill 1775

Bennington 1777

Boston

Saratoga 1777

MA

NEW YORK

RI

CT

New York City

Long Island 1776

Princeton 1777

Monmouth Court House 1778

PENNSYLVANIA

Trenton 1776

Germantown 1777

Brandywine 1777

Philadelphia

NEW JERSEY

ATLANTIC OCEAN

MARYLAND

DELAWARE

VIRGINIA

km 0   50   100
mi 0   50   100

Victory Brings Help from France

When the two armies met, they fought two fierce battles. A brave officer named **Benedict Arnold** led many attacks against the British. The Americans won and forced Burgoyne and more than 5,000 of this soldiers to surrender.

Before the Battle of Saratoga, **Benjamin Franklin** had been trying to get help from France. After the American victory, the French were convinced that the Americans could win. They sent money, soldiers, and a powerful navy to help the Americans. As the war went on, Spain, the Netherlands, and Russia also joined the fight against Britain.

One important French soldier came to America even before the Battle of Saratoga. In August 1777, the wealthy **Marquis de Lafayette** (mahr KEE duh laf ee ET) joined Washington's army. Lafayette was only 19 years old, but he led American soldiers in many battles.

Winter at Valley Forge

The victory at Saratoga was good news for Americans, but there was also troubling news. Washington's army lost two battles in Pennsylvania, and the British captured Philadelphia. The British settled into warm houses there for the winter of 1777. The Continental Army stayed about 20 miles away in Valley Forge, Pennsylvania.

Early Battles The ten battles shown were the major battles during the first years of the war.

SKILL **Reading Maps** Which battles took place in Pennsylvania?

American soldiers suffered at Valley Forge. There were no huts at first, only tents, and men slept on the frozen ground. Food was scarce. Most of the soldiers went barefoot. Many soldiers died of disease.

Washington's leadership helped keep the army going during the difficult times at Valley Forge. He worked hard to get the supplies the army needed. By spring of 1778, his soldiers had more food and were wearing better uniforms.

A Stronger Continental Army

Washington's army was ready to fight when spring came. A German soldier named **Baron Friedrich von Steuben** (SHTOY ben) had joined the army at Valley Forge to train the soldiers.

Von Steuben taught the Americans to march together and use their weapons properly. The men of the Continental Army became good soldiers because of their training at Valley Forge. In their next battle, the Americans fought well against the British army.

With the help of France, and men such as Steuben and Lafayette, it looked as though the United States could win the war.

REVIEW What happened at Valley Forge to make the Continental Army better soldiers?

Lesson Summary

Summer 1776	Washington retreats
December 1776	Victory at Trenton
October 1777	Victory at Saratoga
1777–1778	Winter at Valley Forge

Why It Matters ...

The Continental soldiers fought hard during the difficult early years of the war. They kept alive the Patriots' hope of independence.

Lesson Review

1776 **Battle of Trenton**

1777 **Battle of Saratoga**

1776 1777 1778 1779

1. **VOCABULARY** What happened to the Continental Army in 1776? Write a paragraph, using **retreat** and **victory.**

2. **READING SKILL** What was one **cause** of Washington's success at Trenton?

3. **MAIN IDEA: Citizenship** Give two examples of Washington's leadership during the war.

4. **MAIN IDEA: History** Why was the Battle of Saratoga a turning point in the war?

5. **PEOPLE TO KNOW** Who was **Lafayette**, and how did he help during the war?

6. **TIMELINE SKILL** Which battle came first, the one at Trenton or at Saratoga?

7. **CRITICAL THINKING: Analyze** Why was the help of allies such as the French important to the Americans during the war?

WRITING ACTIVITY Write a newspaper account of Washington crossing the Delaware River. Use the questions *Who?, What?, When?, Where?,* and *Why?* as a guide.

Valley Forge

Valley Forge stands for an army's courage. Why? The story of Valley Forge tells of terrible hardships. During the winter of 1777–1778, Washington's army suffered from cold and hunger. Supplies had run out. Soldiers should have had coats and warm uniforms, but some had only a shirt or a blanket, not enough against the fierce cold. They had little to eat. Instead of milk, meat, or vegetables, they ate "firecake," which was flour and water cooked over a campfire. Many soldiers got sick and died.

Finally in spring, food arrived. General von Steuben came to teach the army how to be better soldiers. In 1778, a well-trained army marched out of Valley Forge.

Those soldiers had not given up. They stayed loyal to Washington, and now they were ready for victory over the British.

This painting shows Washington and his troops on the way to Valley Forge. The artist painted it many years later and knew the story of their trial. The faces show courage. What else do you notice?

Canteens

Soldiers needed canteens for water. For meals at camp, soldiers had simple utensils like the ones below.

"**...Three or four days' bad weather would prove our destruction.**" —George Washington

Uniforms

Notice how ragged many uniforms are. Some soldiers are not even wearing boots. Hats were made of felt, but were not warm enough.

Equipment

Knapsacks held soldiers' belongings. Soldiers also carried up to 60 pounds of equipment. A musket could weigh nearly 10 pounds.

Activities

1. **TALK ABOUT IT** Look at the painting and discuss what it shows about Washington's army.

2. **WRITE ABOUT IT** A motto is a statement to express a goal or a belief. Create a motto for the Continental Army after Valley Forge. Explain why you chose it.

 Technology Learn about other primary sources for this unit at Education Place. www.eduplace.com/kids/hmss05/

Skillbuilder

Read a Battle Map

▶ **VOCABULARY**

battle map

At the Battle of Long Island in 1776, the British army forced the Americans to retreat. Learn more about this important battle by reading a **battle map**. A battle map uses symbols to show how a battle was fought.

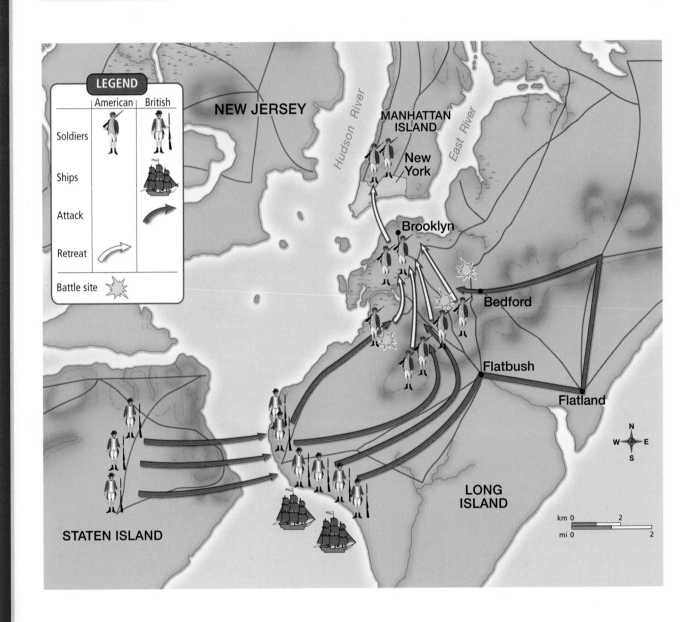

Learn the Skill

Step 1: Read the title and legend. On a battle map, different colors stand for different sides in the battle.

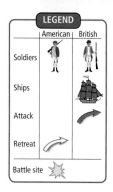

Step 2: Look for the symbols on the map. They show where the soldiers and ships were.

Step 3: Find the arrows on the map. The arrows show you which direction an army or navy moved. When soldiers or ships move towards their enemy, they are attacking. When soldiers move away from their enemy, they are retreating.

Practice the Skill

Study the map of the Battle of Long Island. Use the information on the map to answer the questions about the battle.

1. Which symbol shows the American army at Long Island?

2. Which three towns did British soldiers march through during their attack?

3. About how far, and in what direction, did American soldiers retreat from Bedford to New York?

Apply the Skill

Use the steps above to study the map of the Battle of Antietam on page 454. Then write a brief description of the battle.

Winning the War

1774   1776   1778   1780   1782   1784

1778–1783

VOCABULARY

strategy
traitor
surrender

Vocabulary Strategy

surrender

Notice that **surrender** contains the smaller word **end**. At the end of a war, the losing army surrenders.

READING SKILL

Sequence As you read, list the main events in order.

Build on What You Know Think about how much bigger and stronger you have grown in the past six years. After Valley Forge, it took six more years for the Americans to win the War for Independence. During that time, the Continental Army grew stronger and finally defeated the British army.

The War in the South and West

Main Idea The British invaded the South, but they could not defeat the Patriots there.

After over three years of war in the North, the British had not been able to win. They decided to change their strategy. A **strategy** is a plan of action. In 1779, they made a plan to invade the South with a small army. They thought that the South had more Loyalists than the North did. With support from these Loyalists, the British hoped to win the war.

At first, the new British strategy worked. They captured Savannah, Georgia, and Charleston, South Carolina. They defeated the Americans in every battle they fought. By the summer of 1780, the British controlled Georgia and South Carolina, and many Loyalists had come to help them.

The British also had the help of **Benedict Arnold.** Arnold had been the Patriot hero of the Battle of Saratoga. Later on, he secretly changed sides and became a British general. Patriots were shocked to hear that Arnold had changed sides. Today he is remembered as a traitor. A **traitor** is someone who is not loyal.

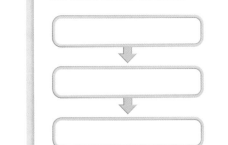

Benedict Arnold He betrayed the Patriot cause and fought for the British.

Patriot Successes

Although the British won many battles in the South, southern Patriots fought back, often using surprise attacks. Groups of soldiers would sneak up on the British, attack, and retreat quickly. Colonel **Francis Marion** was so good at attacking and retreating through swamps that he became known as the Swamp Fox.

The commander of the American army in the South, **Nathanael Greene,** made a plan to wear out the British army. His small army could move faster than the British. Greene forced the British army, led by General **Charles Cornwallis,** to chase him. This tired the British soldiers and used up their supplies of food and gunpowder. The British beat Greene in every major battle, but they could not destroy his army.

"We fight, get beat, rise and fight again," Greene said. In the spring of 1781, Cornwallis had to retreat. Greene's strategy to wear out the British had worked.

The British were losing the war in the West as well. **George Rogers Clark** and about 200 Patriots captured British forts in the Ohio River Valley. After Spain declared war on Britain in 1779, the governor of Louisiana, **Bernardo de Gálvez,** attacked British forts. His army captured forts at Baton Rouge, Natchez, Mobile, and Pensacola.

REVIEW What was Greene's strategy to defeat the British?

Later Battles This map shows the major battles during the last years of the American Revolution.

SKILL **Reading Maps** Which battles took place in 1781?

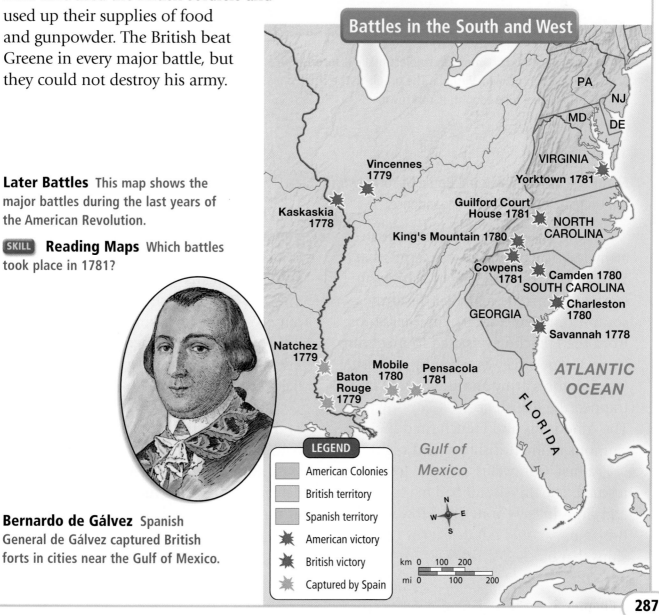

Battles in the South and West

Vincennes 1779

Kaskaskia 1778

PA

NJ

MD

DE

VIRGINIA

Yorktown 1781

Guilford Court House 1781

NORTH CAROLINA

King's Mountain 1780

Cowpens 1781

Camden 1780

SOUTH CAROLINA

GEORGIA

Charleston 1780

Savannah 1778

Natchez 1779

Mobile 1780

Pensacola 1781

Baton Rouge 1779

ATLANTIC OCEAN

FLORIDA

Gulf of Mexico

LEGEND

American Colonies

British territory

Spanish territory

American victory

British victory

Captured by Spain

km 0 100 200

mi 0 100 200

Bernardo de Gálvez Spanish General de Gálvez captured British forts in cities near the Gulf of Mexico.

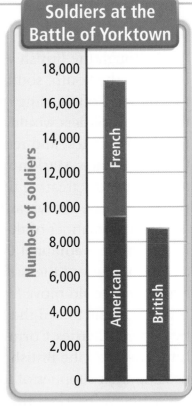

Soldiers at the Battle of Yorktown

Number of soldiers

French / American

British

Attack on Yorktown American soldiers make a surprise attack on a British fort near Yorktown, Virginia. The graph to the right shows the number of soldiers who fought at Yorktown.

SKILL **Reading Graphs** About how many American and French soldiers fought together?

The War Ends

Main Idea By winning the Battle of Yorktown, the United States gained independence.

In the summer of 1781, the British army led by Cornwallis was camped at Yorktown, Virginia. When Washington learned of this, he marched his army south from New York to Virginia. Ships from the French navy sailed to meet him there. Cornwallis was taken by surprise. Washington's army and the French navy trapped the British army at Yorktown. The Americans and French fired their cannons at the British day and night.

At first, Cornwallis expected to be rescued. The British still had many soldiers and ships in New York City. However, the British navy could not defeat the French ships that blocked Yorktown.

After fighting for a week, Cornwallis realized he could not win the battle. He was surrounded by the Americans and the French, and no help was coming. On the morning of October 19, 1781, the British army surrendered at Yorktown. To **surrender** means to give up.

Over 7,000 British soldiers marched out of Yorktown, walking between long lines of French and American soldiers. The British laid down their weapons in a grassy field. The Battle of Yorktown was over.

Yorktown was the last big battle of the War for Independence. The war continued for two more years, but there was little fighting. The Americans had defeated one of the most powerful armies in the world. They had won the war and their independence.

The Treaty of Paris

On September 3, 1783, the United States and Britain signed the Treaty of Paris. The treaty gave Patriots the two things they wanted most. First, **King George III** agreed that the United States of America was an independent nation. Second, the Americans gained land. The United States now reached north to British Canada, west to the Mississippi River, and south to Spanish Florida.

The war was over, but Americans faced new challenges. One challenge was slavery. How could slavery exist in a country that believed in freedom and equality? African Americans began to demand their freedom in court, and some won. Several states passed laws against slavery.

Treaty of Paris 1783

Another challenge for Americans was how they would rule themselves. What kind of government would they create to replace King George III? Americans would have to decide. **Mercy Otis Warren**, a writer, called the new nation "a child just learning to walk." The new nation faced many questions as it took its place in the world.

REVIEW What did the Treaty of Paris say?

Lesson Summary

- The last part of the Revolution was fought in the West and the South.

- The United States won the war with the victory at Yorktown. With the Treaty of Paris in 1783, the United States gained its independence.

Why It Matters ...

By winning the Revolutionary War, Patriots achieved their dream of independence. Americans were free to set up their own government and rule themselves.

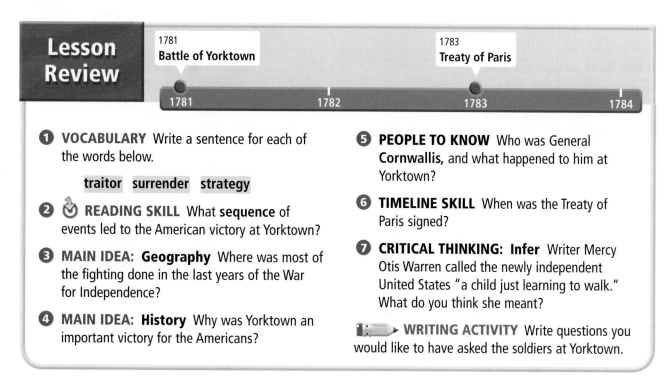

Lesson Review

1781 **Battle of Yorktown**

1783 **Treaty of Paris**

1781   1782   1783   1784

1. **VOCABULARY** Write a sentence for each of the words below.

    traitor   surrender   strategy

2. **READING SKILL** What **sequence** of events led to the American victory at Yorktown?

3. **MAIN IDEA: Geography** Where was most of the fighting done in the last years of the War for Independence?

4. **MAIN IDEA: History** Why was Yorktown an important victory for the Americans?

5. **PEOPLE TO KNOW** Who was General **Cornwallis,** and what happened to him at Yorktown?

6. **TIMELINE SKILL** When was the Treaty of Paris signed?

7. **CRITICAL THINKING: Infer** Writer Mercy Otis Warren called the newly independent United States "a child just learning to walk." What do you think she meant?

WRITING ACTIVITY Write questions you would like to have asked the soldiers at Yorktown.

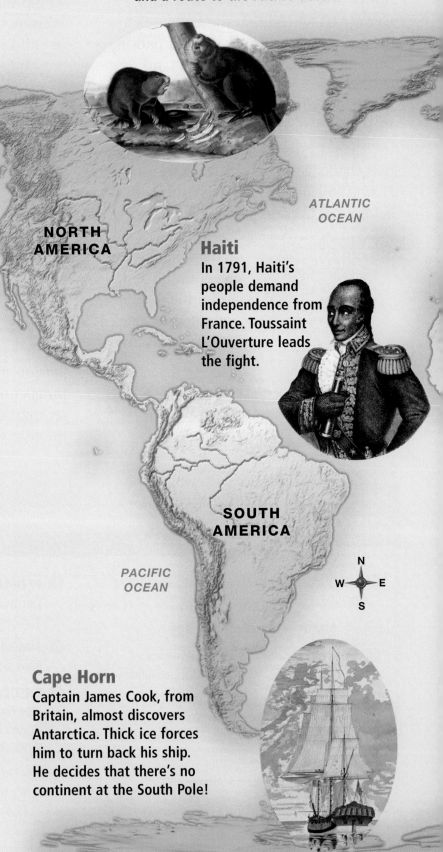

Canada
Britain has control of Canada, and traders explore the land. They are looking for furs and a route to the Pacific Ocean.

A Global View, 1783

The American Revolution is over. What is happening in other lands? The American Revolution brought about a new nation in the late 1700s. Changes were taking place in other parts of the world as well.

Empires were expanding in the late 1700s. Trading around the world increased. Rulers sent explorers to search for new lands and resources. Trade and travel brought an exchange of goods and ideas.

These changes also meant that people were conquered and sometimes enslaved. In some places, people wanted liberty from their rulers. They wanted to govern themselves. Where were these places? Look on the map to find where revolutions were happening.

ATLANTIC OCEAN

NORTH AMERICA

Haiti
In 1791, Haiti's people demand independence from France. Toussaint L'Ouverture leads the fight.

SOUTH AMERICA

PACIFIC OCEAN

Cape Horn
Captain James Cook, from Britain, almost discovers Antarctica. Thick ice forces him to turn back his ship. He decides that there's no continent at the South Pole!

France

The French are unhappy with King Louis XVI. In 1789, they overthrow him in the French Revolution.

Russia

Russia takes more and more land from Europe and Asia. Russia's empress, Catherine the Great, defeats a dangerous rebellion.

China

China's emperor Qianlong and his powerful armies control more land than ever. The population of the Chinese empire doubles in the 1700s.

EUROPE

ASIA

PACIFIC OCEAN

AFRICA

Australia

James Cook, British sea captain, lands in Australia on one of his voyages and is one of the first Europeans to see a kangaroo. The British settle in Australia in 1788.

INDIAN OCEAN

Africa

The Asante Empire trades gold with other African nations and Europe. The empire rules a large area of Africa's west coast.

Activities

1. **MAP IT** Use an atlas map as a guide to draw or trace Haiti and France. About how many miles apart are they? What can you conclude from this fact?

2. **RESEARCH IT** Choose one of the events shown. Find out what kind of government the nation had. How was it alike or different from the government Jefferson described in the Declaration of Independence?

ANTARCTICA

Visual Summary

1.–4. ✏️ Write a description for each main event named below.

| Declaration of Independence, 1776 | Battle of Saratoga, 1777 | Victory at Yorktown, 1781 | Treaty of Paris, 1783 |

_____
_____
_____
_____
_____

Facts and Main Ideas

✔️ **TEST PREP** Answer each question below.

5. **History** Why was *Common Sense* an important document?

6. **Citizenship** Who wrote the Declaration of Independence?

7. **Economics** Why would some farmers and merchants not sell their goods during the war?

8. **History** Why was Yorktown an important victory for the Americans?

9. **Geography** What land did the United States gain in the Treaty of Paris?

Vocabulary

✔️ **TEST PREP** Choose the correct word from the list below to complete each sentence.

independence, p. 262

rights, p. 264

neutral, p. 270

strategy, p. 286

10. In 1776, the colonies declared their _____ from Britain.

11. Some colonists chose to stay _____ instead of joining the Patriots or Loyalists.

12. _____ are freedoms that are protected by law.

13. The _____ of the British army was to invade the South.

1776
Declaration of Independence

1778
Valley Forge

1781
Victory at Yorktown

1783
Treaty of Paris

1775　　　　1777　　　　1779　　　　1781　　　　1783　　　　1785

Apply Skills

✓ **TEST PREP** **Map Skill** Study the battle map below. Then use your map skills to answer each question.

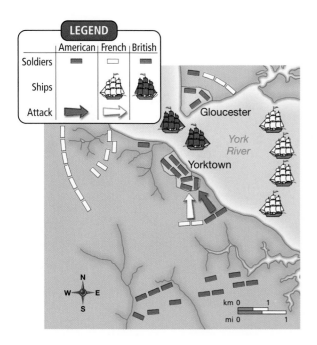

LEGEND

	American	French	British
Soldiers			
Ships			
Attack			

Gloucester

York River

Yorktown

N W E S

km 0　　　　1
mi 0　　　　1

14. Where did the American and French armies attack the British?

　A. Gloucester
　B. York River
　C. Yorktown
　D. Richmond

15. Where were most of the French soldiers?

　A. South of Yorktown
　B. West of Yorktown
　C. East of Yorktown
　D. In Yorktown

Critical Thinking

✓ **TEST PREP** Write a short paragraph to answer each question.

16. **Fact and Opinion** Were the ideas stated in the Declaration of Independence facts or opinions? Explain your answer.

17. **Cause and Effect** The British army had to fight many battles against Nathanael Greene's soldiers in the South. What effect did this have on the British army?

Timeline

Use the Chapter Summary Timeline above to answer the question.

18. In what year did the British and the Americans fight the last major battle of the War for Independence?

Activities

HANDS ON **Art Activity** Create a postage stamp that shows an important event that happened during the American Revolution.

Writing Activity Write a personal essay about a Patriot in this chapter. Describe what he or she did during the war and why you think this person's actions were important.

 Technology
Writing Process Tips
Get help with your essay at
www.eduplace.com/kids/hmss05/

Chapter 9

Creating a Nation

Technology

e • **glossary**
e • **word games**
www.eduplace.com/kids/hmss05/
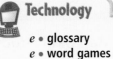

Vocabulary Preview

constitution

During the Revolutionary War, each state government had its own **constitution.** Many of these written plans of government became models for the U.S. Constitution. **page 296**

ratify

To **ratify** the Constitution, nine states had to accept it officially. New Hampshire became the ninth state in June 1788.
page 306

Chapter Timeline

1781
Articles of Confederation

1787
Constitutional Convention

1780   1783   1786

Reading Strategy

Predict and Infer Use this strategy as you read this chapter.

Quick Tip   Look at the pictures in a lesson to predict what it will be about.

amendment

An **amendment** is a change to the Constitution. The first ten amendments, called the Bill of Rights, protect the rights of the people of the United States. **page 316**

inauguration

The ceremony making George Washington President was held in April 1789. This first **inauguration** was in New York City, the capital at the time. **page 321**

1789
George Washington elected

1792
Washington, D.C. founded

1789   1792   1795

A New Nation

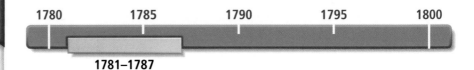

1781–1787

Build on What You Know Have you ever been part of a group whose members worked well together? After the War for Independence, the 13 states did not always work well together. Congress could not make them cooperate.

The Articles of Confederation

Main Idea The Articles of Confederation gave Congress very little power.

During the Revolutionary War, each American colony became a separate state. Each state had its own laws and constitution. A written plan for government is a **constitution**.

Americans did not want to give up power to a strong central government. They had fought the war for the right to self-government. State constitutions gave their citizens the right to make all the laws that would govern them. A **citizen** is an official member of a city, a state, or a nation.

Although the states did not want a strong central government, they needed to work together as one country. The Continental Congress created a plan for a national government. The plan was called the Articles of Confederation. The Articles created a weak national government that left most power with the states. The states accepted the Articles in 1781.

The Articles gave Congress the power to declare war, make peace treaties, and make treaties with other nations, including American Indian nations. It could print and borrow money. There were many powers, however, that Congress did not have. It could not set up an army, control trade, or create taxes.

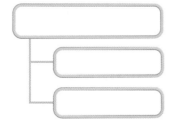

VOCABULARY

constitution
citizen
territory
ordinance

Vocabulary Strategy

| territory

Territory comes from a word that means earth. A territory is a section of land.

READING SKILL

Main Idea and Details
As you read, list details that support the second main idea in the lesson.

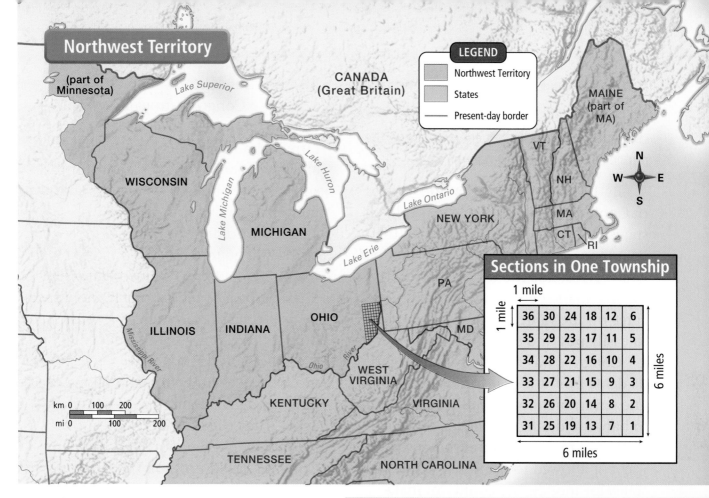

Northwest Territory

(part of Minnesota)

CANADA
(Great Britain)

MAINE
(part of MA)

LEGEND
- Northwest Territory
- States
- Present-day border

Lake Superior

WISCONSIN

Lake Michigan

Lake Huron

MICHIGAN

Lake Ontario

Lake Erie

VT

NH

NEW YORK

MA

CT

RI

ILLINOIS

INDIANA

OHIO

PA

MD

Mississippi River

Ohio River

WEST VIRGINIA

KENTUCKY

VIRGINIA

km 0   100   200
mi 0   100   200

TENNESSEE

NORTH CAROLINA

N W E S

Sections in One Township

1 mile

1 mile

36	30	24	18	12	6
35	29	23	17	11	5
34	28	22	16	10	4
33	27	21	15	9	3
32	26	20	14	8	2
31	25	19	13	7	1

6 miles

6 miles

Townships Land in the Northwest Territory was measured and sold in square plots, as the grid on the map shows. These plots, which formed townships, created fields that looked like a patchwork quilt (right).

The Northwest Territory

Congress had to decide what to do with the land won in the Revolution. This western land was known as the Northwest Territory. A **territory** is land ruled by a national government but which has no representatives in the government.

As settlers moved to the Northwest Territory, Congress made treaties with American Indians to gain control of more land. Then Congress passed two ordinances to organize the Northwest Territory. An **ordinance** is a law.

The first law, the Land Ordinance of 1785, explained how the new land would be measured, divided, and sold.

The second law, the Northwest Ordinance of 1787, explained the government of the Northwest Territory. This law described how a territory could become a state. It also made slavery against the law in the Northwest Territory.

REVIEW What did Congress do to organize the Northwest Territory?

Problems for the New Nation

Main Idea The Articles of Confederation created a government that could not solve the problems facing the new nation.

By 1786, it was clear that the Articles of Confederation could not make the states work together. States printed their own money, and people disagreed about what each state's money was worth. In the free market economy of today, people agree on the value of money, and use it to easily buy and sell goods.

Congress was having trouble paying its debts from the War for Independence. The government owed millions of dollars to banks and other countries. Congress could not raise this money because it was not allowed to tax. It had to ask the states for money, but could not make them pay.

Shays's Rebellion

While Congress struggled, people grew frustrated. In western Massachusetts, farmers had to pay high state taxes. They also owed money to merchants for the supplies they bought. Many did not have money to pay their taxes or debts. Farmers who did not pay could lose their farms and go to jail.

In 1786, a farmer named **Daniel Shays** led a group of about 1,100 farmers in a protest. Shays had been a soldier during the War for Independence.

Shays and the other farmers wanted the state government to stop taking their farms and give them time to pay their debts. They tried to capture weapons belonging to the national government. Congress could not stop the farmers because it did not have an army. State militia defeated the farmers.

Angry Farmers Standing on the courthouse steps, farmers keep the court from holding trials. One of their leaders, Daniel Shays, is shown below.

Daniel Shays

Today, their protest is known as Shays's Rebellion. Shays's Rebellion showed that a weak national government could not keep order. **George Washington** worried that the government was not strong enough to protect people's rights. He asked,

❝ . . . what security has a man for life, liberty, or property? ❞

Many people agreed with Washington. In February 1787, Congress invited the states to send delegates to a meeting in Philadelphia to discuss how to change the Articles of Confederation.

REVIEW Why did farmers in western Massachusetts protest?

George Mason He went to Philadelphia as a delegate from Virginia. Mason wanted a "wise and just government."

Lesson Summary

Articles of Confederation

Congress could	Congress could not
• declare war and peace	• regulate trade
• deal with other nations	• set up army
• print and borrow money	• raise money with taxes
• organize new territories	• force states to obey its laws

Why It Matters . . .

The failure of the Articles of Confederation caused many people to believe that they needed a stronger national government to solve the new nation's problems.

Lesson Review

1780	1781 Articles of Confederation	1782	1783	1784	1785 Land Ordinance	1786 Shays's Rebellion	1787

1 VOCABULARY Use **territory** and **ordinance** in a paragraph that shows what you know about the Northwest Ordinance.

2 READING SKILL Which **details** support the idea that Congress was too weak to stop Shays's Rebellion?

3 MAIN IDEA: Government Why did the states want a weak central government at first?

4 MAIN IDEA: Economics Why did Congress have trouble paying its debts?

5 FACTS TO KNOW What are the Articles of Confederation, and why are they important?

6 TIMELINE SKILL When was the Land Ordinance passed?

7 CRITICAL THINKING: Analyze Do you think the Articles of Confederation needed to be changed? Explain your answer.

✏ WRITING ACTIVITY Write an invitation to the convention to change the Articles of Confederation. Be sure to explain what the Articles achieved, and why the Articles have to be changed.

Chain of Debt

Massachusetts farmers were in trouble. In 1786, many had lost their farms because they could not pay their debts. Farmers had borrowed money to buy goods. Many did not have enough money to repay these loans.

The state of Massachusetts was in trouble, too. To pay the costs of the Revolutionary War, it raised taxes. The taxes put farmers even more into debt. Farmers who could not pay their debts and taxes were brought to court. In western Massachusetts, where Daniel Shays and many other farmers struggled, these court cases, or debt cases, soared into the thousands. Follow the diagram on these pages to see how farmers got into debt and why getting out of debt seemed impossible.

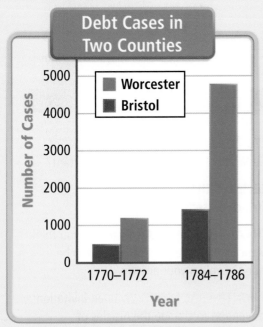

Debt Cases in Two Counties

■ Worcester
■ Bristol

Number of Cases — Year

About how many more cases were there in Worcester County, Massachusetts, between 1784–1786 than between 1770–1772?

Between harvests, farmers borrowed money from shopkeepers to buy goods. The farmers would have to pay for the goods later, after they sold their next harvest.

FARMERS

Farmers often did not have enough money to pay their debts and their taxes. Those who did not pay could lose their farms or go to jail.

Shopkeepers in western Massachusetts borrowed money from wealthy merchants in big cities such as Boston.

Boston merchants borrowed money from banks or wealthy merchant companies in Britain. The former colonies still needed British money to run their businesses.

SHOPKEEPERS

MERCHANTS

To pay their debts to the merchants, shopkeepers demanded the money that the farmers owed them.

The debt went back down the chain. To pay what they owed the British banks, merchants demanded the money shopkeepers owed them.

Activities

1. **THINK ABOUT IT** Who suffered most in the chain of debt? Why?

2. **WRITE ABOUT IT** Write a short dialogue between a farmer and a shopkeeper or between a shopkeeper and a merchant.

Constitutional Convention

1780   1785   1790   1795   1800

1787–1789

VOCABULARY

federal
republic
compromise
ratify

Vocabulary Strategy

republic

Public comes from a word that means people. In a **republic**, the people choose leaders.

READING SKILL

Problem and Solution
Make notes on how delegates solved their disagreements about the Constitution.

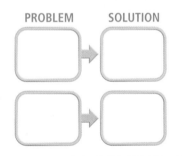

PROBLEM   SOLUTION

Build on What You Know Have you ever solved a problem by giving up one thing to get something else? Delegates who met to change the national government had to give up some things they wanted to solve their differences.

Leaders of the Convention

Main Idea Delegates gathered in Philadelphia to change the way the American government worked.

In the spring of 1787, 55 delegates traveled to Philadelphia. Remember that delegates are chosen to speak for others, or represent them. The delegates came from every state except Rhode Island. They met to discuss how to change the Articles of Confederation. Their meeting has become known as the Constitutional Convention.

The delegates were landowners, business people, and lawyers. Most were wealthy and educated. About 20 were slaveowners. About 30 had fought in the war against Britain. Eight had signed the Declaration of Independence. Many had served in Congress or state government.

Independence Hall Delegates met at Independence Hall in Philadelphia, the same place delegates met in 1776 to declare independence.

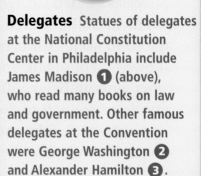

Delegates Statues of delegates at the National Constitution Center in Philadelphia include James Madison **1** (above), who read many books on law and government. Other famous delegates at the Convention were George Washington **2** and Alexander Hamilton **3**.

Such a convention today would include Americans of many different backgrounds. In 1787, though, only white men who owned land were included. No women, African Americans, American Indians, or men who were not landowners took part in the convention.

James Madison of Virginia arrived before the other delegates. He was a member of Congress. Madison wanted to do more than change the Articles. He had a plan for a new system of government. During the convention, Madison took notes. Thanks to these notes, we know much of what people said and did.

George Washington, the hero of the Revolution, came as another Virginia delegate. Ringing bells and cheering crowds greeted him in Philadelphia. **Benjamin Franklin**, representing Pennsylvania, was respected for his wisdom. He had served the United States for many years.

Goals of the Convention

The delegates knew that the Articles of Confederation had to change. As one said,

> 66 If we do not establish a good government . . . we must either go to ruin, or have the work to do over again. 99

The Articles did not give Congress enough power. Some delegates, such as Madison and Washington, wanted a federal system. In a **federal** system, the states share power with the central government, but the central government has more power than the states.

Madison believed that a republic was the only type of government that could keep order and still protect rights. A **republic** is a government in which the citizens elect leaders to represent them. The power in a republic comes from the citizens themselves.

REVIEW What was the advantage of a federal system?

Creating a New Government

Main Idea The delegates all had to give up some of the things they wanted.

The Convention began on May 25, at the start of a very hot summer. The delegates elected George Washington as president of the convention. They also agreed to keep their debates secret. This allowed them to talk openly with each other without being influenced by people who were not part of the convention.

On May 29, **Edmund Randolph**, governor of Virginia, described Madison's plan for the new government. This plan, known as the Virginia Plan, called for a federal system in which the national government had three parts, or branches. Many state governments were already set up this way. One branch, the Congress, would make laws for the nation. Another branch would carry out the laws. Yet another branch, the courts, would settle legal arguments.

Representation

The delegates accepted most of the Virginia Plan, but many did not like one part of it. Madison had suggested that the number of each state's representatives in Congress be based on the state's population. Large states would get more votes in Congress than small states.

The small states did not like this plan. It gave more power to large states. Delegates from the small states created the New Jersey Plan. Like the Articles of Confederation, this plan gave each state one vote, so that small states would have as much power as large states. Delegates argued bitterly about these plans.

Roger Sherman of Connecticut came up with a solution. He suggested dividing Congress into two parts, or houses. Each state would have an equal number of representatives in one house, the Senate. The number of representatives each state sent to the other house, the House of Representatives, would depend on its population. Sherman's suggestion is called the Great Compromise. In a **compromise**, both sides give up something to settle a disagreement. The delegates accepted this compromise, and moved on to other topics.

The Issue of Slavery

Another problem delegates argued about was slavery. Southern delegates wanted slaves to count as part of a state's population. Counting enslaved people would have given their states more representatives in Congress. Other delegates said this was unfair, because slaves were treated as property, not citizens.

Delegates also argued about whether to end the practice of bringing slaves into the United States. Delegates from the southern states said they would not accept the new government unless the slave trade continued.

Arguments over slavery led to another compromise, the Three-Fifths Rule. This rule counted five slaves as three free people. The slave trade was also allowed to continue until 1808. Although some delegates disliked this compromise and wanted to end slavery, they agreed to let it continue so that all states would support the Constitution.

REVIEW Why did delegates argue over representation in Congress?

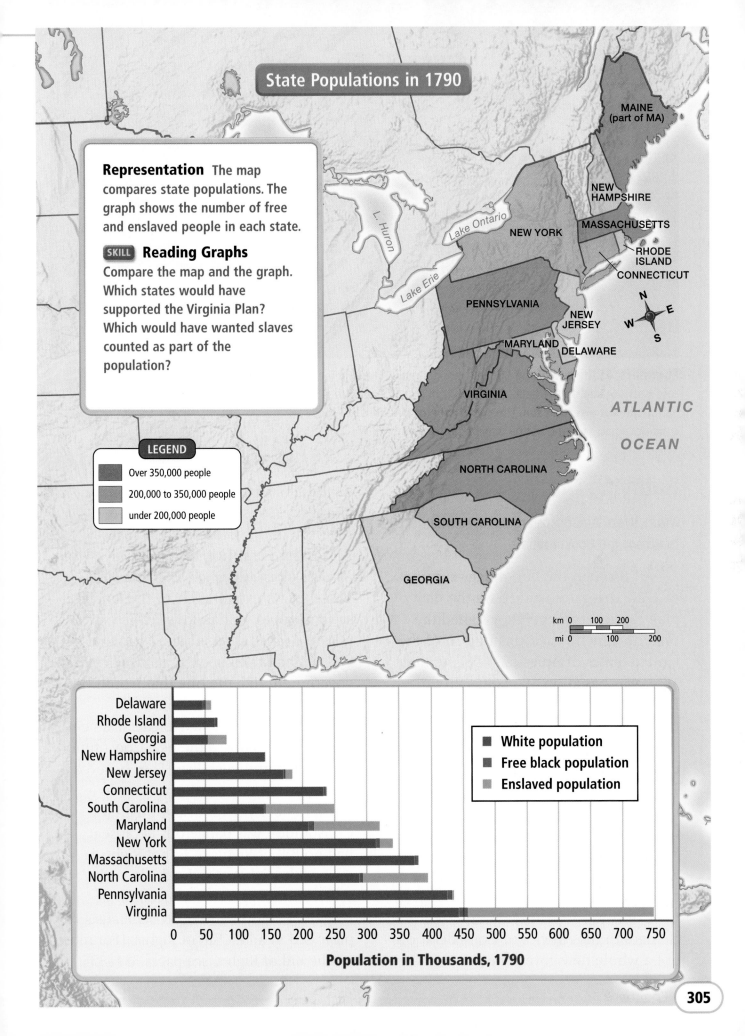

State Populations in 1790

MAINE (part of MA)

NEW HAMPSHIRE

MASSACHUSETTS

NEW YORK

RHODE ISLAND

CONNECTICUT

PENNSYLVANIA

NEW JERSEY

MARYLAND

DELAWARE

VIRGINIA

ATLANTIC OCEAN

NORTH CAROLINA

SOUTH CAROLINA

GEORGIA

L. Huron

Lake Ontario

Lake Erie

Representation The map compares state populations. The graph shows the number of free and enslaved people in each state.

SKILL Reading Graphs
Compare the map and the graph. Which states would have supported the Virginia Plan? Which would have wanted slaves counted as part of the population?

LEGEND
- Over 350,000 people
- 200,000 to 350,000 people
- under 200,000 people

km 0 100 200
mi 0 100 200

Graph: Population in Thousands, 1790

- White population
- Free black population
- Enslaved population

States (top to bottom): Delaware, Rhode Island, Georgia, New Hampshire, New Jersey, Connecticut, South Carolina, Maryland, New York, Massachusetts, North Carolina, Pennsylvania, Virginia

Scale: 0 50 100 150 200 250 300 350 400 450 500 550 600 650 700 750

Population in Thousands, 1790

Founders At the end of the Convention, Benjamin Franklin (center) said that the sun on the back of Washington's chair (right) was a rising and not a setting sun. The completion of the Constitution convinced him that the nation was beginning, not ending.

Ratifying the Constitution

Main Idea Americans argued over whether to accept the Constitution.

All through the hot, muggy summer of 1787, delegates worked on the new plan for government. They signed the final document, the Constitution of the United States of America, on September 17. It was based on Madison's Virginia Plan. Madison has been called the Father of the Constitution.

Before the Constitution could be used, at least nine states had to ratify it. To **ratify** means to accept. In each state, representatives from the towns met to decide whether or not to ratify.

Supporters of the Constitution, who were known as Federalists, faced a big challenge. Many people were shocked by the Constitution. They had expected changes to the Articles of Confederation, not a whole new government.

Federalists had to teach the public about the Constitution. To do this, Madison and two other Federalists, **Alexander Hamilton** and **John Jay**, wrote a series of essays called *The Federalist*. These essays explained how the federal system would work and why the new nation needed it to suceed. They said that the United States needed a strong central government like the one that would be created by the Constitution.

Not everyone wanted a federal system. People who opposed the new Constitution were called Antifederalists. They believed that a strong central government was a threat to liberty. They also thought the Constitution was dangerous because it had no Bill of Rights. A Bill of Rights is a list of the rights of individuals, such as freedom of speech and freedom of religion. Madison and other Federalists promised to add a Bill of Rights. (For more on the Bill of Rights, see pages 334–335.)

Ratification

While Federalists and Antifederalists argued, state representatives met in their own conventions. Delaware was the first state to ratify the Constitution. In June 1788, New Hampshire became the ninth state to ratify. At that point, the Constitution became the country's law. In the end, all 13 states ratified. The United States had a new government.

REVIEW Why did Antifederalists demand a Bill of Rights?

Lesson Summary

In 1787, delegates from the states met in Philadelphia to change the Articles of Confederation. Instead, they wrote a plan for a new government, the Constitution, based on James Madison's Virginia Plan. They made several compromises before agreeing on a final plan. After a long debate between Federalists and Anti-federalists, the Constitution was ratified in June, 1788.

Why It Matters...

The Constitutional Convention created the government the United States still has today.

Bill of Rights This single page lists the 10 amendments written to protect many rights of the people of the United States.

Lesson Review

| MAY 1787 Constitutional Convention | SEPTEMBER 1787 Constitution signed | JUNE 1788 Ninth state ratifies Constitution |

January 1787 — April — July — October — January 1788 — April — July

❶ **VOCABULARY** How do **republic** and **federal** describe the U.S. government? Use both words in your answer.

❷ **READING SKILL** What did the delegates do to **solve** the **problem** of how many representatives each state could have?

❸ **MAIN IDEA: Government** Which compromise did the delegates who wanted slavery agree to?

❹ **MAIN IDEA: Citizenship** Why did Madison, Hamilton, and Jay write *The Federalist*?

❺ **PEOPLE TO KNOW** Why is **James Madison** known as the Father of the Constitution?

❻ **TIMELINE SKILL** How long after the convention did the Constitution become law?

❼ **CRITICAL THINKING: Decision Making** What were some short-term effects of the delegates' decision to continue to allow slavery? What were some long-term effects?

HANDS ON

SPEAKING ACTIVITY Federalists and Antifederalists made many speeches. In a small group, prepare a short speech to convince people to vote for or against the Constitution.

World Constitutions

What are the rules and ideas that guide a nation? In a written constitution, each country lists the rules its citizens are supposed to follow. The U.S. Constitution, ratified in 1788, is the oldest written constitution in the world. It has served as a model for many other countries. At the same time, each constitution is unique. These excerpts from constitutions show what each country values.

People visit the National Archives in Washington, D.C., where they can see the Constitution and the Declaration of Independence.

We, the Japanese people [resolve] that never again shall we be visited with the horrors of war through the action of government.

— Preamble, Constitution of Japan, 1946

The Republic of China, founded on the Three Principles of the People, shall be a democratic republic of the people, by the people, and for the people.

— Article 1, Constitution of Republic of China (Taiwan), 1947

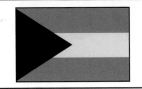

(1) No person shall be held in slavery or servitude.
(2) No person shall be required to perform forced labour.

— Article 18, Constitution of the Bahamas, 1973

Activities tending and undertaken with the intent to disturb peaceful relations between nations, especially to prepare for aggressive war, are unconstitutional.

— Article 26, Constitution of Germany, 1990

Every person has the right to a healthy and ecologically balanced environment.

— Article 50, the Constitution of Costa Rica, 1994

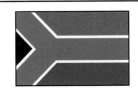

We, the people of South Africa, recognise the injustices of our past; . . . and believe that South Africa belongs to all who live in it, united in our diversity.

— Preamble, Constitution of South Africa, 1996

A nation's history can affect its constitution. For example, both Germany and Japan, which started wars in the 1940s, have constitutions that forbid going to war. In South Africa, the laws used to be very unfair to black people. Now its constitution protects all of its citizens.

Activities

1. **TALK ABOUT IT** Choose one of the excerpts shown here. Tell why you think it is important.

2. **WRITE ABOUT IT** Compare these excerpts to the U.S. Constitution. What similarities do you notice?

Skillbuilder

Understand Point of View

▶ **VOCABULARY**

point of view

Information can come from many different sources, including newspapers, books, and television. Each source of information has one or more points of view. A **point of view** is the way someone thinks about an issue, an event, or a person. A point of view is affected by a person's experiences and beliefs.

Understanding different points of view can help you understand the decisions and behavior of others. It can also help you form your own opinions. Part of being a good citizen is listening to and respecting different points of view.

"Who authorized them to speak the language of We, the People, instead of We, the States?...National Government...will destroy the state governments and swallow the liberties of the people without giving previous notice [warning]."

— Patrick Henry

"We have seen the necessity of the Union, as our bulwark [protection] against foreign danger, as the conservator of peace among ourselves, as the guardian of our commerce [trade]."

— James Madison

Learn the Skill

Step 1: Identify the point of view. What is the subject, and what does the writer or speaker think about it?

_____

Step 2: Identify the source of the information. Do you know of any experiences that may have influenced the writer or speaker?

_____

Step 3: Summarize the writer or speaker's point of view in your own words. If you know about the person's experiences, explain how they might have influenced his or her point of view.

Practice the Skill

Read the passages on page 310 about the debate over whether the national government should have more power than the states. Then answer these questions.

1 What is Patrick Henry's point of view?

2 What is Madison's point of view?

3 How might Madison's experience at the Continental Congress have affected his point of view?

Apply the Skill

Choose a topic below or one of your own. Write a paragraph expressing your point of view on the subject. Describe any personal experiences that affect your point of view.

- Some towns have decided to start and end school later in the day. They are trying to give young people more time to sleep.

- A national helmet law has been suggested. Everyone who uses skates, bikes, and skateboards would need to wear a helmet.

The Constitution

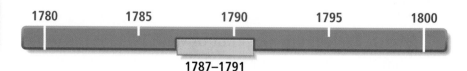

1780   1785   1790   1795   1800

1787–1791

VOCABULARY

democracy
checks and balances
veto
unconstitutional
amendment

Vocabulary Strategy

| amendment |

Find **mend** in amendment. An **amendment** is a way to mend, or fix, a problem.

 READING SKILL

Categorize As you read, list the jobs of each branch of the federal government.

Build on What You Know Builders make a plan before they build a house. The founders of the United States made the Constitution as a plan for the nation's government.

A Plan for Government

Main Idea The Constitution describes how the United States government works.

❝ We the People of the United States . . . ❞

These are the first words of the Constitution, and they have a special meaning. They tell us that our country is a democracy. A **democracy** is a government in which the people have the power to make political decisions. Citizens in a democracy take part in making laws and choosing leaders. In the United States, citizens usually make those decisions through representatives whom they elect.

The United States Constitution is the plan for our democracy. In the Preamble, or beginning, the authors listed their goals for the country. They hoped to create a country where people were safe, could live together in peace, and could have good lives. The rest of the Constitution describes how the government works.

The Constitution
This important document is on display at the National Archives in Washington, D.C.

State of the Union
Once a year, the President gives a speech called the State of the Union Address. The seal (above) is the symbol of the President.

Branches of Government

The Constitution divides the national government into three parts, or branches: the legislative branch, the executive branch, and the judicial branch. Each branch does a different job.

The legislative branch makes laws for the country. This branch is called Congress. Congress has two parts: the Senate and the House of Representatives. Each state elects two senators to the Senate. Each state also elects a certain number of representatives to the House. The number of representatives from each state depends on its population.

Congress has the power to raise money through taxes or by borrowing. It uses this money to pay for goods and services such as an army, roads, and national parks.

The executive branch can suggest laws. It also carries out the laws made by Congress. The head of this branch is the President. United States citizens elect a President every four years. The President is the commander of the United States military.

The judicial branch decides the meaning of laws and whether laws have been followed. Many courts across the nation make up the judicial branch. The highest court is the Supreme Court.

You remember that the Articles of Confederation created a weak federal government. The U.S. Constitution gives the federal government more power, but it does not give its leaders unlimited power. The Constitution is a plan for a limited government. Everyone must follow the law, including those who run the government.

REVIEW What are the jobs of each branch of the national government?

Limits on Government

Main Idea The Constitution puts limits on the power of the government.

James Madison and the other authors of the Constitution created a government with three branches to make sure that the government's powers were limited. No single person or branch has the power to run the United States government alone. Power is divided among the branches.

The delegates to the Constitutional Convention also worried that one branch might become stronger than the other two. They set up checks and balances to keep this from happening.

Checks and balances are a system that lets each branch limit the power of the other two.

The chart below shows examples of checks and balances. The President makes treaties and chooses judges. The President can also **veto,** or reject, laws made by Congress. Congress may reject judges selected by the President and treaties made by the President. Only Congress can declare war. The Supreme Court decides whether laws are unconstitutional. Laws that are **unconstitutional** do not follow rules laid out by the Constitution. If a law is unconstitutional, the law is no longer in effect.

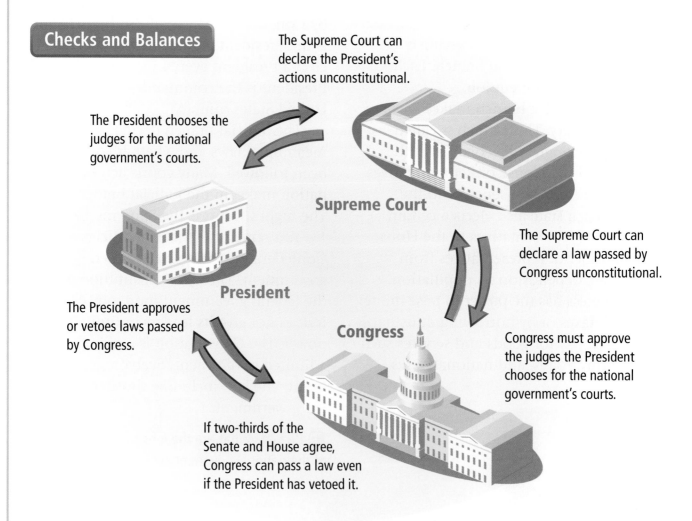

Checks and Balances

The Supreme Court can declare the President's actions unconstitutional.

The President chooses the judges for the national government's courts.

Supreme Court

The Supreme Court can declare a law passed by Congress unconstitutional.

President

The President approves or vetoes laws passed by Congress.

Congress

Congress must approve the judges the President chooses for the national government's courts.

If two-thirds of the Senate and House agree, Congress can pass a law even if the President has vetoed it.

Checks and Balances This diagram shows some of the ways that each branch of the national government can check the power of the other two branches.

The Federal System

The Constitution created a federal system. Remember that under a federal system, the national government and the state governments each have certain powers. This system gives the national government more power than it had under the Articles of Confederation.

The federal government has power over issues that affect the whole country. Its jobs include defending the country, printing money, running the Post Office, and regulating trade between states.

States have more power over local issues. Public education and elections are two state responsibilities. The federal and state governments share certain powers as well. For example, federal and state governments both collect taxes and set up court systems.

Even though the federal government's power is limited, the Constitution makes its laws stronger than state laws. When a state law and a federal law do not agree, the federal law must be obeyed.

REVIEW Why did the authors of the Constitution create checks and balances and a federal system?

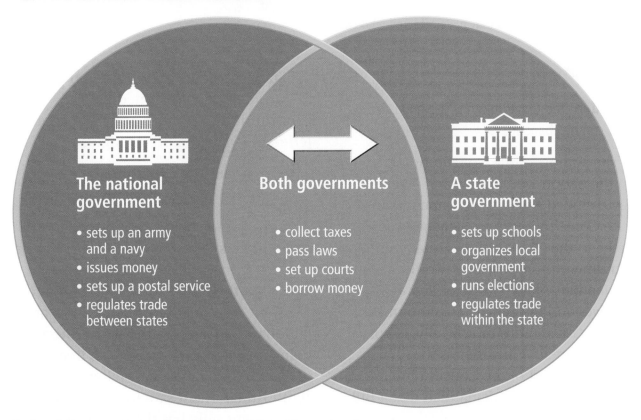

Federal System of Government

The national government
- sets up an army and a navy
- issues money
- sets up a postal service
- regulates trade between states

Both governments
- collect taxes
- pass laws
- set up courts
- borrow money

A state government
- sets up schools
- organizes local government
- runs elections
- regulates trade within the state

Federal System Some powers belong only to the national government, while others belong to state and local governments.

SKILL **Reading Diagrams** What are two powers that the state governments and the national government share?

The Right to Vote Over time, amendments to the Constitution have protected the right to vote for more citizens. The chart on the right shows three amendments that have affected who can vote.

Changing the Constitution

Main Idea The Constitution is designed so that it can be changed.

The authors of the Constitution knew that the nation would grow and change. They included a way to add amendments to the Constitution. An amendment is a change to the Constitution. Usually, an amendment is proposed by two-thirds of the members of the House of Representatives and the Senate. Three-fourths of the states must ratify, or officially accept, the amendment. Only then is the amendment part of the Constitution.

Many Americans demanded that a Bill of Rights be added to the Constitution. People wanted to be sure that the stronger federal government would recognize the rights of individuals.

State constitutions listed the rights of citizens and people wanted the U.S. Constitution to do so as well. **Thomas Jefferson** wanted a Bill of Rights

❝ to guard the people against the federal government . . . ❞

James Madison agreed. He wrote amendments listing rights that were to be protected. In 1791, the 10 amendments known as the Bill of Rights were ratified.

Some of Madison's amendments are famous. The First Amendment protects many important rights, such as freedom of speech and freedom of religion. The Tenth Amendment says that the federal government only has the powers given to it by the Constitution. All other powers belong to the states or to the people.

Speaking Out Americans have often worked together to demand their rights. These women demanded the right to vote.

The Growth of Democracy

In 1790, the Constitution did not protect the rights of all Americans. Thousands of African Americans remained in slavery. Some states allowed only white men who had a certain amount of land or money to vote. The rights of women, African Americans, American Indians, and poor people were not recognized.

Ideas about democracy have changed since 1790, and the Constitution has changed with them. Different groups have fought for their rights and won.

Amendments have been added to the Constitution to protect the voting rights of men and women of all races. Today the equal protection promised by the Constitution is given to more citizens than ever before.

REVIEW Why does the Constitution include a way to make amendments?

Lesson Summary

- The federal government is divided into the legislative, executive, and judicial branches.
- Checks and balances keep any one branch from becoming too powerful.
- The Constitution divides power between the federal government and the states.
- The Constitution can be changed by amendment.

Why It Matters . . .

The Constitution desribes the rules for the government under which you live today.

Lesson Review

1 **VOCABULARY** Use **democracy** and **amendment** in a paragraph about the Constitution.

2 **READING SKILL** Think about the **categories** of jobs the federal government does. What jobs can the legislative branch do that other branches cannot?

3 **MAIN IDEA: Government** Which powers do the states have that the federal government does not have?

4 **MAIN IDEA: Government** What must happen for an amendment to become part of the Constitution?

5 **CRITICAL THINKING: Conclude** Why did the authors of the Constitution want a limited government?

6 **CRITICAL THINKING: Summarize** How do the judicial and executive branches limit the power of the legislative branch?

RESEARCH ACTIVITY Find out who represents you in the Senate and the House of Representatives. The President is also your representative. List these people. Explain what each person's job is and how he or she represents you.

The Liberty Bell

In 1751, Pennsylvania lawmakers had a bell made to celebrate freedom. That year was the 50th anniversary of Pennsylvania's charter. This charter, or official document, promised freedom to people in the colony.

Quakers founded Pennsylvania so they would be free to practice their religious beliefs. They gave people who practiced other beliefs the same freedom. They wrote a verse from the Bible on the bell: "Proclaim LIBERTY throughout the land unto all the inhabitants thereof."

The Bell rang to bring citizens together for important announcements and events. It rang on July 8, 1776 for the first public reading of the Declaration of Independence. It rang when the U.S. Constitution was ratified.

Independence

The Bell rang on July 8, 1776, to call the people of Philadelphia. They listened to Captain John Dixon read aloud the Declaration of Independence.

The Great Train Ride

In 1915, the Bell traveled from Philadelphia to San Francisco by train. In towns and cities along the way, flag-waving crowds greeted the Bell with brass bands.

Liberty Bell Facts

★ ★ ★ ★

Circumference around the lip: 12 feet

Height from lip to crown: 3 feet

Weight: 2080 pounds

Length of clapper: 3 feet, 2 inches

Length of crack: 2 feet, 1/2 inch

Activities

1. **DRAW YOUR OWN** What object would you choose to celebrate freedom on a special anniversary? Draw the object. Explain why it is a symbol of freedom.

2. **ACT IT OUT** More than one million people visit the Liberty Bell each year. Prepare a talk that a tour guide might give visitors about the bell's history.

President Washington

VOCABULARY

inauguration
Cabinet
political party
interest
capital

Vocabulary Strategy

| Cabinet

The President's group of advisors is called the **Cabinet**. Such groups used to meet in small private rooms. Rooms like this were called cabinets.

READING SKILL

Cause and Effect As you read, note results of George Washington's presidency.

Washington's Presidency

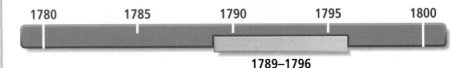

1780   1785   1790   1795   1800

1789–1796

Build on What You Know Are you sometimes nervous when you start something new? Many people are. Even George Washington was not sure he would do a good job as the first President of the United States.

The First President

Main Idea George Washington became the first President under the Constitution.

The United States elected a President for the first time in 1789. The Constitution set up the system for elections. The states chose representatives for a group called the Electoral College. It was the job of the members of the Electoral College to vote for the President. Everyone in the first Electoral College agreed that **George Washington** was the only one for the job. Washington, however, was not sure he would succeed. He wrote,

66 My Countrymen will expect too much from me, 99

Washington knew his actions would set an example for other Presidents to follow. He acted with thought and care.

Souvenirs These buttons celebrated the new Congress and President.

SKILL **Primary Source** What do you think the letters GW on the souvenir stand for?

Inauguration George Washington takes the oath of office at Federal Hall in New York City. Those behind him include Alexander Hamilton and Henry Knox.

Washington's Government

In April 1789, Washington traveled to New York City, where the government met. He was greeted as a hero. An excited crowd watched his inauguration (ihn aw gyur AY shun) in New York City. An inauguration is an official ceremony to make someone President. Washington promised to

66 preserve, protect, and defend the Constitution of the United States. 99

Every President since Washington has made the same promise.

Congress created three departments to help the President run the executive branch. Washington chose people he trusted to run the departments. They were called Secretaries. **Thomas Jefferson** became Washington's Secretary of State.

He would decide how the United States acted toward other countries. Washington picked **Alexander Hamilton** to take care of the nation's finances as Secretary of the Treasury. General **Henry Knox**, who had been in the army with Washington, became Secretary of War. Knox would be in charge of protecting the nation. **Edmund Randolph** became Attorney General. He would see that federal laws were obeyed.

These men often met at Washington's house to advise him. Together, they became known as the President's Cabinet. The Cabinet is a group chosen by the President to help run the executive branch and give advice. Every President since Washington has had a Cabinet.

REVIEW What is the purpose of the Cabinet?

Points of View

Thomas Jefferson and Alexander Hamilton were both in Washington's Cabinet. They argued about the role of the government in the United States.

Jefferson wanted the nation's economy to help the farmers who owned small plots of land. He felt the people should be as free of government control as possible.

Hamilton believed that the nation would be stronger if its economy helped large businesses and trade. He thought that a strong government was necessary to keep order and make rules about trade.

Arguments in the Cabinet

Main Idea Hamilton and Jefferson argued about how the government should act.

Two Cabinet members, Hamilton and Jefferson, often disagreed. Hamilton wanted a strong national government that supported trade and manufacturing. Jefferson felt that the government should be limited so that it could not take away states' rights. He said it should support farming instead of trade.

Jefferson and Hamilton both had followers who formed political parties. A **political party** is a group of people who share similar ideas about government. People supporting Jefferson formed the Democratic-Republican Party. Hamilton's party was known as the Federalist Party.

Hamilton and Jefferson often gave the President opposite advice. For example, Hamilton wanted to start a national bank. He believed it would make the nation wealthier and stronger.

Jefferson was against the idea. He said that the government did not have the power to create the bank. Washington took Hamilton's advice. He approved the law that created a national bank.

The national bank controlled the money of the United States. Customers could keep money in savings accounts there. Today, a savings account is a way to earn money. The bank borrows from savings accounts to make loans. It earns money on the loans by charging interest. **Interest** is what people pay to borrow money. The bank also pays interest for the use of the money to each person who has a savings account.

Hamilton and Jefferson compromised on some problems. Hamilton supported Jefferson's wish to build a new national capital on the Potomac River, between Virginia and Maryland. A **capital** is the city where the government meets. In return, Jefferson agreed to Hamilton's plan to pay the nation's war debts.

President Washington chose the new capital's exact location. **Andrew Ellicott** and **Benjamin Banneker,** both astronomers, measured the land. A French engineer, **Pierre L'Enfant** (lahn FAHN), designed the city. Building began in 1792. The city was named Washington, to honor the President.

After eight years as President, Washington announced his retirement in a farewell address, or speech, to the nation. In his address, he advised people not to form political parties. He felt parties divided people. Washington also wanted the nation to stay out of wars between other countries. Britain and France were at war at this time. Washington refused to take sides. For many years after that, the nation did not take sides in any foreign wars.

George Washington is remembered as a great hero. One of Washington's friends said that he was

> 66 **first in war, first in peace, and first in the hearts of his countrymen.** 99

REVIEW Why did Hamilton and Jefferson disagree about creating a national bank?

Lesson Summary

- George Washington became the first President under the Constitution.
- Disagreements in the Cabinet led to the first political parties.
- Washington agreed to a plan for a national bank and chose the location of a capital city.

Why It Matters . . .

The presidency of George Washington set up traditions that have been followed by all American Presidents.

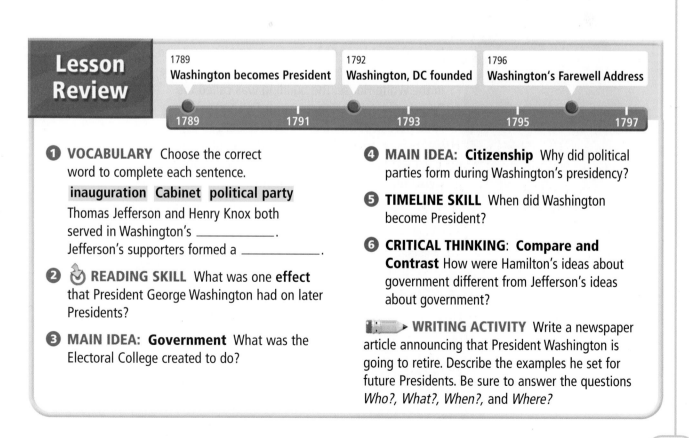

Lesson Review

1789	1792	1796
Washington becomes President	**Washington, DC founded**	**Washington's Farewell Address**

1789   1791   1793   1795   1797

❶ **VOCABULARY** Choose the correct word to complete each sentence.

   inauguration Cabinet political party

   Thomas Jefferson and Henry Knox both served in Washington's _____. Jefferson's supporters formed a _____.

❷ **READING SKILL** What was one **effect** that President George Washington had on later Presidents?

❸ **MAIN IDEA: Government** What was the Electoral College created to do?

❹ **MAIN IDEA: Citizenship** Why did political parties form during Washington's presidency?

❺ **TIMELINE SKILL** When did Washington become President?

❻ **CRITICAL THINKING: Compare and Contrast** How were Hamilton's ideas about government different from Jefferson's ideas about government?

WRITING ACTIVITY Write a newspaper article announcing that President Washington is going to retire. Describe the examples he set for future Presidents. Be sure to answer the questions *Who?, What?, When?,* and *Where?*

Washington, D.C.

Could Washington, D.C. be changed from a small, muddy town to a city as glorious as Paris? A French city planner thought so. Pierre L'Enfant [lahn-FAHN] imagined a great capital city for the United States. Located on the Potomac River, the city would have parks, tree-lined avenues, and grand public buildings. He created a plan for the city in 1791. By 1800, his plan became reality. Washington, D.C. became the capital of the United States. The city center is much as L'Enfant designed it.

Although L'Enfant planned the city, many other people helped make it what it is today. Three of them are shown here.

Abigail Adams

In 1800, First Lady Abigail Adams and her husband, President John Adams, were the first couple to live in the White House. The building was called the President's House, and it wasn't finished yet. Fires were kept burning in the fireplaces to dry the wet plaster on the walls. The large reception room was used to dry laundry. Even so, Abigail Adams called the building a "great castle."

Benjamin Banneker

Benjamin Banneker was a farmer who studied astronomy and other sciences. In 1791, Banneker helped survey, or measure, the land for the new capital city. As part of the job of surveying the land, Banneker set the boundaries for what would be the city. Today, many buildings and organizations are named for Banneker, including a high school in Washington, D.C.

William Thornton

Born in Britain, William Thornton moved to the United States because he admired the ideals of the Revolution. In 1793, he won a contest to design the Capitol Building, where Congress would meet. George Washington liked Thornton's plan for its "grandeur, simplicity, and beauty." The Capitol Building has grown and changed, but it looks like Thornton's basic plan.

This map shows L'Enfant's design for Washington, D.C. The President's House and the Capitol Building still stand where they were shown in his plan.

President's House (White House)

Capitol Building

Activities

1. **DRAW YOUR OWN** Draw a plan for a capital city. What would it look like? What are some of the important buildings in your city? What would you name your city?

2. **PRESENT IT** Research the history of an important building in Washington, D.C. Prepare a short presentation about what you learned.

Visual Summary

1–3. Write a description of each branch of government.

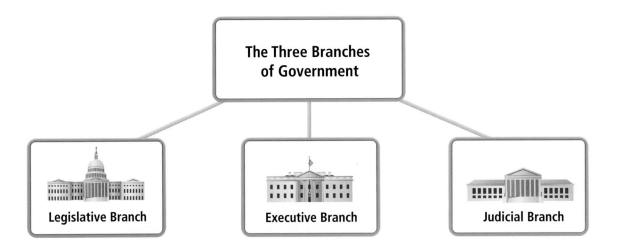

The Three Branches of Government

Legislative Branch

Executive Branch

Judicial Branch

Facts and Main Ideas

TEST PREP Answer each question with information from the chapter.

4. **History** What was Shays's Rebellion?

5. **Government** What was the Great Compromise?

6. **History** Who was James Madison and what did he do at the Constitutional Convention?

7. **Citizenship** Name two rights guaranteed by the Bill of Rights.

8. **Government** What is the purpose of the Cabinet?

Vocabulary

TEST PREP Choose the correct word from the list below to complete each sentence.

constitution, p. 296
compromise, p. 304
political party, p. 322

9. Two sides give up something they want in order to reach a _____.

10. The supporters of Alexander Hamilton formed a _____ and so did the supporters of Thomas Jefferson.

11. Delegates in Philadelphia wrote a new _____ for the United States in 1787.

CHAPTER SUMMARY TIMELINE

1781	1787	1789	1792
Articles of Confederation	Constitutional Convention	Washington elected	Washington, D.C. founded

1780   1783   1786   1789   1792   1795

Apply Skills

✔ **TEST PREP** **Citizenship Skill** Read the quotations below and use what you have learned about point of view to answer each question.

> "The local interests of a state ought, in every case, to give way to the interests of the Union."
>
> — Alexander Hamilton

> "…Some have weakly imagined that it is necessary to annihilate [destroy] the several states, and [give] Congress… government of the continent…. This however, would be impractical."
>
> — *Freeman's Journal* of Philadelphia

12. What was Hamilton's point of view?

   A. States' interests are more important than the interests of the federal government.

   B. The interests of the federal government are more important than states' interests.

   C. The federal government is not important.

   D. States are not important.

13. Describe the point of view expressed by the *Freeman's Journal* in your own words.

Critical Thinking

✔ **TEST PREP** Write a short paragraph to answer each question.

14. **Infer** What effect did the Northwest Ordinance have on settlers?

15. **Problem and Solution** Name two problems caused by the Articles of Confederation. What solutions did delegates at the Constitutional Convention offer?

Timeline

Use the Chapter Summary Timeline above to answer the question.

16. When was the first President elected?

Activities

Drama Activity Prepare a scene of the debate that took place at the Constitutional Convention. Include delegates from both large and small states.

Writing Activity Write a personal essay that George Washington might have written in his autobiography. Describe how he might have felt about being the first President.

Technology
Writing Process Tips
Get help with your personal essay at
www.eduplace.com/kids/hmss05/

Principles *of* DEMOCRACY

★ ★ ★

All nations have governments. A government is a group of people who make and enforce the laws of a political region, such as a country. Just as your school has rules, the nation has laws to govern its citizens.

Life in the United States would be difficult without government. The government sets up ways to choose leaders and makes laws to protect people at home and in the community. Governments run public schools and libraries and print stamps and money. When governments work well, they protect freedom and keep order.

Democratic Government

Governments take many forms. The United States is a democracy. A democracy is a government in which people govern themselves. In a democracy, citizens have the power to make political decisions.

The United States has a form of democracy called representative democracy. That means citizens elect representatives who speak or act for them in making laws.

Majority and Minority

In the United States, the majority of voters usually decides who will win an election. Majority means more than half. Many important decisions are made by majority rule. For example, the majority of lawmakers in Congress must agree on a law before it is passed.

Even though most decisions are made by majority rule, the rights of the minority are protected. Minority means fewer than half. The majority cannot take away the rights of small groups of people to express unpopular views or take part in the government. This limit on majority rule is sometimes called minority rights.

The Rule of Law

The Constitution is the plan for the United States government. It is also the supreme, or highest, law of the United States. Everyone, including the President, must obey the country's laws. This is known as the rule of law. The rule of law is a system in which laws are made by elected representatives, not one or two individuals. The rule of law promises justice to all. In other words, it promises that laws will protect everyone equally.

Two Hundred Years Thousands of balloons were released to celebrate the 200th anniversary of the U.S. Constitution in 1987.

REVIEW What does the rule of law promise to everyone?

Structure
of the
GOVERNMENT

★ ★ ★

The federal government is our national government. The Constitution created a federal government with three branches. These branches, or parts, are the legislative, executive, and judicial branches.

The three branches of government work together, but each branch has its own powers. A system of checks and balances prevents any one branch from having too much power. In this system, each branch limits the power of the other two branches.

For example, the President can veto, or reject, laws passed by Congress. Congress can refuse to approve treaties made by the President. The courts of the judicial branch can rule that laws made by Congress or actions taken by the President are unconstitutional.

All three branches are supposed to work toward the common good of the country's citizens. The common good means what is best for the whole country, not just for a few individuals.

White House

Executive Branch The head of the executive branch is the President. The Vice President and the heads of government departments give advice to the President.

★ proposes, approves, and enforces laws made by Congress

★ makes treaties with other countries

★ leads the military

Capitol

Legislative Branch The legislative branch is called Congress. Congress has two parts: the Senate and the House of Representatives.

★ makes laws

★ raises money by collecting taxes or borrowing money

★ approves the printing of money

★ can declare war

Supreme Court

Judicial Branch The Supreme Court and other courts make up the judicial branch. One Chief Justice and eight Associate Justices serve on the Supreme Court.

★ decides whether laws follow the guidelines of the Constitution

★ decides what laws mean

★ decides whether laws have been followed

REVIEW **Why is it important that a balance of power exist among the three branches of government?**

Levels of Government

★ ★ ★

The federal government is not the only government in the United States. Every state has a government, which is led by a governor. Some decisions are made by the federal government, while others are made by a state government.

Each state is broken into smaller units that have local governments. These units may include counties (parts of states made up of several towns), townships (small parts of counties), cities, and school districts. Local governments take many forms. Some are headed by a mayor. Others are run by a city manager or by a group of people such as a town council.

Federal, state, and local governments have their own powers, but they also share some powers. For example, both the federal and state governments collect taxes, set up courts, and make and enforce laws.

Federal Government

Main Powers

★ prints money

★ declares war

★ runs the postal system

★ makes treaties with other countries

★ collects income taxes

JAN California 200

State Government

★

Main Powers

★ issues licenses, such as marriage licenses and driver's licenses

★ runs elections

★ sets up local governments

★ collects income and sales taxes

Local Government

★

Main Powers

★ provides police and fire protection

★ runs public schools and public libraries (with help from the state)

★ provides public transportation, such as buses and subways

★ collects sales and property taxes

REVIEW Which level of government has the power to run elections?

333

The Bill of Rights

★ ★ ★

The first 10 amendments to the Constitution are called the Bill of Rights. An amendment is an official change or addition to a law. The Bill of Rights is like a promise to the people of the United States. It lists many of the individual rights the U.S. government promises to protect. This chart explains each amendment.

The First Amendment says we have the right to speak our minds.

1 First Amendment The government cannot support any religion above another. It may not prevent people from practicing whichever religion they wish. People have the right to say and write their opinions, and the press has the right to publish them. People can also meet together and ask the government to make changes.

2 Second Amendment Because people may have to fight to protect their country, they may own weapons.

3 Third Amendment People do not have to allow soldiers to live in their homes.

4 Fourth Amendment The police cannot search people or their homes without a good reason.

5 Fifth Amendment People accused of a crime have the right to a fair trial. They cannot be tried more than once for the same crime. Accused people do not have to speak against themselves at a trial.

6 Sixth Amendment People accused of a crime have the right to a speedy, public trial by a jury. A jury is a group of people who hear evidence and make a decision. Accused people also have the right to a lawyer, to be told what crime they are accused of, and to question witnesses.

7 Seventh Amendment People who have a disagreement about something worth more than $20 have the right to a trial by a jury.

8 Eighth Amendment In most cases, accused people can remain out of jail until their trial if they pay bail. Bail is a sum of money they will lose if they don't appear for their trial. Courts cannot demand bail that is too high or punish people in cruel ways.

9 Ninth Amendment People have other rights besides those stated in the Constitution.

10 Tenth Amendment Any powers the Constitution does not give to the federal government belong to the states or the people.

REVIEW List three rights that are protected by the Bill of Rights.

Review
★ ★ ★

Complete two of the following activities.

Art Activity Work with a group to create a poster titled, *What Democracy Means to Me.* Cut out pictures from newspapers and magazines that illustrate some part of government or something government does.

Writing Activity Choose one of the branches of government and write a short report about it. Give an example of how the branch provides for the common good of the American people.

Research Activity A state capital is a city in which a state's government is located. Make a list of every state's capital. Write a fact card for one capital on your list, including its population and the year it was founded.

Writing Activity Find out who your leaders are at each level of government. Write the names of the President and your senators, representatives, and local leaders. Write to a local leader. Ask questions about that person's job.

Speaking Activity The Bill of Rights still matters today. Prepare an oral report on one of the amendments, explaining how it has affected a current event.

Review and Test Prep

Vocabulary and Main Ideas

Write a sentence to answer each question below.

1. Why did American colonists object to the **Proclamation** of 1763?

2. Why were the Americans against paying **taxes** to the British?

3. What was the main difference between the **Patriots** and the **Loyalists?**

4. Why was the American **victory** at Saratoga a turning point of the Revolution?

5. How did the **delegates** to the Constitutional Convention settle their differences?

6. What are the three branches of the **federal** government?

Critical Thinking

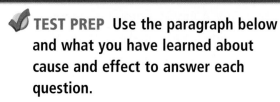 TEST PREP Write a short paragraph to answer each question below.

7. **Drawing Conclusions** Why do you think the Patriots would continue to fight the British even when it seemed that they could not win?

8. **Synthesize** Write a short paragraph explaining how the system of checks and balances protects democracy. Use details from the unit to support your answer.

Apply Skills

TEST PREP Use the paragraph below and what you have learned about cause and effect to answer each question.

> Nine states needed to ratify the new Constitution for it to become law. Some of the states, however, thought the Constitution did not protect people's rights. The Federalists agreed to add a Bill of Rights to the Constitution. Then, all 13 states ratified the Constitution.

9. What caused the Bill of Rights to be added to the Constitution?

   A. Some states wanted to protect people's rights.
   B. Some states did not want a Constitution.
   C. Thirteen states needed to ratify the Constitution.
   D. The Constitution was too short.

10. What was an effect of adding the Bill of Rights to the Constitution?

    A. The government's rights were protected.
    B. The people's rights were taken away.
    C. Thirteen states ratified the Constitution.
    D. Nine states refused to ratify the Constitution.

Unit Activity

The Big Idea

Create a Freedom Fighters Portrait Gallery

- Choose a person mentioned in this unit who fought for freedom.

- Research to find a picture of the person and facts about his or her life.

- Create a portrait, or picture, of the person. Write about his or her life underneath the picture.

- Post the portraits in your classroom.

William Prescott
1726-1795

"Don't one of you fire until you see the whites of their eyes."

- Farmer and brave soldier
- Fought in the French and Indian War and Revolutionary War
- Led the Patriot militia of Bunker Hill

At the Library

You may find these books at your school or public library.

The Boston Tea Party, by Steven Kroll
The events of December 16, 1773, changed the course of American history.

If You Lived at the Time of the American Revolution, by Kay Moore
What was life like for Patriots and Loyalists during the Revolution?

CURRENT   EVENTS

WEEKLY WR READER

Connect to Today

Create a bulletin board about freedom and independence around the world today.

- Find articles that tell about nations of the world and ideals of freedom and independence.

- Write a summary of each article. Draw a picture or map to illustrate each summary.

- Post your illustrated summaries on a bulletin board.

Technology
Get your information for the bulletin board from the Weekly Reader at
www.eduplace.com/kids/hmss05/

Read About It

Look for these Social Studies books in your classroom.

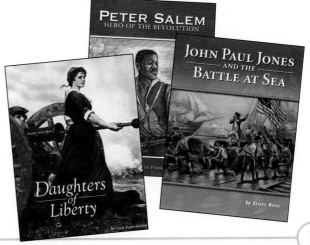

UNIT 5

The New Nation

The Big Idea

What gave the new country its identity?

" *Where liberty is, there is my country.* "

A saying used by Benjamin Franklin

Meriwether Lewis
1774–1809

Thomas Jefferson chose this man to lead the Corps of Discovery across North America. The information that he gathered helped people learn about the West.
page 355

History Makers

Eli Whitney
1765–1825

Can one person change the way goods are made? An American inventer did. Whitney developed ways to produce many goods quickly and at a low cost.

page 379

Susan B. Anthony
1820–1906

Why was this woman arrested for voting? Because in 1782, it was illegal for women to vote in national elections. Anthony spent most of her life fighting for women's rights.

page 391

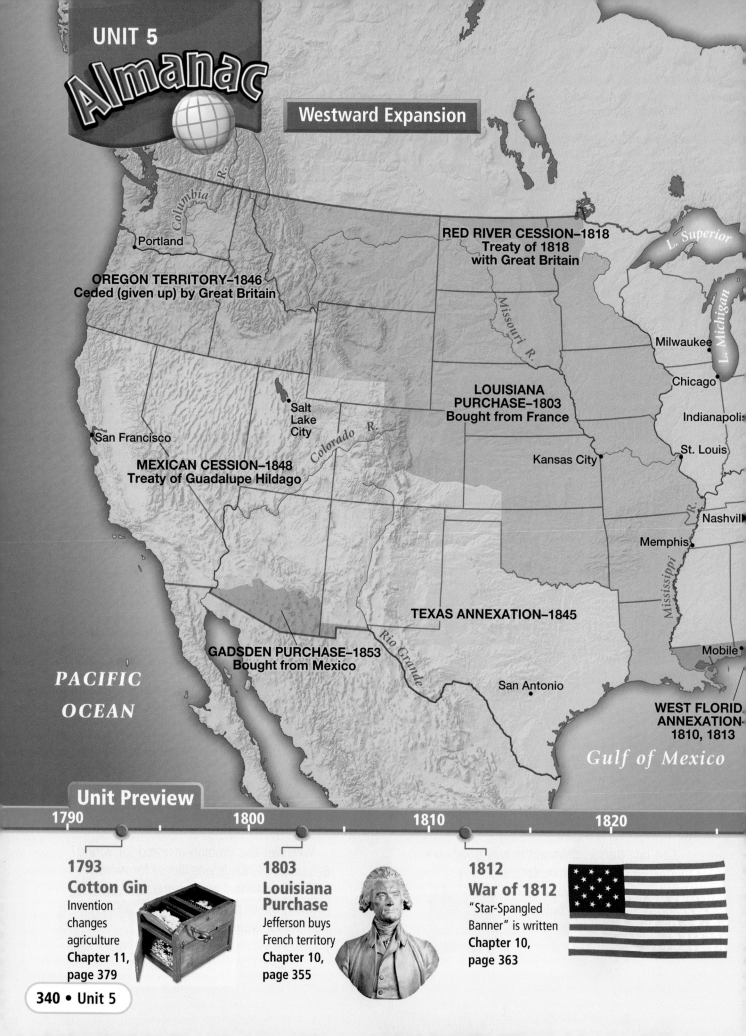

Portland

Columbia R.

OREGON TERRITORY–1846
Ceded (given up) by Great Britain

RED RIVER CESSION–1818
Treaty of 1818
with Great Britain

L. Superior

Missouri R.

L. Michigan

Milwaukee

Chicago

Indianapolis

Salt
Lake
City

Colorado R.

**LOUISIANA
PURCHASE–1803**
Bought from France

St. Louis

San Francisco

Kansas City

MEXICAN CESSION–1848
Treaty of Guadalupe Hildago

Nashvill

Memphis

Mississippi R.

TEXAS ANNEXATION–1845

GADSDEN PURCHASE–1853
Bought from Mexico

Rio Grande

Mobile

*PACIFIC
OCEAN*

San Antonio

**WEST FLORID
ANNEXATION–
1810, 1813**

Gulf of Mexico

Unit Preview

1790	1800	1810	1820

1793
Cotton Gin
Invention
changes
agriculture
Chapter 11,
page 379

1803
**Louisiana
Purchase**
Jefferson buys
French territory
Chapter 10,
page 355

1812
War of 1812
"Star-Spangled
Banner" is written
Chapter 10,
page 363

WEBSTER ASHBURTON
TREATY–1842
**Border adjustment
with Great Britain**

•Portland

•Boston

L. Ontario
•Buffalo

Huron

L. Erie
troit
Cleveland
•Philadelphia
Pittsburgh

•New York

•Baltimore
Washington, D.C.

Ohio R.

UNITED STATES–1783
exington
uisville

•Norfolk

N
NW NE
W E
SW SE
S

•Wilmington

•Atlanta
•Charleston

Savannah

Jacksonville
EAST FLORIDA –1819
**ceded (given up)
by Spain**

ATLANTIC
OCEAN

km 0   150   300
mi 0   150   300

LEGEND
• Major city, 1850

Population Growth, 1800s

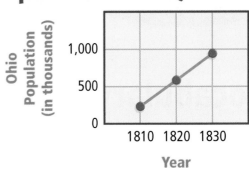

Ohio Population (in thousands)

1,000

500

0
1810 1820 1830
Year

In the early 1800s, people from the eastern states moved to Ohio, which had recently become a state.

Population Growth Today

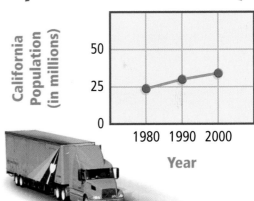

California Population (in millions)

50

25

0
1980 1990 2000
Year

Today people from all over the world move to California because it offers economic opportunities.

CURRENT   EVENTS
WEEKLY (WR) READER

Current events on the web!

Find out about current events that connect with the Big Idea of this unit.
See activities at:
www.eduplace.com/kids/hmss05/

830   1840   1850

1836
Battle of
the Alamo
Texans battle Mexican army
Chapter 11, page 395

1849
Gold Rush
Forty-niners seek fortune in California
Chapter 11, page 402

Chapter 10   The Early Republic

Technology
e • **glossary**
e • **word games**
www.eduplace.com/kids/hmss05/

Vocabulary Preview

canal

A **canal** was a waterway built to make shipping goods easier. The Erie Canal connected the Great Lakes to the Hudson River.
page 346

corps

More than 30 people explored the West with Lewis and Clark. This **corps** was a team of people who worked together.
page 356

Chapter Timeline

1769
Daniel Boone crosses Appalachians

1803
Louisiana Purchase

| 1760 | 1780 | 1800 |

Reading Strategy

Monitor and Clarify Use this strategy to check understanding.

 Quick Tip Stop and ask if the lesson makes sense to you. Reread if you need to.

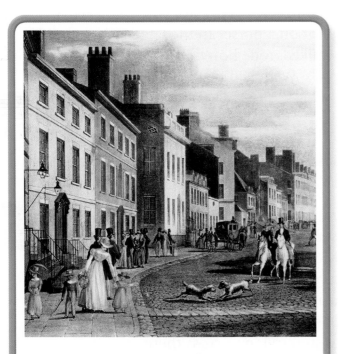

prosperity

After the War of 1812, the Era of Good Feelings began. It was a time of **prosperity.** Many families had enough money for food, clothing, and shelter. **page 364**

campaign

Andrew Jackson was elected President in 1828. His election **campaign** was successful. Voters liked his promise to support ordinary citizens. **page 369**

1812
War of 1812 begins

1838
Trail of Tears

1820

1840

People on the Move

| 1760 | 1780 | 1800 | 1820 | 1840 | 1860 |

1767–1830

Build on What You Know Have you ever taken a ride in a wagon or on a horse? In the late 1700s and early 1800s, people walked, rode horses, or traveled in wagons over bumpy roads. What is different about travel today?

Exploring the Frontier

Main Idea Pioneers explored land west of the Appalachian Mountains in the late 1700s.

The first colonists who came to the British colonies from Europe settled between the Atlantic Ocean and the Appalachian Mountains. This 2,000-mile-long chain of mountains was difficult to cross. Under the Proclamation of 1763, it was against the law for colonists to settle American Indian lands west of the Appalachians. Yet people did not stop trying to cross these mountains. As land in the East filled with farms and towns, settlers looked for new ways to cross the Appalachians.

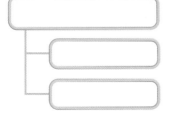

Daniel Boone
He became a hero for his western explorations. This painting shows him leading settlers west.

Daniel Boone

Daniel Boone, a hunter and pioneer, had heard stories about the land west of the Appalachian Mountains. A **pioneer** is one of the first of a group of people to enter or settle a region. In 1769, Boone and several other men followed an American Indian trail through a narrow passage in the Appalachians in Virginia. On the other side of the Cumberland Gap, as this passage was called, they found a land where American Indians farmed and hunted. Boone wanted to live on this land, too.

Boone helped clear a new road through the Cumberland Gap. The route through the mountains was called the Wilderness Road. It stretched 200 miles west. Boone guided families, including his own wife and children, across the Appalachians. Settlers started towns, such as Harrodsburg and Boonesborough, in present-day Kentucky.

Life on the Frontier

Main Idea American settlers made difficult trips across the Appalachians.

By the late 1700s, thousands of people had crossed the Appalachians. They looked for good, inexpensive farmland and new opportunities in the Ohio and Mississippi river valleys.

As settlers went west, they moved into a region known as the frontier. A **frontier** is the edge of a country or settled region. The frontier, and the land beyond it, was already settled by American Indians. Shawnee, Choctaw, Cherokee, and other American Indian nations built villages, farmed, and hunted between the Appalachians and the Mississippi River. Indians and settlers fought over this land on the frontier, but they also borrowed ideas and customs from one another.

REVIEW In which river valleys did people look for farmland on the frontier?

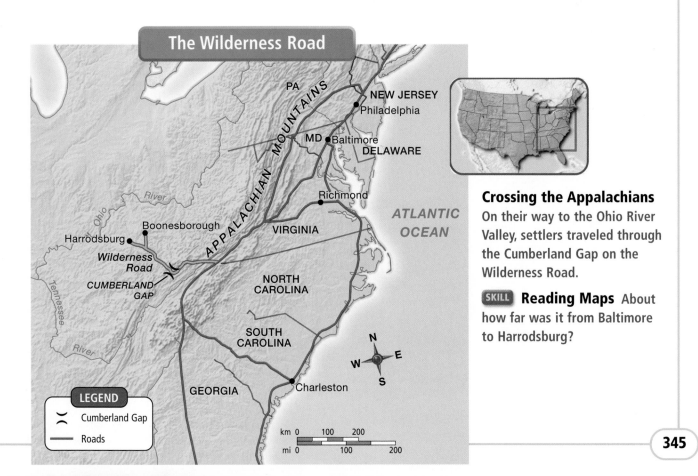

The Wilderness Road

PA
NEW JERSEY
Philadelphia
MD Baltimore
DELAWARE
Richmond
ATLANTIC OCEAN
Boonesborough
Harrodsburg
VIRGINIA
Wilderness Road
CUMBERLAND GAP
NORTH CAROLINA
Ohio River
Tennessee River
SOUTH CAROLINA
N W E S
GEORGIA
Charleston

LEGEND
≍ Cumberland Gap
— Roads

km 0   100   200
mi 0   100   200

Crossing the Appalachians
On their way to the Ohio River Valley, settlers traveled through the Cumberland Gap on the Wilderness Road.

SKILL **Reading Maps** About how far was it from Baltimore to Harrodsburg?

345

Traveling West

Many families who traveled west packed large wagons so full of food and supplies that there was little room for people to ride in them. Early roads were rocky dirt paths, and there were no bridges across rivers. Wagons rolling over the rough roads often broke apart and had to be repaired.

Floating on rivers was faster and more comfortable than traveling over bumpy roads. The Ohio River was the most heavily traveled river. Families, furniture, animals, and equipment floated down the Ohio in flatboats. A **flatboat** was a large rectangular boat partly covered by a roof. Settlers also traveled on canals, such as the Erie Canal, that connected bodies of water. A **canal** is a waterway built for boat travel and shipping.

Flatboats on the Ohio In the early 1820s, about 3,000 flatboats a year floated down the Ohio River.

Making a Home

When pioneers arrived on the frontier, they cut down trees to create a clearing in the woods. They used the logs from these trees to build a house. Inside the house they might have only a table, a bed, a spinning wheel, and a few dishes.

Settlers grew corn and other grains and raised farm animals. Most early settlers grew just enough to feed their families, with no surplus to trade or sell.

Frontier life was hard, especially for women. They lived far from family and friends. Frontier men and women did the same kinds of work as the American Indian men and women who lived nearby. While men went hunting, women took care of their children and farms.

Life was difficult, but many settlers lived better than they had in Europe or in the East. One pioneer wrote: "We were worth nothing when we landed at this place and now we have 1 yoke of oxen, 1 cow, 9 hogs."

Chief Logan

American Indians did not believe that land could be bought or sold. They agreed to sign treaties letting settlers hunt on the land, but not to own it or live on it.

The Iroquois signed one such treaty in 1768. Settlers quickly moved onto the land where Iroquois, Shawnee, Mingo, and other American Indians were living. **Chief Logan** was a Mingo who had always been friendly to the pioneers. In 1774, however, settlers murdered his family.

Chief Logan
This Mingo leader lived in present-day Ohio.

Chief Logan led many attacks against settlers after his family was killed. Like Logan, American Indians would fight with settlers over land for years to come.

REVIEW What kinds of transportation did settlers use to move west?

Lesson Summary

- As the East filled with farms and towns, settlers crossed the Appalachians and built settlements.
- Families traveled west in wagons and on flatboats.
- When settlers moved into areas where American Indians lived, there were conflicts.

Why It Matters ...

Pioneers who crossed the Appalachian Mountains moved the boundaries of American settlement west of the original thirteen colonies.

Lesson Review

| 1769 | | 1774 | |
| Boone crosses Cumberland Gap | | Conflict between settlers and Chief Logan | |

1766 — 1770 — 1774 — 1778

① **VOCABULARY** Write an announcement for a company that provided transportation for settlers in 1821. Use the words **frontier, flatboat,** and **canal.**

② **READING SKILL** Why did settlers make the difficult trip across the Appalachian Mountains? Use **details** in your answer.

③ **MAIN IDEA: History** What were two reasons that some settlers traveled into the Ohio River Valley by flatboat instead of by wagon?

④ **MAIN IDEA: History** What did women do on the frontier?

⑤ **TIMELINE SKILL** When did Daniel Boone travel through the Cumberland Gap?

⑥ **CRITICAL THINKING: Decision Making** An opportunity cost is the thing you give up when you decide to do or have something else. What might have been the opportunity cost for a family who decided to move west across the Appalachians?

ART ACTIVITY Reread the section called "Making a Home." Create a model of a house that a pioneer might have built. Use clay or other materials.

HANDS ON

Flatboat on the Ohio

What was it like to travel on a flatboat? Imagine that it is spring in the year 1816. A pioneer family is traveling down the Ohio River on a **flatboat** along with their animals, furniture, food, and supplies. On the twelfth day of the journey, the children raise an excited shout—Cincinnati is up ahead!

Anne

Tom

Characters

Jonah Rees: farmer

Margaret Rees: farmer

Anne: their 15-year-old daughter

Abby: their 12-year-old daughter

Martin: their 10-year-old son

Susie: their 6-year-old daughter

William Rees: Jonah Rees's brother

Tom: William's 16-year-old son

Granny Rees: mother of
Jonah and William Rees

Keelboat pilot

Tom: Look, cousins! A big town!

Anne: It must be Cincinnati! Mother, please may I go see? I hear it has five thousand people!

Margaret Rees: Be quick about it, Anne. I want to have a look, too. And check if the hens have laid any eggs while you're at it. Granny! It's Cincinnati!

Granny Rees: Yes—I hear all the noise. I'll take a look from one of those crates. Help me up, Martin.

Martin: There you go, Granny. Just look at all those houses!

Abby: What are those buildings near the river?

Tom: Father says there are lots of cotton mills in Cincinnati. I wonder if we'll go ashore. I'd like to see the town.

Anne: I wish we could live here. It looks so cozy and settled.

Abby: Crowded, you mean! I hate to have people breathing down my neck. I can't wait to get to Indiana.

Granny Rees: You sound like your Pa.

Martin: I just hope we're near a settlement with a school and children my age.

Susie: Where are we going to live in Indiana?

Tom: Don't worry. We're buying land from the government.

Anne: Why do we have to move, anyway? Our farm in Pennsylvania was so close to town, so snug, wasn't it?

Abby: That's exactly why.

Granny Rees: She means it was getting too crowded for your Pa. Land is cheap in Indiana, and he got a good price for the farm.

Tom: And my father says he needs a change, too. He says he likes a new challenge. Oh, here's your father.

Jonah Rees: Martin! Have you milked Sally yet? She doesn't sound too happy!

Martin: I'll do it right now!

Margaret Rees: And what about the chickens, Anne?

Anne: I got six eggs. Look.

Margaret Rees: Good. I'll go have a look at Cincinnati. Don't let the fire get too big, and watch for sparks. Are we stopping here, Jonah?

Jonah Rees: No reason to. We don't need anything. The children won't want to leave if we do.

Margaret Rees: The children are a touch homesick. Wouldn't you like to see Cincinnati?

Jonah Rees: I can see it from here. I'd rather get to the land office in Jeffersonville so we can make a claim.

Martin: Look! A keelboat is coming up the river. They're signaling.

Keelboat pilot (shouting): Where are you bound?

William Rees: To Jeffersonville, from Pittsburgh!

Keelboat pilot: Watch for a sandbar below Cincinnati, just past Mill Creek.

William Rees: Much obliged, thank you!

Margaret Rees: Anne, oh no! Check that fire! Get some water! Good—that was close. It was sparking, wasn't it?

Anne: I'm sorry, Mother. We were watching the keelboat and the city, and—

Margaret Rees: Don't fret. We're all getting distracted. Be more careful next time.

William Rees: Jonah, if we're going ashore, we need to bring the boat around now.

Jonah Rees: All right. It seems I'm out-voted. Tom, Anne! Help out, now. Take an oar. We're heading in.

Tom: Cousins, did you hear? We're landing in Cincinnati!

Anne, Abby, Martin, Susie: Hooray!

William Rees: Don't get too worked up, now. We're not staying long.

Jonah Rees: That's right. There's land waiting for us in Indiana!

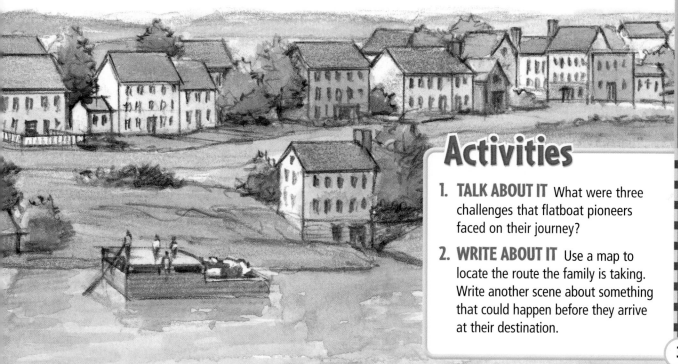

Activities

1. **TALK ABOUT IT** What were three challenges that flatboat pioneers faced on their journey?

2. **WRITE ABOUT IT** Use a map to locate the route the family is taking. Write another scene about something that could happen before they arrive at their destination.

Skillbuilder

Make an Outline

► **VOCABULARY**
outline

In the last lesson, you read about people moving west across the Appalachian Mountains. You can better understand what you read by creating an outline. An outline identifies the main ideas and supporting details of a piece of writing. Making an outline can also help you organize your ideas before writing a report.

Learn the Skill

Step 1: Identify the topic of the piece of writing in a title at the top of your outline.

Step 2: List each main idea with a Roman numeral. Use your own words to express the ideas.

Step 3: List supporting details under each main idea. Indent each detail and place a capital letter in front of it. Use your own words.

Step 4: Repeat Steps 2 and 3 for the other main ideas in the piece of writing.

Title

I. Main Idea
    A. Supporting detail
    B. Supporting detail

II. Main Idea
    A. Supporting detail
    B. Supporting detail

Practice the Skill

Here is an outline of two paragraphs from Lesson 1. Answer the following questions about the outline.

1 What are the two main ideas in the outline?

2 How many supporting details does the first main idea have?

3 What title would you give this outline?

I.   Land travel was difficult
  A. Wagons packed full, little room for people
  B. Poor roads, few bridges
  C. Wagons often needed repairs

II. Water travel was easier
  A. Families, furniture, livestock, equipment floated downriver in flatboats
  B. Canals made travel easier

Apply the Skill

Make an outline of this passage about Daniel Boone.

Daniel Boone was a famous pioneer. He was an expert hunter, trapper, and explorer. Boone guided many families, including his own, through the Cumberland Gap and into Kentucky. There he helped settlers survive in the wilderness. Later, Boone moved his family further west to Missouri, where he lived for the rest of his life.

Boone's adventures were published in a book in 1784. He was soon known around the world for his strength and courage. People began writing biographies and poems about him. Although some of the stories about Boone were not true, he became a legend.

The Nation Grows

1800–1806

VOCABULARY

manufacturer
corps
interpreter
source

Vocabulary Strategy

interpreter

Interpreter includes the word **interpret**. To interpret is to explain. An interpreter explains a language to people who do not speak it.

READING SKILL
Problem and Solution
Chart problems Jefferson faced as President, and how he solved them.

PROBLEM	SOLUTION

Build on What You Know Think of a place that you've never visited. What would you ask someone who had been there? In the early 1800s, President Jefferson sent explorers to parts of the North American continent that he had never seen.

President Jefferson

Main Idea President Thomas Jefferson made the government smaller and the country bigger.

In 1800, **Thomas Jefferson** was elected the nation's third President. He was a member of a different political party than **John Adams,** who had been President before him. When Jefferson took office, the Federalist party gave up its power to the Democratic-Republican party. This change from one party to another was peaceful and democratic. It showed that the plan in the Constitution for electing leaders worked.

Jefferson and the Democratic-Republican party believed states should be stronger than the national government. Jefferson also wanted to help farmers. Federalists disagreed. They wanted a strong national government and laws that would help merchants and manu-facturers. A **manufacturer** is someone who uses machines to make goods.

Thomas Jefferson The third President made the national government smaller by lowering taxes and decreasing the size of the army.

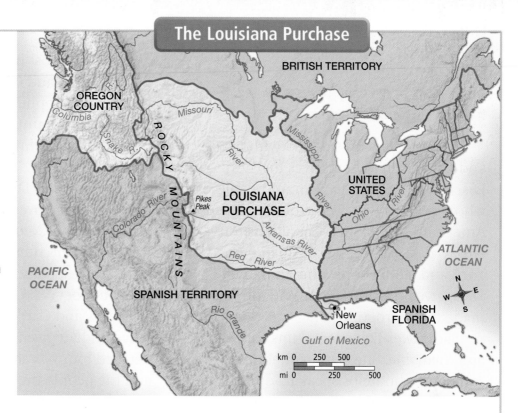

The Louisiana Purchase

BRITISH TERRITORY

OREGON COUNTRY

Columbia R.

Snake R.

Missouri River

ROCKY MOUNTAINS

Pikes Peak

LOUISIANA PURCHASE

Colorado River

Arkansas River

Red River

UNITED STATES

Mississippi River

Ohio River

ATLANTIC OCEAN

PACIFIC OCEAN

SPANISH TERRITORY

Rio Grande

New Orleans

SPANISH FLORIDA

Gulf of Mexico

km 0 250 500
mi 0 250 500

A Growing Nation

Napoleon sold the Louisiana Territory to the United States in 1803 for $15 million, or less than four cents an acre.

SKILL **Reading Maps**

Name the countries that claimed land on the North American continent after the Louisiana Purchase.

Louisiana Purchase

The year Jefferson was elected, a large area of land west of the Mississippi River came under French control. This land, known as Louisiana, had been claimed by the French but was given to Spain in 1763, after the French and Indian War. In 1800, France took control of it again.

The biggest port in Louisiana was the city of New Orleans. American farmers worried that the French would close this port to them.

Jefferson sent representatives to France in 1803. They wanted French ruler **Napoleon Bonaparte** to agree that U.S. farmers could trade through New Orleans.

To the surprise of the Americans, the French offered to sell all of Louisiana because they needed money for a war against Great Britain. Jefferson was eager to add this huge area of land to the United States, so he bought it. The Louisiana Purchase doubled the size of the country, adding about 828,000 square miles, or 530 million acres.

Lewis and Clark

Jefferson had always been interested in science and nature. He was curious about the people, land, plants, and animals in this new territory and beyond. He sent an expedition to explore it.

Jefferson chose **Meriwether Lewis** to lead the expedition. Lewis invited his friend **William Clark** to help. Jefferson asked Lewis and Clark to do three things. First, they were to gather information about the landforms, plants, animals, and climates of the West. Second, he asked them to study the cultures of the western Indians. Finally, he wanted them to explore the Missouri and Columbia rivers. He hoped they would find a water route to the Pacific Ocean.

Lewis and Clark set out from St. Louis in May 1804. More than 30 people, almost all of them soldiers, joined Lewis and Clark on their dangerous journey.

REVIEW Why did Jefferson send representatives to France?

Exploring the West

Main Idea In the early 1800s, explorers traveled into new territory.

The people who traveled with Lewis and Clark called themselves the Corps of Discovery. A **corps** is a team of people who work together. The group included Americans and French-Canadians. An enslaved African American man named **York** and a Shoshone woman named **Sacagawea** (sah KAH guh WEE uh) also made the journey.

Sacagawea collected plants for food and medicine. She was an **interpreter,** or someone who helps speakers of different languages understand each other. Sacagawea could talk with some of the American Indians the Corps met and show that it was a peaceful group.

Perhaps most important, Sacagawea helped Lewis and Clark trade for the horses and supplies they needed to cross the western mountains. Without these horses, the expedition probably would have failed.

The Corps of Discovery traveled up the Missouri River, over the Rocky Mountains, and down the Columbia River to the Pacific Ocean. After traveling about 8,000 miles, the expedition returned to St. Louis in September 1806.

Lewis and Clark completed the tasks Jefferson had given them. They kept detailed journals about the land they saw and the people they met. Even though a direct water route to the Pacific Ocean did not exist, the Corps of Discovery proved it was possible to cross the continent through passes in the Rocky Mountains.

Corps of Discovery Lewis and Clark lead the expedition on its return to St. Louis. Sacagawea, carrying her child, and York follow behind. The United States Mint honored the 200th anniversary of the Lewis and Clark expedition with a new nickel (right).

Zebulon Pike

While Lewis and Clark traveled, another expedition set off into the West. In 1805, **Zebulon Pike** led 20 men up the Mississippi River to look for its source. A source is the place where a river begins. Pike and his men explored from St. Louis to northern Minnesota. They never found the Mississippi's source, but Pike learned a lot about this land.

One year later, Pike explored the Arkansas and Red rivers. These rivers run through the southern part of what was the Louisiana Territory. On that journey, Pike tried to climb a high mountain. He failed, but this peak became known as Pikes Peak, now a famous landmark in Colorado. The journeys of Pike, Lewis, and Clark led the way for pioneers and traders to explore the West.

REVIEW What tasks did Lewis and Clark complete on their expedition?

Lesson Summary

Thomas Jefferson purchased the Louisiana Territory from France in 1803.

Lewis and Clark reached the Pacific Ocean in 1804.

Pike explored the southern part of the Louisiana Purchase in 1806.

Why It Matters ...

President Thomas Jefferson doubled the size of the United States and sent explorers to learn about the western part of the continent.

Lesson Review

1800
Jefferson elected

1803
Louisiana Purchase

1804
Corps of Discovery sets out

1800   1802   1804   1806

1. **VOCABULARY** Match each vocabulary word with its meaning:

   corps   interpreter   source

   (a) team of people; (b) place where a river begins; (c) person who explains a language to others

2. **READING SKILL** How did Jefferson solve the **problem** of wanting to find a water route to the Pacific?

3. **MAIN IDEA: Geography** What did Jefferson do to increase the size of the United States?

4. **MAIN IDEA: History** What was Jefferson's purpose for the Corps of Discovery?

5. **PEOPLE TO KNOW** Who was **Zebulon Pike**, and what areas did he explore?

6. **TIMELINE SKILL** In what year did Jefferson win the presidential election?

7. **CRITICAL THINKING: Draw Conclusions** In 2000, the United States started making one-dollar coins like the one shown on page 356. Why do you think Sacagawea is still honored today?

HANDS ON

ART ACTIVITY Make a poster to persuade people to join the Corps of Discovery. Describe the goals of the expedition and the skills the group needed.

Journey of Discovery

OREGON COUNTRY

PACIFIC OCEAN

Great Falls

Canoe Camp

Fort Clatsop

4

Columbia River

Clearwater River

Camp Fortunate

Shoshone villages

Snake River

They had paddled unmapped rivers and scrambled over mountain passes for more than a year. Finally, the explorers in the Corps of Discovery caught sight of the Pacific Ocean. President Jefferson had asked Lewis and Clark to find a route across the continent to the Pacific. Along the way, they filled their journals with drawings of plants and animals. They described the time that Lewis's dog, Seaman, scared away an attacking bear and the time that Sacagawea saved precious tools and papers from the waters of the Missouri after a boat tipped over.

Lewis and Clark covered thousands of miles. How did the Corps of Discovery travel over this rugged land? Look at the map to find out. Their journey begins on the right side of the map.

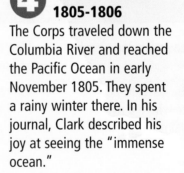

4 **Pacific Ocean, 1805-1806**

The Corps traveled down the Columbia River and reached the Pacific Ocean in early November 1805. They spent a rainy winter there. In his journal, Clark described his joy at seeing the "immense ocean."

3 **Bitterroot Range, 1805**

At Camp Fortunate, Sacagawea helped Lewis and Clark trade for horses with the Shoshone. The explorers needed these horses to cross the steep Bitterroot Range of the Rocky Mountains.

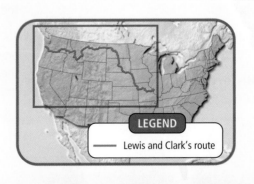

LEGEND

—— Lewis and Clark's route

LEGEND

🛶	Travel by boats		Louisiana Purchase
🏇	Travel by horses		Oregon Country
🚶	Travel by walking		Spanish territory
⛺	American Indian settlement		

② Fort Mandan

Hidatsa and Mandan villages

LOUISIANA PURCHASE

G R E A T   P L A I N S

Missouri River

Mississippi River

START HERE

Camp Dubois
St. Louis

①

Yellowstone River

Missouri River

Platte River

ROCKY MOUNTAINS

② **Fort Mandan, 1804–1805**

After traveling more than a thousand miles, the explorers spent a cold winter at Fort Mandan on the Great Plains.

① **Camp Dubois, 1803–1804**

In May, the Corps of Discovery journeyed up the Missouri River from the point where it joins the Mississippi. The travelers had to paddle or pole their boats to keep moving upriver against the strong current.

Activities

1. **EXPLORE IT** Find the Missouri and Columbia rivers. Follow the route on the map. What places or events made the trip difficult? Why?

2. **WRITE ABOUT IT** Choose one of the photographs. Write a journal entry to describe it. Think about the things the Corps of Discovery needed to do to get past this landmark. List the steps.

The War of 1812

1805   1810   1815   1820   1825   1830

1808–1828

VOCABULARY

prosperity
nationalism
foreign policy

Vocabulary Strategy

nation alism

Look for the word **nation** in **nationalism.** Nationalism means devotion to one's nation, or country.

READING SKILL

Cause and Effect As you read, take notes to show the causes and effects of the War of 1812.

CAUSES	EFFECTS

Build on What You Know What do you feel when you hear the national anthem of the United States? In this lesson, you'll find out when and why this song was written.

Trouble with Britain

Main Idea Conflicts with Britain increased in the early 1800s.

When **James Madison** was elected President in 1808, Britain and France were at war. **Thomas Jefferson** had tried to keep the United States neutral during this war. President Madison also wanted the United States to stay neutral. He hoped that Americans could keep trading with both Britain and France. But conflicts between the United States and Britain made them enemies.

At this time, Britain had a powerful navy. Yet British sailors often worked on American ships because the Americans paid them more money. British officers raided American ships at sea to look for these British sailors. Sometimes they captured American sailors instead and forced them to serve in the British navy. This was called impressment.

Impressment About 5,000 American sailors were forced to serve on British ships between 1803 and 1810.

War Hawks

In 1810, a group in Congress began calling for war against Britain. The group named themselves War Hawks because hawks are seen as aggressive birds. The War Hawks were angry about impressment and even angrier about fighting between American Indians and settlers on the frontier. They believed that people in the British colony of Canada were supplying weapons to American Indians.

The United States government had made treaties that promised it would keep settlers off lands where different groups of American Indians lived. These promises were broken again and again.

Tecumseh (tih CUHM suh), a Shawnee chief, took action. He wanted to unite all the American Indian nations west of the Appalachian Mountains.

Tecumseh and his brother, known as the Prophet, believed that if Indian nations acted together, they could keep settlers away. By 1811, American Indians of many nations had joined Tecumseh.

Tecumseh and nearly 1,000 followers lived near the Tippecanoe River in Indiana Territory. The governor of this territory, **William Henry Harrison**, thought Tecumseh and his followers were a threat. Harrison's army and Tecumseh's followers fought at Tippecanoe. After the Battle of Tippecanoe, Tecumseh went to Canada to join his British allies.

REVIEW Why did Tecumseh want American Indian nations to unite?

Battle of Tippecanoe Tecumseh (right) brought American Indians to Tippecanoe. This painting shows the Battle of Tippecanoe.

Saranac River

Plattsburgh

2

Cumberland Bay

1

Battle of Lake Champlain
September 11, 1814

The Battle of Lake Champlain was an important victory for the United States in the War of 1812. It forced British commanders to return to Canada and give up their plans to invade New York.

1 Early in the morning, British ships sail into Cumberland Bay to attack U.S. ships.

2 At the same time, soldiers fight near the village of Plattsburgh. British and U.S. troops fire cannons at each other across the Saranac River.

Fighting the War

Main Idea In 1812, the United States went to war against Britain.

On June 18, 1812, Congress declared war against Britain. The United States hoped to stop impressment of soldiers and keep the British from helping American Indians who fought with settlers. The United States also wanted to drive the British out of Canada.

Most of the early battles of the war took place near Canada. The U.S. Army tried to invade Canada several times in 1812, but it was badly beaten. The British and their American Indian allies captured Detroit, an important city near the Canadian border.

As the war continued, the United States Army began to win more battles. Captain **Oliver Hazard Perry** forced British ships on Lake Erie to surrender. The Americans recaptured Detroit and chased the British into Canada. There they won a battle on the Thames (tehmz) River. Later, Americans won another important victory at the Battle of Lake Champlain.

Tecumseh was killed in the Battle of the Thames, but many American Indian nations continued his fight. In the South, however, several groups of American Indians fought on the side of the Americans against the British and their allies. In battles in Georgia, the Cherokee, Choctaw, Chickasaw, and some Creek Indians all helped the United States during the War of 1812.

Dolley Madison This First Lady, the wife of President Madison, saved George Washington's portrait.

British Invasions

In August 1814, the British attacked Washington, D.C. As the British Army headed toward the White House, First Lady **Dolley Madison** quickly collected important papers to be taken to safety. She didn't have time to pack most of her family's belongings, but she refused to leave one important item behind—a famous painting of **George Washington** that hung in the White House. After she fled, British forces burned the White House and other buildings in Washington, D.C.

Next, the British moved on to Baltimore. British ships fired cannons at Fort McHenry in Baltimore Harbor, but the U.S. Army did not surrender.

Francis Scott Key, a lawyer, watched the battle. The sight of the American flag flying over the fort in the early morning inspired him to write a poem. This poem was later set to music and became "The Star-Spangled Banner," the country's national anthem.

REVIEW What inspired Francis Scott Key to write the poem that became "The Star-Spangled Banner"?

The End of the War

After two years of fighting, neither Britain nor the United States was winning the war. They agreed to end it.

A peace treaty was signed in 1814 in Ghent, Belgium. The Treaty of Ghent did not give either side any new land. The agreement simply returned things to the way they were before the war started. Canada still belonged to Britain.

News of peace took a long time to reach the United States from Europe. Two weeks after the treaty was signed, a large British force attacked New Orleans. **Andrew Jackson** led an army that forced the British to retreat. Although the war was over, Jackson's brave defense of New Orleans made him a national hero.

Changes to the U.S. Flag

1777 Flag This was the first official U.S. flag. The 13 stars and stripes stood for each of the original 13 states.

1795 Flag The 15 stars and stripes on this flag represented all the states at that time, including Vermont and Kentucky.

1818 Flag The Flag Act of 1818 gave the flag 13 stripes and 20 stars, one for each of the 20 states.

1960 Flag This is the current American flag. It has 13 stripes and 50 stars.

A New Sense of Pride

Main Idea After the War of 1812, people were proud of their country.

The time after the War of 1812 was one of peace and prosperity. **Prosperity** is economic success and security. This period was called the Era of Good Feelings. During these ten years, people had a new sense of **nationalism,** which is a devotion to one's country.

Pride in the United States created more interest in the national flag. In 1818, Congress passed a law about how many stripes and stars would be on the flag. After this law passed, flags had 13 stripes representing the 13 original colonies. The law also said that as each new state joined the nation, a star would be added. Today, the flag has 50 stars.

The Monroe Doctrine

After the War of 1812, the United States wanted to keep European countries out of the Western Hemisphere. President **James Monroe**, who was elected in 1816, worried that European countries would invade the Americas. He was especially worried that Spain might try to take over former colonies in the Americas.

In a speech to Congress in 1823, Monroe warned European countries to stay out of North and South America. He said that in return, the United States would not get involved in fights between European countries. This was a new foreign policy. **Foreign policy** is a government's actions toward other nations. This policy became known as the Monroe Doctrine. A doctrine is an official statement of policy. The Monroe Doctrine warned other countries that the United States might act to protect the Western Hemisphere.

New American Authors

Another sign of growing pride was a new interest in writers from the United States. In 1828, **Noah Webster** published the first dictionary of English that was uniquely American. Until then, people used dictionaries with British English spellings and meanings. Webster's dictionary showed how people in the United States spoke and included words found only in American English. Many words came from American Indian languages.

Two authors, **Washington Irving** and **James Fenimore Cooper,** set their stories in the United States instead of in Europe. Irving wrote "The Legend of Sleepy Hollow," "Rip Van Winkle," and other stories. Cooper wrote many novels. One of the most famous was *The Last of the Mohicans.*

REVIEW How did the law passed in 1818 change the appearance of the national flag?

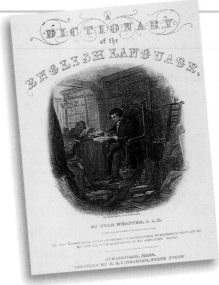

Noah Webster
After about 22 years of research, Webster published this dictionary. It had 70,000 words.

Lesson Summary

- Congress declared war against Britain in June, 1812.
- After the War of 1812, Americans developed a sense of nationalism.
- In the Monroe Doctrine, Monroe warned that the United States might act to protect the Western Hemisphere.

Why It Matters ...

The United States showed it could stand up to Britain and act as a major power after the War of 1812.

Lesson Review

Timeline:
- 1812 **Congress declares war**
- 1814 **British attack Washington, D.C.**
- 1823 **Monroe Doctrine**

(1805 — 1810 — 1815 — 1820 — 1825)

1. **VOCABULARY** Write a paragraph using the word **nationalism** to tell how people showed pride in the United States.

2. **READING SKILL** Why was impressment a **cause** of the War of 1812?

3. **MAIN IDEA: History** Why did the War Hawks want to go to war against Britain?

4. **MAIN IDEA: Culture** How was Webster's dictionary different from British dictionaries?

5. **PEOPLE TO KNOW** Who was **Tecumseh,** and what did he do after the Battle of Tippecanoe?

6. **TIMELINE SKILL** When did the British attack Washington?

7. **CRITICAL THINKING: Analyze** What did Monroe tell Congress in 1823? List the main points of the Monroe Doctrine.

WRITING ACTIVITY Why do you think Dolley Madison wanted to take the portrait of George Washington with her when she fled Washington, D.C.? Write a journal entry she might have written describing the day of the attack.

The National Anthem

Francis Scott Key watches as cannon fire booms in the night sky over Fort McHenry. He is watching from a ship several miles away as the British attack the fort, which is near Baltimore. Key waits for hours to see how the battle will end.

In the early morning, there is a sudden silence. Key looks through his telescope and sees that the American flag still waves over Fort McHenry. He is filled with relief. The United States has not surrendered, and the British have retreated.

Key writes a few lines on the back of a letter to express his feelings of pride. Later he finishes his poem, which he calls "The Defense of Fort McHenry." The poem is printed on September 20, 1814, and people begin singing the first stanza to the tune of an old British song. Both this new song and the American flag itself become known as "The Star-Spangled Banner." In 1931, Key's poem is made the official national anthem of the United States.

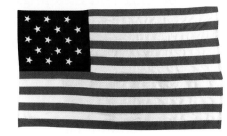

The flag that inspired Francis Scott Key to write his poem was constructed by Mary Young Pickersgill. She made the flag large, to be seen from a distance. It measured 30 feet by 42 feet.

The Star-Spangled Banner

Oh, say can you see, by the dawn's early light,

What so proudly we hailed at the twilight's last gleaming?

Whose broad stripes and bright stars, through the perilous fight,

O'er the ramparts we watched, were so gallantly streaming?

And the rockets' red glare, the bombs bursting in air,

Gave proof through the night that our flag was still there.

O say, does that star-spangled banner yet wave

O'er the land of the free and the home of the brave?

(first stanza of "The Defense of Fort McHenry")

—Francis Scott Key

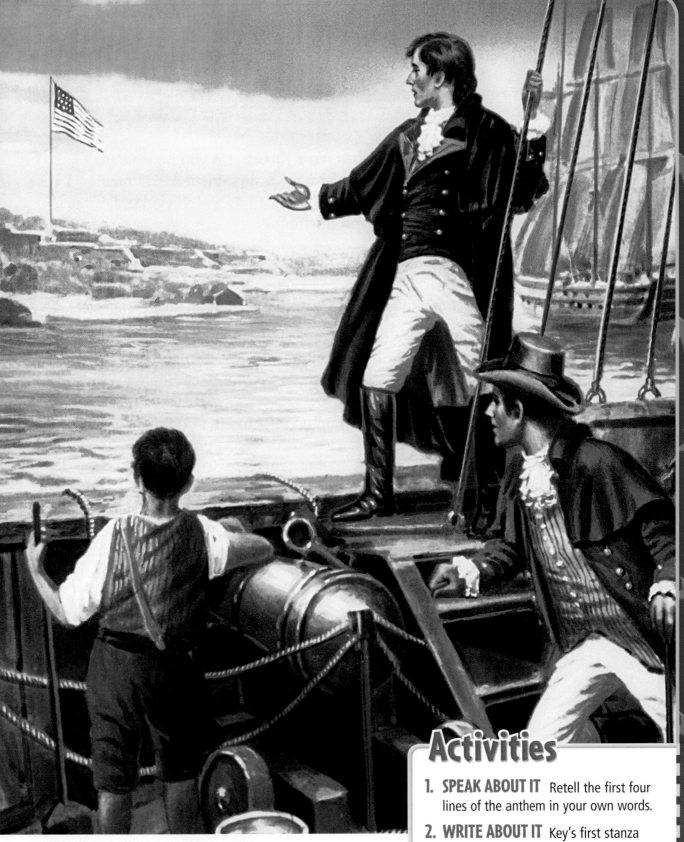

Francis Scott Key gestures toward the American flag. This picture was painted about a hundred years after Key wrote his poem. What feelings do you think the painter was trying to express?

Activities

1. **SPEAK ABOUT IT** Retell the first four lines of the anthem in your own words.

2. **WRITE ABOUT IT** Key's first stanza includes three questions. Write a poem in the form of questions. Describe being relieved, proud, or curious about something.

367

Age of Jackson

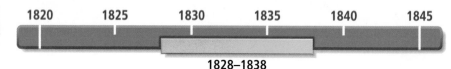

| 1820 | 1825 | 1830 | 1835 | 1840 | 1845 |

1828–1838

VOCABULARY

VOCABULARY

suffrage
campaign
ruling

Vocabulary Strategy

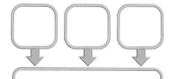

suffrage

Suffrage comes from a word that means to show support. In a democracy, people show support by voting.

READING SKILL

Draw Conclusions Note facts and details about Jackson's actions to help you draw a conclusion about him.

CONCLUSION:

Build on What You Know Do you have a hero, or someone you admire? Many Americans admired **Andrew Jackson** because he was a successful politician who grew up on the frontier.

A New Kind of President

Main Idea Jackson was the first President from the frontier.

The first six people elected President of the United States came from Virginia and Massachusetts. They were all from wealthy families. Andrew Jackson, however, was different.

Jackson grew up on the Carolina frontier. He was poor, but tough and determined. As a young man, Jackson took the Wilderness Trail to Tennessee. In Tennessee, he was a successful lawyer, politician, and business owner. When he became President in 1829, he was the first President to come from a state west of the original thirteen colonies.

After the War of 1812, many people moved to the territories south and west of the original states. When these territories became states, citizens in the new states were guaranteed the right to vote. This right to vote is called **suffrage.**

Jackson's Inauguration
When Jackson was sworn into office, people who admired him traveled to Washington for the ceremony.

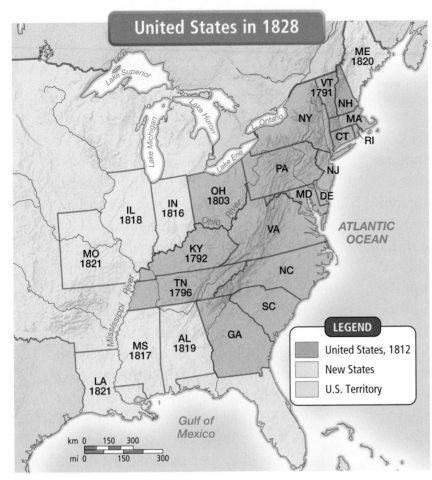

United States in 1828

ME 1820
VT 1791
NH
NY
MA
CT
RI
PA
NJ
OH 1803
MD
DE
IN 1816
IL 1818
Ohio River
VA
MO 1821
KY 1792
NC
TN 1796
SC
MS 1817
AL 1819
GA
LA 1821

Lake Superior
Lake Michigan
Lake Huron
Lake Ontario
Lake Erie
Mississippi River

ATLANTIC OCEAN

Gulf of Mexico

LEGEND
United States, 1812
New States
U.S. Territory

km 0 150 300
mi 0 150 300

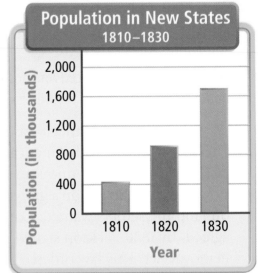

Population in New States 1810–1830

Population (in thousands)

2,000
1,600
1,200
800
400
0

1810 1820 1830
Year

Frontier States Territories became states as more settlers moved west.

SKILL **Reading Graphs** How many people lived in the new states in 1830?

Jackson's Election

Many of these new voters had little money or education. Before this time only white men who owned land or had a certain amount of money could vote. The United States in the 1800s was the only country in the world that gave suffrage to white men who did not own land. Women and most African Americans, however, still could not vote.

In 1828, new voters helped elect Andrew Jackson as President. They liked his campaign message of support for ordinary citizens. A **campaign** is a series of actions taken toward a goal, such as winning a presidential election. Jackson won a huge victory, especially in the new states. People on the frontier were excited to have someone with a background like theirs in the White House.

Jackson and the Bank

President Andrew Jackson took the side of farmers, working people, and frontier settlers. One example of this was his fight against the national bank. The bank had been created while **George Washington** was President. All the government's money was put into the national bank.

Jackson did not like the national bank because poor people could not borrow money from it. He believed that it only helped wealthy people and that it was unfair to those he called "the humble members of society—the farmers, mechanics, and laborers."

In 1833, Jackson ordered the government to take its money out of the national bank and put it in state banks. Three years later the national bank closed.

REVIEW What types of people did Jackson want to help?

Indian Removal Act

Main Idea Jackson forced American Indian nations to move west of the Mississippi.

Settlers moved farther west every year. They often fought with American Indians. Jackson thought that American Indians slowed down the nation's growth by living on land the settlers wanted. Congress agreed. In 1830, Jackson signed the Indian Removal Act. This law ordered all the Indian nations east of the Mississippi River to move west of that river. Families had to leave their homes and businesses behind.

In the Southeast, the United States Army forced Choctaw, Creek, and Chickasaw people to move to present-day Oklahoma. Congress called this area Indian Territory.

Sequoya's Alphabet Sequoya created 85 symbols, one for each syllable in the Cherokee language. Sequoya's alphabet was used for the *Cherokee Phoenix*. This newspaper, first printed in 1828, is still published today.

The Trail of Tears

In Georgia, the Cherokee had added parts of the settlers' culture to their own traditions. Many became farmers. They built roads, schools, and churches. **Sequoya** (sih KWOY uh) invented a writing system for the Cherokee language. The Cherokee published books and a newspaper using this alphabet.

John Ross, a Cherokee chief, led the fight against Indian removal. He went to the Supreme Court, the highest court in the country. The head of the Supreme Court, Chief Justice **John Marshall,** made a ruling. A **ruling** is an official decision. He said that it was against the law to force the Cherokee to move.

President Jackson ignored Marshall's ruling. In 1838, the United States Army forced the Cherokee to make the 1,000-mile trip to Indian Territory. The Cherokee had little to eat. The winter was cold and disease spread quickly. About one-fifth of the Cherokee died along the way. This heartbreaking journey came to be known as the Trail of Tears.

Osceola Fights Back

The United States Army also tried to remove the Seminole from their land in Florida. **Chief Osceola** (AHS ee OH luh) refused to give up his land and convinced many Seminole to join his fight. He and others fought back with surprise attacks. After Chief Osceola was tricked into coming out of hiding to discuss peace, soldiers put him in jail.

Chief Osceola He was a leader in the Seminole Wars in Florida.

Osceola died in prison several months later, but other Seminoles carried on his fight. The struggle of American Indians to keep their homes continued for decades.

REVIEW What did the Cherokee do to fight against removal?

Lesson Summary

By 1828, many small farmers, frontier settlers, and working men had gained suffrage. Their votes helped elect Andrew Jackson. To provide land to frontier settlers, Jackson ordered thousands of American Indians off their land. Their difficult journey west was known as the Trail of Tears.

Why It Matters ...

American Indians were forced to move west, and live in a new environment. Their removal changed the history of people both east and west of the Appalachians.

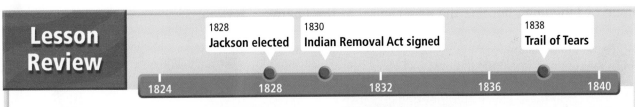

Lesson Review

1828 **Jackson elected**

1830 **Indian Removal Act signed**

1838 **Trail of Tears**

1824   1828   1832   1836   1840

❶ **VOCABULARY** Use the word **suffrage** in a sentence describing who had this right in the early 1800s.

❷ **READING SKILL** Use your notes on Andrew Jackson's actions to **draw** a **conclusion** about his views.

❸ **MAIN IDEA: Government** What new group of voters helped elect Andrew Jackson?

❹ **MAIN IDEA: History** Why were American Indians forced to leave their homelands?

❺ **PEOPLE TO KNOW** Who was **John Marshall**, and what ruling did he make about the Indian Removal Act?

❻ **TIMELINE SKILL** In what year was the Indian Removal Act passed?

❼ **CRITICAL THINKING: Compare and Contrast** How was Andrew Jackson's treatment of frontier settlers different from his treatment of American Indians?

HANDS ON

SPEAKING ACTIVITY Prepare a campaign speech you could act out in support of or against Andrew Jackson for President.

Trail of Tears

The Cherokee had traveled several months when they reached the Mississippi River. Many were sick. Many had died. All were hungry. How their hearts must have ached as they gazed at the ice-clogged waters. No wonder people called the journey "Nunna daul Tsuny," which means "the trail where they cried."

Between 1838 and 1839, about 15,000 Cherokee were forced to leave their homes in the southeastern United States. They traveled more than 800 miles west to what is now the state of Oklahoma, then known as Indian Territory.

The Cherokee were organized into 16 groups. Three groups traveled by steamboat. The rest traveled by foot, horse, and wagon. Their routes are shown on this map.

It took years for the Cherokee to rebuild their lives, but in time, they held elections, built new courthouses and schools, and set up farms. The village of Tahlequah became the new capital of the Cherokee Nation.

LAND ROUTE

MISSOURI

INDIAN TERRITORY

Tahlequah •

ARKANSAS

3

OKLAHOMA

WATER ROUTE

3 Arrival

The last group of Cherokee arrived in the newly created Indian Territory in March 1839. They joined Choctaw, Creek, Chickasaw, and Seminole people who had made similar journeys. They waited under the watchful eyes of U.S. soldiers to find out where they would be allowed to settle.

❶ Forced to Move

In the spring of 1838, thousands of Cherokee were forced to leave their homes. They were held in temporary forts in Tennessee, Alabama, and Georgia. It was hot, and some died before they even left for Oklahoma.

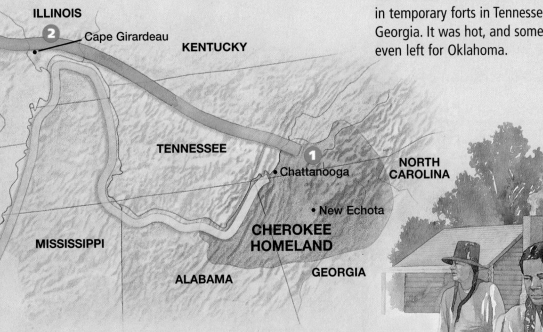

ILLINOIS
❷
Cape Girardeau
KENTUCKY
TENNESSEE
• Chattanooga
❶
NORTH CAROLINA
• New Echota
CHEROKEE HOMELAND
MISSISSIPPI
ALABAMA
GEORGIA

❷ Winter

The first groups of Cherokee reached the Mississippi River in late December. Ice on the river was not solid enough for horses and wagons to cross. The Cherokee camped in the freezing cold for several weeks. Those who survived continued the journey.

Activities

1. **DISCUSS IT** Why do you think the Cherokee call their journey to Indian Territory the Trail of Tears?

2. **WRITE IT** Write a letter that someone in 1838 might have written to President Jackson. Explain why the Indian Removal Act is just or unjust.

Visual Summary

1–4.  Write a description of each item named below.

Wilderness Road

_____
_____
_____
_____

Louisiana Purchase

_____
_____
_____
_____

War of 1812

_____
_____
_____
_____

Trail of Tears

Indian Territory

_____
_____
_____
_____

Facts and Main Ideas

✓ **TEST PREP** Answer each question with information from the chapter.

5. **Geography** Why was the Cumberland Gap a help to pioneers?

6. **History** Who was Chief Logan?

7. **Economics** Why was the Louisiana Purchase an important addition to the United States?

8. **Citizenship** Who wrote "The Star-Spangled Banner" and why?

9. **History** Name one effect of the Indian Removal Act?

Vocabulary

✓ **TEST PREP** Choose the correct word to complete each sentence.

pioneer, p. 345
interpreter, p. 356
foreign policy, p. 364
suffrage, p. 368

10. The Monroe Doctrine said that the _____ of the United States was to stay out of Europe's problems.

11. Daniel Boone was a _____ who led settlers west of the Appalachians.

12. As new states were added to the United States, the settlers were given _____.

13. Sacagawea was sometimes an _____ on the Lewis and Clark expedition.

1769
Boone crosses Appalachians

1803
Louisiana Purchase

1812
War of 1812

1838
Trail of Tears

1760 | 1770 | 1780 | 1790 | 1800 | 1810 | 1820 | 1830 | 1840

Apply Skills

✓ TEST PREP **Study Skill** Read the outline below. Use what you have learned about Andrew Jackson and making an outline to answer each question.

Andrew Jackson
I. Who he was
  A. Grew up poor on the Carolina frontier
  B. Successful lawyer, politician, and business owner
  C.
What he did
  A. Fought against the national bank
  B. Signed the Indian Removal Act

14. Which supporting detail fits best for "C" under the first main idea?

   A. Took the Wilderness Trail to Tennessee

   B. Women and most African Americans were not allowed to vote.

   C. Hero who fought in the War of 1812

   D. Hero who fought in the Revolutionary War

15. What should be placed in front of the second main idea?

   A. A.

   B. B.

   C. I.

   D. II.

Critical Thinking

✓ TEST PREP Write a short paragraph to answer each question.

16. **Cause and Effect** What effect did the movement of pioneers have on American Indians already living on the frontier?

17. **Fact and Opinion** In your opinion, was the War of 1812 worth fighting? Use facts from the chapter to support your opinion.

Timeline

Use the Chapter Summary Timeline above to answer the question.

18. How many years before the Louisiana Purchase did Daniel Boone cross the Appalachian Mountains?

Activities

 Map Activity Make a map showing the route of the Trail of Tears. Label three major landforms or bodies of water on the map.

 Writing Activity Write a description of what pioneers crossing the Appalachian Mountains might have experienced. Describe the weather, the geography, and any challenges they might have faced.

 Technology
Writing Process Tips
Get help with your description at
www.eduplace.com/kids/hmss05/

375

Vocabulary Preview

Technology

e ● **glossary**
e ● **word games**
www.eduplace.com/kids/hmss05/

productivity

New machines increased **productivity.**
Workers produced more goods in a shorter time.
page 379

reform

Both women and men worked for **reform.**
They gave speeches and held meetings to tell
people about ways to improve society.
page 390

Chapter Timeline

1825
Erie Canal opens

1833
National Road completed

1836
Texas wins independence

1825   1830   1835

Reading Strategy

Question Use this strategy as you read the lessons in this chapter.

Quick Tip Stop and ask yourself questions. Do you need to go back and reread?

annexation

People in the independent Republic of Texas voted for **annexation.** Congress also voted to make Texas part of the United States.
page 395

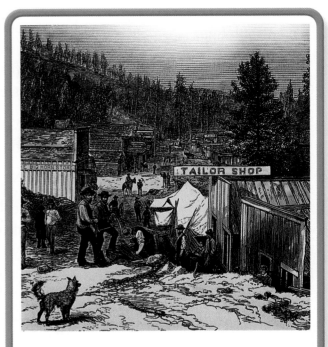

boomtown

During the Gold Rush, people quickly built towns near each new gold mine. These **boomtowns** seemed to spring up overnight.
page 402

1848
Seneca Falls Convention

1840   1845   1850

The Industrial Revolution

1790   1800   1810   1820   1830   1840

1790–1837

Build on What You Know Do you have a chore at home, such as taking out the trash? What if a machine took out the trash twice as fast as you do? During the Industrial Revolution, new machines helped people do things faster.

The Industrial Revolution Begins

Main Idea New inventions brought changes to manufacturing.

In the 1700s, most people were farmers. Cloth, tools, and furniture were made by hand in homes or small shops. By the early 1800s, people began making cloth and other goods in factories. New forms of transportation moved people and goods faster than ever before. These changes in manufacturing and transportation are called the Industrial Revolution.

The Industrial Revolution started in Britain. Inventors created machines for the British textile industry. **Textile** means cloth or fabric. These machines spun cotton into yarn much faster than the old hand-powered spinning wheel, or spinning ginny.

In 1790, a British mechanic named **Samuel Slater** opened the first cotton-spinning mill in the United States. He built machines like the ones he used in Britain. His mill was set on a river in Rhode Island. Water power drove the machines in the mill.

Cotton Before cotton could be spun, the seeds deep inside the cotton (right) had to be removed.

Eli Whitney

New machines turned cotton into yarn very quickly, but getting cotton ready for the mills took a long time. A lot of work went into cleaning the seeds from cotton so it could be spun. In 1793, **Eli Whitney** invented a cotton engine, or cotton gin. Its wire teeth cleaned cotton very quickly.

Cotton was soon the nation's largest export. Cotton production rose from less than 2 million pounds per year in 1790 to 60 million pounds per year in 1805.

A few years after inventing the cotton gin, Whitney was hired to make 10,000 guns for the U.S. government. At that time, guns were made by hand. A part made for one gun would not fit in another gun. To make guns quickly and at less cost, Whitney used interchangeable parts. **Interchangeable parts** are parts made by a machine to be exactly the same in size and shape. Any part could then fit into any gun of the same design. If one part of a gun broke, a new part could replace it.

Cotton Gin With the help of Whitney's invention (below), cotton production increased during the period from 1790–1830.

SKILL **Reading Graphs** How many pounds of cotton were produced in 1830?

Mass Production

Whitney used a system of mass production to make the guns. Mass is another word for "many." **Mass production** means making many products at once. Instead of one person making a complete gun, each worker put together the same section of many guns. Fitting together the same parts over and over was faster than making a single gun from start to finish.

Manufacturers used interchangeable parts and mass production to make many types of tools and machines. The new ways of making goods increased the productivity of the whole United States. **Productivity** is the amount of goods and services produced by workers in a certain amount of time.

REVIEW What did Whitney do to manufacture guns more quickly and cheaply?

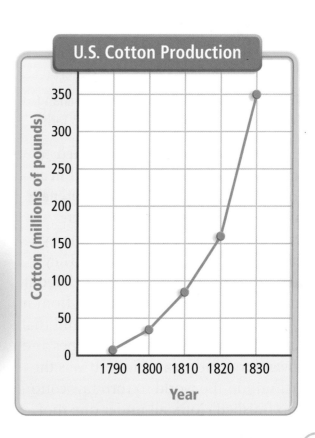

U.S. Cotton Production

Cotton (millions of pounds) / Year

Lowell Factories These workers use machines that prepare cotton for spinning. Labels like the one on the right showed that the cloth was made in the Lowell Mills.

CASSIMERES
EXTRA HEAVY
LOWELL MILLS
FOR MEN'S WEAR.

Machines Bring Change

Main Idea The Industrial Revolution changed the way people worked in mills and on farms.

In 1814, an entrepreneur named **Francis Cabot Lowell** built a mill near Boston, Massachusetts. An **entrepreneur** takes risks to start a business. Entrepreneurs can lose money and time by starting and running a business. They take risks because they are excited about an idea and hope to earn money from it.

Lowell's idea was to build a mill that had both cotton-spinning machines and power looms to weave cloth. It was the first mill in the world to turn raw cotton into finished cloth, all under one roof.

Lowell's factory was a great success. Within five years, the mill was spinning 30 miles of cloth a day. Other cotton and wool factories soon opened. New England became the center of a growing textile industry.

Many people went to work in these factories. Their lives and workdays changed as they found jobs in the mill towns. Before the Industrial Revolution, Americans did different kinds of work on their own farms or in small workshops. In factories built during the Industrial Revolution, people did the same task, over and over, all day long.

Working in the Lowell Mills

The workers in the first textile mills were girls and young women from the New England countryside. They left home to earn money for themselves and their families. Some were as young as 10 years old.

Mill workers lived in boardinghouses. Their workday began at 5:00 A.M. and ended at 7:00 P.M., with only one hour of free time. They still found time to take classes, learn new languages, and write poems, stories, and essays. They published these in a magazine called *The Lowell Offering*.

One mill worker, **Lucy Larcom**, became a well-known writer and teacher. Later in her life, she wrote about what it was like to work in the Lowell mills. She described:

66 **The buzzing and hissing and whizzing of pulleys and rollers and spindles and flyers....** 99

Changes on the Farm

The Industrial Revolution changed life for people who stayed on farms, too. In 1831, **Cyrus McCormick** built a horse-drawn reaper. A reaper has sharp blades that cut grain. Harvesting an acre of wheat by hand took about 20 hours. McCormick's reaper did the same job in less than an hour.

In 1837, **John Deere**, a blacksmith from Illinois, invented the steel plow. This plow could cut through tough soil that would break a wooden plow. Deere's invention made it easier for farmers to plow thick soil on prairies and plains.

REVIEW In what ways did the workday change for many people during the Industrial Revolution?

Cyrus McCormick
He planned, built, and tested his first reaper in just six weeks.

LIGHT DRAFT. SUPERIOR DESIGN.

"OUR FIELD IS THE WORLD."

CLEAN AND RAPID CUTTER.

McCORMICK No. 2 IRON MOWER

McCormick Harvesting Machine Co., Chicago.

ESTABLISHED 1831.

McCormick's Reaper
This advertisement, showing a reaper from 1875, illustrates how the machine helped farmers quickly cut wheat.

SKILL **Reading Visuals**
What does the advertisement say to persuade the reader to buy a McCormick reaper?

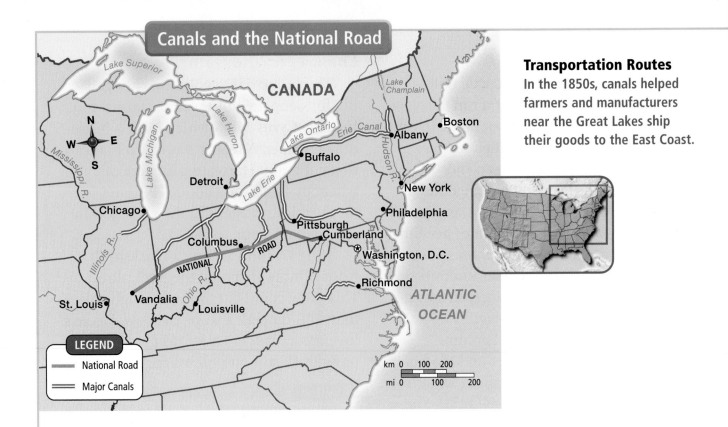

Canals and the National Road

CANADA

Lake Superior
Lake Huron
Lake Michigan
Lake Ontario
Lake Erie
Lake Champlain

Mississippi R.
Illinois R.
Ohio R.

N W E S

Chicago
Detroit
Buffalo
Erie Canal
Albany
Boston
Hudson R.
New York
Philadelphia
Pittsburgh
Cumberland
Columbus
ROAD
NATIONAL
Washington, D.C.
Richmond
St. Louis
Vandalia
Louisville

ATLANTIC OCEAN

LEGEND
National Road
Major Canals

km 0 100 200
mi 0 100 200

Transportation Routes
In the 1850s, canals helped farmers and manufacturers near the Great Lakes ship their goods to the East Coast.

Changes in Transportation

Main Idea People and goods traveled faster in the 1800s.

In the early 1800s, settlers headed west in search of land. At the same time, factories and farms produced more goods to be shipped to distant cities to be sold.

Overland travel was slow, difficult, and expensive. Early roads were narrow dirt paths barely wide enough for a horse and carriage. Rain turned roads to mud. Snow and ice blocked roads in winter.

In 1811, the federal government began building the National Road to connect Ohio with the East. By 1833, the new road stretched from Cumberland, Maryland, to Columbus, Ohio. It was wide and paved with flat stones. The National Road, which later went as far as Vandalia, Illinois, became the most heavily traveled road in the United States. Towns and businesses, such as blacksmith shops and inns, were built along the roadsides.

Steamboats and Canals

On August 9, 1807, Americans watched a strange-looking boat travel up the Hudson River. **Robert Fulton's** new steam-powered boat was making its first trip from New York City to Albany, New York, in a record 32 hours. The boat's paddlewheel powered it against the flow of water. Until then, boats needed oars, wind, or water currents to move. No one had ever seen a steamboat. Within a few years, however, steamboats were widely used on rivers.

Because roads were so poor at this time, rivers and canals were the fastest and cheapest ways to ship goods. Canals are waterways built for travel and shipping. In 1825, the Erie Canal opened. This canal connected the Hudson River to Lake Erie. More canals were built throughout the East. By 1840, more than 3,000 miles of canals crossed the eastern part of the nation.

Railroads

Wagons on new roads, steamboats on rivers, and barges on canals all changed transportation. But the steam locomotive created even greater changes. Trains pulled by steam locomotives were fast. They could go up and down hills effortlessly. A trip from New York City to Albany, New York, took 32 hours by steamboat. It took only 10 hours by train.

By 1850, the nation had 9,000 miles of railroad track. New tracks were added every day. Soon factories and farmers could ship their goods to almost any city or town in the country by train.

REVIEW Why were steam locomotives better than other forms of transportation?

Lesson Summary

- The Industrial Revolution came to the United States in the late 1700s.

- New inventions increased productivity and changed the way people worked in factories and on farms.

- New roads, canals, steamboats, and steam locomotives made travel and shipping cheaper and faster.

Why It Matters ...

The Industrial Revolution changed the way people worked and the goods that were produced in the United States.

Fulton's Steamboat

Lesson Review

1793	1814	1825
Whitney invents cotton gin	**Lowell builds mill**	**Erie Canal opened**

1790   1800   1810   1820   1830

❶ **VOCABULARY** Which vocabulary word is a synonym, or has the same meaning, as *cloth*?

    productivity   textile   entrepreneur

❷ **READING SKILL** Using your chart, write a paragraph about how one **problem** in the early 1800s was solved by new machines.

❸ **MAIN IDEA: Economics** How did mass production increase productivity?

❹ **MAIN IDEA: History** In what way was Fulton's steamboat different from other boats?

❺ **PEOPLE TO KNOW** Who was **Eli Whitney,** and how did his invention increase cotton production?

❻ **TIMELINE SKILL** How many years after the invention of the cotton gin did Lowell build his mill?

❼ **CRITICAL THINKING: Evaluate** Why is the Industrial Revolution a good name for the period of 1790 to 1840?

HANDS ON

DRAMA ACTIVITY With a partner, act out a scene between two cotton mill workers discussing mass production.

Inside a Cotton Mill

Bales of Cotton
Workers rip open huge bales of cotton weighing about 500 pounds. The raw cotton is run through machines that clean and sort the cotton fibers.

How does cotton become cloth?

The process involves many steps, including cleaning, spinning, and weaving the cotton. The first cotton mills only spun cotton into yarn. Weavers wove yarn into cloth in homes or small shops. When Francis Cabot Lowell put power looms in his Massachusetts textile factory, he made it possible to do all of the steps of making cloth in one building.

The cloth-making process began on the bottom floor of the mill. After the raw cotton was cleaned, cotton fibers were carded, or combed into loose ropes. These ropes were spun into thread on the second floor of the mill. Next, the thread was prepared for weaving. This process, called warping, took place on the third floor. Finally, the thread was woven into finished cloth. Each of these steps required a different machine.

The mill's machines used water power. Lowell's company built canals along the Merrimack River. The canals carried rushing water to the mills where it turned waterwheels. The waterwheels were attached to belts that powered the machines in the factory.

Spinning

Loose strings of cotton are spun into yarn or thread. The thread is wound onto wooden sticks called bobbins.

Weaving

Looms turn yarn into cloth by weaving thousands of threads under and over each other.

Activities

1. **TALK ABOUT IT** Look at the pictures of workers and machines. Which step do you think took the most time? Why?

2. **DESCRIBE IT** Look at the picture and read the captions. Write the steps for making cloth in a numbered list. Use your list to write a paragraph describing how cloth is made.

385

Study Skills

Find and Evaluate Sources

▶ **VOCABULARY**
research

In Lesson 1, you read about the Industrial Revolution. To learn more about that time period, you can do research. Research is the search for facts. These steps will help you to use encyclopedias and websites to research a topic.

Learn the Skill

Step 1: Form a question about what you want to research.

Step 2: Identify a key word or phrase in your question. Key words are the most important words.

- **Encyclopedias** — Look in the volume that includes the first letter of your key word. If there is no information on that topic, look for a list of related topics or try another key word.

- **The Internet** — Use a search engine. When you type your key word into a search engine, it will show you a list of websites related to the word. If those websites aren't helpful, try another key word or phrase.

Step 3: Evaluate your sources to see if they are reliable and accurate. Use these questions to evaluate them:

- What is the purpose of the source? Is it designed to teach, to entertain, or to sell?

- Is the source written by an expert or an average person?

- Is the information correct? Check it in another source.

Step 4: Make sure the sources answer your original question. If they do not, look for new sources. If they do, take notes.

Practice the Skill

Think of a question about the Industrial Revolution that you would like to research. Find an encyclopedia article and a website that provide the information you want. Then answer the questions.

1 What related articles listed after the encyclopedia entry might also be helpful?

2 What information about the author and the website lead you to believe that they are reliable?

3 How are the two articles similar? How are they different?

Apply the Skill

Using the two sources you found, write a paragraph that answers your research question about the Industrial Revolution.

Immigrants and Reformers

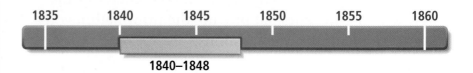
VOCABULARY

famine
reform
temperance
injustice

Vocabulary Strategy

re**form**

The prefix **re-** in **reform** means again. Reform forms something again, or changes it. People who worked for reform wanted to change society.

READING SKILL

Compare and Contrast
Chart the similarities and differences between German and Irish immigrants.

GERMAN   IRISH

Build on What You Know You may have celebrated St. Patrick's Day by wearing green. Irish immigrants brought this holiday to the United States.

German and Irish Immigrants

Main Idea Millions of German and Irish immigrants came to the United States in the mid-1800s.

People had been moving to North America from European countries since the 1500s. They were immigrants, that is, people who move to another country to live. Between 1840 and 1860, the numbers of immigrants rose sharply. About four million Europeans came to the United States during this time. Almost half of these immigrants were Irish. About one-third were German. The rest came from other parts of Europe.

European Immigration
1840–1860

Other European Countries 24%

Germany 34%

Ireland 42%

SKILL **Reading Graphs**
What percentage of immigrants coming to the United States between 1840 and 1860 were German?

Why They Came

Irish and German people learned about what to expect in the United States from relatives who lived there. They were told of the land and job opportunities that could be found across the Atlantic Ocean.

Thousands of Germans left Europe because of war and crop failures. When they arrived in the United States, many Germans settled in the Midwest where land was plentiful. Those who had the money, education, and skills bought land and started farms. Some found work in midwestern cities such as Chicago, St. Louis, and Milwaukee.

The Irish Potato Famine caused many Irish people to leave their country. **Famine** is a widespread shortage of food. Potatoes were the main source of food for the poor in Ireland. When a disease destroyed Ireland's potato crop in 1846, more than a million Irish people died.

Irish Immigration Immigrants wait to board ships to the United States. The city names on the signs show where these immigrants are going.

Finding Work

Over the next 10 years, about 1.5 million people left Ireland and came to the United States. When they arrived, most didn't have enough money to buy land or even to leave the port cities in which they landed. Irish men and women settled in the cities of the Northeast to work in factories, as household servants, or as builders of canals and railroads.

Some people disliked immigrants because their customs seemed unusual. Many immigrants worked for very little money because they needed jobs. People in cities often thought immigrants were taking jobs away from them.

Immigrants were not the only people who wanted jobs. Blacksmiths, weavers, and other craftspeople were losing work. Goods they had made by hand, such as tools and cloth, were now produced at lower cost in factories. Rural people left farms and workshops to find jobs in cities.

REVIEW Why did Irish immigrants usually stay in northeastern cities, while most Germans moved to the Midwest?

389

Making a Better Society

Main Idea In the 1800s, people tried to improve society by joining reform movements.

Beginning in the 1820s, a rise in religious feeling spread throughout the United States. Thousands of people joined Christian churches. This widespread religious movement was called the Second Great Awakening.

During the Second Great Awakening, many people were inspired to change society. Society is all the people living in the same country.

People worked to improve society through reform. **Reform** is an action that makes something better. Several important reform movements came about at this time, including the antislavery and temperance movements. **Temperance** means controlling or cutting back on the drinking of alcohol.

Seneca Falls Convention

Religion wasn't the only cause of reform movements. Many women who worked for reform, especially in the antislavery movement, realized they also faced injustice. **Injustice** means unfair treatment that abuses a person's rights. For example, women were not allowed to speak to an audience that included men. They had to be silent in public meetings.

Women could not vote either. Only a small number of low-paying jobs were available to women. In most states, a married woman could not own property or keep the money she earned. Everything she had belonged to her husband.

Courageous women spoke out against this injustice, but few people listened. Then, in 1848, a group of women held a convention in Seneca Falls, New York, to discuss their rights. Nearly 300 people attended this meeting. The convention marked the beginning of the women's rights movement.

Elizabeth Cady Stanton was the leader of the Seneca Falls Convention. Drawing on the words of the Declaration of Independence, which says that "all men are created equal," Stanton said,

66 all men and women are created equal. 99

Many excited discussions followed her bold speech.

Seneca Falls In the 1800s, reformers held conventions to gather support. Here, Elizabeth Cady Stanton addresses the crowd at the Seneca Falls Convention and calls for rights for women.

Susan B. Anthony joined Stanton as a movement leader. Anthony traveled across the country, giving powerful speeches and working to change laws.

Many felt that a woman's role should not change. Newspapers published attacks against Stanton, Anthony, and others in the women's rights movement. The attacks did not stop women from joining the movement.

REVIEW Why did women reformers decide to start a movement to protect their own rights?

Susan B. Anthony
She and Elizabeth Cady Stanton founded several organizations that fought for women's rights.

Lesson Summary

Millions of German and Irish immigrants came to America in the mid-1800s. Cities and jobs changed as people moved to cities from farms and other countries in search of work. During the Second Great Awakening, people worked for important reform movements, including temperance, antislavery, and women's rights. Women demanded recognition of their rights at the Seneca Falls Convention of 1848.

Why It Matters ...

In the 1800s, women and other reformers began working for change in growing numbers. They led the way for others to work to improve society.

Lesson Review		1846 Irish Potato Famine		1848 Seneca Falls Convention
	1845	1846	1847	1848

❶ **VOCABULARY** Explain why people joined **reform** movements. Use the word **injustice** in your answer.

❷ **READING SKILL** Use your chart to write a paragraph on one **similarity** and one **difference** between the Irish and German immigrants.

❸ **MAIN IDEA: History** Why did the Irish Potato Famine cause Irish people to leave their country?

❹ **MAIN IDEA: Culture** What was the Second Great Awakening?

❺ **PEOPLE TO KNOW** Why did **Elizabeth Cady Stanton** and **Susan B. Anthony** work for women's rights?

❻ **TIMELINE SKILL** In what year was Ireland's potato crop destroyed?

❼ **CRITICAL THINKING: Decision Making** For someone living in Ireland in the 1840s what were the costs and benefits of deciding to move to the United States?

✏️ **WRITING ACTIVITY** Write a newspaper headline and a brief article about the Seneca Falls Convention. Tell *Who?, What?, Where?, When?,* and *Why?*

The Reform Movements

"We'll have our rights … and you can't stop us from them." Sojourner Truth spoke those forceful words at a women's rights convention in 1853. Some people disagreed with Truth, an African American woman. Others nodded their heads in agreement as she spoke.

Sojourner Truth was a reformer in the mid-1800s. Reformers held conventions all over the United States so that they could meet others who shared their views and work together to meet their goals.

The antislavery movement was one of the first important reform movements. It led to many others. Many reformers took part in several movements. For example, antislavery leader Frederick Douglass also attended women's rights conventions. Courageous men and women encouraged one another to fight the injustices of their times.

Change came slowly. People fought for these causes for decades, and women did not win the right to vote in national elections until 1920, more than 70 years after Elizabeth Cady Stanton and others demanded suffrage.

Education

Old buildings, short school years, and a lack of teacher training caused problems in public schools in the early 1800s.

Women's Rights

Women worked for recognition of their right to vote, own property, and earn money.

Mental Health

Until the 1840s, mentally ill people were locked up in jails. Reform leaders worked to improve conditions for the mentally ill.

Temperance

People who drank too much alcohol caused problems in their families and workplaces. Temperance workers wanted to make selling alcohol illegal.

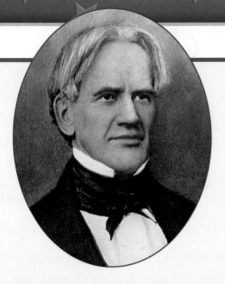

Horace Mann
He led efforts to provide textbooks, increase pay and training for teachers, and build schoolhouses. Mann also worked in the temperance and mental health movements.

Elizabeth Cady Stanton and Susan B. Anthony
After they met in 1851, they worked together to improve women's rights for the rest of their lives. While Anthony traveled and gave speeches, Stanton stayed at home with her family and organized their campaigns.

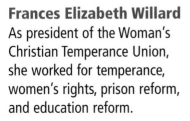

Dorothea Dix
She led a movement to help mentally ill people. Dix wrote state leaders to say mentally ill people should not be punished and put in jail, and she founded hospitals for their care.

Frances Elizabeth Willard
As president of the Woman's Christian Temperance Union, she worked for temperance, women's rights, prison reform, and education reform.

Activities

1. **THINK ABOUT IT** How did reform leaders show good citizenship?

2. **CHART IT** Research one of the people described. Make a chart or timeline of major events or accomplishments in the life of that person.

Texas and the Mexican War

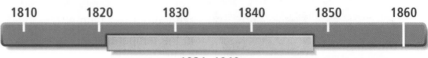

1810   1820   1830   1840   1850   1860

1821–1848

Build on What You Know You know that American colonists fought for independence from Britain during the American Revolution. When Texas was part of Mexico, Texans also fought a war for independence.

The Texas Revolution

Main Idea Americans and Mexicans in Texas fought for independence from the Mexican government.

In 1821, the first settlers from the United States arrived in Texas in search of inexpensive land. Texas was then a part of Mexico. The leader of these settlers was **Stephen Austin.** Within ten years, there were more Americans than Mexicans in Texas. Mexico passed laws to stop settlers from moving to Texas, but they continued to come.

These new settlers did not always obey Mexican laws. For example, Texas settlers brought slaves with them from the United States even though slavery was illegal in Mexico. Because of differences over slavery and other issues, the settlers wanted to break away from Mexico.

Stephen Austin Called the "Father of Texas," Austin set up the first American colony in Texas.

The Fighting Begins

Many Tejanos (teh HAHN ohs), as the Mexicans who lived in Texas were called, also wanted to break away from Mexico. They did not like laws made by **Antonio López de Santa Anna,** Mexico's President. Tejanos and Texans rebelled against Mexico to win independence.

In early 1836, Santa Anna led a large army to San Antonio to stop this rebellion. His goal was to capture the Alamo, an old mission that was used as a military fort. Fewer than 200 American Texans and Tejanos defended the fort. During the Battle of the Alamo, most of them were killed.

Meanwhile, Texan leaders voted to officially declare independence from Mexico and form the Republic of Texas. They chose **Sam Houston** to lead their army. He was an experienced soldier who had fought alongside **Andrew Jackson** in the War of 1812.

Houston led a surprise attack on Santa Anna's army at San Jacinto (sahn hah SEEN toh). At that battle, Texans shouted

66 Remember the Alamo! 99

as they defeated Mexican troops and captured Santa Anna. To gain his freedom, Santa Anna agreed to give Texas its independence.

The Republic Becomes a State

The Republic of Texas held its first election in September 1836. Texans elected Sam Houston as their president. They made slavery legal, and they voted to join the United States. Texans had not wanted to be part of Mexico, but they were in favor of annexation by the United States. **Annexation** is the act of joining two countries or pieces of land together.

Martin Van Buren, the U.S. President, was against annexation. He feared it would lead to war with Mexico because Mexico wanted Texas back. He also did not want to add a new state that allowed slavery. Many Americans were against slavery.

Supporters of annexation argued that it was the nation's destiny to expand west. They believed the United States should spread across the entire North American continent, from the Atlantic Ocean to the Pacific Ocean. This belief is called **manifest destiny.** Manifest means obvious, and destiny is what will happen in the future. People who supported manifest destiny thought that Texas should become part of the United States. In 1845, when **James Polk** became President, Congress voted to annex Texas.

REVIEW Why didn't President Van Buren want to annex Texas?

The Alamo
This former mission is where the Battle of the Alamo took place. It still stands in San Antonio, Texas.

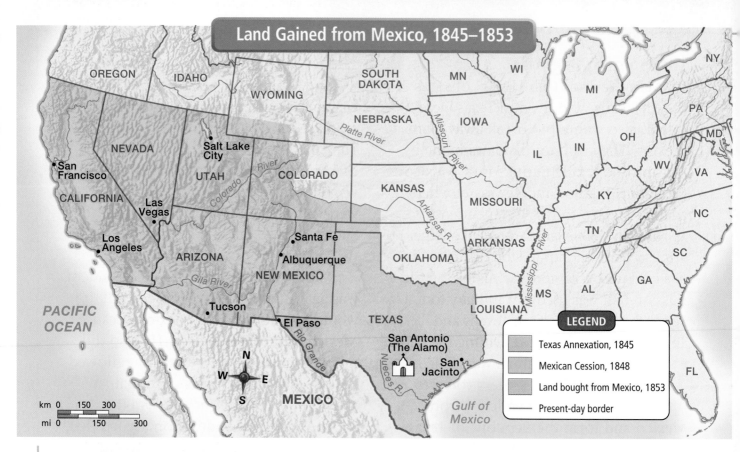

Land Gained from Mexico, 1845–1853

OREGON
IDAHO
WYOMING
SOUTH DAKOTA
MN
WI
MI
NY
PA
NEBRASKA
IOWA
OH
MD
NEVADA
Salt Lake City
UTAH
COLORADO
IL
IN
WV
VA
San Francisco
Colorado River
KANSAS
MISSOURI
KY
NC
CALIFORNIA
Las Vegas
Arkansas R.
ARKANSAS
TN
SC
Los Angeles
ARIZONA
Santa Fe
Albuquerque
NEW MEXICO
OKLAHOMA
MS
AL
GA
PACIFIC OCEAN
Tucson
Gila River
El Paso
TEXAS
LOUISIANA
FL
Rio Grande
San Antonio (The Alamo)
San Jacinto
Nueces R.
MEXICO
Gulf of Mexico
Platte River
Missouri River
Mississippi River

LEGEND
Texas Annexation, 1845
Mexican Cession, 1848
Land bought from Mexico, 1853
Present-day border

km 0 150 300
mi 0 150 300

A Growing Nation The United States gained present-day California, Nevada, Utah, and parts of Colorado, Arizona, New Mexico, and Wyoming after the Mexican War.

SKILL **Reading Maps** Which river forms the border between Mexico and Texas?

War with Mexico

Main Idea After Texas became a state, the United States went to war with Mexico.

When Texas joined the United States, Mexico wanted the border between Texas and Mexico to be at the Nueces (NWEH sehs) River. President Polk wanted the boundary to be the Rio Grande (REE oh GRAHN deh), a river that lay 150 miles south of the Nueces. The Rio Grande boundary would give the United States more land. The Mexican government would not agree to this border. Polk sent soldiers led by General **Zachary Taylor** into Texas and asked Congress to declare war with Mexico. Congress declared war on May 13, 1846.

The Mexican War was fought on three fronts. A **front** is where fighting takes place in a war. The first front was in northern Mexico. The second was in New Mexico where American soldiers captured Santa Fe and then headed west to help the U.S. Navy take control of California. The third front was in southern Mexico. U.S. soldiers invaded Mexico by sea and marched inland to capture Mexico City in September 1847.

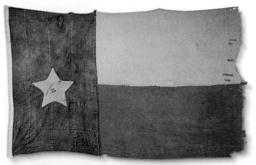

Lone Star State The Republic of Texas chose this flag in 1839.

The Treaty of Guadalupe Hidalgo

After the U.S. Army captured Mexico City, Mexico's leaders agreed to discuss a peace treaty. In 1848, the United States and Mexico signed the Treaty of Guadalupe Hidalgo (gwah dah LOO peh ee DAHL goh). Mexico agreed to accept the annexation of Texas and the Rio Grande as the border between Texas and Mexico. Mexico was also forced to turn over a large area of land called the Mexican Cession. A **cession** is something that is given up.

The United States paid Mexico $15 million for the cession. Mexicans living on this land were allowed to become citizens of the United States. Laws protected them from losing their property, but these laws were often ignored. Many new American citizens lost their land.

REVIEW What did Mexico agree to under the Treaty of Guadalupe Hidalgo?

Lesson Summary

1820s	United States settlers come to Texas

1836	Texas war for independence

1845	Texas annexed by United States

1846	United States goes to war with Mexico

Why It Matters ...

Texas, California, and nearly all of the present-day American Southwest became part of the United States after the Mexican War.

Lesson Review

1836
Battle of the Alamo

1845
Texas annexed

1848
Mexican Cession

1836 — 1840 — 1844 — 1848

1 VOCABULARY Match each vocabulary word with its meaning:

cession   annexation   front

(a) the act of joining land; (b) something that is given up; (c) where fighting takes place in a war

2 READING SKILL What happened at the Battle of San Jacinto? Use **details** from the lesson in your answer.

3 MAIN IDEA: History Why was slavery a cause of conflict between American settlers and the Mexican government?

4 MAIN IDEA: Geography Why did the United States declare war against Mexico?

5 PEOPLE TO KNOW Who was **Sam Houston,** and which two positions did he hold in Texas?

6 TIMELINE SKILL When did the Mexican Cession happen?

7 CRITICAL THINKING: Infer Why do you think Texas wanted to be annexed by the United States? Explain your answer.

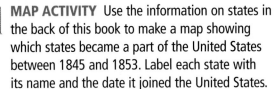

HANDS ON

MAP ACTIVITY Use the information on states in the back of this book to make a map showing which states became a part of the United States between 1845 and 1853. Label each state with its name and the date it joined the United States.

AT THE ALAMO

Who took part in the fierce 13-day attack on the Alamo? The painting shows the Mexican leader, Santa Anna, and his troops attacking the mission in 1836. Nearly all those who defended the Alamo lost their lives, including Davy Crockett, a famous pioneer. Two survivors who saw the fight were Susanna Wilkerson Dickinson and Juan Seguin.

Davy Crockett 1786–1836

A well-known hunter and trapper, Davy Crockett was the subject of many tall tales. One writer said Crockett could "run faster, jump higher, squat lower, dive deeper, stay under longer, and come out drier, than any man in the whole country." He was elected to Congress, where he voted against President Andrew Jackson's Indian Removal Act.

Crockett went to Texas to help his friend Sam Houston fight for independence from Mexico. Crockett hoped to become a political leader in the independent Texas. He lost his life at the Battle of the Alamo, but his courage in the face of death inspired others.

Susanna Wilkerson Dickinson   1814–1883

Susanna Dickinson lived at the Alamo. Her husband, a soldier, was killed in the battle, but she and her baby survived. Mexican soldiers found them, and Santa Anna gave her money and a blanket for her journey home. He also ordered her to deliver a letter to Sam Houston. Santa Anna wanted Dickinson to tell about the defeat of the Texans at the Alamo. He hoped the story would terrify those who were fighting for Texas independence. It didn't. Six weeks later, the Texans defeated Santa Anna.

Juan Seguin   1806–1890

Juan Seguin was a Mexican Texan, or Tejano, from a wealthy family in San Antonio. As an army captain in the Texas revolution, Seguin helped force Santa Anna's troops out of San Antonio in 1835. The next year he joined the troops defending the Alamo. When Santa Anna attacked, Seguin was told to run from the fort and get help. That order probably saved his life. He fought against Santa Anna again at the battle of San Jacinto.

Later, when Texas became independent, Seguin served in the state senate. As a senator, he worked to have the laws of the new republic printed in Spanish. From 1841 to 1842, Seguin was the mayor of San Antonio.

Activities

1. **TALK ABOUT IT** Which of these people could tell the best story of the battle of the Alamo? Why do you think so?

2. **PRESENT IT** Write a speech that someone might give at a ceremony to present an Award for Courage to one of these three people.

 Technology Visit Education Place for more biographies of people in this unit. www.eduplace.com/kids/hmss05/

Moving West

Build on What You Know What made you choose the last book you read? Maybe you heard about it from a friend. Settlers in the 1840s heard exciting things about the West and decided to move there.

Trails West

Main Idea Pioneers made difficult journeys to settle in the West.

In 1824, Crow Indians showed a trapper a way through the Rocky Mountains that was wide enough for wagons. The route was called the South Pass. By the end of the 1850s, thousands of people had traveled through the South Pass on a route known as the Oregon Trail.

The Oregon Trail was about 2,000 miles long. It started in Missouri and stretched west across the Rocky Mountains to present-day Oregon. In some places, the trail was wide and open. When it crossed rivers and mountains, the path became very narrow.

Marcus and **Narcissa Whitman** were two of the first pioneers to travel the Oregon Trail. They were missionaries who settled in eastern Oregon in 1836. They wanted to teach American Indians about Christianity. The Whitman mission became a place where travelers could rest.

John Frémont explored parts of the West and helped make maps of the Oregon Trail. He wrote reports describing the beauty of the land. People on the Oregon Trail used Frémont's maps and reports as guides.

Narcissa Whitman She was the first American woman to travel through the South Pass.

Traveling West Settlers traveled in wagon trains for safety and to keep each other company on the long trip.

Wagon Trains

The first large group of about 1,000 people set out on the Oregon Trail in 1843. They came from Ohio, Indiana, Illinois, Kentucky, and Tennessee. They were looking for good, inexpensive land.

Pioneers on the Oregon Trail traveled by wagon train. A **wagon train** was a line of covered wagons that moved together. Oxen, mules, or horses pulled each wagon.

Travelers on the Oregon Trail faced injuries, diseases, and bad weather. Lack of food and water were problems, too. One woman described the trail in her journal:

> 66 **Not a drop of water, nor a spear of grass to be seen, nothing but barren hills, bare and broken rock, sand and dust.** 99

Despite the hardships, many people settled in Oregon.

President **James Polk** believed in manifest destiny. He wanted Oregon to belong to the United States. At the time, Oregon was claimed by both the United States and Britain. In 1846, Polk signed a treaty with Britain to set the border between the western United States and Canada. The land south of this border became the Oregon Territory in 1848.

Pioneers also took other trails to the West. People who traveled on the Mormon Trail were members of the Church of Jesus Christ of Latter-Day Saints. Members of this church, which was founded in 1830 in New York, were called Mormons.

Some people opposed the Mormons' teachings and would not allow them to practice their religion. In 1847, Mormon leader **Brigham Young** took his people west. They settled in present-day Utah.

REVIEW Why did the first large group of people set out on the Oregon Trail?

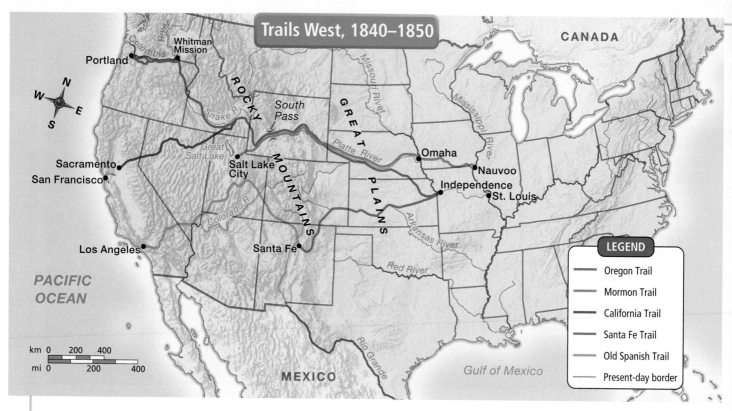

Trails West, 1840–1850

Whitman Mission

Portland

ROCKY MOUNTAINS

South Pass

GREAT PLAINS

Snake R.

Great Salt Lake

Sacramento

San Francisco

Salt Lake City

Missouri River

Mississippi River

Platte River

Omaha

Nauvoo

Independence

St. Louis

CANADA

Colorado R.

Los Angeles

Santa Fe

Arkansas River

Red River

PACIFIC OCEAN

Rio Grande

MEXICO

Gulf of Mexico

km 0 200 400
mi 0 200 400

LEGEND
— Oregon Trail
— Mormon Trail
— California Trail
— Santa Fe Trail
— Old Spanish Trail
— Present-day border

Overland Trails This map shows the trails most settlers traveled to get to the West. The trails led pioneers along rivers and through mountain passes.

SKILL **Reading Maps** Which trail ends in Sacramento?

The California Gold Rush

Main Idea Thousands rushed to California to dig for gold in the mid-1800s.

Before the 1700s, California Indians lived in villages where they hunted, gathered plants, and fished. When California became part of New Spain, many American Indians were forced to live and work on Spanish missions.

When Mexico gained independence in 1821, California became part of it. Californios, as Mexican citizens in California were called, built large ranches on old mission lands. American Indians were forced to work on the ranches. In 1848, when California joined the United States, Californios could become U.S. citizens. Very little changed for the American Indians living there.

That same year, gold was discovered in California. Thousands of people from the United States, Mexico, China, Europe, and South America rushed to California to dig for gold. These people became known as forty-niners. A **forty-niner** was a miner who went to California around 1849.

During the California Gold Rush, more than 250,000 people poured into California. A **gold rush** takes place when many people hurry to the same area to look for gold. Boomtowns sprang up near the gold mines. A **boomtown** is a town whose population booms, or grows very quickly. Merchants and traders in boomtowns sold food and clothing to the miners. People in boomtowns published newspapers and opened banks and inns. Lawyers found work settling arguments.

Forty-Niners Miners dug for gold with picks and shovels.

After the Gold Rush

The California Gold Rush lasted only about five years. Though a few miners found gold, most did not. Some forty-niners went back home, but thousands stayed and settled in California.

The gold rush changed California. Miners and farmers killed California Indians and took over their land. Newcomers also forced many Californio property owners off their land.

Cities such as San Francisco grew. By 1850, only two years after becoming a U.S. territory, California had enough people to become a state. The new state included American Indians and people from Mexico, China, South America, Europe, and other parts of the United States.

REVIEW Who lived in the boomtowns around the gold mines?

Lesson Summary

- Missionaries, farmers, and other settlers traveled west in wagon trains.
- The discovery of gold in 1848 brought thousands of people to California.
- Growth in California led to conflicts with American Indians and Californios.

Why It Matters...

In their search for land, religious freedom, and gold, pioneers started new towns in many present-day western states.

Lesson Review

1843	1847	1848
First wagon train to Oregon	Mormons arrived in Utah	Gold discovered in California

1840 1842 1844 1846 1848 1850 1852

1 **VOCABULARY** Choose the vocabulary word that correctly completes the sentence below.

boomtowns   forty-niners   wagon trains

In 1849, _____ rushed to California for gold.

2 **READING SKILL** Choose one reason why settlers moved west from your chart, and write a summary of what **effect** these settlers had on the country.

3 **MAIN IDEA: History** Why did the Whitmans settle in eastern Oregon?

4 **MAIN IDEA: History** List two changes that took place in California after the gold rush ended.

5 **PEOPLE TO KNOW** Who was **John Frémont**, and how did he help settlers travel west?

6 **TIMELINE SKILL** How many years after the first group of settlers traveled to Oregon did the Mormons arrive in Utah?

7 **CRITICAL THINKING: Evaluate** What economic reason would a banker, innkeeper, or shopkeeper have for moving to a California boomtown during the gold rush?

WRITING ACTIVITY Write a journal entry that a person traveling in a wagon train might have written. Describe the hardships he or she might have faced.

Wagons West!

There wasn't much room in a covered wagon for passengers. People packed as many belongings as they could for their new homes. They brought quilts and bedding, tools, lanterns, and staple foods—flour, sugar, salt, dried beef, rice, and coffee, for example. Water was stored in large wooden barrels, which were refilled along the way.

Wagons were so crammed with supplies that pioneers and their children might have to walk alongside or behind their wagons. In the photograph, the people are walking the Mormon Trail the way their pioneer ancestors did. They might be singing a pioneer song popular in the 1850s:

" *For some must push, and some must pull*
As we go marching up the hill!
So merrily on our way we go,
Until we reach the Valley, O! "

①
Household Goods

②
Treasures

① Household Goods
Everyday items such as candles, scissors, and medicines were brought along for emergencies.

② Treasures
Dishes, books, games, and toys were reminders of home. If they made the wagon too heavy, they had to be left behind.

③ Pioneer Kitchens
When the wagons stopped for meals, pioneers built a cooking fire and unpacked the kettle, skillet, and other wares for making food.

④ Tools
Wagon repairs were often needed, and pioneers also needed tools for building their new homes and barns.

④ **Tools**

③ **Pioneer Kitchens**

Activities

1. **EXPLORE IT** Look at the items in the painting. What else would people need on a long journey across the country?

2. **WRITE A SCHEDULE** Think about a 24-hour period on a wagon train. What would people do? How many times would they pack and unpack? Write a schedule for a typical day on the trail.

Visual Summary

1.–4.  Write a description of each event named below.

Erie Canal, 1825

_____
_____
_____
_____

Seneca Falls, 1848

_____
_____
_____
_____

Treaty of Guadalupe, 1848

_____
_____
_____
_____

Gold Rush, 1849

_____
_____
_____
_____

Facts and Main Ideas

✓ **TEST PREP** Answer each question with information from the chapter.

5. **Economics** What was the effect of interchangeable parts on the production of guns and other products?

6. **History** Why did some U. S. citizens feel that immigrants might take away their jobs?

7. **History** Why did settlers in Texas want independence from Mexico?

8. **Geography** Where did the Oregon Trail start and where did it end?

9. **Citizenship** Why did California have such a diverse population when it became a state?

Vocabulary

✓ **TEST PREP** Choose the correct word from the list below to complete each sentence.

entrepreneur, p. 380
reform, p. 390
annexation, p. 395
boomtown, p. 402

10. The temperance movement was a _____ movement that tried to make life better for people.

11. San Francisco was a _____ that grew during the California Gold Rush.

12. Francis Cabot Lowell was an _____ who took the risk of starting a cotton mill.

13. People in favor of _____ wanted Texas to become part of the United States.

1825
Erie Canal opens

1833
National Road completed

1836
Texas wins independence

1848
Seneca Falls Convention

1825   1830   1835   1840   1845   1850

Apply Skills

☑ **TEST PREP Reading and Thinking Skill** Read the paragraph below. Then evaluate the source to answer each question.

No one needs Robert Fulton's steamboat. The boats are ugly and dangerous. I don't think travelers care whether they can get from New York City to Albany in five or ten days. I've made the trip many times, and if a boat cannot make the trip one day, it can just wait for the winds to pick up the next day. In my opinion, we don't need steamboats at all.

14. What key word might have been used to find this source?
   A. Albany
   B. New York City
   C. Steamboats
   D. Erie Canal

15. Which of the following suggests that the article is not reliable?
   A. It supports facts you read in a textbook.
   B. It presents more opinions than facts.
   C. It presents many sides of an argument.
   D. It supports its arguments with facts.

Critical Thinking

☑ **TEST PREP** Write a short paragraph to answer each question.

16. **Synthesize** How were the experiences of Tejanos and Californios similar?

17. **Fact and Opinion** Which invention discussed in this chapter was the most important? Support your opinion with facts from the chapter.

Timeline

Use the Chapter Summary Timeline above to answer the question.

18. How many years after the opening of the Erie Canal was the National Road completed?

Activities

Science Activity Think about an invention from the last 100 years. Find out more about it. Make a drawing or model to show how it works.

Writing Activity Write a persuasive essay that Susan B. Anthony or Elizabeth Cady Stanton might have written to explain her views on women's rights.

Technology
Writing Process Tips
Get help with your essay at
www.eduplace.com/kids/hmss05/

Review and Test Prep

Vocabulary and Main Ideas

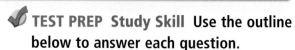 **TEST PREP** Write a sentence to answer each question.

1. Why was traveling on a **flatboat** easier than traveling in a wagon in the early 1800s?

2. How did Sacagawea's skill as an **interpreter** help Lewis and Clark?

3. In what way did President Monroe change U.S. **foreign policy** in 1823?

4. What did Francis Cabot Lowell do to help New England become a center of the **textile** industry?

5. List three kinds of **injustice** women faced in the 1800s.

6. Why did settlers often travel by **wagon train** when moving west?

Critical Thinking

TEST PREP Write a short paragraph to answer each question.

7. **Infer** In the early 1800s, a British settler said, "Old America seems to be breaking up and moving westward." What did the settler mean by that?

8. **Evaluate** Explain the ways in which transportation improved during the Industrial Revolution. Describe methods of transportation used before and after 1800.

Apply Skills

TEST PREP Study Skill Use the outline below to answer each question.

> I. Changes in Manufacturing
>   A. Slater's Cotton-spinning mill
>   B. Whitney's cotton gin
>   C. Interchangable parts
>   D. Mass Production
> II. Changes in Transportation
>   A. The National Road
>   B. The Erie Canal
>   C. Steam locomotives

9. Which of the following topics is the title of the outline?

   A. Changes in Manufacturing
   B. The National Road
   C. The Industrial Revolution
   D. Changes in Transportation

10. Which supporting detail could be added under the main idea "Changes in Transportation"?

    A. Fulton's steamboat
    B. Lowell's mill
    C. Deere's steel plow
    D. McCormick's reaper

Unit Activity

The Big Idea

Write a Poem about Being an American

- Brainstorm a list of details about what it means to be an American.

- Use your ideas in a poem. The first line might ask, "What does it mean to be an American?" The following lines might answer the question.

- Illustrate your poem and read it aloud.

To be an American

What does it mean to be an American?

At the Library

You may find these books at your school or public library.

The Flag Maker by Susan C. Bartoletti
A Baltimore girl helped make the flag that inspired "The Star-Spangled Banner."

Animals on the Trail with Lewis and Clark by Dorothy Henshaw Patent
Lewis and Clark identified dozens of animals on their 1804–1806 expedition.

Connect to Today

Create a poster about people who are trying to improve the United States today.

- Find articles about current reformers, or people who are trying to improve the United States.

- Write a summary of each article. Draw a picture to illustrate each summary.

- Arrange your summaries on a poster, and display it in your classroom.

Technology
Get information for the poster from the Weekly Reader at
www.eduplace.com/kids/hmss05/

Read About It

Look for these Social Studies Independent Books in your classroom.

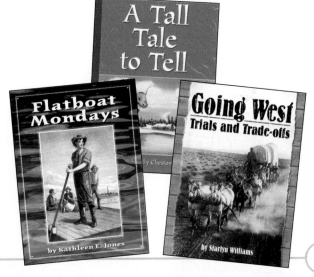

A Tall Tale to Tell

Flatboat Mondays
by Kathleen E. Jones

Going West
Trials and Trade-offs
by Starlyn Williams

UNIT 6

The Civil War

The Big Idea

What makes a good leader?

In 1865, Abraham Lincoln said that the country should act,

"With malice toward none, with charity for all . . ."

Harriet Tubman
1820?–1913

Why would someone risk her life over and over again? Tubman knew what slavery was like, and she wanted to help others to reach freedom, as she had.
page 427

Harriet Tubman

Black Heritage USA 13c

History Makers

Abraham Lincoln
1809–1865

Lincoln's election angered southern states so much that they broke away from the Union. Yet no President had ever worked as hard to keep the nation together.
page 440

Booker T. Washington
1856–1915

This teacher helped former slaves gain new skills. At his Tuskegee Institute in Alabama, students of all ages learned to make and grow the things they needed.
page 484

Seattle

WASHINGTON
TERRITORY

Columbia R.

Portland

Fort
Walla Walla

OREGON

Snake R.

Fort
Boise

Fort
Hall

Fort
Benton

Fort Union

DAKOTA TERRITORY

MINNESOTA

L. Superior

MICHIGA

WISCONSIN

L. Michigan

Fort Pierre

Missouri R.

IOWA

Chicago

INDIA

St. Louis

ILLINOIS

Fort
Bridger

NEVADA
TERRITORY

UTAH
TERRITORY

San Francisco

CALIFORNIA

Fort Laramie

Fort Randall

NEBRASKA TERRITORY

Platte R.

Fort
Kearny

Fort Riley

Fort
Leavenworth

KANSAS

Colorado R.

COLORADO
TERRITORY

Bent's
New Fort

Arkansas R.

MISSOURI

Los Angeles

Fort
Defiance

Santa Fe

Fort
Union

NEW MEXICO
TERRITORY

San Diego

Fort Yuma

Pecos R.

INDIAN
TERRITORY

Fort
Smith

ARKANSAS

MISSISSIPPI

Fort
Belknap

Brazos R.

LOUISIANA

New Orleans

Fort
Davis

R.

TEXAS

Rio Grande

PACIFIC
OCEAN

Gulf of
Mexico

Unit Preview

1830   1840   1850   1860

1831
**Abolitionism
Grows**
William Lloyd Garrison
publishes *The Liberator*
**Chapter 12,
page 425**

1857
**Dred Scott
Decision**
Slavery is legal
in territories
**Chapter 12,
page 434**

1861
**Fort
Sumter**
Civil War
begins
**Chapter 12,
page 445**

Map labels

MAINE

VERMONT

NEW HAMPSHIRE

Boston
MASSACHUSETTS

NEW YORK

L. Ontario

Huron

L. Erie

RHODE ISLAND

CONNECTICUT

New York

PENNSYLVANIA

NEW JERSEY

Philadelphia

Baltimore

OHIO

Washington, D.C.

DELAWARE

MARYLAND

Cincinnati

WEST VIRGINIA

isville

NTUCKY

VIRGINIA

ATLANTIC OCEAN

NORTH CAROLINA

NNESSEE

SOUTH CAROLINA

N NE E SE S SW W NW

GEORGIA

BAMA

FLORIDA

LEGEND

- Union
- Slave states not seceding
- Confederacy
- Territories
- 🌱 Cotton growing area
- Textile mill
- Western fort
- Boundary of the Confederacy

0 150 300

i 0 150 300

Timeline

1870

1880

1863
Emancipation Proclamation
Lincoln declares end to slavery
Chapter 13, page 456

1870
15th Amendment
African Americans gain right to vote
Chapter 13, page 476

Connect to Today

North and South, 1860s

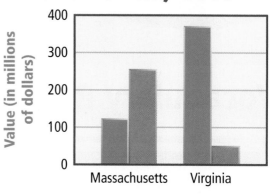

Value (in millions of dollars)

400
300
200
100
0

Massachusetts   Virginia

■ farms   ■ manufactured goods

In 1860, states in the North and South had very different economies.

North and South Today

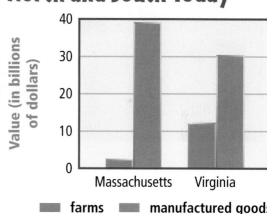

Value (in billions of dollars)

40
30
20
10
0

Massachusetts   Virginia

■ farms   ■ manufactured goods

In 1860, Virginia's economy depended on farming. What is its economy like today?

CURRENT EVENTS

WEEKLY (WR) READER

Current events on the web!

Find out about current events that connect with the Big Idea of this unit.
See activities at:
www.eduplace.com/kids/hmss05/

Technology

e • **glossary**
e • **word games**
www.eduplace.com/kids/hmss05/

Vocabulary Preview

states' rights

John C. Calhoun favored **states' rights.** He wanted states to have more power than the federal government. **page 419**

abolitionist

An **abolitionist** was someone who fought to end slavery. Sojourner Truth gave powerful speeches about the cruelty of slavery. **page 424**

Chapter Timeline

1831
Nat Turner's Rebellion

1852
Uncle Tom's Cabin written

| 1830 | 1835 | 1840 | 1845 | 1850 |

Reading Strategy

Predict and Infer Before you read each lesson, use this strategy.

Look at each lesson title and the pictures. What do you think you will learn about?

fugitive

Many people believed it was wrong to return an escaped **fugitive** to slavery. Harriet Beecher Stowe wrote *Uncle Tom's Cabin* in protest over the Fugitive Slave Law. **page 434**

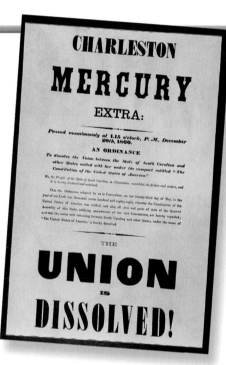

secession

After the **secession** of 11 southern states, war broke out between the North and the South. States that left the Union formed the Confederacy. **page 440**

1859
John Brown's raid

1861
Civil War begins

1855   1860   1865

Worlds Apart

| 1760 | 1780 | 1800 | 1820 | 1840 | 1860 | 1880 |

1793–1860

VOCABULARY

tariff
states' rights
sectionalism

Vocabulary Strategy

sectionalism

Find the word **section** in **sectionalism**. Sectionalism is loyalty to one section, or part, of a country.

READING SKILL

Compare and Contrast
What differences were there between the North and South in the early 1800s? Write them down as you read.

NORTH	SOUTH

Build on What You Know When people have very different ideas from one another, it can seem as if they live in separate worlds. In the early 1800s, the South and the North were worlds apart from each other in many ways.

Slavery in the United States

Main Idea Slavery grew in the South after the invention of the cotton gin.

Slavery had a long history in the United States. The thirteen colonies had all allowed slavery, though slaves were less common in the North than in the South. After the War for Independence, several northern states passed laws to abolish, or end, slavery. Southern states chose not to.

At the Constitutional Convention, some delegates tried to stop slavery in all states. As one delegate said, slavery did not fit with "the principles of the Revolution."

The Growth of Slavery

George Mason, a slaveowner from Virginia, called slavery a "national sin." Delegates at the Continental Congress could not agree to end slavery. Many hoped that it would soon die out. However, changes in southern farming caused slavery to grow in coming years.

After the invention of the cotton gin in 1793, southern farmers wanted more enslaved people to work in their cotton fields. The cotton gin made cotton much easier to produce. At the same time, the value of cotton was rising. New textile mills in Britain and New England needed more cotton, and the South could grow it.

Cotton became the South's most important crop. By 1840, the South was growing most of the world's cotton. Plantation owners used their profits to buy more land and more slaves. Slavery grew rapidly. In 1790, there were about 800,000 enslaved people in the South. By 1860, there were nearly four million.

Resistance to Slavery

Sometimes enslaved people fought against slaveowners. In Virginia in 1831, an enslaved African American named **Nat Turner** led a rebellion against slave owners. He and his followers killed 59 people before being stopped by the local militia. After Nat Turner's Rebellion, southern states passed laws to control both enslaved and free blacks. For example, black ministers were no longer allowed to preach without a white person present. By the 1850s, slaves and free blacks had fewer rights than ever.

Slavery became a source of deep conflict between the North and South. Many southerners argued that slavery was too important to their economy to give up. Some people in the North argued that slavery kept the country's economy from growing faster. They also believed that slavery was unfair and wrong.

REVIEW What led to the growth of slavery in the early 1800s?

Cotton Plantations

1. Enslaved people worked in the fields, picking cotton.

2. Cotton was packed into bales before being shipped.

3. Many plantations were near the Mississippi River, where steamboats carried the cotton south to New Orleans.

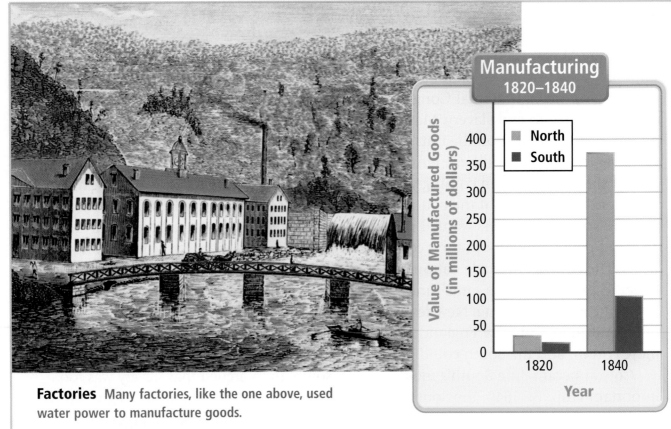

Manufacturing 1820–1840

Factories Many factories, like the one above, used water power to manufacture goods.

SKILL **Reading Graphs** What was the value of goods made in the North in 1840?

North and South

Main Idea The many differences between the North and South divided the two regions.

The North and the South had different economies. The South's economy was agricultural, or mostly based on farming. Some southerners worked on large cotton plantations. Many more had small farms and grew food crops such as corn, or raised cattle and pigs. These farmers usually had only a few enslaved people or none at all.

Northern states had many farmers as well, but the economy of the North was changing. Cities in the North were growing quickly and factories were being built throughout the region. In factories, people made textiles, shoes, tools, and other goods. By 1860, fewer than half of people in the North were farmers.

The Tariff

The different economies in the North and South led to disagreements between the regions about tariffs. A **tariff** is a tax on imported goods.

Between 1816 and 1832, Congress passed high tariffs on goods made outside the country. British textiles, for example, became very expensive. The only cloth most people could afford came from the mills of New England.

Congress used tariffs to help American manufacturing. Tariffs were good for northern industry, but they did not help the South, where there was less industry. Southerners, like all consumers, had to pay higher prices for manufactured goods they wanted, such as steel and cloth. When prices of these goods went up, southerners blamed it on tariffs and the North.

States' Rights

One southerner who argued against tariffs was **John C. Calhoun** of South Carolina. Calhoun was Vice President in 1828. He believed the Constitution did not allow the federal government to create tariffs. He argued for states' rights. **States' rights** is the idea that states, not the federal government, should make the final decisions about matters that affect them. Calhoun believed that states had the right to veto tariffs. States' rights became a popular idea in the South.

Disagreements over slavery, tariffs, and other economic issues increased sectionalism in the North and South. Loyalty to one part of the country is called **sectionalism.** As conflicts grew, it seemed that many people cared more about their own section of the country than for the country as a whole.

REVIEW Why did southerners dislike tariffs?

Lesson Summary

Slavery grew with the demand for cotton.

Tariffs helped the growing number of northern factories.

The North and South argued over slavery, tariffs, and states' rights.

Why It Matters ...

The North and South were headed toward war. It began with arguments about slavery and the power of the national and state governments.

John C. Calhoun
He became a U.S. senator after serving as Vice President. Calhoun argued for slavery and states' rights.

Lesson Review

1793
Cotton gin invented

1831
Nat Turner's Rebellion

1790   1800   1810   1820   1830   1840

1. **VOCABULARY** Show that you understand the meaning of **sectionalism** and **states' rights** by using these words in a paragraph about disagreements between the North and South.

2. **READING SKILL** What were the views on slavery in the South and North? Use your notes to **compare** and **contrast.**

3. **MAIN IDEA: Economics** Why did cotton become the South's most important crop?

4. **MAIN IDEA: Economics** What did tariffs do to help northern industries?

5. **TIMELINE SKILL:** When was Nat Turner's Rebellion?

6. **CRITICAL THINKING: Infer** Tell what you think might have happened if the cotton gin had not been invented.

WRITING ACTIVITY Write one or two math questions based on the graph on page 418. Trade questions with a partner and try to answer your partner's questions.

King Cotton

In the 1840s and 1850s, cotton was called "king." It was the most valuable crop raised in the South and an important part of the North's growing industrial economy. In some years, more than two million bales of cotton were harvested. Bales weighed about 500 pounds. All that cotton was turned into shirts, pants, jackets, and other useful products.

Each step of the process of turning cotton into clothing was done separately by workers who did only that step. This specialization made each part of the process faster. As the cotton industry became more productive, people could buy more and more cotton goods.

1 Working in the Fields Cotton grows in the South's fertile soil and mild climate. It is often grown on large plantations and picked by enslaved workers.

3 Unloading at the Docks Bales of cotton arrive in northern ports such as Boston. The North has most of the nation's mills, including some of the biggest in the world.

5 Train Delivery The finished cloth is loaded onto trains and shipped to buyers throughout the United States and other countries.

2 **Shipping North** Bundled into bales, the cotton is sent by wagon and steamboat to port cities such as New Orleans and Charleston. Then it is loaded onto ships and sent to the North and to other countries.

4 **Weaving the Thread** The cotton arrives at the mills. There, it is spun into thread and woven into cloth by women and girls working at huge spinning and weaving machines.

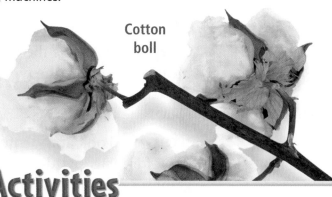

Cotton boll

Activities

1. **DISCUSS IT** Use the pictures to compare all of the different places cotton traveled, from when it was picked to the finished cloth.

2. **REPORT IT** Where does cotton come from today? Using library resources, research cotton and write a summary of what you find out.

421

Compare Bar, Line, and Circle Graphs

▶ **VOCABULARY**
bar graph
line graph
circle graph

Graphs can give you a better understanding of historical information, such as the importance of cotton to the United States economy. Different kinds of graphs present different kinds of information.

- **Bar graphs** compare amounts of things.

- **Line graphs** show changes over time.

- **Circle graphs** illustrate how a part compares with the whole.

Together, these graphs can show overall patterns. The steps below will help you to read and describe information from these three kinds of graphs.

Learn the Skill

Step 1: Read the title and identify the kind of graph. The title tells you about the subject and purpose of each graph.

Step 2: Examine the labels. They explain the units of measurement and the type of information presented.

Step 3: Look at the information on each of the graphs. Look for increases, decreases, or sudden changes on line graphs. Compare amounts on bar graphs and the parts of the whole on circle graphs. How is the information on the three graphs related?

Compare the information on the bar, line, and circle graphs by answering the following questions.

1 How is the information on the three graphs related?

2 How does the information on the bar graph differ from the facts in the other two graphs?

3 On the line graph, what 10-year period had the greatest change in cotton production?

4 Based on your reading of Lesson 1 and the circle graph, what crop was exported more than any other crop in 1860? Why?

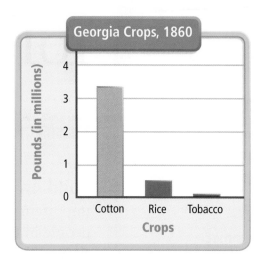

Georgia Crops, 1860

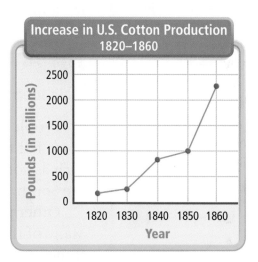

Increase in U.S. Cotton Production 1820–1860

Apply the Skill

Write a paragraph describing cotton production in the United States and Georgia in 1860. In your paragraph, include data from each of the three graphs.

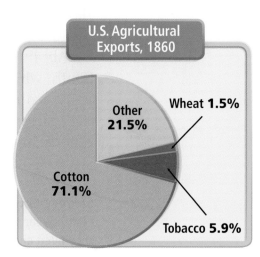

U.S. Agricultural Exports, 1860

The Struggle for Freedom

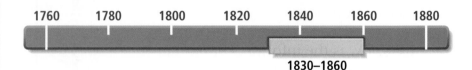

1760   1780   1800   1820   1840   1860   1880

1830–1860

Build on What You Know Think about how important freedom is to you. In the early 1800s, not all people in the United States were free. Many lived in slavery. They struggled to win freedom, with help from the antislavery movement.

The Antislavery Movement

Main Idea Groups against slavery formed in the mid-1800s.

People could not agree about the issue of slavery. Some felt that slavery was needed to grow cash crops such as cotton and tobacco. As cotton farming spread in the South, they wanted slavery to spread as well.

Other people felt it was wrong to enslave people. Many of them became abolitionists. An **abolitionist** is someone who joined the movement to abolish, or end, slavery. Most abolitionists felt that slavery went against the ideas of Christianity.

Abolitionists included people in the North and South, whites and free blacks, men and women. They wrote pamphlets and traveled across the country, speaking against slavery. The abolitionist movement grew quickly in the 1830s and 1840s.

VOCABULARY

abolitionist
discrimination
Underground Railroad

Vocabulary Strategy

abolitionist

Abolitionist comes from the word **abolish**. Abolitionists were people who wanted to abolish, or end, slavery.

 READING SKILL

Problem and Solution
Look for solutions abolitionists found to fight slavery.

PROBLEM   SOLUTIONS

Slavery →

Slavery Some enslaved people had to wear tags that told where they lived and what they did.

SKILL **Primary Sources** What city is stamped on this tag?

William Lloyd Garrison
"I will not retreat a single inch —
AND I WILL BE HEARD," Garrison
wrote in *The Liberator*.

Frederick Douglass
After escaping to the North,
Douglass raised enough
money to buy his freedom.

Sojourner Truth
When she preached against
slavery, she attracted
large crowds.

Leading Abolitionists

In 1831, **William Lloyd Garrison** began printing an antislavery newspaper called *The Liberator*. In it, he demanded that all enslaved people be freed.

Frederick Douglass was a well-known black abolitionist. Douglass had escaped from slavery. He was a writer and often spoke to white audiences about slavery. He told one audience,

> 66 I can tell you what I have seen with my own eyes, felt on my own person, and know to have occurred in my own neighborhood. 99

Sojourner Truth, another important abolitionist, had also been born into slavery. Truth spoke in favor of abolition and women's rights.

Sarah Grimké (GRIM kee) and **Angelina Grimké** of South Carolina saw the cruelty of slavery from another point of view. They were daughters of a slave-owner. As adults, the sisters moved north and spoke out against slavery.

Free Blacks

By 1860, about 500,000 free blacks lived in the United States. About half lived in the North, half in the South.

Free blacks in the South often faced discrimination. **Discrimination** is the unfair treatment of particular groups. State laws limited the rights of free blacks. For example, they could not travel without permission or meet in groups without a white person present.

African Americans in the North also faced discrimination. However, they could travel freely, organize groups, and publish newspapers. These rights made it possible for free blacks in the North to work openly against slavery. Free black leaders joined whites in creating the American Anti-Slavery Society in 1833. This group called for the immediate end of slavery. Many free blacks gave money to the group. *The Liberator* also received most of its money from free blacks.

REVIEW What did free blacks in the North do to convince people that slavery was wrong?

The Underground Railroad

Main Idea The Underground Railroad helped people escape from slavery.

Some abolitionists worked in secret to help slaves escape to freedom. They set up a system known as the Underground Railroad. The **Underground Railroad** was a series of escape routes and hiding places to bring slaves out of the South.

Runaways, the people who fled slavery, could head for the North and Canada, or go south to Florida, Mexico, or the Caribbean.

Runaways often walked at night. Sometimes they hid in carts driven by members of the Underground Railroad. Escaping took great courage. Runaways who were caught would be punished and returned to slavery.

Escape to Freedom The Underground Railroad was not really underground, and not really a railroad. It was the routes that led slaves to freedom.

Underground Railroad

LEGEND

Routes of escape

Slave states in 1860

Free states in 1860

Harriet Tubman This photograph shows Harriet Tubman (left) with a group of enslaved people she helped to escape.

Stations and Conductors

Free blacks gave most of the money and did most of the work to support the Underground Railroad. Members of the Railroad gave food, clothing, and medical aid to runaways. They hid them until it was safe to move on. Hiding places were known as stations. "Conductors" guided runaways on to the next station.

The most famous conductor was **Harriet Tubman**, who escaped from slavery in Maryland. She then returned 19 times to lead others to freedom. Each time, she risked being caught and enslaved again. Tubman helped about 300 people escape to the North. She became a symbol of the abolitionist movement.

REVIEW What was the purpose of the Underground Railroad?

Lesson Summary

Abolitionists worked to end slavery. Free blacks and women played important roles in the abolitionist movement. Many people worked against slavery by helping enslaved people escape to freedom on the Underground Railroad.

Why It Matters ...

As abolitionists struggled to free enslaved people, they convinced others that slavery was wrong.

Lesson Review

1831
The Liberator first published

1833
American Anti-Slavery Society founded

| 1830 | 1831 | 1832 | 1833 | 1834 | 1835 |

❶ **VOCABULARY** Use the words below to write a short paragraph about the fight against slavery.

    abolitionist   Underground Railroad

❷ **READING SKILL** What was one **solution** used to fight slavery?

❸ **MAIN IDEA: History** In what ways were Frederick Douglass and Sojourner Truth alike?

❹ **MAIN IDEA: Geography** Where did the Underground Railroad take runaways?

❺ **PEOPLE TO KNOW** Who was **Sojourner Truth,** and what did she do to fight slavery?

❻ **TIMELINE SKILL:** How long after *The Liberator* was the American Anti-Slavery Society founded?

❼ **CRITICAL THINKING: Decision Making** What were the possible consequences for Harriet Tubman when she helped slaves escape along the Underground Railroad? Why do you think people like her made the decision to help runaways?

RESEARCH ACTIVITY Research an abolitionist you read about in the lesson. Look for characteristics such as courage or persistence. Write a short report about his or her life.

Stealing Freedom

by Elisa Carbone

This story is based on the life of a real person, Ann Weems, an enslaved servant who lived in the Maryland home of Charles Price in the 1850s. Ann, age thirteen, hopes to be freed. A lawyer, Jacob Bigelow, promised to help her escape on the Underground Railroad. But tonight a man whom Ann saw at the county fair has kidnapped her from the Prices and bundled her into the back of a carriage. She has been riding in the carriage a long time. Where is he taking her?

✳

The horse stopped. In an instant, Ann threw off the blanket and grasped the handle of the carriage door. But the man leaped so quickly from his seat, he was already standing over her.

"I told you to stay covered!" He threw the blanket over her head and lifted her in it, his arms tight as a vise around her chest. Ann's mouth bumped against something bony—his shoulder? She opened her mouth wide and, blanket and all, bit him as hard as she could.

The man yelped and dropped her. She landed on her rump and struggled to get untangled from the blanket. He grabbed her again and, this time with no blanket to cushion him, she bit down on his arm.

A door opened and a slice of yellow light brightened the dark street.

"Help!" Ann cried.

But the blanket came down over her head again.

"Are you mad?" It was another man's hushed voice. "The constable patrols this street every hour all night!"

"The wench bit me!"

Ann found herself being held tightly by two pairs of strong hands.

"Just get her inside."

She heard a door shut and as it did, her heart sank. She was trapped.

"You've scared her half to death, is what you've done."

"I got her here, ain't I?" came the voice of her captor.

The blanket was lifted off her head. A hand grasped hers and helped her to her feet. She blinked, uncomprehending. She was standing in the foyer of a narrow row house. One candle flickered on a table nearby. In the dancing light she saw the stubbly face of the tobacco-chewing man from the fair. He was calmly picking his teeth. When she turned to see the other man who'd helped him drag her inside, she let out a yelp and stepped back, her hands covering her mouth. It was Jacob Bigelow.

"Welcome to my home," said Mr. Bigelow.

Ann took in a sharp breath. "You're . . . I mean . . ." She pointed to the other man. "He's . . ."

Mr. Bigelow smoothed the sweaty hair away from her forehead. "There will be time for explanation," he said. "Are you in one piece?"

She nodded.

Mr. Bigelow handed the man a fat wad of paper money. "You got her here safely. Now be off before the constable comes by to find out why there's a brawl going on in my foyer at three A.M."

The man tipped his hat to Ann and slipped out the door.

"I apologize for his conduct," said Mr. Bigelow, "but often it's only the roughest sort who are willing to do such risky work. And I'm sure you understand why we had to do it this way."

Ann screwed up her face. "I don't think I understand anything," she said, bewildered.

Mr. Bigelow helped her to a chair in the parlor, carrying the candle with them. She sat stiff and uncomfortably. It was the first time she'd ever sat in a parlor.

"We had to steal you from your master this way," he said.

Ann felt a quiver go from her throat to her belly as it dawned on her what had actually happened this night.

"You see—" Mr. Bigelow adjusted his spectacles. "If you'd known that you were escaping, you would not have played the part so convincingly. But as it was, if you'd been taken up by the sheriff, what would you have told him?"

"That I'd been kidnapped!"

"Exactly," said Mr. Bigelow. "And you would have been returned to your master without harm or suspicion."

Ann's eyes widened as the plan began to make sense.

"And if anyone has seen you, the rumor mill will serve us well. You were not seen running away. You were being carried away against your will."

Ann rubbed the bump on her head—what a small price to pay for a clean escape! "Thank you," she said. She held her hands together toward him in a gesture like prayer. "Thank you so much."

Mr. Bigelow pressed his fingertips together. "Ah, yes," he said. "A lawyer by day, a lawless kidnapper by night. It's a wonder I get any sleep at all."

There was the sound of footsteps in the street. They stopped briefly outside the door, then moved on.

"That's Sergeant Orme on his parol," Mr. Bigelow said quietly. "I'd better show you to the guest quarters now."

He led Ann into the hallway and, with one wiry eyebrow raised, pointed to the ceiling. "There you are," he said. "The most comfortable lodging in town for kidnapping victims."

The candlelight flickered and Ann squinted at the place where he'd pointed. All she could see was wide ceiling boards that fit tightly together. Was he playing a joke on her?

Mr. Bigelow hummed as he opened a nearby closet and pulled out a ladder.

Then he climbed up and pushed carefully on the ceiling. Ann's mouth dropped open as a piece of the ceiling lifted up and he slid it aside.

"Up you go," he said, stepping down off the ladder. He gave her the candle.

Ann climbed up until her head entered a stuffy, attic-like room. She lifted the candle and saw a pitcher of water, a dish of corn bread, a straw mat and quilt, and a chamber pot over in the corner. She looked down at Mr. Bigelow. "No one will know I'm here!" she exclaimed.

"My thoughts exactly," he replied.

Ann scrambled up, then lay on her stomach to peer down before closing up the opening. "May I know his name?" she asked. "The man who brought me here?" He had given her several hours of terror and a rather large bump on her head, but he had, in fact, been her savior. She wanted to remember him.

Mr. Bigelow rested one foot on the bottom rung of the ladder. "The Powder Boy," he answered. "He takes both gunpowder and fugitives on his sailing vessel. Of course, that's not his real name, but that is how he's known on the road—and since you are now a passenger on the road, that is how you should know him."

The Powder Boy. She would never forget. She looked quizzically at Mr. Bigelow. "The road?" she asked, shaking her head slightly.

"The Underground Railroad. You have just begun to ride it, my dear. I am one of the conductors, and this is your first stop. It runs all the way to Canada."

Canada. She felt the quiver run through her again. She could not turn back now. And Canada was so far away.

They said good night, and Ann slid the ceiling boards back into place. They fit perfectly. The hiding place must have been built, she thought, like a hidden closet behind one of the upstairs bedrooms.

When she blew out the candle the room went quite dark. Her stomach had been through too much this night for her to eat the corn bread, but she drank thirstily from the pitcher. The air was hot and close. Sweat dripped down her neck as she lay on the mat. Her heart pounded in her ears with a new rhythm—one she'd never heard before. It said, "I'm free, I'm free, I'm free . . . ."

Activities

1. **TALK ABOUT IT** Why was Ann kidnapped? What do you think of Joseph Bigelow's plan?

2. **MAP IT** Where will Ann go next? Plan a route that Ann might follow from Baltimore, Maryland to Canada. Show the route on a map. Mark places on the map where she might stop along the Underground Railroad.

Compromise and Conflict

1760   1780   1800   1820   1840   1860   1880

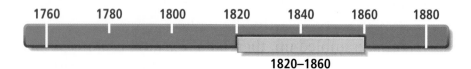

1820–1860

VOCABULARY

slave state
free state
Union
popular sovereignty
fugitive

Vocabulary Strategy

fugitive

Fugitive and refuge come from a word meaning to flee. A fugitive flees to find refuge, or safety.

READING SKILL

Cause and Effect Note the causes that made the conflict over slavery grow worse.

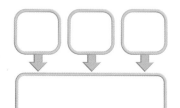

Build on What You Know To solve a disagreement, you give a little to get something back. That is a compromise. During the 1800s, Congress made several compromises over slavery to keep the country together.

Would Slavery Spread?

Main Idea Congress had to decide whether to allow slavery in new territories and states.

The United States grew in the 1800s. The Louisiana Purchase and the Mexican War had opened new lands to settlers. Congress set up governments for these lands, and some of the regions became territories. When a territory's population was large enough, it could become a state.

Congress had to decide whether to allow slavery in each territory. Territories that allowed slavery became slave states. A **slave state** permitted slavery. Territories where slavery was illegal became free states. A **free state** did not permit slavery. For a time, Congress tried to keep an equal number of free and slave states.

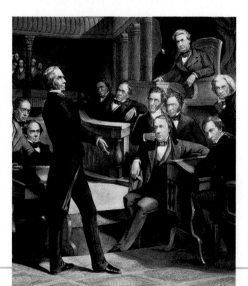

Henry Clay Known as the Great Compromiser, Kentucky senator Henry Clay tried to keep arguments over slavery from dividing the nation.

Compromises in Congress

Through the first half of the 1800s, Congress argued over which territories would have slavery. Northerners wanted free states to have a majority of representatives in Congress, so they could pass laws against slavery. Southerners wanted more slave states.

Missouri wanted to join the Union as a slave state in 1820. The **Union** is another name for the United States. To satisfy both sides, Congress created the Missouri Compromise. It accepted Missouri as a slave state and Maine as a free state. Congress then created an invisible line across the rest of the territories. Only territories south of that line would allow slavery.

Congress continued to debate the spread of slavery into new territories. In the Compromise of 1850, Congress allowed settlers in some territories to make the decision for themselves. The right of people to make political decisions for themselves is called **popular sovereignty.**

In 1854, Congress passed the Kansas-Nebraska Act. This law gave popular sovereignty to the Kansas and Nebraska territories. Abolitionists opposed the act because it allowed slavery north of the line created in the Missouri Compromise. Settlers supporting and opposing slavery rushed into Kansas. Both sides wanted to win the vote on whether to allow slavery. Soon the two sides fought for control of the territory. In 1861, Kansas joined the Union as a free state.

REVIEW What compromises did Congress make as the nation grew?

Growth and Compromise Compromises in Congress affected where slavery was allowed.

SKILL Reading Maps Which state joined the Union as a free state in 1850?

MISSOURI COMPROMISE, 1820

LEGEND
- Free state or territory
- Slave state or territory
- Decision on slavery left to territory

COMPROMISE OF 1850

KANSAS-NEBRASKA ACT, 1854

Harriet Beecher Stowe
Her book, *Uncle Tom's Cabin*, described the suffering of slaves. Many people in the North began to feel new sympathy for enslaved people after reading the book.

The Growing Crisis

Main Idea Events in the 1850s made the split between the North and South worse.

As part of the Compromise of 1850, Congress passed the Fugitive Slave Law, which upset northerners. A **fugitive** is a person who is running away. The law said that slaves who had escaped to the North had to be returned to slavery. The Fugitive Slave Law also ordered citizens to help catch fugitives. Many northerners refused to obey the law.

Harriet Beecher Stowe, a writer from New England, was against the Fugitive Slave Law. She decided to write a story describing the cruelty of slavery. Her book, *Uncle Tom's Cabin*, sold 300,000 copies in one year. Stowe pointed out in the book that slavery was not just the South's problem. It was the nation's problem. *Uncle Tom's Cabin* convinced many northerners that slavery was wrong. Some southerners insisted that Stowe's picture of slavery was false. The arguments over the book pushed the North and South further apart.

Dred Scott

A legal case about slavery came to the Supreme Court in 1857. **Dred Scott,** an enslaved man from Missouri, asked the court for his freedom. Scott argued that he should be free because he had once lived in Illinois, a free state, and Wisconsin, a free territory. The Supreme Court disagreed. It said that enslaved people were property, and that living in a free state did not make them citizens. The Supreme Court also said that the government could not keep slavery out of any territory, because that would prevent slaveowners from moving their property to new territories.

The Dred Scott decision was a victory for slaveowners. It meant that slavery had to be legal in all territories, even if most settlers did not want it. Abolitionists feared that slavery would spread over the whole country.

Dred Scott

Attack at Harpers Ferry

John Brown's Raid

An abolitionist named **John Brown** decided to fight slavery on his own. In 1859, he tried to start a rebellion against slavery by attacking a U.S. Army post at Harpers Ferry, Virginia. Soldiers quickly surrounded his group and captured Brown. The government accused Brown of treason. At his trial, he insisted that he had done "no wrong but right." Brown was found guilty and hanged. Many northerners saw Brown as a hero. Southerners saw him as a violent man out to destroy their way of life.

By 1860, the North and South were deeply divided. As antislavery feeling grew stronger in the North, some southerners argued that they should leave the Union to protect their way of life.

REVIEW Why did John Brown attack Harpers Ferry?

Lesson Summary

Americans disagreed about whether slavery should be allowed to spread.

Congress tried to settle the slavery issue with a series of compromises.

The Fugitive Slave Law and John Brown's raid drove the North and South further apart.

Why It Matters ...

Over time, it became much harder for Americans to compromise over slavery. This conflict started to split the nation.

Lesson Review

1852 — *Uncle Tom's Cabin* written

1857 — **Dred Scott decision**

1859 — **John Brown's raid**

1852 — 1854 — 1856 — 1858 — 1860

1. **VOCABULARY** Write a short paragraph, using the words **free state, slave state,** and **fugitive** to describe the United States in the 1850s.

2. **READING SKILL** What **effect** did the Kansas-Nebraska Act of 1854 have on the conflict over slavery?

3. **MAIN IDEA: Government** Why did the Fugitive Slave Law upset some people in the North?

4. **MAIN IDEA: Government** What did the Dred Scott decision say?

5. **TIMELINE SKILL** What important event took place in 1859?

6. **PEOPLE TO KNOW** What effect did **Harriet Beecher Stowe's** book have on the debate over slavery?

7. **CRITICAL THINKING: Infer** Why did the compromises made in Congress fail to end the conflict over slavery?

WRITING ACTIVITY John Brown's raid on Harpers Ferry was an important event in the debate over slavery. Write a news report telling people what happened and why it happened.

A Troubling Law

Was the Fugitive Slave Law a bad law? The setting is dusk in a northern town in 1850. Citizens have gathered to decide how to respond to the new **Fugititve** Slave Law, meant to help slave owners. Should people in free states follow it or resist it?

Characters

Annabella Smith: teacher

Charlotte Pressman: elderly writer

Patrick James: stable owner

John Chase: storekeeper

Mary Chase: storekeeper

Edward Lester: law student

James Eglin: printer

Catherine Giles: baker

Annabella Smith: I have bad news. Robert Simms has been arrested — taken from his house last night!

John Chase: What happened? What was his offense?

Charlotte Pressman: I'm sure he did nothing wrong. We all know Robert. He has lived in this town for five years since he came here from Virginia.

Patrick James: It's that new slave law! He will be dragged back to slavery unless we do something.

Edward Lester: It is a very troubling law. It strikes a blow to the heart of our efforts to free people.

John Chase: That's easy for you to say, Edward. Mary and I are storekeepers, and radical talk about abolition isn't good for business.

Patrick James: But Simms worked in our town, John, and he is a human being.

Mary Chase: I used to say that slavery was a southern evil, no concern of mine. I live in a free state. But this new law…

Catherine Giles: This law is a danger to all of us. I am a free woman, born of free parents. But because I am black, I could be kidnapped and sold into slavery, and there would be no help for me.

James Eglin: It's true! I ran away from slavery. I earn an honest living as a printer. Now the law says my old master can come after me, and you have to help him.

Charlotte
Pressman

Annabella
Smith

Annabella Smith: Help him?

James Eglin: And if my old master catches me, I don't get a trial. I can't speak in my own defense. Just his word alone can send me back in chains.

Edward Lester: Did you know that the judge who hears the case is paid $5 when he frees a fugitive and $10 when he sends him back to slavery?

Annabella Smith: We must disobey this law. We must help Mr. Simms.

John Chase: I hear the punishment for helping a fugitive is a $1,000 fine or six months in jail.

James Eglin: That's nothing compared to a person's freedom.

John Chase: A thousand dollars is still a lot of money. If I spent six months in jail, my business would collapse.

Patrick James: I am willing to risk it.

Edward Lester

Mary Chase

ABOLITION

Meeting Tonight

ewbury Hall

:00 p.m

LAW

Charlotte Pressman: The question is, what can we do? It's too late to hide him. He has already been caught.

Patrick James: Then we must rescue him by force. Don't look so shocked! It has already happened in Boston. A group broke into the courthouse and rescued a fugitive.

John Chase

James Eglin: It wouldn't be easy. My uncle says a slaveowner and his hunters tried to capture some fugitives in Pennsylvania. People were badly wounded. A man died.

Annabella Smith: This could be dangerous.

Catherine Giles: It could lead to terrible violence.

Edward Lester: Then we will set out to rescue Mr. Simms without violence. We will gather a group large enough to overpower the guards and try to persuade them to let Robert go. We will carry no firearms.

James Eglin: I will do it.

Patrick James: You know I will.

Mary Chase: So will I.

John Chase: What if you get hurt? What if you are thrown in jail? I just don't know what to do.

Mary Chase: This is a free state, John. We cannot let the slaveholders take away our freedom.

Charlotte Pressman: I will defy this law, no matter what may come of it!

Activities

1. **THINK ABOUT IT** In what ways do you think the townspeople showed **courage**?

2. **WRITE ABOUT IT** Write a letter to the editor of a newspaper in 1850 telling your beliefs about the Fugitive Slave Law.

Civil War Begins

| 1840 | 1845 | 1850 | 1855 | 1860 | 1865 | 1870 |

1854–1861

VOCABULARY

secession
Confederacy
civil war

Vocabulary Strategy

Confederacy

A confederation is a group that unites for a purpose. The **Confederacy** was a confederation formed by 11 southern states.

READING SKILL

Sequence As you read, note in order the events that began the Civil War.

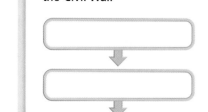

Build on What You Know You know that strong beliefs can make a difference in people's lives. President Abraham Lincoln strongly believed that the Union should not be allowed to split apart. When southern states tried to leave the Union, Lincoln went to war to stop them.

Abraham Lincoln

Main Idea Many people joined a new political party that opposed the spread of slavery.

By 1860, the conflict over slavery was becoming worse. **John Brown's** raid on Harpers Ferry in 1859 had worried people in the South. They thought abolitionists wanted to start a slave rebellion. Some southerners believed secession was the only way to protect their states' rights and continue as a slave-owning region. When part of a country leaves or breaks off from the rest it is called **secession.**

Northerners were upset as well. Many disliked the Kansas-Nebraska Act and the **Dred Scott** decision. They feared that slavery would spread across the country. Some formed a new political party, the Republican Party. Republicans wanted to keep slavery out of the territories. **Abraham Lincoln** was a famous Republican. In these difficult years, he became one of the most important leaders the United States has ever had.

Abraham Lincoln He earned a reputation for hard work and honesty.

Log cabin This is a copy of the cabin where Lincoln was born. As a boy, he studied math, grammar, spelling, and history. A page of his math homework is on the right.

Lincoln's Early Years

Abraham Lincoln was born in a small cabin in Kentucky, a slave state. His father was a farmer there. The family later moved to Indiana and then to Illinois, both free states. As a boy, Lincoln worked hard on his father's farm. He did not have much time to go to school. He loved reading, though, and read all the books he could.

Lincoln did not want to be a farmer. He studied law and became a lawyer. Lincoln also wanted to be a member of the Illinois legislature. He first won an election at age 25 and served four terms. Each term was for two years.

Later, Lincoln served one term as a representative in the United States Congress. He argued against allowing slavery to expand into new territories. After his time in Congress, Lincoln returned to his job as a lawyer.

REVIEW Why did some southerners want their states to leave the Union?

Lincoln's Campaigns

Main Idea Abraham Lincoln opposed slavery when he ran for the Senate and for President.

After Congress passed the Kansas-Nebraska Act, Lincoln decided to run for office again. In 1858, he ran for the Senate in Illinois as a Republican against **Stephen Douglas.** The two men held seven debates. In the debates, they argued about slavery.

Lincoln saw slavery as a "moral, social, and political evil." He argued that the United States could not go on forever divided by slavery. He said,

> 66 A house divided against itself cannot stand. I believe this government cannot endure [last] permanently half slave and half free. . . . It will become all one thing, or all the other. 99

Douglas wanted popular sovereignty in the territories. He did not believe slavery was wrong and thought it should be legal if people wanted it. Douglas also thought the country could remain split over slavery. He asked, "Why can it not exist divided into free and slave states?"

Lincoln hated slavery, but he did not think that the national government had the power to end slavery in slave states. The Constitution did not mention slavery. He said, "I have no purpose . . . to interfere with the institution of slavery in the states where it exists. I believe I have no lawful right to do so."

Although Lincoln did not argue for abolition, he wanted to keep slavery from spreading into the territories. Like many Republicans, Lincoln believed that slavery would end on its own if it were not allowed to spread across the country.

A Divided Nation

Lincoln lost the election to Douglas, but the debates made Lincoln famous. Reporters printed what the two men said. Across the country, people read Lincoln's words. Many northerners agreed with his views on slavery. In the South, people saw him as an enemy.

In 1860, the country held an election for President. The Democratic Party was split and could not agree on only one candidate. Northern Democrats chose Stephen Douglas. Southern Democrats chose **John Breckinridge** of Kentucky. Breckinridge owned slaves. He wanted slavery allowed in all the territories.

The Republican Party chose Abraham Lincoln as its candidate. Lincoln was the only candidate against slavery. He had support in the North, but very little in the South. In 10 southern states, voters were not given Lincoln's name as a choice.

Lincoln won the election, but the result showed how divided Americans were. He did not win in a single southern state. To southerners, Lincoln's election was a disaster. One southern newspaper called it "the greatest evil that has ever befallen [happened to] this country."

Many southerners felt that the federal government had become too powerful. When the government passed tariffs or tried to limit slavery, southerners argued that their states' rights were under attack. With Lincoln as President, they feared that the government would grow stronger and that Lincoln would try to end slavery. They believed that secession was the only way to protect their rights.

REVIEW Why did southerners see Lincoln as an enemy?

THE CAMPAIGN IN ILLINOIS.
THE LAST JOINT DEBATE.
DOUGLAS AND LINCOLN AT ALTON.
5,000 TO 10,000 PERSONS PRESENT!

Lincoln–Douglas Debates

The seven debates made history, attracting large crowds each time. The newspaper headline tells of their last one, which was on October 15, 1858. After two months of traveling around the state of Illinois and debating, Lincoln spoke these famous lines...

"Has anything ever threatened the existence of this Union save and except this very institution of slavery? That is the real issue."

Antislavery Medals, 1860s

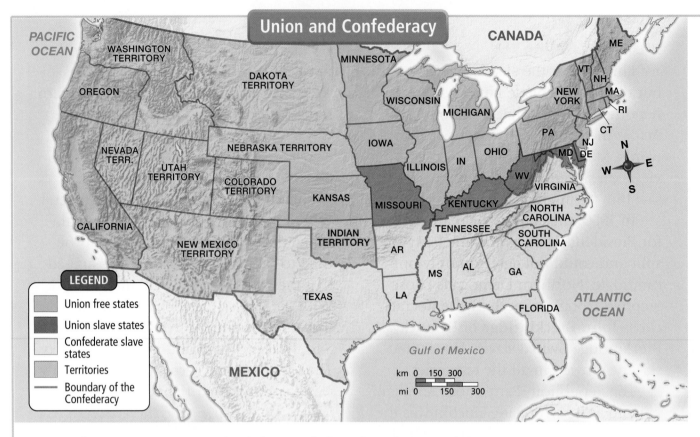

Union and Confederacy

LEGEND
- Union free states
- Union slave states
- Confederate slave states
- Territories
- Boundary of the Confederacy

Secession Eleven slave states decided to secede from the Union. Four slave states chose to stay in the Union. **SKILL** **Reading Maps** How many states were part of the Union?

Secession Begins

Main Idea Eleven southern states left the Union and formed their own government.

South Carolina withdrew from the Union first. People there voted to leave the Union on December 20, 1860. Mississippi, Florida, Alabama, Georgia, Louisiana, and Texas soon did the same.

On February 4, 1861, delegates from the seven states met in Montgomery, Alabama. They voted to form their own confederation. In this confederation, the states would have more power than the central government. These states called themselves the Confederate States of America, or the **Confederacy.** The delegates elected **Jefferson Davis** as President.

Attack on Fort Sumter

President Lincoln was determined to find a way to hold the country together. "We are not enemies, but friends," he said. "We must not be enemies."

It was too late. In Charleston, South Carolina, the state militia had surrounded Fort Sumter, a federal fort with United States soldiers inside. The Confederate government wanted control of the fort, but Lincoln refused to surrender it. Instead, he sent a ship with supplies to the fort.

Jefferson Davis After serving as an officer in the Mexican War, he became a senator from Mississippi and argued for states' rights.

Lincoln wanted to show that he would not give in to the Confederacy. However, he also did not want to start a war. He hoped that the southern states would return to the Union peacefully.

Confederate leaders saw the refusal to surrender of Fort Sumter as an act of war. They ordered cannons to fire on the fort. The first shot was fired on April 12, 1861.

The cannons fired on Fort Sumter for 34 hours. At last, the soldiers in the fort had to surrender. The attack on Fort Sumter marked the beginning of the Civil War. A **civil war** is a war between two groups or regions within a nation.

Fort Sumter

President Lincoln called for 75,000 soldiers to fight the rebellion. Some states refused to send men to help Lincoln. Arkansas, North Carolina, Tennessee, and Virginia joined the Confederacy instead. Citizens in the North and the South prepared to fight.

REVIEW What event began the Civil War?

Lesson Summary

- Americans who opposed slavery formed the Republican Party.
- Abraham Lincoln became famous for his speeches against slavery.
- After Lincoln's election, southern states began to leave the Union.

Why It Matters ...

For the first time in United States history, states tried to leave the Union. This began a terrible war.

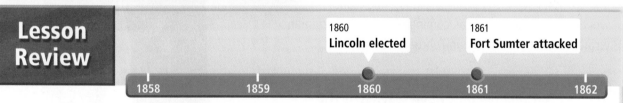

Lesson Review

1858	1859	1860 **Lincoln elected**	1861 **Fort Sumter attacked**	1862

❶ **VOCABULARY** Use **secession** and **civil war** in a paragraph describing the election of 1860.

❷ **READING SKILL** Use your **sequence** chart to tell what happened after the election of 1860.

❸ **MAIN IDEA: Citizenship** What were Lincoln's reasons for wanting to keep slavery out of the territories?

❹ **MAIN IDEA: History** Why were southerners upset about Lincoln's election?

❺ **TIMELINE SKILL** In what year did the Confederates attack Fort Sumter?

❻ **PEOPLE TO KNOW** Who was **Jefferson Davis?** What was his role in the Confederacy?

❼ **CRITICAL THINKING: Infer** Why do you think Virginia, North Carolina, Arkansas, and Tennessee waited before joining the Confederacy?

HANDS ON **SPEAKING ACTIVITY** Lincoln and Douglas helped make debating an important part of American politics. With a partner, prepare a short debate on a topic in the news today.

Blue and Gray

"I fear our happy days are gone," wrote Sarah Rousseau Espey of Alabama in her diary in March, 1861. The threat of war was tearing the United States apart. States, towns, and even families were divided over which side to support. Only a few people guessed how terrible the war would be.

Americans in the North and South wrote many letters and diary entries expressing their feelings about the causes of the war and what had to be done. Many of these letters have been saved. Today, we can read the words and think about how the writers felt.

Confederate Soldier After South Carolina and six other southern states seceded, Americans wondered whether war was coming. One young Virginian wrote home to his mother in February 1861:

" I believe we will have war with the North in less than sixty days…I am a man who knows my rights…One of those rights is secession…But like that gallant Henry [Patrick Henry] who rose in rebellion against the mightiest empire on earth my words are 'give me liberty or give me death.' "

—John H. Cochran

Gray
Confederate soldiers often wore uniforms that were gray, or a shade of brown called butternut.

Union Soldier Once the Confederacy fired on Fort Sumter, people all across the North prepared for war. A young man on his way to join the Union army wrote to the people of his home town in Middle Spring, Pennsylvania:

" I think it is my duty as well as those of my neighbors to go and join with those that have gone before; and help to fight the battles of our country…And every young single man that is healthy and will not go when his country needs him is either a coward or a rebel and I don't care which. No good country loving Patriot will stay at home when he hears of his country's flag being trampled in the dust by the Southern confederacy. "

—George Traxler

Blue

At the beginning of the war Union soldiers wore many different uniforms, but soon they all wore blue.

Activities

1. **TALK ABOUT IT** How are the Union and Confederate uniforms the same? How are they different? Why are the differences important?

2. **WRITE ABOUT IT** Write a personal narrative from the point of view of one of the letter writers. Describe his feelings about going to war. Include setting, events, and other people.

 Technology Learn about other primary sources for this unit at Education Place. www.eduplace.com/kids/hmss05/

447

Visual Summary

1–3. ✏️ Write a description of each event named below.

Conflicts before the Civil War	
Nat Turner's Rebellion	
Attack on Harpers Ferry	
Attack on Fort Sumter	

Facts and Main Ideas

✅ **TEST PREP** Answer each question with information from the chapter.

4. **Economics** What happened to slavery as states grew more cotton?

5. **History** What effect did Nat Turner's rebellion have on southerners and their opinion of freedom for African Americans?

6. **Geography** What were the results of the Kansas-Nebraska Act?

7. **History** How did the Underground Railroad help people escape slavery?

8. **Government** Why were many southerners unhappy when Abraham Lincoln was elected President?

Vocabulary

✅ **TEST PREP** Choose the correct word from the list below to complete each sentence.

> **tariff,** p. 418
> **popular sovereignty,** p. 433
> **fugitive,** p. 434

9. In some territories, settlers had _____ and decided for themselves whether to allow slavery.

10. When Congress passed a _____, people had to pay higher prices for imported goods.

11. An escaped slave was called a _____.

1831
Nat Turner's rebellion

1852
Uncle Tom's Cabin written

1859
John Brown's raid

1861
Civil War begins

1830 1835 1840 1845 1850 1855 1860 1865

Apply Skills

 TEST PREP Chart and Graph Skill

Use the graphs about African American population before the Civil War to answer each question.

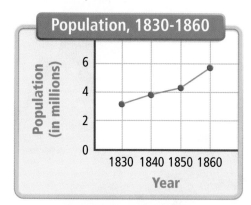

Population, 1830-1860

Population (in millions)

6
4
2
0

1830 1840 1850 1860
Year

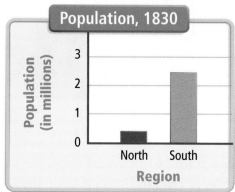

Population, 1830

Population (in millions)

3
2
1
0

North   South
Region

12. Which statement is most accurate?

A. The number of African Americans in the North grew quickly.

B. The number of African Americans in the North and South was equal in 1830.

C. The number of African Americans decreased over time.

D. The number of African Americans in the South was greater than in the North.

13. What do the two graphs have in common?

Critical Thinking

 TEST PREP Write a short paragraph to answer each question.

14. Cause and Effect What were the causes of sectionalism in the United States?

15. Compare and Contrast In what way was Abraham Lincoln's view of slavery different from that of Stephen Douglas?

Timeline

Use the Chapter Summary Timeline above to answer the question.

16. Which events took place during the 1850s?

Activities

Research Activity With a partner, find out more about an abolitionist in this chapter. Write and illustrate a short biography of that person.

Writing Activity Write a dialogue for a story in which a member of the Underground Railroad asks friends to help rescue enslaved people. Have the characters discuss the dangers and importance of the work.

 Technology
Writing Process Tips
Get help with your story at
www.eduplace.com/kids/hmss05/

Technology

e • **glossary**
e • **word games**
www.eduplace.com/kids/hmss05/

Vocabulary Preview

emancipation

In 1862, President Lincoln ordered the **emancipation** of all the slaves in the Confederacy. He declared that they were free.
page 456

civilian

The war touched the lives of everyone, whether soldier or **civilian.** Family photographs were a comfort to civilians who stayed at home.
page 462

Chapter Timeline

1863
Battle of Gettysburg

1865
Civil War ends

1860   1865   1870

Reading Strategy

Summarize Use this strategy to focus on important ideas.

Review the main ideas. Then look for important details that support those ideas.

telegraph

Generals used the **telegraph** to give President Lincoln information about the war. Their messages traveled quickly over wires. **page 467**

sharecropping

After the war, many African Americans began **sharecropping.** They gave the owner of the land they farmed a share of the crops they raised. **page 482**

1877
Reconstruction ends

1881
Tuskegee Institute opens

875   1880   1885

A Nation at War

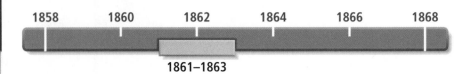

| 1858 | 1860 | 1862 | 1864 | 1866 | 1868 |

1861–1863

Build on What You Know Have you ever started a task that was harder than it seemed at first? At the start of the Civil War, both sides thought they could win quickly. Soon, they knew that winning would be far from easy.

VOCABULARY

border states
casualties
draft
emancipation

Vocabulary Strategy

draft

Draft is a homograph, a word with more than one meaning. In this lesson, it means a system for bringing people into the military.

READING SKILL

Classify List the advantages and disadvantages that the North and the South had at the start of the war.

NORTH	SOUTH

North Against South

Main Idea The Union and Confederacy had different strengths.

When the Civil War began, 11 southern states seceded and formed the Confederacy. Four other slave states, Missouri, Kentucky, Maryland, and Delaware, stayed in the Union. Slave states that stayed in the Union were known as **border states.**

The North had many advantages in the war. About 22 million people lived in the North. The South only had around nine million people, and about one-third of them were enslaved and could not become soldiers. The North had more factories for making weapons and supplies. It also had more railroad lines than the South. Soldiers and supplies could move quickly by railroad.

The Confederate states had some advantages, too. Most of the fighting took place in the South, and Confederate soldiers were defending land they knew. The South also had excellent military leaders, such as General **Robert E. Lee.**

General Lee He was a skilled and respected Confederate general who had fought in the Mexican War.

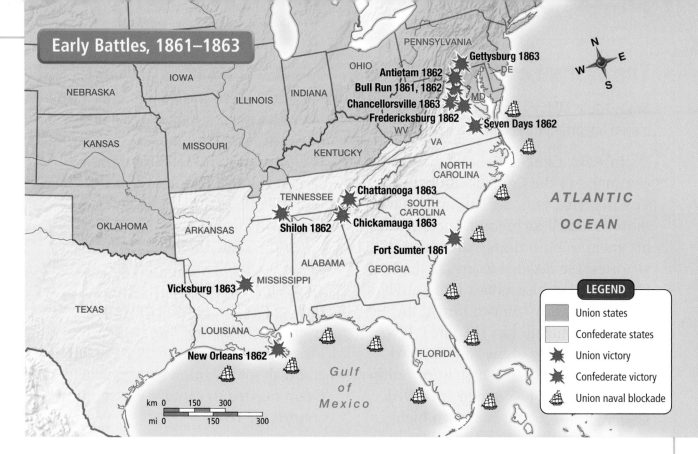

Early Battles, 1861–1863

OHIO
IOWA
NEBRASKA
ILLINOIS INDIANA
KANSAS
MISSOURI
KENTUCKY
OKLAHOMA
ARKANSAS
TENNESSEE
TEXAS
MISSISSIPPI
LOUISIANA
ALABAMA GEORGIA
PENNSYLVANIA
Gettysburg 1863
Antietam 1862
Bull Run 1861, 1862
Chancellorsville 1863
Fredericksburg 1862
WV
Seven Days 1862
VA
NORTH CAROLINA
Chattanooga 1863
SOUTH CAROLINA
Shiloh 1862 Chickamauga 1863
Fort Sumter 1861
Vicksburg 1863
New Orleans 1862
FLORIDA
Gulf of Mexico
ATLANTIC OCEAN

km 0   150   300
mi 0   150   300

LEGEND
Union states
Confederate states
Union victory
Confederate victory
Union naval blockade

Early Battles The Union plan to block Confederate ports and attack by land was called the Anaconda Plan, after a snake that squeezes its prey.

SKILL **Reading Maps** In which state were most of the Confederate victories?

Plans for War

Union leaders created a strategy, or plan, to defeat the South. The navy would block southern seaports so that the Confederacy could not trade with other countries. The navy would also take control of the Mississippi River. Then the Union army would attack in the East and West at the same time.

The South's strategy was to fight off northern attacks until the Confederacy could survive as a separate nation. Southerners knew that many people in the North were already against the war. If the Union lost too many battles, northerners might give up. Southerners also hoped for help from Britain and France because those countries needed southern cotton.

The War in the East

At the start of the war, both sides expected a quick, easy victory. Thousands of men from the North and South joined the Union and Confederate armies.

In July 1861, a Union army marched south from Washington. Its goal was to capture the Confederate capital of Richmond, Virginia, about 100 miles away. On July 21, the two armies fought at a stream called Bull Run, near the town of Manassas. Both sides fought hard all day. At the end of the battle, called the First Battle of Bull Run, the Union army retreated in a panic. The battle was worse than expected. People began to realize that the war would not end soon.

REVIEW What was the Confederacy's plan for winning the war?

The War's Leaders

Main Idea Military and political leaders played important roles during the war.

In 1862, General Robert E. Lee took command of the Confederate army in Virginia. That year, the Union tried twice more to attack Richmond. Lee defeated his enemies both times. After these victories, Lee decided to invade the North. He led his soldiers into Maryland. The Union army stopped him at the Battle of Antietam (an TEE tam). It was the deadliest day of the war. The two armies suffered 22,000 casualties. Soldiers who are killed or wounded are called **casualties.** Lee's army had such high casualties that he returned to Virginia.

Battle of Antietam Look at the map and the description on the next page to learn more about this fierce battle.

The War in the West

In the West, the Union army and navy had more success. General **Ulysses S. Grant** led a Union army south from Illinois into Tennessee. He captured several Confederate forts along the way. In the Battle of Shiloh, he defeated a large Confederate army.

At the same time, the Union navy sailed up the Mississippi River and attacked New Orleans. By early 1863, the only major Confederate town left on the river was Vicksburg, Mississippi. From Vicksburg's cliffs, Confederate soldiers could shoot at Union ships on the river. Grant needed to capture Vicksburg to control the river.

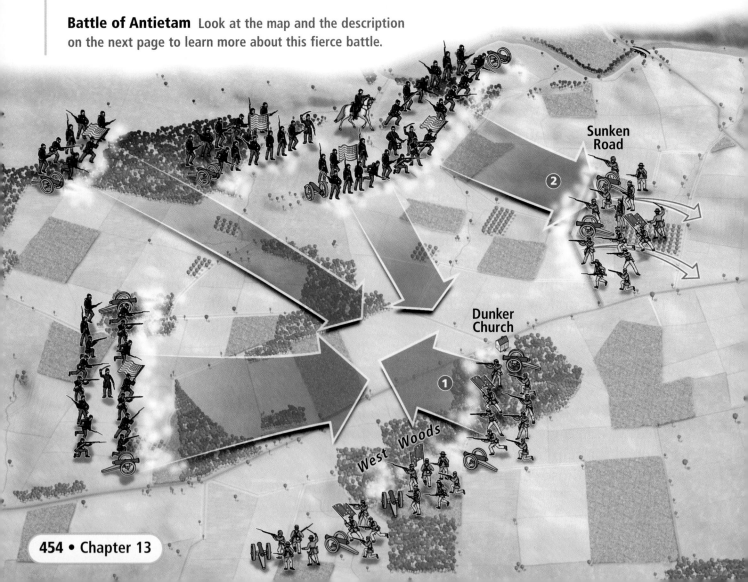

Sunken Road

Dunker Church

West Woods

The Governments Respond

Jefferson Davis, the president of the Confederacy, faced many problems. The Union blockade closed most Confederate ports. The South had trouble getting enough food, weapons, or money to fight. Not enough people wanted to join the army. To find more soldiers, Davis had to start a draft. During a **draft,** a government selects people to serve in the military. The Confederate states often ignored Jefferson Davis's orders.

President **Abraham Lincoln** also faced challenges. As the number of casualties rose, he had to work hard to win support for the war.

Like the Confederacy, the Union had to start a draft. Rich people could pay to get out of the draft. This upset people who could not afford the money and those who were against the war. In New York City, people opposed to the draft started a riot that lasted for days. A riot is a violent protest. The government had to send in thousands of soldiers to stop the riots.

REVIEW Why did people in the North oppose the draft?

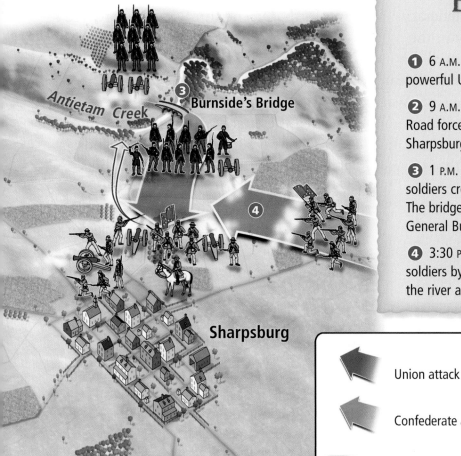

Antietam Creek

Burnside's Bridge

Sharpsburg

Battle of Antietam
September 17, 1862

1 6 A.M. – 9 A.M. Confederate soldiers fight off three powerful Union attacks near the Dunker Church.

2 9 A.M. – 1 P.M. Union attacks on the Sunken Road force Confederate soldiers to retreat toward Sharpsburg. Both sides suffer many casualties.

3 1 P.M. – 3 P.M. After hours of fighting, Union soldiers cross Antietam Creek and attack Sharpsburg. The bridge is later renamed for their commander, General Burnside.

4 3:30 P.M. Confederate soldiers take the Union soldiers by surprise, forcing them to retreat back across the river and saving Lee's army from defeat.

LEGEND

Union attack

Confederate attack

Union retreat

Confederate retreat

Union soldier

Confederate soldier

Union General McClellan

Confederate General Lee

Turning Points

Main Idea Events in 1863 helped the Union become stronger in the Civil War.

At the start of the war, President Lincoln's only goal was to keep the Union together. He did not plan to free enslaved people. By 1862, however, he changed his mind. Many people in the North wanted him to end slavery, and freeing enslaved people could weaken the Confederacy. He also hoped that freed slaves would work to help the Union.

Lincoln put the Emancipation Proclamation into effect on January 1, 1863. **Emancipation** is the freeing of enslaved people. This proclamation declared that slaves in the Confederacy were free. It did not end slavery in the border states. Confederates ignored the new law. The North would have to defeat the South to free the slaves. The Civil War had started as a war to save the Union. The Emancipation Proclamation made it a war to end slavery in the South.

Vicksburg and Gettysburg

In 1863, the Union won two important battles. In the West, General Grant's army surrounded Vicksburg and fired cannons into the town for six weeks. On July 4, Vicksburg surrendered. The Union now controlled the Mississippi River. This cut off Texas and Arkansas from the rest of the South.

The Union also won a major battle in the East. After stopping two more attacks on Richmond, General Lee decided to invade the Union again. He marched north into Pennsylvania. The Union army met Lee's soldiers on July 1, near the town of Gettysburg.

For two days the armies battled back and forth. On the third day, Lee ordered a final attack. Nearly 14,000 Confederate soldiers charged across open fields towards the Union army.

The Union soldiers were ready. They stopped the attack with rifle and cannon fire. The heavy fire killed or wounded about half of the Confederate soldiers. Lee's weakened army had to retreat.

July 1863 was the turning point of the war. The Union victories at Vicksburg and Gettysburg gave the Union a better chance of winning.

Emancipation Proclamation
President Lincoln decided to issue the proclamation to free the slaves. This is a copy that was made so that people could put it up in their homes and schools.

Later that year, President Lincoln gave a short speech at Gettysburg, known as the Gettysburg Address. He declared that the Union was fighting to make sure that American democracy would survive. The speech is famous as a powerful statement about the purpose of the Civil War.

REVIEW Why was the victory at Vicksburg important to the Union?

Lesson Summary

At first, the Confederacy won most battles in the East, while the Union won battles in the West. However, victories at Vicksburg and Gettysburg gave the Union the advantage in the war.

Why It Matters...

With the Emancipation Proclamation, the Civil War became a fight to end slavery in the Confederate States.

Gettysburg This painting shows the Confederate attack on the third day of the battle. The attack is known as Pickett's Charge, after one of the generals who led it.

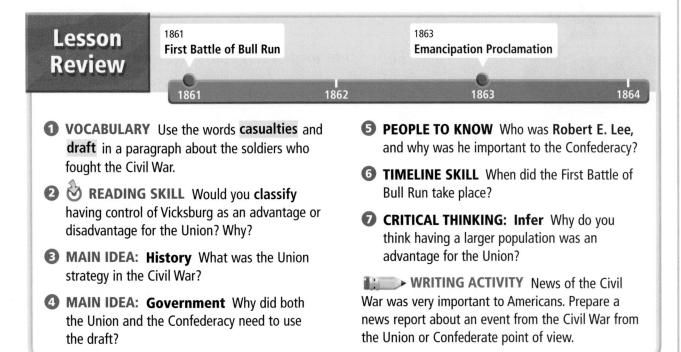

Lesson Review

1861		1863	
First Battle of Bull Run		**Emancipation Proclamation**	
1861	1862	1863	1864

① **VOCABULARY** Use the words **casualties** and **draft** in a paragraph about the soldiers who fought the Civil War.

② **READING SKILL** Would you **classify** having control of Vicksburg as an advantage or disadvantage for the Union? Why?

③ **MAIN IDEA: History** What was the Union strategy in the Civil War?

④ **MAIN IDEA: Government** Why did both the Union and the Confederacy need to use the draft?

⑤ **PEOPLE TO KNOW** Who was **Robert E. Lee**, and why was he important to the Confederacy?

⑥ **TIMELINE SKILL** When did the First Battle of Bull Run take place?

⑦ **CRITICAL THINKING: Infer** Why do you think having a larger population was an advantage for the Union?

WRITING ACTIVITY News of the Civil War was very important to Americans. Prepare a news report about an event from the Civil War from the Union or Confederate point of view.

Primary Source

The GETTYSBURG ADDRESS

The speech President Lincoln gave on that November day in 1863 was short. It took him barely two minutes to read it. The speech that came before his had lasted for two hours. But Americans still remember the Gettysburg Address more than 140 years later.

Lincoln gave the address just four months after the Battle of Gettysburg. In a ceremony honoring the Union soldiers who had died in the battle, Lincoln spoke about the meaning of the war and its terrible cost. His words captured the feelings of Americans as they struggled to meet a serious danger to their country.

① *Four score and seven years ago our fathers brought forth on this continent, a new nation, conceived in Liberty, and dedicated to the proposition that all men are created equal.*

② *Now we are engaged in a great civil war, testing whether that nation, or any nation so conceived and so dedicated, can long endure.*

③ *We are met on a great battle-field of that war. We have come to dedicate a portion of that field, as a final resting place for those who here gave their lives that that nation might live. It is altogether fitting and proper that we should do this.*

④ But, in a larger sense, we can not dedicate—we can not consecrate—we can not hallow—this ground. The brave men, living and dead, who struggled here, have consecrated it, far above our poor power to add or detract. The world will little note, nor long remember what we say here, but it can never forget what they did here. It is for us the living, rather, to be dedicated here to the unfinished work which they who fought here have thus far so nobly advanced. It ⑤ is rather for us to be here dedicated to the great task remaining before us—that from these honored dead we take increased devotion to that cause for which they gave the last full measure of devotion—that we here highly resolve that these dead shall not have died in vain—that this nation, under God, shall have a new birth of freedom—and that government of the people, by the people, for the people, shall not perish from the earth.

① Eighty-seven years ago, our nation was founded on the ideals of freedom and equality.

② Now we are fighting a war to see if our nation and our ideals can survive.

③ We are here to honor soldiers who died fighting in this war.

④ The best way we can honor them is to stay dedicated to our ideals.

⑤ We promise to uphold freedom so that our democracy will survive.

Activities

1. **TALK ABOUT IT** What do you think Lincoln meant by "unfinished work"?

2. **WRITE ABOUT IT** Explain why you think Lincoln's speech is famous today. Choose two of his ideas and write a one-page paper about why they are still important.

 Technology Learn about other primary sources for this unit at Education Place. www.eduplace.com/kids/hmss05/

The Human Face of War

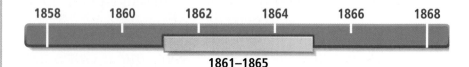

1858   1860   1862   1864   1866   1868

1861–1865

Build on What You Know Have you ever missed someone or waited for a card from a friend or family member? If you have, then you know part of what it was like to live during the Civil War. During the war, soldiers and their families missed each other's company.

The Soldier's Life

Main Idea Soldiers in the Civil War faced problems other than fighting battles.

Men from all parts of the country fought in the Civil War. Many hoped for excitement and glory. Instead, they found terror in battle and boredom in camp. A **camp** is a group of temporary shelters, such as tents.

Soldiers read, sang, or wrote letters to pass the time in camp. Some put on shows or printed newspapers. They loved to get letters. "It made the boys shout with Joy to heare from home once more," wrote one soldier.

Food in the army was usually poor. Union soldiers grew tired of eating the same food almost every day. However, Confederate soldiers suffered more because they often did not have enough to eat.

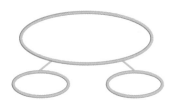
Camp Life Soldiers in camp often slept on the ground in tents, with nothing to sit on but the ground or wooden boxes.

New Soldiers African American soldiers fought for the Union in many battles. Several won the Congressional Medal of Honor, shown at right, for their courage.

Who Were the Soldiers?

Civil War soldiers came from many different backgrounds. At first, almost all were white and born in the United States. As the war went on, the Union allowed African Americans to join the army. About 180,000 African Americans served in the Union army. They fought in many battles, including Vicksburg.

Immigrants also joined the Union army. They included people from Germany, Ireland, and Italy. American Indians fought on both sides.

Thousands of boys went into battle even though they were too young. Some served as drummers who sent signals to soldiers in battle. Hundreds of women on both sides disguised themselves as men and joined the army. Women also worked as spies for one side or the other.

Casualties of War

The Civil War was the deadliest war in American history. Rifles could shoot farther and more accurately than ever before. Casualties were much higher than people had expected. However, battle was not the only danger of war. Disease killed twice as many soldiers as the fighting did.

Women helped care for the sick and wounded. More than 3,000 northern women served as nurses. One was **Clara Barton,** who later founded the American Red Cross. Southern women also cared for wounded soldiers in hospitals and in their homes.

The Civil War affected the lives of most Americans. Soldiers had to face the dangers of battle and disease, as well as the boredom of camp life. Thousands of families lost loved ones.

REVIEW What did women on both sides of the war do to help their side?

On the Home Front

Main Idea The Civil War was difficult for people at home, especially in the South.

Many soldiers left families behind when they went to war. Those families were part of the home front. When a country is at war, the **home front** is all the people who are not in the military. Soldiers and their families did not want to be separated. "My Dear Dear Father," wrote the daughter of one officer, "I do miss you so much. . . ." With men gone, women took on new tasks. They ran farms and businesses. Thousands of women sewed uniforms, knitted socks, made bandages, and raised money for their armies.

Most of the battles in the Civil War took place in the South. Few people in the North could see the war happening. The new technology of photography let civilians see what the war looked like. A **civilian** is a person who is not in the military. **Mathew Brady** took pictures of soldiers, camp life, and battlefields. He showed his photographs in the North. Civilians there saw that war was much worse than they had realized.

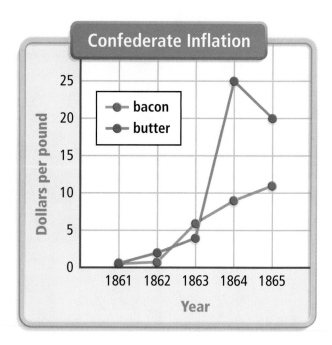

Confederate Inflation

Dollars per pound / *Year* — ● bacon, ● butter (1861, 1862, 1863, 1864, 1865)

Inflation Food and other necessary goods became too expensive for many southerners to afford. **SKILL** **Reading Graphs** How expensive was butter in 1864?

The Southern Home Front

Life on the home front was especially hard in the South. Their farms became battlefields. Their cities, homes, and barns were destroyed.

In the South, soldiers and civilians often did not have enough to eat. Inflation, or a rise in prices, made food very expensive. The money printed by the Confederate government became almost worthless. A barrel of flour that cost $6 in 1861 might cost $1,000 in 1865. In Richmond and other towns, hungry women attacked shops in search of food.

Enslaved people in the South suffered as well, but most still welcomed the war. The Emancipation Proclamation in 1863 gave them the hope of freedom.

Money Each Confederate state printed its own money. Because of inflation, most of the bills became almost worthless.

Juneteenth African American communities celebrate Juneteenth. This parade was held in Austin, Texas, where it is a yearly event.

Some enslaved people only learned of the proclamation at the end of the war. News of the Emancipation Proclamation reached Texas on June 19, 1865. This day became a day of celebration. Known as Juneteenth, June 19 is still celebrated in Texas and other parts of the country as the day slavery ended.

REVIEW What happened to prices in the South during the Civil War?

Lesson Summary

- During the war soldiers faced danger in battle and from disease.
- Soldiers came from many different backgrounds.
- The Civil War affected the lives of all Americans, not just soliders.

Why It Matters ...

During the Civil War, Americans lived through of the hardest years in the nation's history.

Lesson Review

1 **VOCABULARY** Write a pargraph about the lives of ordinary people during the Civil War. Use **home front** and **civilian** in your paragraph.

2 **READING SKILL** Use the details in the chart on page 462 to explain why life was hard during the Civil War.

3 **MAIN IDEA: History** What made camp life hard for Civil War soldiers?

4 **MAIN IDEA: Citizenship** In what ways did women contribute to the war effort?

5 **PEOPLE TO KNOW** Who was **Mathew Brady** and what did he do during the Civil War?

6 **CRITICAL THINKING: Draw Conclusions** Use information you have learned to tell why women and children joined the army on both sides.

7 **CRITICAL THINKING: Analyze** What was the point of view of enslaved people in the South toward the war? How was it different from the view of most other southerners?

MAP ACTIVITY Trace a map of the United States. Identify the states that fought in the Civil War. Use different colors for the Union, the Confederacy, and the border states.

Courageous Women

Many women are remembered today for their role in the Civil War. Few women fought, but many on both sides did take part in the war. Some braved serious dangers to nurse wounded soldiers on the battlefields. Others took risks by acting as spies. For many, especially in the South, simply living through the war took courage.

CLARA BARTON
1821–1912

When Clara Barton volunteered as a Union army nurse, she saw that hospitals had no medicines or bandages. She wrote letters to newspapers asking people to make donations. When she arrived at battlefields with loads of supplies, she sometimes risked her life. But the troops cheered. "I went in while the battle raged," she once recalled. After the war, in 1881, she was asked to start the American Red Cross, an organization that still helps people in times of war and peace.

ELIZABETH VAN LEW
1818 – 1890

Even before the Civil War began, Elizabeth Van Lew opposed slavery. She lived in Virginia, a southern state, and she convinced her mother to free the family's slaves. During the war, Van Lew became a spy for the Union army. She got important information from Confederate sources. She asked former slaves to carry her secret coded messages in hollow eggshells or in the soles of their shoes. In 1865, when Union troops arrived in Richmond, Van Lew flew the Union flag for all to see.

MARY CHESNUT
1823 – 1886

Mary Chesnut kept a diary during the Civil War. She was a wealthy South Carolinian whose husband was a Confederate general. In her diary, she described the collapse of the Confederate government. She recorded the thoughts and fears of people involved in the war, including her own true beliefs—she was against slavery. Her writing is valued today as a full portrait of the Confederacy, and a rich source of information for historians.

Activities

1. **TALK ABOUT IT** Discuss how each of these women showed **courage** during the Civil War.

2. **DEBATE IT** Do you think it was harder or easier for women to take part in the war than for men? Debate your opinion. Support your opinion with facts.

 Technology Visit Education Place for more biographies of people in this unit. www.eduplace.com/kids/hmss05/

465

The War Ends

VOCABULARY

telegraph
total war
desert

Vocabulary Strategy

telegraph

The prefix **tele-** in the word
telegraph means "far away."
A telegraph sends messages
to distant places.

READING SKILL
Predict Outcomes
As you read, make a prediction
about how the Civil War will
finally end.

PREDICTION

OUTCOME

Build on What You Know To finish a job, you need
to have enough supplies. In the Civil War, the Union had
more soldiers, weapons, and food than the Confederacy.
These supplies helped the Union win the war.

Union Victories

Main Idea The Union tried to force the South to surrender by
destroying southerners' resources.

By the end of 1863, the Union had won several
important battles in the Civil War. Victories at Vicksburg
and Gettysburg gave northerners hope of winning the
war. But the Confederate armies were still fighting hard.
To end the war, the North had to destroy the South's
ability to fight.

President Lincoln needed a tough army general to
defeat the South. He chose **Ulysses S. Grant.** Grant
proved in the West that he could fight hard. Lincoln
made him the commander of all Union armies.

Grant planned to lead an army into Virginia to defeat
General **Robert E. Lee's** army
and capture Richmond. Grant
also ordered General **William
Tecumseh Sherman** to lead
the Union army in Tennessee.
Sherman planned to attack
Atlanta, Georgia, a major
Confederate city.

General Grant Little
known before the war, he
became famous for his
determination to win.

Later Battles, 1864–1865

PENNSYLVANIA
MARYLAND
DELAWARE
ILLINOIS INDIANA OHIO WEST VIRGINIA
Wilderness 1864
Spotsylvania 1864
Cold Harbor 1864
Appomattox Court House 1865
Petersburg 1864–1865
VIRGINIA
Ohio River
KENTUCKY
NORTH CAROLINA
ATLANTIC OCEAN
Nashville 1864 TENNESSEE
Franklin 1864
Chattanooga
SOUTH CAROLINA
Columbia
Atlanta 1864 Atlanta
Charleston
Mississippi River
ALABAMA GEORGIA
Savannah
MISSISSIPPI
Mobile Bay 1864
New Orleans
FLORIDA

Gulf of Mexico

km 0 150 300
mi 0 150 300

LEGEND
Union states
Confederate states
Union victory
Confederate victory
No clear victory
Sherman's route

Later Battles This map shows the major battles from the last two years of the Civil War. During their march through Georgia, Union soldiers wrecked railroads (above) by bending the rails.

Sherman's March

Sherman began his attack on Atlanta in May 1864. His experienced soldiers quickly marched into Georgia. The Confederates fought all summer, but Sherman's army captured Atlanta in September. Sherman sent a message to President Lincoln by telegraph. A **telegraph** is a machine that sends electric signals over wires. Sherman's message said, "Atlanta is ours, and fairly won." That summer, the Union navy won another important battle by capturing Mobile Bay in Alabama.

Lincoln welcomed these victories. He was running for reelection in 1864 and worried about losing. He needed military victories like Atlanta and Mobile Bay to gain voters' support.

From Atlanta, Sherman's army marched to Savannah, on Georgia's coast. This march became known as the March to the Sea. Along the way, the soldiers destroyed anything southerners needed for the war. They stole food, killed animals, and wrecked factories and railroad tracks. Sherman used total war to make southerners so tired of fighting that they would give up. **Total war** is the strategy of destroying an enemy's resources.

After reaching Savannah, Sherman's army turned north once again destroying everything in its path. One woman described how the soldiers "roamed about setting fire to every house . . ."

REVIEW Why did Sherman decide to use total war against the South?

467

Grant and Lee

Main Idea Grant's attacks in Virginia wore down Lee's army and forced it to surrender.

While Sherman marched into Georgia in 1864, Grant led a huge army toward Richmond, Virginia. He was opposed by Robert E. Lee's army. Lee was a brilliant general who had defeated larger armies. Grant's strength was his determination. He kept attacking, even after a defeat.

Lee used all of his skill to fight off Grant's army. The Union suffered terrible losses, but Grant kept attacking. His attacks wore down the Confederate army in a series of battles. Lee was forced farther and farther south.

In June 1864, the two armies faced each other near Richmond. They stayed there for almost a year. Neither side could defeat the other. However, the Union army was growing stronger.

Lee's Surrender

The Union's resources helped Grant. He received a steady supply of food and equipment. The North sent thousands more soldiers to join his army. President Lincoln said, "We have more men now than we had when the war began."

At the same time, Lee's army was struggling. The Confederate government had no more soldiers or supplies to send Lee. Confederate soldiers went hungry, and some began to desert. To **desert** means to leave the army without permission.

By early April 1865, Lee's army was too weak to defend Richmond any longer. Lee retreated. The Union army captured Richmond and chased Lee's army west. Finally, near a town called Appomattox Court House, Lee made a hard decision. His starving army was nearly surrounded. He had to surrender. He said,

> 66 **There is nothing left for me to do but go and see General Grant...** 99

Surrender Lee surrendered to Grant on April 9, 1865 at Appomattox Court House. "We are all Americans," one of Grant's officers told Lee afterwards.

Lee's Chair

On April 9, 1865, Grant and Lee met in a home in the village of Appomattox Court House. Grant said that Lee's soldiers could go home. Lee agreed to surrender. Grant then sent 25,000 meals to the hungry Confederate soldiers.

Grant told his soldiers not to celebrate. "The war is over," he said. "The rebels are our countrymen again." A few days later, Lee's soldiers marched past the Union army to surrender. As they passed, the Union soldiers saluted their old enemies.

News of Lee's surrender spread quickly. In Washington, people celebrated in the streets. Confederate soldiers in North Carolina surrendered to Sherman. Fighting continued in a few places, but by late June all was quiet. The war was over at last.

REVIEW Why did Lee have to surrender?

Lesson Summary

> General Sherman used total war to destroy the South's ability to fight.

> General Lee's army could not get enough food or equipment.

> Lee had to surrender to General Grant.

Why It Matters ...

The victory of the Union made certain that the United States would remain one nation.

Lesson Review

1864
Grant invades Virginia

1865
Lee surrenders

1864 — 1865 — 1866

❶ **VOCABULARY** Choose the correct word to complete each sentence.

   total war   telegraph   desert

   Sherman used the _____ to communicate with President Lincoln. Lee's army shrank as his soldiers began to _____.

❷ **READING SKILL** Check your **prediction**. Compare it to the description in the lesson of how the war ends.

❸ **MAIN IDEA: History** What was Sherman's plan for making the South surrender?

❹ **MAIN IDEA: Economics** In what way did lack of resources affect the Confederate army?

❺ **PEOPLE TO KNOW** Who was **Ulysses S. Grant**, and why was he important during the Civil War?

❻ **TIMELINE SKILL** In what year did Grant invade Virginia?

❼ **CRITICAL THINKING: Decision Making** What were the effects of Sherman's decision to march from Atlanta to Savannah?

HANDS ON **MATH ACTIVITY** At Appomattox Court House, the Union army had about 103,000 soldiers and the Confederate army had about 28,000 soldiers. How many more soldiers did the Union have? Draw a bar graph to compare the size of the two armies.

A Global View, 1865

During the 1860s, the Civil War changed life for most Americans. At the same time, changes were taking place elsewhere. Powerful nations in Europe tried to conquer land in other continents. Some countries grew more wealthy. People in other countries rebelled against their leaders and governments.

New technology made travel and communication easier, so trade among continents grew. Goods and ideas spread more quickly than ever before. Look on the map to see what was happening around the world.

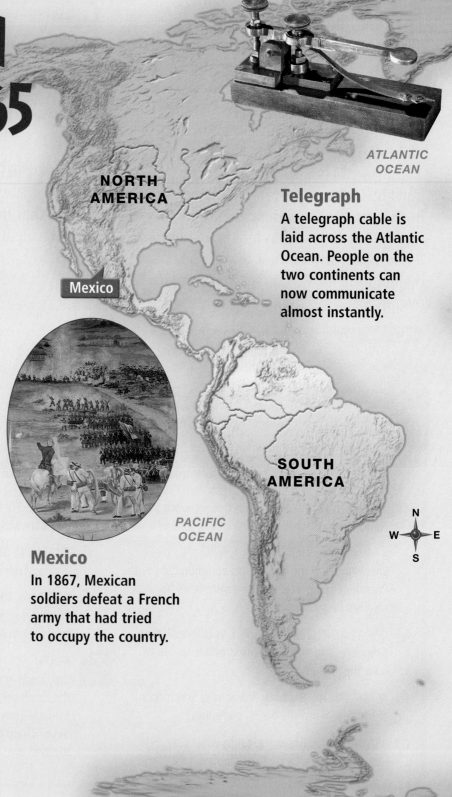

NORTH AMERICA

Mexico

ATLANTIC OCEAN

PACIFIC OCEAN

SOUTH AMERICA

Telegraph

A telegraph cable is laid across the Atlantic Ocean. People on the two continents can now communicate almost instantly.

Mexico

In 1867, Mexican soldiers defeat a French army that had tried to occupy the country.

Italy

Italy, which had been made up of many small states, is united for the first time in almost 1,500 years.

EUROPE

Italy

Egypt

AFRICA

India

The British government takes over large parts of India. India is ruled by Britain until 1947.

ASIA

India

PACIFIC OCEAN

Egypt

The Suez Canal opens in 1869. Ships traveling between Europe and Asia no longer have to sail all the way around Africa.

INDIAN OCEAN

Australia

The discovery of gold in Australia brings thousands of new settlers to the colonies there.

AUSTRALIA

ANTARCTICA

Activities

1. **TALK ABOUT IT** How do you think the Suez Canal or a telegraph across the Atlantic Ocean changed people's lives?

2. **CREATE IT** Find out the different ways people could travel and communicate in 1865. Make a poster comparing travel and communication in 1865 and today.

Reconstruction

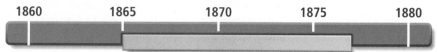

1860   1865   1870   1875   1880

1865–1877

VOCABULARY

**Reconstruction
assassination
Freedmen's Bureau
impeach**

Vocabulary Strategy

Reconstruction

Find the word **construct** in **Reconstruction.** When you reconstruct something, you construct, or build, it again.

READING SKILL
Draw Conclusions
Use facts and details to come to a conclusion about how Reconstruction affected people's lives.

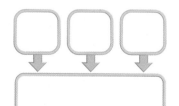

Build on What You Know Have you ever had a moment when you knew that your life has changed forever? That is a turning point. The Civil War was a turning point for the United States. After the war, the nation would never be the same again.

Plans for Reconstruction

Main Idea President Lincoln and Congress disagreed about how to rebuild the South.

As the Civil War ended, Americans faced a great challenge. When the South tried to leave the Union, the nation had nearly split apart. During Reconstruction, the country had to be reunited. The period when the South rejoined the Union is called **Reconstruction.**

Reconstruction was a difficult time. Americans could not agree on how to bring the South back into the Union. Some wanted to make it easy for southern states to rejoin. They hoped that the nation could be almost the way it had been before the war.

Many northerners felt differently. They were bitter about the war and blamed the South for it. Some of them wanted to use Reconstruction to punish the South.

President Lincoln Saving the Union was Lincoln's greatest concern. He wanted to reunite the nation quickly.

Funeral Train
Large crowds gathered for parades honoring President Lincoln after his death.

President **Lincoln** did not want to punish the South. He asked northerners to forget their anger. Lincoln said,

> 66 With malice [meanness] toward none, with charity for all . . . let us strive on [try] to finish the work we are in, to bind up the nation's wounds . . . 99

Lincoln planned to let the defeated states set up new state governments and rejoin the Union quickly.

Many people disagreed with Lincoln, especially the Radical Republicans. These senators and representatives wanted to greatly change the South. For example, they hoped to use Reconstruction to protect the rights of African Americans. Because they disagreed with the President, Republicans in Congress wanted to control Reconstruction.

Lincoln's Death

Before Lincoln and Congress could agree on a plan, disaster struck. On the evening of April 14, 1865, Lincoln went to a play at Ford's Theater in Washington. **John Wilkes Booth**, an actor, crept up behind Lincoln. Booth supported the Confederacy and was angry about the South's defeat. He pulled out a gun and shot the President. Abraham Lincoln died the next day.

Lincoln's assassination shocked the nation. **Assassination** is the murder of an important leader. Lincoln had become a hero to many people. His death filled them with sadness. They would miss his leadership during the difficult years of Reconstruction.

REVIEW What was Lincoln's plan for Reconstruction?

Reconstruction

Main Idea Congress took control of Reconstruction from President Andrew Johnson.

After Lincoln's death, Vice President **Andrew Johnson** of Tennessee became President. Johnson put Lincoln's plan for Reconstruction into action in 1865. The southern states quickly set up new state governments. The federal government forced them to abolish slavery in their state constitutions. At the same time, though, most southern states passed harsh laws called Black Codes. The Black Codes limited the rights of former slaves to travel, vote, and work in certain jobs.

Radical Republicans in Congress were unhappy about the Black Codes. President Johnson upset them more by allowing southern states to elect former Confederate leaders to Congress.

Congress fought back. Members voted not to let the new southern representatives join Congress. They passed a law to protect the rights of freedmen, who were the people freed from slavery. Congress also created the Freedmen's Bureau. The **Freedmen's Bureau** provided food, clothing, medical care, and legal advice to poor blacks and whites. It set up hospitals and schools and found jobs for many.

Reconstruction The mural below shows several scenes from Reconstruction: **1** Students attend a new school opened by the Freedmen's Bureau. **2** Radical Republicans impeach President Johnson. **3** African Americans vote for the first time. **4** African Americans serve in Congress.

Congress Takes Control

In 1867, Congress began its own Reconstruction plan. It put the South under military rule. Soldiers from the national army marched into the region. When they arrived, they forced southern states to obey Congress. The states had to allow all men, including blacks, to vote.

After taking over Reconstruction, Congress tried to remove President Johnson. In 1868, the House of Representatives voted to impeach Johnson. To **impeach** means to charge a government official with a crime. They accused him of breaking one of their new laws. Congress almost forced Johnson out of office, but they did not succeed, and he finished his presidency.

Carpetbaggers and Scalawags

Some southerners supported the Republicans during Reconstruction. They were unpopular with southerners. Southerners who helped the government during Reconstruction were known as scalawags. Scalawag was a slang word for an old worthless horse.

Many northerners traveled south during Reconstruction. Some wanted to help rebuild the South, but others just wanted to make money. These people were known as carpetbaggers, because they often carried suitcases made of carpet material. Southerners disliked carpetbaggers and did not want them there.

REVIEW Why were soldiers sent to the South?

The Constitution Changes

Main Idea Congress changed the Constitution to protect the rights of African Americans.

During Reconstruction, Congress created three new amendments to the Constitution. The new amendments gave the national government more power over the states. They also protected the rights of African Americans.

The first of the new amendments, the Thirteenth Amendment, ended slavery throughout the United States. In 1865, the states ratified the amendment, which means they approved it.

Black Codes still limited the rights of African Americans. To protect those rights, Congress passed the Fourteenth Amendment, which gave citizenship to African Americans. It said that a citizen's life, liberty, or property cannot be taken away without a fair trial. This is called "due process of law." It also said that all citizens must be treated equally under the law.

Almost every southern state refused to ratify the Fourteenth Amendment. They did not want the national government to interfere with their state laws. Congress declared that southern states had to ratify the Fourteenth Amendment to rejoin the Union. The states then agreed to the demands of Congress.

A year later, Congress passed the Fifteenth Amendment, guaranteeing African American men the right to vote. The Fifteenth Amendment had an effect right away. African Americans began taking part in government. Religious leaders, former soldiers, and others ran for office. Some became leaders in community and state government.

Many African Americans served in state legislatures. They worked to create the first public schools for whites and blacks in the South. Seventeen African Americans joined the United States Congress. **Blanche K. Bruce** and **Hiram Revels** of Mississippi became two of the first black senators.

Three New Amendments

Thirteenth Amendment

The Thirteenth Amendment declared that slavery would not be allowed to exist in the United States. It ended the long argument in the United States over whether slavery should be legal.

Fourteenth Amendment

The Fourteenth Amendment declared that the states could not limit the rights of citizens. States could not take away life, liberty, or property without due process of the law, or deny equal protection of the law.

Fifteenth Amendment

The Fifteenth Amendment gave all men the right to vote, no matter what their skin color was or if they had been enslaved. However, women were still not allowed to vote until the 1920s.

The Struggle for Rights Continues

The amendments passed during Reconstruction helped all Americans. They protected people's rights and made laws fairer. For example, the Fourteenth Amendment requires both the federal and the state governments to treat all citizens equally and fairly.

The amendments, however, did not solve all of the nation's problems. Some people, both in the North and in the South, did not want African Americans to vote or to have equal rights.

Hiram Revels
He served in the Mississippi state senate, and later became the first African American elected to the U.S. Senate.

Sometimes laws protecting rights were ignored. The struggle for equality would continue for African Americans.

REVIEW Why did Congress pass the Fourteenth Amendment?

Lesson Summary

- Congress and President Lincoln had different plans for Reconstruction.
- President Lincoln was assassinated just after the war ended.
- Congress took control of Reconstruction from President Johnson.
- Three important amendments were ratified during Reconstruction.

Why It Matters ...

During Reconstruction, the nation's laws became fairer, with new constitutional protection for citizens' rights and freedoms.

Lesson Review

1865	1868	1870
Lincoln assassinated	Congress impeaches Johnson	15th Amendment

1865 —— 1867 —— 1869 —— 1871

❶ **VOCABULARY** Write a paragraph about the actions of the United States government after the Civil War, using the words **Reconstruction, Freedmen's Bureau,** and **impeach.**

❷ **READING SKILL** Review your **conclusion.** What effect do you think Reconstruction had on the lives of freedmen?

❸ **MAIN IDEA: Government** Why did Congress fight against President Johnson?

❹ **MAIN IDEA: Citizenship** What right did the Fifteenth Amendment protect for African American men?

❺ **PEOPLE TO KNOW** Why was **Andrew Johnson** important after Lincoln's death?

❻ **TIMELINE SKILL** What did Congress do in 1868?

❼ **CRITICAL THINKING: Infer** How do you think Reconstruction might have been different if President Lincoln had not been assassinated?

HANDS ON **RESEARCH ACTIVITY** The Fourteenth Amendment guarantees due process of law and equal protection under the law. Use library or Internet resources to find out more about this amendment and create a mural explaining it.

The South After the War

After the Civil War, the economy of the United States grew faster than ever before. The South, however, did not see as much growth as other regions. Manufacturing in the South grew more slowly than in the rest of the country. Southern farmers struggled to produce as much as they had before the war.

The economy of the South suffered for many reasons. The region lost two-thirds of its wealth. Many young men who would have been farmers or workers lost their lives in the war. The war ruined homes, farms, machinery, factories, and railroads.

People in the South worked hard to rebuild their homes, cities, and factories. Cities such as Atlanta, Richmond, and Charleston became centers of trade and industry again.

Charleston (above) was left in ruins by the end of the Civil War. However, people rebuilt quickly. By 1893, Charleston (below) had grown into a large and busy city.

In 1870, the value of a southern farm was only one-third of what it had been before the war.

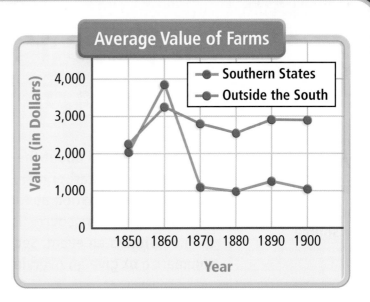

Average Value of Farms

Value (in Dollars)

- Southern States
- Outside the South

Year
1850 1860 1870 1880 1890 1900

The economy of the South improved after the war. However, the value of goods made in the South remained lower than in the rest of the country.

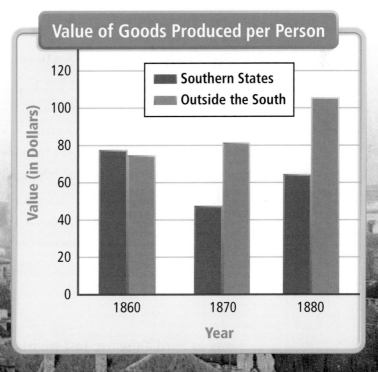

Value of Goods Produced per Person

Value (in Dollars)

- Southern States
- Outside the South

Year
1860 1870 1880

Activities

1. **THINK ABOUT IT** Why do you think so much property was destroyed in the South, but not in the North?

2. **MAKE YOUR OWN** Look at the line graph of farm values. Make a bar graph showing farm values.

Skillbuilder

Compare Primary and Secondary Sources

► **VOCABULARY**

primary source

secondary source

People learned about the death of President Lincoln from two types of sources: primary and secondary. A **primary source** is firsthand information about an event, a place, or a time period. A **secondary source** is information from someone who did not witness an event. Secondary sources sometimes summarize or give an overview of what happened.

The New York Herald

J. Wilkes Booth, the Actor, the Alleged Assassin of the President

War Department – Washington, April 15, 1865 – 1:30 a.m. – Major General Dix, New York:

This evening, at about 9:30 p.m., at Ford's Theatre [Washington, D.C.], the President, while sitting in his private box with Mrs. Lincoln,...was shot by an assassin, who suddenly entered the box and approached behind the President.

The assassin then leaped upon the stage, brandishing [waving] a large dagger or knife, and made his escape in the rear of the theatre.

...I was at Ford's theatre last night, seated in the left hand side nearly opposite the President's box. About half past ten I heard a shot. I thought it was in the play. A man appeared in front of the President's box and got upon the stage swinging himself down partly by the curtains and partly jumping. I noticed he had a large dagger in his left hand I think. He appeared to stagger but recovered himself. He held the dagger up just as he got upon the stage and said in a tragical tone very clearly...sic semper tyrannis [thus always to tyrants].

- Will T. Kent, testimony given to Supreme Court
  on April 15, 1865

Learn the Skill

Step 1: Read the sources. Look for clue words such as *I* and *my*, which are sometimes used in primary sources.

Step 2: Identify the information as a primary or secondary source. Ask yourself, Who wrote the information? Was the writer at the event?

Step 3: Make a list of the similarities and differences in the sources. Does the primary source give a different account of the event than the secondary source? What information did you learn from each source?

Practice the Skill

Read the two accounts of President Lincoln's assassination on page 480. Then answer these questions.

❶ Is the news article a primary or a secondary source? How do you know?

❷ Is Will T. Kent's account a primary or a secondary source? How do you know?

❸ What facts do the two accounts share?

❹ What differences do you see between sources?

Apply the Skill

Find an example of a primary source in a book, newspaper, or magazine article. Then find an article that is an example of a secondary source. In a paragraph, explain how you identified each one.

The Challenge of Freedom

1860	1865	1870	1875	1880	1885	1890

1865–1881

VOCABULARY

sharecropping
Jim Crow
segregation

Vocabulary Strategy

share**cropping**

In **sharecropping,** a farmer only gets to keep a part, or **share,** of a crop and gives the rest to the landowner.

READING SKILL
Problem and Solution
Take notes to identify the problems facing African Americans after the Civil War and their solutions.

PROBLEMS	SOLUTIONS

Build on What You Know You know how important freedom is to people in the United States. Millions of African Americans were free after the Civil War. Freedom brought new opportunities, but also new challenges.

Freedom and Hardship

Main Idea Freed African Americans looked for ways to make a living after the end of slavery.

" **No more iron chain for me, no more, no more!** "

African Americans sang with joy to celebrate their new freedom. Reconstruction was a time of hope for them. Slavery had ended at last. They had the chance to make new lives for themselves.

Freedom was exciting, but it was not easy. Newly freed African Americans had to struggle to make a living. They also had to prepare for their new roles as full citizens. They worked to educate themselves and took part in politics. However, times were hard in the South and some people did not want African Americans to be truly free.

Sharecropping This photograph shows sharecroppers at work in the fields they rent from a landowner.

The Rise of Sharecropping

Reconstruction ended the plantation system in the South, leaving many people there very poor. Freed people wanted to farm for themselves. However, few had enough money to buy land.

Landowners set up a system called sharecropping that let poor whites and former slaves become farmers. In **sharecropping,** poor farmers used a landowner's fields. In return, the farmer gave the landowner a share of the crop. Landowners often loaned sharecroppers tools and seeds as well.

Sharecropping gave African Americans some independence. It also kept poor farmers in debt. After selling their crops, many sharecroppers did not have enough money to pay the landowners what they owed. They had to keep borrowing and could not get out of debt. Sharecropping made it hard for poor farmers to save money and provide a good life for their families.

Responses to Reconstruction

Reconstruction angered some people in the South. They opposed the new laws that protected African Americans' rights. They also disliked having federal soldiers in the South to enforce the laws.

Some people wanted to stop African Americans from taking part in government. They formed secret organizations, such as the Ku Klux Klan. The Ku Klux Klan threatened, beat, and even killed African Americans to keep them from voting. The Ku Klux Klan also attacked people who helped African Americans. In 1871, African Americans in Kentucky asked Congress for protection. They described the Klan's "riding nightly over the country . . . robbing, whipping . . . and killing our people."

REVIEW Why did many freed African Americans become sharecroppers?

Debts Landowners often charged high prices. This chart shows how much a sharecropper might owe after a year of hard work.

SKILL **Reading Charts** How much more did this farmer need to earn to make a profit?

Sharecropper's Account for the Year 1870

Money Borrowed		Money Earned		Debt
Food	-$83.25	Cotton	+$90.45	
Clothing	-$64.75			
Farm Supplies	-$75.08			
Medicine	-$2.17			
TOTAL:	-$225.25		+$90.45	-$134.80

The End of Reconstruction

Main Idea African Americans worked and studied to overcome new laws that limited their rights.

People grew disappointed with Reconstruction over time. They did not feel that it had successfully reunited the nation. In 1877, the new President, **Rutherford B. Hayes**, ended Reconstruction and ordered government soldiers to leave the South. Without protection, many African Americans were unable to vote and they lost their political power.

Southern states began passing Jim Crow laws. **Jim Crow** was a nickname for laws that kept African Americans separate from other Americans. These laws made segregation legal. **Segregation** is the forced separation of the races. Jim Crow laws segregated schools, hospitals, and even cemeteries. States usually spent less money on schools and hospitals for African Americans.

New Schools

African Americans did not want to let Jim Crow laws ruin their hopes for the future. Many believed that education would give them a chance for a better life. Eager students filled the new schools and colleges for African Americans that opened in the South. Churches in the North sent money and teachers to support these new schools. African American churches in the South also took a leading role. These churches became important centers in African American communities.

In 1881, a former slave named **Booker T. Washington** opened the Tuskegee Institute in Alabama. All of Tuskegee's students and teachers were African Americans. Washington believed that African Americans would receive equal treatment in time if they were educated and learned useful skills. Students at the Tuskegee Institute studied writing, math, and science. They also learned trades such as printing, carpentry, and farming.

Tuskegee Schools such as the Tuskegee Institute (right) gave African Americans the education they had not received under slavery. Booker T. Washington, (below) was the president of Tuskegee.

The most famous teacher at Tuskegee was **George Washington Carver**. Carver studied how to improve the lives of poor southern farmers. He taught them to grow crops such as peanuts, pecans, and sweet potatoes instead of cotton.

Carver invented over 300 products made from peanuts. His inventions included peanut butter, peanut cheese, and peanut milk. Carver's discoveries helped farmers across the South.

REVIEW What was the purpose of the Tuskegee Institute?

Lesson Summary

- Many freed African Americans became sharecroppers.
- The Ku Klux Klan used violence to stop African Americans from voting.
- Reconstruction ended when government soldiers left the South in 1877.
- After Reconstruction, Jim Crow laws required segregation in many public places in the South.

Why It Matters...

Reconstruction did not solve all of the nation's problems. After Reconstruction, African Americans had to continue their struggle for freedom.

George Washington Carver
He worked at the Tuskegee Institute for more than 40 years. He invented new products that could be made from common crops.

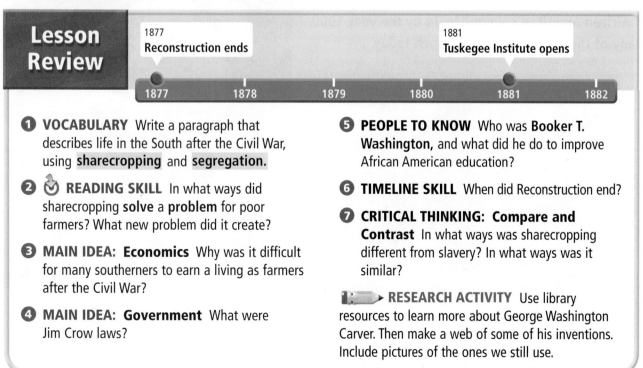

Lesson Review

1877 Reconstruction ends				1881 Tuskegee Institute opens	
1877	1878	1879	1880	1881	1882

❶ **VOCABULARY** Write a paragraph that describes life in the South after the Civil War, using **sharecropping** and **segregation.**

❷ 📖 **READING SKILL** In what ways did sharecropping **solve** a **problem** for poor farmers? What new problem did it create?

❸ **MAIN IDEA: Economics** Why was it difficult for many southerners to earn a living as farmers after the Civil War?

❹ **MAIN IDEA: Government** What were Jim Crow laws?

❺ **PEOPLE TO KNOW** Who was **Booker T. Washington,** and what did he do to improve African American education?

❻ **TIMELINE SKILL** When did Reconstruction end?

❼ **CRITICAL THINKING: Compare and Contrast** In what ways was sharecropping different from slavery? In what ways was it similar?

✏️ **RESEARCH ACTIVITY** Use library resources to learn more about George Washington Carver. Then make a web of some of his inventions. Include pictures of the ones we still use.

African American Education

The Freedmen's Bureau closed, but African Americans kept their schools open. After the Civil War, the Freedmen's Bureau gave money to set up schools and colleges for African Americans in the South. The head of the bureau said that they helped start 4,239 schools. More than 240,000 students attended these schools.

When the Freedmen's Bureau closed in 1872, African Americans raised money to keep their schools open. Their efforts increased the number of African American colleges to 34 by the year 1900. Many of these schools are still open today.

A Freedmen's Bureau School

Tuskegee One of the most famous Freedmen's Bureau schools was the Tuskegee Institute, shown above. It specialized in practical education. Students learned skills such as shoemaking, carpentry, and cabinetmaking.

The Institute Grows

The Institute started in a small building. By 1888, the Institute covered 540 acres and had more than 400 students.

Long Days at School

Students at the Institute studied and worked as many as 16 hours per day.

Activities

1. **MAKE YOUR OWN** Create a poster that might have appeared in the 1870s to raise money for a new African American college.

2. **WRITE ABOUT IT** What courses do you think would have been important for elementary school students to learn in the 1870s? Write a brief description of a typical school day.

Visual Summary

1–4. Write a description of each item named below.

Emancipation Proclamation, 1863	Jim Crow Laws	Three New Amendments	Tuskegee Institute

_____	_____	_____	_____
_____	_____	_____	_____
_____	_____	_____	_____
_____	_____	_____	_____

Facts and Main Ideas

TEST PREP Answer each question with information from the chapter.

5. **Citizenship** What were the effects of the Civil War on civilians in the South?

6. **Geography** Why did the Union army want to control the Mississippi River?

7. **History** Why did General Robert E. Lee decide to surrender?

8. **Economics** What were some advantages and disadvantages of sharecropping?

9. **Government** Why did Congress create the Freedmen's Bureau?

Vocabulary

TEST PREP Choose the correct word to complete each sentence.

draft, p. 455
home front, p. 462
total war, p. 467
segregation, p. 484

10. People who are not in the military when a country is at war are part of the _____.

11. After the Civil War, some states passed laws making _____ legal.

12. Sherman used the strategy of destroying an enemy's resources known as _____.

13. Jefferson Davis started a _____ to get enough soldiers for his army.

CHAPTER SUMMARY TIMELINE

| 1863 | 1865 | | 1877 | 1881 |
| Battle of Gettysburg | Civil War ends | | Reconstruction ends | Tuskegee Institute opens |

| 1860 | 1865 | 1870 | 1875 | 1880 | 1885 |

Apply Skills

✔ **TEST PREP** **Study Skill** Read the quotes about the final charge at Gettysburg to answer the question.

> We saw the enemy with colors [flags] flying…until this moment I had not gazed upon so grand a sight as was presented by that beautiful mass of grey.
>
> — Thomas Galwey, Union soldier

> About 13,000 troops advanced across an open field and up Cemetery Ridge in what has become known as "Pickett's Charge."…Only a few of the Southern troops reached the top of the ridge.
>
> — from the *World Book* encyclopedia article for the Battle of Gettysburg

14. What does the first source tell you that the second source does not?
    A. who led the charge
    B. when the charge took place
    C. how many soldiers were in the battle
    D. how the charge looked to the soldiers

15. How do you know that the *World Book* article is a secondary source?

Critical Thinking

✔ **TEST PREP** Write a short paragraph to answer each question.

16. **Analyze** In what ways was life during the war harder in the South than it was in the North?

17. **Categorize** What two categories could you use to group the following?

    Abraham Lincoln, Robert E. Lee, Jefferson Davis, Ulysses S. Grant, William T. Sherman

Timeline

Use the Chapter Summary Timeline above to answer the question.

18. Did the Civil War end before or after the end of Reconstruction?

Activities

Music Activity During the Civil War, songs were written and sung about victory, about missing home, and other topics. Write the words or music for a song about an event in this chapter.

Writing Activity Write a short story about the first day for students at a Freedmen's School in the South. Include details about what life was like after the Civil War.

Technology
Writing Process Tips
Get help with your story at
www.eduplace.com/kids/hmss05/

Review and Test Prep

Vocabulary and Main Ideas

✓ **TEST PREP** Write a sentence to answer each question.

1. What issues increased **sectionalism** in the United States during the early 1800s?

2. Why was **popular sovereignty** an important issue as the United States grew?

3. Why did some people in the South argue for **secession**?

4. What did the **Emancipation Proclamation** say?

5. What did General Sherman's army do when it used **total war** against the South?

6. How did **segregation** and **Jim Crow** laws affect life for African Americans?

Critical Thinking

✓ **TEST PREP** Write a short paragraph to answer each question.

7. **Contrast** In what ways was life in the South after the Civil War different from life before the Civil War?

8. **Synthesize** Explain how the Thirteenth, Fourteenth, and Fifteenth Amendments changed the U.S. Constitution. Use details from the unit to support your answer.

Apply Skills

✓ **TEST PREP** **Study Skill** Use the two sources about John Brown's raid on Harpers Ferry below to answer each question.

…before me stood four men, three armed with Sharpe's rifles. …I was then told that I was a prisoner.
— Colonel Washington, Harpers Ferry, 1859

The next appearance… was at the house of the Colonel Lewis Washington, a large farmer and slave-owner. …A party [group] rousing Colonel Washington, told him he was their prisoner…
— R.M. DeWitt, New York, 1859

9. What piece of information tells you that Colonel Washington's account is a primary source?

   A. the description of the type of rifles
   B. the words "I was"
   C. the description of the number of men
   D. the date it was written

10. What does the secondary source tell you that the primary source does not?

   A. what time the event occurred
   B. where the event took place
   C. who Colonel Washington was
   D. why Colonel Washington was taken prisoner

Unit Activity

Write a News Report

- Choose an event in this unit in which one person led others.

- Do research to find out more about the event.

- Write a news report describing the event, the leader, and how well you think this person led others.

- Illustrate your news report and share it with the class.

☆ **News Report** ☆
Battle of Gettysburg

On July 1, the Union and Confederate armies began fighting in Gettysburg, Pennsylvania. The battle lasted for three days. George Meade led the Union army, and Robert E. Lee led the Confederate army.

At the Library

Check your school or public library for these books.

Only Passing Through: The Story of Sojourner Truth by Anne Rockwell

Sojourner Truth was one of the most powerful voices in the abolitionist movement.

Lincoln: A Photobiography by Russell Freedman

This biography of Lincoln includes photos and excerpts from Lincoln's own writing.

CURRENT EVENTS
WEEKLY (WR) READER

Connect to Today

Create a poster about the leaders of different countries today.

- Find articles about the leader of another country.

- Write a short biography of this leader. Draw or find a picture of him or her.

- Display your poster in your classroom.

Technology

Get information for the poster from the Weekly Reader at **www.eduplace.com/kids/hmss05/**

Read About It

Look for these Social Studies Independent Books in your classroom.

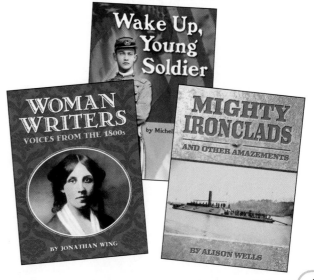

Wake Up, Young Soldier
by Michel...

WOMAN WRITERS
VOICES FROM THE 1800s
BY JONATHAN WING

MIGHTY IRONCLADS
AND OTHER AMAZEMENTS
BY ALISON WELLS

UNIT 7

Transforming the Nation

The Big Idea

How can people change the world they live in?

" If there is no struggle, there is no progress."

Frederick Douglass, 1857

Chief Joseph
1840?–1904

How far did this man walk in search of freedom? Chief Joseph led the Nez Perce on a journey of more than 1,200 miles to escape being forced onto a reservation.
page 524

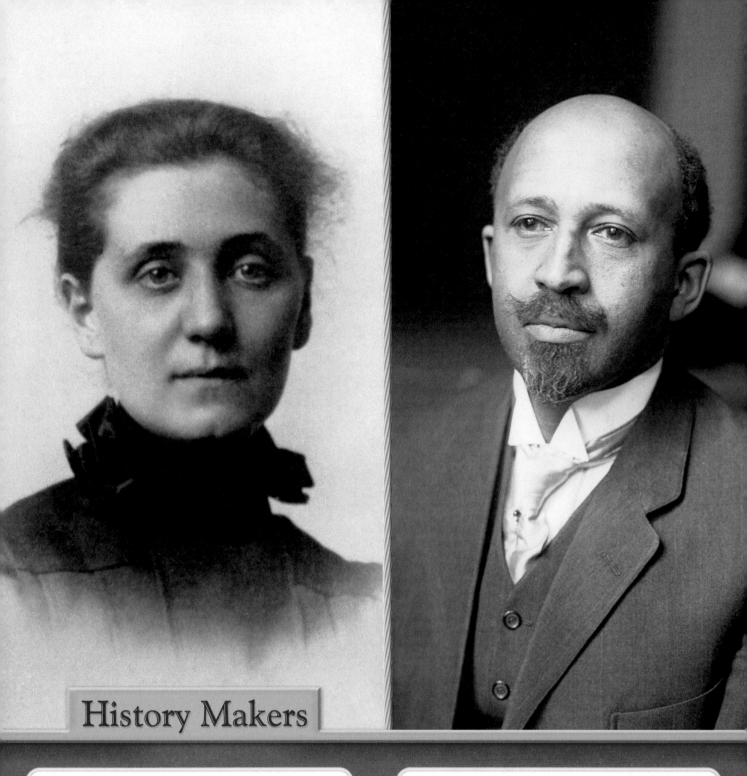

History Makers

Jane Addams
1860–1935

As a young woman, Jane Addams wanted to change the lives of immigrants. She founded Hull House, a settlement house in Chicago that provided services to people in need.

page 551

W.E.B. Du Bois
1868–1963

This man led the fight for equal rights for African Americans. Almost 100 years ago, he started an organization that is still working for people's rights today.

page 557

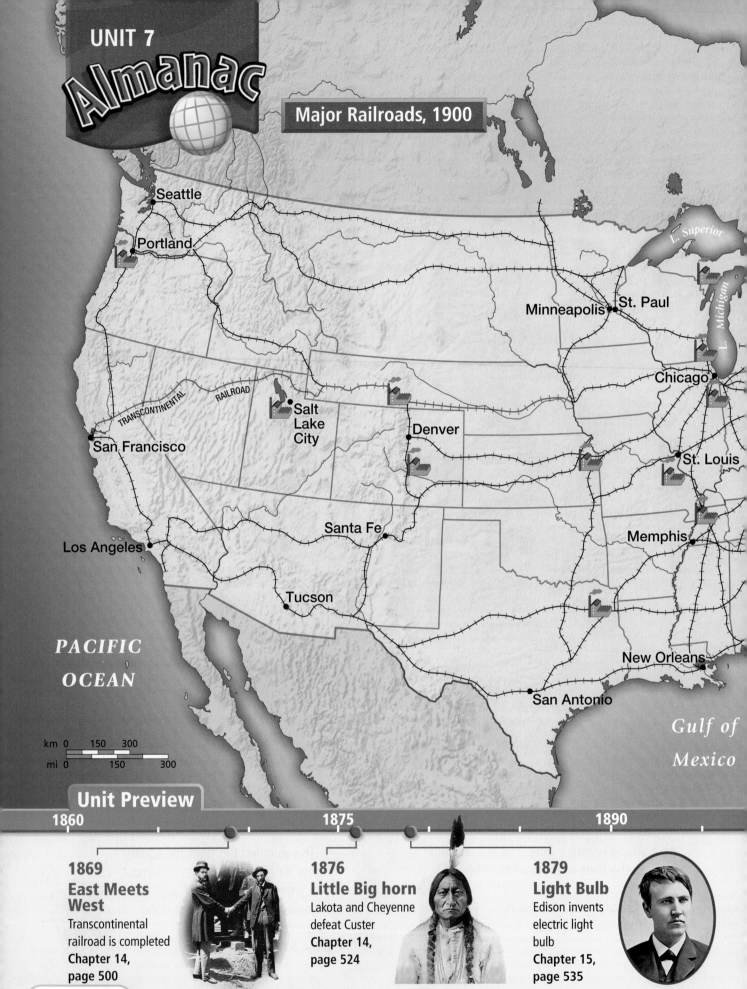

Seattle

Portland

L. Superior

Minneapolis

St. Paul

L. Michigan

Chicago

TRANSCONTINENTAL   RAILROAD

Salt Lake City

Denver

St. Louis

San Francisco

Santa Fe

Memphis

Los Angeles

Tucson

PACIFIC

OCEAN

New Orleans

San Antonio

Gulf of

Mexico

km 0   150   300

mi 0   150   300

Unit Preview

1860

1875

1890

1869
East Meets West

Transcontinental railroad is completed

Chapter 14, page 500

1876
Little Big horn

Lakota and Cheyenne defeat Custer

Chapter 14, page 524

1879
Light Bulb

Edison invents electric light bulb

Chapter 15, page 535

Boston

Buffalo

Detroit

L. Ontario

L. Erie

Cleveland · Pittsburgh

Cincinnati

New York

Philadelphia

Baltimore

Huron

**ATLANTIC
OCEAN**

Atlanta

Savannah

N
NE
NW
E
W
SE
SW
S

LEGEND

+++ Major Railroad

+++ Transcontinental Railroad,
completed 1869

Iron or steel mill

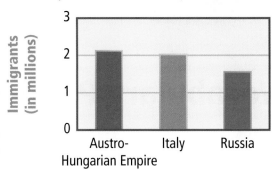

Connect to Today

Immigration, Early 1900s

Immigrants (in millions)

3
2
1
0

Austro-Hungarian Empire · Italy · Russia

Country

In the early 1900s, most immigrants came from eastern and southern Europe.

Immigration Today

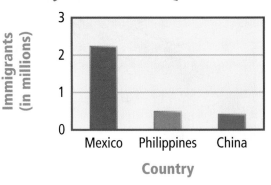

Immigrants (in millions)

3
2
1
0

Mexico · Philippines · China

Country

Today, most immigrants come from Latin America and Asia.

Which bar graph shows more immigrants coming to the United States?

CURRENT EVENTS

WEEKLY (WR) READER

Current events on the web!

Find out about current events that connect with the content of this unit.
See activities at:
www.eduplace.com/kids/hmss05/

1905   1920

**1909
NAACP
Founded**

African Americans struggle for equality
**Chapter 15,
page 556**

**1920
19th Amendment**

Women gain the right to vote
**Chapter 15,
page 556**

Chapter 14

Changes on the Plains

Technology

e • **glossary**
e • **word games**
www.eduplace.com/kids/hmss05/

Vocabulary Preview

transcontinental

In 1869, the first **transcontinental** railroad was completed. People could travel and send goods across the continent.
page 500

homestead

Settlers paid a small amount of money for a home and land on the Great Plains. After five years, they became the owners of their **homestead.** page 507

Chapter Timeline

1862
Homestead Act

1869
Transcontinental Railroad

1876
Battle of the Little Bighorn

1860   1865   1870   1875

Reading Strategy

Monitor and Clarify Check your understanding with this strategy.

Quick Tip Stop and check that you understand what you are reading. Reread, if you need to.

railhead

Ranchers brought the cattle they wanted to sell to towns called **railheads.** These towns were located at the beginning or end of railroad tracks. **page 515**

habitat

Buffalo once lived on the Great Plains in large numbers. The grasslands of the plains were their **habitat.**
page 525

1887
Dawes Act

1880   1885   1890

Linking East and West

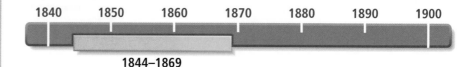

| 1840 | 1850 | 1860 | 1870 | 1880 | 1890 | 1900 |

1844–1869

Build on What You Know Have you ever had to wait for news from friends or family? In the early 1800s, people often waited weeks to receive messages from far away.

The Telegraph Helps Communication

Main Idea The telegraph made it much faster to send messages over long distances.

In the early 1800s, letters and news traveled by horse, stagecoach, or steamboat. It could take days or weeks to send a message from one city to another. Newspaper stories might be weeks old by the time they were printed.

In 1844, **Samuel Morse** amazed people by sending a message from Washington, D.C., to Baltimore, Maryland, in seconds. Morse used a telegraph to send his message. A telegraph is a machine that sends electric signals over wire telegraph lines. Morse invented a code of dots and dashes to send such messages.

Samuel Morse Morse is shown here holding an early version of his telegraph. The chart shows Morse Code, which uses electric signals to stand for letters of the alphabet.

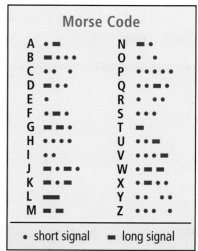

Morse Code

A	• ▬	N	▬ •
B	▬ • • •	O	• •
C	• • •	P	• • • • •
D	▬ • •	Q	• • ▬ •
E	•	R	• • •
F	• ▬ •	S	• • •
G	▬ ▬ •	T	▬
H	• • • •	U	• • ▬
I	• •	V	• • • ▬
J	▬ • ▬ •	W	• ▬ ▬
K	▬ • ▬	X	• ▬ • •
L	▬	Y	• • • •
M	▬ ▬	Z	• • • •

• short signal   ▬ long signal

At that time, the telegraph was the quickest way to send a message over long distances. Many companies built telegraph lines throughout the country. By October 1861, over 20,000 miles of telegraph wires carried messages from the East Coast to the West Coast.

Few inventions had changed people's lives as greatly as the telegraph. People could tell each other about important events soon after they took place.

Reporters used the telegraph to send stories to their newspapers. Other people used it to send messages to family and friends. Bankers used it to get business information. During the Civil War, generals sent battle plans by telegraph.

A Transcontinental Railroad

Main Idea Transcontinental railroads made traveling and shipping easier and faster.

Remember that many pioneers were heading west by the 1840s. Some were searching for gold. Others were looking for new places to settle. To get to the West, many people sailed around South America. Others traveled as far as they could on railroads and then continued overland in wagons pulled by horses, mules, or oxen. When people go overland they travel on land. Either way, the trip was slow, unsafe, and expensive.

REVIEW How did people travel west in the 1840s?

Transcontinental Railroad This railroad linked California to places east of the Mississippi River.

SKILL **Reading Charts** About how many weeks longer did it take to travel from coast to coast by ship than by the first transcontinental railroad?

Transcontinental Travel, 1869

Method of Travel	Travel Time
Ship	Six months
Railroad and wagon	Five months
Transcontinental railroad	Eight days

Major U.S. Railroads, 1869

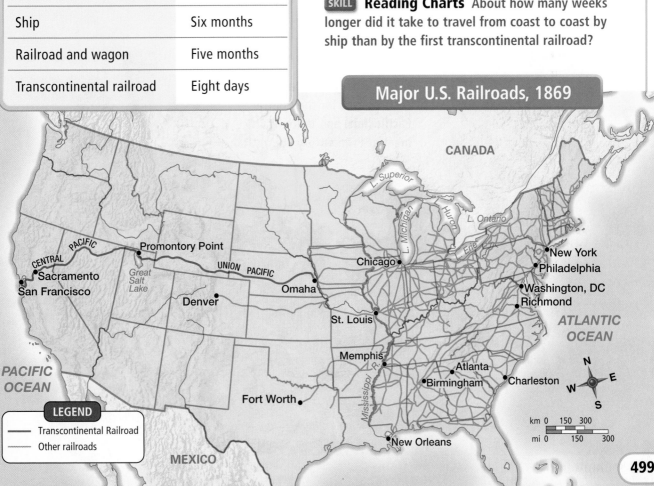

LEGEND
— Transcontinental Railroad
— Other railroads

Two Railroad Companies

A group of entrepreneurs in California planned to earn money by building a transcontinental railroad. A **transcontinental** railroad is a railroad that crosses a continent. This railroad would make travel easier from California to the East. The group asked Congress to help by giving them money and land.

In 1862, Congress passed the Pacific Railway Act. This law said the government could loan money to the Union Pacific and the Central Pacific railroad companies. Congress told the Union Pacific to build a railroad from east to west, starting in Nebraska. The Central Pacific was to build a railroad from west to east, starting in California. Rails built by the two companies would meet to create a transcontinental railroad.

After the Civil War, the Union Pacific hired thousands of former soldiers and freed African Americans. Irish immigrants also moved west to work on the railroad.

The Central Pacific hired many Chinese workers. Thousands of Chinese had come to California to search for gold. The Chinese faced prejudice from other railroad workers. **Prejudice** is an unfair, negative opinion that can lead to unjust treatment. The Chinese were paid less than other workers. Sometimes they were given dangerous jobs such as using explosives to blast away rock.

On May 10, 1869, both tracks were joined at Promontory Point, Utah. Railroad officials tapped spikes of gold and silver into the last piece of track. Then two railroad locomotives, one traveling west, the other traveling east, slowly moved forward until they met.

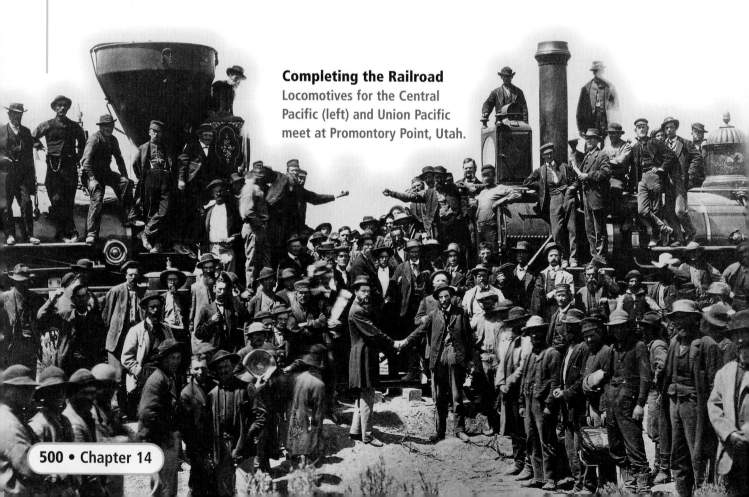

Completing the Railroad
Locomotives for the Central Pacific (left) and Union Pacific meet at Promontory Point, Utah.

The Effects of the Railroads

Telegraph wires instantly carried the exciting news from Promontony Point throughout the United States. People around the country held parades and gave speeches to celebrate. The 1,800-mile transcontinental railroad was finally finished.

This railroad was the first of several transcontinental railroads that would be built in the United States. These railroads made it easier to move people and goods across the country.

Transcontinental railroads helped settlers in the West earn money by shipping their goods to markets. Trains carried cattle and wheat and other western crops to eastern cities. Western farmers and ranchers could sell their products for more money in the East, where there were more people and fewer farms.

In the East, businesses and factories used the railroads to ship clothing, tools, and other goods to western towns and mining camps.

REVIEW What kinds of goods were shipped on transcontinental railroads?

Lesson Summary

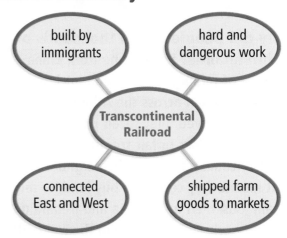

Why It Matters...

Improvements in communication and transportation helped unite the country and made the economy of the West grow.

Lesson Review

1844 Morse sends telegraph message	1862 Pacific Railway Act	May 10, 1869 Transcontinental Railroad

1840   1850   1860   1870   1880

❶ VOCABULARY Use the words **prejudice** and **transcontinental** in a paragraph about Chinese railroad workers.

❷ READING SKILL Review the predictions you made. Who used the new railroad?

❸ MAIN IDEA: Technology List three ways people used the telegraph in the 1800s.

❹ MAIN IDEA: Economics In what ways did the transcontinental railroad make it easier for settlers in the West to earn money?

❺ PLACES TO KNOW Where did the Central Pacific and Union Pacific meet to finish the first transcontinental railroad?

❻ TIMELINE SKILL How many years after Congress passed the Pacific Railway Act was the first transcontinental railroad finished?

❼ CRITICAL THINKING: Decision Making What were some short-term effects of the decision to build the transcontinental railroad? What were some long-term effects?

MATH ACTIVITY If two people left the East on June 1, 1869, one traveling by ship and the other by transcontinental railroad, when would each arrive in California? Use the chart on page 499 to find the answer. Ask a partner two more math questions using information from this chart.

HANDS ON

Railroad Workers

Why did people travel thousands of miles from their homelands? Some came from China, crossing the Pacific in the hope of finding gold to send back home. Others came from Ireland, driven across the Atlantic by famine.

Once they arrived, they faced prejudice and discrimination. Discrimination means unfair treatment. For these immigrants it meant they could not live in the neighborhoods where others lived. It meant they could not buy land, or mine gold, or work in certain jobs. Men from China and Ireland did hard and dangerous work, such as building the railroads that would someday link every corner of the United States.

As Irish workers built the Union Pacific Railroad, they sang this song. "Tay" means tea, and the U.P. railway is the Union Pacific.

Drill, my heroes, drill
Drill all day, no sugar in your tay
Workin' on the U.P. railway.

Transcontinental
railroad workers

By 1867, 90 percent of the workers on the Central Pacific Railroad were Chinese immigrants. The company paid the 12,000 Chinese workers about two-thirds of what it paid other workers. When the Chinese refused to work unless they were treated fairly, the company cut off food to their camp. After the railroads were built, Chinese workers still faced unfair treatment. Many went to work in factories in San Francisco.

Activities

1. **TALK ABOUT IT** What planning might it take to build the track shown in this picture?

2. **CHART IT** Find out what kinds of work Chinese immigrants did after the railroads were built. Show your findings on a chart.

503

Skillbuilder

Read a Time Zone Map

▶ VOCABULARY

time zone

International Date Line

Before railroads became widespread, every town decided on its own time. When trains made fast, long-distance travel possible, people needed a way to handle time differences. A system of 24 time zones was set up around the globe. A **time zone** is a region that shares the same time. By understanding time zones on a map, you can figure out the day and time in any part of the world.

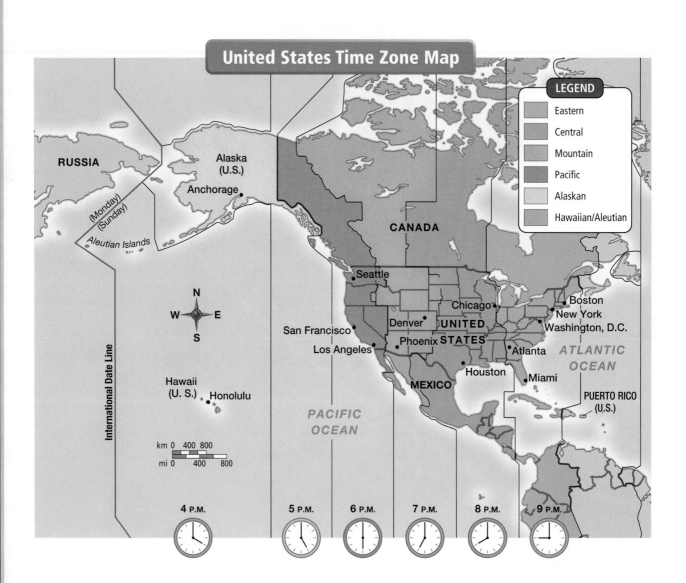

United States Time Zone Map

LEGEND

Eastern
Central
Mountain
Pacific
Alaskan
Hawaiian/Aleutian

4 P.M.   5 P.M.   6 P.M.   7 P.M.   8 P.M.   9 P.M.

Learn the Skill

Step 1: Find the time zones on the map. The legend tells you the name of each one.

Step 2: Note the time difference for each zone. For example, when you move one time zone to the west, the time is one hour earlier.

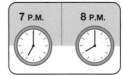

Step 3: Find the **International Date Line.** It is an imaginary line that marks where the date changes. For example, if it is noon on Friday in the time zone on the west side of the Line, it is noon on Thursday in the time zone on the east side of the Line.

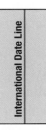

Practice the Skill

Use the time zone map to answer these questions.

1 In what time zone is Chicago, Illinois?

2 If it is 3 P.M. in Houston, Texas, what time is it in San Francisco, California, and in Atlanta, Georgia?

3 If it is Tuesday and you cross the International Date Line traveling east, what day does it become?

Apply the Skill

Suppose you live in San Francisco, California, and your cousin lives in Boston, Massachusetts. By what time would you need to call your cousin if she goes to bed at 9 P.M.?

Life on the Great Plains

1840   1850   1860   1870   1880   1890   1900

1862–1890

Build on What You Know Have you ever seen people rush to buy something because the price has been lowered? During the late 1800s, settlers rushed to the Great Plains because land was inexpensive.

Settling the Great Plains

Main Idea During the late 1800s, large numbers of settlers moved onto the Great Plains and started farming.

The Great Plains are in the middle of the United States. They stretch from Texas to Canada and from east of the Rocky Mountains to the Mississippi River. This vast area is mostly flat and covered by grasses. It has few trees and gets less than 20 inches a year of rain. At first, most settlers moving west passed through the Great Plains without stopping. They thought the dry land would be bad for farming and that they would have trouble building homes or fences because wood was hard to find.

Land for Sale This railroad company pamphlet was used to sell millions of acres of land.

SKILL **Primary Source** Read the advertisement. Where is the land located?

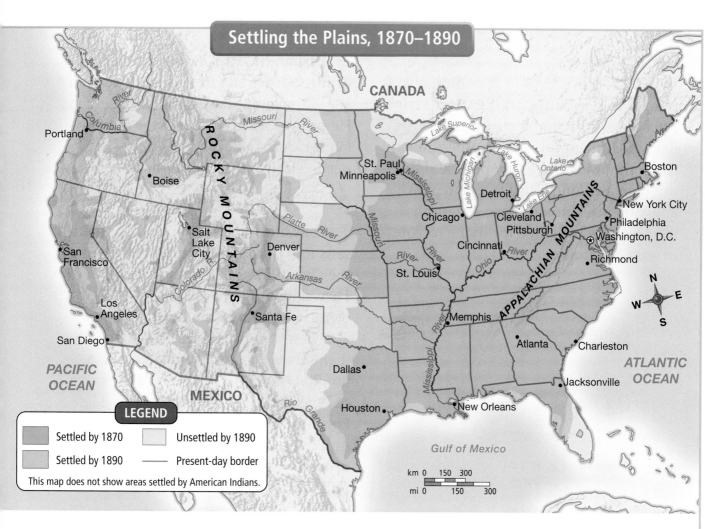

Settling the Plains, 1870–1890

LEGEND
- Settled by 1870
- Settled by 1890
- Unsettled by 1890
- Present-day border

This map does not show areas settled by American Indians.

km 0 150 300
mi 0 150 300

Moving West Large areas of the United States were still unsettled after 1870. **SKILL** **Reading Maps** By what year was most of the land east of the Mississippi river settled?

The Homestead Act

Farmers began to settle the Great Plains after Congress passed a law called the Homestead Act in 1862. A **homestead** is a settler's home and land. The Homestead Act offered 160 acres of land to adults who were citizens or who wanted to become United States citizens. To claim land, settlers had to pay a small amount of money and farm the land for five years. After that, it was theirs.

Many settlers came from the eastern United States, where good farmland was expensive. People who couldn't afford to buy good land in the East moved to the Great Plains.

Europeans also wanted to farm on the Great Plains. Most farms in Europe were only a few acres, much smaller than farms on the Great Plains. Land was much easier to buy in the United States.

European settlers came to the Great Plains from Germany, Sweden, Norway, Denmark, and the Netherlands. For a time, some parts of the Great Plains had more European-born people than people born in the United States. Between 1860 and 1890, the population of Nebraska alone had increased by over a million.

REVIEW Why did settlers from Europe and the East move to the Great Plains?

The Exodusters

African Americans in the South also wanted to start farms on the Great Plains. After Reconstruction ended in the 1870s, life was difficult for African Americans in the South. Most were very poor and did not own any land. They faced prejudice and violence. Some African Americans were attacked or killed for trying to vote or start businesses.

Benjamin "Pap" Singleton was an African American who visited Kansas in 1873. Singleton liked Kansas very much. He printed advertisements for Kansas land. He said that African Americans needed to leave the South because

> 66 **starvation is staring us in the face.** 99

Tens of thousands of African Americans moved to Kansas and other parts of the Great Plains between 1877 and 1879. They started towns where they made their own laws and felt safe from injustice.

These African American settlers called themselves **Exodusters,** after *Exodus*, a book of the Bible. *Exodus* tells the story of how the people of ancient Israel left Egypt to escape slavery. Many African Americans felt that they were like the people of Israel. They, too, were trying to find a place to be free.

New Settlers The Speese family was among the thousands of Exodusters who settled on the Great Plains. This photo was taken in Nebraska in 1888.

Settlers Face Hardships

Main Idea Settlers had to learn new ways of farming on the Great Plains.

Settlers had different reasons for moving to the Great Plains, but once there, they all shared the same hardships. The area's harsh climate made life difficult.

Winters were long and bitterly cold. Temperatures could sink as low as 40 degrees below zero. Blizzards of snow and wind could last for days. Spring often brought violent thunderstorms, heavy rains, floods, tornados, and hailstones as big as baseballs.

Summers were hot and dry and droughts were common. A **drought** is a long period with little or no rain. This extreme dry weather could destroy crops for many years in a row because plants did not get the water they needed.

During dry weather, farmers had to watch out for prairie fires. Flames from campfires or lightning strikes could quickly spread across miles of prairie grasslands. Settlers even had to worry about grasshoppers. Millions of the insects appeared on the Great Plains in the 1870s. They ate crops, clothing, and even the wood handles of farm tools.

Some homesteaders thought that life on the Great Plains was too difficult and moved away. One Kansas settler said that he did not want to stay in a land

> **66 where it rains grasshoppers, fire, and destruction. 99**

Other settlers stayed and adapted to the Great Plains. They found ways to adjust to the environment.

REVIEW Why was life on the Great Plains so difficult?

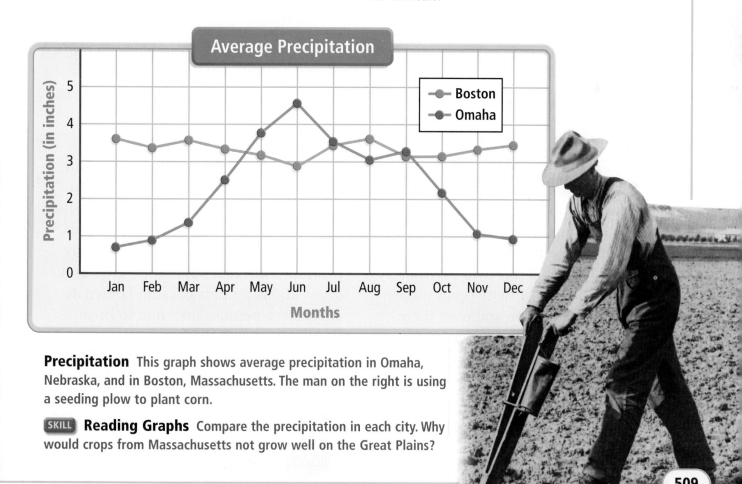

Precipitation This graph shows average precipitation in Omaha, Nebraska, and in Boston, Massachusetts. The man on the right is using a seeding plow to plant corn.

SKILL **Reading Graphs** Compare the precipitation in each city. Why would crops from Massachusetts not grow well on the Great Plains?

Homesteaders Settlers used natural resources and new machines to adapt to the Great Plains.

Settlers Adapt to the Great Plains

The first problem settlers faced was how to build a house. Wood was very scarce on the Great Plains, so most settlers made their first homes out of sod. Sod is grass-covered dirt held together by a thick mass of roots. Settlers cut pieces of sod from the prairie and used them like bricks. Sod kept the settlers' homes cool in summer and warm in winter. Unfortunately, sod also leaked during rainstorms. Sometimes snakes and other small animals dug through the sod walls.

Sod was much harder to plow than the soil of the eastern United States or Europe. Farmers had to slice through the thick sod before they could plant seeds. They used iron or steel plows to slowly push into the ground. Some plows broke. Great Plains farmers became known as **sodbusters** because they had to break through so much thick soil.

Life in a sod house could get lonely. If a sodbuster family needed help from a neighbor, or just wanted some company, they might have to travel for miles.

Growing Crops

Another challenge sodbusters faced was finding crops that would grow in such a dry climate. The wheat that grew in the eastern United States grew poorly on the Great Plains. Farmers tried seeds brought to the United States by European settlers. These seeds came from the dry grasslands of Eastern Europe. The wheat grown with these seeds was even better than wheat grown in the East.

Because there was little rainfall, farmers carried water from streams or springs. Settlers who lived far from streams dug deep wells and pumped water by hand. Both ways of getting water were difficult and took a lot of time. Settlers who could afford windmills attached them to the pumps in their wells. Wind power operated the water pumps and made getting water easier.

Farmers could not hire extra workers because few people lived on the Great Plains. Nearly all the early settlers were part of homesteading families.

New and improved farming machines replaced extra workers. Machines such as plows, planters, reapers, and threshers made it faster and easier to grow crops.

In 1840, it took 35 hours of work to produce an acre of wheat. In 1880, after better farm machines had been invented, producing an acre of wheat took only 20 hours. These machines made farmers more productive. They could farm more land and grow more wheat.

REVIEW How did settlers adapt to the lack of extra workers on the Great Plains?

Lesson Summary

Large numbers of farmers settled the Great Plains in the late 1800s. Most came from Europe and the eastern and southern United States. The climate of the Great Plains was harsh, but many settlers adapted.

Why It Matters ...

Farmers turned the Great Plains into vast fields of wheat.

Lesson Review

1 **VOCABULARY** Write a paragraph about the Great Plains using **homestead, drought,** and **sodbuster.**

2 **READING SKILL** How did settlers solve the **problem** of getting water for their crops? Describe their **solutions**.

3 **MAIN IDEA: Geography** Describe the climate of the Great Plains.

4 **MAIN IDEA: History** In what ways did settlers adapt to the Great Plains?

5 **PEOPLE TO KNOW** Who were the **Exodusters,** and why did they move to Kansas?

6 **CRITICAL THINKING: Draw Conclusions** Do you think Congress wanted people to settle on the Great Plains? Why or why not?

7 **CRITICAL THINKING: Generalize** Settlers had to adapt to life on the Great Plains. Why is learning to adapt to new and difficult situations an important skill?

WRITING ACTIVITY Many settlers on the Great Plains wrote to relatives in other parts of the United States and Europe. Write a description that a settler might have sent to a relative about life on the Great Plains.

Sod Houses

Without trees or stones, what did homesteaders use to build their houses? One resource they used was the prairie soil, or sod, around them. They cut sod into blocks and stacked them like bricks. Houses were small, sometimes one room with a hanging quilt to divide it.

Settlers might live in their "soddy" for six or seven years. When they had enough money to buy lumber, they built a wooden house. Then the old soddy became a home for farm animals.

Walls
Thick sod walls, two rows thick, kept soddies cool in summer and warm in winter. Prairie grass and roots helped hold the sod together. Sometimes bugs fell into the house.

Roof

Builders put woven sticks under hay or grass. On top of that was a layer of sod. The roof couldn't be as thick as the walls; it would be too heavy. So when the rains came, it leaked.

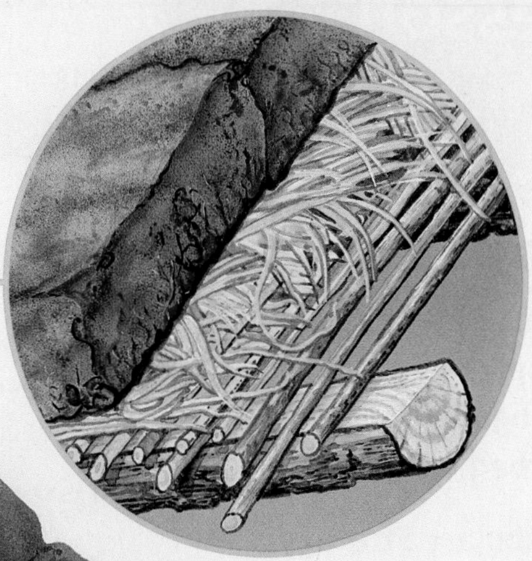

Activities

1. **EXPLORE IT** Talk about what it would be like to live in a one-room sod house like the one shown here.

2. **WRITE ABOUT IT** Research climate in the Great Plains. Write two diary entries describing what it would be like to live in a sod house during two different seasons.

513

Cattle Ranchers

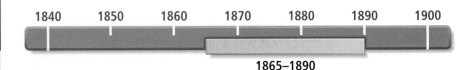

Build on What You Know You may have seen exciting movies or paintings about cowhands. A cowhand's work, however, was mostly hard, dirty, and boring.

Texas Cattle

Main Idea In the 1800s, ranchers in Texas raised and sold longhorn cattle.

In the 1860s, millions of wild longhorn cattle lived on the Texas plains. Longhorns were tough, strong animals that were first brought to North America by Spanish settlers. The cattle could live far from water and shelter, eating nothing but grass.

Remember that Texas had been part of Mexico, which was once ruled by Spain. After Texas became part of the United States in 1845, Mexicans in Texas became U.S. citizens. Many Mexican Americans faced prejudice from other Americans. Some had their lands taken away. But vaqueros (vah KEH rohs), or Mexican cowhands, were respected for their skill at herding cattle. Vaqueros taught their methods of herding on horseback to other cowhands and ranchers in the Southwest.

VOCABULARY

demand
supply
railhead
barbed wire

Vocabulary Strategy

barbed wire

A **barb** is a sharp point. **Barbed wire** is wire with sharp points attached to it.

READING SKILL
Cause and Effect Note the reasons why cattle drives began and ended.

CAUSE	EFFECT

Vaqueros at Work This painting shows vaqueros leading a herd of cattle. These cowhands often took care of thousands of cattle.

Demand and Supply The point on this graph where the demand and supply lines meet shows where the amount of cattle that sellers are willing to supply equals the amount that buyers demand. This point is what the price would be.

SKILL Reading Graphs
What would be the price of cattle if the supply were at 30,000?

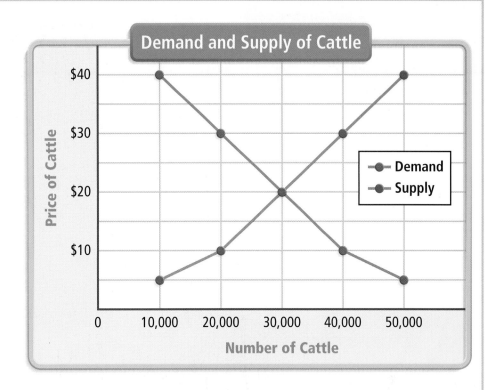

Demand and Supply of Cattle

Price of Cattle

$40
$30
$20
$10

Demand
Supply

0   10,000   20,000   30,000   40,000   50,000

Number of Cattle

Demand and Supply for Cattle

There were many cattle in Texas but few people to buy them. Cattle sold in Texas for only about $4 each. People in the eastern and northern United States wanted cattle products such as beef and leather. Cattle sold in those regions for about $40 each.

The price of cattle was partly set by demand and supply. **Demand** is the amount of something that people want to buy at certain prices. When the price of something is low, people usually want to buy more of it.

Supply is the amount of something that people want to sell at certain prices. When the price of something is high, people want to produce and sell more of it. Demand and supply affect the price of nearly everything that is bought and sold—not just cattle.

The Cattle Drives

Main Idea Cowhands led cattle to railroads, where the cattle were shipped to eastern and northern cities.

Texas ranchers wanted to sell their cattle in the regions where they could get the highest prices. They shipped their cattle to eastern and northern cities. To get to these cities, the cattle first had to be led to railheads. A **railhead** is a town where railroad tracks begin or end. At the railheads, cattle were loaded onto trains.

Railheads were often hundreds of miles away from the cattle ranches. Beginning in the 1860s, cowhands led cattle to the railheads. These cattle drives took weeks or months to complete. Cattle drives followed trails where water and grass were available.

REVIEW Why did Texas cattle ranchers want to sell their animals in the East and North?

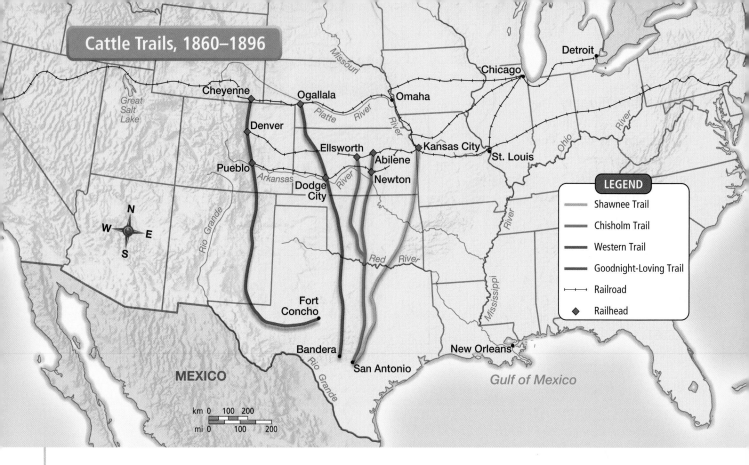

Cattle Trails, 1860–1896

Great Salt Lake

Cheyenne

Denver

Pueblo

Ogallala

Platte River

Omaha

Chicago

Detroit

Missouri River

Ellsworth

Abilene

Newton

Kansas City

St. Louis

Ohio River

Arkansas River

Dodge City

Rio Grande

Red River

Fort Concho

Bandera

San Antonio

New Orleans

Mississippi River

MEXICO

Gulf of Mexico

Rio Grande

LEGEND

Shawnee Trail
Chisholm Trail
Western Trail
Goodnight-Loving Trail
Railroad
Railhead

km 0   100   200
mi 0   100   200

Cattle Trails Five major cattle trails led from Texas to Great Plains railheads.
SKILL **Reading Maps** Which major rivers did the cattle trails cross?

Life on the Drives

Life on the cattle drives was hard. The work was sometimes dangerous, often boring, and always dirty. A dozen cowhands had to care for about 3,000 longhorns. Cowhands spent 10 to 14 hours a day on horseback. They rode slowly next to the herd to keep the cattle together. Usually nothing much happened. When cattle were startled by lightning or sudden noises, however, they might stampede, or run away. A cattle stampede was dangerous. Riders had to race after the cattle to round them up again. Lost cattle meant lost money.

Nat Love was a cowhand who wrote about a stampede at night. He asked readers to imagine

66 chasing an immense [big] herd of maddened [upset] cattle which we could hear but could not see . . . It was the worst night's ride I ever experienced. 99

Cowhands slept on the ground, wrapped in blankets. At night, they took turns guarding the herd from animals and thieves. By the end of a cattle drive, the cowhands were exhausted. They were happy to reach the railheads where their journey ended.

Nat Love Many cowhands were African American or Mexican. Love wrote a book about his cowhand adventures.

The End of the Drives

The cattle drives lasted for only about 20 years, from the late 1860s to the late 1880s. They ended for several reasons.

The first reason was the invention of barbed wire. **Barbed wire** is twisted wire with a sharp barb, or point, every few inches. Barbed wire fences, put up by new settlers, blocked the cattle trails that crossed the Great Plains.

The next reason was the growth of railroads. After railroads were built in Texas in the 1870s, ranchers used nearby railheads to ship cattle to eastern cities. They no longer had to drive their cattle hundreds of miles to reach a railhead.

Another reason was that by the mid-1880s, too many cattle grazed on crowded ranges. There was not enough grass to feed all the cattle. Sheepranchers also wanted this scarce land for their flocks.

Finally, during the terrible winter of 1886–1887, freezing cold temperatures killed thousands of cattle. Cattle were still very important in Texas, but by the 1890s, the days of the long cattle drives were over.

REVIEW What led to the end of the big cattle drives?

Lesson Summary

- Cattle ranchers sent their herds on long cattle drives to railheads so that the cattle could be shipped to the East and North.
- The price of cattle was affected by demand and supply.
- By the 1890s, big cattle drives had mostly ended.

Why It Matters ...

Cattle drives lasted for only about 20 years, a short time in U.S. history. Yet people still think of cattle drives when they think of the West.

Lesson Review

1 VOCABULARY Choose the correct word to complete each sentence.

demand supply

The price of milk was so low that the _____ fell.
The _____ for cheap land was high.

2 🔄 **READING SKILL** What effect did railroads have on the beginning and ending of cattle drives?

3 MAIN IDEA: Geography Why did the cattle business develop in Texas?

4 MAIN IDEA: Economics Use demand and supply to explain why Texas ranchers sent their longhorns on cattle drives.

5 CRITICAL THINKING: Summarize What was the life of a cowhand like?

6 CRITICAL THINKING: Infer When the supply of a product is large, people often have to sell it for a low price. What would probably happen to that product's price if the supply decreased?

MUSIC ACTIVITY Cowhands sang songs about life on the cattle drives. Using library resources, find a cowhand song. Act out the song and describe what it is about.

IN THE DAYS OF THE
VAQUEROS

by Russell Freedman

Mexican vaqueros are known as the first cowhands of America. They rode across the open range looking for stray cattle. Their work was often hard. Sometimes they went without food, and they often slept on the ground. The vaqueros developed a style of dress that fit their rugged way of life.

In the early days, the vaquero wore any clothes he happened to own, but as the years passed, he developed a distinct and practical way of dressing. While his clothing varied from one region to the next, according to the terrain he rode, and changed appearance over the years, it always singled him out as a working cowhand.

To shield his head and eyes from the Mexican sun, he wore a sombrero, from the word *sombrear,* "to shade"—a wide-brimmed hat made of straw, leather, or felt. Held in place with a *barbiquejo,* a chin strap, it often was decorated with a colorful band. A sombrero might have a low flat crown with a straight stiff brim, or a tall crown, several inches high, with a soft floppy brim. Whatever its shape, it was always impressively large, with a brim wide enough to shade the wearer's face.

Because of its practicality, the big wide-brimmed hat became a familiar cowboy trademark.

Under his sombrero, the vaquero wore a kerchief tied over his head. His hair was parted in the middle and brushed back into a long braid that might hang down his back, or be folded up and tucked under his hat.

A vaquero usually carried a brightly colored sarape, or poncho, which was thrown over his shoulder like a shawl or carried on the back of his saddle. A sarape offered protection when it rained and warmth when it was cold. It served as a bed at night when the vaquero slept under the stars. Waved wildly in the air, it was used to haze cattle during roundups and stampedes.

When the gold rush ended, cattle raising in California began a slow decline as ranches gradually gave way to farms. But on the sparsely settled Texas prairie, cattle were multiplying faster than anyone could count. These animals had descended from herds left behind by missionaries who had gone back to Spain, and from herds abandoned by Mexican ranch owners who had fled across the Rio Grande when Texas broke away from Mexico, leaving both their cattle and their vaqueros behind.

Texas cattle were not at all like the tame and docile animals that Anglo settlers in Texas were accustomed to raising back East. These cattle were as wild as buffalo and antelope, and now millions of them were wandering around loose. They clustered together in bunches, hiding in thickets by day and running by night. They could go days without water. Their sense of smell was keener than a deer's. And they had long, sharp, dangerous horns.

If a man tried to approach on foot, a bull would paw the earth, toss his head in anger, lower his horns, and charge. The animals could be approached only on horseback. And even then, bulls often tried to attack both man and horse.

American settlers considered the wild cattle they found in Texas fair game, free for the taking. Yet they had little idea how to manage large numbers of fierce, far-ranging longhorns. Most of the early Texas settlers were farmers who raised a few cattle on the side. They had never practiced large-scale ranching, as the Spaniards and Mexicans had on their ranchos and haciendas.

A Mexican vaquero, photographed around 1900 in Berino, New Mexico

Handling wild cattle on the open range was new to the Americans but old to the Mexican vaqueros. And so the Americans turned to the vaqueros for help. "They are universally acknowledged to be the best hands that can be [found] for the management of cattle, horses, and other livestock," a Texas settler reported.

Mexican vaqueros still living in Texas began to capture mustangs for the newcomers and round up wild steers. As the Americans watched the vaqueros work, they too became skilled at taming mustangs and roping steers. In this way, the North American cowboy learned his trade from the Mexican vaquero.

Activities

1. **TALK ABOUT IT** Look closely at the painting on page 519. What skills does the vaquero need to catch the horse? What tools does he need?

2. **PRESENT IT** Prepare an oral report or multimedia presentation on the vaqueros. Include what the settlers learned from them.

Conflicts on the Plains

VOCABULARY

reservation
habitat
extinct
assimilate

Vocabulary Strategy

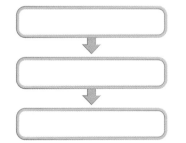

| assimilate |

To **assimilate** a group is to make it fit in or be similar. Think of "similar" when you read the word assimilate.

READING SKILL

Sequence As you read, list the main events in order. Think about the connection between the events.

Build on What You Know You have learned that there were many conflicts as settlers moved onto American Indian lands in the eastern United States. The same thing happened years later as settlers moved onto the Great Plains.

War on the Plains

Main Idea American Indians and soldiers fought on the Great Plains during the late 1800s.

Beginning in the 1840s, more and more settlers moved west in search of land or gold. They built towns and dug mines. They divided land where American Indians already lived into farms and ranches.

The U.S. government built roads and railroads to help these settlers. Officials tried to convince Plains Indians to sell land and move to reservations. A **reservation** is land that the government set aside for American Indians. Congress promised that reservations would remain Indian land.

Plains Indians did not want to live on reservations. They felt the reservations were too small. Some reservations were far from the lands American Indians hunted on and called home.

Plains Buffalo Indians used the meat, skin, bones, and other parts of bison, or buffalo, to provide most of what they needed.

Sand Creek This painting shows the Colorado militia attacking a Cheyenne village near Sand Creek. **SKILL** **Reading Visuals** What details does the artist show about this battle?

Government officials hoped that Plains Indians would move to reservations and become farmers. People of Indian nations such as the Lakota and Arapaho did not want to farm. They were nomads, which means they moved from place to place to find food and water. They rode horses over miles of open prairie to hunt bison. Bison, also known as buffalo, provided Plains Indians with most of what they needed, such as food and clothing. Without large areas of land, Plains Indians would not be able to find the resources they needed to live.

Plains Indians fought soldiers who tried to force them onto reservations. Sometimes they attacked settlers and miners to make them leave Indian territory. Most of this fighting on the Great Plains happened in the 1860s and 1870s.

Sand Creek

In 1864, volunteer fighters of the Colorado militia attacked a Cheyenne village near Sand Creek, Colorado. The Cheyenne were asleep when the attack began. **Chief Black Kettle** raised a white flag and an American flag to surrender. The soldiers ignored him and killed almost half of the men, women, and children in the village.

After the Sand Creek Massacre, many Plains Indians thought that peace with the U.S. government was impossible.

Fighting among Indians, soldiers, and settlers increased after Sand Creek. By the 1870s, however, most Indian nations had been forced onto reservations. Only a few nations, including the Lakota and the Cheyenne, were still fighting for their land and traditions.

REVIEW Why did Plains Indians need large areas of land?

523

Battle of the Little Bighorn

The Black Hills of South Dakota and Wyoming are sacred, or holy, to the Lakota. In the early 1870s, a lieutenant colonel named **George Custer** led soldiers to the Black Hills and found gold. Thousands of Lakota and Cheyenne gathered to protect the Black Hills.

In June 1876, Custer and his soldiers tried to force the Lakota and Cheyenne onto a reservation. The soldiers attacked them at their village on the Little Bighorn River in Montana. Led by **Crazy Horse, Gall,** and **Sitting Bull,** the Lakota and Cheyenne won what became known as the Battle of the Little Bighorn. All of the U.S. soldiers were killed.

Little Bighorn was one example of how American Indians fought efforts to move them to reservations. The Nez Perce of Oregon resisted being moved to Idaho.

Chief Joseph was among those who tried to lead the Nez Perce to Canada. The Nez Perce fought several battles with the soldiers before they surrendered, 30 miles from the Canadian border in 1877.

Within a few years, all the Plains Indian nations were on reservations.

Wounded Knee

In the late 1880s, Plains Indians hoped for some way to improve their lives. Many of them began to follow a religion called the Ghost Dance. This religion taught that the buffalo would return and dead Indians would come back to life. As more and more Plains Indians turned to the Ghost Dance, government officials worried that the Ghost Dancers would start another war.

Chief Joseph (right) Government soldiers chased Chief Joseph and the Nez Perce for 1600 miles, through Idaho, Wyoming, and Montana. The photograph below shows a Plains Indian village in the late 1800s.

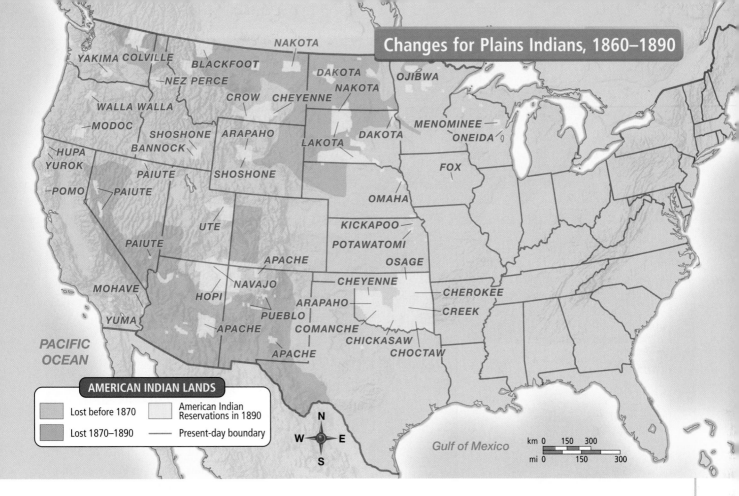

Changes for Plains Indians, 1860–1890

YAKIMA COLVILLE
BLACKFOOT
NEZ PERCE
NAKOTA
DAKOTA
OJIBWA
NAKOTA
CROW CHEYENNE
WALLA WALLA
MODOC
SHOSHONE ARAPAHO
DAKOTA
MENOMINEE
ONEIDA
BANNOCK
LAKOTA
HUPA
YUROK
PAIUTE
SHOSHONE
FOX
POMO
PAIUTE
OMAHA
UTE
KICKAPOO
POTAWATOMI
PAIUTE
APACHE
OSAGE
MOHAVE
NAVAJO
CHEYENNE
HOPI
ARAPAHO
CHEROKEE
PUEBLO
CREEK
YUMA
APACHE
COMANCHE
CHICKASAW
PACIFIC
OCEAN
APACHE
CHOCTAW

AMERICAN INDIAN LANDS

Lost before 1870

American Indian Reservations in 1890

Lost 1870–1890

Present-day boundary

N W E S

Gulf of Mexico

km 0   150   300
mi 0   150   300

Indian Lands By 1870, American Indians had already lost most of their lands to the U.S. government. **SKILL** **Reading Maps** What color is used on this map to show reservation lands in 1890?

When Sitting Bull became a Ghost Dancer, government officials sent police to arrest him. During the struggle, Sitting Bull was killed.

Sitting Bull's death frightened the Ghost Dancers. They were afraid that they would be killed as well. Led by **Chief Big Foot,** many Ghost Dancers went to hide in the Badlands of South Dakota.

U.S. soldiers captured Big Foot and his followers near Wounded Knee Creek. On the morning of December 29, 1890, the soldiers tried to take the Indians' guns. In the fighting that followed, the soldiers killed women and children, as well as men. This event became known as the Massacre at Wounded Knee.

Destruction of the Buffalo

Reservations changed Indian life. So did the destruction of the buffalo. At one time, millions of buffalo lived on the Great Plains. As more people crossed the Great Plains, wagon trails and railroad tracks cut across buffalo habitat. A **habitat** is the area where an animal or plant normally lives or grows.

The settlers killed buffalo for meat. Their cattle carried diseases that were deadly to the buffalo. Hunters shot buffalo for sport or for the skins, which were made into coats or leather products.

As more and more settlers moved onto the Great Plains, buffalo herds kept shrinking. Soon the buffalo were nearly extinct. When a certain type of plant or animal becomes **extinct** it no longer exists. By 1889, only about 1,000 buffalo were left.

REVIEW Why did the buffalo herds shrink?

Before

After

Indian Schools The children above were students at an Indian school in Pennsylvania around 1900.

Before and After At Indian schools, students had to cut their hair and could not wear their traditional clothing. These photos show the same three Navajo children before and after they entered an Indian school.

Government Policy

Main Idea Government officials tried to force American Indians to change their way of life.

Even though Plains Indians were on reservations, government officials were afraid of more fighting. They hoped Indians would be less likely to fight if they gave up their old ways. Reformers and lawmakers tried to make American Indians assimilate into American life. **Assimilate** means changing a group's culture and traditions so that it blends with a larger group.

One way the government tried to force American Indians to change was to make religious practices such as the Ghost Dance illegal. Another way was to send children to schools where they were not allowed to speak American Indian languages or wear traditional clothing.

In 1887, Congress passed the Dawes Act to make American Indians become farmers. This law took reservation land away from Indian nations and split it into smaller pieces. Some of this land was given to individual American Indians to farm. The rest was sold to settlers.

People of a few Indian nations knew how to farm, but most did not. Farming was not a part of their culture. Even American Indians who knew how to farm had little success with the poor farmland on reservations. The only way many American Indians could survive was to accept food from the federal government.

Assimilation did not work well. Most Plains Indians were unhappy on reservations. Crazy Horse said,

> 66 **We preferred hunting to a life of idleness [laziness] on the reservation, where we were driven against our will. . . All we wanted was peace and to be left alone.** 99

REVIEW What did the Dawes Act do to reservation land?

Lesson Summary

- The federal government gave settlers the lands promised to Plains Indians.
- American Indians fought with U.S. soldiers, but they were defeated and forced onto reservations.
- Plains Indians depended on the buffalo for food, but settlement of the Great Plains destroyed buffalo herds.
- Government officials made laws to force American Indians to change their way of life.

Why It Matters . . .

Decisions made by the U.S. government in the late 1800s changed American Indian cultures. Today, however, on many reservations, American Indian work to preserve their traditions.

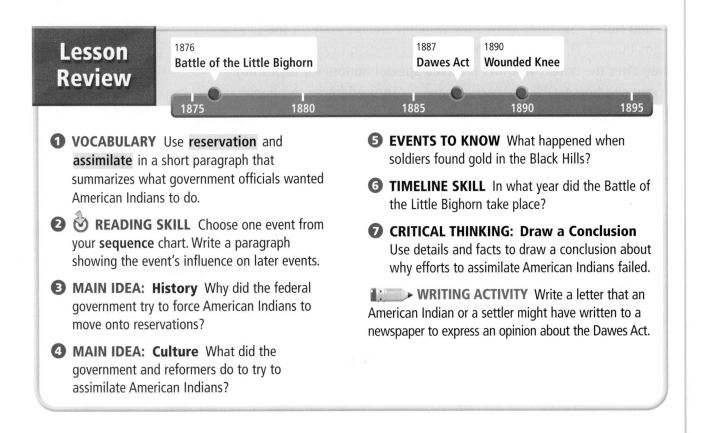

Lesson Review

1876 **Battle of the Little Bighorn**

1887 **Dawes Act**

1890 **Wounded Knee**

1875   1880   1885   1890   1895

1 VOCABULARY Use **reservation** and **assimilate** in a short paragraph that summarizes what government officials wanted American Indians to do.

2 READING SKILL Choose one event from your **sequence** chart. Write a paragraph showing the event's influence on later events.

3 MAIN IDEA: History Why did the federal government try to force American Indians to move onto reservations?

4 MAIN IDEA: Culture What did the government and reformers do to try to assimilate American Indians?

5 EVENTS TO KNOW What happened when soldiers found gold in the Black Hills?

6 TIMELINE SKILL In what year did the Battle of the Little Bighorn take place?

7 CRITICAL THINKING: Draw a Conclusion Use details and facts to draw a conclusion about why efforts to assimilate American Indians failed.

WRITING ACTIVITY Write a letter that an American Indian or a settler might have written to a newspaper to express an opinion about the Dawes Act.

Battle of the Little Bighorn

How do we know what happened at the Battle of the Little Bighorn in 1876? Lakota, Cheyenne, and Arapaho Indians who survived the battle told stories about it. These stories were later recorded by historians. Some survivors drew pictures to tell about the battle.

Red Horse, a Lakota who was at the Little Bighorn, drew what he saw. He used colored pencils and ink to create a series of 41 pictures on large sheets of paper. These drawings are an important primary source.

Red Horse's pictures show how valuable horses were to the Plains Indians. This drawing shows warriors leading cavalry horses away after the battle. Warriors received special honors for capturing an enemy's horse. Often a warrior gave a captured horse to people in his village.

USA 13c — Crazy Horse

Crazy Horse
1840?–1877

Crazy Horse was a Lakota leader who refused to accept life on a reservation. Crazy Horse led a charge against Custer during the Battle of the Little Bighorn.

Sitting Bull
1831?–1890

After Little Bighorn, Sitting Bull led his followers to Canada. He returned to the United States, where he was forced to live on a reservation, but he kept working for justice for the Lakota.

George Armstrong Custer
1839–1876

Custer fought in the Civil War. He began fighting American Indians in 1867. He had such confidence in his abilities as an Indian fighter that he thought he would win at the Little Bighorn.

Activities

1. **THINK ABOUT IT** What can you find out about the Lakota by looking at the drawing on this page?

2. **WRITE ABOUT IT** List three ways that this picture shows that horses were important to the Lakota.

Technology Visit Education Place for more primary sources.
www.eduplace.com/kids/hmss05

529

Visual Summary

1–4. Write a description of the four items in the web below.

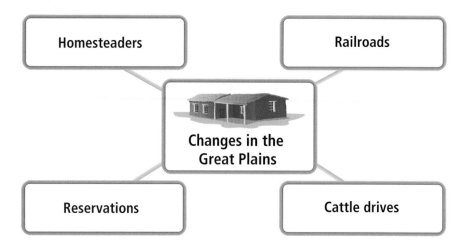

Homesteaders

Railroads

Changes in the Great Plains

Reservations

Cattle drives

Facts and Main Ideas

TEST PREP Answer each question with information from the chapter.

5. **Technology** Why was the invention of the telegraph important to the United States?

6. **Economics** What were two effects of the transcontinental railroad on the United States?

7. **History** Why did Exodusters move to the Great Plains?

8. **History** What brought about the end of the cattle drives?

Vocabulary

TEST PREP Choose the correct word to complete each sentence.

prejudice, p. 500
drought, p. 509
demand, p. 515

9. Some railroad workers who felt _____ toward Chinese workers treated them unfairly.

10. Ranchers wanted to sell their cattle where the _____ and price for beef were high.

11. The hot and dry weather on the Plains often created a _____.

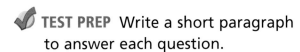

1862
Homestead Act

1876
Battle of the Little Bighorn

1887
Dawes Act

1860 1865 1870 1875 1880 1885 1890

Apply Skills

 TEST PREP Map Skill Use the time zone map below to answer each question.

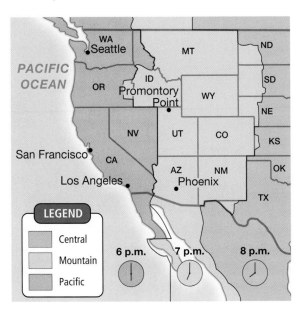

WA
Seattle
MT
ND

PACIFIC OCEAN
OR
ID
Promontory
Point
WY
SD

NV
UT
CO
NE

San Francisco
CA
KS

Los Angeles
AZ
NM
Phoenix
OK

TX

LEGEND

Central
Mountain
Pacific

6 p.m. 7 p.m. 8 p.m.

12. If the Central Pacific Railroad workers started working at 8 A.M. in Nevada, what time was it in California?

   A. 7 A.M.

   B. 10 A.M.

   C. 8 A.M.

   D. 9 A.M.

13. If golden spikes were tapped into the track at Promontory Point, Utah, around 11:45 A.M., what time was it in Seattle, Washington?

   A. around 12:45 P.M.

   B. around 5:45 P.M.

   C. around 8:45 A.M.

   D. around 10:45 A.M.

Critical Thinking

 TEST PREP Write a short paragraph to answer each question.

14. Decision Making What would be the costs and benefits of a European immigrant's decision to settle on the Great Plains?

15. Draw Conclusions Which event in this chapter do you think caused the biggest changes on the Great Plains? Explain your conclusions.

Timeline

Use the Chapter Summary Timeline above to answer the question.

16. How many years after the Homestead Act was the Dawes Act passed?

Activities

HANDS ON

Art Activity Create an invitation to a celebration of the completion of the transcontinental railroad.

Writing Activity Think of two questions about the sodbusters that you would like answered. Write two paragraphs of a research report answering the questions.

Technology
Writing Process Tips
Get help with your research report at
www.eduplace.com/kids/hmss05/

Chapter 15

Big Business and Big Cities

Technology

e • **glossary**
e • **word games**
www.eduplace.com/kids/hmss05/

Vocabulary Preview

labor union

Workers formed the first **labor union** to demand change from big companies. Union members acted as a group to get more pay and better working conditions. **page 538**

tenement

Immigrants came to the United States with little money for food and rent. Most lived in crowded and unsafe buildings called **tenements.** **page 544**

Chapter Timeline

1869
First labor union

1882
Chinese Exclusion Act

1860   1870   1880   1890

Reading Strategy

Summarize Use this strategy to focus on important information.

Quick
Tip
Take notes as you read. Then highlight the most important information.

rapid transit

Electricity made it possible for people to travel quickly on streetcars and subways. These **rapid transit** systems were built in many large cities. **page 550**

progressive

Jane Addams was a **progressive.** She started a community center that helped people in Chicago improve their lives. **page 554**

1909
NAACP founded

1920
Nineteenth Amendment

1900   1910   1920

The Rise of Big Business

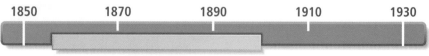

| 1850 | 1870 | 1890 | 1910 | 1930 |

1856–1900

Build on What You Know You probably enjoy talking to your friends and relatives on the phone. In the late 1800s, the telephone was a brand-new invention. Few Americans had one.

A Time of Invention

Main Idea Inventions of the late 1800s changed people's lives.

The last half of the 1800s was full of wonderful inventions. These inventions allowed people to do things that had been impossible before, such as recording sound. New machines saved time and money and improved life for many people.

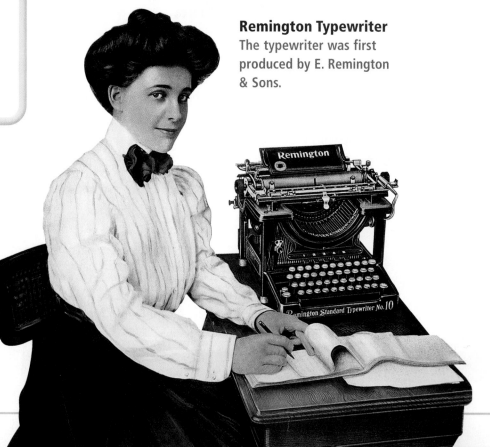

Remington Typewriter
The typewriter was first produced by E. Remington & Sons.

Alexander Graham Bell In his laboratory in Boston, Bell (left) works on his new invention, the telephone. His assistant is Thomas Watson.

Inventions for Home and Work

In 1872, **Elijah McCoy** invented an oil cup. The oil cup kept trains and other machines running longer by dripping oil over moving parts.

In 1874, E. Remington & Sons became the first company to make and sell typewriters. Office workers saved time by typing letters and reports.

In 1867, **Margaret Knight** invented a machine that made paper bags with a flat bottom, so they could hold more. Her paper-bag-making machine is still in use.

Granville Woods Woods improved the telephone, telegraph, and transportation systems. His inventions made streetcars like the one below faster and safer.

Alexander Graham Bell invented the telephone in 1876. Workers in large buildings used the telephone to talk to people on other floors. People at home used telephones to talk to friends and relatives hundreds of miles away.

Thomas Edison created over 1,000 inventions. In 1877, he invented the phonograph, or record player. For the first time, sounds such as music and speech could be recorded and played back.

Edison developed the electric light bulb in 1879. Before electric lighting, people used gaslights. These lights were smoky and could start fires. Electric lights were cleaner, safer, and brighter than gas lamps. They kept city streets bright and allowed factories and shops to stay open after dark.

These inventions affected the way businesses operated. Some inventions kept machines running longer, or made it possible for workers to do more work. During the last half of the 1800s, new inventions allowed businesses to change and grow.

REVIEW In what ways did inventions of the late 1800s save time?

Steel Mills Andrew Carnegie (left) was an entrepreneur, a person who takes risks to start a business. He owned many steel mills. The painting above shows workers inside a steel mill.

Big Business

Main Idea Businesses in the late 1800s produced more goods, hired more people, and earned more money than before.

In 1856, British scientist **Henry Bessemer** invented a process to make steel. The Bessemer process made steel much less expensive to produce.

Andrew Carnegie was one of the first people in the United States to use the Bessemer process. He built a factory that used the Bessemer process to make steel rails for railroads. Steel rails lasted much longer than the iron rails that other American factories sold. Railroad companies bought Carnegie's steel rails, and his business grew. To help his steel company succeed, Carnegie bought fuel companies, railroads, and ships.

Because he owned these companies, he could get fuel for his factories and shipping for his goods at a lower price. By 1900, Carnegie's steel company produced about one quarter of all the steel made in the United States.

Corporations

Andrew Carnegie's steel company was big, but **John D. Rockefeller's** oil company was even larger. In 1870, Rockefeller formed the Standard Oil Company, which made products such as fuel and lamp oil. Standard Oil was a corporation. A **corporation** is a business in which many people own shares, or parts, of the business. Corporations pay part of their profits to their share owners. A profit is the money earned by a business after all the costs of machinery, workers, and raw materials are paid.

Companies Grow Larger

Corporations such as Standard Oil grew and became more common in the late 1800s. A corporation could raise money by selling lots of shares to many people. Business owners wanted to raise money to build factories and buy expensive machines. A small business could not afford the factories or machines needed to produce many products.

Another way Standard Oil grew was by buying other oil companies. It soon controlled 90 percent of the oil sold in the United States. One reason Rockefeller bought these companies was to reduce competition. **Competition** occurs when more than one business tries to sell the same goods or service.

When there is competition, a company has to keep prices low and quality high to get customers to buy its goods. When there is little competition, consumers have fewer choices about where to get the goods and services they want. A company with few competitors may raise prices or provide poor service.

Rockefeller bought so many oil companies that Standard Oil almost became a monopoly. A **monopoly** is a company that has no competition. Entrepreneurs such as Carnegie and Rockefeller earned large profits for their companies. They were accused, however, of using business practices that hurt consumers and smaller businesses.

Both Carnegie and Rockefeller became philanthropists. A philanthropist is a person who gives money to projects that help other people. Carnegie and Rockefeller believed wealthy people should use some of their money for good causes. Carnegie paid for libraries in nearly 3,000 towns. He gave away about $350 million. Rockefeller donated over $500 million to schools, colleges, churches, and hospitals.

REVIEW What is a monopoly?

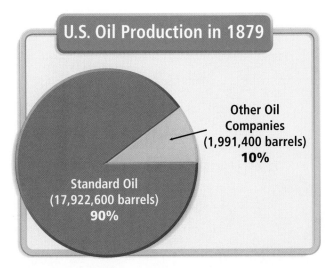

U.S. Oil Production in 1879

Other Oil Companies (1,991,400 barrels) **10%**

Standard Oil (17,922,600 barrels) **90%**

Oil Production In 1879, Standard Oil controlled most of the oil production in the United States. Rockefeller (right) became one of the richest people in the United States as a result.

Workers' Lives Change

Main Idea Workers united to improve working conditions.

In the late 1800s, businesses used mechanization to speed up the process of producing goods. Mechanization is the use of machines to do work. Machine-made goods could be sold at lower prices than handmade goods.

Consumers bought large quantities of these inexpensive machine-made products. Businesses made more goods and hired more workers to run the machines. Factories and businesses grew bigger. Some had thousands of workers.

Workers in factories did the same thing for ten or twelve hours a day, six days a week. Few factories had safe working conditions and many workers were injured or killed in accidents.

The Labor Movement

Factory workers were poorly paid. Many families struggled to pay for a place to live and food to eat. Children as young as 10 to 15 years old worked because their families needed the money they earned.

Anyone who complained about poor pay or bad working conditions could be fired. Workers formed labor unions so they could act as a group and have more power. A **labor union** is an organization of workers that tries to improve pay and working conditions for its members.

The Knights of Labor was the first large labor union. It was formed in 1869. Its goals were safer working conditions and an eight-hour workday. The Knights of Labor also wanted to stop businesses from hiring children. The labor union used strikes to try to force business owners to make changes. During a **strike,** workers refuse to work.

Striking Workers Labor unions included workers from different countries. The striking workers in this photo hold signs written in several languages.

SKILL **Reading Visuals**
Read the English signs in the photo. What do the workers want?

Some workers thought the Knights of Labor was not doing enough. In 1886, these workers formed the American Federation of Labor (AFL). They elected **Samuel Gompers** as the AFL's president. The AFL was a large group of trade unions. A trade union is an organization of workers who do the same type of job, such as plumbing, or are in the same industry, such as steelworking. Trade unions in the AFL wanted better wages, safer conditions in the workplace, and shorter workdays.

Samuel Gompers
An immigrant from England, Gompers believed that workers needed to act together to improve their working conditions.

The first labor unions did not have much success. Strikes failed when businesses fired the strikers. People were hurt or killed in fights between police or soldiers and striking workers. Powerful monopolies often blocked progress for workers. Labor unions, however, continued to bring workers together.

REVIEW Why did workers form labor unions?

Lesson Summary

- In the late 1800s, many inventions changed people's lives.
- Businesses became larger and earned bigger profits.
- Workers formed labor unions to improve poor working conditions.

Why It Matters ...

Inventions allowed people to save time and made life easier. Changes in business created more profits and led to the first labor unions.

Lesson Review

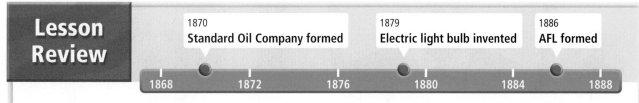

1870 Standard Oil Company formed	1879 Electric light bulb invented	1886 AFL formed

1868 — 1872 — 1876 — 1880 — 1884 — 1888

1 **VOCABULARY** Which of the following does not describe Standard Oil?
corporation   monopoly   labor union

2 **READING SKILL** Use the information you **classified** under the column of inventions to write a summary paragraph about changes in the late 1800s.

3 **MAIN IDEA: Technology** Why was the electric light bulb such an important invention?

4 **MAIN IDEA: Economics** What did John D. Rockefeller do to make his oil company grow?

5 **PEOPLE TO KNOW** Who was **Samuel Gompers**?

6 **TIMELINE SKILL** How long before the AFL began was the Standard Oil Company formed?

7 **CRITICAL THINKING: Infer** Why do you think that most business owners did not like labor unions?

HANDS ON
ART ACTIVITY Make a Then and Now poster. Use images from library resources to show an invention from the late 1800s and what it looks like today.

Electric Lights

In 1900, few homes had electric lights. Most had gaslight. Electric lights were brighter than gaslights and they could be placed anywhere in a room. Gaslights could not be moved because they were connected to gas lines in walls and ceilings. Gas could explode, so children could not turn lights on or off by themselves. People were eager to have safe, convenient electric lights.

When most homes were wired for electric lights, new inventions such as toasters and refrigerators began to be widely used.

Thomas Edison

As a boy, Thomas Alva Edison was fascinated by electricity. When he was fifteen, he rescued the son of an electric telegraph operator from being run over by a train. The operator rewarded Edison by teaching him to use a telegraph. Edison invented many electric devices, including the light bulb, in 1879. He also set up electric stations all over the United States so that people could have electric lights in their homes.

Lewis Latimer

Like Edison, Lewis Latimer was interested in the inventions of his time. He drew the diagrams for Alexander Graham Bell's telephone. He became an inventor and went to work for the U. S. Electric Lighting Company. There, Latimer made several improvements to the light bulb. Latimer later went to work for Edison. Latimer wrote a book to explain how electric lights work.

Robert   3/8/21

1. Why are electric light bulbs so much
better then gas?
Electric light bulbs are bright the gaslights,
cleaner the gaslights, and you can put them
anywhere in your home.

2. Why are electric lights so portable?
They don't need gas lines, which most
house didn't have. Most homes these
days are wired for electric lights.

3. Do electric lights make the air all
stuffy and uncomfortable? No
No, gaslights used oxygen to work, which
made rooms stuffy. Electric lights only
need electricity, so your rooms stay
breathable.

Comfortable Gaslights used up oxygen and made rooms stuffy. With electric lights, windows could be open or closed.

Clean
Electric lights did not cause soot or dust. Ceilings, carpets, and furniture stayed clean.

Bright
Electric lights made it easier for people to read after dark. Electric lights were bright and lamps could be placed next to chairs. In one town, people checked out eight times as many library books after electric lights were used as they had before.

Activities

1. **TALK ABOUT IT** What things do you like to do that would be harder or impossible to do without electric lights?

2. **WRITE ABOUT IT** List three questions that a person who has never had electric lights might ask about them. Answer the questions.

Immigrants in America

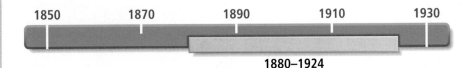

| 1850 | 1870 | 1890 | 1910 | 1930 |

1880–1924

Build on What You Know Do you know anyone who has moved to your neighborhood from another place? Many people moved to the United States about 100 years ago.

Arriving in America

Main Idea Millions of immigrants moved to the United States in the late 1800s and early 1900s.

About 25 million immigrants moved to the United States in the years between 1880 and 1924. Most immigrants before 1880 came from Ireland, Germany, England, Sweden, Denmark, and other countries of northern or western Europe. The newer immigrants, however, were usually from southern or eastern Europe. They came from Italy, Russia, Hungary, Greece, and Poland. Some also came from Mexico.

Immigrants were looking for work. Growing businesses like those of **Andrew Carnegie** and **John D. Rockefeller** offered plenty of jobs. Some immigrants also came to escape war or persecution. **Persecution** is unfair treatment or punishment. For example, many Jews in eastern Europe were hurt or killed because of their religion. Jewish people hoped to escape persecution by moving to the United States.

Most immigrants found greater political freedom in America as well. A man from Slovenia expressed immigrants' feelings when he said,

❝ In America everything was possible. ❞

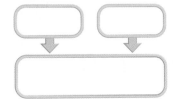

Immigration Stations

Once immigrants arrived in the United States, they went through immigration stations, such as Ellis Island in New York Harbor. Government workers at the stations asked newcomers about where they planned to live and work. Doctors examined the immigrants to be sure they didn't have diseases that could spread to others. Almost all European immigrants who came to the United States were allowed to enter.

Coming to America Immigrants fill a ship crossing the Atlantic Ocean. These children (right) are coming to the United States from Italy.

Asians moved to the United States to find jobs, too. Large numbers of Chinese immigrants first arrived on the West Coast in the 1850s. They also had to go through immigration stations, such as Angel Island in San Francisco Bay. They faced more prejudice than European immigrants. Asian immigrants on Angel Island had to stay for weeks, months, or even years before being allowed to enter the United States. About 25 percent were forced to return to their home countries.

REVIEW In what ways were Asian immigrants treated differently than immigrants from Europe?

Living in a New Country

Main Idea Many immigrants moved to large cities and worked in factories.

After entering the United States, most immigrants settled near family or friends. Immigrant communities in big cities grew quickly. In some cities whole neighborhoods were made up of a single ethnic group. An **ethnic group** is a group of people who share a culture or language. In ethnic neighborhoods, immigrants spoke their native languages, practiced their religions, and kept their country's customs.

Immigrants' lives were not easy. Some worked in dangerous steel mills. Others had jobs in noisy and dirty factories where they sewed clothing or made thread. Nearly all worked long hours for low pay, making so little money they could barely buy food for themselves or their families.

Many newcomers lived in tenements. A **tenement** is a poorly built apartment building. Tenements were crowded and unsafe. They often had no windows or running water. Several families might live in one small apartment.

Hard Times for Immigrants

As neighborhoods changed, immigrants faced prejudice from people who were frightened by unfamiliar languages and customs. Employers liked to hire immigrants because they worked hard for little pay. For the same reason, some people worried about losing their jobs to immigrants and wanted immigration stopped.

Anna Rosenberg Born in Hungary, Rosenberg was the first female Assistant Secretary of Defense for the United States.

Immigrant Neighborhoods

LEGEND
- Chinese
- Syrian, Turkish, Greek
- Russian, Polish, other Eastern Europeans
- Italian
- Irish
- German

Hudson River

14TH STREET

CANAL STREET

BROADWAY

BOWERY STREET

East River

N W E S

km 0 .25 .5
mi 0 .25 .5

New York City This map shows ethnic neighborhoods in New York City in 1920.

SKILL Reading Maps Which ethnic groups lived along Canal Street?

Laws Against Immigration

In 1882, Congress limited immigration by passing the Chinese Exclusion Act. This law excluded, or kept out, almost all new Chinese immigrants. Later laws limited the number of people from other countries. In 1921 and 1924, Congress passed laws that greatly lowered the number of Europeans allowed into the United States. These same laws also kept out most people from Asia.

Laws made it hard for immigrants to enter the United States, and they faced prejudice when they arrived. Immigrants overcame these hardships and helped the United States become one of the richest and fastest-growing countries in the world. They constructed thousands of miles of railroad tracks, dug deep coal mines, and worked in factories.

REVIEW What did immigrants do to help the United States grow?

Lesson Summary

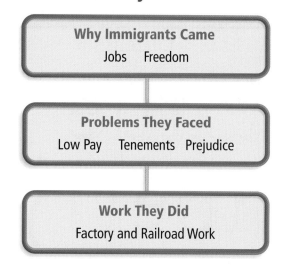

Why Immigrants Came
Jobs   Freedom

Problems They Faced
Low Pay   Tenements   Prejudice

Work They Did
Factory and Railroad Work

Why It Matters ...

The United States today includes the great-grandchildren of immigrants who came in search of freedom and better lives in the 1800s and early 1900s.

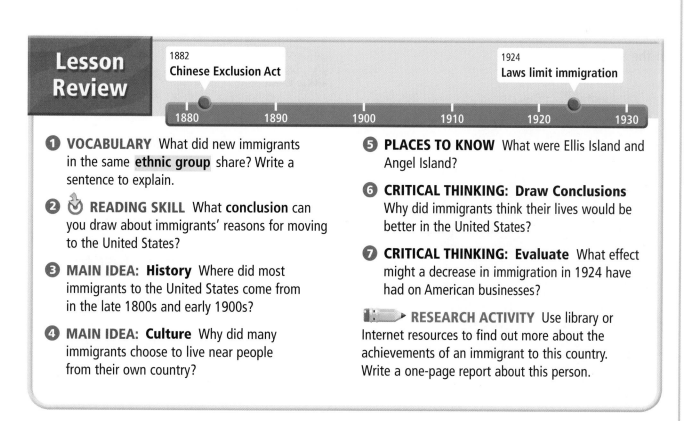

Lesson Review

1882
Chinese Exclusion Act

1924
Laws limit immigration

1880   1890   1900   1910   1920   1930

1. **VOCABULARY** What did new immigrants in the same **ethnic group** share? Write a sentence to explain.

2. **READING SKILL** What **conclusion** can you draw about immigrants' reasons for moving to the United States?

3. **MAIN IDEA: History** Where did most immigrants to the United States come from in the late 1800s and early 1900s?

4. **MAIN IDEA: Culture** Why did many immigrants choose to live near people from their own country?

5. **PLACES TO KNOW** What were Ellis Island and Angel Island?

6. **CRITICAL THINKING: Draw Conclusions** Why did immigrants think their lives would be better in the United States?

7. **CRITICAL THINKING: Evaluate** What effect might a decrease in immigration in 1924 have had on American businesses?

RESEARCH ACTIVITY Use library or Internet resources to find out more about the achievements of an immigrant to this country. Write a one-page report about this person.

Statue of Liberty

French sculptor Frédéric Auguste Bartholdi loved America. He wanted to build an enormous statue as a symbol of the long friendship between France and the United States.

Bartholdi called the 225-ton statue "Liberty Enlightening the World," but today it is known as the Statue of Liberty. It stands in New York harbor. It is a symbol of friendship between nations, of hope for immigrants, and of freedom for all Americans.

Poet Emma Lazarus was invited to write a poem about the statue. Her words are engraved on the statue's base.

" *Give me your tired, your poor,*

Your huddled masses yearning to breathe free,

The wretched refuse of your teeming shore.

Send these, the homeless, tempest-tost to me.

I lift my lamp beside the golden door! "

—Emma Lazarus

Torch

The right arm and torch were completed first. By 1949, the torch's lamps beamed 13,000 watts of light. The torch is a symbol of freedom.

Crown

The seven spikes on the crown stand for the seven seas and seven continents.

Tablet

The tablet in Liberty's left hand is engraved with July 4, 1776, in Roman numerals.

▲ Making the Statue of Liberty

Bartholdi and his assistants started by making clay models of the statue. They created models that were larger and larger until they made a model that was as big as the final statue—151 feet high.

Activities

1. **THINK ABOUT IT** Why do people visit the Statue of Liberty today?

2. **DESIGN YOUR OWN** Draw your idea for a monument about citizenship. What words of inspiration would be on the monument? What parts of the monument would be symbols? Use captions to explain the symbols.

547

Growing Cities

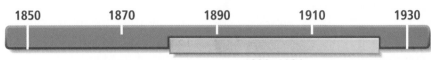

1850　　　1870　　　1890　　　1910　　　1930

1880–1924

Build on What You Know When you think about cities, do you think about millions of people and very tall buildings? In the late 1800s, millions of people moved to cities and built the first tall buildings.

Moving to Cities

Main Idea Cities in the United States grew quickly in the late 1800s and early 1900s.

Most of the millions of immigrants who came to the United States between 1880 and 1910 lived and worked in cities. Many people who lived on farms or in small towns also moved to urban areas during this time. There were not many jobs for them in the rural United States. Fewer farm workers were needed after new machines increased productivity on farms.

Urban Growth By 1910, nearly 50 million people lived in cities.

SKILL **Reading Graphs** What percentage of people in the United States lived in cities in 1910?

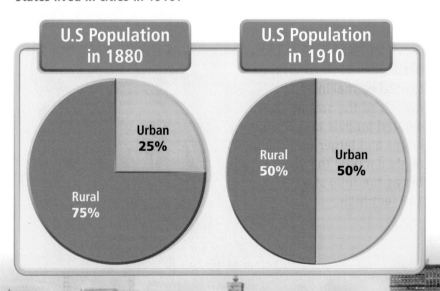

U.S Population in 1880

Urban 25%

Rural 75%

U.S Population in 1910

Rural 50%

Urban 50%

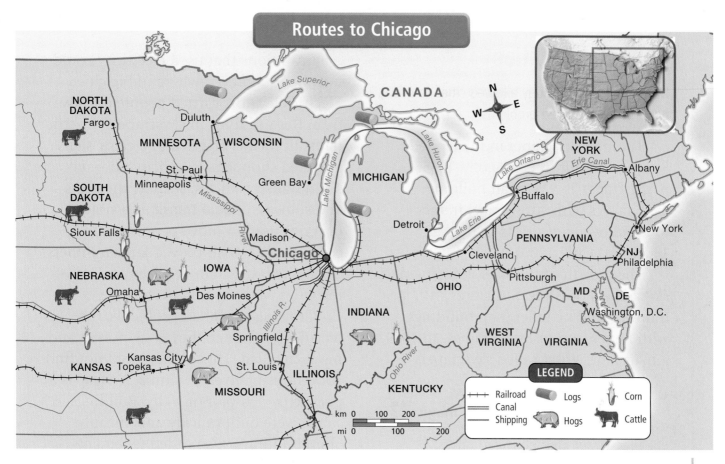

Chicago's Resources This map shows Chicago and its nearby natural resources and transportation routes.

A Good Location

During the late 1800s, cities grew as businesses and factories became larger. One city, Chicago, grew quickly because of its location near transportation routes, natural resources, and Lake Michigan. Transportation routes such as rivers and a canal linked the city to the Illinois and Mississippi rivers. Railroads and boats brought logs from northern forests to the city. They also carried wheat, corn, and cattle from western farms and ranches.

Chicago, 1913

Factories in Chicago cut logs into lumber. Mills turned wheat and corn into food. Stockyards held thousands of animals. A **stockyard** is a fenced area where large numbers of animals, such as pigs and cattle, are kept until they are used as food or moved to another place.

Many people moved to Chicago to find jobs in the city's growing factories and shops. Between 1870 and 1920, the population of Chicago grew from about 300,000 to about 2.7 million.

REVIEW Why did so many people move to cities in the late 1800s and early 1900s?

Changes in Cities

Main Idea Technology allowed cities to grow, but crowding caused problems.

The first skyscraper in the United States was built in Chicago in 1885. A **skyscraper** is a very tall building. Skyscrapers with strong steel frames towered over city streets in the late 1800s and early 1900s.

The growth of the steel industry made skyscrapers possible. Structures with steel frames could be taller than buildings with heavy iron or brick frames. In 1889, a magazine writer called skyscrapers

> 66 **tower-like structures that have sprung up as if by magic.** 99

Electricity also changed cities. Inventors **Thomas Edison** and **Nikola Tesla** thought of new ways to make electricity and send it through wires.

Inventions that used electricity could now be found everywhere in big cities. Electric elevators carried people quickly from floor to floor in skyscrapers. Electric lights lit theater stages and electric signs attracted shoppers. Electricity powered rapid transit vehicles, such as streetcars and subways. **Rapid transit** is a system of trains used to move people around cities. Rapid transit moved large numbers of people faster than ever before. Growing cities were exciting places.

Growing cities had problems, too. As cities got busier, they grew noisier and more crowded. Those who could not find good housing lived in slums. A **slum** is a poor, crowded part of a city. Buildings in slums were built quickly and cheaply. Slum buildings, also called tenements, were not safe. They could catch fire easily, and many had no fire escapes.

Electric Streetcars

Electric Sign

Electricity By the early 1900s, city streets were full of signs and streetcars powered by electricity. Nikola Tesla (above), an immigrant from Croatia, found ways to send electricity through wires.

Helping Each Other

City people, especially immigrants, helped each other find jobs and places to live. Reformers helped as well.

Jane Addams and **Ellen Gates Starr** were reformers who opened Hull House in Chicago in 1889. Hull House was one of the first settlement houses in the United States. A **settlement house** is a community center for people in cities.

Jane Addams Reformers such as Addams helped immigrants.

People came to Hull House to learn English, get medical care, or find jobs. Hull House had clubs for girls and boys. Working mothers left babies in the Hull House nursery. Reformers in other cities liked the work Hull House did and they started settlement houses themselves.

REVIEW What kinds of help did immigrants find in settlement houses?

Lesson Summary

- In the late 1800s and early 1900s, immigrants and people from rural areas moved to cities.
- Technology changed urban life.
- Settlement houses helped people in cities solve their problems.

Why It Matters ...

During the late 1800s and early 1900s, skyscrapers and electricity made cities start to look more like they do today.

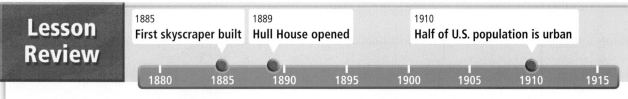

Lesson Review

1885 First skyscraper built	1889 Hull House opened	1910 Half of U.S. population is urban

1880 1885 1890 1895 1900 1905 1910 1915

1 **VOCABULARY** Write a description of cities in the late 1800s and early 1900s, using **skyscraper**, **slum**, and **rapid transit**.

2 **READING SKILL** What was the **effect** of electricity on rapid transit?

3 **MAIN IDEA: Geography** Why did Chicago grow quickly in the late 1800s and early 1900s?

4 **MAIN IDEA: History** What problems did people face in growing cities?

5 **PEOPLE TO KNOW** What did **Thomas Edison** and **Nikola Tesla** do to change cities?

6 **TIMELINE SKILL** How many years after the first skyscraper was built were half of all Americans living in cities?

7 **CRITICAL THINKING Decision Making** For a farmer in the late 1800s, what were some of the consequences of the decision to move from the farm to the city?

WRITING ACTIVITY Write a newspaper editorial from 1889 about the work of Hull House for the citizens of Chicago.

STEEL CITY

Pittsburgh was just the right place to produce steel. It had two major rivers. It had natural resources nearby, such as coal. Steel was in demand in the late 1800s and early 1900s. The nation needed steel for railroads, bridges, skyscrapers, and factories. Pittsburgh soon got the nickname "Steel City."

Iron ore and a mineral called lime were the ingredients used to make steel. Tons of coal were burned to melt the ore, and the smoke blackened the skies of Pittsburgh as the city grew. Rivers and railroads carried raw materials into the city and carried finished steel out of it.

The number of Pittsburgh steel and iron workers increased by how many between 1880 and 1910?

The Carnegie Steel Company owned these Pittsburgh factories, shown in the early 1900s.

① **Smokestacks**
Smoke from burning coal blows into the sky. Rain carries some of this pollution back into the river.

② **River** Boats take coal up the Monongahela River, pictured above. The city's other major river is the Allegheny.

Activities

1. **TALK ABOUT IT** Discuss how you think the making of steel changed Pittsburgh.

2. **WRITE ABOUT IT** Write a paragraph describing the scene in the picture.

Time of Reform

1850　　　1870　　　1890　　　1910　　　1930

1900–1920

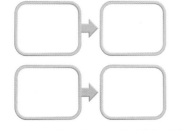
Build on What You Know You have probably tried to fix something that wasn't working well. In the early 1900s, people called progressives wanted to fix what they thought was wrong with the country.

The Progressives

Main Idea Progressives tried to improve life in the United States.

As cities and businesses grew, more adults and children went to work in factories. Jobs in factories were not always safe. People could slip on dirty floors or get hurt while working with unsafe machines.

Factories dumped dirt and poisons into city water. Smokestacks blew soot and smoke into city air. People who lived near factories got sick from drinking dirty water and breathing dirty air.

Progressives wanted to make cities and factories cleaner and safer. **Progressives** were reformers. They did not always agree with one another, but most thought governments should make laws to protect workers, consumers, and citizens' rights.

Working Children
Some children worked long hours in factories. This girl is making stockings.

Making Changes

Progressives wrote about workers who were hurt in accidents. They took pictures of children working in unsafe places. They convinced state lawmakers to protect workers and keep children from working.

Progressives who wrote about the need for change were called muckrakers. Muck is something dirty or unpleasant. A muckraker is someone who "rakes up," or points out, unpleasant truths.

In 1906, a muckraker named **Upton Sinclair** published his book, *The Jungle*. This fictional description was based on Sinclair's observations of unsafe and dirty conditions in meatpacking plants. It told about the use of chemicals to cover the taste of rotten meat. Sinclair wrote,

66 **There was never the least attention paid to what was cut up for sausage . . . rats, bread, and meat would go into the hoppers [containers] together.** 99

Government Reforms

President **Theodore Roosevelt** worked with Congress to pass two laws in 1906 to make food safer. The Pure Food and Drug Act and the Meat Inspection Act stated that medicine and foods had to be made without harmful chemicals. The factories where they were made had to be clean.

Roosevelt also wanted to preserve wilderness areas. He was influenced by **John Muir,** a conservationist who believed that natural areas were precious resources. Muir took President Roosevelt to visit present-day Yosemite (yoh SEHM ih tee) National Park in California in 1903. After seeing Yosemite, Roosevelt set aside millions of acres for national parks and wilderness areas.

REVIEW What did the Pure Food and Drug Act and the Meat Inspection Act do to make food safer?

Constitutional Amendments

Progressives' Goal	Result	What It Did
Make people who earned more money pay more of the cost of government	16th Amendment	Allowed Congress to pass an income tax
Allow voters to choose their lawmakers	17th Amendment	Allowed citizens to elect senators
Reduce violence and crime they thought was caused by drinking alcohol	18th Amendment	Made it against the law to make or sell alcoholic beverages
Allow women to vote	19th Amendment	Recognized the right of women aged 21 or older to vote

Progressive Amendments Between 1913 and 1920, the time known as the Progressive Era, Congress passed several amendments to the Constitution.

SKILL **Reading Charts** What did the 19th Amendment do?

Working for Equal Rights

Main Idea In the early 1900s, women and African Americans worked to gain equal rights.

New laws helped workers and made food safer. Yet women and African Americans could not vote in many states. They also faced discrimination in getting jobs and education. For example, most colleges and universities did not take women or African American men as students.

Voting Rights for Women

Women first called for the right to vote before the Civil War. They wanted Congress to amend the Constitution to recognize this right. In 1878, Congress voted against such an amendment. Leaders of the women's suffrage movement, however, did not give up. Women such as **Carrie Chapman Catt** gave speeches and wrote letters to lawmakers. Thousands of women marched in protest in New York, Chicago, and Washington, D.C.

For decades, women fought for suffrage. They won the right to vote in a few states, but they could not vote in national elections. Finally, Congress passed the Nineteenth Amendment, which guaranteed women the right to vote. In 1920, two-thirds of the states approved the amendment and it became law.

Women's Suffrage On a crowded street in 1916, women march for the right to vote. Women worked hard to win the support of President Wilson for their cause.

Struggle for Racial Equality

In the early 1900s, African Americans, Mexican Americans, American Indians, and Asian Americans faced prejudice when they applied for jobs or tried to rent or buy homes. Some states had laws that kept people in these groups from voting, or forced their children to go to separate schools. Many organizations fought against unfair laws and prejudice.

The National Association for the Advancement of Colored People (NAACP) was founded in 1909 to work for equality for African Americans. Advancement means improvement. "Colored People" was a term used at the time for African Americans.

One of the NAACP's leaders was **W.E.B. Du Bois.** Du Bois was an African American writer and professor. His writings on African American life helped persuade many Americans that change was needed. **Booker T. Washington** was another African American leader. He started a school to educate and give job training to southern African Americans.

Around 1910, a growing number of African Americans left the south for jobs in northern cities. In the early 1920s, the Ku Klux Klan, the group that attacked African Americans, grew larger.

W.E.B. Du Bois
He worked for equal rights for African Americans.

The Klan's increasing violence made life even more difficult for southern African Americans. Between 1910 and 1930, about 1.5 million African Americans left the rural South. Most went North to work in large factories and businesses. This movement of people became known as the Great Migration.

REVIEW What is the NAACP and what is its purpose?

Lesson Summary

During the early 1900s, progressives wanted laws to protect workers, consumers, and citizens' rights. Laws were passed to make food safer and conserve land. Women won the right to vote. Many organizations, including the NAACP, fought prejudice and injustice.

Why It Matters ...

The laws that progressives worked for made life in the United States safer and more just.

Lesson Review

| 1905 | 1906 | 1907 | 1908 | 1909 | 1910 |

1906 **Pure Food and Drug Act**

1909 **NAACP founded**

1 **VOCABULARY** Write a paragraph about the Pure Food and Drug Act and the Meat Inspection Act, using **progressives** and **muckraker.**

2 **READING SKILL** What was the **solution** to the **problem** of women not being allowed to vote?

3 **MAIN IDEA: History** Name three things progressives tried to change in the early 1900s.

4 **MAIN IDEA: Citizenship** What did Booker T. Washington do for African Americans in the South?

5 **PEOPLE TO KNOW** What did **Theodore Roosevelt** do to support conservation?

6 **TIMELINE SKILL** When was the NAACP started?

7 **CRITICAL THINKING: Synthesize** Why were progressives important to millions of people in the United States?

HANDS ON **ART ACTIVITY** Create a poster that a person in the early 1900s might have made about voting rights for women.

The Great Migration

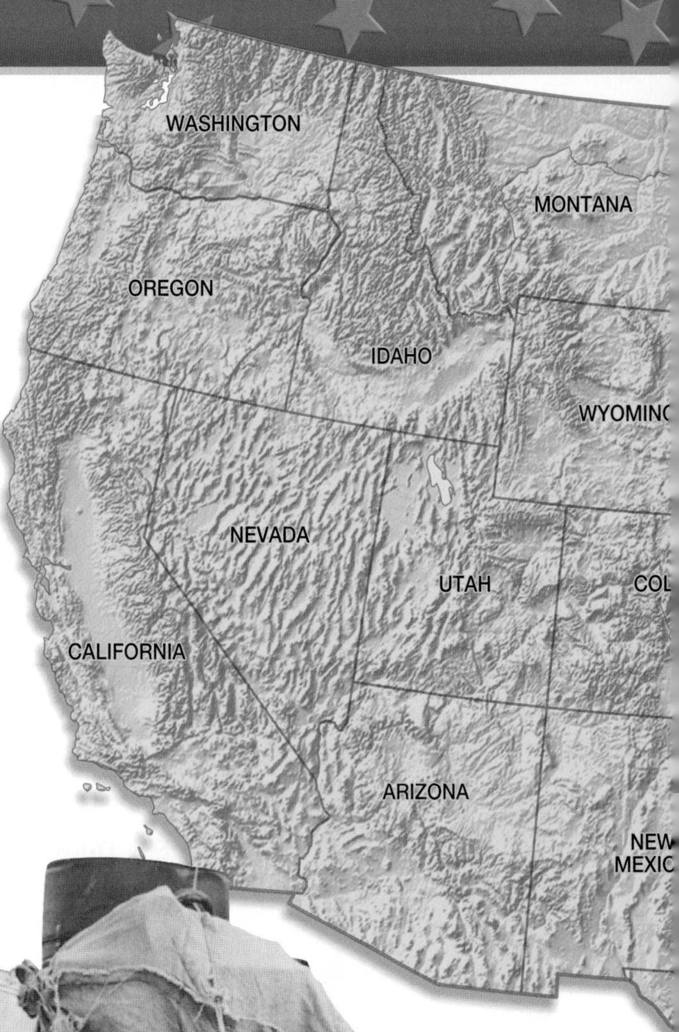

Why did millions of African Americans leave their homes in the South? The answer is jobs and opportunities. Jobs in steel mills and railroad yards and in the automobile, meatpacking, and food processing plants of the North and Midwest paid much better than jobs open to African Americans in the South.

Although African Americans faced prejudice in the North, they had new opportunities, too. Adults could vote. Children could go to public schools.

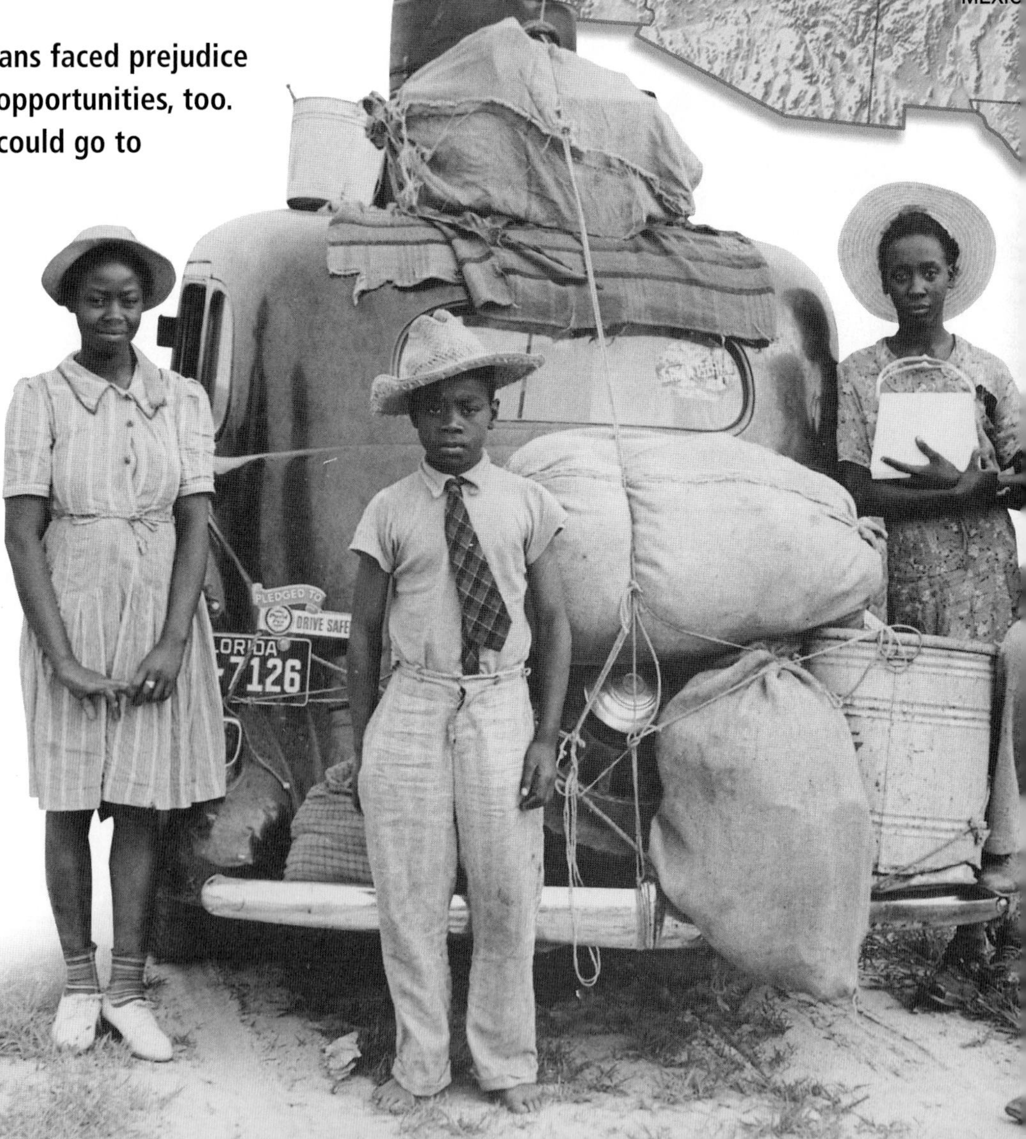

WASHINGTON

MONTANA

OREGON

IDAHO

WYOMING

NEVADA

UTAH   COL

CALIFORNIA

ARIZONA

NEW
MEXIC

Ready to Leave
The Great Migration occurred in several waves from the 1910s through the 1950s. This family is moving north in 1940.

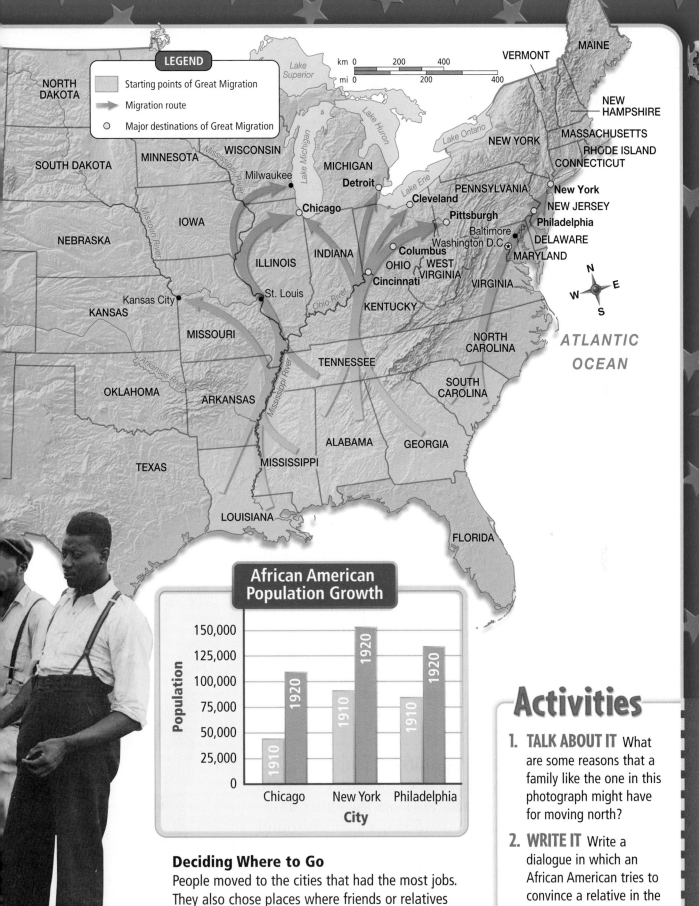

LEGEND

Starting points of Great Migration

→ Migration route

○ Major destinations of Great Migration

km 0   200   400
mi 0   200   400

NORTH DAKOTA
SOUTH DAKOTA
MINNESOTA
WISCONSIN
Milwaukee
Lake Superior
Lake Michigan
Lake Huron
Lake Ontario
MICHIGAN
Detroit
Lake Erie
Cleveland
VERMONT
MAINE
NEW HAMPSHIRE
NEW YORK
MASSACHUSETTS
RHODE ISLAND
CONNECTICUT
New York
NEW JERSEY
Philadelphia
DELAWARE
MARYLAND
NEBRASKA
IOWA
Chicago
ILLINOIS
INDIANA
OHIO
Columbus
Cincinnati
WEST VIRGINIA
Pittsburgh
PENNSYLVANIA
Baltimore
Washington D.C.
VIRGINIA
Mississippi River
Missouri River
St. Louis
Ohio River
KENTUCKY
Kansas City
KANSAS
MISSOURI
Arkansas River
OKLAHOMA
ARKANSAS
TENNESSEE
NORTH CAROLINA
SOUTH CAROLINA
Mississippi River
TEXAS
LOUISIANA
MISSISSIPPI
ALABAMA
GEORGIA
FLORIDA
ATLANTIC OCEAN

N W E S

African American Population Growth

Population

150,000
125,000
100,000
75,000
50,000
25,000
0

1910 | 1920 — Chicago
1910 | 1920 — New York
1910 | 1920 — Philadelphia

City

Deciding Where to Go
People moved to the cities that had the most jobs. They also chose places where friends or relatives were already living.

Activities

1. **TALK ABOUT IT** What are some reasons that a family like the one in this photograph might have for moving north?

2. **WRITE IT** Write a dialogue in which an African American tries to convince a relative in the South to move North.

Reading and Thinking Skills

Skillbuilder

Identify Fact and Opinion

▶ **VOCABULARY**
fact
opinion

When you study social studies, it helps to be able to identify the difference between fact and opinion. A **fact** is a piece of information that can be proved. Proof can come from sources such as observation, books, or artifacts. Facts answer questions such as *Who, What, When,* and *Where.* An **opinion** is a personal belief. It expresses someone's thoughts or feelings and cannot be proved.

Learn the Skill

Step 1: Read the piece of writing. Look for specific names, events, dates, and numbers. These often signal facts.

Step 2: Look for theories, feelings, and thoughts. These are opinions. Sometimes opinions contain phrases such as *I believe* or *I think.* Other opinion words are *might, could, should,* and *probably.* The words *best, worst, greatest,* or *extremely* also signal opinions.

Step 3: Identify the purpose of the writing. What does the writer want you to do or believe? Does the writer have a reason to try to make the facts sound different from what they really are?

Practice the Skill

Read the following statements. Then identify each one as a fact or an opinion. Explain how you made your decision.

1 It seems to me that the Pure Food and Drug Act was terrible for the business of meat factories.

2 Creating and protecting national parks is the best thing a President can do for the country.

3 When the NAACP was created, its members worked to educate people about the unfair treatment of African Americans. They made speeches, started a newspaper, and handed out flyers.

Apply the Skill

Read the following paragraph about women's suffrage and the Nineteenth Amendment. Identify the facts and opinions. Then explain your choices. What did the writer want you to believe?

Women had been calling for suffrage since the Seneca Falls Convention in 1848. It was surprising that by the end of World War I, women still were not allowed to vote. During the war, thousands of women filled the jobs of men who had gone off to fight. They worked in airplane factories, drove trucks, and operated elevators. These women put an end to the silly argument that women should stay in the home and let men do the voting. In 1920, the Nineteenth Amendment was passed, guaranteeing women the right to vote.

Visual Summary

1.–4. Write a description of how each person below improved others' lives.

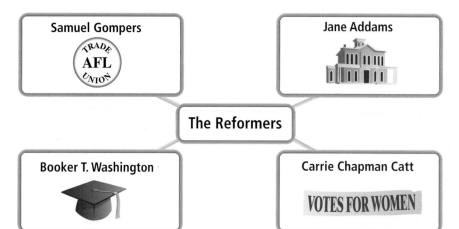

Samuel Gompers

TRADE **AFL** UNION

Jane Addams

The Reformers

Booker T. Washington

Carrie Chapman Catt

VOTES FOR WOMEN

Facts and Main Ideas

✔ TEST PREP Answer each question with information from the chapter.

5. **Economics** What did John D. Rockefeller do to make Standard Oil grow?

6. **Citizenship** Why did immigrants settle in ethnic neighborhoods?

7. **Geography** Why did the location of Chicago cause it to grow quickly?

8. **History** What new kinds of technology helped cities grow?

9. **Government** What did women do to gain support for the Nineteenth Amendment?

Vocabulary

✔ TEST PREP Choose the correct word from the list below to complete each sentence.

corporation, p. 536
persecution, p. 542
rapid transit, p. 550
progressives, p. 554

10. Some immigrants came to the United States to escape _____.

11. People own shares, or parts, of a _____.

12. Reformers like Upton Sinclair were _____ who wanted to improve society.

13. Streetcars and subways are part of a _____ system.

1869
First labor union

1882
Chinese Exclusion Act

1909
NAACP founded

1920
Nineteenth Amendment

1860   1870   1880   1890   1900   1910   1920

Apply Skills

TEST PREP **Reading and Thinking Skill** Read the paragraph below from *The Bitter Cry of the Children* by John Spargo. Then use what you have learned about fact and opinion to answer each question.

> I shall never forget my first visit to a glass factory…The boys employed, [were] about forty in number, at least ten of whom were less than twelve years of age…The hours of labor for the "night shift" were from 5:30 P.M. to 3:30 A.M.…The work of these…boys was by far the hardest of all.

14. Which of the following is an opinion?

 A. About 40 boys were employed.

 B. Ten boys were less than twelve years old.

 C. Boys worked from 5:30 P.M. to 3:30 A.M.

 D. The work of these boys was by far the hardest of all.

15. Which of the following best summarizes what Spargo wants you to believe about child labor?

 A. Children worked hard jobs for long hours.

 B. Child labor laws protected children.

 C. Visitors did not see the worst sights.

 D. Children only worked at night.

Critical Thinking

TEST PREP Write a short paragraph to answer each question.

16. **Cause and Effect** Why did labor unions organize strikes?

17. **Infer** What changes did the Great Migration bring to the lives of African Americans?

Timeline

Use the Chapter Summary Timeline above to answer the question.

18. What events took place in the 1800s?

Activities

Speaking Activity Prepare a speech for a reformer living in the late 1800s. Choose a problem, such as unsafe factories, and suggest a solution.

Writing Activity Learn more about one of the inventions of the late 1800s, such as the oil cup, typewriter, or telephone. Write a description of the invention, explaining its effect on life in the United States.

Technology
Writing Process Tips
Get help with your description at
www.eduplace.com/kids/hmss05/

Review and Test Prep

Vocabulary and Main Ideas

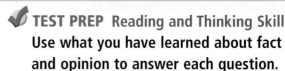 **TEST PREP** Write a sentence to answer each question.

1. What effect did **transcontinental railroads** have on life in the United States?

2. What did the U.S. government do to make American Indians **assimilate?**

3. In what way does **competition** help to keep prices low?

4. Why did workers believe that **labor unions** were important?

5. Why did new immigrants to the United States often live with members of **ethnic groups?**

6. Who was Upton Sinclair and why was he called a **muckraker?**

Critical Thinking

TEST PREP Write a short paragraph to answer each question.

7. **Evaluate** Do you think immigrants' lives were better or worse after they arrived in the United States? Why or why not?

8. **Cause and Effect** How was the growth of cities a cause of the Progressive movement?

Apply Skills

TEST PREP Reading and Thinking Skill
Use what you have learned about fact and opinion to answer each question.

> Settlers on the Great Plains faced many hardships. Winter temperatures could sink to 40° below zero. No one should have to live with that kind of freezing weather. Summers were hot and dry. Millions of grasshoppers ate the crops. The settlers probably wanted to live someplace else. But they had no right to complain, because land was so inexpensive.

9. Which statement is a fact?

    A. Settlers had no right to complain.

    B. Winter temperatures could sink to 40° below zero.

    C. Summers were pleasantly cool.

    D. No one should have to live with that kind of freezing weather.

10. Which statement is an opinion?

    A. Millions of grasshoppers ate the crops.

    B. Settlers on the Plains faced many hardships.

    C. The settlers probably wanted to live someplace else.

    D. Summers were hot and dry.

Unit Activity

The Big Idea

Create a Web of Change

- Choose one event that you read about in this unit and place it in the center of a Web of Change.

- Research other events or other changes that were caused by that central event.

- Draw lines from the central event to the effects it caused.

- Post your Web of Change in your class.

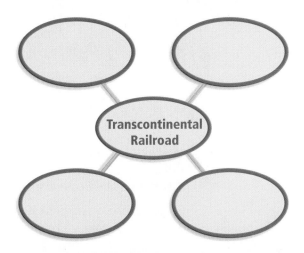

Transcontinental Railroad

At the Library

You may find these books at your school or public library.

Kids on Strike! by Susan C. Bartoletti
Working children of the early 1900s joined together to demand better working conditions.

Rodzina by Karen Cushman
Twelve-year-old Polish immigrant Rodzina traveled on an orphan train bound for California.

CURRENT EVENTS
WEEKLY (WR) READER

Connect to Today

Create a bulletin board that connects an important event from this unit to events going on today.

- Choose an event or topic from the unit, such as new inventions, and write a description of it. Then find articles about a similar topic.

- Write a paragraph or draw a picture showing the connections between the events.

- Display your articles, paragraphs, and illustrations on a bulletin board.

Technology
Get information for your bulletin board from the Weekly Reader at
www.eduplace.com/kids/hmss05/

Read About It

Look for these Social Studies Independent Books in your classroom.

I Care: American Reformers

Angel Island and the Land of Promise
by Julia Jones

"What Shall Workers Do?"
By Toby Ng

UNIT 8

The Twentieth Century

The Big Idea

How do different people show their courage?

"The only thing we have to fear is fear itself."

President Franklin D. Roosevelt,
First Inaugural Address, 1933

Charles Lindbergh
1902–1974

Would you be willing to travel on a journey that no one else had ever taken before? This pilot did so, and "Lucky Lindy" became a hero to people all over the world.
page 589

History Makers

Franklin D. Roosevelt
1882–1945

After millions of people lost their jobs during the Great Depression, Roosevelt offered Americans a "New Deal." His programs helped the nation survive this hard time.
page 594

Rosa Parks

Rosa Parks spent years working for justice for African Americans. She showed her courage when she challenged state laws and refused to give up her seat in the front of a bus.
page 627

UNIT 8
Almanac

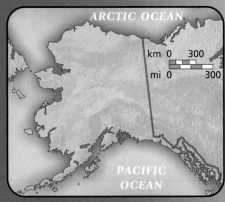

Major Events, 1900–1970

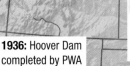

1941: Carving of Mount Rushmore completed

▲ *Mt. Rushmore*

1962: Cesar Chavez organizes farm workers

1936: Hoover Dam completed by PWA

1930: Dust Bowl Migration

PACIFIC OCEAN

ARCTIC OCEAN

km 0   300
mi 0   300

PACIFIC OCEAN

km 0   150   300
mi 0   150   300

km 0   50 100
mi 0   50   100

PACIFIC OCEAN

Unit Preview

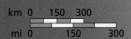

| 1910 | 1920 | 1930 | 1940 |

1914
World War I Begins

Alliances draw countries into war
Chapter 16, page 579

1929
Great Depression Begins

Millions face hunger and unemployment
Chapter 16, page 592

1939
World War II Begins

Allies fight against Axis
Chapter 16, page 601

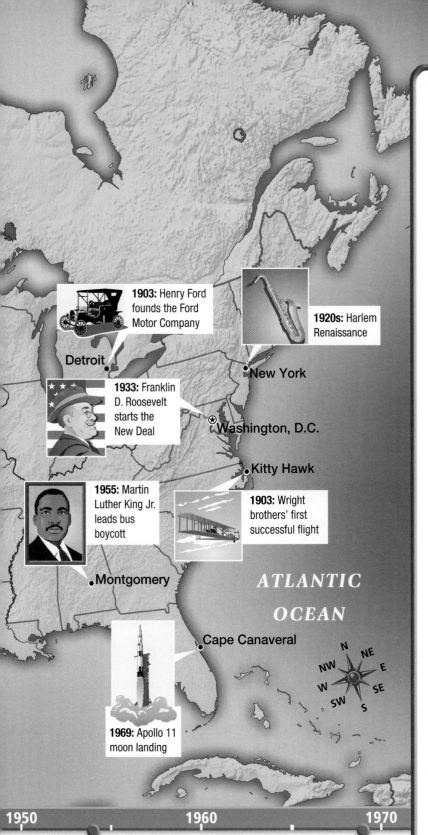

1903: Henry Ford founds the Ford Motor Company

1920s: Harlem Renaissance

Detroit

New York

1933: Franklin D. Roosevelt starts the New Deal

⊛ Washington, D.C.

Kitty Hawk

1955: Martin Luther King Jr. leads bus boycott

1903: Wright brothers' first successful flight

Montgomery

ATLANTIC

OCEAN

Cape Canaveral

N
NW NE
W E
SW SE
S

1969: Apollo 11 moon landing

1950   1960   1970

1954
Brown vs. Board of Education
Segregation ruled unconstitutional
Chapter 17, page 627

1969
Moon Landing
Astronauts land on moon
Chapter 17, page 633

Connect to Today

Top Exports in 1970

Export	Value (billions of $)
Machinery	11.6
Chemicals	3.8
Vehicles	3.2

The top export, machinery, was worth three times as much as the next export, chemicals.

Top Exports Today

In 2001, the United States' top export was computers and electronics. The value of these exports was about $72.1 billion.

How much more was the value of the top export in 2001 than in 1970?

CURRENT EVENTS
WEEKLY (WR) READER

Current events on the web!

Find out about current events that connect with the Big Idea of this unit.
See activities at:
www.eduplace.com/kids/hmss05/

Chapter 16

Becoming a World Power

Technology

e • **glossary**
e • **word games**
www.eduplace.com/kids/hmss05/

Vocabulary Preview

alliance

In the early 1900s, Britain, France, and Russia formed an **alliance.** They agreed to defend one another if attacked.

page 578

armistice

When World War I ended, people celebrated the **armistice** with parades. People were glad the war was over.

page 583

Chapter Timeline

1898
Spanish-American War

1914
World War I begins

1895   1905   1915

Reading Strategy

Question To check that you understand the text, use this strategy as you read.

Ask yourself whether you understand what you have just read. What do you need to know more about?

division of labor

The automobile industry uses **division of labor.** Each worker does one part of the job of building a car.

page 586

war bond

During World War II, an American could show patriotism by purchasing a **war bond.** The United States government sold bonds to pay for the war. **page 602**

1929
Stock market crash

1939
World War II begins

925

1935

1945

New Territories

| 1860 | 1870 | 1880 | 1890 | 1900 | 1910 | 1920 |

1867–1914

Build on What You Know Have you noticed that people like to show others what they can do? At the end of the 1800s, many Americans wanted to show the world how powerful the United States had become.

The Nation Expands

Main Idea The United States added the territories of Alaska and Hawaii.

By the late 1800s, railroads and factories had made the United States economy strong. Some Americans wanted the United States to expand its economic power in the world. Government leaders looked for new territories that would increase the country's wealth.

Alaska

In 1867, the United States was still recovering from the Civil War. Few people were thinking about adding new land to the country. Then Russia offered to sell its colony of Alaska to the United States. This was a huge area of land twice the size of Texas. Secretary of State **William Seward** convinced Congress to buy Alaska. Most people believed that buying Alaska was foolish. They called Alaska "Seward's Folly."

People would not think Seward was foolish for long. In 1896, gold was found in Canada near Alaska. Gold hunters rushed to Canada, and soon the gold rush spread into the land Seward had bought. Thousands of people went to Alaska hoping to get rich. Very few discovered gold. What people did discover was that Alaska's fish, forests, and minerals were worth far more than its gold. Buying Alaska no longer seemed a folly.

VOCABULARY

imperialism
isthmus

Vocabulary Strategy

imperialism

Imperial and empire are related words. When people practice imperialism, they are building empires.

 READING SKILL

Compare and Contrast
Take notes to contrast three different ways in which the United States expanded.

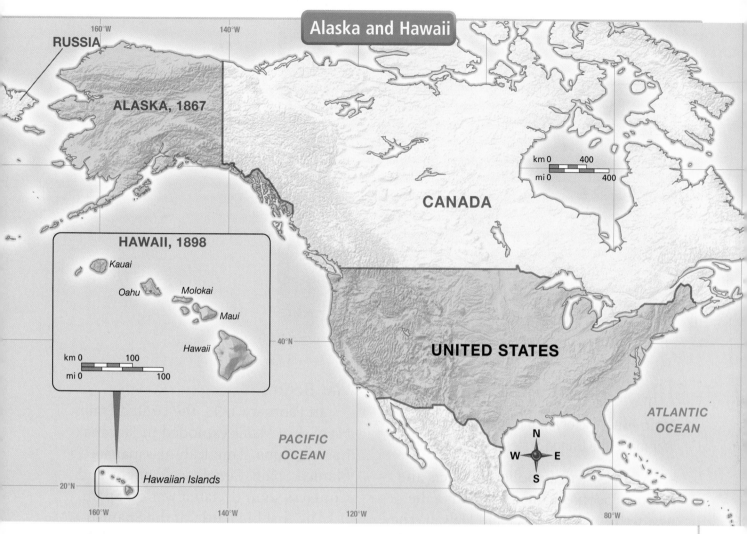

RUSSIA

160°W

140°W

ALASKA, 1867

km 0   400
mi 0   400

CANADA

HAWAII, 1898

Kauai

Oahu   Molokai

Maui

km 0   100
mi 0   100

Hawaii

40°N

UNITED STATES

ATLANTIC
OCEAN

PACIFIC
OCEAN

N
W   E
S

Hawaiian Islands

20°N

160°W   140°W   120°W   80°W

New Territories Alaska was bought in 1867. Hawaii became a territory in 1898. Both joined the United States as the 49th and 50th states in 1959.

SKILL **Reading Maps** Which line of longitude is closest to both Hawaii and Alaska?

Hawaii

Hawaii is a series of large islands in the Pacific Ocean about 2,500 miles west of California. The original Hawaiians settled there over 1,500 years ago. The first Americans to come to the island were mostly traders and missionaries. They arrived in the late 1700s. Later, Americans set up large plantations to grow cash crops such as sugar cane and pineapple. By the late 1800s, planters owned most of the land and businesses in Hawaii. Many Hawaiians were unhappy about the planters' power.

In the early 1890s, Hawaii's **Queen Liliuokalani** (luh lee uh oh kuh LAH nee)

wanted to give control of the land back to native Hawaiians. The wealthy plantation owners feared the queen's plans. They led a revolt against her in 1893. After the revolt ended, Americans in Hawaii asked to join the United States.

REVIEW How did Alaska and Hawaii become United States territories?

Queen Liliuokalani
The Hawaiian ruler was forced from power in 1893.

573

The *Maine* This painting shows the U.S. Navy ship *Maine* exploding in February 1898, in Havana harbor, Cuba. Two officers on the ship are pictured at the top.

The Spanish-American War

Main Idea Victory in the Spanish-American War made the United States a world power.

Many American political leaders and business people wanted more than the new territories of Alaska and Hawaii. They wanted to control colonies overseas to use as a base for more world trade. Some people believed the United States had begun a policy of imperialism. When nations build empires by starting colonies, it is called **imperialism.** A conflict with Spain gave the United States the overseas territories many people wanted.

In the 1890s, Spain held colonies in Cuba and Puerto Rico in the Caribbean Sea. It also controlled the Philippine (FIHL uh peen) Islands and Guam (GWAHM) in the Pacific Ocean. Spain barely had enough soldiers and ships to control its faraway colonies.

In 1895, the people of Cuba revolted. American newspapers wrote about Spain's cruel treatment of Cubans. Although not all the reports were true, they turned many Americans against Spain.

War Begins

In February 1898, the United States Navy ship *Maine* exploded in Havana harbor, Cuba. American newspapers blamed Spain. People were angry, and Congress soon declared war on Spain.

The first big battle of the Spanish-American War was not fought in Cuba. It was fought thousands of miles away in Spain's Philippine Islands. In a fierce fight, the U.S. Navy sank most of Spain's warships. This was a big defeat for Spain.

When the war with Spain began, **Theodore Roosevelt** was the Assistant Secretary of the United States Navy. To help fight the Spanish, he formed a volunteer fighting group called the Rough Riders. In Cuba, the Rough Riders were joined by a group of African American soldiers known as the Buffalo Soldiers. Together they won the battle of San Juan Hill.

After the victory at San Juan Hill, the U.S. Navy destroyed Spanish ships as they tried to escape Cuba. Spain surrendered, and in August 1898 agreed to give Puerto Rico, the Philippines, and Guam to the United States.

Building the Panama Canal

After the war, Theodore Roosevelt became President. He wanted to build a canal in Central America to speed up travel between the Atlantic and Pacific oceans. The canal had to be built at the narrowest point in Central America, the Isthmus of Panama. An **isthmus** (IHS muhs) is a narrow strip of land that links two larger pieces of land.

Panama was part of the nation of Colombia. Colombia refused to turn over the land to the United States.

Theodore Roosevelt He was President during the building of the Panama Canal.

Roosevelt helped Panama gain its independence from Colombia. The new nation of Panama then agreed to let the United States build the canal.

In 1914, after ten years of work, the canal opened. It shortened the trip between the two coasts of the United States by thousands of miles and helped increase the nation's trade.

REVIEW Where did most of the fighting take place in the Spanish-American War?

Lesson Summary

By the early 1900s, Alaska and Hawaii had become part of the United States. Victory in the Spanish-American War gave the nation the colonies of Guam, Puerto Rico, and the Philippines. President Roosevelt had the Panama Canal built as a trade route.

Why It Matters ...

The United States became a stronger leader in the world after the Spanish-American War.

Lesson Review

1867 Seward buys Alaska	1898 United States adds Hawaii	1914 Panama Canal opens

1860 — 1880 — 1900 — 1920

1. **VOCABULARY** Show the meaning of **isthmus** by using it in a paragraph about Panama.

2. **READING SKILL Contrast** how the United States gained Alaska and Hawaii with how it gained Spanish territories.

3. **MAIN IDEA: History** Why did some U.S. leaders want more overseas territories?

4. **MAIN IDEA: Economics** What was the main reason for building the Panama Canal?

5. **PEOPLE TO KNOW** Who was **Theodore Roosevelt,** and what did he do during the Spanish-American War?

6. **TIMELINE SKILL** How long after Hawaii became a United States territory did the Panama Canal open?

7. **CRITICAL THINKING: Decision Making** Which countries around the world were affected by the United States' decision to go to war with Spain? How were they affected?

HANDS ON

MATH ACTIVITY Find out about how long it takes to travel from New York to San Francisco by ship. Compare the time it takes with and without using the Panama Canal. Calculate the difference. Put your information in a chart.

PANAMA CANAL

The Panama Canal changed the geography of an entire region. How? The builders of the Panama Canal faced an almost impossible job on the isthmus of Panama. They had to dig and blast through 50 miles of jungle, swamp, and mountains to build a canal that would connect the Atlantic and Pacific Oceans. When the canal opened in 1914, it was said to be one of the greatest engineering achievements in history.

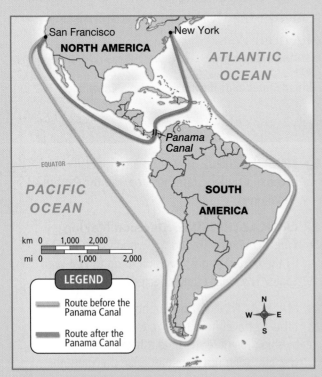

San Francisco · New York
NORTH AMERICA
ATLANTIC OCEAN
Panama Canal
EQUATOR
PACIFIC OCEAN
SOUTH AMERICA

km 0 1,000 2,000
mi 0 1,000 2,000

LEGEND
Route before the Panama Canal
Route after the Panama Canal

N W E S

The Panama Canal turned a 13,000-mile trip into a trip of fewer than 5,200 miles.

Machinery

Enormous steam shovels were used to dig the canal. Billions of tons of rock and earth were hauled away in 4,000 wagons pulled by 160 steam locomotives.

Workers

More than 45,000 people worked for ten years on the canal. The use of dynamite and heavy machinery made the work dangerous.

Health and Climate

Workers lived in buildings like these. They slept with fine nets around their beds to protect them from mosquitoes. Thousands of workers died from the jungle heat, accidents, and disease during the building of the canal.

Trade

In 1914, the new 51-mile-long channel sped up the flow of people and goods. Today, hundreds of ships pass through the canal daily, carrying goods from all over the world.

Activities

1. **EXPLORE IT** Put yourself in this picture. Talk about what it would be like to be working on the canal.

2. **CHART IT** Use a world map to estimate distances between four countries for ships using the Panama Canal. Then estimate distances between the same countries for ships not using the canal. Show the differences on a chart.

World War I

1913   1914   1915   1916   1917   1918   1919

1914–1918

VOCABULARY

alliance
trench warfare
armistice
isolationism

Vocabulary Strategy

alliance

When you read the word **alliance,** think of ally. An ally is a friend or helper. An alliance is an agreement one ally makes with another.

READING SKILL

Sequence List in order the events that led to World War I.

[ ]
↓
[ ]
↓
[ ]

Build on What You Know Have you ever had to do something you really didn't want to do because a friend needed your help? Most Americans didn't want to get involved in a war in Europe, but when allies in Europe needed help, the United States joined the war.

War in Europe

Main Idea European nations fought each other in a world war.

In the early 1900s, strong feelings of nationalism were growing in Europe. Nationalism is the belief that your country is better than other countries. Leaders in Britain, France, Germany, and Italy competed with one another to make their countries world powers. These countries raced to establish colonies in Africa and Asia. To protect their empires, the countries made their armies and navies stronger. This contest for power made it very hard for European nations to live in peace.

As countries in Europe built up their armies, they also made alliances with one another. An **alliance** is an agreement between nations to work together and defend each other.

Military Buildup
German army troops stand at attention for their leader Kaiser Wilhelm III.

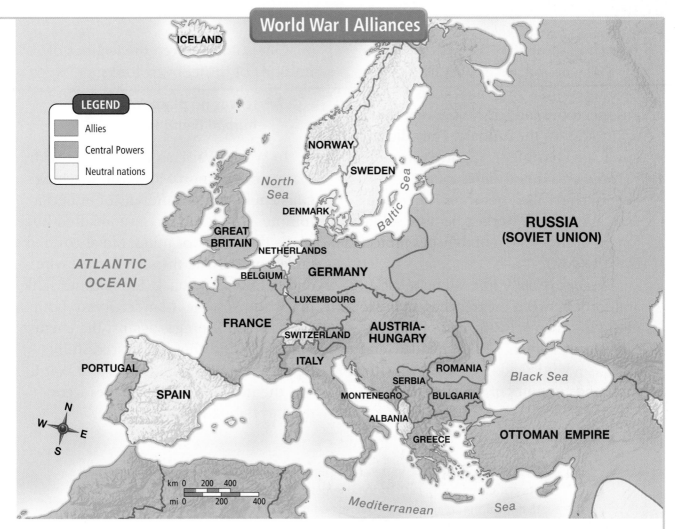

World War I Alliances

LEGEND
- Allies
- Central Powers
- Neutral nations

ICELAND

NORWAY

SWEDEN

North Sea

DENMARK

Baltic Sea

RUSSIA (SOVIET UNION)

GREAT BRITAIN

NETHERLANDS

ATLANTIC OCEAN

BELGIUM

GERMANY

LUXEMBOURG

FRANCE

SWITZERLAND

AUSTRIA-HUNGARY

PORTUGAL

ITALY

ROMANIA

Black Sea

SERBIA

SPAIN

MONTENEGRO

BULGARIA

ALBANIA

GREECE

OTTOMAN EMPIRE

km 0   200   400
mi 0   200   400

Mediterranean Sea

World War I The Allies included Great Britain, France, and Russia. Germany and Austria-Hungary led the Central Powers. **SKILL** **Reading Maps** Which European nations were neutral during World War I?

Britain, France, and Russia decided to form an alliance. The countries in this alliance became known as the Allies. Germany and Austria-Hungary formed another alliance known as the Central Powers. The two alliances competed with each other for land and power.

Instead of bringing peace, these alliances pushed Europe closer to war. If one of the Allies got into a fight with one of the Central Power countries, all the other alliance members would have to join the fight.

In 1914, the country of Austria-Hungary declared war on Serbia. Soon the other members of the Allies and Central Powers declared war on each other. World War I had begun. It was a world war because it involved so many countries of the modern world.

REVIEW What were two major causes of World War I?

World War I Newspaper headlines from August 1914 talked about the beginning of World War I.

Trench Warfare

Many people were eager for war. Because of the strong nationalism in Europe, thousands of young men signed up to serve in the military. They did not know how terrible the fighting would be.

Soldiers on both sides fought from long ditches called trenches. The fighting was called trench warfare because soldiers fought from a system of trenches protected by barbed wire.

For four years, soldiers fought back and forth between the trenches, trying to defeat the enemy. By the end of the war, millions of soldiers had been killed, and European battlefields were covered with thousands of miles of trenches.

One soldier voiced the feelings of millions of his fellow soldiers:

> 66 It was no place for a human being to be . . . 99

In World War I, soldiers fought with many new weapons. Powerful machine guns could shoot hundreds of bullets a minute. New kinds of cannons fired huge shells that went for miles. Metal-covered tanks could break through barbed wire and help troops attack. Submarines sank many ships in the Atlantic Ocean. Both sides used poison gas against the enemy. The **Wright** brothers had successfully flown a plane in 1903, but World War I was the first time that airplanes were used to fight a major war.

Life in the Trenches In trench warfare, soldiers lived where they fought. They ate out of mess kits, such as the one below on the left. Notice the wooden fencing that lined the trenches in the photos on this page and the next.

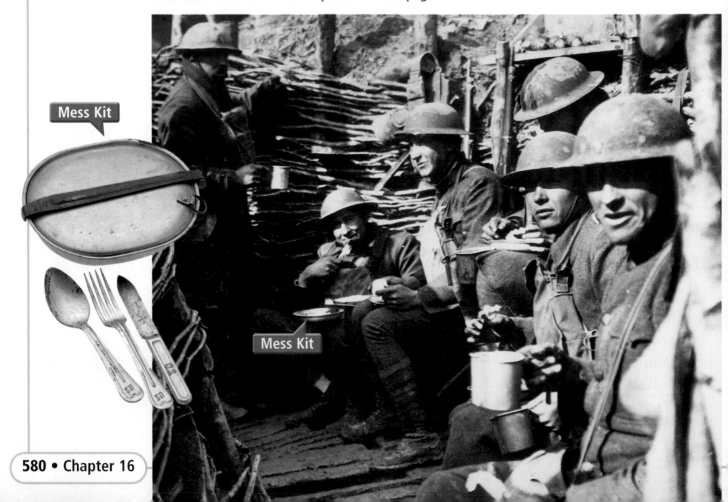

Mess Kit

Mess Kit

America Enters the War

Main Idea The United States helped the Allies win World War I.

When the war started, most people wanted the United States to stay out. Then German submarines, also called U-boats, started sinking British ships in the Atlantic Ocean. No American lives had been lost until a German submarine sank the *Lusitania* on May 7, 1915. The *Lusitania* was a British passenger ship with many Americans on board. People at home were shocked and angry, but most did not want to go to war.

After sinking the *Lusitania*, Germany agreed not to attack any more passenger ships. In 1917, however, Germany broke this promise and began attacks on American ships.

Soon afterwards, President **Woodrow Wilson** asked Congress to declare war on the Central Powers. He said,

❝ The world must be made safe for democracy. ❞

When the United States entered the war in 1917, the soldiers of the Allies had already been fighting for more than three years. The weary Allies welcomed the supplies and the confident spirit brought by a million U.S. troops.

Many groups of people served in World War I. Nearly 367,000 African Americans entered military service, as well as many Mexican Americans, American Indians, and women.

REVIEW What was trench warfare?

Steel Helmet

Rifle

Trench

The Home Front

Soldiers fighting in the trenches of Europe needed lots of food and supplies. They needed small weapons, such as pistols, and large weapons, such as cannons. They needed uniforms, rifles, and helmets. Civilian workers made all of these things. They produced more supplies during the war than any country ever had in history.

Civilians also supported the soldiers by eating less food and using less fuel at home. The government decided to allow only limited amounts of certain goods to each person. For example, civilians were asked not to eat meat on Tuesdays. The government used the food people saved to help feed the soldiers.

So many men went to war that there were not enough workers in the nation's factories. This shortage of workers brought opportunities for women. Many women took jobs that had been open only to men. For example, women made weapons in factories, repaired cars, delivered the mail, and directed traffic.

Building a Ship Thousands of African Americans helped with the war effort. In this photo, champion riveter Charles Knight (left) puts together a ship with bolts called rivets.

During the war, thousands of African Americans left the South to work in northern cities, such as Chicago and Detroit, where the factories were. African Americans earned more money working in factories in the North than they could earn in the South. They also earned respect because they were helping to win the war. Even so, African Americans still faced prejudice in both the North and the South.

Supporting the War Women work in a rifle factory during World War I. People had strong feelings of patriotism, as the flag hanging from the ceiling shows.

Treaty of Versailles

The United States joined the fighting late, but its troops and supplies made a difference. The Allies won the war. On November 11, 1918, the Allies and the Central Powers signed an armistice. An **armistice** is an agreement to stop fighting. Today, November 11 is called Veteran's Day. This national holiday honors Americans who fought in wars, including World War I.

After the armistice, leaders of the Allies and Central Powers gathered in Versailles (vehr SY), France. This historic meeting was held to discuss a peace treaty. President **Woodrow Wilson** wanted the treaty to include an organization in which all nations of the world would work together for peace. It was called the League of Nations.

Wilson returned home with a peace treaty that included plans for the United States to join the League of Nations. The Senate did not approve the treaty. After the war, many Americans felt that they had done enough for other nations.

There was a growing feeling of isolationism in the United States. **Isolationism** means that a country stays out of other countries' affairs. The United States decided not to join the League of Nations.

REVIEW What caused the shortage of workers in the United States during World War I?

Lesson Summary

- In 1914, the Allies and the Central Powers went to war in Europe.
- The United States joined the Allies in 1917 and sent soldiers to Europe.
- Civilians at home worked hard to support the war.
- In 1918, the Allies and the Central Powers ended the war by signing the Treaty of Versailles.

Why It Matters ...

At the time, World War I was the largest and most destructive war that had ever been fought. The war changed the lives of millions of people.

Lesson Review

| 1914 WWI begins | 1915 *Lusitania* sunk | 1917 U.S. enters WWI | 1918 WWI ends |

1914   1916   1918   1920

1. **VOCABULARY** Write a paragraph about World War I. Use the words **alliance, trench warfare,** and **armistice.**

2. **READING SKILL** Which event followed the sinking of the *Lusitania* and why? Use your **sequence** chart to explain your answer.

3. **MAIN IDEA: Technology** Describe the new kinds of weapons soldiers used in World War I.

4. **MAIN IDEA: Citizenship** In what ways did United States civilians help fight the war?

5. **PEOPLE TO KNOW** Who was **Woodrow Wilson**, and what was his role in World War I?

6. **TIMELINE SKILL** When did World War I end?

7. **CRITICAL THINKING: Analyze** What was the purpose of the League of Nations?

WRITING ACTIVITY Write a letter that a soldier living in the trenches during World War I might have written home. Write about what living in the trenches was like.

Over There!

How did a popular song help win a war? In April, 1917, headlines blared the news: The United States had declared war on Germany and entered World War I. Europeans had been fighting for almost three years, and the Allies badly needed the help of American soldiers.

On a train to New York City, American songwriter George M. Cohan read those war headlines. Cohan was famous for patriotic songs such as "You're a Grand Old Flag" and "Yankee Doodle Dandy." Now a new patriotic song began to form in his mind. It was a song to inspire Americans to join the war effort. He built the chorus around a simple three-note bugle call. The title "Over There" came to him.

The song's message was a simple one: "We're coming! Help is on the way!" The message lit a fire of determination in people, inspiring many Americans to enlist in the army.

American soldiers on a ship heading to Europe.

Over There

George M. Cohan

Refrain

① O-ver there,___ o-ver there,___ Send the word, send the word o-ver there,___ That the ② Yanks are com-ing, the Yanks are com-ing, The drums rum - tum-ming ev - 'ry where.___ So pre-pare,___ say a prayer___ Send the word, send the word to be - ware,___ ③ We'll be o - ver, we're com - ing o - ver, And we won't come ④ back 'til it's o - ver o - ver there. O - ver there.

---

① *Over there* means across the ocean in Europe, especially France, where most of the fighting was taking place.

② A message of encouragement to the Allies that the "Yanks"—the Americans—were on their way.

③ A warning to the enemies to watch out.

④ A proud claim that Americans would not come home until the war was over.

▲ "Over There" became the most popular song of World War I and was even translated into French. By the end of the war, more than two million copies of the sheet music for the song had been sold.

Activities

1. **THINK ABOUT IT** Why do you think "Over There" was translated into French?

2. **REPORT IT** Interview someone who lived in the time of World War II or the Vietnam War. Ask about war songs. Then write the title of one song and explain its purpose.

 Technology Find more primary sources at Education Place. www.eduplace.com/kids/hmss05/

The 1920s

1918   1920   1922   1924   1926   1928   1930

1920–1929

VOCABULARY

assembly line
division of labor
credit

Vocabulary Strategy

assembly line

To **assemble** means to put together. An **assembly line** is a line of people or machines that puts a product together.

READING SKILL
Problem and Solution
Write down how Henry Ford solved the problem of producing many cars quickly.

PROBLEM   SOLUTION

Build on What You Know After you finish some hard work, what do you want to do? You probably just want to relax and have fun. That's how many Americans felt after working hard to win World War I.

A Growing Economy

Main Idea The American economy boomed during the 1920s.

The 1920s were years of wealth and peace for most Americans. The economy grew, and the United States became one of the richest nations in history. Most people had more money and more time to spend it.

The Automobile Industry

The automobile industry grew rapidly in the 1920s. The most successful car maker was **Henry Ford.** The Ford Motor Company was the largest car company in the world. A key to Ford's success was changing the way cars were assembled, or made.

Ford used assembly lines to increase production. An **assembly line** is a line of workers and equipment that puts a product together piece by piece. As parts move down the assembly line, each group of workers does one specific job. When workers perform different parts of a large task, it is called **division of labor.**

Henry Ford and other car makers sold millions of cars in the 1920s. As the supply of cars went up, the price of each car came down. The booming car industry helped the steel, rubber, and oil companies grow.

Henry Ford Millions of Americans bought his Model T cars.

Consumer Goods and Credit

In the 1920s, factories made consumer goods in record numbers. To buy these products, many people used credit. Buying on **credit** means buying an item today, but paying for it later with small payments. In exchange for paying a little bit at a time, buyers agree to pay more than the original price of the item. The cost of borrowing money is called interest. Paying with credit was easier than paying all at once with cash. Credit allowed many families to own homes for the first time. But using credit also increased people's debt, which means they owed money.

Americans believed that the economy would keep growing, and they looked for ways to make more money. Many people invested their dollars in things they thought would become more valuable, such as land or paintings. Although not everyone invested in these ways, most people felt very positive about the growth of the economy. President **Calvin Coolidge** said,

> 66 . . . the chief business of the American people is business. 99

REVIEW How did credit change the way people paid for goods?

Car Sales, 1921–1929

Year	
1921	🚗🚗
1925	🚗🚗🚗🚗
1929	🚗🚗🚗🚗🚗

🚗 = 1 million cars

The Model T A Model T Ford car moves to the end of its assembly line. The pictograph (left) shows the increase in car sales during the 1920s.

Body is put on car

Next car follows in line

Conveyer belt pulls car along

Jazz In this photo, a band plays jazz music. Notice the mix of different instruments: trombone, trumpet, and saxophone. Ma Rainey is the singer. The cartoon on the magazine cover shows how much fun it was to play jazz.

A Changing Society

Main Idea New ways of life and new forms of entertainment changed American society in the 1920s.

The American economy wasn't the only thing changing in the 1920s. Daily life was fast-paced and exciting. The 1920s became known as the Roaring Twenties. People felt life was roaring along like a speeding car.

People moved to cities in large numbers to look for jobs in factories and new businesses. For the first time, more Americans lived in cities than in the countryside.

The Roaring Twenties were also a time of change for many women. Young women, called flappers, changed women's fashions. They cut their hair short and wore knee-length skirts. More women took jobs in business and industry.

Women did things most had not done before, such as play sports, drive a car, or fly an airplane. Most important of all, women won the right to vote. In 1920, women voted in a national election for the first time.

In the 1920s, hundreds of thousands of African Americans moved from rural parts of the South to big industrial cities in the North. They left to find jobs in cities such as Chicago and Detroit. They formed new communities in places such as Harlem in New York City. Many great African American writers, musicians, and artists lived in Harlem. Their work created what would later be called the Harlem Renaissance.

Thousands of Mexicans also migrated north into the United States from Mexico. Many of them worked in Texas and California on large vegetable and fruit farms.

New Kinds of Entertainment

A popular music heard in Harlem and cities around the country was jazz. This new kind of music began among African American musicians. Radio allowed millions of people to listen to jazz music. The 1920s were also called the Jazz Age.

Radio helped make new heroes. In 1927, **Charles Lindbergh** was the first person to fly an airplane alone across the Atlantic Ocean. Radio spread the news. **Amelia Earhart** and **Bessie Coleman** were famous pilots, too.

Movies, like radio, became popular in the 1920s. People all over the country saw the same movies. Because of movies and radio, Americans from many different backgrounds and parts of the country started to have more in common.

REVIEW In what ways did the lives of American women change in the 1920s?

Lesson Summary

The 1920s were a time of growth for the United States economy, including the automobile industry. People used credit to buy consumer goods. Women changed how they lived and worked, and new kinds of entertainment brought people together.

Why It Matters ...

The 1920s gave men and women more freedom to try new things and go new places.

Amelia Earhart She was the first woman to fly alone across the Atlantic Ocean.

Lesson Review

1925
Height of Harlem Renaissance

1927
Lindbergh crosses Atlantic

1925 — 1926 — 1927 — 1928

❶ **VOCABULARY** How did the **assembly line** depend on **division of labor?**

❷ **READING SKILL** In what way did Henry Ford **solve** the **problem** of needing to make cars more quickly?

❸ **MAIN IDEA: History** Why were the 1920s called the Roaring Twenties?

❹ **MAIN IDEA: Economics** How did some families use credit during the 1920s?

❺ **PEOPLE TO KNOW** Who was **Amelia Earhart** and what did she do?

❻ **TIMELINE SKILL** When did Charles Lindbergh make history?

❼ **CRITICAL THINKING: Categorize** What were new forms of entertainment in the 1920s?

HANDS ON

SPEAKING ACTIVITY Find out more about Charles Lindbergh's flight. Prepare a news report that a radio announcer might have given about it.

THE Harlem Renaissance

In the 1920s, the air of Harlem, in New York City, seemed full of poetry and the rhythms of jazz. A new generation of African American musicians and writers was getting people's attention.

African American poets, novelists, painters, and musicians came together in Harlem and other cities to share their ideas and their art. They showed how they felt about being black in a white world. They wrote about discrimination, their anger over slavery, and their need for equality. The movement spread to other cities. This outpouring of talent resulted in books, poems, operas, and plays—many of which are read and performed today.

The poets Georgia Johnson and Langston Hughes got their start during this period. Hughes loved listening to jazz and the blues. He wrote much of his poetry so it could be spoken to a jazz beat.

GEORGIA DOUGLAS JOHNSON (1886–1966)

Georgia Douglas Johnson began her career as a school teacher. She published her first book of poems in 1918. She said she wore a writing tablet and pencil on a string around her neck, "so when an idea, a word, a line for a poem comes, I jot it down." Johnson invited young writers to her Washington, D.C. home and encouraged them. Many famous writers came, including Langston Hughes.

Souvenir

A little hour of sunshine,
　　A little while of joy,
We winnow in our harvesting
　　From all the world's alloy.

None, none, are so benighted,
　　Who journey up life's hill,
But have some treasured memory,
　　Which lives all vibrant still.

— *Georgia Douglas Johnson*

Dream Variations

To fling my arms wide
In some place of the sun,
To whirl and to dance
Till the white day is done.
Then rest at cool evening
Beneath a tall tree
While night comes on gently
　　Dark like me—
That is my dream!

To fling my arms wide
In the face of the sun,
Dance! Whirl! Whirl!
Till the quick day is done.
Rest at pale evening . . .
A tall, slim tree . . .
Night coming tenderly
　　Black like me.

—*Langston Hughes, 1926*

LANGSTON HUGHES (1902–1967)

Langston Hughes was born in Missouri. He began writing poetry in eighth grade and was selected class poet. Hughes first came to New York to study engineering, but soon gained recognition for his poetry. He once worked in a restaurant and left three poems on a table where a famous poet was dining. Impressed, the poet helped Hughes get his poems published. Hughes wrote books of poetry, plus stories, novels, plays, musicals, and operas— a total of around 60 books.

King Oliver Creole Jazz Band, 1923

Activities

1. **TALK ABOUT IT** Listen to someone read aloud "Dream Variations." Explain how the poem is like music.

2. **WRITE ABOUT IT** Choose one of the poems on these pages. Write a paragraph explaining what the poem means to you.

The Great Depression

1928   1930   1932   1934   1936   1938   1940

1929–1939

VOCABULARY

stock market
unemployment
depression

Vocabulary Strategy

unemployment

Employ means to give someone a job. The prefix **-un** means not. Unemployment means not being employed, or not working.

 READING SKILL

Cause and Effect As you read, list possible causes for the Great Depression.

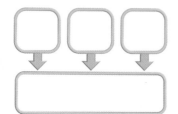

Build on What You Know Have you heard people use the terms "good times" and "hard times"? The 1930s were "hard times," and many people needed help.

Hard Times for Americans

Main Idea The Great Depression caused factory closings, job losses, and hunger throughout the United States.

For most of the 1920s, the United States economy grew. Many people felt it was a good time to invest their money in businesses. One way to do this was to buy stocks in a company. A stock is a small part, or share of ownership, of a company. Stocks are sold in the stock market. The **stock market** is where people can buy and sell shares of a company's stock.

When a company does well, the value of its stock usually goes up. Then people who own stocks make money. When a company does poorly, the value of its stock usually goes down. Stockowners then lose money. When the value of many stocks drops suddenly, this is called a stock market crash.

The Depression Begins

By the end of the 1920s, the United States economy had begun to slow down. Then, on October 24, 1929, the American stock market crashed. Stockowners panicked. Many sold their shares for whatever price they could get. Prices fell so low that many stocks became worthless. Thousands of people lost all the money they had.

The Effects of the Great Depression

After the stock market crash, the economy became even weaker. Stores could not sell all their goods, and factories did not need as many workers. Bank closings shook people's confidence in the economy. People lost their savings. Many businesses closed, and unemployment began to rise. **Unemployment** is the number of people without a job.

This time of high unemployment and hardship became known as the Great Depression. A **depression** is a period when many people can't find work, and many others have no money to keep businesses going. The Great Depression was the worst depression in United States history.

Without jobs, many people could not continue to make payments on their homes and lost ownership of them.

Thousands of hungry people lined up at community kitchens each day to get free bread or a bowl of soup. The lack of jobs forced over 500,000 Mexicans and Mexican Americans to move to Mexico.

Many farmers could not make enough money to keep on farming and went out of business. When a severe drought struck the Great Plains in the early 1930s, farmers' lives became even harder. So little rain fell that many farmers in Kansas, Oklahoma, Texas, Colorado, and New Mexico could not grow crops. The soil was so dry that windstorms whipped up clouds of dust that could block out the sun. This area in the middle of the United States became known as the Dust Bowl.

REVIEW What made unemployment go up during the Great Depression?

Dust Bowl Farmers migrated west, looking for a place to start a new life. **SKILL** **Reading Maps** Name three states in the area that was hardest hit by the Dust Bowl.

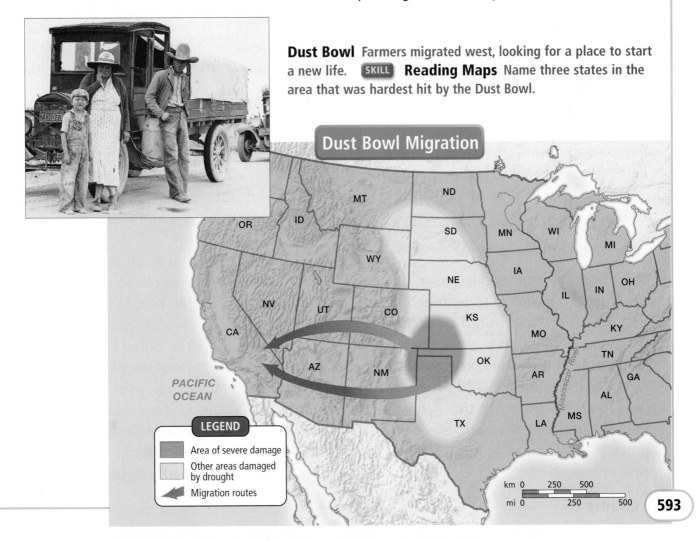

Dust Bowl Migration

LEGEND
- Area of severe damage
- Other areas damaged by drought
- Migration routes

PACIFIC OCEAN

km 0 250 500
mi 0 250 500

Cleaning Up In this photograph, WPA workers are cleaning up after a flood. Notice the sandbags that were used to keep out water.

The New Deal

Main Idea New Deal programs helped many Americans find work during the Great Depression.

Franklin D. Roosevelt was elected President in 1932. He believed that the government should try to help end the Depression. When he took office, the new President tried to give hope to the American people. He said,

> 66 **The only thing we have to fear is fear itself.** 99

The President promised to create government programs to help people who were suffering from the effects of the Great Depression.

Roosevelt called his programs the New Deal. Some New Deal programs gave food and shelter to those in need. Others put people to work. Congress quickly passed most of Roosevelt's programs into law.

Eleanor Roosevelt, the President's wife, worked hard to help the country during the Depression. She felt strongly that the government should assist people. She said,

> 66 **Government has a responsibility to defend the weak.** 99

The First Lady spoke out for the rights of workers and children. She wanted equal treatment for African Americans. She also worked with the President to improve his New Deal programs.

One New Deal program was the Public Works Administration (PWA). It created jobs by hiring people to work on public projects, such as improving roads and keeping up parks. Some PWA projects employed thousands of people. In one of the largest PWA projects, workers built electric plants on the Tennessee River in Tennessee, Alabama, and Kentucky. The Works Progress Administration (WPA) was another New Deal program.

A New Deal program called Social Security gave money to people who were unemployed, or who had stopped working at age 65. Social Security still exists today.

The New Deal did not end the Great Depression. In 1939, millions of Americans were still out of work. Even so, Roosevelt's New Deal gave people hope and strengthened their faith in democracy. People saw how a President and Congress could work together during hard times.

REVIEW What kinds of projects did the PWA hire people to work on?

Lesson Summary

The worst depression in United States history began after the stock market crash of 1929. Businesses and factories closed. Workers lost their jobs. Farmers in the Dust Bowl had to leave their homes and farms. President Roosevelt's New Deal gave food and jobs to the unemployed.

Why It Matters ...

The United States government helped American citizens get through an economic depression and created government programs that still exist today.

Franklin D. Roosevelt He had a disease that affected his ability to walk. Here he talks to a young friend named Ruthie Bie while holding his dog, Fala.

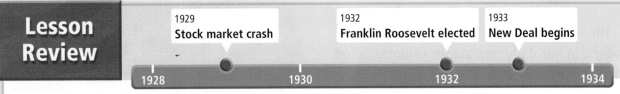

Lesson Review	1929 Stock market crash	1932 Franklin Roosevelt elected	1933 New Deal begins
1928	1930	1932	1934

❶ **VOCABULARY** Write a paragraph about the Great Depression. Use **stock market** and **depression** in separate sentences.

❷ 🕐 **READING SKILL** List three **effects** of the Great Depression on the United States.

❸ **MAIN IDEA: Economics** What happened to the stock market at the beginning of the Great Depression?

❹ **MAIN IDEA: History** Why was the Great Depression a difficult time for many people?

❺ **PEOPLE TO KNOW** Who was **Franklin D. Roosevelt** and what did he do?

❻ **TIMELINE SKILL** How many years after the stock market crash did the New Deal begin?

❼ **CRITICAL THINKING: Infer** Why is the Social Security program still in use today?

📝 **WRITING ACTIVITY** Write a description of what a big dust storm might have looked and felt like. Include information about what the dust did to homes and fields.

Eleanor Roosevelt

1884–1962

Champion of Equality

Eleanor Roosevelt believed in the equality of blacks and whites and all people.

Why was she admired for her knowledge, wisdom, and courage? Eleanor Roosevelt saw firsthand how citizens lived, and she listened to their concerns. During the worst times of the Depression, she traveled and met with southern blacks and migrant workers to find out about their struggles. She would talk over her experiences with her husband, President Franklin D. Roosevelt. Though she could not make laws, she could help shape New Deal programs.

She also shared her ideas with millions of readers. In her daily newspaper column, called "My Day," Roosevelt wrote about the rights of African Americans and women. She described the need for fair housing and fair working conditions.

In 1946, President Truman chose her to head the United Nations Human Rights Commission. In 1961, President John F. Kennedy made her head of the Commission on the Status of Women.

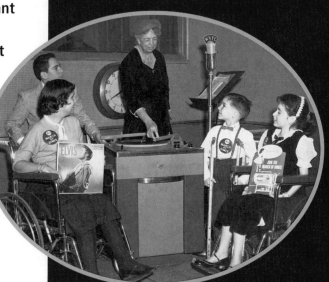

Concern for Others

Roosevelt often visited children with disabilities. Her own husband had overcome a disability.

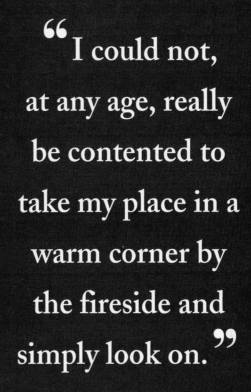

"I could not, at any age, really be contented to take my place in a warm corner by the fireside and simply look on."

—Eleanor Roosevelt

Activities

1. **TALK ABOUT IT** How did Eleanor Roosevelt work for **fairness** for other people?

2. **RESEARCH IT** Find out what happened in 1949 when Eleanor Roosevelt asked Marian Anderson to sing at the Lincoln Memorial. Use resources in your library.

 Technology Read more biographies at Education Place. www.eduplace.com/kids/hmss05/

Skillbuilder

Read Population Maps

Historians and geographers often want to know where people lived in the past and where they live now. Population maps can help. A **population map** shows where people live. By comparing population maps from two different time periods, you can see how settlement patterns have changed.

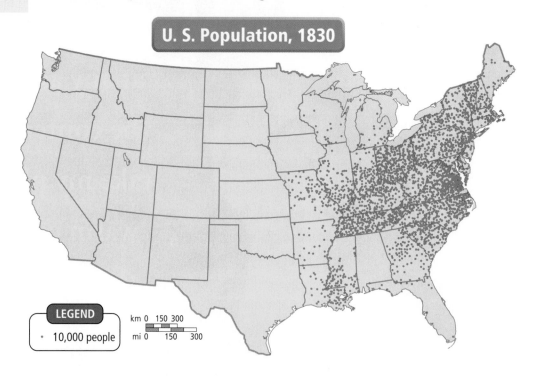

U. S. Population, 1830

LEGEND

· 10,000 people

km 0 150 300
mi 0 150 300

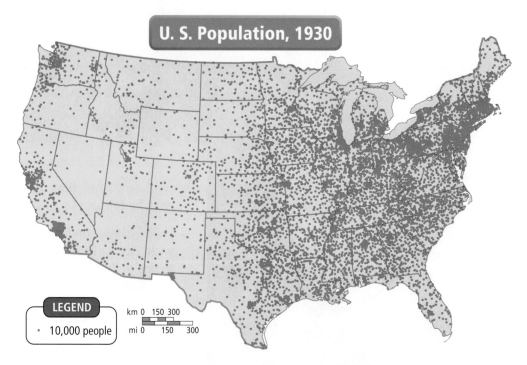

U. S. Population, 1930

LEGEND

· 10,000 people

km 0 150 300
mi 0 150 300

Learn the Skill

Step 1: Look at the two maps. Read each title. What is the subject and time period of each map?

U. S. Population, 1830

Step 2: Read the legend. It shows the number of people represented by each dot.

LEGEND

· 10,000 people

Step 3: Look at the dots on the maps. Areas with a lot of dots close together have many people living close together. Areas that have dots farther apart have fewer people.

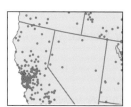

Step 4: Compare the two maps.

Practice the Skill

Use the two maps on page 598 to answer these questions.

1 Which regions of the country had the most people in 1830?

2 Which regions of the country had the fewest people in 1930?

3 Which regions of the country show the greatest population growth over time?

Apply the Skill

In a paragraph, describe the major changes in the United States settlement patterns between 1830 and 1930. Use information from the maps, as well as what you have learned about the history of this time period to explain some of these changes.

World War II

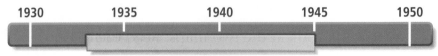

1930	1935	1940	1945	1950

1933–1945

VOCABULARY

dictator
war bonds
internment camp
atomic bomb
concentration camp

Vocabulary Strategy

dictator

To dictate is to give orders. The suffix **-or** makes the word a person. A **dictator** is a person who gives orders.

READING SKILL

Sequence List in order the events in World War II.

1	
2	
3	
4	

Build On What You Know Have you ever worked on a class project that needed everyone's help to complete? In World War II, almost every citizen of the United States contributed to winning the war.

The Road to War

Main Idea The rise of dictators helped lead to World War II.

Nations around the world had serious problems during the 1930s. The Great Depression damaged their economies. Millions of people in Europe and Asia were unemployed and hungry. People began to look to strong leaders to solve their problems.

The Rise of Dictators

A German leader named **Adolf Hitler** said he could solve his country's problems. He led a political party called the National Socialists, or Nazis. Hitler told the German people that they had not been treated fairly after World War I. He also blamed Jewish people for many of Germany's problems and stirred up hatred against them.

In 1933, the Nazis took power in Germany. Hitler soon ruled as a dictator. A **dictator** is a ruler who has total power over a country and its people. Once in power, Hitler increased his persecution of the Jews. Nazi soldiers arrested many Jews and sent them to prison.

Hitler and Mussolini The two men, Mussolini on the left and Hitler on the right, ruled their countries as dictators.

World War II in Europe, 1939

LEGEND
- Axis nations
- Allies

NORWAY
FINLAND
SWEDEN
ESTONIA
DENMARK
LATVIA
LITHUANIA
North Sea
Baltic Sea
IRELAND
GREAT BRITAIN
NETHERLANDS
English Channel
BELGIUM
GERMANY
POLAND
RUSSIA (SOVIET UNION)
CZECHOSLOVAKIA
ATLANTIC OCEAN
FRANCE
SWITZ.
AUSTRIA
HUNGARY
ROMANIA
ITALY
PORTUGAL
SPAIN
YUGOSLAVIA
BULGARIA
Black Sea
ALBANIA
TURKEY
GREECE
Mediterranean Sea

km 0 200 400
mi 0 200 400

Europe in World War II This map shows the Axis nations and the Allies in Western Europe and North Africa at the beginning of World War II.

SKILL **Reading Maps** How many countries were part of the Axis in 1939?

Italy and Japan also turned to dictators. **Benito Mussolini** (moo soh LEE nee) had taken control of Italy. In Japan, military leaders ruled the country. Germany and Italy formed an alliance in 1936. These countries called themselves the Axis Powers, or Axis. These leaders of the Axis wanted to take over Europe.

In September 1939, Hitler's army invaded Poland. In response, Poland, Britain, and France declared war on Germany, and World War II began. The countries fighting Germany were known as the Allied Powers, or Allies. Later, the Soviet Union joined the Allies and helped them fight the German army.

At the beginning of the war, most Americans believed in isolationism. They remembered World War I and hoped to avoid fighting in Europe again.

In 1940, Japan joined the Axis. Japan wanted to enlarge its empire. Japanese troops had taken over part of China. Japanese leaders next wanted to control East Asia and the islands of the Pacific Ocean. Only the U.S. Navy at Pearl Harbor in Hawaii was close enough to stop Japan's plans. The Japanese military decided to destroy the U.S. Pacific Fleet in a surprise attack.

REVIEW Why didn't the United States join the Allies in 1939?

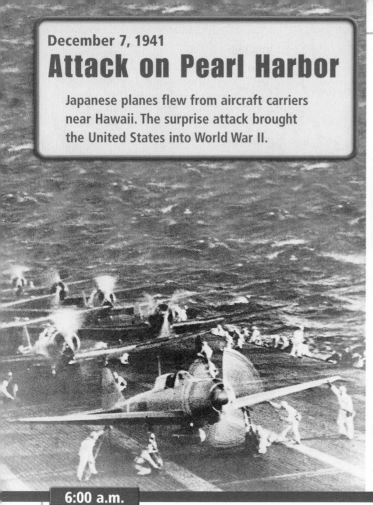

6:00 a.m.

Attack Begins Japanese planes take off from an aircraft carrier in the Pacific Ocean.

7:55 a.m.

Japanese Planes Attack Japanese bombers begin destroying the Pacific Fleet.

America Goes to War

Main Idea The attack on Pearl Harbor brought the United States into World War II.

On December 7, 1941, Japanese airplanes bombed Pearl Harbor in Hawaii. They blew up dozens of American military ships and airplanes. The Pacific Fleet was almost completely destroyed. President **Franklin D. Roosevelt** called the day of the attack "a date which will live in infamy." Infamy means that something is known as evil.

The United States immediately declared war on Japan and joined the Allies. The Axis countries of Germany and Italy responded by declaring war on the United States.

Supporting the War

World War II affected everyone in the United States. Millions of people, including nearly 7 million women, worked in factories that produced war supplies. Children helped, too, by collecting old tires and pieces of metal that could be used by wartime factories.

The United States government asked people to buy war bonds. **War bonds** were loans to the federal government. The money from the bonds was used to help pay for the war. The government promised to pay back Americans more money than the bonds had cost. Buying war bonds was a way for people to show patriotism during a difficult time.

10:00 a.m.

Ships are Burning The attack at Pearl Harbor took people completely by surprise. The bombs set many ships on fire.

Japanese Americans

After the attack at Pearl Harbor, many Japanese Americans wanted to support their country. Thousands joined the military and fought bravely. Even so, some people feared that the Japanese Americans who stayed at home might help Japan. Because of this fear, President Roosevelt issued orders that forced over 110,000 Japanese American men, women, and children to live in internment camps. An **internment camp** is a place where prisoners are held during wartime. Two thirds of the people in the camps were United States citizens. Many Japanese Americans were kept in the camps until almost the end of the war.

Fighting the War

Main Idea The Allies defeated the Axis in World War II.

World War II was fought in three major areas. In Europe and North Africa, the Allies fought Germany and Italy. In the Pacific, the Allies fought Japan. More than 15 million American men and women served in the Allied forces. This number included one million African Americans, about 300,000 Mexican Americans, as well as thousands of American Indians and Asian Americans.

REVIEW What action did the United States take after the attack on Pearl Harbor?

D-day

When the United States entered World War II, Germany and Italy had already conquered much of Europe. To win the war, the Allies had to strike back.

The Allies invaded Europe on June 6, 1944, known as D-day. Nearly 200,000 Allied troops landed in northern France. This huge force, followed by millions more troops, pushed back the German army.

By mid-September 1944, the Allies had freed much of France and Belgium. Led by General **Dwight D. Eisenhower**, American and British troops moved toward Germany from the west. Soviet troops attacked Germany from the east.

By April 1945, the Allies were approaching the capital of Germany, Berlin. Soviet troops fought a fierce battle to take the city. On May 7, 1945, Germany surrendered. The war in Europe was over.

The War in the Pacific

While the Allies fought Axis troops in Europe, the war against Japan continued in the Pacific.

By the summer of 1945, American forces were close enough to invade Japan. United States leaders feared that many people would die in an invasion. They chose a different plan. The United States had developed a secret weapon, an atomic bomb. An **atomic bomb** is a powerful bomb that can destroy an entire city.

On August 6, 1945, an American plane dropped an atomic bomb on the Japanese city of Hiroshima. The powerful explosion killed nearly 100,000 people. Three days later, the United States dropped an atomic bomb on Nagasaki, another Japanese city. Japan quickly surrendered. World War II was over.

Island Hopping Allied soldiers fought to win back important Japanese islands and to use them as bases from which to reach Japan. This was called island hopping.

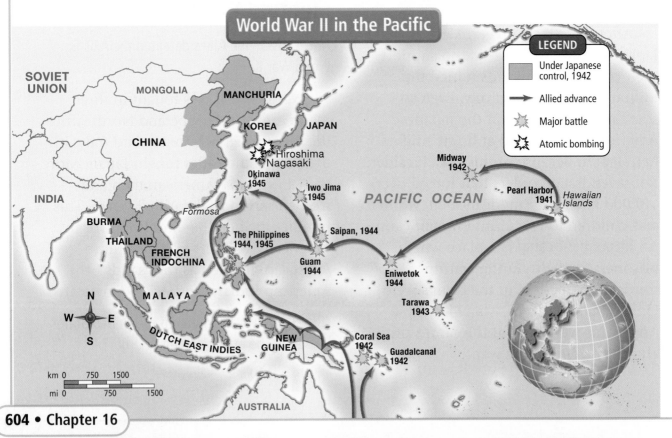

World War II in the Pacific

LEGEND

Under Japanese control, 1942

Allied advance

Major battle

Atomic bombing

SOVIET UNION
MONGOLIA
MANCHURIA
KOREA
JAPAN
CHINA
Hiroshima
Nagasaki
Okinawa 1945
INDIA
Formosa
Iwo Jima 1945
PACIFIC OCEAN
Midway 1942
Pearl Harbor 1941
Hawaiian Islands
BURMA
THAILAND
FRENCH INDOCHINA
The Philippines 1944, 1945
Saipan, 1944
Guam 1944
Eniwetok 1944
MALAYA
Tarawa 1943
DUTCH EAST INDIES
NEW GUINEA
Coral Sea 1942
Guadalcanal 1942
km 0 750 1500
mi 0 750 1500
AUSTRALIA

Concentration Camp
Prisoners at a concentration camp stare through a fence.

The Holocaust

As the fighting ended, Allied troops discovered one of the worst horrors of the war. In Europe, the Nazis had forced Jews and other people that they blamed for Germany's problems into concentration camps. A **concentration camp** is a place where large numbers of people are held prisoner and forced to work. Over 12 million people, about six million of them Jews, died in concentration camps. This mass murder is known as the Holocaust.

REVIEW What did the United States military do to force Japan to surrender?

Lesson Summary

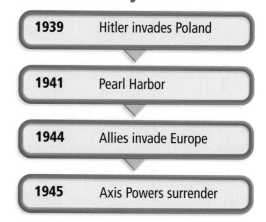

1939	Hitler invades Poland
1941	Pearl Harbor
1944	Allies invade Europe
1945	Axis Powers surrender

Why It Matters ...

In World War II, the United States helped the Allies defeat dictators in Germany, Italy, and Japan.

Lesson Review

| 1939 WWII begins | 1941 Pearl Harbor attacked | | 1944 D-day | 1945 WWII ends |

1939   1941   1943   1945

1. **VOCABULARY** Write a short paragraph to describe how people at home helped defeat a **dictator** by buying **war bonds.**

2. **READING SKILL** Looking at your **sequence** chart, choose an event, and explain why you think it was important in World War II.

3. **MAIN IDEA: History** Which countries formed the Axis? Which were the Allies?

4. **MAIN IDEA: Economics** How did World War II affect the daily lives of Americans?

5. **PEOPLE TO KNOW** Who was **Adolf Hitler**?

6. **TIMELINE SKILL** How many years after the attack on Pearl Harbor did Japan surrender?

7. **CRITICAL THINKING: Predict** Tell what you think might have happened if Japan had not attacked Pearl Harbor. Would the United States still have entered the war?

HANDS ON

INTERVIEW ACTIVITY Prepare interview questions that you would want to ask someone who lived during World War II. Compare and share them in a small group.

D-DAY

Paratroopers
D-day began with thousands of paratroopers landing behind enemy lines to help the invasion.

The largest and most powerful sea invasion in history was about to begin. It was D-day. On June 6, 1944, over 150,000 Allied troops waited anxiously in southern England. Crossing the English Channel in boats loaded with troops would be tough. The Channel often had high wind and waves.

Early in the morning, under cover of darkness, close to 6,500 ships and landing craft headed into the rough waters for France. At the same time, hundreds of Allied war ships and bombers pounded German troops in France.

The Allied troops landing in Normandy met fierce German resistance, but they fought with great courage. They gained control of the beaches, and by the end of June, about 850,000 Allied troops had arrived in France.

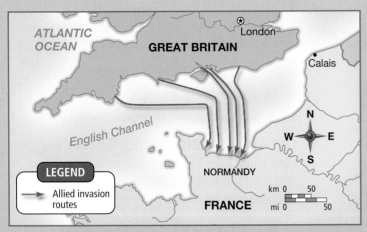

Troops from the United States, Canada, and Great Britain crossed the English Channel. They landed at five different beaches.

Landing Craft
Landing craft could motor right onto the beach to unload soldiers, tanks, and vehicles.

Greeting French Citizens
People were overjoyed when they saw the Allied soldiers, who had come to take back France from the Nazis.

Activities

1. **TALK ABOUT IT** Look at the pictures of the landing craft used to carry troops across the English Channel. Why do you think the Allies were worried about bad weather?

2. **PRESENT IT** Find information about U.S. General Dwight D. Eisenhower or British General Bernard Montgomery. Share your findings in an oral report.

607

Visual Summary

1.–3. Write what you learned about each person named below.

Presidents	
Theodore Roosevelt	
Woodrow Wilson	
WORK **PROGRAM** **WPA** Franklin D. Roosevelt	

Facts and Main Ideas

TEST PREP Answer each question with information from the chapter.

4. **Geography** What territories did the United States gain as a result of the Spanish-American War?

5. **Government** Why did the United States decide not to join the League of Nations?

6. **History** What were two new kinds of entertainment that people enjoyed during the 1920s?

7. **Economics** What was the New Deal?

8. **History** In which war did the Holocaust take place?

Vocabulary

TEST PREP Choose the correct word from the list below to complete each sentence.

alliance, p. 578
armistice, p. 583
unemployment, p. 593

9. During the Great Depression, _____ was very high.

10. On November 11, 1918, the Allies and the Central Powers signed an _____.

11. Before World War I, Germany and Austria-Hungary formed an _____ called the Central Powers.

CHAPTER SUMMARY TIMELINE

1898 Spanish-American War	1914 World War I begins	1929 Stock market crash	1939 World War II begins

1890   1900   1910   1920   1930   1940   1950

Apply Skills

✔ TEST PREP **Map Skill** Study the 1890 population map below. Then use what you have learned about reading a population map to answer each question.

LEGEND

· 10,000 people

12. What does each dot represent?

    A. 1,000 people

    B. 5,000 people

    C. 10,000 people

    D. 100,000 people

13. What conclusion can you draw from the 1890 map?

    A. More people lived in the Southwest than in the Southeast.

    B. More people lived in the Northwest than the Northeast.

    C. Most people lived in the western half of the country.

    D. Most people lived in the eastern half of the country.

Critical Thinking

✔ TEST PREP Write a short paragraph to answer each question.

14. **Cause and Effect** The Depression brought hard times to millions of people across the country. What were two effects of the Great Depression?

15. **Summarize** How did people at home help the war effort during the two world wars?

Timeline

Use the Chapter Summary Timeline above to answer this question.

16. How many years after World War I began did World War II begin?

Activities

 Art Activity Make a diagram that explains how an assembly line works. Include the term **division of labor**.

 Writing Activity Write a persuasive essay to encourage the United States to enter World War I, or to warn the country against the war. Be sure to give the reasons for your opinion.

 Technology **Writing Process Tips** Get help with your essay at www.eduplace.com/kids/hmss05/

Chapter 17

Americans Face Changes

Technology

e • **glossary**
e • **word games**
www.eduplace.com/kids/hmss05/

Vocabulary Preview

capitalism

The United States economy is based on **capitalism.** People and businesses, not the government, decide what goods and services to make and sell. **page 612**

veteran

When soldiers came home from the war, families welcomed them. Each soldier who left the army to return to civilian life became a **veteran.** **page 620**

Chapter Timeline

1945
United Nations formed

1954
School desegregation ordered

1945   **1950**   **1955**

Reading Strategy

Predict and Infer As you read each lesson, use this strategy.

 Quick Tip Look at the pictures to predict what a lesson will be about.

nonviolent protest

African Americans used **nonviolent protest** to change unjust laws. Many college students protested by sitting at lunch counters that did not serve African Americans. **page 627**

space race

The Soviet Union and the United States competed in the **space race.** Both tried to be the first to send people into space and land on the moon. **page 633**

1965
U.S. enters Vietnam War

1969
First moon landing

1960　　　　　　　**1965**　　　　　　　**1970**

The Cold War

1945   1950   1955   1960   1965

1945–1962

Build on What You Know You know that countries usually use armies, not words, to fight wars. During the Cold War, the United States and the Soviet Union fought mostly with words, but sometimes conflicts did break out.

Superpowers at War

Main Idea   After World War II, the United States and the Soviet Union entered a conflict called the Cold War.

The United States and the Soviet Union were the world's strongest nations after World War II. They were called superpowers. In the years following World War II, the two superpowers fought a war of words and ideas called the Cold War.

The two nations had different forms of government. The Soviet Union was a communist country. Under **communism,** the government controls production and owns the nation's natural and capital resources. This kind of economy is called a command economy. Communist governments often tell people where to live and what work to do. Soviet citizens had few freedoms. There was no democracy.

The United States is a capitalist country. In **capitalism,** ordinary people and businesses control the production of goods and services. People in the United States decide for themselves where to live and what work to do. United States citizens are part of a democracy and have many freedoms.

Soviet Flag The hammer and sickle shown on this flag were symbols of the communist government.

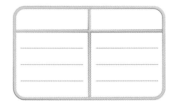

The Cold War Begins

The Cold War began in Europe as World War II came to an end. The Soviet Union gained control of Eastern Europe and set up communist governments there. A communist government also took over in China in 1949.

Western leaders saw the spread of communism as a threat to freedom and wanted to stop it. In 1947, President **Harry S. Truman** told Congress, "I believe that we must assist free people to work out their own destinies [futures] in their own way."

After World War II, the Soviet Union controlled the eastern half of Germany. The United States, Britain, and France governed the western half. Germany's capital city of Berlin was in Soviet territory. The city itself was divided into East Berlin and West Berlin, with the Soviets in control of East Berlin.

The Soviet Union and Eastern Europe

After World War II, the Soviet Union took over countries in Eastern Europe.

In June 1948, the Soviet Union tried to force the United States, Great Britain, and France to leave West Berlin. The Soviets blocked off all the roads and railroads that led into the city. The United States and Great Britain and France rescued West Berlin with the Berlin Airlift. Each day airplanes brought thousands of tons of supplies to the trapped people. Finally, in May 1949, the Soviet Union lifted the blockade. Years later, in 1961, the Soviet Union built the Berlin Wall to divide the communist part of Berlin from the rest of the city.

During the tense early years of the Cold War, a new international organization called the United Nations, or UN, was formed. In 1945, more than 50 nations joined together to try to keep peace in the world. The United Nations faced many difficult challenges during the 1950s.

REVIEW What was the Berlin Airlift just before the Cold War began?

The Cold War

LEGEND
- Communist countries
- Non-Communist countries

NORWAY, SWEDEN, Baltic Sea, North Sea, Moscow, IRELAND, GREAT BRITAIN, DENMARK, SOVIET UNION, London, NETHER-LANDS, Berlin, POLAND, BELGIUM, EAST GERMANY, Warsaw, ATLANTIC OCEAN, Paris, LUX., WEST GERMANY, CZECHOSLOVAKIA, FRANCE, SWITZ., AUSTRIA, HUNGARY, ROMANIA, ITALY, YUGOSLAVIA, Black Sea, PORTUGAL, SPAIN, Rome, BULGARIA, ALBANIA, GREECE, TURKEY, Mediterranean Sea

km 0 200 400
mi 0 200 400

North and South Korea Korea was divided along the cease-fire line in 1953. **SKILL** **Reading Maps** Identify the capitals of North and South Korea.

Cold War Conflicts

Main Idea The Korean War and the Cuban Missile Crisis were two major conflicts of the Cold War.

After World War II, the Korean Peninsula in Asia was divided into North and South Korea. North Korea became a communist country. South Korea was a capitalist country. In June 1950, the North Korean army invaded South Korea. The United Nations sent troops to help South Korea. General **Douglas MacArthur** led the UN army. Soldiers from 16 nations joined the fight. The United States sent the most soldiers.

UN troops pushed the North Korean army back almost to the border with China. China reacted by sending several hundred thousand soldiers to help North Korea. The fighting dragged on, and thousands of soldiers died. The war became unpopular in the United States. In 1953, the war ended without either side winning. Korea is still divided today.

By the time the Korean War ended, the United States and the Soviet Union were in a nuclear arms race. An **arms race** is a contest between nations to build bigger and more powerful weapons. Nuclear arms are atomic bombs and missiles. People feared that a nuclear war between the Soviet Union and the United States would destroy the whole world.

In 1959, **Fidel Castro** took power in Cuba, an island nation just 90 miles south of Florida. The Soviet Union helped Castro set up a communist government there. The United States then ended all contact with Cuba.

The Cuban Missile Crisis

In October 1962, the United States discovered that the Soviet Union was secretly sending missiles to Cuba. The missiles were large enough to carry an atomic bomb and could easily have reached the United States. Fearing a surprise attack, President **John F. Kennedy** ordered a blockade of Cuba. United States warships surrounded Cuba and stopped weapons from getting in or out.

Kennedy hoped the blockade would force the Soviet Union to remove its missiles. At first, the Soviet Union refused. For six days, a nuclear war seemed possible. Then the Soviet Union agreed to take its missiles out of Cuba.

The United States lifted the blockade. What came to be known as the Cuban Missile Crisis ended peacefully.

REVIEW What did Kennedy do to end the Cuban Missile Crisis?

The Cuban Missile Crisis President Kennedy (right) meets with his brother, Attorney General Robert Kennedy in October 1962.

Lesson Summary

- The Cold War between the superpowers of the Soviet Union and the United States began soon after World War II.

- During the Berlin Airlift, the United States, Britain, and France flew food and supplies into West Berlin.

- In 1950, North Korea and China fought United States and UN forces in the Korean War.

- In 1962, the Cuban Missile Crisis could have led to a nuclear war between the Soviet Union and United States.

Why It Matters ...

For many years, the Cold War between the United States and the Soviet Union increased the fear of a nuclear war.

Lesson Review

1950
Korean War starts

1962
Cuban Missile Crisis

1945　　1950　　1955　　1960　　1965

1 **VOCABULARY** Write a paragraph about the Cold War, using the terms **arms race** and **communism.**

2 **READING SKILL** In what ways was personal freedom **different** under capitalism and Soviet communism?

3 **MAIN IDEA: History** What were two major conflicts of the Cold War?

4 **MAIN IDEA: Geography** What part of Europe did the Soviet Union control after World War II?

5 **PLACES TO KNOW** What happened in Korea in the Cold War?

6 **TIMELINE SKILL** How many years before the Cuban Missile Crisis did the Korean War start?

7 **CRITICAL THINKING: Infer** Why was the Cuban Missile Crisis so dangerous?

WRITING ACTIVITY The Berlin Airlift happened at the beginning of the Cold War. Write a paragraph giving your opinion about the decision to fly supplies into West Berlin. Support your answer with reasons.

The Berlin Airlift

All roads are blocked. Nothing can come in, and nothing can go out. Food, fuel, and medicines are running out, and people wonder how long they and their neighbors can survive.

This happened in West Berlin in the summer of 1948. The Soviet Union had cut off all routes into the city by land and water. The people of West Berlin were hostages to the Soviet blockade.

There was still one way into West Berlin—by air. In just two days, the United States, Great Britain, and France began an emergency airlift. Planes flew over West Berlin day and night, dropping supplies by parachute. For the next year, pilots delivered more than 2,300,000 tons of supplies to people in West Berlin in over 278,000 flights. The planes brought something else to West Berlin during the airlift. They brought hope to the tired, hungry people of that city.

The Candy Hero

An American pilot named Gail S. Halvorsen became known as the "Candy Bomber" during the airlift, because he dropped candy to German children from his aircraft. He had another nickname, as well. As a signal to children on the ground, he would wiggle the wings of his plane. Soon Halvorsen began receiving letters addressed to "Uncle Wiggly Wings."

Special Delivery A young boy holds a box of candy, complete with parachute, dropped by Uncle Wiggly Wings.

Supplies Delivered in Berlin Airlift (in tons)

Food:	536,705
Coal:	1,586,029
Other:	202,775
Total:	2,325,509

Which supply did the Allies deliver the most? Why?

Activities

1. **THINK ABOUT IT** How did "Uncle Wiggly Wings" show that he was a **caring** person?

2. **WRITE ABOUT IT** Berlin lived through some of the most frightening events of the 20th century. Use your library to find out more about Berlin from 1950 to today. Write a story about one important event.

Skillbuilder

Make a Timeline

▶ **VOCABULARY**

timeline

A **timeline** shows events in the order that they happened. Placing important dates on a timeline can help you to organize and understand what you read.

Learn the Skill

Step 1: Look back at the lesson you just read. Make a list of four important events from the lesson. Put the events in order, listing the earliest event first.

1945	End of World War II
1945	United Nations founded
1948	Berlin Airlift
1950	Start of Korean War

Step 2: Timelines are divided into sections that show equal periods of time. Draw a horizontal line and divide it into equal sections. Label the end of each section with a year.

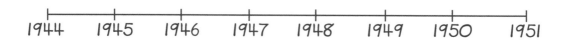

1944　1945　1946　1947　1948　1949　1950　1951

Step 3: Place each event on the timeline on the date it occurred. When two events happened in the same year, stack them one above the other.

End of World War II
United Nations founded　　　　Berlin Airlift　　　Start of Korean War

1944　1945　1946　1947　1948　1949　1950　1951

Read the following paragraph about the Korean War and answer the questions. Then make a timeline of the events.

> In 1950, North Korean troops invaded South Korea. The United States convinced the United Nations (UN) to defend South Korea. The UN troops pushed the North Koreans out of South Korea and far into the north. Then China sent soldiers to help the North Korean army. By 1951, the Chinese and North Koreans had forced the UN troops back to the South Korean border. Finally, in 1953, the two sides agreed to stop fighting. Neither side had won.

1 In the paragraph, how many events have dates?

2 Which event came first?

3 Which event came last?

4 How much time is there between the first and last event?

Apply the Skill

Make your own timeline. Reread Chapter 16, Lesson 4, on pages 592–595. List three events in the lesson. Then create a timeline that includes those events.

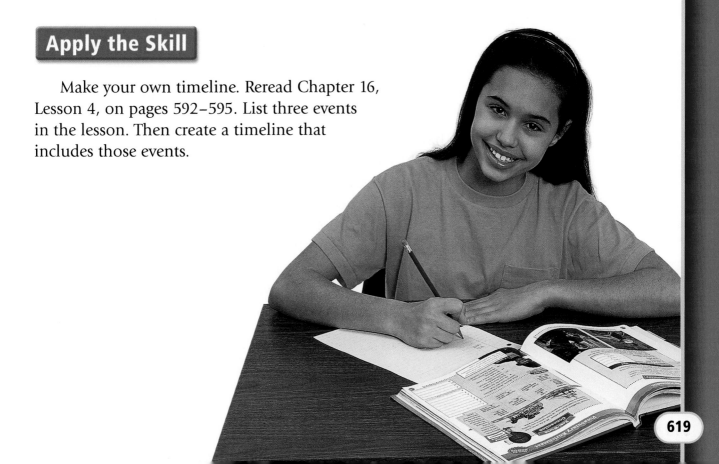

Life in the 1950s

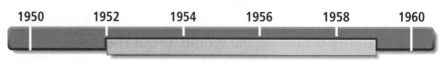

Build on What You Know You have seen household items such as dishwashers and televisions in stores. In the 1950s, many people went to department stores to buy televisions and dishwashers for the first time.

Post-War Prosperity

Main Idea The economic boom of the 1950s gave families in the United States more choices about what they could buy.

In 1952, General **Dwight D. Eisenhower** was elected President. He was a popular war hero who had led the Allied troops in Europe during World War II. People called him Ike and wore buttons that said "I Like Ike."

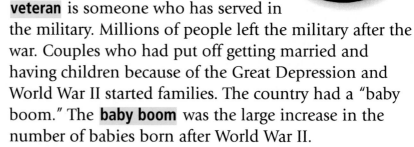

The United States economy grew rapidly under Eisenhower's leadership. The economic boom of the 1950s was created by World War II veterans and their families. A **veteran** is someone who has served in the military. Millions of people left the military after the war. Couples who had put off getting married and having children because of the Great Depression and World War II started families. The country had a "baby boom." The **baby boom** was the large increase in the number of babies born after World War II.

During the 1950s the population of the United States grew by over 28 million people. More babies were born in the period between 1949 and 1953 than had been born in the previous 30 years!

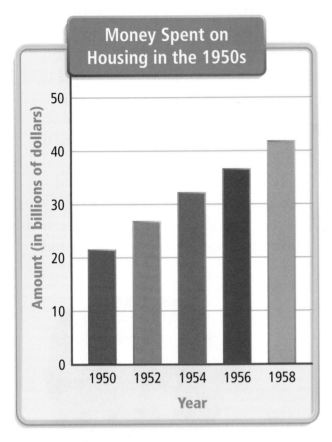

Money Spent on Housing in the 1950s

Amount (in billions of dollars)

50	
40	
30	
20	
10	
0	

Year: 1950, 1952, 1954, 1956, 1958

Housing In the 1950s, people spent more and more money on housing. Millions of families moved into homes in housing developments such as this.

SKILL **Reading Graphs** How much was spent on housing in 1954?

New Choices for Consumers

One effect of the baby boom was a shortage of houses. The population grew so fast that there weren't enough homes for people to live in. Builders responded by building large housing developments. The houses in the communities often looked alike and were built very close together. Most of the developments were built outside cities, where land was less expensive. The government lent money to millions of veterans so that they could buy these homes in the suburbs.

Factories and businesses could barely keep up with the demand for items such as washing machines and clothes dryers.

In 1950, consumers spent 191 billion dollars on consumer goods. By 1959, they had spent almost twice as much.

As businesses grew, workers earned more income. (Money earned is called income.) Families had more choices about what to buy, and many created a budget. A **budget** is a plan for saving and spending income. Income can be saved in places such as a bank savings account. Income can be used to pay expenses, such as buying a home or a car. Income can also be spent on entertainment, such as a movie or a baseball game.

REVIEW What did families use budgets for?

Cultural Changes

Main Idea Cars, television, and young people shaped much of 1950s culture.

In the 1950s, cars became much more important in people's lives. Families living in the suburbs had to drive almost everywhere. They bought cars in record numbers and loved to use them. They drove to national parks, such as Yellowstone. They watched movies at drive-in movie theaters. They ate at drive-in burger restaurants where food was served by people on roller skates. They even went to drive-in ice cream shops for dessert. Shopping centers outside city centers became very popular.

Television became much more important in people's lives in the 1950s. Television made it easy for them to see new places without leaving their homes.

Before television, people either listened to the radio or read the newspaper to get the news. With television, families could see faraway events as they happened. People watched soap operas such as "Guiding Light" during the day and comedy shows such as "I Love Lucy" at night.

Television and radio also helped rock 'n' roll become popular in the 1950s. The new music used electric guitars, had a powerful beat, and was usually loud.

Television and Cars Actress Lucille Ball (right) and her television show were popular. The photo below shows people having lunch at a drive-in restaurant.

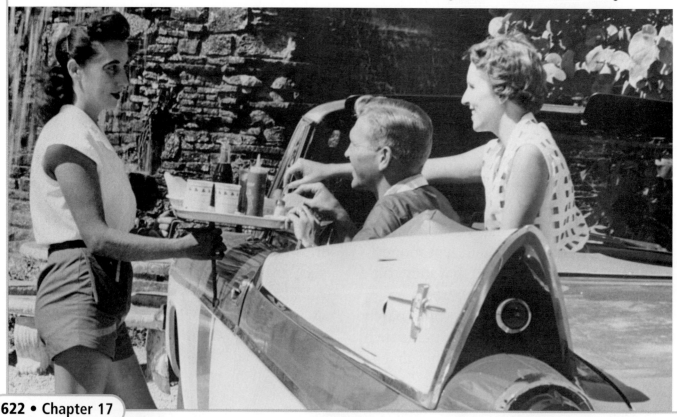

Many teenagers loved rock 'n' roll. Huge crowds of young people screamed and cheered for singers such as **Chuck Berry** and **Elvis Presley.** Some people doubted that rock 'n' roll would last. But the 1950s were only the beginning. Rock 'n' roll continued to grow and change into new kinds of music that people still listen to today.

REVIEW In what new ways did people use their cars during the 1950s?

Lesson Summary

After World War II, returning veterans created a baby boom and the economy grew. People bought houses, cars, and consumer goods. The popularity of television and rock 'n' roll changed entertainment in the United States.

Why It Matters...

In the 1950s, cars, living in suburbs, and television became even more important in the daily life of Americans. They continue to be important today.

Chuck Berry He was one of the most popular musicians in the country in the 1950s.

Lesson Review

1 VOCABULARY Match each vocabulary word with its meaning.

veteran baby boom budget

(a) person who served in a war (b) plan for saving and spending income (c) increase in number of children born after World War II.

2 READING SKILL What did families do to plan saving and spending money? Use your list of details to find the answer.

3 MAIN IDEA: History What did the returning veterans do that helped the 1950s economy?

4 MAIN IDEA: Economics What kind of products did people buy in the 1950s?

5 PEOPLE TO KNOW What made President **Dwight Eisenhower** so popular?

6 CRITICAL THINKING: Decision Making For a family in the 1950s, what might have been the opportunity cost of the decision to buy a new car? Remember that an opportunity cost is the thing you give up when you decide to do or have something else.

WRITING ACTIVITY Write a rock 'n' roll song about the 1950s. Use what you have learned about how people loved cars and television.

The Baby Boom

Babies! Millions and millions of new babies! How would all these new babies affect the American economy?

In the 1950s, the United States population grew by over 30 million in just 10 years.

This rapid increase in population had a powerful impact on the U.S. economy. It created a large demand for new houses. Between 1950 and 1960, over 15 million new homes were built.

All over the country, thousands of people found work in the home-building industry. Millions more worked to meet the demand for the materials needed to build and furnish new homes for baby boom families. Factories poured out appliances, televisions, and furniture.

As the baby boom generation grew up, the demand for new goods and services continued, helping to create one of the longest periods of economic growth in U.S. history.

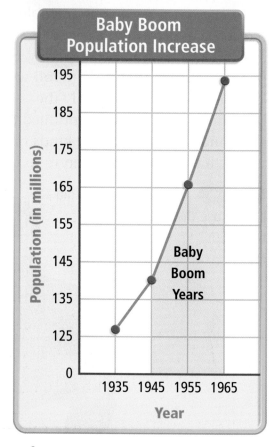

Baby Boom Population Increase

Population (in millions)

Baby Boom Years

Year

Baby Boom You can see on the chart that the population grew faster and faster after the end of World War II.

In the 1950s, more babies were born in America than at any other time in its history.

New Homes This view from the air shows new homes in the 1950s. Mass production was used to build inexpensive homes. That is why they all look similar.

New Housing

New Homes (in thousands)

2,000
1,750
1,500
1,250
1,000
750
500
250
0

1945 1950 1955 1960 1965

Year

Housing Boom The difference between 1945 and 1950 is huge. Compare this graph to the graph on page 624. How are they related?

Activities

1. **LIST IT** Make a list of the furniture and other things a family might need to set up a new house.

2. **DESIGN IT** What invention would help families today? Write a description of your invention and sketch it.

Civil Rights

1950   1955   1960   1965   1970   1970

1954–1965

VOCABULARY

civil rights
desegregation
nonviolent protest

Vocabulary Strategy

desegregation

The prefix **de-** in the word **desegregation** means "the opposite of." Desegregation is the antonym of segregation, the separation of races.

READING SKILL

Cause and Effect Take notes on the effects of the civil rights movement on laws in the United States.

CIVIL
RIGHTS
MOVEMENT

Build on What You Know When a problem is hard to solve, you may need to try something new. In the 1950s and 1960s, African Americans found new ways to gain greater recognition of their rights.

The Movement Begins

Main Idea In the 1950s, United States Supreme Court decisions changed segregation laws.

The end of slavery was not the end of inequality for African Americans. Nearly 100 years after the Civil War, black Americans still struggled for freedom. State laws and discrimination greatly limited their civil rights. Civil rights are the rights that countries guarantee their citizens. Some civil rights are the right to vote, the right to equal treatment, and the right to speak out.

Linda Brown In 1954, Linda Brown (front) and her parents brought a case against school segregation to the United States Supreme Court, and won. Here, she is seated in class.

Segregation Ends

In the early 1950s, many places in the United States were segregated. Segregated means separated by racial or ethnic group. In some cities, African Americans could not use the same restaurants and schools as whites. Segregation was legal, but many people believed that it should not be. Segregation took away the important civil right of equal treatment. African Americans went to court to end this inequality.

In 1954, the parents of a girl named **Linda Brown** went to court against the Board of Education of Topeka, Kansas. Linda's parents said that she was not getting the same education as white students. The Supreme Court decided that segregation was unconstitutional. The Court ordered desegregation of all public schools. **Desegregation** means ending the separation of people by racial or ethnic group.

The governments of some states did not want to obey the Supreme Court's decision. In 1957, President **Dwight Eisenhower** had to send soldiers to protect African American students enrolling in an all-white high school in Little Rock, Arkansas.

African Americans worked hard to end segregation in other places, too. In Montgomery, Alabama, in 1955, an African American woman named **Rosa Parks** refused to give up her seat on a bus. City law in Montgomery stated that African Americans had to sit in their own section, usually at the back of the bus. The police arrested Parks for not giving up her seat to a white man.

Members of Rosa Parks's church asked African Americans in Montgomery to boycott, or not use, the buses.

Rosa Parks Her courageous act inspired the civil rights movement.

For over a year, the city's African Americans walked, rode bicycles, and shared cars instead of riding the bus.

Dr. **Martin Luther King Jr.,** a young minister from Atlanta, Georgia, helped lead the boycott. King believed in nonviolent protest. **Nonviolent protest** is a way of bringing change without using violence. King said that even if people were hurt or arrested, they must not fight back. King's strong religious faith, and the faith of many other protesters, helped them hold on to that idea. They did not use violence or give up. In late 1956, the Supreme Court ruled that segregation on buses was illegal.

REVIEW What was the goal of the Montgomery Bus Boycott?

We Will Not Leave This photo shows a sit-in at a lunch counter in Charlotte, North Carolina in 1960.

Civil Rights Victories

Main Idea African Americans and other ethnic groups gained many civil rights in the 1960s.

In 1960 in Greensboro, North Carolina, four African American college students sat at a "whites only" lunch counter and refused to leave until they were served. This kind of protest was known as a sit-in. African Americans held sit-ins in about 54 cities. The sit-ins forced the stores to make a choice—close down or treat African Americans equally. For the first time, many stores agreed to serve African Americans.

In 1963, Congress was discussing a bill to end segregation in the United States. To show support for the bill, Martin Luther King Jr. and other civil rights leaders organized a protest march in Washington, D.C. Over 200,000 people took part. King gave his most famous speech at the march. He said,

66 **I have a dream that my four little children will one day live in a nation where they will not be judged by the color of their skin, but by the content of their character.** 99

Martin Luther King Jr.'s "I Have a Dream" speech and the March on Washington got more people to join the civil rights movement.

President **Lyndon B. Johnson** worked with Congress to pass the Civil Rights Act of 1964. The law banned segregation at school, work, and in public places such as restaurants and theaters. The next year, Congress made further progress toward recognizing the rights of all Americans. The Voting Rights Act of 1965 made it illegal to prevent or hinder citizens from voting because of their racial or ethnic backgrounds.

In 1968, only five years after the March on Washington, Martin Luther King Jr. was assassinated. This sad event did not stop the civil rights movement. People of diverse backgrounds— Christians and Jews, Northerners and Southerners, Latinos, American Indians, and Asian Americans—joined the struggle for civil rights. The American people were sending a clear message to Congress.

The civil rights movement inspired other groups to work for change. In the early 1960s, **Cesar Chavez** and **Dolores Huerta** (hoo EHR tah) formed a farm workers union. They improved conditions for farm workers in California.

Voting African Americans line up to vote in Alabama.

Women also worked for equal rights. American Indian groups in the 1960s took bold action to get back their land. All of these groups continued working for equal rights in the years ahead.

REVIEW What did the March on Washington do to help the civil rights movement?

Lesson Summary

- The Supreme Court declared school segregation laws unconstitutional.
- Sit-ins and other nonviolent protests helped end segregation in the South.
- The Civil Rights Act ended segregation in public places.
- The Voting Rights Act made it illegal to stop people from voting.

Why It Matters...

The struggle for civil rights caused the creation of new laws that protect important rights such as the right to vote.

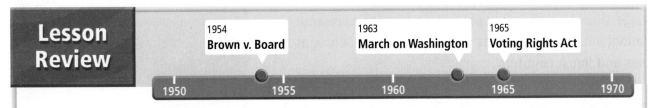

Lesson Review

1954 **Brown v. Board**

1963 **March on Washington**

1965 **Voting Rights Act**

1950 — 1955 — 1960 — 1965 — 1970

① **VOCABULARY** Choose the correct words to complete this sentence:

civil rights desegregation nonviolent protest

Martin Luther King Jr. used _____ to fight for the _____ of African Americans.

② **READING SKILL** Write one **effect** of lunch counter sit-ins.

③ **MAIN IDEA: History** What court case in the 1950s won a victory over segregation?

④ **MAIN IDEA: Citizenship** Give two examples of civil rights that are guaranteed by the Constitution.

⑤ **PEOPLE TO KNOW** Who was **Rosa Parks,** and what did she do to help end segregation?

⑥ **TIMELINE SKILL** How many years passed after the March on Washington before the Voting Rights Act?

⑦ **CRITICAL THINKING: Evaluate** Is nonviolent protest a powerful way to bring about change? Explain your answer.

HANDS ON

ART ACTIVITY Think about people who fought for civil rights such as the right to equal treatment and the right to vote. Create a picture of a civil rights leader and show what he or she did.

Biography

Dr. Martin Luther King Jr.

(1929–1968)

It is August 28th, 1963. Thousands of people have marched from the Washington Monument to the Lincoln Memorial. Folk singers have performed, and civil rights leaders have spoken to the crowd. Now Dr. Martin Luther King Jr. steps forward to the podium.

Dr. King has written part of the speech only hours ago. He has given other parts before. He looks out at the crowd. So many people have joined together in one place in the cause of equality and justice.

Throughout his life, Dr. King worked for civil rights for all Americans. He was dedicated to bringing about change through nonviolent protest. In Montgomery and Birmingham, he led boycotts and protests to desegregate buses and lunch counters.

As Dr. King begins to speak, the people cheer. Of the many speeches given on this day, this is the one that most will remember. People join hands as they listen to his message of freedom.

Major Achievements

1957
Travels thousands of miles and gives over 200 speeches

1963
Leads March on Washington and gives "I Have a Dream" speech

1963
Meets with President Kennedy about civil rights

"When we allow freedom to ring, when we let it ring from every village and every hamlet, from every state and every city, we will be able to speed up that day when all God's children, black men and white men, Jews and Gentiles, Protestants and Catholics, will be able to join hands and sing in the words of the old Negro spiritual: "Free at last! Free at last! Thank God Almighty, we are free at last!"

— From the speech "I Have a Dream"

1964
Wins Nobel Peace Prize

1965
Leads march
from Selma to
Montgomery

Activities

1. **LIST IT** List the ways that Dr. King worked for **fairness** for all Americans.

2. **WRITE ABOUT IT** Read King's speech at the back of this book. Choose a part of the speech and write about what it means to you.

 Technology Read about other biographies at Education Place.
www.eduplace.com/kids/hmss05/

631

Life in the 1960s

| 1955 | 1960 | 1965 | 1970 | 1975 | 1980 |

1960–1975

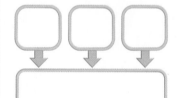
Build on What You Know On television, you've probably seen the Space Shuttle take off and land. Imagine a time when human flight in space was still a dream. In the 1960s, this dream finally came true.

Presidents Kennedy and Johnson

In 1960, voters elected **John F. Kennedy** President. He was the youngest person and first Roman Catholic ever elected to the office. Kennedy urged Americans to serve their nation by helping people in need. He said,

> **❝ . . . ask not what your country can do for you, but what you can do for your country. ❞**

President Kennedy believed that citizens could make society better and inspired many people across the United States. Thousands of young people volunteered for his Peace Corps program. The Peace Corps sends volunteers to teach children, help grow food, and develop businesses in countries around the world. The Peace Corps still exists today.

President John F. Kennedy
This photo shows President Kennedy's young son, John Jr., peeking out from under his father's desk.

The Space Race Begins

While Kennedy was President, the United States competed in a space race. The **space race** was the competition between the United States and the Soviet Union to send people into space.

The Soviet Union won the first major victory. In 1957, a Soviet rocket sent *Sputnik I* into outer space. *Sputnik I* was the first manufactured object to circle Earth. In April of 1961, Soviet cosmonaut **Yuri Gagarin** (yoo ree guh GAHR ihn) became the first person to circle Earth in a space capsule.

A month after Gagarin's flight, astronaut **Alan Shepard** was the first American to go into outer space. In February of 1962, astronaut **John Glenn** circled Earth for six hours.

President Kennedy promised that the United States would reach the moon before the Soviet Union did. On July 20th, 1969, astronauts **Neil Armstrong** and **Buzz Aldrin** landed on the moon. For the first time in history, a human being had set foot on another world.

Man on the Moon An astronaut stands on the surface of the moon. His spacecraft is reflected on the surface of his helmet.

Lyndon B. Johnson The Texas Senator became Kennedy's Vice President, and President after Kennedy was killed.

President Kennedy did not live to see the moon landing. He was assassinated in 1963 in Dallas, Texas. Americans were shocked and saddened by the sudden death of the popular young President. Vice President **Lyndon Baines Johnson** was sworn in as President later that day.

President Johnson worked to improve the lives of people who were in need through his Great Society programs. Some programs built houses or paid for medical care. Others prepared young children for school.

REVIEW Who won the race to send a person into space?

The Vietnam War

Vietnam is located in Southeast Asia. Like Korea, Vietnam was split into two countries, a communist one in the North and a capitalist one in the South. North Vietnam supported communist fighters who were trying to take over South Vietnam. Leaders in the United States were worried about communism spreading to South Vietnam. At first, the United States only sent advisors and military supplies to help South Vietnam. Later, the United States began sending its soldiers to fight in what became known as the Vietnam War.

Divisions at Home

By 1968, the United States had about 500,000 troops fighting in Vietnam. There was a sharp difference of opinion over whether the United States should have troops in Vietnam. Some people believed that the United States should not interfere in a civil war between the people of North and South Vietnam. Others argued that the United States had to stop communism wherever it was.

On college campuses many students protested the war. As the war became more unpopular, large crowds of all ages gathered for demonstrations. A **demonstration** is a gathering of people who want to express their opinion to the public and the government. People for and against the war held demonstrations in cities around the country.

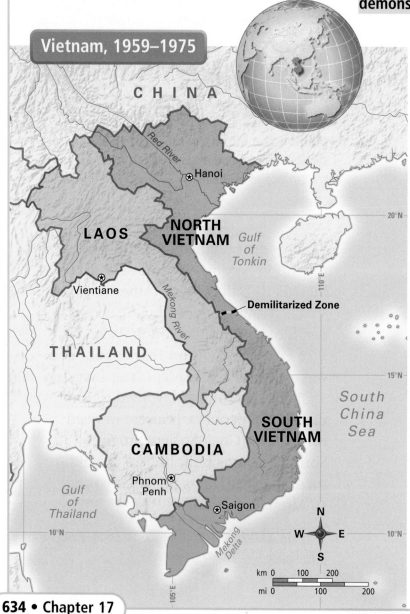

Vietnam, 1959–1975

CHINA

Red River

Hanoi

20°N

LAOS

NORTH VIETNAM

Gulf of Tonkin

Vientiane

110°E

Mekong River

Demilitarized Zone

THAILAND

15°N

South China Sea

SOUTH VIETNAM

CAMBODIA

Phnom Penh

Gulf of Thailand

10°N

Saigon

Mekong Delta

N
W   E
S

105°E

km 0   100   200
mi 0   100   200

Southeast Asia Fighting spread from North and South Vietnam to Cambodia and Laos to the west.

SKILL **Reading Maps** Identify the capitals of North and South Vietnam.

Landing in Vietnam American troops used helicopters to move around quickly.

Getting Out of Vietnam

Richard Nixon became President in January 1969. He started to bring troops home. At the same time, United States planes increased the bombing of North Vietnam and began bombing Cambodia, the nation west of South Vietnam. Many communist fighters had bases there.

In 1973, North Vietnam, South Vietnam, and the United States signed a cease-fire. A **cease-fire** is an agreement to stop all fighting. U.S. soldiers returned home, but once this happened, the communists renewed the fighting. Two years later, North Vietnam defeated South Vietnam.

For a long time after the war ended, people felt its effects. Over 55,000 American soldiers and millions of Vietnamese had died. The nation had lost its battle to stop communism in Vietnam.

REVIEW Why did many people in the United States protest against the war in Vietnam?

Lesson Summary

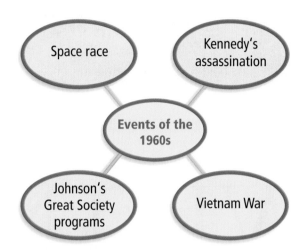

Why It Matters ...

In the 1960s the exploration of space began a new era of discovery. People saw Earth in a completely new way. The United States fought a major war in Southeast Asia.

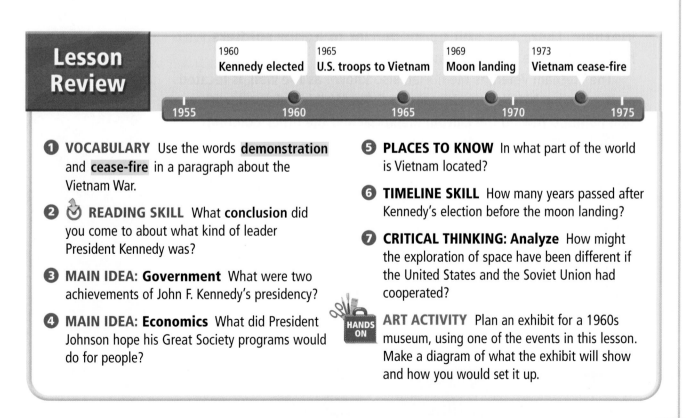

Lesson Review

1960	1965	1969	1973
Kennedy elected	U.S. troops to Vietnam	Moon landing	Vietnam cease-fire

1955   1960   1965   1970   1975

1 VOCABULARY Use the words **demonstration** and **cease-fire** in a paragraph about the Vietnam War.

2 READING SKILL What **conclusion** did you come to about what kind of leader President Kennedy was?

3 MAIN IDEA: Government What were two achievements of John F. Kennedy's presidency?

4 MAIN IDEA: Economics What did President Johnson hope his Great Society programs would do for people?

5 PLACES TO KNOW In what part of the world is Vietnam located?

6 TIMELINE SKILL How many years passed after Kennedy's election before the moon landing?

7 CRITICAL THINKING: Analyze How might the exploration of space have been different if the United States and the Soviet Union had cooperated?

HANDS ON

ART ACTIVITY Plan an exhibit for a 1960s museum, using one of the events in this lesson. Make a diagram of what the exhibit will show and how you would set it up.

THE

VIETNAM

VETERANS

MEMORIAL

Nearly ten years after the last American troops had left Vietnam, there was still no memorial to honor soldiers who had died there. In 1982, a memorial was built.

The Vietnam Veterans Memorial, also known as the Wall, is located on the National Mall in Washington, D.C. The Wall is V-shaped, with one side pointing toward the Lincoln Memorial and the other pointing toward the Washington Monument.

The name of each American who died or was missing during the Vietnam War is on the Wall. The soldiers' names are grouped by their time of service in Vietnam to make it easier for veterans to find the names of people who served with them.

The polished black granite of the Wall reflects the grass and trees around the monument. The quiet atmosphere makes the Vietnam Veterans Memorial a place to remember and respect those who gave their lives in service to their country.

Maya Lin

The Vietnam Veterans Memorial was designed by Maya Lin from Ohio. She was 21 when she won a competition for the best memorial design at the age of 21. Lin designed the Memorial to work peacefully with the landscape. She hoped it would help people to heal after the war.

Activities

1. **THINK ABOUT IT** How did Maya Lin show **respect** for veterans in her design of the Vietnam Veterans Memorial?

2. **WRITE IT** Poetry is a way to honor events and sacrifices. Write a short poem about the soldiers honored by the memorial.

637

Visual Summary

1–4.  Write a description of each event named below.

Baby Boom, 1950s	Cuban Missile Crisis, 1962	March on Washington, 1963	Moon Landing, 1969
	 Cuba	 Civil Rights	

Facts and Main Ideas

✔ **TEST PREP** Answer each question with information from the chapter.

5. **Geography** During the Cold War, what three countries were divided into North and South or East and West?

6. **Economics** Why did the economy grow when World War II veterans came home?

7. **History** What effect did the growth of suburbs have on the use of cars?

8. **Citizenship** What was the Voting Rights Act of 1965?

9. **Government** Why were North and South Vietnam at war?

Vocabulary

✔ **TEST PREP** Choose the correct word from the list below to complete each sentence.

capitalism, p. 612
budget, p. 621
desegregation, p. 627
demonstration, p. 634

10. Many civil rights groups worked for the _____ of schools.

11. A _____ can help you make decisions about spending and saving income.

12. People living under _____ can choose what goods to make and sell.

13. Students would often hold a _____ to voice their opinions about the Vietnam War.

1945
United Nations formed

1954
School desegregation

1965
U.S. enters Vietnam War

1969
First moon landing

1945   1950   1955   1960   1965   1970

Apply Skill

 TEST PREP **Chart and Graph Skill**
Read the paragraph below and answer each question about making a timeline.

> After World War II ended, the Soviet Union wanted the Allies to leave West Berlin. In June 1948, the Soviets began a blockade. They stopped all land, river, and rail traffic. In October, the British and Americans joined forces to deliver supplies to the people of West Berlin. The Soviet Union ended the blockade in May 1949. The United States and Great Britain continued the Berlin Airlift until September 1949.

14. Which event would be first on a timeline made from the information above?

   A. delivery of supplies

   B. end of the airlift

   C. end of the blockade

   D. beginning of the blockade

15. If you made a timeline for the paragraph above, into what segments would you divide it?

   A. days

   B. months

   C. years

   D. decades

Critical Thinking

TEST PREP Write a short paragraph to answer each question.

16. **Cause and Effect** What effect did Rosa Parks's refusal to move to the back of the bus have on segregation in Montgomery?

17. **Infer** Why do you think the space race was important to the United States?

Timeline

Use the Chapter Summary Timeline above to answer the question.

18. Which events happened in the 1960s?

Activities

 Research Activity Find out more about fads of the 1950s, such as poodle skirts, hula hoops, or Cinerama. Create a bulletin board display of these fads for your classroom.

 Writing Activity Write a persuasive essay to tell others why they should use a budget. Give reasons to support your argument.

 Technology
Writing Process Tips
Get help with your essay at
www.eduplace.com/kids/hmss05/

Vocabulary and Main Ideas

✓ **TEST PREP** Write a sentence to answer each question.

1. Why did some people describe actions of the U.S. government in the early 20th century as **imperialism?**

2. In what way did **alliances** help to start World War I?

3. What was one thing that people used **credit** for in the 1920s?

4. In what way was **unemployment** related to the Great Depression of the 1930s?

5. What is a **veteran?**

6. How is power divided in a government ruled by a **dictator?**

Critical Thinking

✓ **TEST PREP** Write a short paragraph to answer each question.

7. **Compare and Contrast** What are some ways in which World War I and World War II were alike and different?

8. **Synthesize** Explain how the New Deal helped people in the United States during the Great Depression. Use details from the unit to support your answer.

Apply Skills

✓ **TEST PREP** **Chart and Graph Skill** Use the following paragraph and what you have learned about making a timeline to answer each question.

The space race began in 1957 when the Soviet Union launched Sputnik I. In 1961, the Soviet Union sent Yuri Gagarin into space. The following year, John Glenn became the first American to orbit the earth. In 1969, the United States successfully sent men to the moon. That event made many people feel that the United States had won the space race.

9. If you were making a timeline of the events in this paragraph, which would be the best date to place at the beginning of your timeline?

   A. 1940

   B. 1955

   C. 1960

   D. 1965

10. Which two events would be closest to each other on your timeline?

    A. Sputnik and the moon landing

    B. Sputnik and Gagarin flight

    C. Gagarin flight and Glenn flight

    D. Glenn flight and moon landing

Unit Activity

Create and Present a Courage Award

- Choose a person mentioned in this unit whom you think showed great courage.

- Write a sentence or two telling why this person deserves an award for courage.

- Tape the sentence on construction paper and illustrate or decorate it as a certificate.

- Present your award by reading your certificate aloud.

★ Courage ★
ROSA PARKS

Rosa Parks showed great courage when she refused to go stand in the back of the bus.

At the Library

You may find this book at your school or public library.

The Voice that Challenged a Nation by Russell Freedman

African American opera singer Marian Anderson used her voice to help bring racial equality to our nation.

CURRENT EVENTS
WEEKLY (WR) READER

Connect to Today

Make a display of people in the news who have courage.

- Find articles describing the actions of at least two courageous people.

- Find photographs or draw pictures of the people you chose.

- Below each picture, write a sentence or two describing that person's courageous acts.

- Discuss with a partner why you chose each person.

Technology
Get information for the display from the Weekly Reader at **www.eduplace.com/kids/hmss05/**

Read About It

Look for these Social Studies Independent Books in your classroom.

TURN UP THE RADIO

Thurgood Marshall and Civil Rights
by Jerome Foster

THE NAVAJO CODE TALKERS
by Joy E. Dickerson

UNIT 9

Linking to the Present

The Big Idea

What do all people in the United States share?

> " *America is woven of many strands. Our fate is to become one, and yet many.* "

Ralph Ellison, twentieth-century author

Dolores Huerta

What did this teacher do to help her students? She left teaching to start the Farm Workers Association. By improving working conditions for farm workers, she helped their children, too.
page 651

History Makers

Ronald Reagan

The 40th President of the United States made many Americans feel confident and positive about their country. Reagan strengthened the U.S. military and helped to end the Cold War. **page 653**

Daniel Inouye

This son of immigrants showed his patriotism when he fought in World War II. As a senator for more than 40 years, he has worked to improve education and health care for all Americans. **page 694**

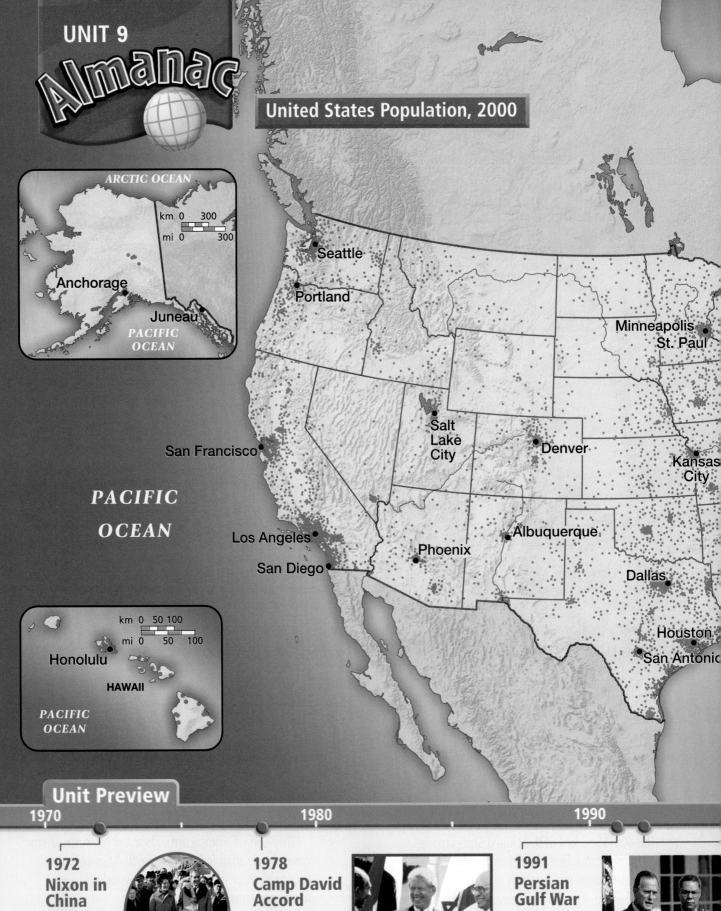

UNIT 9

Almanac

United States Population, 2000

ARCTIC OCEAN

km 0 300
mi 0 300

Anchorage

Juneau

PACIFIC OCEAN

Seattle

Portland

Minneapolis
St. Paul

PACIFIC

OCEAN

San Francisco

Salt
Lake
City

Denver

Kansas
City

Los Angeles

Phoenix

Albuquerque

San Diego

Dallas

Houston

San Antonio

km 0 50 100
mi 0 50 100

Honolulu

HAWAII

PACIFIC OCEAN

Unit Preview

1970   1980   1990

1972
Nixon in China
First President to visit China
Chapter 18, page 648

1978
Camp David Accord
Carter works for Middle East peace
Chapter 18, page 652

1991
Persian Gulf War
U.S. forces Iraq out of Kuwait
Chapter 18, page 659

Map Labels

Superior
L. Michigan
L. Huron
L. Erie
L. Ontario

Detroit
Cleveland
Chicago
Philadelphia
New York
Boston
Cincinnati
Washington, D.C.
Norfolk
St. Louis
Nashville
Charlotte
Memphis
Atlanta
New Orleans
Miami

ATLANTIC OCEAN

Gulf of Mexico

N NE E SE S SW W NW

km 0 150 300
mi 0 150 300

Timeline

2000

2010

1992
NAFTA Signed
Canada, U.S., and Mexico agree to free trade
Chapter 19, page 684

2001
September 11
Terrorists attack the United States
Chapter 18, page 674

Connect to Today

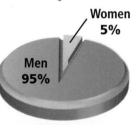

Women's Education, 1970

1970
Estimated number of women receiving law degrees: 805

Women 5%
Men 95%

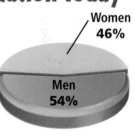

Women's Education Today

2000
Estimated number of women receiving law degrees: 17,511

Women 46%
Men 54%

Today, there are almost as many women getting law degrees as men.

How might other careers have changed during the same time period?

CURRENT EVENTS
WEEKLY WR READER

Current events on the web!

Find out about current events that connect with the content of this unit.
See activities at:
www.eduplace.com/kids/hmss05/

Our Nation and the World

Technology

e • **glossary**
e • **word games**
www.eduplace.com/kids/hmss05/

Vocabulary Preview

accord

President Carter convinced leaders of Israel and Egypt to sign a peace agreement. This important **accord** is called the Camp David Accord. **page 652**

coalition

The United States and its UN allies formed a group to fight in the Persian Gulf. This **coalition** of countries won the war. **page 659**

Chapter Timeline

1974	1980	1989
Richard Nixon resigns	Ronald Reagan elected	Fall of the Berlin Wall

1970　　1975　　1980　　1985　　1990

Reading Strategy

Monitor and Clarify As you read the lessons in this chapter, use this strategy to check your understanding.

Stop and ask yourself whether what you are reading makes sense. Reread, if you need to.

free-trade agreement

Nations make a **free-trade agreement** to increase trade with other countries. A treaty on trade removes tariffs, making it easier and less expensive to trade. **page 669**

popular vote

The vote of each citizen is counted in the **popular vote.** This number gives the total votes received by each candidate. **page 672**

1992
Bill Clinton elected

2001
September 11 attacks

1995　　2000　　2005

Challenges of the 1970s

1970   1975   1980   1985   1990   1995   2000   2005

1970–1979

Build on What You Know When you start school
each year, you face a lot of changes: a new grade, a new
teacher, and new classmates. Changes in the 1970s
included two new Presidents and several new rights
movements.

The Nixon Years

Main Idea The major events in Nixon's presidency included
his trip to China, the oil crisis, and Watergate.

In 1968, **Richard Nixon** was elected President. Nixon
focused on world events for much of his presidency. His
biggest success was improving the United States' relations
with the two largest communist countries: China and the
Soviet Union. The United States had not traded with China
since 1949, when China became communist. In 1972,
Nixon became the first U.S. President to visit China,
where he met with Chinese leader **Mao Zedong.** This
meeting led to more contact and trade between the
two countries.

That same year,
Nixon traveled to the
Soviet Union. He and
Soviet leaders signed
an agreement to limit
the number of nuclear
weapons each country
made.

Nixon in China While in China,
Nixon toured the Great Wall of China,
an important cultural landmark.

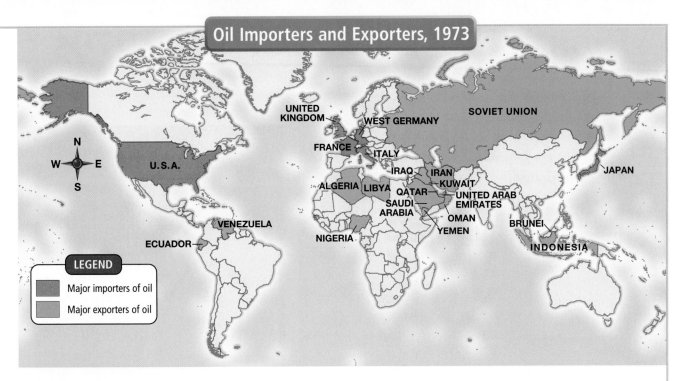

Oil Importers and Exporters, 1973

LEGEND
- Major importers of oil
- Major exporters of oil

Oil Trade The United States is one of the biggest oil importers in the world.

SKILL **Reading Maps** What are three other big oil imports?

The Oil Crisis

Not all international relationships went well during Nixon's presidency. In 1973, a war started in the Middle East. The countries of Egypt and Syria attacked the country of Israel.

The United States was Israel's ally during the war. Many of the oil-producing countries in the Middle East supported Egypt and Syria. These countries decided to punish the United States for helping Israel. They knew the United States imported their oil, so they decided to produce much less oil. When the supply of oil went down, the price went up.

The rise in oil prices caused the price of gasoline and other fuels to go up. Because businesses had to pay more for fuel to make or transport their products, they charged their customers more. This caused an overall increase in prices, which is called inflation. The oil crisis ended after five months, but inflation remained a problem for many more years.

Nixon Resigns

The president faced another problem. In 1972, Nixon, a Republican, ran for reelection. Some people working for his reelection broke into the Democratic Party's offices in the Watergate building in Washington, D.C. They were caught stealing information from the Democrats.

Nixon said he did not know about the break-in. Investigators learned that he had lied and was trying to cover up the crime. The whole event became known as Watergate.

In 1974, Nixon resigned as President because of the Watergate scandal. To **resign** means to give up your job. He was the first U.S. President ever to resign. Vice President **Gerald Ford** took over as President. He urged Americans to put Watergate behind them, saying,

❝ Our long national nightmare is over. ❞

REVIEW Which events caused inflation during the 1970s?

RIGHTS MOVEMENTS OF THE 1970s

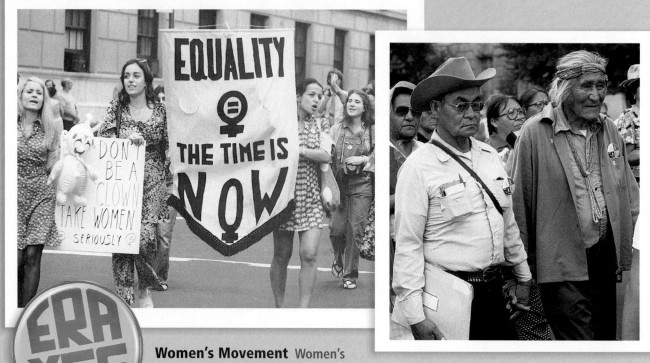

Women's Movement Women's rights groups held marches in cities around the country, including Washington, D.C.

American Indian Rights After protests by American Indians, the government formed a committee to solve problems facing Indian nations.

A Time of Change

Main Idea In the 1970s, women, farm workers, American Indians, and other groups worked for equal rights.

During the 1970s, different groups of people wanted the government to protect their rights. Women had won the right to vote in 1919. By the 1970s, however, women still did not have the same rights as men. For example, men usually were paid more than women for the same kind of work. Some businesses hired men instead of women, even though the women who wanted the jobs were just as qualified as the men.

Women of the 1970s spoke out. Leaders such as **Gloria Steinem** wrote books and essays with strong views about the importance of equality.

Women's Rights

Many women supported the National Organization of Women (NOW) in its fight for women's rights. NOW worked hard to pass an amendment to the Constitution, called the Equal Rights Amendment (ERA). This amendment would have guaranteed rights for women. However, the Equal Rights Amendment did not pass and become law.

The women's movement succeeded in many ways. The number of women serving in state legislatures doubled between 1975 and 1988. By the late 1980s, 40 out of 50 states had laws requiring equal pay for men and women doing the same work. Many women began holding jobs in business and government that had been open only to men.

Farm Workers' Rights Cesar Chavez (holding sign) urged people not to buy fruits and vegetables grown on farms with bad working conditions.

THE CONSUMER REVOLT

FIFTY CENTS   DECEMBER 12, 1969

TIME

RALPH NADER

Consumer Rights Ralph Nader led the movement to protect consumers from unsafe products.

Other Groups Seek Rights

American Indians, many of whom lived on reservations, faced problems, too. Most reservations did not provide good health care and education. Many had high unemployment. American Indian groups wanted more control over what happened on their reservations.

American Indians also wanted the U.S. government to honor earlier treaties it had signed with them. These treaties had promised to protect the rights of Indians and honor their sacred lands. In the 1970s, the government returned sacred land in New Mexico to the Taos Pueblo Indians, recognized Indian fishing rights in Washington State, and settled land claims in Alaska.

Migrant workers were another group working for their rights. A **migrant worker** is a person who moves from place to place to find work, mostly on farms. Big farm companies paid migrant workers very little and did not provide health care. **Cesar Chavez** (SAY sahr CHAH vehz) and **Dolores Huerta** (doh LOH rehs WEHR tah) led the migrant workers movement in California. Migrant workers' protests forced some farm companies to improve working conditions.

Another group, led by **Ralph Nader,** worked to protect consumers' rights. Those efforts helped create laws to improve the quality and safety of consumer products, such as cars.

REVIEW What were two goals of the Indian rights movement?

The Carter Years

Main Idea President Carter struggled with inflation at home while he encouraged peace in the Middle East.

By 1976, people in the United States were angry with the government because of Watergate and inflation. Voters wanted a change. In the presidential election that year, Democrat **Jimmy Carter** from Georgia ran against Ford. During the election, Carter promised to end scandals in government. Carter won the election and became the nation's 39th President.

Like Nixon, President Carter was more successful dealing with problems between nations than problems in the United States. In 1978, he invited the leaders of Israel and Egypt to a meeting at Camp David in Maryland. The two countries had been enemies for 30 years, but Carter helped get their leaders to sign a peace agreement. This achievement was known as the Camp David Accord. An **accord** is another word for agreement.

Economic Problems

Carter also struggled with the problem of inflation in the United States. To solve the problem, he tried to limit government spending and raise taxes, but his approach did not work. Oil-producing countries in the Middle East raised the price of oil again. By 1980, oil prices were more than double the price in 1977, when Carter became President.

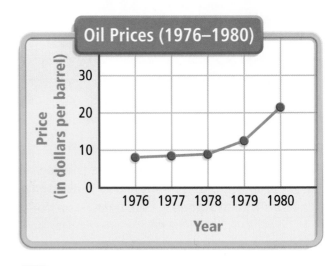

Oil Prices (1976–1980)

(Price in dollars per barrel; Year: 1976, 1977, 1978, 1979, 1980)

SKILL **Reading Graphs** About how much did the price of oil increase between 1978 and 1980?

The Camp David Accord
President Carter (center) helped Anwar Sadat, President of Egypt (left), and Menachem Begin, Prime Minister of Israel (right), sign a peace agreement.

By the end of Carter's term, people in the United States wanted a change in government again. Republican **Ronald Reagan** ran for President in 1980 and won the election.

After leaving office, Carter continued to work for peace and human rights around the world. This work and the Camp David Accord helped him win the Nobel Peace Prize in 2002.

REVIEW What were President Jimmy Carter's successes?

Lesson Summary

- Watergate forced President Nixon to resign.
- Women, American Indians, migrant workers, and other groups worked for their rights.
- President Carter helped create the Camp David Accord that led to peace between Israel and Egypt.
- During the 1970s, inflation caused economic problems.

Why It Matters . . .

The changes in the United States during the 1970s still affect the way Americans think about their rights and their government.

Nobel Peace Prize
This prize is awarded each year to people who have contributed to world peace.

Lesson Review

1972 Watergate break-in		1974 Nixon resigns		1976 Carter elected	
1972	1973	1974	1975	1976	1977

❶ **VOCABULARY** Choose a word to complete each sentence below.

   resign   accord

   Carter helped Israel and Egypt sign an ____.
   Nixon had to ____ as President.

❷ **READING SKILL** What did lower oil production in the Middle East lead to in the United States?

❸ **MAIN IDEA: Citizenship** What changes did the women's movement bring in the 1970s?

❹ **MAIN IDEA: History** What event started Watergate?

❺ **PEOPLE TO KNOW** Who was **Gerald Ford** and what did he do in 1974?

❻ **CRITICAL THINKING: Generalize** What could you say was true of all the groups who fought for their rights during the 1970s?

❼ **CRITICAL THINKING: Draw Conclusions** What effect did Watergate have on people in the United States?

SPEAKING ACTIVITY Prepare notes for a short speech about equal rights. Include reasons why equality is important and how to work for it.

Women's Rights Movement

For much of our history, women's rights were unprotected. In the early 1800s, they were prevented from voting or holding political office. They had far fewer chances than men to get an education. If a woman owned property, it became her husband's when she married.

People's views of women's rights have changed a great deal in the past two hundred years. Today, women vote and hold political offices. They attend college as often as men and work as doctors, lawyers, and business leaders. The changes in women's rights did not come all at once. Look at this timeline to see some of the most important steps in the march toward women's equality in American life.

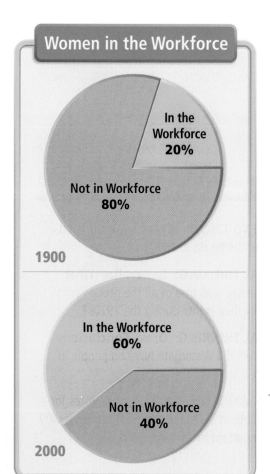

Women in the Workforce

In the Workforce
20%

Not in Workforce
80%

1900

In the Workforce
60%

Not in Workforce
40%

2000

1878
Lawmakers defeat an amendment giving women the vote. The amendment is reintroduced in every session of Congress until 1919, when it passes.

1890
Thirty-three states protect women's right to keep their own property when they marry.

1840   1880

1848
Elizabeth Cady Stanton (below) helped organize the first women's rights convention held in Seneca Falls, New York.

◀ How much did the percentage of women in the workforce grow in the 20th Century?

1963
Betty Friedan (above) writes a book, *The Feminine Mystique*, which helps start the modern women's movement.

1963
Congress passes the Equal Pay Act, requiring equal pay for men and women doing the same jobs.

1981
Sandra Day O'Connor (above) becomes the first woman appointed to the U.S. Supreme Court.

1920
The 19th Amendment guarantees equal voting rights for women.

VOTE
BALLOT BOX
League of Women Voters

1920   1960   2000

1917
Jeanette Rankin (below) of Montana becomes the first woman elected to the U.S. Congress.

1976
U.S. military academies admit women.

Activities

1. **TALK ABOUT IT** If you were helping to pass the 19th Amendment, what would you say to leaders in Congress?

2. **ASK ABOUT IT** Interview a woman you know who remembers an event on this timeline. Ask why the event was important and what details she remembers. Write a one-page report of the interview.

The 1980s

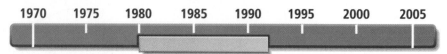

| 1970 | 1975 | 1980 | 1985 | 1990 | 1995 | 2000 | 2005 |

1980–1992

VOCABULARY

deregulation
deficit
coalition

Vocabulary Strategy

deficit

Deficit is the antonym of surplus. A surplus is more than what is needed. A deficit is less than what is needed.

READING SKILL

Main Idea and Details
Note the details that support the first main idea.

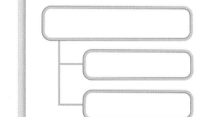

Build on What You Know Have you ever been walking and not sure you were on the right path? Many people in the United States felt this way in 1980. They elected Ronald Reagan to change the direction of the country.

Reagan Becomes President

Main Idea President Reagan cut taxes and government spending on many programs, while building a stronger military.

For many people, the late 1970s were a time of disappointment. The United States faced many challenges, including a weak economy. When **Ronald Reagan** ran for President in 1980, he tried to change the country's mood. He spoke about

❝ the great confident roar of American progress. ❞

Before Reagan, many Presidents tried to use government programs as a way to help people. For example, President Johnson's Great Society programs used government money to pay for health care, job training, and housing. Presidents in the 1960s and 1970s kept those programs and added new ones of their own.

President Reagan People in the United States knew Ronald Reagan as a popular actor before he became President.

Reagan's Economic Ideas

Reagan had a different view of government. He wanted to spend less money on some government programs because he believed that many programs did not work well. For example, some large government housing projects failed to give safe, comfortable homes to people who moved into them. Reagan also thought that people had become too dependent on the government. He said, "Government is not the solution to our problems; government is the problem."

Reagan also believed that a strong economy would help people more than government programs could. He wanted to use the government to help businesses grow. At the end of his term as President, 20 million more Americans had jobs than when he took office.

To help businesses be more productive, Reagan removed many government rules about what businesses could or could not do. Removing these rules is called **deregulation.** Because government rules often cost businesses money, deregulation helped slow inflation.

Military Spending

During Reagan's presidency, the government spent less money on some government programs and much more money on the military. Reagan believed that a strong military would keep the United States safe during the Cold War with the Soviet Union.

Building up the military, however, was expensive. The added spending left the United States with a large budget deficit. When the government spends more money than it collects in taxes in a particular year, it has a **deficit,** or shortage. In the 1980s, the deficit grew to the highest it had ever been.

REVIEW Why did President Reagan spend government money on the military?

U. S. Deficit

National Debt
A billboard in New York City showed how much the national debt increased every second. The debt is the sum of all yearly deficits.

SKILL **Reading Charts**
About how much did the deficit change between 1980 and 1988?

International Events

Main Idea After the Cold War ended, the United States fought a war in the Middle East.

The Soviet Union was in serious trouble in the 1980s. Its command economy could not provide enough jobs, goods, and housing for most people. Its failing economy made it impossible to pay the cost of the arms race. Soviet leaders had spent a large amount of money building expensive weapons.

Mikhail Gorbachev (mihkh uh EEL GAWR buh chawv) became the Soviet leader in 1985. Gorbachev decided to slow down the arms race by building a better relationship with the United States.

The Cold War Ends

Reagan and Gorbachev first met in 1985. They met several more times over the next two years to discuss ending the arms race. In 1987, they signed a treaty that lowered the number of nuclear weapons each country had. Slowly, the Cold War was ending.

In 1988, **George Bush** was elected President. Bush had been Reagan's Vice President for eight years. While Bush was President, the Soviet government and economy became weaker and weaker.

Soviet weakness gave the people in Eastern Europe and the Soviet Union the chance to break free from their communist rulers. Large groups of people joined protests in the streets of Eastern European cities. One by one, the communist governments in Eastern Europe fell from power. The most dramatic example was when the Berlin Wall came down and East and West Germany were reunited.

Finally, the Soviet Union itself fell apart. Many of its regions split away to form independent countries. The Russian people elected a new, non-communist government, and the Cold War was over.

Germany Reunited The Berlin Wall separated East Germany from West Germany for 28 years. In 1989, people on both sides of the wall helped bring it down and reunite the nation.

George Bush and Colin Powell As a top advisor under President Bush (left), General Powell (right) was in charge of the Persian Gulf War.

The Persian Gulf War

Although the Cold War was over, President Bush faced a new conflict in the Middle East. **Saddam Hussein** (SAHD uhm hoo SAYN) was the leader of Iraq. In 1990, his army invaded the neighboring country of Kuwait. Hussein planned to capture that country's oil fields.

Bush asked other countries in the United Nations to form a coalition to stop Iraq. A **coalition** is a group of allies that work together to achieve a goal.

In 1991, the United States led the coalition in a war against Iraq. The Persian Gulf War lasted about seven weeks. The coalition won the war quickly using advanced weapons and highly trained soldiers. Hussein remained in power, which worried leaders in the United States in the years to come.

REVIEW How did President Reagan help end the Cold War?

Lesson Summary

Reagan increased military spending and created a large deficit. During Bush's presidency, the Cold War ended.

Why It Matters ...

The Cold War ended when communists lost control of Eastern Europe and the Soviet Union.

Lesson Review

1980 Reagan elected				1988 Bush elected		1991 Gulf War
1980	1982	1984	1986	1988	1990	1992

❶ **VOCABULARY** Write a short paragraph about the economy under Ronald Reagan, using **deficit** and **deregulation.**

❷ **READING SKILL** What were Reagan's economic ideas that guided the way he spent government money?

❸ **MAIN IDEA: History** Which countries were reunited after the fall of the Berlin Wall?

❹ **MAIN IDEA: History** What was the cause of the Persian Gulf War?

❺ **PEOPLE TO KNOW** Who was **Mikhail Gorbachev?**

❻ **TIMELINE SKILL** For how long was Ronald Reagan President?

❼ **CRITICAL THINKING: Decision Making** What were the consequences of President Reagan's decision to spend large amounts of money on the military?

DRAMA ACTIVITY Write a short script to act out a meeting between Reagan and Gorbachev as they worked to end the Cold War.

The Fall of Communism

In the mid-1980s, few people guessed that the Cold War would end in just a few years. The conflict between the United States and the Soviet Union had lasted for 40 years.

By the late 1980s, however, Soviet-style communism was in crisis. Its economy could no longer compete with the market economies of democratic nations. As its economy failed, Soviet political strength also collapsed.

In Eastern Europe, nations such as Poland broke free from Soviet control. Soon the Soviet Union itself broke apart and several republics became independent nations. Mikhail Gorbachev, the Soviet leader, knew these changes would greatly affect the world. "The Cold War is over," he said. "We are experiencing a turning point in international affairs."

Latvia

Latvia became a free nation after years of being part of the Soviet Union. In one town, citizens pulled down a statue of Vladimir Lenin, a founder of the Soviet Union.

Poland

During the 1980s, Lech Walesa led Solidarity, a union that opposed Poland's communist government. In 1990, he was elected President of Poland.

Russia
U.S. President Ronald Reagan and Soviet leader Mikhail Gorbachev met in 1988 to discuss common interests. Here they are standing in Red Square in Moscow, Russia's capital city.

LEGEND

Russia, 1991

Countries formerly under Soviet control

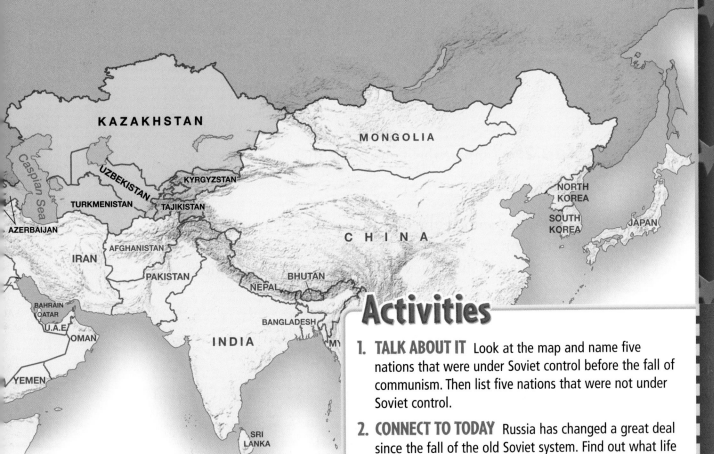

R U S S I A

KAZAKHSTAN

MONGOLIA

Caspian Sea

UZBEKISTAN

KYRGYZSTAN

TURKMENISTAN

TAJIKISTAN

AZERBAIJAN

NORTH KOREA

SOUTH KOREA

JAPAN

AFGHANISTAN

C H I N A

IRAN

PAKISTAN

BHUTAN

NEPAL

BAHRAIN
QATAR

BANGLADESH

U.A.E.

OMAN

INDIA

MY

YEMEN

SRI LANKA

Activities

1. **TALK ABOUT IT** Look at the map and name five nations that were under Soviet control before the fall of communism. Then list five nations that were not under Soviet control.

2. **CONNECT TO TODAY** Russia has changed a great deal since the fall of the old Soviet system. Find out what life is like in Russia today. Write a one-page report.

Skillbuilder

Compare Maps with Different Scales

▶ **VOCABULARY**

map scale

A map scale compares distance on a map to distance in the real world. People use maps with different scales for different reasons. Sometimes, you may need to see many details on a map or a small area of land. Other times, you need to see a large area or don't need many details. The two maps on the next page have different scales and show different information.

Learn the Skill

Step 1: Read the scales on the two maps. For each map, see how many miles equal one inch.

Map A   Map B

Step 2: Compare the scales. Note the differences.

Step 3: Compare the information on the two maps. What information does each map show? Which map gives a broad view of a large area, and which focuses on a smaller location?

Step 4: Think about what you want to learn. Identify which map presents the information you need.

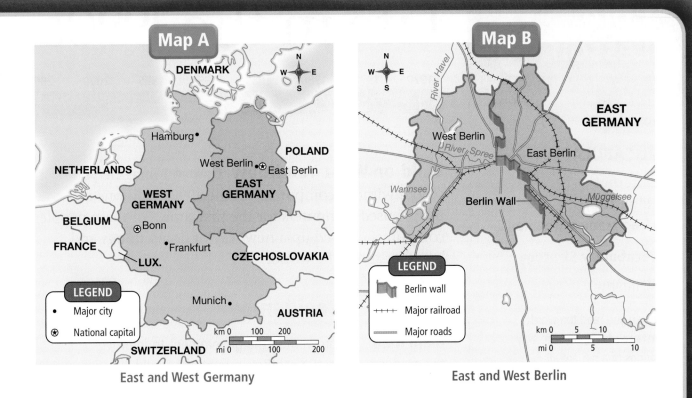

Map A

DENMARK

Hamburg•

POLAND

West Berlin •⊛•East Berlin

NETHERLANDS

WEST
GERMANY

EAST
GERMANY

BELGIUM

⊛Bonn

FRANCE

•Frankfurt

LUX.

CZECHOSLOVAKIA

LEGEND

• Major city

⊛ National capital

Munich•

AUSTRIA

km 0   100   200

mi 0   100   200

SWITZERLAND

East and West Germany

Map B

River Havel

West Berlin

EAST
GERMANY

River Spree

East Berlin

Wannsee

Berlin Wall

Müggelsee

LEGEND

Berlin wall

Major railroad

Major roads

km 0   5   10

mi 0   5   10

East and West Berlin

Practice the Skill

Use the two maps above to answer these questions.

1 What is the map scale for Map A?

2 What is the map scale for Map B?

3 Which map would you use to find the distance from Munich to East Berlin? Use a ruler to find that distance.

4 Which map would you use to find the approximate length of the Berlin Wall? Use a ruler and a piece of string to find that length.

Apply the Skill

Compare the two resource maps on pages 15 and 549. Write a paragraph explaining when and why you might use each of the maps. Be sure to describe the map scale, the amount of detail, and the purpose of each map.

Life in the 1990s

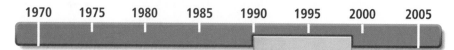

| 1970 | 1975 | 1980 | 1985 | 1990 | 1995 | 2000 | 2005 |

1990–1999

Build on What You Know Can you imagine your
school without computers? In the 1990s, millions of
people used computers for the first time. For these people,
computers opened up a new way of doing things and
learning about the world.

Clinton's Presidency

Main Idea Clinton wanted the government to improve
the economy and settle conflicts around the world.

The victory in the Persian Gulf War made **George
Bush** a popular President. By 1992, however, the United
States' economy had stopped growing. Many people lost
their jobs. As unemployment grew, Bush lost support.

In 1992, **Bill Clinton** defeated Bush in the presidential
election. During his election campaign, Clinton told voters
that the government should focus on the economy now
that the Cold War was over.

Clinton and Albright President Clinton chose Madeleine Albright
to be Secretary of State, the most important job a woman had ever
held in government.

Clinton's Economic Ideas

Clinton was a Democrat. In many ways he was like earlier Democratic Presidents. He believed the government should use social programs to help people in the United States. However, the budget deficit from the 1980s made it hard to spend money on new programs. Also, the Republicans who controlled Congress did not want more government programs. For these reasons, Clinton asked for only small increases in spending for education, health care, and other public services.

The economy grew again during Clinton's years as President. Inflation remained low. Businesses hired more workers. With more people working, the government collected more taxes. By 1998, the budget deficit had turned into a budget surplus. When the government collects more money than it spends, the money left over is a surplus.

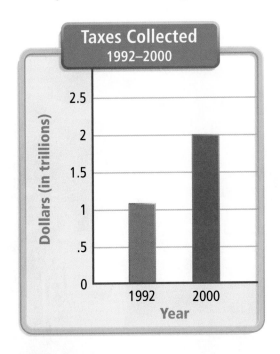

Taxes Collected
1992–2000

Dollars (in trillions)

Year

SKILL **Reading Graphs** About how much more money did the government collect in 2000 than in 1992?

World Events

Clinton acted as a peacemaker in several conflicts around the world. In Northern Ireland, Catholics and Protestants had been fighting for many decades. In 1998, Clinton helped with peace talks there. He also tried to end conflict in the Middle East.

The Balkan region in eastern Europe was another trouble spot during Clinton's presidency. Fighting there started when the former communist country of Yugoslavia split apart. Several ethnic groups battled each other as they tried to form new nations in the area. In the 1990s, the United States and other countries sent soldiers to try to stop the fighting.

Clinton Impeached

Clinton was reelected in 1996. His second term as President was hurt by a scandal. Some people in the United States believed that the President had lied in court about his private life. The House of Representatives voted to impeach him. To impeach means to charge a government official with a crime or other serious wrongdoing.

Clinton became the second President ever to be impeached. The first one was **Andrew Johnson** in 1868. The Senate held a trial to decide whether Clinton was guilty. They found him not guilty.

REVIEW In which places did President Clinton help settle conflicts?

A Changing Economy

Main Idea During the 1990s, the economy grew quickly.

During the 1990s, the United States had the longest period of economic growth in its history. The economic boom lasted for 10 years. Many people had more income to save, spend, or invest. In 2000, the stock market reached an all-time high.

Changes in computer technology boosted the economy in the 1990s. Inventors made computers, better, faster, and less expensive. One inventor named **Bill Gates** developed computer programs to use in homes, classrooms, and businesses. Another inventor, **Marc Andreesen,** developed programs that allowed people to view websites on the Internet. The **Internet** links computers around the world with each other.

New Technology

Millions of people bought computers for the first time in the 1990s. As the technologies improved, people found new uses for their computers. Through the Internet, they began to shop, send e-mail, and get information of all kinds.

The growing computer industry was part of a boom for high-tech (high-technology) businesses. **High-tech** businesses develop or use the most recent knowledge and equipment. They make products such as cellular phones and Internet software.

New technologies have made the U.S. economy more productive. Computers play a big role in most businesses. For example, computers now control much of the work on car assembly lines. Computer control makes production quicker, safer, and less expensive.

Computer Evolution

1946

ENIAC ENIAC was the first electronic digital computer. It weighed 30 tons and filled a large room. Even though it was a breakthrough at that time, it had less computing power than a digital watch does today.

Changes in Jobs

As the United States economy changed, jobs changed, too. During the 1990s, the number of people working in service jobs increased. People with service jobs provide information or perform tasks for others. For example, banks provide checking and savings accounts to people and lend money to businesses and consumers.

At the same time, the number of people who worked in manufacturing decreased. Computers and other machines helped businesses produce more goods with fewer workers. Some companies moved their factories overseas, where they could make their products at a lower cost. Farmers also used more machinery to grow food, so fewer workers were needed on farms.

Service Jobs

Number of Jobs (in millions): 0, 10, 20, 30, 40, 50
Year: 1990, 2000

SKILL **Reading Graphs** About how many more people worked in service jobs in 2000 than in 1990?

The changing economy gave many people new opportunities. People with more education benefited the most. They had the skills and knowledge that they needed to become more productive. Many of these people saw their wealth grow quickly in the 1990s.

REVIEW What effect did computers have on the economy in the 1990s?

1977

Desktop The Apple II was the first desktop computer manufactured in large numbers for use at home.

1993

PDA These tiny computers were first sold in 1993. They run on batteries and hook up to personal computers. They can send and receive e-mail, search the Internet, and play movies and music.

1981

Laptop Companies started creating computers that could be carried around and placed anywhere, including someone's lap.

A Connected World

Main Idea Technology, transportation, and trade have helped create a world where countries depend on one another.

During the 1990s, new technologies changed people's lives all over the world. Improved communication and better transportation brought individuals around the world closer than ever before.

New technologies, such as the Internet and cellular phones, made this change possible. Today, we take high-tech communication for granted, but communication has not always been so quick and easy. In the 1830s, it took four weeks for news to travel by ship between the United States and England.

Individuals now learn about events all over the world almost as soon as they happen. They can communicate with others no matter where they are. Some have even used telephones and computers on Mount Everest, the tallest mountain on Earth.

Transportation and Trade

Today, airplanes take people and products to any place in the world. Between 1985 and 1999, the number of Americans traveling to other countries nearly doubled. People coming to the United States from other countries grew by the same amount.

Better communication and transportation have increased trade among nations. With more trade, nations have become more interdependent. To be interdependent means to depend, or rely, on each other. Many American businesses trade and work closely with companies in other nations. In the automobile and computer industries, for example, parts are imported from many countries. The natural resources and materials that go into these parts come from even more countries.

Inside a Car Businesses around the world cooperate to make many of the products people use today.

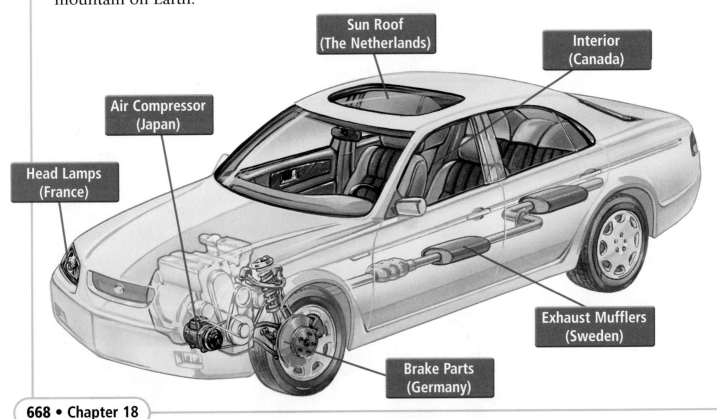

Sun Roof
(The Netherlands)

Interior
(Canada)

Air Compressor
(Japan)

Head Lamps
(France)

Exhaust Mufflers
(Sweden)

Brake Parts
(Germany)

Trade Agreements

Since the end of World War II, the United States has worked to increase international trade through free-trade agreements. A **free-trade agreement** is a treaty between countries that trade with each other. These agreements remove the taxes or tariffs that countries charge each other when they trade products. Without taxes, imported products cost less. When imported products cost less, consumers are more likely to buy them.

During the 1990s, leaders in the United States, Canada, and Mexico signed free-trade agreements. The agreements made trading less expensive among the three countries. The agreements also opened up new markets for each country's products.

REVIEW In what ways did better communication change life for people during the 1990s?

Lesson Summary

- During the 1990s, the economy grew quickly.
- Clinton tried to settle conflicts in Northern Ireland, the Middle East, and Yugoslavia.
- Computers and high-tech businesses contributed to the economic boom.
- The world became more interdependent because of better technology and increased trade.

Why It Matters . . .

The technologies developed during the 1990s will have effects on people and businesses for years to come.

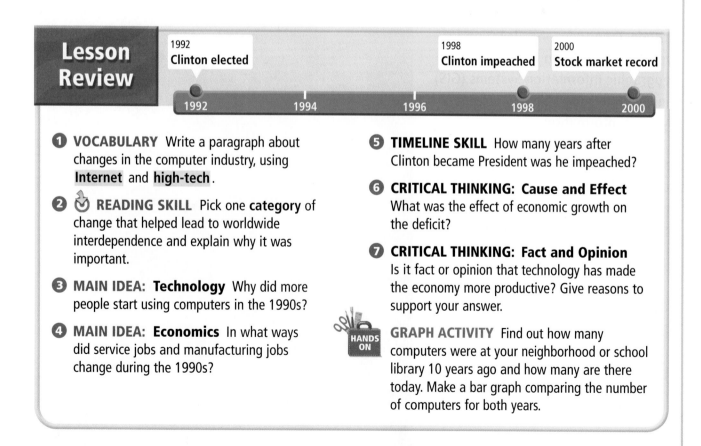

Lesson Review

1992 **Clinton elected**

1998 **Clinton impeached**

2000 **Stock market record**

1992 — 1994 — 1996 — 1998 — 2000

❶ **VOCABULARY** Write a paragraph about changes in the computer industry, using **Internet** and **high-tech**.

❷ **READING SKILL** Pick one **category** of change that helped lead to worldwide interdependence and explain why it was important.

❸ **MAIN IDEA: Technology** Why did more people start using computers in the 1990s?

❹ **MAIN IDEA: Economics** In what ways did service jobs and manufacturing jobs change during the 1990s?

❺ **TIMELINE SKILL** How many years after Clinton became President was he impeached?

❻ **CRITICAL THINKING: Cause and Effect** What was the effect of economic growth on the deficit?

❼ **CRITICAL THINKING: Fact and Opinion** Is it fact or opinion that technology has made the economy more productive? Give reasons to support your answer.

HANDS ON

GRAPH ACTIVITY Find out how many computers were at your neighborhood or school library 10 years ago and how many are there today. Make a bar graph comparing the number of computers for both years.

High-Tech Geography

Where am I? The question seems simple, but the answer has not always been easy. Explorers and navigators need to know exactly where they are on Earth. Old technologies gave them only part of the answer. But in the 1990s, highly detailed maps and images of the world became possible.

A **high-tech** geography system called the Global Positioning System (GPS) uses satellites orbiting Earth to send information to computers on land. The information provides the latitude, longitude, and elevation for every square yard on Earth's surface. Geographic Information Systems (GIS) can combine several maps to create layers of information.

There are many uses for such detailed information. GIS can help track wildlife migrations and plan transportation in cities. Firefighters also use GIS to battle forest fires.

This smokejumper is headed into a fire zone in Montana.

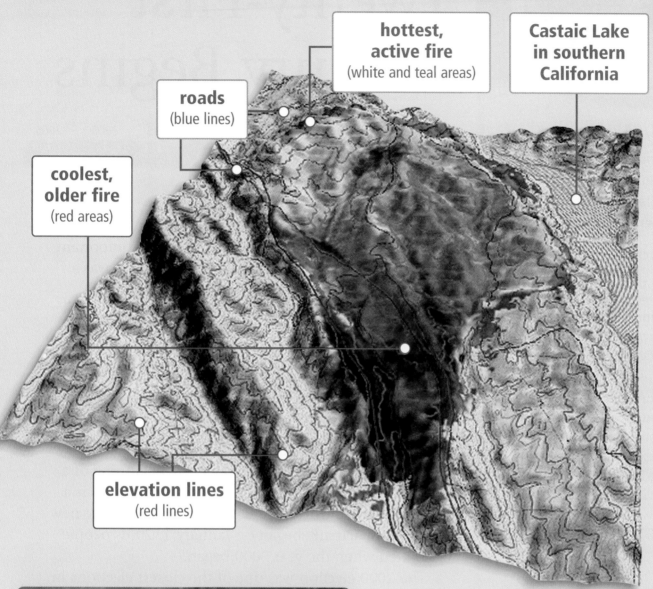

hottest, active fire
(white and teal areas)

Castaic Lake in southern California

roads
(blue lines)

coolest, older fire
(red areas)

elevation lines
(red lines)

▲ This infared color image was made using GIS technology. Combined with a roadmap, it lets firefighters know the best routes for moving people away from the fire.

Smokejumpers use new technology to decide where to dig trenches to contain the fire.

Activities

1. **TALK ABOUT IT** Discuss other kinds of emergencies in which having a detailed map could save lives.

2. **PRESENT IT** Find out how new technologies can help track wildlife migrations or plan transportation in cities. Present the information in a report.

Twenty-First Century Begins

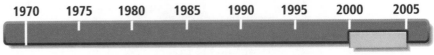
2000–2005

VOCABULARY

millennium
popular vote
Electoral College
terrorism

Vocabulary Strategy

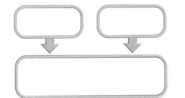

popular vote

Popular means "of the people." The **popular vote** is the vote of the people.

READING SKILL

Cause and Effect As you read, take notes on the reasons for the outcome of the 2000 presidential election.

Build on What You Know Many people celebrate each birthday, but some birthdays seem more important than others. Many people felt that the year 2000 was a special birthday for the whole world.

The 2000 Election

Main Idea The year 2000 brought one of the biggest parties ever and an unusual presidential election.

On December 31, 1999, people spent New Year's Eve listening to music, dancing, and watching fireworks. Parties around the world celebrated the beginning of a new century and a new millennium. A **millennium** is a period of 10 centuries, or 1,000 years. Although the new millennium actually began on January 1, 2001, people celebrated when the year 2000 began.

The 2000 election was one of the closest elections in United States history. The Democratic candidate was **Al Gore**, the Vice President under President Clinton. The Republican candidate was **George W. Bush**. He was the son of former President **George Bush**.

New Year's 2000 The New Year's celebrations of 2000 were some of the biggest ever.

Popular versus Electoral Votes

A presidential election has two steps. The first step is the popular vote. The **popular vote** is the vote of individuals. The next step is the Electoral College. The **Electoral College** is made up of representatives, called electors, from each state who vote for the President and Vice President.

The candidate who wins a state's popular vote wins all of that state's Electoral College votes. To become President, a candidate must win the Electoral College vote. Under this system, it is possible for a candidate to win the popular vote but lose the electoral vote.

On election night in 2000, both the popular and electoral votes were very close. With only Florida's vote left to be counted, Gore had a slight lead. Whoever won in Florida would become President. Bush won the first count. The race was so close, however, that Florida had to recount the votes. Then Bush and Gore disagreed about whether the votes in Florida were properly counted.

George W. Bush He won one of the closest presidential elections in U.S. history.

The disagreement turned into a legal battle. The Supreme Court decided that the votes in Florida would not be counted a third time. The Court's decision made the first recount in Florida official. Bush had won that count, so he won Florida's electoral votes and became President. This was the first time in U.S. history that the Supreme Court judged the voting for a presidential election.

REVIEW What is the difference between the popular vote and the electoral vote?

Electoral Votes, 2000

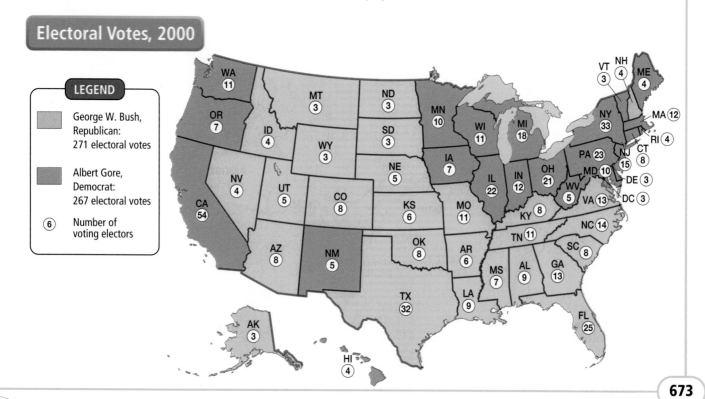

LEGEND

George W. Bush, Republican: 271 electoral votes

Albert Gore, Democrat: 267 electoral votes

6 Number of voting electors

WA 11
OR 7
MT 3
ND 3
MN 10
VT 3
NH 4
ME 4
NY 33
MA 12
ID 4
SD 3
WI 11
MI 18
RI 4
WY 3
PA 23
NJ 15
CT 8
NV 4
NE 5
IA 7
IL 22
IN 12
OH 21
MD 10
DE 3
UT 5
CO 8
WV 5
VA 13
DC 3
CA 54
KS 6
MO 11
KY 8
NC 14
AZ 8
NM 5
OK 8
AR 6
TN 11
SC 8
MS 7
AL 9
GA 13
TX 32
LA 9
FL 25
AK 3
HI 4

Attack on the Nation

Main Idea The terrorist attacks of September 11, 2001, started a new era for the people and government of the United States.

On September 11, 2001, several acts of terrorism were carried out against the United States. **Terrorism** is the use of violence against ordinary people to achieve a political goal.

On that day, terrorists hijacked four airplanes. They crashed two planes into the World Trade Center in New York City. The two buildings caught fire and fell. Terrorists crashed a third plane into the Pentagon, the nation's military headquarters outside of Washington, D.C. The fourth plane crashed in Pennsylvania.

Nearly 3,000 innocent people were killed in these attacks. The United States found out that the terrorists belonged to a group from the Middle East called al-Qaeda (al KY duh). Their leader was **Osama bin Laden** (oh SAH mah bihn LAH dehn). Bin Laden and his followers strongly opposed the United States' involvement in the Middle East.

Bush told the military to prepare for war. He said,

> 66 **While the price of freedom and security is high, it is never too high. Whatever it costs to defend our country, we will pay.** 99

Afghanistan and Iraq Both countries are in the Middle East region.

SKILL **Reading Maps** Where is Afghanistan located in relation to Iraq?

Middle East Region

Black Sea

Caspian Sea

Mediterranean Sea

TURKEY

SYRIA

LEBANON

ISRAEL

JORDAN

IRAQ

KUWAIT

IRAN

AFGHANISTAN

PAKISTAN

EGYPT

BAHRAIN

QATAR

OMAN

SAUDI ARABIA

UNITED ARAB EMIRATES

OMAN

Persian Gulf

Red Sea

Arabian Sea

INDIAN OCEAN

YEMEN

N
W E
S

km 0   250   500
mi 0   250   500

LEGEND
- - - Disputed border

War in Afghanistan and Iraq

Osama bin Laden's headquarters was in the country of Afghanistan in southwest Asia. Bush accused the government of Afghanistan of hiding bin Laden and his followers. In October, 2001, the United States led a coalition of nations into a war in Afghanistan.

The war lasted for three months. The United States defeated Afghanistan's government and military but did not capture bin Laden. New leaders in Afghanistan formed a government that was supported by the United States.

In 2003, Bush turned his attention to the nation of Iraq in the Middle East. **Saddam Hussein** was still in power there. During the 1990s, the United Nations tried to inspect places in Iraq to see whether Hussein had destroyed his most dangerous weapons. Bush did not believe that Hussein had disarmed. He worried that Iraq's weapons could be used to attack neighboring countries or the United States.

In March, 2003, the United States went to war in Iraq. After defeating Hussein's army, the U.S. military stayed in Iraq to help form a new Iraqi government. Saddam Hussein was found and arrested in December, 2003.

REVIEW How did the United States respond to the terrorist attacks of September 11, 2001?

Lesson Summary

2000	George W. Bush elected President
September 11, 2001	Terrorist attacks
2001	War in Afghanistan
2003	War in Iraq

Why It Matters...

The terrorist attacks of September 11, 2001, deeply affected people in the United States and the world.

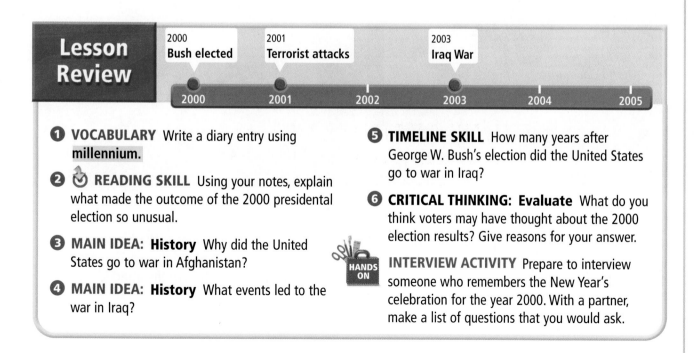

Lesson Review

| 2000 Bush elected | 2001 Terrorist attacks | | 2003 Iraq War | | |
| 2000 | 2001 | 2002 | 2003 | 2004 | 2005 |

❶ **VOCABULARY** Write a diary entry using **millennium.**

❷ 🕐 **READING SKILL** Using your notes, explain what made the outcome of the 2000 presidental election so unusual.

❸ **MAIN IDEA: History** Why did the United States go to war in Afghanistan?

❹ **MAIN IDEA: History** What events led to the war in Iraq?

❺ **TIMELINE SKILL** How many years after George W. Bush's election did the United States go to war in Iraq?

❻ **CRITICAL THINKING: Evaluate** What do you think voters may have thought about the 2000 election results? Give reasons for your answer.

HANDS ON

INTERVIEW ACTIVITY Prepare to interview someone who remembers the New Year's celebration for the year 2000. With a partner, make a list of questions that you would ask.

9/11 HEROES

News of the attacks on September 11, 2001, shocked the nation. As thousands of New Yorkers fled the city, hundreds of police and firefighters rushed to the burning World Trade Center to help survivors. Search and rescue teams went to New York City from all over the country, along with emergency medical crews. For these professionals, responding to this act of terrorism was the hardest job in their careers.

Ordinary citizens wanted to help, too. Truckers and work crews came to remove the tons of rubble from the collapsed buildings. Volunteers donated blankets, food, and other goods for people affected by the tragedy. Many people raised money for the effort. Together, people worked to comfort their fellow citizens and help them recover from the terrible blow.

Kids Step Forward

Students collected money to help the victims of the attacks. At a Saltillo, Mississippi, elementary school, students raised $971.00 in one day.

Run for Funds

This Michigan firefighter went to Washington, D.C., to take part in a fundraising race. The race was dedicated to the victims of the attacks.

On the Scene
Three firefighters raise the United States flag at the World Trade Center shortly after the 9/11 attacks.

©2001 The Record (Bergen County, NJ), www.groundzerospirit.org

Activities

1. DRAW IT Many people have ideas for a memorial for the victims of the September 11th attacks. Draw your idea for a memorial.

2. WRITE ABOUT IT The students from Saltillo, Mississippi, deserved a thank you note for their hard work. Write a letter the mayor of New York City might have written to them.

Visual Summary

1.–4. 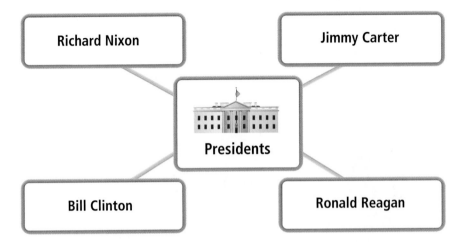 Describe what you learned about each President named below.

Richard Nixon

Jimmy Carter

Presidents

Bill Clinton

Ronald Reagan

Facts and Main Ideas

✓ **TEST PREP** Answer each question with information from the chapter.

5. **Citizenship** Name two groups of people who worked for equal rights in the 1970s.

6. **Government** Why did President Carter win the Nobel Peace Prize?

7. **History** Which two leaders signed agrements that led to the end of the arms race?

8. **Economics** Which three countries are part of NAFTA?

9. **Government** In what way was the 2000 presidential election unusual?

Vocabulary

✓ **TEST PREP** Choose the correct word from the list below to complete each sentence.

resign, p. 649
deficit, p. 657
high-tech, p. 666
terrorism, p. 674

10. Many _____ inventions led to improvements in medicine and business.

11. The use of violence against ordinary people to achieve a political goal is called _____.

12. Richard Nixon was the first U.S. President ever to _____.

13. The government spent more than it collected in taxes, which created a _____.

CHAPTER SUMMARY TIMELINE

1974
Nixon resigns

1980
Reagan elected

1989
Fall of the Berlin Wall

2001
September 11 attacks

1970   1975   1980   1985   1990   1995   2000   2005

Apply Skills

 TEST PREP Map Skill Compare the map of Afghanistan below to the map of the Middle East region on page 674. Then answer each question.

14. What can you learn from the map above that you can't learn from the map on page 674?

  A. the distance between Kabul and Kandahar

  B. the major rivers in the Middle East

  C. the locations of battles in the war in Afghanistan

  D. the distance between the capitals of Iran and Iraq

15. Which map would you use to learn the names of the countries that border Saudi Arabia?

Critical Thinking

 TEST PREP Write a short paragraph to answer each question.

16. **Cause and Effect** What were the effects of the rise in oil prices in the 1970s?

17. **Summarize** How has the world become more interdependent in recent years?

Timeline

Use the Chapter Summary Timeline above to answer the question.

18. Was Reagan elected before or after the fall of the Berlin Wall?

Activities

Interview Activity With a partner, write a set of questions you might want to ask one of the people named in chapter 18. Use *who, what, where, when, why,* and *how* questions.

Writing Activity Write a persuasive essay to a student explaining why he or she will need a good education to succeed in an interdependent world.

Technology
Writing Process Tips
Get help with your essay at
www.eduplace.com/kids/hmss05/

Chapter 19

America Today and Tomorrow

Technology

e • **glossary**
e • **word games**
www.eduplace.com/kids/hmss05/

Vocabulary Preview

province

The United States is made up of 50 states, but Canada has political regions called **provinces.** Each province has a capital and a government.
page 682

heritage

The ideals of democracy and human rights are part of the history of the United States. The Liberty Bell is a symbol of this **heritage.**
page 693

Chapter Timeline

1821
Mexican independence

1867
Canadian independence

1800   1850   1900

Reading Strategy

Summarize As you read, use the summarize strategy to focus on important ideas.

Quick Tip It helps to reread sections and put them in your own words.

responsibility

Americans have many rights. They also have a **responsibility** to follow the laws of the United States.
page 700

volunteer

People, no matter what their age, can help others by being a **volunteer.** Doing work to help others without being paid is an American tradition. **page 700**

1992
NAFTA signed

1950   2000

Neighbors in North America

| 1500 | 1600 | 1700 | 1800 | 1900 | 2000 |

1521–present

Build on What You Know You and your neighbors share the same street. The United States and its neighbors, Canada and Mexico, share the same continent. The three countries also share similar histories.

Canada

Main Idea The United States and Canada have similar histories and are important trading partners.

Canada is the United States' neighbor to the north. Canada is large in area, but it has only 32 million people. In comparison, the United States is smaller in area, but it has 285 million people. Canada's capital is Ottawa. The country has three territories and ten provinces. A **province** is a political region of a country that is similar to a state.

Canada and the United States share a 4,000-mile border that stretches from the Atlantic Ocean to the Pacific Ocean and along the eastern side of Alaska. Thousands of cars and trucks from both the United States and Canada cross the border every day.

Canadian Flag The maple leaf symbolizes the land and people of Canada. Red and white are Canada's official colors.

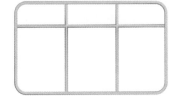

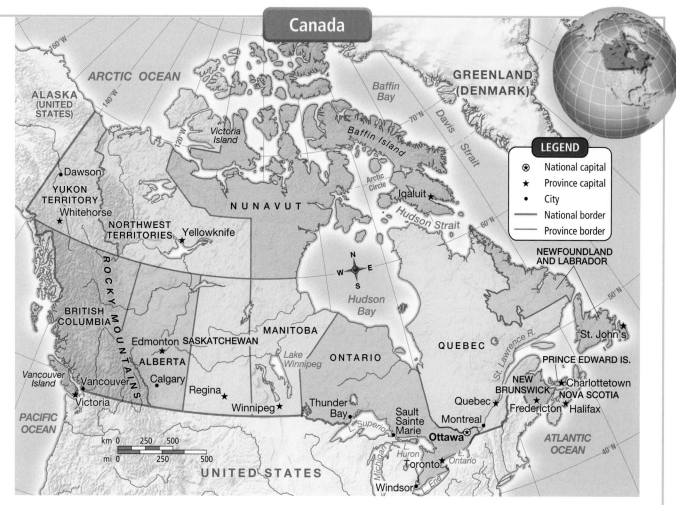

Our Northern Neighbor Canada is the second largest country in area in the world.

Canada's History and Culture

The history of Canada is similar to the history of the United States. The first people to live in Canada were native peoples, such as the Cree, Huron, and the Inuit, who are also known as Eskimos. Like the United States, Canada was colonized by Europeans. At first, the colonists were mainly French. In 1754, France and Britain began a war for control of North America. France lost, and the British gained control of Canada.

In 1867, Canada separated from Britain and became a self-governing country. It has a representative democracy, with powers divided between the provinces and a federal government. Canada also belongs to the Commonwealth of Nations, a group of countries that were once part of the British Empire.

The French influence is still strong in Canada, especially in the province of Quebec. In Quebec, most people speak French or both French and English. Throughout Canada, French and English are official languages.

Native peoples are an important part of Canadian society. The Inuit have their own territory called Nunavut.

Canada also has many immigrants from Europe, Asia, and South and Central America. In Canada, one out of six people is an immigrant. With so many immigrants, Canada is a multi-cultural society. **Multicultural** means having many cultural traditions.

REVIEW Why is French one of the two official languages in Canada?

Ottawa, Canada's Capital Canada's representatives meet in the Parliament building in Ottawa. Street signs in parts of Canada are in both French and English.

Canada and the United States

In 1992, Canada signed the North American Free Trade Agreement (NAFTA) with the United States and Mexico. NAFTA is an agreement among these three countries to increase trade. The agreement says that the countries will remove tariffs and taxes for the products they sell to each other. Today, the United States and Canada trade more with each other than with any other countries.

The United States buys oil, electricity, lumber, car parts, and paper from Canada. The United States sells cars, machines, chemicals, and other products to Canada. The two nations also work together to deal with environmental problems that affect both countries.

One example is reducing pollution that blows from the American Midwest into Canada. They also work together to improve the quality of the water in the Great Lakes. The Great Lakes form part of the border between the two countries.

Canada's Exports

Fish/shellfish	
Oil	
Natural gas	
Lumber/wood products	
Farm animals and products	

SKILL **Readings Charts** Which of Canada's exports are taken from the ground?

Mexico

Main Idea Mexico was colonized by the Spanish, but it has been an independent country since 1821.

Mexico is the United States' neighbor to the south. The 2,000-mile border between the United States and Mexico stretches from California to Texas. About 103 million people live in Mexico. Mexico City is the capital of Mexico and is one of the largest cities in the world.

The country has 31 states and one federal district. In northern Mexico, the land includes a central plateau with basins and ranges. This area is warm and dry. The south has mountains and tropical rain forests that cross Mexico's southern border with Belize and Guatemala.

Mexico's History

Mexico has a rich history. The Mayas and Aztecs were some of the first peoples in Mexico. They built large, beautiful cities and used technologies, such as irrigation, that were advanced for their time. Irrigation helped them have large farms.

Spanish explorers began coming to Mexico in the early 1500s. In 1521, Mexico became a Spanish colony. Like the United States, Mexico fought a war for its independence. In 1821, Mexico defeated the Spanish and became an independent country. Since 1910, Mexico has had a representative government that gives a lot of power to the President.

REVIEW How and when did Mexico gain its independence?

Our Southern Neighbor Mexico is the most populated Spanish-speaking country in the world. **SKILL** **Reading Maps** Which Mexican states border the United States?

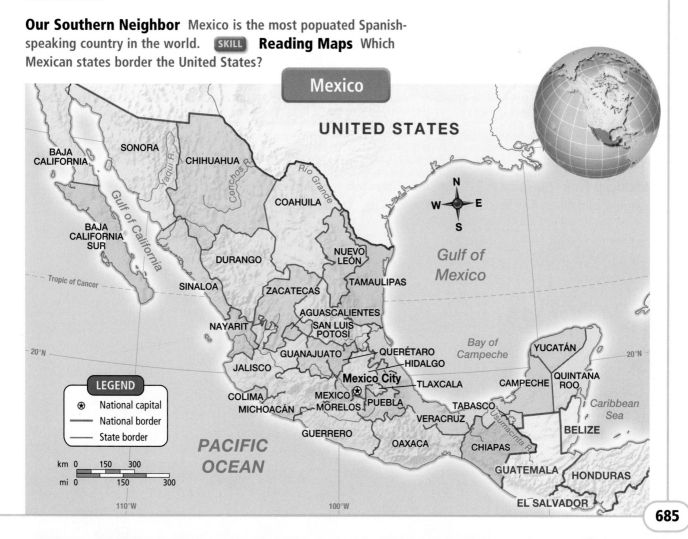

Mexican Culture

Mexico's people have a Spanish and Indian heritage. Most Mexicans are mestizo (meh STEE zoh), which means people of both Spanish and Mexican Indian ancestry. Spanish is the official language, but many Indian languages are also spoken. Most Mexicans are Catholics, and the Catholic Church has shaped Mexico's culture in many ways.

Many Mexicans live in small villages in the countryside, where farming is an important part of life. Even more Mexicans live in busy modern cities. Most Mexican cities have a Spanish-style central square or plaza. Art inspired by the country's Indian heritage decorates many public places.

Mexican Flag The three stripes symbolize from left to right independence, religion, and union. The flag flies over Mexico City's central plaza (below).

Mexico and the United States

Mexico and the United States have different cultures, but the two countries have had close contact for more than 150 years. Because much of the southwestern United States was once part of Mexico, Mexican arts, food, and building styles are common in California, Texas, Arizona, and New Mexico.

Many Mexicans immigrate to the United States. Immigration provides workers for the U.S. economy and gives jobs to Mexicans. Immigration can cause problems, however, especially when it is done illegally. The two countries work together to try to reduce illegal immigration across their shared border.

Mexico and the United States have important economic ties. Since the 1970s, businesses in the United States and other countries have built factories in Mexico near the U.S. border. This kind of factory is called a **maquiladora** (mah kee lah DOH rah). Thousands of Mexicans work in maquiladoras. They put together cars, televisions, computers, and other products that are sold all over the world.

NAFTA

In 1992, Mexico signed NAFTA with the United States and Canada. Afterward, its trade with the two countries greatly increased. Today, Mexico's most important trading partner is the United States. Mexico is the United States' second most important trading partner after Canada.

Mexico's Exports

Farm crops	
Oil	
Farm animals and products	
Precious metals	
Iron	

SKILL **Reading Charts** Which of Mexico's exports are the same as Canada's exports?

The United States buys oil and minerals from Mexico. It sells machines, car parts, and farm equipment to Mexico. Partly because of NAFTA, the three countries will have close ties for a long time to come.

REVIEW What are some of Mexico's connections with the United States?

Lesson Summary

- British and French cultures are part of daily life in Canada.
- Spanish and Mexican Indian cultures are part of daily life in Mexico.
- Canada, Mexico, and the United States signed NAFTA to increase trade among the three countries.

Why It Matters...

The United States, Canada, and Mexico are neighbors in North America. They all gain from trade and cultural sharing across the borders.

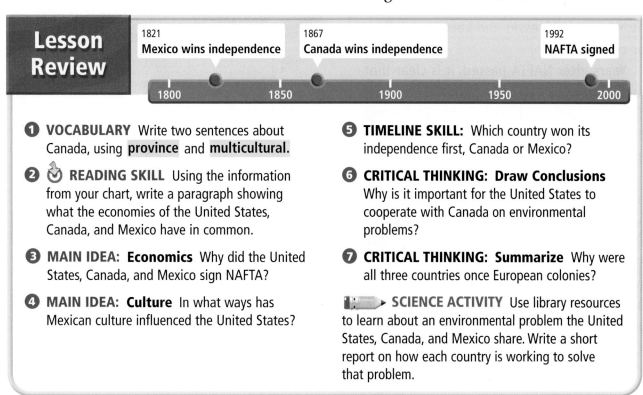

Lesson Review

1821 **Mexico wins independence**

1867 **Canada wins independence**

1992 **NAFTA signed**

1800 1850 1900 1950 2000

① **VOCABULARY** Write two sentences about Canada, using **province** and **multicultural.**

② **READING SKILL** Using the information from your chart, write a paragraph showing what the economies of the United States, Canada, and Mexico have in common.

③ **MAIN IDEA: Economics** Why did the United States, Canada, and Mexico sign NAFTA?

④ **MAIN IDEA: Culture** In what ways has Mexican culture influenced the United States?

⑤ **TIMELINE SKILL:** Which country won its independence first, Canada or Mexico?

⑥ **CRITICAL THINKING: Draw Conclusions** Why is it important for the United States to cooperate with Canada on environmental problems?

⑦ **CRITICAL THINKING: Summarize** Why were all three countries once European colonies?

SCIENCE ACTIVITY Use library resources to learn about an environmental problem the United States, Canada, and Mexico share. Write a short report on how each country is working to solve that problem.

THE EFFECTS OF NAFTA

Before NAFTA was signed into law, no one knew how free trade would affect the U.S. economy. Plenty of people had opinions, though. Some people warned that Americans would lose jobs if trade became freer. They predicted that more companies would move their factories to Mexico.

Most economists believed NAFTA would be good for each country. They believe free trade helps businesses and keeps prices low for consumers.

Years after NAFTA passed, it is clear that North American trade has grown. Between 1993 and 2001, total trade between Canada, Mexico, and the United States more than doubled.

Most leaders in Canada, Mexico, and the United States have been pleased by the increase in trade. However, some report that NAFTA has not helped to create enough jobs. Other nations will watch NAFTA's effects carefully. If free trade works in North America, they may want similar agreements with the United States.

LUMBER Canada's forests are the largest in North America. Wood and wood products from those forests are important exports.

Trade between the U.S. and Canada
1993–2001

- Exports to Canada
- Imports from Canada

Canada is our nation's biggest trading partner. About how many billions more in exports were traded from 1993 to 2001?

AUTOMOBILES Cars and car parts are important to North American trade. Car parts from the United States are put together in this Mexican factory.

OIL In recent years, Mexico has become a leading oil exporter. Most of its oil exports go to its NAFTA trading partners.

Trade between the U.S. and Mexico
1993–2001

- Exports to Mexico
- Imports from Mexico

Dollars (in Billions)

150
125
100
75
50
25
0

1993 1995 1997 1999 2001

Year

After NAFTA, Mexican imports to the United States more than tripled between 1993 and 2001.

Activities

1. **LIST IT** List three questions to ask other students about the information in the charts.

2. **GRAPH IT** Create a bar graph from the line graphs, comparing Canadian and Mexican trade with the United States.

689

Citizenship Skills

Skillbuilder

Resolve Conflicts

▶ VOCABULARY

conflict

In Lesson 1, you read about how the United States works with Canada and Mexico to resolve and avoid conflicts. A **conflict** is a disagreement. To resolve, or settle, a conflict, people sometimes need to compromise. Use the steps below to help resolve conflicts.

Learn the Skill

Step 1: Describe the conflict.

Your class has decided to give the school a gift, but you cannot agree on what to give.

Step 2: Identify what each person or group wants and why they want it. Look for shared goals.

One group wants to donate musical instruments to the school band. A second group wants to buy art supplies and paint a mural. A third group wants to give books to the library.

Step 3: Brainstorm possible solutions. Look for more than one way to make the most people happy.

The class could split the money between buying a few musical instruments and painting a small mural. You could instead think of a fourth gift that would please everyone.

Step 4: Compromise and agree to one of the solutions. Some people may have to change what they want in order to resolve the conflict.

Practice the Skill

Read about a brief conflict between the United States and Canada. Then answer the questions about how it was resolved.

> The governments of Canada and the United States wanted a way for large ships to travel more easily from the Atlantic Ocean to the Great Lakes. In the early 1950s, Canada began building dams and canals on the St. Lawrence River. However, it became too expensive for Canada to complete the work alone. The United States agreed to help but wanted to control the project. Canada did not want the United States to have complete control.
>
> The two governments compromised. Each country agreed to build different parts of the waterway. Each government would then take part of the profits from the project. In June, 1959, Queen Elizabeth of Great Britain and President Eisenhower opened the St. Lawrence Seaway.

1 What was the conflict between Canada and the United States?

2 How were the goals of the two countries similar?

3 In what way was the solution a compromise?

Apply the Skill

Use your library or the Internet to research a conflict between two groups in the United States today. Identify the conflict and the goals of each side. Then suggest and evaluate possible resolutions of the conflict.

United States Today

VOCABULARY

refugee
heritage
motto

Vocabulary Strategy

heritage

The words **heritage** and **inherit** are related.
A heritage is something you receive, or inherit, from your family or culture.

READING SKILL

Cause and Effect What happened as a result of the change in United States immigration laws in 1965? Take notes as you read.

CAUSE   EFFECT

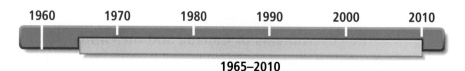

| 1960 | 1970 | 1980 | 1990 | 2000 | 2010 |

1965–2010

Build on What You Know You know that each of your classmates has special ideas, talents, likes, and dislikes. Each person contributes to your class. The same is true for the United States. There are almost 300 million people living in the United States, and each person contributes to the country in some way.

A Nation of Immigrants

Main Idea Immigrants come to the United States from all over the world.

Throughout its history, the United States has attracted many millions of immigrants. Some people come to the United States to escape poverty and to make a better life. Others come as refugees looking for political or religious freedom. A **refugee** is a person who escapes war or other danger and seeks safety in another country.

A Diverse Nation In the United States, about one out of ten people are immigrants. Many more are children or grandchildren of immigrants.

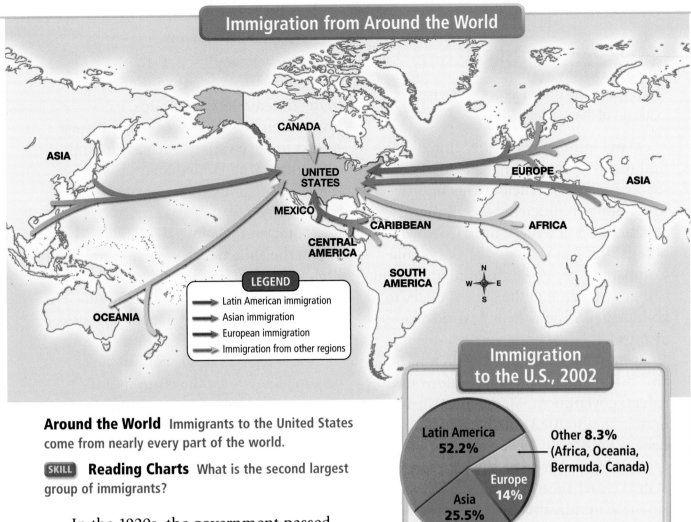

Immigration from Around the World

CANADA

ASIA

UNITED STATES

EUROPE

ASIA

MEXICO

CARIBBEAN

AFRICA

CENTRAL AMERICA

SOUTH AMERICA

OCEANIA

LEGEND
- Latin American immigration
- Asian immigration
- European immigration
- Immigration from other regions

Immigration to the U.S., 2002

- Latin America 52.2%
- Other 8.3% (Africa, Oceania, Bermuda, Canada)
- Europe 14%
- Asia 25.5%

Around the World Immigrants to the United States come from nearly every part of the world.

SKILL Reading Charts What is the second largest group of immigrants?

In the 1920s, the government passed laws that limited immigration to the United States. From the 1920s to the 1960s, most immigrants came from only Europe or Mexico. In 1965, Congress passed a new law, allowing more immigrants from Latin America, Asia, the West Indies, and Africa to come to the United States.

Spanish-speaking immigrants come from Central and South America and from the Caribbean region. In the 1960s, when Cuba became a communist country, Cuban refugees came to the United States. During the 1980s, refugees fled wars in El Salvador and Nicaragua and settled in this country.

Today, about one-fourth of immigrants to the United States are Asian. They come from countries such as India, China, and the Philippines.

Where Immigrants Settle

Immigrants often settle in communities where other people from their home countries live. Most of these communities are in cities. Los Angeles, New York, Chicago, and other cities attract large groups of immigrants.

Many immigrants from Latin America settle in California, Texas, and Florida. Like all immigrants, Latin Americans influence the government and culture in the places where they settle. For example, many Cuban immigrants have settled in Miami. Cuban Americans affect the politics, economy, and culture of Miami and Florida.

REVIEW Why did immigration to the United States change after 1965?

Many People, One Nation

Main Idea The United States is one nation made up of many peoples.

Many immigrants to the United States find the freedom they need to start successful careers. Their talents improve the country in different ways. **Roberto Goizueta** was a refugee from Cuba who became the President of The Coca-Cola Company. **I. M. Pei** is an immigrant from China who came to the United States to go to college. Today he is a world-famous architect.

Immigrants and their children have also made important contributions to the federal government. **Madeleine Albright** immigrated to the United States from eastern Europe. In 1996, President Bill Clinton chose her to be the Secretary of State. **Daniel Inouye** is the son of Japanese immigrants and a senator from Hawaii. He is the third longest-serving member of the Senate.

Ethnic Diversity

Because the United States has so many different ethnic groups, its population is very diverse. To be diverse means to have variety, such as cultural differences. The United States is also the most religiously diverse country in the world.

Ethnic and religious diversity is one of the United States' greatest strengths. Each individual brings talents, skills, and knowledge to the nation. Each ethnic group adds its art, food, language, music, and customs to United States culture.

Some regions of the country have become known for the customs and traditions brought there by immigrants. For example, bluegrass music in the Appalachian Mountain region was influenced by the music of Scots-Irish immigrants. Today, bluegrass is heard and enjoyed all over the United States and is now a part of our national culture.

Roberto Goizueta He led an international company with branches in more than 200 countries.

Madeleine Albright She was the first woman to hold the job of Secretary of State.

I. M. Pei He designed part of the National Gallery in Washington, D. C.

Our Common Heritage

Although the United States has a lot of diversity, all of its people share a democratic heritage. A **heritage** is something that is passed down from one generation to the next. The Constitution and Bill of Rights are part of that heritage. This shared heritage helps unite our large population.

One motto of the United States is:

66E pluribus unum. 99

A **motto** is a short statement that explains an ideal or a goal. This phrase means "out of many, one."

"E pluribus unum" is written on coins and government buildings across the United States. The motto is a reminder that the original thirteen colonies formed one country. Today, fifty states form one democratic nation, with a culture that is as rich and diverse as the people who live in it.

> **REVIEW** What do all U.S. citizens share?

Motto on Money
American coins are a daily reminder of the motto "E pluribus unum."

Lesson Summary

After immigration laws changed in 1965, more immigrants started coming to the United States from Latin America, Asia, and Africa. Many of them come to escape poverty or war and to make a better life. They add to the country's society, politics, and economy. In addition to diverse cultures, people in the United States share a common democratic heritage.

Why It Matters ...

Because of the country's diversity, people in the United States have the opportunity to learn about different cultures.

Lesson Review

1965
Immigration laws change

| 1960 | 1970 | 1980 | 1990 | 2000 | 2010 |

1. **VOCABULARY** Write a paragraph about immigration to the United States, using **refugee** and **heritage.**

2. **READING SKILL** In what way did the change in immigration laws in 1965 affect immigration from Asian countries?

3. **MAIN IDEA: Geography** Look at the chart on page 693. From which area do most immigrants to the United States come?

4. **MAIN IDEA: Citizenship** What does "E pluribus unum" mean and what meaning does it have for the United States today?

5. **PEOPLE TO KNOW** Who is **Daniel Inouye** and what has he done in public life?

6. **CRITICAL THINKING: Synthesize** What are some contributions immigrants make to United States society?

7. **CRITICAL THINKING: Decision Making** What were the effects of the government's decision in 1965 to change immigration laws?

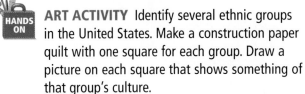

ART ACTIVITY Identify several ethnic groups in the United States. Make a construction paper quilt with one square for each group. Draw a picture on each square that shows something of that group's culture.

In America

★ ★ ★

What is the experience of immigrants or their children in the United States? These poems show the points of view of people from many cultures.

What is a Green Card? To begin with, it is not green. It is the size of a driver's license and gives a person permission from the government to live and work permanently in the United States.

Speak Up

by Janet S. Wong

You're Korean, aren't you?

Yes.

Why don't you speak Korean?

Just don't, I guess.

Say something Korean.

I don't speak it.
I can't.

C'mon. Say something.

Halmoni. Grandmother.
Haraboji. Grandfather.
Imo. Aunt.

Say some other stuff.
Sounds funny.
Sounds strange.

Hey, let's listen to you for a change.

Listen to me?

Say some foreign words.

But I'm American, can't you see?

Your family came from somewhere else.
Sometime.

But I was born here.

So was I.

Green Card Fever

by Bobbi Katz

NEW AMERICANS
Coast to Coast, 1995

We come from
  Haiti,
   Nevis,
    Pakistan,
   India,
    Afghanistan—
    Romania,
   El Salvador,
  China,
  Cuba,
 Ecuador—
  Ghana,
   Mali,
    Katmandu—
   the Phillippines,
    St. Kitts,
     Peru—
      Thailand,
      Israel,
       Palestine,
      Turkey,
     Greece,
    the Levantine—
   Guatemala,
  Mexico …

We ALL know where we want to go!
Working, striving, trying hard—
  where life depends on a
   GREEN CARD!

Activities

1. **TALK ABOUT IT** Read aloud the words of each character in "Speak Up." Then discuss what it feels like to be that character.

2. **WRITE YOUR OWN** Write a poem that is a conversation between a recent immigrant and someone whose grandparents were immigrants.

Citizenship and Democracy

Build on What You Know You know that a car needs an engine to run. Democracy is the engine that keeps the United States running. The actions and choices of people in the United States give the nation and the government the power to move forward.

VOCABULARY

naturalization
register
responsibility
volunteer

Vocabulary Strategy

responsibility

Responsibility, meaning duty, is related to "respond." Citizens in a democracy must respond to their duties.

READING SKILL

Classify As you read, put information under these two category headings: Rights and Responsibilities.

Citizenship

Main Idea Living in a democracy brings rights and duties.

Being a citizen of a democracy like the United States is special. In most countries throughout history, ordinary people have had no role in their government. This is true for some countries even today. In a democracy, all people have a role. The choices they make help shape the government and culture.

One thing that is special about democracy is that its citizens have many rights. Rights are freedoms protected by law. The United States government is supposed to guarantee and protect these rights.

People who come to the United States from other countries can become citizens and vote. They go through a legal process called naturalization. **Naturalization** is the process of becoming a citizen by learning the laws of the country and the rights and duties of citizens.

A Guide to Naturalization

Studying Citizenship Immigrants going through naturalization study the laws and history of the United States using a book like this one.

Voting and Other Rights

Voting is one of the most important rights American citizens have. By voting, citizens help choose leaders and give direction to the government. At age 18, citizens can register to vote. To **register** means to sign up. Citizens also have the right to run for political office.

The Bill of Rights is made up of the first ten amendments to the Constitution. These amendments include the right to speak freely, the right to practice any religion, and the right to a fair trial in court.

Protecting Rights

The federal government protects other rights of citizens that are not listed in the Bill of Rights. These include economic rights, such as the right to own property and businesses. The government has also passed laws to protect people from discrimination in jobs and housing. For example, the Fair Housing Act says that property owners, bank officials, and others cannot discriminate against people who are buying or renting houses or apartments because of their race, religion, or other reasons.

REVIEW At what age can citizens register to vote?

Rights of Citizens

Vote
Join groups of your choice
Express opinions freely
Practice religion of choice
Have a fair trial
Own property and businesses
Not be discriminated against in jobs and housing

Naturalization Ceremony These immigrants are about to become United States citizens. When they do, they will enjoy all the rights listed in the chart to the left.

Responsibilities of Citizens

Personal	Civic
These actions improve your life and the lives of others.	These actions help make a democratic system work.
Educate yourself	Vote
Respect others	Obey laws
Help in your community	Pay taxes
Set a good example	Serve on juries

Two Kinds of Duties
It should be up to citizens to improve their own lives and the lives of others. They must also work to preserve the government.

SKILL Reading Charts
What kind of responsibility is paying taxes?

Citizens' Responsibilities

Main Idea Citizens in a democracy have important responsibilities.

In the United States, citizens have a lot of freedom. That does not mean people can do anything they want. Along with rights, citizens also have a responsibility to the country. A **responsibility** is a duty that someone is expected to fulfill.

In a democracy, it is up to the people to create an orderly and caring society. Representatives of the people write the nation's laws. Everyone must then obey the laws. When people obey laws, they help build a safe community. When they disobey laws, they often hurt others and make the community a dangerous place. Obeying the law is an important duty that puts the common good of the country first.

Paying taxes is another important responsibility. Taxes help our government pay for public goods and services. These goods and services include public parks, police, firefighters, roads, and many others. Citizens also have responsibilities to serve on juries in law courts and to vote. Men over the age of 18 have the responsibility of registering for the military.

Responsibilities of Young People

Young people have responsibilities as citizens, too. They are expected to go to school. The knowledge that students gain in school helps prepare them to make thoughtful decisions about public issues and to be good citizens.

Every day, government officials make decisions about issues such as safety, pollution, and schools. Citizens cannot expect their government to do everything, however. Ordinary people can also do their part by becoming volunteers. A **volunteer** helps other people without being paid. Volunteers help make their communities better places to live.

Young people can volunteer in hundreds of ways. For example, a third-grade class in Maryland collects gifts for children who need to stay at the local hospital. Leslie Lenkowsky, who is the leader of the Corporation for National and Community Service, said:

66 Organizations of every type in every community depend on the time and talent of volunteers. 99

Preserving Democracy

The future of the United States depends on the strength of its democracy. In a democracy, all citizens have a responsibility to be involved in the life of their communities and country. Some citizens do this by becoming active in politics. Other citizens vote, stay informed about issues, or run for political office.

Speaking Out Even before young people can vote, they can express their opinions to political leaders.

Being informed helps young people make good choices when, as adults, it comes time to vote. In big and small ways, each person can contribute to democracy and make the United States a better country.

REVIEW In what ways can learning about issues prepare young people to be good citizens?

Lesson Summary

- Being a citizen of a democracy means having rights and responsibilities.
- The Bill of Rights lists many of the rights United States citizens have.
- Citizens also have responsibilities to help create an orderly, caring society.
- Even though they cannot vote, young people have responsibilities to their communities and country.

Why It Matters ...

Good citizenship is necessary for a strong country and for safe communities.

Lesson Review

❶ **VOCABULARY** Use **naturalization** and **register** in a paragraph. Explain why these terms are important for citizenship.

❷ 📝 **READING SKILL** Use your notes to explain how citizens' responsibilities help preserve democracy.

❸ **MAIN IDEA: Government** In what way are taxes used to help maintain a democracy?

❹ **MAIN IDEA: Citizenship** Why is obeying the law important for the common good?

❺ **FACTS TO REMEMBER** What part of the Constitution lists many of the rights of United States citizens?

❻ **CRITICAL THINKING: Fact and opinion** Is it fact or opinion that government protects the rights of citizens? Give reasons for your answer.

❼ **CRITICAL THINKING: Draw Conclusions** Why is it important for citizens to vote?

✏️ **CITIZENSHIP ACTIVITY** Write a personal essay explaining why it is necessary for citizens to be involved in their communities.

Citizen Sara

What rights and responsibilities go along with being a citizen? Sara has just turned 18; now she can **register** to vote. Her brother Will goes to Town Hall with her, and they see examples of democracy in action.

TV Reporter

Characters

Sara: age 18

Will: her brother, age 10

Supporter #1

Supporter #2

Supporter #3

TV Reporter

Senior Citizen

Frankie: Will's friend, age 11

Lisa: Will's friend, age 10

Mr. Addison: the principal of Will's school

Town Clerk

Petitioner

Senior
Citizen

Sara: I am so excited, Will.

Will: You already told me.

Sara: I know, but I have to say it again. I'm on my way to register to vote for the first time! I can't believe it!

Will: I can't believe I agreed to come along just to take your picture.

Sara: It's history! A photo for my scrapbook.

Will: Hey, what's happening over there?

Supporters: (*chanting*) More money for schools! More money for schools!

Sara: Oh, this must be about Question 3 that the town will be voting on.

Supporter #1: Say "yes" to raising more money for our schools!

Supporter #2: Say "yes" to keeping programs such as Art and Spanish!

Supporter #3: Say "yes" to a better education for our kids!

Will: Look, a TV reporter is interviewing someone. (*He takes a picture.*)

TV Reporter: What is your opinion about Question 3?

Senior Citizen: I don't like to lose those programs. But if the vote is yes, the town is going to raise our taxes again! Some of us can't afford to pay more taxes.

Will: We'd better go, Sara. The clerk's office closes in a half hour.

Sara: That's why being a citizen is great. Each of us gets to express our opinion. I guess I'd better find out more about Question 3. I want to make a good decision when I vote on it next month.

Will: Let's cut through Ames Park. It's faster.

Sara: Okay. Hey, look at all those people in the park. What's going on?

Frankie: Yo, Will! Did you forget?

Lisa: Today is "Keep Ames Park Beautiful Day!"

Mr. Addison: That's right. It's our big **volunteer** cleanup effort.

Sara: Wow! It looks like a lot of townspeople turned out today.

Mr. Addison: The more the merrier, Sara! Are you two going to join us?

Will: Uh…sure! Look, I even brought my camera!

Mr. Addison

Sara

Will

Sara: But first he has to take my picture. I'm on my way to register to vote.

Mr. Addison: Good for you, Sara! We'll see both of you later.

Will: There's no escaping now.

Sara: Oh, come on. It feels good when you give your time to make your community better.

Will: I know. I'm just kidding. Look, here we are at Town Hall.

Frankie

Sara: The town clerk's office is through this door.

Town Clerk: Hello, can I help you?

Sara: Yes, please! I'm here to register to vote.

Town Clerk: May I see your identification? Fill out this form and sign at the bottom.

Will: (*Taking their picture*) Say cheese!

Town Clerk: You're all set, Sara. Now remember—and I tell this to everyone— a vote is a citizen's most powerful tool. Use it well.

Sara: I will, starting next month!

Will: Congratulations, sis. I have to say, I'm a little envious. (*They walk outside.*)

Petitioner: Excuse me, would you mind signing our petition? We want to convince the town government to put a stoplight at Elm and South Streets.

Will: I'll sign that petition!

Sara: That's the spirit, Citizen Will.

Will: Thanks, Citizen Sara. Now let's go clean up the park.

Activities

1. **TALK ABOUT IT** How do Sara and Will show their sense of responsibility?

2. **WRITE ABOUT IT** As a citizen, what issues do you care about? Choose a national or local issue and write a letter to a government official about it.

705

Visual Summary

1.–3. Write a description for the three topics named below.

Life in the United States	
NAFTA **Trade with Canada and Mexico**	
Diverse Population	
Rights and Responsibilities	

Facts and Main Ideas

✓ **TEST PREP** Answer each question with information from the chapter.

4. **History** What effect did the 1965 immigration laws have on immigration to the United States?

5. **Citizenship** What are two rights and two responsibilities that citizens of the United States have?

6. **History** Which European nation controlled Mexico until 1821?

7. **Citizenship** Why is the diversity of the United States one of its strengths?

8. **Economics** Which nations signed NAFTA?

Vocabulary

✓ **TEST PREP** Choose the correct word from the list below to complete each sentence.

province, p. 682
refugee, p. 692
register, p. 698

9. A person who escapes war and seeks safety in another country is a _____.

10. When U.S. citizens turn 18, they can _____ to vote.

11. Quebec is a _____ of Canada where French influence is still strong.

1821
Mexico's independence

1867
Canada's independence

1992
NAFTA

1800   1850   1900   1950   2000

Apply Skills

✓ **TEST PREP** **Citizenship Skill** Read the paragraph below and use what you have learned about resolving conflicts to answer each question.

> Rivers are part of the border between the United States and Mexico. Floods and pollution affect cities in both countries. The International Boundary and Water Commission works in both countries to prevent floods and to build sewage treatment plants. By cooperating, the countries make sure they both have clean water.

12. What issue might cause conflict between the United States and Mexico?

A. Floods and pollution affect the United States.

B. Floods and pollution affect both countries.

C. Floods and pollution affect neither country.

D. Sewage treatment plants are too expensive to run.

13. Why is an international organization a good way to resolve a conflict?

A. It does what is best for the United States.

B. It does what is best for Mexico.

C. It does what is best for both countries.

D. It does what is best for the world.

Critical Thinking

✓ **TEST PREP** Write a short paragraph to answer each question.

14. **Compare and Contrast** How are the United States and Canada alike and different?

15. **Synthesize** What role does government play in guarding the rights of citizens?

Timeline

Use the Chapter Summary Timeline above to answer the question.

16. Which country gained independence first, Canada or Mexico?

Activities

Citizenship Activity Find out about contributions that an ethnic group has made to life in the United States. Look at topics such as customs, holidays, and music. Then create an information sheet.

Writing Activity Write a personal narrative about a time when you met your responsibilities as a citizen. You may wish to describe your work as a volunteer.

Technology
Writing Process Tips
Get help with your essay at
www.eduplace.com/kids/hmss05/

Vocabulary and Main Ideas

✔ **TEST PREP** Write a sentence to answer each question.

1. Why did **migrant workers** and other groups fight for their rights in the 1970s?

2. What effect did **free-trade agreements** have on the U.S. economy in the 1990s?

3. Why did the **popular vote** and the **Electoral College** vote create a conflict in the 2000 presidential election?

4. What is the **heritage** that all U.S. citizens share, and why is it important?

5. Why is it important for people to **register** to vote?

6. What rights and **responsibilities** do U.S. citizens have?

Critical Thinking

✔ **TEST PREP** Write a short paragraph to answer each question.

7. **Evaluate** Why was the end of the Cold War an important event in American history?

8. **Cause and Effect** What has been the effect of immigration on the culture of the United States? Use details from the unit to support your answer.

Apply Skills

✔ **TEST PREP** Map Skill Use the map of North and South America to answer each question about map scales.

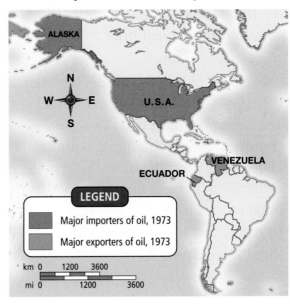

9. What can you learn from this map that you can't learn from the map of Canada on page 683?

   A. the distance from Quebec to Toronto
   B. the names of the provinces of Canada
   C. the distance from Venezuela to Alaska
   D. the oil producing provinces in Canada

10. What can you learn from the map on page 683 that you can't learn from this map?

    A. the name of the largest country in South America
    B. the names of the Great Lakes
    C. the distance from Ottawa to Mexico City
    D. the major oil producing countries in North America

Unit Activity

The Big Idea

Create a Poster for American Unity

- Brainstorm a list of beliefs, activities, and qualities that Americans share.
- Create a poster illustrating one or more items on your list.
- Write a heading and captions to go with your poster.
- Display your poster in your classroom.

At the Library

You may find these books at your school or public library.

Coming to America: A Muslim Family's Story by Bernard Wolf

What is life like for a family that has recently immigrated to the United States from Egypt?

In Defense of Liberty: The Story of America's Bill of Rights by Russell Freedman

This history of the Bill of Rights gives examples of how it applies to today's world.

CURRENT EVENTS
WEEKLY (WR) READER

Connect to Your Community

Design a volunteer project that your class can do together.

- Find articles about volunteer projects that students are doing around the country.
- Find out about issues and in your school or community. Who or what needs your help?
- Design a volunteer project to deal with the issue or help solve the problem. Present it to your class.

 Technology

Get information about volunteer projects from the Weekly Reader at **www.eduplace.com/kids/hmss05/**

Read About It

Look for these Social Studies Independent Books in your classroom.

References

Citizenship Handbook

Resources

Pledge of Allegiance

*I pledge allegiance to the flag
of the United States of America
and to the Republic for which it stands,
one Nation under God, indivisible,
with liberty and justice for all.*

Spanish

Prometo lealtad a la bandera
de los Estados Unidos de América,
y a la república que representa,
una nación bajo Diós, indivisible,
con libertad y justicia para todos.

Russian

Я даю клятву верности флагу
Соединённых Штатов Америки
и стране, символом которой
он является, народу, единому
перед Богом, свободному
и равноправному.

Tagalog

Ako ay nanunumpa ng katapatan
sa bandila ng Estados Unidos
ng Amerika, at sa Republikang
kanyang kinakatawan, isang
Bansang pumapailalim sa isang
Maykapal hindi nahahati, may
kalayaan at katarungan para
sa lahat.

Arabic

ادين بالولاء لعلم الولايات المتحده الامريكيه و الى
الجمهوريه التي تمثلها و دولة واحدة تؤمن باللة و
متحدة تمنح الحرية و العدالة للجميع

Chinese

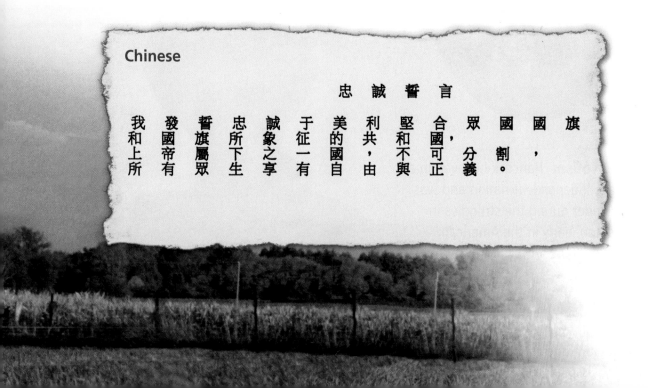

忠　誠　誓　言

旗
國
，
國
割
眾
分
義
合
國
可
正
利
共
堅
和
，
不
由
與
美
的
國
自
于
征
一
有
誠
象
之
享
忠
所
下
生
誓
旗
屬
眾
發
國
帝
有
我
和
上
所

Character Traits

Character includes feelings, thoughts, and behaviors. A character trait is something people show by the way they act. To act bravely shows courage, and courage is one of several character traits.

Positive character traits, such as honesty, caring, and courage, lead to positive actions. Character traits are also called "life skills." Life skills can help you do your best, and doing your best leads to reaching your goals.

Character Traits

Hilda Perera
Caring Perera has won many awards for her writing. Hilda Perera Day in Florida recognizes her lifelong work to bring literature to all children.

John Hancock
Patriotism Hancock believed in a new, independent nation and was a leader during the struggles in Boston, early in the American Revolution.

Courage means acting bravely. Doing what you believe to be good and right, and telling the truth, requires courage.

Patriotism means working for the goals of your country. When you show national pride, you are being patriotic.

Responsibility is taking care of work that needs to be done. Responsible people are reliable and trustworthy, which means they can be counted on.

Respect means paying attention to what other people want and believe. The "golden rule," or treating others as you would like to be treated, shows thoughtfulness and respect.

Fairness means working to make things fair, or right, for everyone. Often one needs to try again and again to achieve fairness. This requires diligence, or not giving up.

Civic virtue is good citizenship. It means doing things, such as cooperating and solving problems, to help communities live and work well together.

Caring means noticing what others need and helping them get what they need. Feeling concern or compassion is another way to define caring.

Historical Documents

Pilgrims are shown writing the Mayflower Compact while still aboard the ship.

The Mayflower Compact (1620)

"*. . . We whose names are underwritten, . . . Having undertaken, for the Glory of God, and Advancement of the Christian Faith, and Honor of our King and Country, a Voyage to plant the first Colony in the northern Parts of Virginia; Do by these Presents, solemnly and mutually, in the Presence of God and one of another, covenant and combine ourselves together into a civil Body Politick, for our better Ordering and Preservation, and Furtherance of the Ends aforesaid: And by Virtue hereof do enact, constitute, and frame such just and equal Laws, Ordinances, Acts, Constitutions, and Officers, from time to time, as shall be thought most meet and convenient for the general Good of the Colony; unto which we promise all due Submission and Obedience. . . .*"

Mr. John Carver	Mr. Samuel Fuller	Edward Tilly
Mr. William Bradford	Mr. Christopher Martin	John Tilly
Mr. Edward Winslow	Mr. William Mullins	Francis Cooke
Mr. William Brewster	Mr. William White	Thomas Rogers
Isaac Allerton	Mr. Richard Warren	Thomas Tinker
Myles Standish	John Howland	John Ridgdale
John Alden	Mr. Steven Hopkins	Edward Fuller
John Turner	Digery Priest	Richard Clark
Francis Eaton	Thomas Williams	Richard Gardiner
James Chilton	Gilbert Winslow	Mr. John Allerton
John Craxton	Edmund Margesson	Thomas English
John Billington	Peter Brown	Edward Doten
Joses Fletcher	Richard Britteridge	Edward Liester
John Goodman	George Soule	

Pitt's Speech to Parliament on the Stamp Act (1766)

"*The Americans have not acted in all things with prudence and temper. They have been wronged. They have been driven to madness by injustice. Will you punish them for the madness you have occasioned? Rather let prudence and temper come first from this side. I will undertake for America, that she will follow the example. . . .*

Upon the whole, I will beg leave to tell the House what is really my opinion. It is, that the Stamp-Act be repealed absolutely, totally, and immediately; that the reason for the repeal should be assigned, because it was founded on an erroneous principle."

William Pitt

Historical Documents

Burke's Speech to Parliament on Conciliation with America (1775)

"*The proposition is peace. Not peace through the medium of war; not peace to be hunted through the labyrinth of intricate and endless negotiations . . . It is simple peace, sought in its natural course and in its ordinary haunts. . . .*

Let the colonies always keep the idea of their civil rights associated with your government — they will cling and grapple to you, and no force under heaven will be of power to tear them from their allegiance. But let it be once understood that your government may be one thing and their privileges another, that these two things may exist without any mutual relation — the cement is gone, the cohesion is loosened, and everything hastens to decay and dissolution. . . .

Magnanimity in politics is not seldom the truest wisdom; and a great empire and little minds go ill together."

Edmund Burke

In the Declaration of Independence, the colonists explained why they were breaking away from Britain. They believed they had the right to form their own country.

Members of the Continental Congress are shown signing the Declaration of Independence.

The opening part of the Declaration is very famous. It says that all people are created equal. Everyone has certain basic rights that are "unalienable." That means that these rights cannot be taken away. Governments are formed to protect these basic rights. If a government does not do this, then the people have a right to begin a new one.

Forming a new government meant ending the colonial ties to the king. The writers of the Declaration listed the wrongs of King George III to prove the need for their actions.

Colonists said the king had not let the colonies make their own laws. He had limited the people's representation in their assemblies.

The Declaration of Independence

In Congress, July 4, 1776

The unanimous declaration of the thirteen United States of America

Introduction*

When, in the course of human events, it becomes necessary for one people to dissolve the political bonds which have connected them with another, and to assume, among the powers of the earth, the separate and equal station to which the laws of nature and of nature's God entitle them, a decent respect to the opinions of mankind requires that they should declare the causes which impel them to the separation.

Basic Rights

WE hold these truths to be self-evident: That all men are created equal, that they are endowed by their Creator with certain unalienable rights; that among these are life, liberty, and the pursuit of happiness; that, to secure these rights, governments are instituted among men, deriving their just powers from the consent of the governed; that whenever any form of government becomes destructive of these ends, it is the right of the people to alter or to abolish it, and to institute new government, laying its foundation on such principles, and organizing its powers in such form, as to them shall seem most likely to effect their safety and happiness. Prudence, indeed, will dictate that governments long established should not be changed for light and transient causes; and accordingly all experience hath shown that mankind are more disposed to suffer, while evils are sufferable, than to right themselves by abolishing the forms to which they are accustomed. But when a long train of abuses and usurpations, pursuing invariably the same object, evinces a design to reduce them under absolute despotism, it is their right, it is their duty, to throw off such government, and to provide new guards for their future security. Such has been the patient sufferance of these colonies; and such is now the necessity which constrains them to alter their former systems of government. The history of the present King of Great Britain is a history of repeated injuries and usurpations, all having in direct object the establishment of an absolute tyranny over these states. To prove this, let facts be submitted to a candid world.

Charges Against the King

HE has refused his assent to laws, the most wholesome and necessary for the public good.

HE has forbidden his governors to pass laws of immediate and pressing importance, unless suspended in their operation till his assent should be obtained; and, when so suspended, he has utterly neglected to attend to them.

HE has refused to pass other laws for the accommodation of large districts of people, unless those people would relinquish the right of representation in the legislature, a right inestimable to them, and formidable to tyrants only.

HE has called together legislative bodies at places unusual, uncomfortable, and distant from the depository of their public records, for the sole purpose of fatiguing them into compliance with his measures.

HE has dissolved representative houses repeatedly, for opposing, with manly firmness his invasions on the rights of the people.

*Titles have been added to the Declaration to make it easier to read. These titles are not in the original document.

HE has refused for a long time, after such dissolutions, to cause others to be elected; whereby the legislative powers, incapable of annihilation, have returned to the people at large for their exercise; the state remaining in the mean time, exposed to all the dangers of invasions from without and convulsions within.

HE has endeavored to prevent the population of these states; for that purpose obstructing the laws for the naturalization of foreigners; refusing to pass others to encourage their migration hither, and raising the conditions of new appropriations of lands.

HE has obstructed the administration of justice, by refusing his assent to laws for establishing judiciary powers.

HE has made judges dependent on his will alone, for the tenure of their offices, and the amount of payment of their salaries.

HE has erected a multitude of new offices, and sent hither swarms of officers to harass our people and eat out their substance.

HE has kept among us, in times of peace, standing armies, without the consent of our legislatures.

HE has affected to render the military independent of, and superior to, the civil power.

HE has combined with others to subject us to a Jurisdiction foreign to our constitution and unacknowledged by our laws, giving his assent to their acts of pretended legislation:

FOR quartering large bodies of armed troops among us;

FOR protecting them, by a mock trial, from punishment for any murders which they should commit on the inhabitants of these states;

FOR cutting off our trade with all parts of the world;

FOR imposing taxes on us without our consent;

FOR depriving us, in many cases, of the benefits of trial by jury;

FOR transporting us beyond seas, to be tried for pretended offenses;

FOR abolishing the free system of English laws in a neighboring province, establishing therein an arbitrary government, and enlarging its boundaries, so as to render it at once an example and fit instrument for introducing the same absolute rule into these colonies;

FOR taking away our charters, abolishing our most valuable laws, and altering fundamentally the forms of our governments;

FOR suspending our own legislatures, and declaring themselves invested with power to legislate for us in all cases whatsoever.

HE has abdicated Government here, by declaring us out of his protection and waging war against us.

HE has plundered our seas, ravaged our coasts, burned our towns, and destroyed the lives of our people.

HE is at this time transporting large armies of foreign mercenaries to complete the works of death, desolation, and tyranny, already begun with circumstances of cruelty and perfidy scarcely paralleled in the most barbarous ages, and totally unworthy the head of a civilized nation.

HE has constrained our fellow-citizens, taken captive on the high seas, to bear arms against their country, to become the executioners of their friends and brethren, or to fall themselves by their hands.

The king had made colonial assemblies meet at unusual times and places. This made going to assembly meetings hard for colonial representatives.

In some cases the king stopped the assembly from meeting at all.

The king tried to stop people from moving to the colonies and into new western lands.

The king prevented the colonies from choosing their own judges. Instead, he sent over judges who depended on him for their jobs and pay.

The king kept British soldiers in the colonies, even though the colonists had not asked for them.

King George III

The king and Parliament had taxed the colonists without their consent. This was one of the most important reasons the colonists were angry at Britain.

The colonists felt that the king had waged war on them.

The king had hired German soldiers and sent them to the colonies to keep order.

British soldiers became a symbol of British misrule to many colonists.

The colonists said that they had asked the king to change his policies, but he had not listened to them.

HE has excited domestic insurrections amongst us, and has endeavored to bring on the inhabitants of our frontiers, the merciless Indian savages, whose known rule of warfare is an undistinguished destruction of all ages, sexes, and conditions.

Response to the King

IN every stage of these oppressions we have petitioned for redress in the most humble terms; Our repeated petitions have been answered only by repeated injury. A prince, whose character is thus marked by every act which may define a tyrant, is unfit to be the ruler of a free people.

NOR have we been wanting in our attentions to our British brethren. We have warned them from time to time, of attempts by their legislature to extend an unwarrantable jurisdiction over us. We have reminded them of the circumstances of our emigration and settlement here. We have appealed to their native justice and magnanimity; and we have conjured them, by the ties of our common kindred, to disavow these usurpations, which, would inevitably interrupt our connections and correspondence. They, too, have been deaf to the voice of justice and of consanguinity. We must, therefore, acquiesce in the necessity which denounces our separation, and hold them, as we hold the rest of mankind, enemies in war, in peace, friends.

Independence

The writers declared that the colonies were free and independent states, equal to the world's other states. They had the powers to make war and peace and to trade with other countries.

WE, therefore, the representatives of the United States of America, in General Congress Assembled, appealing to the Supreme Judge of the world for the rectitude of our intentions, do, in the name and by authority of the good people of these colonies, solemnly publish and declare, that these United Colonies are, and of right ought to be, FREE AND INDEPENDENT STATES; that they are absolved from all allegiance to the British crown, and that all political connection between them and the state of Great Britain is, and ought to be, totally dissolved; and that, as free and independent states, they have full power to levy war, conclude peace, contract alliances, establish commerce, and do all other acts and things which independent states may of right do. And for the support of this declaration, with a firm reliance on the protection of Divine Providence, we mutually pledge to each other our lives, our fortunes, and our sacred honor.

The signers pledged their lives to the support of this Declaration. The Continental Congress ordered copies of the Declaration of Independence to be sent to all the states and to the army.

Congress ordered copies of the Declaration of Independence to be sent to all the states and to the army.

NEW HAMPSHIRE
Josiah Bartlett
William Whipple
Matthew Thornton

MASSACHUSETTS
John Hancock
John Adams
Samuel Adams
Robert Treat Paine
Elbridge Gerry

NEW YORK
William Floyd
Philip Livingston
Francis Lewis
Lewis Morris

RHODE ISLAND
Stephen Hopkins
William Ellery

NEW JERSEY
Richard Stockton
John Witherspoon
Francis Hopkinson
John Hart
Abraham Clark

PENNSYLVANIA
Robert Morris
Benjamin Rush
Benjamin Franklin
John Morton
George Clymer
James Smith
George Taylor
James Wilson
George Ross

DELAWARE
Caesar Rodney
George Read
Thomas McKean

MARYLAND
Samuel Chase
William Paca
Thomas Stone
Charles Carroll
of Carrollton

NORTH CAROLINA
Willam Hooper
Joseph Hewes
John Penn

VIRGINIA
George Wythe
Richard Henry Lee
Thomas Jefferson
Benjamin Harrison
Thomas Nelson, Jr.
Francis Lightfoot Lee
Carter Braxton

SOUTH CAROLINA
Edward Rutledge
Thomas Heyward, Jr.
Thomas Lynch, Jr.
Arthur Middleton

CONNECTICUT
Roger Sherman
Samuel Huntington
William Williams
Oliver Wolcott

GEORGIA
Button Gwinnett
Lyman Hall
George Walton

The Constitution of the United States

Preamble*

We the people of the United States, in order to form a more perfect Union, establish justice, insure domestic tranquility, provide for the common defense, promote the general welfare, and secure the blessings of liberty to ourselves and our posterity, do ordain and establish this Constitution for the United States of America.

ARTICLE I
Legislative Branch

SECTION 1. CONGRESS

All legislative powers herein granted shall be vested in a Congress of the United States, which shall consist of a Senate and House of Representatives.

SECTION 2. HOUSE OF REPRESENTATIVES

1. **Election and Term of Members** The House of Representatives shall be composed of members chosen every second year by the people of the several States, and the electors in each State shall have the qualifications requisite for electors of the most numerous branch of the State Legislature.

2. **Qualifications** No person shall be a representative who shall not have attained to the age of twenty-five years, and been seven years a citizen of the United States, and who shall not, when elected, be an inhabitant of that State in which he shall be chosen.

3. **Number of Representatives per State** Representatives ~~and direct taxes~~** shall be apportioned among the several States which may be included within this Union, according to their respective numbers, ~~which shall be determined by adding to the whole number of free persons, including those bound to service for a term of years, and excluding Indians not taxed, three fifths of all other persons.~~ The actual enumeration shall be made within three years after the first meeting of the Congress of the United States, and within every subsequent term of ten years, in such manner as they shall by law direct. The number of representatives shall not exceed one for every thirty thousand, but each State shall have at least one representative; ~~and until such enumeration shall be made, the State of New Hampshire shall be entitled to choose three, Massachusetts eight, Rhode Island and Providence Plantations one, Connecticut five, New York six, New Jersey four, Pennsylvania eight, Delaware one, Maryland six, Virginia ten, North Carolina five, South Carolina five, and Georgia three.~~

4. **Vacancies** When vacancies happen in the representation from any State, the executive authority thereof shall issue writs of election to fill such vacancies.

5. **Special Powers** The House of Representatives shall choose their speaker and other officers; and shall have the sole power of impeachment.

*The titles of the Preamble, and of each article, section, clause, and amendment have been added to make the Constitution easier to read. These titles are not in the original document.

**Parts of the Constitution have been crossed out to show that they are not in force any more. They have been changed by amendments or they no longer apply.

Preamble The Preamble, or introduction, states the purposes of the Constitution. The writers wanted to strengthen the national government and give the nation a more solid foundation. The Preamble makes it clear that it is the people of the United States who have the power to establish or change a government.

Congress Section 1 gives Congress the power to make laws. Congress has two parts, the House of Representatives and the Senate.

Election and Team Members Citizens elect the members of the House of Representatives every two years.

Qualifications Representatives must be at least 25 years old. They must have been United States citizens for at least seven years. They also must live in the state they represent.

Number of Representatives per State The number of representatives each state has is based on its population. The biggest states have the most representatives. Each state must have at least one representative. An enumeration, or census, must be taken every 10 years to find out a state's population. The number of representatives in the House is now fixed at 435.

George Washington watches delegates sign the Constitution.

Americans often use voting machines on election day.

Number, Term, and Selection of Members In each state, citizens elect two members of the Senate. This gives all states, whether big or small, equal power in the Senate. Senators serve six year terms. Originally, state legislatures chose the senators for their states. Today, however, people elect their senators directly. The Seventeenth Amendment made this change in 1913.

Qualifications Senators must be at least 30 years old and United States citizens for at least nine years. Like representatives, they must live in the state they represent.

President of the Senate The Vice President of the United States acts as the President, or chief officer, of the Senate. The Vice President votes only in cases of a tie.

Impeachment Trials If the House of Representatives impeaches, or charges, an official with a crime, the Senate holds a trial. If two-thirds of the senators find the official guilty, then the person is removed from office. The only President ever impeached was Andrew Johnson in 1868. He was found not guilty.

Election of Congress Each state decides where and when to hold elections. Today congressional elections are held in even-numbered years, on the Tuesday after the first Monday in November.

Annual Sessions The Constitution requires Congress to meet at least once a year. In 1933, the 20th Amendment made January 3rd the day for beginning a regular session of Congress.

Organization A quorum is the smallest number of members that must be present for an organization to hold a meeting. For each house of Congress, this number is the majority, or more than one-half, of its members.

SECTION 3. SENATE

1. *Number, Term, and Selection of Members* The Senate of the United States shall be composed of two senators from each State, chosen by the Legislature thereof, for six years; and each Senator shall have one vote.

2. *Overlapping Terms and Filling Vacancies* Immediately after they shall be assembled in consequence of the first election, they shall be divided as equally as may be into three classes. ~~The seats of the senators of the first class shall be vacated at the expiration of the second year, of the second class at the expiration of the fourth year, and of the third class at the expiration of the sixth year, so~~ that one-third may be chosen every second year; ~~and if vacancies happen by resignation, or otherwise, during the recess of the legislature of any State, the executive thereof may make temporary appointments until the next meeting of the legislature, which shall then fill such vacancies.~~

3. *Qualifications* No person shall be a senator who shall not have attained to the age of thirty years, and been nine years a citizen of the United States, and who shall not, when elected, be an inhabitant of that State for which he shall be chosen.

4. *President of the Senate* The Vice President of the United States shall be President of the Senate, but shall have no vote, unless they be equally divided.

5. *Other Officers* The Senate shall choose their other officers, and also a President pro tempore, in the absence of the Vice President, or when he shall exercise the office of the President of the United States.

6. *Impeachment Trials* The Senate shall have the sole power to try all impeachments. When sitting for that purpose, they shall be on oath or affirmation. When the President of the United States is tried, the Chief Justice shall preside: and no person shall be convicted without the concurrence of two-thirds of the members present.

7. *Penalties* Judgment in cases of impeachment shall not extend further than to removal from office, and disqualification to hold and enjoy any office of honor, trust, or profit under the United States: but the party convicted shall nevertheless be liable and subject to indictment, trial, judgement and punishment, according to law.

SECTION 4. ELECTIONS AND MEETINGS

1. *Election of Congress* The times, places and manner of holding elections for senators and representatives, shall be prescribed in each State by the legislature thereof; but the Congress may at any time by law make or alter such regulations, except as to the places of choosing Senators.

2. *Annual Sessions* The Congress shall assemble at least once in every year, ~~and such meeting shall be on the first Monday in December,~~ unless they shall by law appoint a different day.

SECTION 5. RULES OF PROCEDURE

1. *Organization* Each house shall be the judge of the elections, returns and qualifications of its own members, and a majority of each shall constitute a quorum to do business; but a smaller number may adjourn from day to day, and may be authorized to compel the attendance of absent members, in such manner, and under such penalties as each house may provide.

2. **Rules** *Each house may determine the rules of its proceedings, punish its members for disorderly behavior, and, with the concurrence of two-thirds, expel a member.*

3. **Journal** *Each house shall keep a journal of its proceedings, and from time to time publish the same, excepting such parts as may in their judgement require secrecy; and the yeas and nays of the members of either house on any question shall, at the desire of one-fifth of those present, be entered on the journal.*

4. **Adjournment** *Neither house, during the session of Congress, shall, without the consent of the other, adjourn for more than three days, nor to any other place than that in which the two houses shall be sitting.*

SECTION 6. PRIVILEGES AND RESTRICTIONS

1. **Pay and Protection** *The senators and representatives shall receive a compensation for their services, to be ascertained by law, and paid out of the treasury of the United States. They shall in all cases, except treason, felony and breach of the peace, be privileged from arrest during their attendance at the session of their respective houses, and in going to and returning from the same; and for any speech or debate in either house, they shall not be questioned in any other place.*

2. **Restrictions** *No senator or representative shall, during the time for which he was elected, be appointed to any civil office under the authority of the United States, which shall have been created, or the emoluments whereof shall have been increased during such time; and no person holding any office under the United States, shall be a member of either house during his continuance in office.*

SECTION 7. MAKING LAWS

1. **Tax Bills** *All bills for raising revenue shall originate in the House of Representatives; but the Senate may propose or concur with amendments as on other bills.*

2. **Passing a Law** *Every bill which shall have passed the House of Representatives and the Senate, shall, before it became a law, be presented to the President of the United States; if he approve, he shall sign it, but if not, he shall return it, with his objections, to that house in which it shall have originated, who shall enter the objections at large on their journal, and proceed to reconsider it. If after such reconsideration two-thirds of that house shall agree to pass the bill, it shall be sent, together with the objections, to the other house, by which it shall likewise be reconsidered, and if approved by two-thirds of that house, it shall become a law. But in all such cases the votes of both houses shall be determined by yeas and nays, and the names of the persons voting for and against the bill shall be entered on the journal of each house respectively. If any bill shall not be returned by the president within ten days (Sundays excepted) after it shall have been presented to him, the same shall be a law, in like manner as if he had signed it, unless the Congress by their adjournment prevent its return, in which case it shall not be a law.*

3. **Orders and Resolutions** *Every order, resolution, or vote to which the concurrence of the Senate and House of Representatives may be necessary (except on a question of adjournment) shall be presented to the President of the United States; and before the same shall take effect, shall be approved by him, or, being disapproved by him, shall be repassed by two-thirds of the Senate and House of Representatives, according to the rules and limitations prescribed in the case of a bill.*

Rules Each house can make rules for its members and expel a member by a two-thirds vote.

Journal The Constitution requires each house to keep a record of its proceedings. *The Congressional Record* is published every day. It includes parts of speeches made in each house and allows any person to look up the votes of his or her representative.

Pay and Protection Congress sets the salaries of its members, and they are paid by the federal government. No member can be arrested for anything he or she says while in office. This protection allows members to speak freely in Congress.

Restrictions Members of Congress cannot hold other federal offices during their terms. This rule strengthens the separation of powers and protects the checks and balances system set up by the Constitution.

Tax Bills A bill is a proposed law. Only the House of Representatives can introduce bills that tax the people.

Passing a Law A bill must be passed by the majority of members in each house of Congress. Then it is sent to the President. If the President signs it, the bill becomes a law. If the President refuses to sign a bill, and Congress is in session, the bill becomes law ten days after the President receives it.

The President can also veto, or reject, a bill. However, if each house of Congress repasses the bill by a two-thirds vote, it becomes a law. Passing a law after the President vetoed it is called overriding a veto. This process is an important part of the checks and balances system set up by the Constitution.

Orders and Resolutions Congress can also pass resolutions that have the same power as laws. Such acts are also subject to the President's veto.

Taxation Only Congress has the power to collect taxes. Federal taxes must be the same in all parts of the country.

Commerce Congress controls both trade with foreign countries and trade among states.

Naturalization and Bankruptcy Naturalization is the process by which a person from another country becomes a United States citizen. Congress decides the requirements for this procedure.

Coins and Measures Congress has the power to coin money and set its value.

Copyrights and Patents Copyrights protect authors. Patents allow inventors to profit from their work by keeping control over it for a certain number of years. Congress grants patents to encourage scientific research.

Declaring War Only Congress can declare war on another country.

Militia Today the Militia is called the National Guard. The National Guard often helps people after floods, tornadoes, and other disasters.

National Capital Congress makes the laws for the District of Columbia, the area where the nation's capital is located.

Necessary Laws This clause allows Congress to make laws on issues, such as television and radio, that are not mentioned in the Constitution.

SECTION 8. POWERS DELEGATED TO CONGRESS

1. **Taxation** *The Congress shall have the power to lay and collect taxes, duties, imposts, and excises, to pay the debts and provide for the common defense and general welfare of the United States; but all duties, imposts and excises shall be uniform throughout the United States;*

2. **Borrowing** *To borrow money on the credit of the United States;*

3. **Commerce** *To regulate commerce with foreign nations, and among the several States, and with the Indian tribes;*

4. **Naturalization and Bankruptcy** *To establish an uniform rule of naturalization, and uniform laws on the subject of bankruptcies throughout the United States;*

5. **Coins and Measures** *To coin money, regulate the value thereof, and of foreign coin, and fix the standard of weights and measures;*

6. **Counterfeiting** *To provide for the punishment of counterfeiting the securities and current coin of the United States;*

7. **Post Offices** *To establish post offices and post roads;*

8. **Copyrights and Patents** *To promote the progress of science and useful arts by securing for limited times to authors and inventors the exclusive right to their respective writings and discoveries;*

9. **Courts** *To constitute tribunals inferior to the Supreme Court;*

10. **Piracy** *To define and punish piracies and felonies committed on the high seas, and offenses against the law of nations;*

11. **Declaring War** *To declare war, grant letters of marque and reprisal, and make rules concerning captures on land and water;*

12. **Army** *To raise and support armies, but no appropriation of money to that use shall be for a longer term than two years;*

13. **Navy** *To provide and maintain a navy;*

14. **Military Regulations** *To make rules for the government and regulation of the land and naval forces;*

15. **Militia** *To provide for calling forth the militia to execute the laws of the Union, suppress insurrections and repel invasions;*

16. **Militia Regulations** *To provide for organizing, arming and disciplining the militia, and for governing such part of them as may be employed in the service of the United States, reserving to the States respectively the appointment of the officers, and the authority of training the militia according to the discipline prescribed by Congress;*

17. **National Capital** *To exercise exclusive legislation in all cases whatsoever, over such district (not exceeding ten miles square) as may, by cession of particular states, and the acceptance of Congress, become the seat of the government of the United States, and to exercise like authority over all places purchased by the consent of the legislature of the State in which the same shall be, for the erection of forts, magazines, arsenals, dock-yards, and other needful buildings;—and*

18. **Necessary Laws** *To make all laws which shall be necessary and proper for carrying into execution the foregoing powers, and all other powers vested by this Constitution in the government of the United States, or in any department or officer thereof.*

SECTION 9. POWERS DENIED TO CONGRESS

1. **Slave Trade** ~~The migration or importation of such persons as any of the States now existing shall think proper to admit, shall not be prohibited by the Congress prior to the year 1808, but a tax or duty may be imposed on such importation, not exceeding ten dollars for each person.~~

2. **Habeas Corpus** The privilege of the writ of habeas corpus shall not be suspended, unless when in cases of rebellion or invasion the public safety may require it.

3. **Special Laws** No bill of attainder or ex post facto law shall be passed.

4. **Direct Taxes** ~~No capitation or other direct tax shall be laid, unless in proportion to the census or enumeration herein before directed to be taken.~~

5. **Export Taxes** No tax or duty shall be laid on articles exported from any State.

6. **Ports** No preference shall be given by any regulation of commerce or revenue to the ports of one State over those of another; nor shall vessels bound to, or from, one State, be obliged to enter, clear, or pay duties in another.

7. **Regulations on Spending** No money shall be drawn from the treasury, but in consequence of appropriations made by law; and a regular statement and account of the receipts and expenditures of all public money shall be published from time to time.

8. **Titles of Nobility and Gifts** No title of nobility shall be granted by the United States: and no person holding any office or profit or trust under them, shall, without the consent of the Congress, accept of any present, emolument, office, or title, of any kind whatever, from any king, prince, or foreign state.

SECTION 10. POWERS DENIED TO THE STATES

1. **Complete Restrictions** No State shall enter into any treaty, alliance, or confederation; grant letters of marque and reprisal; coin money; emit bills of credit; make anything but gold and silver coin a tender in payment of debts; pass any bill of attainder, ex post facto law, or law impairing the obligation of contracts, or grant any title of nobility.

2. **Partial Restrictions** No State shall, without the consent of the Congress, lay any imposts or duties on imports or exports, except what may be absolutely necessary for executing its inspection laws; and the net produce of all duties and imposts, laid by any State on imports or exports, shall be for the use of the treasury of the United States; and all such laws shall be subject to the revision and control of the Congress.

3. **Other Restrictions** No State shall, without the consent of Congress, lay any duty of tonnage, keep troops, or ships of war in time of peace, enter into any agreement or compact with another State, or with a foreign power, or engage in war, unless actually invaded, or in such imminent danger as will not admit of delay.

ARTICLE II
Executive Branch

SECTION 1. PRESIDENT AND VICE PRESIDENT

1. **Term of Office** The executive power shall be vested in a President of the United States of America. He shall hold his office during the term of four years, and together with the Vice President, chosen for the same term, be elected as follows:

2. **Electoral College** Each State shall appoint, in such manner as the legislature thereof may direct, a number of electors, equal to the whole number of senators and representatives to which the State may be entitled in the Congress; but no

---

Slave Trade This clause was another compromise between the North and the South. It prevented Congress from regulating the slave trade for 20 years. Congress outlawed the slave trade in 1808.

Habeas Corpus A writ of habeas corpus requires the government either to charge a person in jail with a particular crime or let the person go free. Except in emergencies, Congress cannot deny the right of a person to a writ.

Ports When regulating trade, Congress must treat all states equally. Also, states cannot tax goods traveling between states.

Regulations on Spending Congress controls the spending of public money. This clause checks the President's power.

Complete Restrictions The Constitution prevents the states from acting like individual countries. States cannot make treaties with foreign nations. They cannot issue their own money.

Partial Restrictions States cannot tax imports and exports without approval from Congress.

Other Restrictions States cannot declare war. They cannot keep their own armies.

Term of Office The President has the power to carry out the laws passed by Congress. The President and the Vice President serve four-year terms.

Electoral College A group of people called the Electoral College actually elects the President. The number of electors each state receives equals the total number of its representatives and senators.

senator or representative, or person holding an office of trust or profit under the United States, shall be appointed an elector.

Election Process Originally, electors voted for two people. The candidate who received the majority of votes became President. The runner-up became Vice President. Problems with this system led to the 12th Amendment, which changed the electoral college system.

Today electors almost always vote for the candidate who won the popular vote in their states. In other words, the candidate who wins the popular vote in a state also wins its electoral votes.

3. *Election Process* ~~The electors shall meet in their respective States, and vote by ballot for two persons, of whom one at least shall not be an inhabitant of the same State with themselves. And they shall make a list of all the persons voted for, and of the number of votes for each; which list they shall sign and certify, and transmit sealed to the seat of the government of the United States, directed to the President of the Senate. The President of the Senate shall, in the presence of the Senate and House of Representatives, open all the certificates, and the votes shall then be counted. The person having the greatest number of votes shall be the President, if such number be a majority of the whole number of electors appointed; and if there be more than one who have such majority, and have an equal number of votes, then the House of Representatives shall immediately choose by ballot one of them for President; and if no person have a majority, then from the five highest on the list the said house shall in like manner choose the President. But in choosing the President, the votes shall be taken by States, the representation from each State having one vote; a quorum for this purpose shall consist of a member or members from two thirds of the States, and a majority of all the States shall be necessary to a choice. In every case, after the choice of the President, the person having the greatest number of votes of the electors shall be the Vice-President. But if there should remain two or more who have equal votes, the Senate shall choose from them by ballot the Vice-President.~~

Time of Elections Today we elect our President on the Tuesday after the first Monday in November.

4. *Time of Elections* The Congress may determine the time of choosing the electors, and the day on which they shall give their votes; which day shall be the same throughout the United States.

Qualifications A President must be at least 35 years old, a United States citizen by birth, and a resident of the United States for at least 14 years.

5. *Qualifications* No person except a natural-born citizen, ~~or a citizen of the United States at the time of the adoption of this Constitution,~~ shall be eligible to the office of President; neither shall any person be eligible to that office who shall not have attained to the age of thirty-five years, and been fourteen years a resident within the United States.

Vacancies If the President resigns, dies, or is impeached and found guilty, the Vice President becomes President. The 25th Amendment replaced this clause in 1967.

6. *Vacancies* ~~In case of the removal of the President from office, or of his death, resignation, or inability to discharge the powers and duties of the said office, the same shall devolve on the Vice-President, and the Congress may by law provide for the case of removal, death, resignation, or inability, both of the President and Vice-President, declaring what officer shall then act as President, and such officer shall act accordingly, until the disability be removed, or a President shall be elected.~~

Salary The President receives a yearly salary that cannot be increased or decreased during his or her term. The President cannot hold any other paid government positions while in office.

7. *Salary* The President shall, at stated times, receive for his services a compensation, which shall neither be increased nor diminished during the period for which he shall have been elected, and he shall not receive within that period any other emolument from the United States, or any of them.

Oath of Office Every President must promise to uphold the Constitution. The Chief Justice of the Supreme Court usually administers this oath.

8. *Oath of Office* Before he enter on the execution of his office, he shall take the following oath or affirmation:—"I do solemnly swear (or affirm) that I will faithfully execute the office of President of the United States, and will to the best of my ability, preserve, protect and defend the Constitution of the United States."

SECTION 2. POWERS OF THE PRESIDENT

Military Powers The President is the leader of the country's military forces.

1. *Military Powers* The President shall be commander in chief of the army and navy of the United States, and of the militia of the several States, when called into the actual service of the United States; he may require the opinion, in writing, of the principal officer in each of the executive departments, upon any subject relating to the duties of their respective offices, and he shall have power to

grant reprieves and pardons for offenses against the United States, except in cases of impeachment.

2. Treaties and Appointments He shall have power, by and with the advice and consent of the Senate, to make treaties, provided two-thirds of the Senators present concur; and he shall nominate, and by and with the advice and consent of the Senate, shall appoint ambassadors, other public ministers and consuls, judges of the Supreme Court, and all other officers of the United States, whose appointments are not herein otherwise provided for, and which shall be established by law: but the Congress may by law vest the appointment of such inferior officers, as they think proper, in the President alone, in the courts of law, or in the heads of departments.

3. Temporary Appointments The President shall have power to fill up all vacancies that may happen during the recess of the Senate, by granting commissions which shall expire at the end of their next session.

SECTION 3. DUTIES

He shall from time to time give to the Congress information of the State of the Union, and recommend to their consideration such measures as he shall judge necessary and expedient; he may on extraordinary occasions, convene both houses, or either of them, and in case of disagreement between them with respect to the time of adjournment, he may adjourn them to such time as he shall think proper; he shall receive ambassadors and other public ministers; he shall take care that the laws be faithfully executed, and shall commission all the officers of the United States.

SECTION 4. IMPEACHMENT

The President, Vice President, and all civil officers of the United States, shall be removed from office on impeachment for, and conviction of, treason, bribery, or other high crimes and misdemeanors.

ARTICLE III
Judicial Branch

SECTION 1. FEDERAL COURTS

The judicial power of the United States shall be vested in one Supreme Court, and in such inferior courts as the Congress may from time to time ordain and establish. The judges, both of the Supreme and inferior courts, shall hold their offices during good behaviour, and shall, at stated times, receive for their services, a compensation, which shall not be diminished during their continuance in office.

SECTION 2. AUTHORITY OF THE FEDERAL COURTS

1. General Jurisdiction The judicial power shall extend to all cases, in law and equity, arising under this Constitution, the laws of the United States, and treaties made, or which shall be made, under their authority; to all cases affecting ambassadors, other public ministers and consuls; to all cases of admiralty and maritime jurisdiction; to controversies to which the United States shall be a party; to controversies between two or more States; between a State and citizens of another State; between citizens of different States; between citizens of the same State claiming lands under grants of different States, and between a State, or the citizens thereof, and foreign states, citizens or subjects.

Treaties and Appointments The President can make treaties with other nations. However, treaties must be approved by a two-thirds vote of the Senate. The President also appoints Supreme Court Justices and ambassadors to foreign countries. The Senate must approve these appointments.

Duties The President must report to Congress at least once a year and make recommendations for laws. This report is known as the State of the Union address. The President delivers it each January.

Impeachment The President and other officials can be forced out of office only if found guilty of particular crimes. This clause protects government officials from being impeached for unimportant reasons.

Federal Courts The Supreme Court is the highest court in the nation. It makes the final decisions in all of the cases it hears. Congress decides the size of the Supreme Court. Today it contains nine judges. Congress also has the power to set up a system of lower federal courts. All federal judges may hold their offices for as long as they live.

General Jurisdiction Jurisdiction means the right of a court to hear a case. Federal courts have jurisdiction over such cases as those involving the Constitution, federal laws, treaties, and disagreements between states.

The President delivers the State of the Union address each year.

The Supreme Court One of the Supreme Court's most important jobs is to decide whether laws that pass are constitutional. This power is another example of the checks and balances system in the federal government.

Trial by Jury The Constitution guarantees everyone the right to a trial by jury. The only exception is in impeachment cases, which are tried in the Senate.

Definition People cannot be convicted of treason in the United States for what they think or say. To be guilty of treason, a person must rebel against the government by using violence or helping enemies of the country.

Official Records Each state must accept the laws, acts, and legal decisions made by other states.

Privileges States must give the same rights to citizens of other states that they give to ther own citizens.

Return of a Person Accused of a Crime If a person charged with a crime escapes to another state, he or she must be returned to the original state to go on trial. This act of returning someone from one state to another is called extradition.

Every American has a right to a trial by jury. Jurors' chairs are shown below.

---

*2. **The Supreme Court** In all cases affecting ambassadors, other public ministers and consuls, and those in which a State shall be party, the Supreme Court shall have original jurisdiction. In all the other cases before mentioned, the Supreme Court shall have appellate jurisdiction, both as to law and fact, with such exceptions, and under such regulations as the Congress shall make.*

*3. **Trial by Jury** The trial of all crimes, except in cases of impeachment, shall be by jury; and such trial shall be held in the State where the said crimes shall have been committed; but when not committed within any state, the trial shall be at such place or places as the Congress may by law have directed.*

SECTION 3. TREASON

*1. **Definition** Treason against the United States shall consist only in levying war against them, or in adhering to their enemies, giving them aid and comfort. No person shall be convicted of treason unless on the testimony of two witnesses to the same overt act, or on confession in open court.*

*2. **Punishment** The Congress shall have power to declare the punishment of treason, but no attainder of treason shall work corruption of blood, or forfeiture except during the life of the person attainted.*

ARTICLE IV
Relations Among the States

SECTION 1. OFFICIAL RECORDS

Full faith and credit shall be given in each state to the public acts, records and judicial proceedings of every other State. And the Congress may by general laws prescribe the manner in which such acts, records, and proceedings shall be proved, and the effect thereof.

SECTION 2. PRIVILEGES OF THE CITIZENS

*1. **Privileges** The citizens of each State shall be entitled to all privileges and immunities of citizens in the several states.*

*2. **Return of a Person Accused of a Crime** A person charged in any State with treason, felony, or other crime, who shall flee from justice, and be found in another State, shall on demand of the executive authority of the State from which he fled, be delivered up, to be removed to the State having jurisdiction of the crime.*

*3. **Return of Fugitive Slaves** ~~No person held to service or labor in one State, under the laws thereof, escaping into another, shall, in consequence of any law or regulation therein, be discharged from such service or labor, but shall be delivered up on claim of the party to whom such service or labor may be due.~~*

SECTION 3. NEW STATES AND TERRITORIES

1. **New States** *New states may be admitted by the Congress into this Union; but no new State shall be formed or erected within the jurisdiction of any other State, nor any State be formed by the junction of two or more States, or parts of States, without the consent of the legislatures of the States concerned, as well as of the Congress.*

2. **Federal Lands** *The Congress shall have power to dispose of and make all needful rules and regulations respecting the territory or other property belonging to the United States; and nothing in this Constitution shall be so construed as to prejudice any claims of the United States, or of any particular State.*

SECTION 4. GUARANTEES TO THE STATES

The United States shall guarantee to every State in this Union a republican form of government, and shall protect each of them against invasion; and on application of the legislature, or of the executive (when the legislature cannot be convened) against domestic violence.

ARTICLE V
Amending the Constitution

The Congress, whenever two-thirds of both houses shall deem it necessary, shall propose amendments to this Constitution, or, on the application of the legislatures of two-thirds of the several States, shall call a convention for proposing amendments, which, in either case, shall be valid to all intents and purposes, as part of this Constitution, when ratified by the legislatures of three-fourths of the several States, or by conventions in three-fourths thereof, as the one or the other mode of ratification may be proposed by the Congress; provided, that no amendment which may be made prior to the year 1808, shall in any manner affect the first and fourth clauses in the ninth section of the first article; and that no State, without its consent, shall be deprived of its equal suffrage in the Senate.

ARTICLE VI
General Provisions

1. **Public Debt** *All debts contracted and engagements entered into, before the adoption of this Constitution, shall be as valid against the United States under this Constitution, as under the Confederation.*

2. **Federal Supremacy** *This Constitution, and the laws of the United States which shall be made in pursuance thereof; and all treaties made, or which shall be made, under the authority of the United States, shall be the supreme law of the land; and the judges in every State shall be bound thereby, anything in the Constitution or laws of any State to the contrary notwithstanding.*

3. **Oaths of Office** *The senators and representatives before mentioned, and the members of the several State legislatures, and all executive and judicial officers, both of the United States, and of the several States, shall be bound by oath or affirmation to support this Constitution; but no religious test shall ever be required as a qualification to any office or public trust under the United States.*

New States Congress has the power to create new states out of the nation's territories. All new states have the same rights as the old states. This clause made it clear that the United States would not make colonies out of its new lands.

Guarantees to the State The federal government must defend the states from rebellions and from attacks by other countries.

Amending the Constitution An amendment to the Constitution may be proposed either by a two-thirds vote of each house of Congress or by a national convention called by Congress at the request of two-thirds of the state legislatures. To be ratified, or approved, an amendment must be supported by three-fourths of the state legislatures or by three-fourths of special conventions held in each state.

Once an amendment is ratified, it becomes part of the Constitution. Only a new amendment can change it. Amendments have allowed people to change the Constitution to meet the changing needs of the nation.

Federal Supremacy The Constitution is the highest law in the nation. Whenever a state law and a federal law are different, the federal law must be obeyed.

Oaths of Office All state and federal officials must take an oath promising to obey the Constitution.

ARTICLE VII
Ratification

The ratification of the conventions of nine States shall be sufficient for the establishment of this Constitution between the States so ratifying the same.

Done in Convention by the unanimous consent of the States present the seventeenth day of September in the year of our Lord one thousand seven hundred and eighty-seven and of the independence of the United States of America the twelfth. In witness whereof we have hereunto subscribed our names.

George Washington, President and deputy from Virginia

Ratification The Constitution went into effect as soon as nine of the 13 states approved it.

Each state held a special convention to debate the Constitution. The ninth state to approve the Constitution, New Hampshire, voted for ratification on June 21, 1788.

DELAWARE
George Read
Gunning Bedford, Junior
John Dickinson
Richard Bassett
Jacob Broom

MARYLAND
James McHenry
Daniel of St. Thomas Jenifer
Daniel Carroll

VIRGINIA
John Blair
James Madison, Junior

NORTH CAROLINA
William Blount
Richard Dobbs Spaight
Hugh Williamson

SOUTH CAROLINA
John Rutledge
Charles Cotesworth
  Pinckney
Charles Pinckney
Pierce Butler

GEORGIA
William Few
Abraham Baldwin

NEW HAMPSHIRE
John Langdon
Nicholas Gilman

MASSACHUSETTS
Nathaniel Gorham
Rufus King

CONNECTICUT
William Samuel Johnson
Roger Sherman

NEW YORK
Alexander Hamilton

NEW JERSEY
William Livingston
David Brearley
William Paterson
Jonathan Dayton

PENNSYLVANIA
Benjamin Franklin
Thomas Mifflin
Robert Morris
George Clymer
Thomas FitzSimons
Jared Ingersoll
James Wilson
Gouverneur Morris

Delegates wait for their turn to sign the new Constitution.

AMENDMENTS TO THE CONSTITUTION

AMENDMENT I (1791)*
Basic Freedoms

Congress shall make no law respecting an establishment of religion, or prohibiting the free exercise thereof; or abridging the freedom of speech, or of the press; or the right of the people peaceably to assemble, and to petition the government for a redress of grievances.

AMENDMENT II (1791)
Weapons and the Militia

A well-regulated militia, being necessary to the security of a free State, the right of the people to keep and bear arms, shall not be infringed.

AMENDMENT III (1791)
Housing Soldiers

No soldier shall, in time of peace, be quartered in any house, without the consent of the owner, nor in time of war, but in a manner to be prescribed by law.

AMENDMENT IV (1791)
Search and Seizure

The right of the people to be secure in their persons, houses, papers, and effects, against unreasonable searches and seizures, shall not be violated, and no warrants shall issue, but upon probable cause, supported by oath or affirmation, and particularly describing the place to be searched, and the persons or things to be seized.

AMENDMENT V (1791)
Rights of the Accused

No person shall be held to answer for a capital, or otherwise infamous crime, unless on a presentment or indictment of a grand jury, except in cases arising in the land or naval forces, or in the militia, when in actual service in time of war or public danger; nor shall any person be subject for the same offense to be twice put in jeopardy of life or limb; nor shall be compelled in any criminal case to be a witness against himself, nor be deprived of life, liberty, or property, without due process of law; nor shall private property be taken for public use without just compensation.

AMENDMENT VI (1791)
Right to a Fair Trial

In all criminal prosecutions, the accused shall enjoy the right to a speedy and public trial, by an impartial jury of the State and district wherein the crime shall have been committed, which district shall have been previously ascertained by law, and to be informed of the nature and cause of the accusation; to be confronted with the witnesses against him; to have compulsory process for obtaining witnesses in his favor, and to have the assistance of counsel for his defense.

AMENDMENT VII (1791)
Jury Trial in Civil Cases

In suits at common law, where the value in controversy shall exceed twenty dollars, the right of trial by jury shall be preserved, and no fact tried by a jury shall be otherwise reexamined in any court of the United States, than according to the rules of the common law.

Amendments to the Constitution

Basic Freedoms The government cannot pass laws that favor one religion over another. Nor can it stop people from saying or writing whatever they want. The people have the right to gather openly and discuss problems they have with the government.

Weapons and the Militia This amendment was included to prevent the federal government from taking away guns used by members of state militias.

Housing Soldiers The army cannot use people's homes to house soldiers unless it is approved by law. Before the American Revolution, the British housed soldiers in private homes without permission of the owners.

Search and Seizure This amendment protects people's privacy in their homes. The government cannot search or seize anyone's property without a warrant, or a written order, from a court. A warrant must list the people and the property to be searched and give reasons for the search.

Rights of the Accused A person accused of a crime has the right to a fair trial. A person cannot be tried twice for the same crime. This amendment also protects a person from self-incrimination, or having to testify against himself or herself.

Right to a Fair Trial Anyone accused of a crime is entitled to a quick and fair trial by jury. This right protects people from being kept in jail without being convicted of a crime. Also, the government must provide a lawyer for anyone accused of a crime who cannot afford to hire a lawyer.

Jury Trial in Civil Cases Civil cases usually involve two or more people suing each other over money, property, or personal injury. A jury trial is guaranteed in large lawsuits.

---

*The date after each amendment indicates the year the amendment was ratified.

Bail and Punishment Courts cannot treat people accused of crimes in ways that are unusually harsh.

Powers Reserved to the People The people keep all rights not listed in the Constitution.

Powers Reserved to the States Any rights not clearly given to the federal government by the Constitution belong to the states or the people.

Suits Against the States A citizen from one state cannot sue the government of another state in a federal court. Such cases are decided in state courts.

Election of the President and Vice President Under the original Constitution, each member of the Electoral College voted for two candidates for President. The candidate with the most votes became President. The one with the second highest total became Vice President.

The 12th Amendment changed this system. Members of the electoral college distinguish between their votes for the President and Vice President. This change was an important step in the development of the two party system. It allows each party to nominate its own team of candidates.

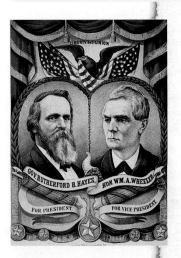

The Twelfth Amendment allowed parties to nominate teams of candidates, as this campaign poster shows.

AMENDMENT VIII (1791)
Bail and Punishment

Excessive bail shall not be required, nor excessive fines imposed, nor cruel and unusual punishments inflicted.

AMENDMENT IX (1791)
Powers Reserved to the People

The enumeration in the Constitution, of certain rights, shall not be construed to deny or disparage others retained by the people.

AMENDMENT X (1791)
Powers Reserved to the States

The powers not delegated to the United States by the Constitution, nor prohibited by it to the States, are reserved to the States respectively, or to the people.

AMENDMENT XI (1795)
Suits Against States

The judicial power of the United States shall not be construed to extend to any suit in law or equity, commenced or prosecuted against one of the United States by citizens of another State, or by citizens or subjects of any foreign State.

AMENDMENT XII (1804)
Election of the President and Vice President

The electors shall meet in their respective States and vote by ballot for President and Vice President, one of whom, at least, shall not be an inhabitant of the same State with themselves; they shall name in their ballots the person voted for as President, and in distinct ballots the person voted for as Vice President, and they shall make distinct lists of all persons voted for as President, and of all persons voted for as Vice President, and of the number of votes for each, which lists they shall sign and certify, and transmit sealed to the seat of the government of the United States, directed to the President of the Senate; the President of the Senate shall, in the presence of the Senate and House of Representatives, open all the certificates and the votes shall then be counted; the person having the greatest number of votes for President, shall be the President, if such number be a majority of the whole number of electors appointed; and if no person have such majority, then from the persons having the highest numbers not exceeding three on the list of those voted for as President, the House of Representatives shall choose immediately, by ballot, the President. But in choosing the President, the votes shall be taken by States, the representation from each State having one vote; a quorum for this purpose shall consist of a member or members from two-thirds of the States, and a majority of all the States shall be necessary to a choice. And if the House of Representatives shall not choose a President whenever the right of choice shall devolve upon them, before the fourth day of March next following, then the Vice President shall act as President, as in case of the death or other constitutional disability of the President. The person having the greatest number of votes as Vice President, shall be the Vice President, if such number be a majority of the whole number of electors appointed, and if no person have a majority, then from the two highest numbers on the list, the Senate shall choose the Vice President; a quorum for the purpose shall consist of two-thirds of the whole number of senators, and a majority of the whole number shall be necessary to a choice. But no person constitutionally ineligible to the office of President shall be eligible to that of Vice President of the United States.

AMENDMENT XIII (1865)
End of Slavery

SECTION 1. ABOLITION

Neither slavery nor involuntary servitude, except as a punishment for crime whereof the party shall have been duly convicted, shall exist within the United States, or any place subject to their jurisdiction.

SECTION 2. ENFORCEMENT

Congress shall have power to enforce this article by appropriate legislation.

AMENDMENT XIV (1868)
Rights of Citizens

SECTION 1. CITIZENSHIP

All persons born or naturalized in the United States, and subject to the jurisdiction thereof, are citizens of the United States and of the State wherein they reside. No State shall make or enforce any law which shall abridge the privileges or immunities of citizens of the United States; nor shall any State deprive any person of life, liberty, or property, without due process of law; nor deny to any person within its jurisdiction the equal protection of the laws.

SECTION 2. NUMBER OF REPRESENTATIVES

Representatives shall be apportioned among the several States according to their respective numbers, counting the whole number of persons in each State, excluding Indians not taxed. But when the right to vote at any election for the choice of electors for President and Vice President of the United States, representatives in Congress, the executive and judicial officers of a State, or the members of the legislature thereof, is denied to any of the male inhabitants of such State, being twenty-one years of age, and citizens of the United States, or in any way abridged, except for participation in rebellion, or other crime, the basis of representation therein shall be reduced in the proportion which the number of such male citizens shall bear to the whole number of male citizens twenty-one years of age in such State.

SECTION 3. PENALTY FOR REBELLION

No person shall be a senator or representative in Congress, or elector of President and Vice President, or hold any office, civil or military, under the United States, or under any State, who, having previously taken an oath, as a member of Congress, or as an officer of the United States, or as a member of any State legislature, or as an executive or judicial officer of any State, to support the Constitution of the United States, shall have engaged in insurrection or rebellion against the same, or given aid or comfort to the enemies thereof. But Congress may by a vote of two-thirds of each house, remove such disability.

SECTION 4. GOVERNMENT DEBT

The validity of the public debt of the United States, authorized by law, including debts incurred for payment of pensions and bounties for services in suppressing insurrection or rebellion, shall not be questioned. But neither the United States nor any State shall assume or pay any debt or obligation incurred in aid of insurrection or rebellion against the United States, or any claim for the loss or emancipation of any slave; but all such debts, obligations and claims shall be held illegal and void.

This etching shows a group of former slaves celebrating their emancipation.

Abolition This amendment ended slavery in the United States. It was ratified after the Civil War.

Citizenship This amendment defined citizenship in the United States. "Due process of law" means that no state can deny its citizens the rights and privileges they enjoy as United States citizens. The goal of this amendment was to protect the rights of the recently freed African Americans.

Number of Representatives This clause replaced the Three-Fifths Clause in Article 1. Each state's representation is based on its total population. Any state denying its male citizens over the age of 21 the right to vote will have its representation in Congress decreased.

Penalty of Rebellion Officials who fought against the Union in the Civil War could not hold public office in the United States. This clause tried to keep Confederate leaders out of power. In 1872, Congress removed this limit.

Government Debt The United States paid all of the Union's debts from the Civil War. However, it did not pay any of the Confederacy's debts. This clause prevented the southern states from using public money to pay for the rebellion or from compensating citizens who lost their enslaved persons.

SECTION 5. ENFORCEMENT

The Congress shall have power to enforce, by appropriate legislation, the provisions of this article.

AMENDMENT XV (1870)
Voting Rights

SECTION 1. RIGHT TO VOTE

The right of citizens of the United States to vote shall not be denied or abridged by the United States or by any State on account of race, color, or previous condition of servitude.

SECTION 2. ENFORCEMENT

The Congress shall have power to enforce this article by appropriate legislation.

AMENDMENT XVI (1913)
Income Tax

The Congress shall have power to lay and collect taxes on incomes, from whatever sources derived, without apportionment among the several States, and without regard to any census or enumeration.

AMENDMENT XVII (1913)
Direct Election of Senators

SECTION 1. METHOD OF ELECTION

The Senate of the United States shall be composed of two senators from each State, elected by the people thereof, for six years; and each senator shall have one vote. The electors in each State shall have the qualifications requisite for electors of the most numerous branch of the State legislatures.

SECTION 2. VACANCIES

When vacancies happen in the representation of any State in the Senate, the executive authority of such State shall issue writs of election to fill such vacancies: Provided, that the legislature of any State may empower the executive thereof to make temporary appointments until the people fill the vacancies by election as the legislature may direct.

SECTION 3. EXCEPTION

This amendment shall not be so construed as to affect the election or term of any Senator chosen before it becomes valid as part of the Constitution.

AMENDMENT XVIII (1919)
Ban on Alcoholic Drinks

SECTION 1. PROHIBITION

After one year from the ratification of this article the manufacture, sale, or transportation of intoxicating liquors within, the importation thereof into, or the exportation thereof from the United States and all territory subject to the jurisdiction thereof for beverage purposes is hereby prohibited.

SECTION 2. ENFORCEMENT

The Congress and the several States shall have concurrent power to enforce this article by appropriate legislation.

Right to Vote No state can deny its citizens the right to vote because of their race. This amendment was designed to protect the voting rights of African Americans.

Income Tax Congress has the power to tax personal incomes.

Direct Election of Senators In the original Constitution, the state legislatures elected senators. This amendment gave citizens the power to elect their senators directly. It made senators more responsible to the people they represented.

The Prohibition movement used posters like this to reach the public.

Prohibition This amendment made it against the law to make or sell alcoholic beverages in the United States. This law was called prohibition. Fourteen years later, the 21st Amendment ended Prohibition.

SECTION 3. RATIFICATION

This article shall be inoperative unless it shall have been ratified as an amendment to the Constitution by the legislatures of the several States, as provided in the Constitution, within seven years from the date of the submission hereof to the States by Congress.

AMENDMENT XIX (1920)
Women's Suffrage

SECTION 1. RIGHT TO VOTE

The right of citizens of the United States to vote shall not be denied or abridged by the United States or by any State on account of sex.

SECTION 2. ENFORCEMENT

The Congress shall have power to enforce this article by appropriate legislation.

AMENDMENT XX (1933)
Terms of Office

SECTION 1. BEGINNING OF TERMS

The terms of the President and Vice-President shall end at noon on the 20th day of January, and the terms of senators and representatives at noon on the 3rd day of January, of the years in which such terms would have ended if this article had not been ratified; and the terms of their successors shall then begin.

SECTION 2. SESSIONS OF CONGRESS

The Congress shall assemble at least once in every year, and such meeting shall begin at noon on the 3rd day of January, unless they shall by law appoint a different day.

SECTION 3. PRESIDENTIAL SUCCESSION

If, at the time fixed for the beginning of the term of the President, the President-elect shall have died, the Vice President-elect shall become President. If a President shall not have been chosen before the time fixed for the beginning of his term, or if the President-elect shall have failed to qualify, then the Vice President-elect shall act as President until a President shall have qualified; and the Congress may by law provide for the case wherein neither a President-elect nor a Vice President-elect shall have qualified, declaring who shall then act as President, or the manner in which one who is to act shall be selected, and such person shall act accordingly until a President or Vice President shall have qualified.

SECTION 4. ELECTIONS DECIDED BY CONGRESS

The Congress may by law provide for the case of the death of any of the persons from whom the House of Representatives may choose a President whenever the right of choice shall have devolved upon them, and for the case of the death of any of the persons from whom the Senate may choose a Vice President whenever the right of choice shall have devolved upon them.

SECTION 5. EFFECTIVE DATE

Sections 1 and 2 shall take effect on the 15th day of October following the ratification of this article.

Ratification The amendment for Prohibition was the first one to include a time limit for ratification. To go into effect, the amendment had to be approved by three-fourths of the states within seven years.

Women's Suffrage This amendment gave the right to vote to all women 21 years of age and older.

This 1915 banner pushed the cause of women's suffrage.

Beginning of Terms The President and Vice President's terms begin on January 20th of the year after their election. The terms for senators and representatives begin on January 3rd. Before this amendment, an official defeated in November stayed in office until March.

Presidential Succession A President who has been elected but has not yet taken office is called the President-elect. If the President-elect dies, then the Vice President-elect becomes President. If neither the President-elect nor the Vice President-elect can take office, then Congress decides who will act as President.

President Kennedy delivers his inaugural address in 1961.

SECTION 6. RATIFICATION

This article shall be inoperative unless it shall have been ratified as an amendment to the Constitution by the legislatures of three fourths of the several States within seven years from the date of its submission.

AMENDMENT XXI (1933)
End of Prohibition

SECTION 1. REPEAL OF EIGHTEENTH AMENDMENT

The eighteenth article of amendment to the Constitution of the United States is hereby repealed.

SECTION 2. STATE LAWS

The transportation or importation into any State, territory, or possession of the United States for delivery or use therein of intoxicating liquors, in violation of the laws thereof, is hereby prohibited.

SECTION 3. RATIFICATION

This article shall be inoperative unless it shall have been ratified as an amendment to the Constitution by conventions in the several States, as provided in the Constitution, within seven years from the date of the submission hereof to the States by the Congress.

AMENDMENT XXII (1951)
Limit on Presidential Terms

SECTION 1. TWO-TERM LIMIT

No person shall be elected to the office of the President more than twice, and no person who has held the office of President, or acted as President, for more that two years of a term to which some other person was elected President shall be elected to the office of the President more than once. But this article shall not apply to any person holding the office of President when this article was proposed by the Congress, and shall not prevent any person who may be holding the office of President, or acting as President, during the term within which this article becomes operative from holding the office of President or acting as President during the remainder of such term.

SECTION 2. RATIFICATION

This article shall be inoperative unless it shall have been ratified as an amendment to the Constitution by the legislatures of three fourths of the several States within seven years from the date of its submission to the States by the Congress.

AMENDMENT XXIII (1961)
Presidential Votes for Washington, D.C.

SECTION 1. NUMBER OF ELECTORS

The District constituting the seat of government of the United States shall appoint in such manner as the Congress may direct:

A number of electors of President and Vice President equal to the whole number of senators and representatives in Congress to which the District would be entitled if it were a State, but in no event more than the least populous State; they shall be in addition to those appointed by the States, but they shall be considered, for the purposes of the election of President and Vice President, to be elec-

End of Prohibition This amendment repealed, or ended, the 18th Amendment. It made alcoholic beverages legal once again in the United States. However, states can still control or stop the sale of alcohol within their borders.

Two-Term Limit George Washington set a precedent that Presidents should not serve more than two terms in office. However, Franklin D. Roosevelt broke the precedent. He was elected President four times between 1932 and 1944. Some people feared that a President holding office for this long could become too powerful. This amendment limits Presidents to two terms in office.

Presidential Votes for Washington, D.C. This amendment gives people who live in the nation's capital a vote for President. The electoral votes in Washington D.C., are based on its population. However, it cannot have more votes than the state with the smallest population. Today, Washington, D.C. has three electoral votes.

tors appointed by a State; and they shall meet in the District and perform such duties as provided by the twelfth article of amendment.

SECTION 2. ENFORCEMENT

The Congress shall have power to enforce this article by appropriate legislation.

AMENDMENT XXIV (1964)
Ban on Poll Taxes

SECTION 1. POLL TAXES ILLEGAL

The right of citizens of the United States to vote in any primary or other election for President or Vice President, for electors for President or Vice President, or for senator or representative in Congress, shall not be denied or abridged by the United States or any State by reason of failure to pay any poll tax or other tax.

SECTION 2. ENFORCEMENT

The Congress shall have power to enforce this article by appropriate legislation.

AMENDMENT XXV (1967)
Presidential Succession

SECTION 1. VACANCY IN THE PRESIDENCY

In case of the removal of the President from office or of his death or resignation, the Vice President shall become President.

SECTION 2. VACANCY IN THE VICE PRESIDENCY

Whenever there is a vacancy in the office of the Vice President, the President shall nominate a Vice President who shall take office upon confirmation by a majority vote of both houses of Congress.

SECTION 3. DISABILITY OF THE PRESIDENT

Whenever the President transmits to the President pro tempore of the Senate and the Speaker of the House of Representatives his written declaration that he is unable to discharge the powers and duties of his office, and until he transmits to them a written declaration to the contrary, such powers and duties shall be discharged by the Vice President as Acting President.

SECTION 4. DETERMINING PRESIDENTIAL DISABILITY

Whenever the Vice President and a majority of either the principal officers of the executive departments or of such other body as Congress may by law provide, transmit to the President pro tempore of the Senate and the Speaker of the House of Representatives their written declaration that the President is unable to discharge the powers and duties of his office, the Vice President shall immediately assume the powers and duties of the office as Acting President.

Thereafter, when the President transmits to the President pro tempore of the Senate and the Speaker of the House of Representatives his written declaration that no inability exists, he shall resume the powers and duties of his office unless the Vice President and a majority of either the principal officers of the executive departments or of such other body as Congress may by law provide, transmit within four days to the President pro tempore of the Senate and the Speaker of the House of Representatives their written declaration that the President is unable to discharge the powers and duties of his office. Thereupon Congress shall decide

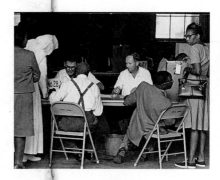

African Americans vote in Selma, Alabama, in 1966.

Ban on Poll Taxes A poll tax requires a person to pay a certain amount of money to register to vote. These taxes were used to stop poor African Americans from voting. This amendment made any such taxes illegal in federal elections.

Vacancy in the Vice Presidency If the Vice President becomes President, he or she may nominate a new Vice President. This nomination must be approved by both houses of Congress.

Disability of the President This section tells what happens if the President suddenly becomes ill or is seriously injured. The Vice President takes over as Acting President. When the President is ready to take office again, he or she must tell Congress.

the issue, assembling within 48 hours for that purpose if not in session. If the Congress, within 21 days after receipt of the latter written declaration, or, if Congress is not in session, within 21 days after Congress is required to assemble, determines by two-thirds vote of both houses that the President is unable to discharge the powers and duties of his office, the Vice President shall continue to discharge the same as Acting President; otherwise, the President shall resume the powers and duties of his office.

AMENDMENT XXVI (1971)
Voting Age

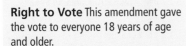

Right to Vote This amendment gave the vote to everyone 18 years of age and older.

SECTION 1. RIGHT TO VOTE

The right of citizens of the United States, who are 18 years of age or older, to vote shall not be denied or abridged by the United States or by any state on account of age.

SECTION 2. ENFORCEMENT

The Congress shall have power to enforce this article by appropriate legislation.

AMENDMENT XXVII (1992)
Congressional Pay

No law, varying the compensation for the services of the senators and representatives, shall take effect, until an election of representatives shall have intervened.

Limit on Pay Raises This amendment prohibits a Congressional pay raise from taking effect during the current term of the Congress that voted for the raise.

The voting age was lowered to 18 in 1971.

from *The Federalist* (No. 10) (1787)

The two great points of difference between a democracy and a republic are: first, the delegation of the government, in the latter, to a small number of citizens selected by the rest; secondly, the greater number of citizens and greater sphere of country, over which the latter may be extended.

The effect of the first difference is, on the one hand, to refine and enlarge the public views, by passing them through the medium of a chosen body of citizens, whose wisdom may best discern the true interest of their country and whose patriotism and love of justice will be least likely to sacrifice it to temporary or partial considerations. . . .

By enlarging too much the number of electors, you render the representative too little acquainted with all their local circumstances and lesser interests; as by reducing it too much, you render him unduly attached to these, and too little fit to comprehend and pursue great and national objects. . . .

Extend the sphere and you take in a greater variety of parties and interests; you make it less probable that a majority of the whole will have a common motive to invade the rights of other citizens.

The Star-Spangled Banner (1814)

O say, can you see, by the dawn's early light,
What so proudly we hailed at the twilight's last gleaming,
Whose broad stripes and bright stars, through the perilous fight,
O'er the ramparts we watched were so gallantly streaming?
And the rockets' red glare, the bombs bursting in air,
Gave proof through the night that our flag was still there.
O say, does that Star-Spangled Banner yet wave
O'er the land of the free and the home of the brave?

On the shore, dimly seen through the mists of the deep,
Where the foe's haughty host in dread silence reposes,
What is that which the breeze, o'er the towering steep,
As it fitfully blows, half conceals, half discloses?
Now it catches the gleam of the morning's first beam,
In full glory reflected now shines on the stream;
'Tis the Star-Spangled Banner, O long may it wave
O'er the land of the free and the home of the brave!

O thus be it ever when free men shall stand
Between their loved homes and the war's desolation!
Blest with vict'ry and peace, may the heav'n-rescued land
Praise the Power that hath made and preserved us a nation.
then conquer we must, for our cause it is just,
And this be our motto: 'In God is our trust.'
And the Star-Spangled Banner in triumph shall wave
O'er the land of the free and the home of the brave.

Francis Scott Key wrote "The Star-Spangled Banner" in 1814 while aboard ship during the battle of Fort McHenry. The gallantry and courage displayed by his fellow countrymen that night inspired Key to pen the lyrics to the song that officially became our national anthem in 1931.

John F. Kennedy was the 35th President of the United States.

from President John F. Kennedy's Inaugural Address (1961)

"*In your hands, my fellow citizens, more than mine, will rest the final success or failure of our course. Since this country was founded, each generation of Americans has been summoned to give testimony to its national loyalty. The graves of young Americans who answered the call to service surround the globe.*

Now the trumpet summons us again—not as a call to bear arms, though arms we need—not as a call to battle, though embattled we are—but a call to bear the burden of a long twilight struggle, year in and year out, 'rejoicing in hope, patient in tribulation'—a struggle against the common enemies of man: tyranny, poverty, disease, and war itself.

Can we forge against these enemies a grand and global alliance, North and South, East and West, that can assure a more fruitful life for all mankind? Will you join in that historic effort? . . .

And so, my fellow Americans: ask not what your country can do for you—ask what you can do for your country.

My fellow citizens of the world: ask not what America will do for you, but what together we can do for the freedom of man."

President Kennedy gives a speech. Jackie Kennedy is at his left.

from Martin Luther King Jr.'s "I Have a Dream" Speech (1963)

In August 1963, while Congress debated civil rights legislation, Martin Luther King Jr. led a quarter of a million demonstrators on a march on Washington. On the steps of the Lincoln Memorial he gave a stirring speech in which he told of his dream for America.

"I say to you today, my friends, that in spite of the difficulties and frustrations of the moment I still have a dream. It is a dream deeply rooted in the American dream.

I have a dream that one day this nation will rise up and live out the true meaning of its creed: 'We hold these truths to be self-evident; that all men are created equal.'

I have a dream that one day on the red hills of Georgia the sons of former slaves and the sons of former slaveowners will be able to sit down together at the table of brotherhood. . . .

I have a dream that my four little children will one day live in a nation where they will not be judged by the color of their skin but by the content of their character.

I have a dream today. . . .

. . . From every mountainside, let freedom ring.

When we let freedom ring, when we let it ring from every village and every hamlet, from every state and every city, we will be able to speed up that day when all of God's children, black men and white men, Jews and Gentiles, Protestants and Catholics, will be able to join hands and sing in the words of the old Negro spiritual, 'Free at last! Free at last! Thank God Almighty, we are free at last!'"

Historical Documents

Presidents of the United States

George Washington 1

(1732–1799)
President from: 1789–1797
Party: Federalist
Home state: Virginia
First Lady: Martha Dandridge Custis Washington

John Adams 2

(1735–1826)
President from: 1797–1801
Party: Federalist
Home state: Massachusetts
First Lady: Abigail Smith Adams

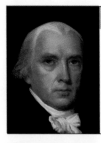

Thomas Jefferson 3

(1743–1826)
President from: 1801–1809
Party: Democratic-Republican
Home state: Virginia
First Lady: Martha Jefferson Randolph (daughter)

James Madison 4

(1751–1836)
President from: 1809–1817
Party: Democratic-Republican
Home state: Virginia
First Lady: Dolley Payne Todd Madison

James Monroe 5

(1758–1831)
President from: 1817–1825
Party: Democratic-Republican
Home state: Virginia
First Lady: Elizabeth Kortright Monroe

John Quincy Adams 6

(1767–1848)
President from: 1825–1829
Party: Democratic-Republican
Home state: Massachusetts
First Lady: Louisa Catherine Johnson Adams

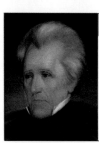

Andrew Jackson 7

(1767–1845)
President from: 1829–1837
Party: Democratic
Home state: Tennessee
First Lady: Emily Donelson (late wife's niece)

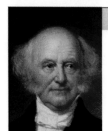

Martin Van Buren 8

(1782–1862)
President from: 1837–1841
Party: Democratic
Home state: New York
First Lady: Angelica Singleton Van Buren (daughter-in-law)

William Henry Harrison 9

(1773–1841)
President: 1841
Party: Whig
Home state: Ohio
First Lady: Jane Irwin Harrison (daughter-in-law)

John Tyler 10

(1790–1862)
President from: 1841–1845
Party: Whig
Home state: Virginia
First Lady: Letitia Christian Tyler

U.S. Presidents

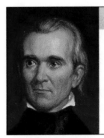

James K. Polk ⑪

(1795–1849)
President from: 1845–1849
Party: Democratic
Home state: Tennessee
First Lady: Sarah Childress Polk

Andrew Johnson ⑰

(1808–1875)
President from: 1865–1869
Party: Democratic
Home state: Tennessee
First Lady: Eliza McCardle Johnson

Zachary Taylor ⑫

(1784–1850)
President from: 1849–1850
Party: Whig
Home state: Louisiana
First Lady: Margaret Mackall Smith Taylor

Ulysses S. Grant ⑱

(1822–1885)
President from: 1869–1877
Party: Republican
Home state: Illinois
First Lady: Julia Dent Grant

Millard Fillmore ⑬

(1800–1874)
President from: 1850–1853
Party: Whig
Home state: New York
First Lady: Abigail Powers Fillmore

Rutherford B. Hayes ⑲

(1822–1893)
President from: 1877–1881
Party: Republican
Home state: Ohio
First Lady: Lucy Ware Webb Hayes

Franklin Pierce ⑭

(1804–1869)
President from: 1853–1857
Party: Democratic
Home state: New Hampshire
First Lady: Jane Means Appleton Pierce

James A. Garfield ⑳

(1831–1881)
President: 1881
Party: Republican
Home state: Ohio
First Lady: Lucretia Rudolph Garfield

James Buchanan ⑮

(1791–1868)
President from: 1857–1861
Party: Democratic
Home state: Pennsylvania
First Lady: Harriet Lane (niece)

Chester A. Arthur ㉑

(1830–1886)
President from: 1881–1885
Party: Republican
Home state: New York
First Lady: Mary Arthur McElroy (sister)

Abraham Lincoln ⑯

(1809–1865)
President from: 1861–1865
Party: Republican
Home state: Illinois
First Lady: Mary Todd Lincoln

Grover Cleveland ㉒ ㉔

(1837–1908)
President from: 1885–1889 and 1893–1897
Party: Democratic
Home state: New York
First Lady: Frances Folsom Cleveland

U.S. Presidents

Benjamin Harrison **23**

(1833–1901)
President from: 1889–1893
Party: Republican
Home state: Indiana
First Lady: Caroline Lavina Scott
Harrison

William McKinley **25**

(1843–1901)
President from: 1897–1901
Party: Republican
Home state: Ohio
First Lady: Ida Saxton McKinley

Theodore Roosevelt **26**

(1858–1919)
President from: 1901–1909
Party: Republican
Home state: New York
First Lady: Edith Kermit Carow
Roosevelt

William Howard Taft **27**

(1857–1930)
President from: 1909–1913
Party: Republican
Home state: Ohio
First Lady: Helen Herron Taft

Woodrow Wilson **28**

(1856–1924)
President from: 1913–1921
Party: Democratic
Home state: New Jersey
First Lady: Edith Bolling Galt Wilson

Warren G. Harding **29**

(1865–1923)
President from: 1921–1923
Party: Republican
Home state: Ohio
First Lady: Florence Kling Harding

Calvin Coolidge **30**

(1872–1933)
President from: 1923–1929
Party: Republican
Home state: Massachusetts
First Lady: Grace Anna Goodhue
Coolidge

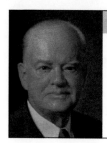

Herbert Hoover **31**

(1874–1964)
President from: 1929–1933
Party: Republican
Home state: California
First Lady: Lou Henry Hoover

Franklin Delano Roosevelt **32**

(1882–1945)
President from: 1933–1945
Party: Democratic
Home state: New York
First Lady: Anna Eleanor Roosevelt
Roosevelt

Harry S. Truman **33**

(1884–1972)
President from: 1945–1953
Party: Democratic
Home state: Missouri
First Lady: Elizabeth Virginia Wallace
Truman

Dwight D. Eisenhower **34**

(1890–1969)
President from: 1953–1961
Party: Republican
Home state: New York
First Lady: Mamie Geneva Doud
Eisenhower

John F. Kennedy **35**

(1917–1963)
President from: 1961–1963
Party: Democratic
Home state: Massachusetts
First Lady: Jacqueline Lee Bouvier
Kennedy

U.S. Presidents

Lyndon Baines Johnson 36

(1908–1973)
President from: 1963–1969
Party: Democratic
Home state: Texas
First Lady: Claudia Alta (Lady Bird)
Taylor Johnson

Richard M. Nixon 37

(1913–1994)
President from: 1969–1974
Party: Republican
Home state: New York
First Lady: Thelma Catherine (Pat)
Ryan Nixon

Gerald R. Ford 38

(1913–)
President from: 1974–1977
Party: Republican
Home state: Michigan
First Lady: Elizabeth Bloomer Ford

Jimmy Carter 39

(1924–)
President from: 1977–1981
Party: Democratic
Home state: Georgia
First Lady: Rosalynn Smith Carter

Ronald Reagan 40

(1911–)
President from: 1981–1989
Party: Republican
Home state: California
First Lady: Nancy Davis Reagan

George Bush 41

(1924–)
President from: 1989–1993
Party: Republican
Home state: Texas
First Lady: Barbara Pierce Bush

William Clinton 42

(1946–)
President from: 1993–2001
Party: Democratic
Home state: Arkansas
First Lady: Hillary Rodham Clinton

George W. Bush 43

(1946–)
President from: 2001–
Party: Republican
Home state: Texas
First Lady: Laura Welch Bush

Biographical Dictionary

The page number after each entry refers to the place where the person is first mentioned. For more complete references to people, see the Index.

A

Adams, Abigail 1744–1818, Patriot in the American Revolution (p. 266).

Adams, John 1735–1826, 2nd President of the United States, 1797–1801 (p. 241).

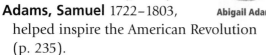

Abigail Adams

Adams, Samuel 1722–1803, helped inspire the American Revolution (p. 235).

Addams, Jane 1860–1935, social worker who founded Hull House (p. 551).

Albright, Madeleine K. 1937–, first female Secretary of State for the United States (p. 664).

Aldrin, Buzz 1930–, American astronaut; first person, with Neil Armstrong, to walk on the moon (p. 633).

Armistead, James 1748–1830, Patriot hero who spied on the British army (p. 271).

Armstrong, Neil 1930–, American astronaut; first person to set foot on the moon (p. 633).

Andreessen, Mark 1971–, inventor who developed programs allowing people to surf the Internet (p. 666).

Anthony, Susan B. 1820–1906, reformer who fought for women's rights (p. 391).

Arnold, Benedict 1741–1801, general in American Revolution; committed treason (p. 280).

Attucks, Crispus 1723–1770, former slave; killed in the Boston Massacre (p. 240).

Austin, Stephen 1793–1836, settler in Texas; supported Texas statehood (p. 394).

B

Balboa, Vasco Núñez de 1475–1519, Spanish explorer (p. 100).

Ball, Lucille 1911–1989, popular television actress and star of "I Love Lucy" (p. 622).

Banneker, Benjamin 1731–1806, helped survey Washington, D.C. (p. 323).

Barela, Casimiro 1847–1920, Mexican American who served in the Colorado State Senate for 25 years; member of the Colorado Constitutional Convention.

Bartholdi, Frédéric-Auguste 1834–1904, French sculptor who created the Statue of Liberty (p. 546).

Barton, Clara 1821–1912, nurse in Civil War; began American Red Cross (p. 461).

Begay, Fred 1932–, Navajo nuclear physicist (p. 59).

Begin, Menachem 1913–1992, prime minister of Israel who signed Camp David Accord (p. 652).

Bell, Alexander Graham 1847–1922, invented the telephone (p. 535).

Berkeley, John 1602–1678, proprietor, with George Carteret, of the New Jersey colony (p. 188).

Berry, Chuck 1926–, rock 'n' roll musician (p. 623).

Bessemer, Henry 1813–1898, English scientist; invented process to convert iron to steel (p. 536).

Big Foot ?–1890, Ghost Dancer leader captured at Wounded Knee Creek (p. 525).

bin Laden, Osama 1957–, leader of al-Qaeda organization (p. 674).

Black Kettle 1807?–1868, Cheyenne chief attacked at Sand Creek Massacre (p. 523).

Bolívar, Simón 1783–1830, helped free several South American countries from Spain.

Simón Bolívar

Bonaparte, Napoleon 1769–1821, French ruler who agreed to the Louisiana Purchase (p. 355).

Boone, Daniel 1734–1820, frontiersman who cut trail into Kentucky (p. 345).

Booth, John Wilkes 1838–1865, assassinated Abraham Lincoln (p. 473).

Braddock, Edward 1695–1755, British general; defeated during French and Indian War (p. 232).

Bradford, William 1590–1657, governor of Plymouth Colony (p. 138).

Brady, Mathew 1823?–1896, American photographer during the Civil War (p. 462).

Brant, Joseph 1742–1807, Mohawk chief who fought for the British (p. 271).

Breckinridge, John 1760–1806, supported spread of slavery; ran against Abraham Lincoln for President (p. 443).

Brown, John 1800–1859, abolitionist who led rebellion at Harpers Ferry (p. 435).

Brown, Linda 1943–, African American student who won Supreme Court decision forcing desegregation (p. 626).

Bruce, Blanche K. 1841–1898, African American planter and politician (p. 476).

Burgoyne, John 1723–1792, British general defeated at the Battle of Saratoga (p. 280).

Bush, George 1924–, 41st President of the United States, 1989–1993 (p. 658).

Bush, George W. 1946–, 43rd President of the United States, son of President George Bush (p. 672).

Cabeza de Vaca, Álvar Núñez 1490?–1557?, Spanish explorer (p. 109).

Cabot, John 1450–1499, English explorer; reached Newfoundland (p. 123).

Cabral, Pedro Alvarez 1467–1520, explorer who claimed Brazil for Portugal (p. 100).

Calhoun, John C. 1782–1850, politician who supported slavery and states' rights (p. 419).

Calvert, Cecilius 1605–1675, Catholic leader of the Maryland colony; also called Lord Baltimore (p. 203).

Campbell, Ben Nighthorse 1933–, Northern Cheyenne chief and U.S. Senator.

Ben Nighthorse Campbell

Carnegie, Andrew 1835–1919, entrepreneur in the steel industry; philanthropist (p. 536).

Carter, Jimmy 1924–, 39th President of the United States, 1977–1981 (p. 652).

Carteret, George 1610?–1680, proprietor, with John Berkeley, of the New Jersey colony (p. 188).

Cartier, Jacques 1491–1557, French explorer; sailed up St. Lawrence River (p. 123).

Carver, George Washington 1864–1943, teacher at Tuskegee Institute who used his discoveries to help farmers (p. 484).

Castro, Fidel 1926–, communist leader of Cuba who took power in 1959 (p. 614).

Catt, Carrie Chapman 1859–1947, leader of women's suffrage movement (p. 556).

Charles I 1600–1649, king of England, 1625–1649; granted charters for Massachusetts and Maryland colonies (p. 203).

Charles II 1630–1685, king of England, 1660–1685; son of King Charles I who formed Carolina and New Hampshire colonies (p. 188).

Chavez, Cesar 1927–1993, labor leader; founded the United Farm Workers Union (p. 629).

Dennis Chavez

Chavez, Dennis 1888–1962, first Hispanic American elected to the U.S. Senate.

Chesnut, Mary 1823–1886, lived in South Carolina and kept a diary during Civil War (p. 465).

Clark, George Rogers 1752–1818, captured three British forts during Revolutionary War (p. 287).

Clark, William 1770–1838, explored Louisiana Purchase with Lewis (p. 355).

Clay, Henry 1777–1852, proposed the Missouri Compromise and the Compromise of 1850 (p. 432).

Clinton, William J. 1946–, 42nd President of the United States, 1993–2001 (p. 664).

Cohan, George M. 1878–1942, American songwriter who wrote popular patriotic songs such as "Yankee Doodle Dandy" (p. 584).

Coleman, Bessie 1892–1926, aviator who became the first African American woman to earn a pilot's license (p. 589).

Columbus, Christopher 1451–1506, Italian navigator; reached the Americas (p. 96).

Cook, James 1728–1779, British sea captain who explored Australia, New Zealand, and Antarctica (p. 288).

Coolidge, Calvin 1872–1933, 30th President of the United States, 1923–1929 (p. 587).

Cooper, James Fenimore 1789–1851, novelist and historian; wrote stories about the American frontier (p. 365).

Cornwallis, Charles 1738–1805, English general in Revolutionary War; surrendered to Americans in 1781 (p. 287).

Coronado, Francisco Vázquez de 1510–1554, Spanish conquistador (p. 106).

Cortés, Hernán 1485–1547, Spanish conquistador (p. 104).

Crazy Horse 1849?–1877, Lakota chief who defeated Custer at Little Bighorn (p. 524).

Crockett, Davy 1786–1836, pioneer and member of Congress; died at the Alamo (p. 398).

Custer, George 1839–1876, army officer killed at Little Bighorn in battle sometimes called Custer's Last Stand (p. 524).

da Verrazano, Giovanni 1485–1528, Italian sea captain who explored the east coast of North America for France (p. 123).

Davis, Jefferson 1808–1889, president of Confederacy during Civil War (p. 444).

Dawes, William 1745–1799, Patriot who rode with Paul Revere (p. 251).

de Avilés, Pedro Menéndez 1519–1574, founder of St. Augustine (p. 111).

de Champlain, Samuel 1567–1635, French explorer; founded Quebec in 1608 (p. 123).

Deere, John 1804–1886, inventor of the steel plow in 1837 (p. 381).

de Soto, Hernando 1500?–1542, Spanish explorer (p. 106).

Dias, Bartholomeu 1450?–1500, Portuguese navigator (p. 93).

Dickinson, Susanna Wilkerson 1814–1883, survivor of the Battle of the Alamo (p. 399).

Dix, Dorothea 1802–1887, reformer who worked to improve care for the mentally ill (p. 393).

Douglas, Stephen 1813–1861, supported popular sovereignty; ran against Abraham Lincoln for senate and President (p. 442).

Douglass, Frederick 1817–1895, abolitionist and writer; escaped from slavery (p. 392).

Drake, Francis 1540–1596, English sea captain and privateer; leader of English naval victory against Spanish Armada (p. 124).

Du Bois, W.E.B. 1868–1963, educator who helped create the NAACP (p. 557).

Earhart, Amelia 1897–1937, aviator who became the first woman to fly across the Atlantic Ocean (p. 589).

Edison, Thomas A. 1847–1931, inventor of the light bulb, the moving-picture camera, and the phonograph (p. 535).

Eddy, Mary Baker 1821–1910, religious leader; founder of the Christian Science Church.

Edwards, Jonathan 1703–1758, religious leader; Puritan minister (p. 178).

Eisenhower, Dwight D. 1890–1969, general in U.S. Army; 34th President of the United States, 1953–1961 (p. 604).

Mary Baker Eddy

Elizabeth I 1533–1603, queen of England, 1558–1603; supported Walter Raleigh's colonization of Virginia (p. 124).

Equiano, Olaudah 1745–1797, West African taken into slavery; was freed and became abolitionist in England (p. 176).

Espey, Sarah Rousseau 1815–1898, lived in Alabama and kept a diary during Civil War (p. 446).

Estevanico ?–1539, enslaved African who traveled on Spanish explorations (p. 109).

Ferdinand 1452–1516, king of Spain who paid for Columbus's voyage to find a westward route to Asia (p. 96).

Ford, Gerald 1913–, 38th President of the United States, 1974–1977 (p. 649).

Ford, Henry 1863–1947, automobile manufacturer; made cars on assembly line (p. 586).

Franklin, Benjamin 1706–1790, printer, writer, publisher, scientist, and inventor (p. 190).

Franklin, Deborah 1708–1774, wife of Benjamin Franklin (p. 237).

Frémont, John 1813–1890, explorer of the West who helped make maps of the Oregon Trail (p. 400).

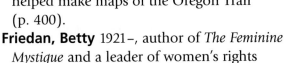

Benjamin Franklin

Friedan, Betty 1921–, author of *The Feminine Mystique* and a leader of women's rights movement (p. 655).

Fulton, Robert 1765–1815, engineer; built first profitable steamboat (p. 382).

Gagarin, Yuri 1934–1968, Soviet cosmonaut; first person to travel in space (p. 633).

Gage, Thomas 1721–1787, leader of British Army during Revolutionary War (p. 251).

Gall 1840–1894, Lakota chief who fought at Little Bighorn (p. 524).

Gálvez, Bernardo de 1746–1786, Spanish colonial administrator (p. 287).

Gama, Vasco da 1460–1524, Portuguese navigator (p. 93).

Garrison, William Lloyd 1805–1879, reformer and abolitionist (p. 425).

Gates, Bill 1955–, inventor who developed computer programs for use in homes, classrooms, and businesses (p. 666).

George III 1738–1820, king of England, 1760–1820; supported British policies that led to American Revolution (p. 204).

Glenn, John 1921–, first American astronaut to orbit the earth; U.S. Senator (p. 633).

Goddard, Mary Katherine 1738–1816, printer of the Declaration of Independence (p. 264).

Goizueta, Roberto 1931–1998, Cuban immigrant who became president of The Coca-Cola Company (p. 694).

Gompers, Samuel 1850–1924, founder of the AFL (American Federation of Labor) (p. 539).

Gorbachev, Mikhail 1931–, last president of the former Soviet Union (p. 658).

Gore, Al 1948–, Vice President under President Clinton; ran for President against George W. Bush (p. 672).

Grant, Ulysses S. 1822–1885, 18th President of the United States, 1869–1877; Union general in Civil War (p. 454).

Greene, Nathanael 1742–1786, American general in South during Revolutionary War (p. 287).

Grimke, Angelina 1805–1879, abolitionist and supporter of women's rights (p. 425).

Grimke, Sarah 1792–1873, abolitionist and supporter of women's rights (p. 425).

Gutenberg, Johannes 1400?–1468?, inventor of the printing press (p. 90).

Hale, Nathan 1755–1776, Patriot spy during Revolutionary War (p. 279).

Halvorsen, Gail 1920–, American pilot during Berlin Airlift (p. 617).

Hamilton, Alexander 1755–1804, contributor to *The Federalist;* first Secretary of the Treasury (p. 306).

Hancock, John 1737–1793, first signer of Declaration of Independence (p. 265).

Harrison, William Henry 1773–1841, 9th President of the United States, 1841–1841; defeated Tecumseh at Tippecanoe (p. 361).

Hart, Nancy Morgan 1735?–1830, Patriot (p. 272).

Hays, Mary Ludwig 1754–1832, Patriot who helped fight in the Revolutionary War (p. 272).

He, Zheng 1371–1433, Chinese explorer who traveled throughout Asia and Africa (p. 85).

Henry 1394–1460, Portuguese prince who started a school for navigation (p. 92).

Henry, Patrick 1736–1799, Revolutionary leader and orator (p. 235).

Hiawatha 14th c.–?, Onondaga who spread messages of peace among the Haudenosaunee (p. 70).

Hitler, Adolf 1889–1945, Nazi leader of Germany during World War II (p. 600).

Hooker, Thomas 1586–1647, founder of Hartford, Connecticut, in 1636 (p. 168).

Houston, Samuel 1793–1863, first president of Republic of Texas (p. 395).

Hudson, Henry ?–1611, English navigator; gave name to Hudson River (p. 124).

Huerta, Dolores 1930–, labor leader; founded United Farm Workers Union with Cesar Chavez (p. 651).

Hughes, Langston 1902–1967, poet during the Harlem Renaissance (p. 590).

Hurston, Zora Neale 1891?–1960, writer during the Harlem Renaissance.

Hussein, Saddam 1937–, former leader of Iraq (p. 659).

Hutchinson, Anne 1591?–1643, Puritan who challenged church leaders (p. 167).

Zora Neale Hurston

Inouye, Daniel 1924–, senator from Hawaii; son of Japanese immigrants (p. 694).

Irving, Washington 1783–1859, writer of humorous tales, history, and biography (p. 365).

Isabella 1451–1504, queen of Spain, 1474–1504; supported and financed Columbus (p. 96).

Jackson, Andrew 1767–1845, 7th President of the United States, 1829–1837; encouraged Western expansion (p. 364).

James I 1566–1625, king of England, 1603–1625; gave charter to Virginia Company (p. 131).

James, Duke of York 1633–1701, brother of King Charles II and proprietor of New York colony (p. 188).

Jay, John 1745–1829, contributor to *The Federalist*; Chief Justice, U.S. Supreme Court (p. 306).

Jefferson, Thomas 1743–1826, 3rd President of the United States, 1801–1809; wrote Declaration of Independence (p. 264).

Johnson, Andrew 1808–1875, 17th President of the United States, 1865–1869; impeached, then acquitted (p. 474).

Johnson, Georgia Douglas 1886–1966, African American poet during the Harlem Renaissance (p. 590).

Johnson, Lyndon 1908–1973, 36th President of the United States, 1963–1969; took office after Kennedy was assassinated (p. 628).

Jolliet, Louis 1645–1700, French-Canadian explorer; sailed down Mississippi River with Jacques Marquette (p. 147).

Joseph 1840?–1904, Nez Perce chief who tried to lead his people to Canada to escape white settlement (p. 524).

Katz, Bobbi 1933–, poet, writer, and children's author (p. 697).

Kennedy, John F. 1917–1963, 35th President of the United States, 1961–1963 (p. 596).

Kennedy, Robert F. 1925–1968, U.S. attorney general (p. 615).

Key, Francis Scott 1779–1843, writer of *Star-Spangled Banner* (p. 363).

Khan, Kublai 1215–1294, Mongol emperor in China (p. 84).

King, Martin Luther, Jr. 1929–1968, civil rights leader (p. 267).

Knight, Margaret 1838–1914, inventor of a machine that made paper bags (p. 535).

Knox, Henry 1750–1806, first U.S. Secretary of War (p. 255).

Kosciuszko, Thaddeus 1746–1817, Polish engineer who helped the Continental Army (p. 280).

Kwan, Mei-Po geographer (p. 27).

L'Enfant, Pierre 1754–1825, French city planner who designed Washington, D.C. (p. 324).

L'Ouverture, Toussaint 1743?–1803, leader of Haiti's fight for independence (p. 288).

Lafayette, Marquis de 1757–1834, French; fought in American Revolution (p. 280).

Larcom, Lucy 1824–1893, mill worker who became a well-known writer and teacher (p. 381).

La Salle, Robert 1643–1687, French explorer; claimed land around Mississippi River for king of France (p. 147).

las Casas, Bartolomé de 1474–1566, Spanish missionary opposed to slavery (p. 112).

Latimer, Lewis 1848–1928, inventor who made improvements on the light bulb (p. 540).

Lazarus, Emma 1849–1887, wrote poem that appears on Statue of Liberty's base (p. 546).

Lee, Richard Henry 1732–1794, delegate to Continental Congress (p. 263).

Lee, Robert E. 1807–1870, commander of Confederacy (p. 452).

Lenin, Vladimir 1870–1924, a founder of the Soviet Union (p. 660).

Lewis, Meriwether 1774–1809, explored Louisiana Purchase with Clark (p. 355).

Liliuokalani 1838–1917, last queen of Hawaii (p. 573).

Lin, Maya 1959–, Chinese American designer of the Vietnam Veterans Memorial (p. 637).

Lincoln, Abraham 1809–1865, 16th President of the United States; issued Emancipation Proclamation; assassinated (p. 440).

Lindbergh, Charles 1902–1974, first person to fly alone nonstop across Atlantic Ocean (p. 589).

Locke, John 1632–1704, English philosopher whose ideas inspired Declaration of Independence (p. 264).

Logan 1725–1780, Mingo chief (p. 347).

Louis XIV 1638–1715, king of France, 1643–1715; Louisiana Territory in North America was named in his honor (p. 147).

Love, Nat 1854–1921, cowboy (p. 516).

Lowell, Francis Cabot 1775–1817, built first complete cotton spinning and weaving mill in the United States (p. 380).

Ma, Yo Yo 1955–, Chinese American cellist (p. 89).

MacArthur, Douglas 1880–1964, general who commanded the UN army in the Korean War (p. 614).

Madison, Dolley 1768–1849, wife of James Madison; first lady during War of 1812 (p. 363).

Madison, James 1751–1836, 4th President of the United States (p. 303).

Magellan, Ferdinand 1480?–1521, Portuguese explorer (p. 100).

Malinche 1500?–1531, Aztec interpreter and guide for Cortés in 1519 (p. 105).

Mankiller, Wilma 1945–, Cherokee chief; first woman chief of a major American Indian nation.

Mann, Horace 1796–1859, educator who reformed public schools (p. 393).

Marion, Francis 1732?–1795, commander in American Revolution (p. 287).

Wilma Mankiller

Marquette, Jacques 1637–1675, French explorer; sailed down Mississippi River (p. 147).

Marshall, John 1755–1835, Chief Justice of U.S. Supreme Court (p. 370).

Marshall, Thurgood 1908–1993, lawyer who argued Linda Brown's case; first African American appointed to U.S. Supreme Court.

Masayesva, Victor Jr. 1951–, Hopi filmmaker and artist (p. 59).

Thurgood Marshall

Mason, George 1725–1792, Virginia delegate at the Constitutional Convention (p. 299).

Massasoit 1580–1661, Wampanoag chief who made peace with the Pilgrims (p. 138).

McCormick, Cyrus 1809–1884, inventor of a horse-drawn reaper that made harvesting wheat faster (p. 381).

McCoy, Elijah 1843–1929, inventor of the oil cup, which kept machines running longer (p. 535).

Metacomet ?–1676, American Indian leader, known as King Philip to British (p. 168).

Mink, Patsy Takemoto 1927–2002, first Asian American woman elected to U.S. Congress.

Minuit, Peter 1589?–1638, founder of New Amsterdam and New Sweden (p. 144).

Patsy Takemoto Mink

Moctezuma 1480?–1520, Aztec emperor during Spanish conquest of Mexico (p. 44).

Monroe, James 1758–1831, 5th President of the United States, 1817–1825 (p. 364).

Morse, Samuel 1791–1872, invented telegraph code called Morse Code (p. 498).

Mott, Lucretia 1793–1880, directed first women's rights convention at Seneca Falls.

Muir, John 1838–1914, conservationist who argued for preservation of Yosemite National Park (p. 555).

Musa, Mansa ?–1337, Muslim ruler of Mali empire, 1312–1337 (p. 87).

Mussolini, Benito 1883–1945, Fascist leader of Italy during World War II (p. 600).

N

Nader, Ralph 1934–, leader of consumers' rights movement (p. 651).

Nixon, Richard 1913–1994, 37th President of the United States from 1969 until he resigned in 1974 (p. 648).

North, Frederick 1732–1792, leader of the British Parliament; passed Coercive Acts (p. 242).

Novello, Antonia 1944–, first woman and first Hispanic elected U.S. surgeon general.

Antonia Novello

O

O'Connor, Sandra Day 1930–, first woman appointed to U.S. Supreme Court (p. 655).

Oglethorpe, James 1696–1785, founder of Georgia (p. 204).

Oñate, Juan de 1549?–1624?, explorer and colonizer of New Mexico (p. 111).

Osceola 1800?–1838, American Indian leader in Florida (p. 371).

P

Paine, Thomas 1737–1809, wrote *Common Sense*, urging a declaration of independence (p. 262).

Parks, Rosa 1913–, African American who refused to obey segregation laws in Alabama (p. 627).

Pei, I. M. 1917–, famous architect who emigrated from China (p. 694).

Penn, William 1644–1718, founder of Pennsylvania (p. 189).

Rosa Parks

Perry, Oliver Hazard 1785–1819, American naval captain who defeated British fleet on Lake Erie during War of 1812 (p. 363).

Philip II 1527–1598, king of Spain, 1556–1598; leader of Spanish Armada (p. 124).

Pickersgill, Mary Young 1776–1857, made the flag that inspired the *Star-Spangled Banner* (p. 366).

Pike, Zebulon 1779–1813, explorer of western frontier; founded Pikes Peak (p. 357).

Pinckney, Eliza Lucas 1722–1793, introduced growing of indigo (blue dye) in South (p. 211).

Pitt, William 1708–1778, leader of the British Parliament (p. 230).

Pocahontas 1595?–1617, Powhatan who married colonist John Rolfe (p. 132).

Polk, James 1795–1849, 11th President of the United States, 1845–1849 (p. 395).

Polo, Marco 1254–1324, Italian merchant who worked in China and wrote a book about his travels (p. 84).

Ponce de Léon, Juan 1460?–1521, Spanish explorer of Florida (p. 106).

Pontiac ?–1769, Ottowa chief; united several American Indian nations (p. 230).

Popé ?–1692, Pueblo leader who led a revolt against Spanish settlers in 1680 (p. 113).

Powell, Colin 1937–, top advisor to President George Bush and Secretary of State under President George W. Bush (p. 659).

Prescott, Samuel 1751–1777?, Patriot who rode with Paul Revere (p. 251).

Prescott, William 1726–1795, Patriot leader at Bunker Hill (p. 253).

Presley, Elvis 1935–1977, rock 'n' roll musician (p. 623).

R

Randolph, Edmund 1753–1813, U.S. Attorney General and Secretary of State (p. 304).

Rainey, Gertrude Pridgett 1886–1939, known as "Ma Rainey," considered the first great blues singer (p. 588).

Rankin, Jeanette 1880–1973, first woman elected to U.S. Congress (p. 655).

Reagan, Ronald 1911–, 40th President of the United States, 1981–1989 (p. 656).

Revels, Hiram R. 1822–1901, African American Senator during Reconstruction (p. 476).

Revere, Paul 1735–1818, rode from Boston to Lexington to warn Patriots that the British were coming (p. 241).

Rivera, Diego 1886–1957, Mexican artist whose murals decorate the National Palace in Mexico City (p. 44).

Rockefeller, John D. 1839–1937, entrepreneur and creator of Standard Oil Co. (p. 536).

Rolfe, John 1585–1622, English colonist; married Pocahontas (p. 132).

Roosevelt, Eleanor 1884–1962, fought for rights of women, children, and African Americans; wife of President Franklin D. Roosevelt (p. 594).

Roosevelt, Franklin D. 1882–1945, 32nd President of the United States, 1933–1945 (p. 594).

Roosevelt, Theodore 1858–1919, 26th President of the United States, 1901–1909 (p. 555).

Rosenberg, Anna 1902–1983, first female Assistant Secretary of Defense for the United States (p. 544).

Ross, Betsy 1752–1836, maker of flags during the American Revolution.

Ross, John 1790–1866, Cherokee chief who led the fight against American Indian removal (p. 370).

S

Sacagawea 1787?–1812, Shoshone interpreter for Lewis and Clark (p. 356).

Sadat, Anwar 1918–1981, president of Egypt who signed Camp David Accord (p. 652).

Salem, Peter 1750–1816, Patriot who fought at Battle of Bunker Hill in 1775 (p. 271).

Salk, Jonas 1914–1995, inventor of vaccine that treats polio.

Jonas Salk

Salomon, Haym 1740–1785, banker who gave Continental Army money (p. 271).

Sampson, Deborah 1760–1827, Patriot woman who fought as a soldier (p. 272).

Santa Anna, Antonio López de 1795–1876, Mexican general and president during Texas revolution (p. 395).

Scott, Dred 1795?–1858, enslaved African American who sued for his freedom (p. 434).

Seguin, Juan 1806–1890, fought for Texas independence and served in Texas state senate (p. 399).

Sequoya 1770?–1843, American Indian scholar; studied Cherokee (p. 370).

Serra, Junípero 1713–1784, Spanish priest who explored California (p. 111).

Seward, William Henry 1801–1872, U.S. Secretary of State responsible for Alaska purchase (p. 572).

Shays, Daniel 1747?–1825, led a rebellion of Massachusetts farmers (p. 298).

Shepard, Alan 1923–1998, first American astronaut to travel in space (p. 633).

Sherman, Roger 1721–1793, member of Constitutional Convention (p. 304).

Sherman, William Tecumseh 1820–1891, Union general in Civil War (p. 466).

Silko, Leslie Marmon 1948–, Laguna Pueblo writer and teacher (p. 58).

Sinclair, Upton 1878–1968, muckraker who wrote *The Jungle,* a novel about meatpacking plants (p. 555).

Singleton, Theresa archaeologist who studies slavery (p. 217).

Singleton, Benjamin 1809–1892, leader of the Exodusters who encouraged African Americans to move to Kansas (p. 508).

Sitting Bull 1834?–1890, Lakota chief; fought at Battle of Little Bighorn (p. 524).

Slater, Samuel 1768–1835, set up cotton mill in Rhode Island (p. 378).

Smith, John 1580–1631, leader of Jamestown colony (p. 131).

Squanto ?–1622?, Wampanoag who taught the Pilgrims to farm, hunt, and fish (p. 138).

Stanton, Elizabeth Cady 1815–1902, organized first women's rights conference in Seneca Falls (p. 390).

Starr, Ellen Gates 1859–1940, reformer who helped open Hull House (p. 551).

Steinem, Gloria 1934–, a leader of women's rights movement (p. 650).

Steuben, Baron Friedrich von 1730–1794, Prussian soldier; trained American soldiers for Revolution (p. 281).

Stowe, Harriet Beecher 1811–1896, author of *Uncle Tom's Cabin* (p. 434).

Stuyvesant, Peter 1610?–1672, governor of New Netherland (p. 145).

Taylor, Zachary 1784–1850, 12th President of the United States, 1849–1850; general in Mexican War (p. 396).

Tecumseh 1768?–1813, Shawnee chief; killed fighting for the British in War of 1812 (p. 361).

Tesla, Nikola 1856–1943, invented ways to create and send electricity (p. 550).

Thornton, William 1759–1828, designer of the Capitol building in Washington, D.C. (p. 325).

Truman, Harry S. 1884–1972, 33rd President of the United States, 1945–1953 (p. 613).

Truth, Sojourner 1797?–1883, abolitionist and supporter of women's rights (p. 392).

Tubman, Harriet 1821?–1913, helped enslaved African Americans to freedom (p. 427).

Turner, Nat 1800–1831, led rebellion of enslaved people (p. 417).

Van Buren, Martin 1782–1862, 8th President of the United States, 1837–1841, opposed the annexation of Texas (p. 395).

Van Lew, Elizabeth 1818–1890, spied for Union during Civil War (p. 465).

Vespucci, Amerigo 1454–1512, Italian explorer who first determined that land west of Europe was a new continent; America was named for him (p. 100).

Waldseemuller, Martin 1475?–1522, published first map in 1507 to show the American continent was separate from Asia (p. 102).

Walesa, Lech 1943–, leader of Solidarity; elected president of Poland after fall of communist government (p. 660).

Warren, Mercy Otis 1728–1814, author of political works (p. 250).

Washington, Booker T. 1856?–1915, first president of Tuskegee Institute (p. 484).

Washington, George 1732–1799, commanded Continental armies during Revolution; first President of the United States, 1789–1797 (p. 228).

Webster, Noah 1758–1843, wrote first American dictionary (p. 365).

Wheatley, Phillis 1753?–1784, African American poet (p. 272).

White, John ?–1593, leader of Roanoke colony (p. 130).

Whitefield, George 1714–1770, popular Great Awakening minister (p. 178).

Whitman, Marcus 1802–1847, missionary and pioneer in Oregon territory (p. 400).

Whitman, Narcissa 1808–1847, missionary and pioneer in Oregon territory (p. 400).

Whitney, Eli 1765–1825, inventor of the cotton gin (p. 379).

Wilhelm II 1859–1941, known as "Kaiser Wilhelm;" leader of Germany during World War I (p. 578).

Willard, Frances Elizabeth 1839–1898, president of the Women's Christian Temperance Union (p. 393).

Williams, Roger 1603?–1683, founder of Rhode Island in 1636 (p. 167).

Wilson, Woodrow 1856–1924, 28th President of the United States, 1913–1921 (p. 581).

Winthrop, John 1588–1649, first governor of the Massachusetts Bay Colony (p. 138).

Wong, Janet S. 1962–, poet and children's author (p. 696).

Wood, William 1956–, geographer for the U.S. government (p. 27).

Woods, Granville 1856–1910, inventor who made improvements to the telephone, telegraph, and streetcars (p. 535).

Wright, Dawn 1961–, oceanographer (p. 26).

Granville Woods

Young, Brigham 1801–1877, Mormon leader; settled in Utah (p. 401).

York 1770–?, African American who traveled with Lewis and Clark (p. 356).

Zedong, Mao 1893–1976, leader of communist China (p. 648).

Zenger, John Peter 1697–1746, was acquitted in landmark freedom-of-the-press trial in 1734.

Biographical Dictionary

FACTS TO KNOW
The 50 United States

ALABAMA

22nd
Heart of Dixie

Population: 4,500,752
Area: 52,423 square miles
Admitted: December 14, 1819

ALASKA

49th
The Last Frontier

Population: 648,818
Area: 656,424 square miles
Admitted: January 3, 1959

ARIZONA

48th
Grand Canyon State

Population: 5,580,811
Area: 114,006 square miles
Admitted: February 14, 1912

ARKANSAS

25th
The Natural State

Population: 2,725,714
Area: 53,182 square miles
Admitted: June 15, 1836

CALIFORNIA

31st
Golden State

Population: 35,484,453
Area: 163,707 square miles
Admitted: September 9, 1850

COLORADO

8th
Centennial State

Population: 4,550,688
Area: 104,100 square miles
Admitted: August 1, 1876

CONNECTICUT

5th
Constitution State

Population: 3,483,372
Area: 5,544 square miles
Admitted: January 9, 1788

DELAWARE

1st
First State

Population: 817,491
Area: 2,489 square miles
Admitted: December 7, 1787

FLORIDA

27th
Sunshine State

Population: 17,019,068
Area: 65,758 square miles
Admitted: March 3, 1845

GEORGIA

4th
Peach State

Population: 8,684,715
Area: 59,441 square miles
Admitted: January 2, 1788

HAWAII

50th
The Aloha State

Population: 1,257,608
Area: 10,932 square miles
Admitted: August 21, 1959

IDAHO

43rd
Gem State

Population: 1,366,332
Area: 83,574 square miles
Admitted: July 3, 1890

ILLINOIS

21st
The Prairie State

Population: 12,653,544
Area: 57,918 square miles
Admitted: December 3, 1818

INDIANA

19th
Hoosier State

Population: 6,195,643
Area: 36,420 square miles
Admitted: December 11, 1816

IOWA

29th
Hawkeye State

Population: 2,944,062
Area: 56,276 square miles
Admitted: December 28, 1846

KANSAS

34th
Sunflower State

Population: 2,723,507
Area: 82,282 square miles
Admitted: January 29, 1861

KENTUCKY

15th
Bluegrass State

Population: 4,117,827
Area: 40,411 square miles
Admitted: June 1, 1792

LOUISIANA

18th
Pelican State

Population: 4,496,334
Area: 51,843 square miles
Admitted: April 30, 1812

MAINE

23rd
Pine Tree State

Population: 1,305,728
Area: 35,387 square miles
Admitted: March 15, 1820

MARYLAND

7th
Old Line State

Population: 5,508,909
Area: 12,407 square miles
Admitted: April 28, 1788

MASSACHUSETTS

6th
Bay State

Population: 6,433,422
Area: 10,555 square miles
Admitted: February 6, 1788

MICHIGAN

26th
Great Lakes State

Population: 10,079,985
Area: 96,810 square miles
Admitted: January 26, 1837

MINNESOTA

32nd
North Star State

Population: 5,059,375
Area: 86,943 square miles
Admitted: May 11, 1858

MISSISSIPPI

20th
Magnolia State

Population: 2,881,281
Area: 48,434 square miles
Admitted: December 10, 1817

MISSOURI

24th
Show Me State

Population: 5,704,484
Area: 69,709 square miles
Admitted: August 10, 1821

MONTANA

41st
Treasure State

Population: 917,621
Area: 147,046 square miles
Admitted: November 8, 1889

NEBRASKA

37th
Cornhusker State

Population: 1,739,291
Area: 77,358 square miles
Admitted: March 1, 1867

NEVADA

36th
Sagebrush State

Population: 2,241,154
Area: 110,567 square miles
Admitted: October 31, 1864

NEW HAMPSHIRE

9th
Granite State

Population: 1,287,687
Area: 9,351 square miles
Admitted: June 21, 1788

NEW JERSEY

3rd
Garden State

Population: 8,638,396
Area: 8,722 square miles
Admitted: December 18, 1787

NEW MEXICO

47th
Land of Enchantment

Population: 1,874,614
Area: 121,598 square miles
Admitted: January 6, 1912

NEW YORK

11th
Empire State

Population: 19,190,115
Area: 54,475 square miles
Admitted: July 26, 1788

NORTH CAROLINA

12th
Tarheel State

Population: 8,407,248
Area: 53,821 square miles
Admitted: November 21, 1789

NORTH DAKOTA

39th
Peace Garden State

Population: 633,837
Area: 70,704 square miles
Admitted: November 2, 1889

OHIO

17th
Buckeye State

Population: 11,435,798
Area: 44,828 square miles
Admitted: March 1, 1803

OKLAHOMA

46th
Sooner State

Population: 3,511,532
Area: 69,903 square miles
Admitted: November 16, 1907

OREGON

33rd
Beaver State

Population: 3,559,596
Area: 98,386 square miles
Admitted: February 14, 1859

PENNSYLVANIA

2nd
Keystone State

Population: 12,365,455
Area: 46,058 square miles
Admitted: December 12, 1787

RHODE ISLAND

13th
Ocean State

Population: 1,076,164
Area: 1,545 square miles
Admitted: May 29, 1790

SOUTH CAROLINA

8th
Palmetto State

Population: 4,147,152
Area: 32,007 square miles
Admitted: May 23, 1788

SOUTH DAKOTA

40th
Coyote State

Population: 764,309
Area: 77,121 square miles
Admitted: November 2, 1889

TENNESSEE

16th
Volunteer State

Population: 5,841,748
Area: 42,146 square miles
Admitted: June 1, 1796

TEXAS

28th
Lone Star State

Population: 22,118,509
Area: 261,914 square miles
Admitted: December 29, 1845

UTAH

45th
Beehive State

Population: 2,351,467
Area: 84,904 square miles
Admitted: January 4, 1896

VERMONT

14th
Green Mountain State

Population: 619,107
Area: 9,615 square miles
Admitted: March 4, 1791

VIRGINIA

10th
Old Dominion

Population: 7,386,330
Area: 42,769 square miles
Admitted: June 25, 1788

WASHINGTON

42nd
Evergreen State

Population: 6,131,445
Area: 71,303 square miles
Admitted: November 11, 1889

WEST VIRGINIA

35th
Mountain State

Population: 1,810,354
Area: 24,231 square miles
Admitted: June 20, 1863

WISCONSIN

30th
Badger State

Population: 5,472,299
Area: 65,503 square miles
Admitted: May 29, 1848

WYOMING

44th
Equality State

Population: 501,242
Area: 97,818 square miles
Admitted: July 10, 1890

DISTRICT OF COLUMBIA

No nickname

Population: 563,384
Area: 68 square miles
Incorporated: 1802

Geographic Terms

basin
a round area of land surrounded by higher land

bay
part of a lake or ocean extending into the land

coast
the land next to an ocean

coastal plain
a flat, level area of land near an ocean

delta
a triangular area of land formed by deposits at the mouth of a river

desert
a dry area where few plants grow

▲ **glacier**
a large ice mass that moves slowly down a mountain or over land

gulf
a large body of sea water partly surrounded by land

harbor
a sheltered body of water where ships can safely dock

hill
a raised area of land, smaller than a mountain

island
a body of land surrounded by water

isthmus
a narrow strip of land connecting two larger bodies of land

lake
a body of water surrounded by land

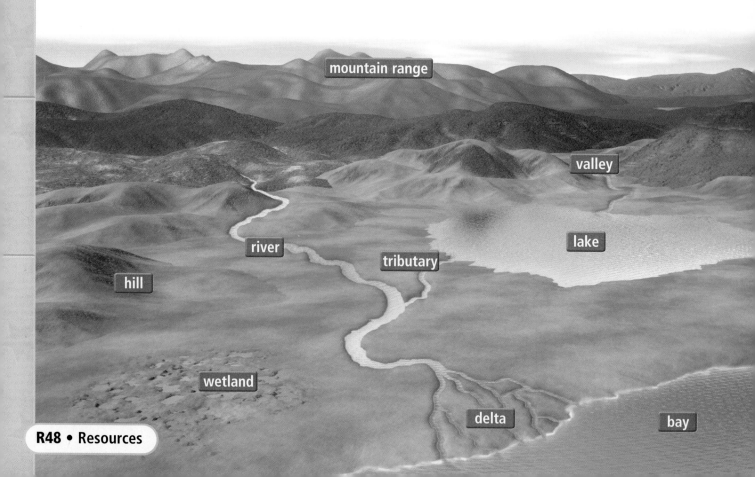

mountain range

valley

lake

river

tributary

hill

wetland

delta

bay

mesa
a wide flat-topped mountain with steep sides, found mostly in dry areas

mountain
a steeply raised mass of land, much higher than the surrounding country

mountain range
a row of mountains

ocean or sea
a salty body of water covering a large area of the earth

plain
a large area of flat or nearly flat land

plateau
a large area of flat land higher than the surrounding land

prairie
a large, level area of grassland with few or no trees

river
a large stream that runs into a lake, ocean, or another river

sea level
the level of the surface of the ocean

strait
a narrow channel of water connecting two larger bodies of water

tree line
the area on a mountain above which no trees grow

tributary
a river or stream that flows into a larger river

valley
low land between hills or mountains

volcano
an opening in the earth through which lava and gases from the earth's interior escape

wetland
a low area saturated with water

Atlas

The World: Political

ALB.	—Albania
AZER.	—Azerbaijan
BOS. & HERZ.	—Boznia & Herzegovina
CEN. AFR. REP.	—Central African Republic
DEM. REP. OF CONGO	—Democratic Republic of Congo
FR.	—France
IT.	—Italy
LIECH.	—Liechtenstein
LUX.	—Luxembourg
NETH.	—Netherlands
N.Z.	—New Zealand
REP. OF CONGO	—Republic of Congo
SERB. & MONT.	—Serbia & Montenegro
SLOV.	—Slovenia
SWITZ.	—Switzerland
U.A.E.	—United Arab Emirates
U.K.	—United Kingdom
U.S.	—United States

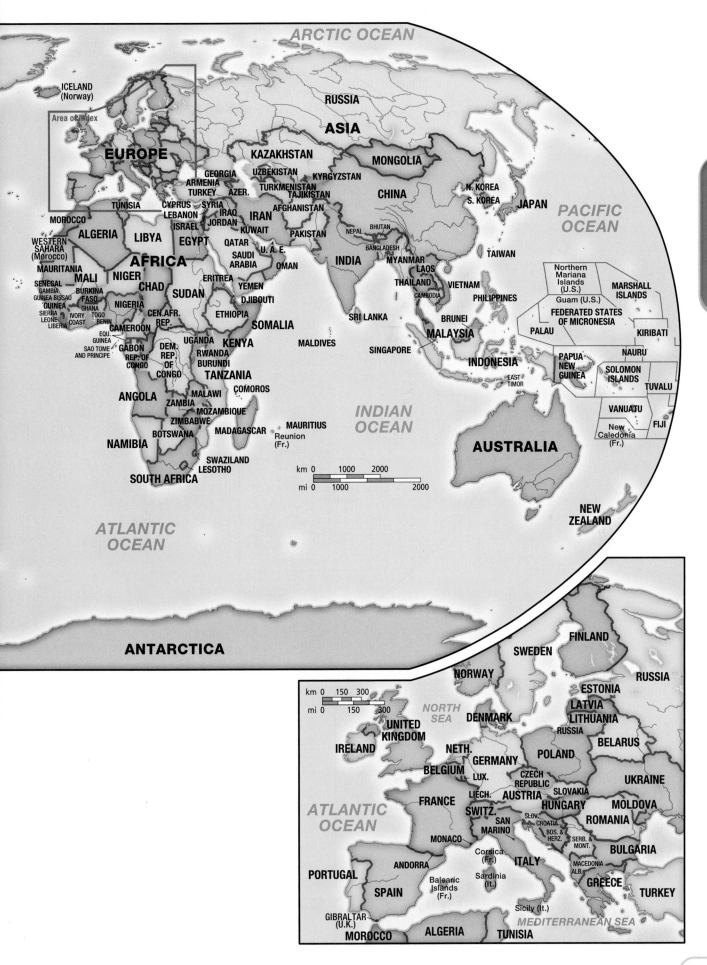

ICELAND
(Norway)

Area of Index

EUROPE

RUSSIA

ASIA

KAZAKHSTAN

GEORGIA
ARMENIA
TURKEY
AZER.
UZBEKISTAN
KYRGYZSTAN
MONGOLIA

TAJIKISTAN

CYPRUS
SYRIA
TUNISIA
LEBANON
IRAQ
ISRAEL
JORDAN
IRAN
AFGHANISTAN
CHINA

N. KOREA
S. KOREA
JAPAN

PACIFIC
OCEAN

MOROCCO

ALGERIA
LIBYA
EGYPT
KUWAIT
QATAR
SAUDI
ARABIA
U.A.E.
OMAN
PAKISTAN
NEPAL
BHUTAN
BANGLADESH
INDIA
MYANMAR
LAOS
TAIWAN

WESTERN
SAHARA
(Morocco)

MAURITANIA
MALI
NIGER
CHAD
SUDAN
ERITREA
YEMEN
DJIBOUTI
THAILAND
VIETNAM
CAMBODIA
PHILIPPINES

Northern
Mariana
Islands
(U.S.)

MARSHALL
ISLANDS

AFRICA

SENEGAL
GAMBIA
GUINEA BISSAU
GUINEA
SIERRA
LEONE
LIBERIA
BURKINA
FASO
GHANA
TOGO
BENIN
IVORY
COAST
NIGERIA
CEN.AFR.
REP.
ETHIOPIA
SOMALIA
SRI LANKA
BRUNEI
MALAYSIA
SINGAPORE
Guam (U.S.)
FEDERATED STATES
OF MICRONESIA
PALAU
KIRIBATI

EQU.
GUINEA
SAO TOME
AND PRINCIPE
CAMEROON
GABON
DEM.
REP.
OF
CONGO
REP. OF
CONGO
UGANDA
RWANDA
BURUNDI
KENYA
MALDIVES
INDONESIA
EAST
TIMOR
PAPUA
NEW
GUINEA
SOLOMON
ISLANDS
NAURU
TUVALU

TANZANIA

ANGOLA
MALAWI
ZAMBIA
MOZAMBIQUE
ZIMBABWE
COMOROS
INDIAN
OCEAN
VANUATU
New
Caledonia
(Fr.)
FIJI

MAURITIUS
Reunion
(Fr.)

NAMIBIA
BOTSWANA
MADAGASCAR
AUSTRALIA

SWAZILAND
LESOTHO
SOUTH AFRICA

km 0   1000   2000
mi 0   1000   2000

NEW
ZEALAND

ATLANTIC
OCEAN

ANTARCTICA

Atlas

FINLAND

SWEDEN

NORWAY

RUSSIA

ESTONIA
LATVIA
LITHUANIA
RUSSIA
BELARUS

km 0 150 300
mi 0   150   300

NORTH
SEA

DENMARK

UNITED
KINGDOM

NETH.
GERMANY
POLAND

IRELAND

BELGIUM
LUX.
CZECH
REPUBLIC
SLOVAKIA
UKRAINE

LIECH.
AUSTRIA
HUNGARY
MOLDOVA

FRANCE
SWITZ.
SAN
MARINO
SLOV.
CROATIA
BOS. &
HERZ.
ROMANIA

ATLANTIC
OCEAN

MONACO
SERB. &
MONT.
BULGARIA

ANDORRA
Corsica
(Fr.)
ITALY
MACEDONIA
ALB.

PORTUGAL

Balearic
Islands
(Fr.)
Sardinia
(It.)
GREECE
TURKEY

SPAIN

Sicily (It.)

GIBRALTAR
(U.K.)
MEDITERRANEAN SEA

MOROCCO
ALGERIA
TUNISIA

R51

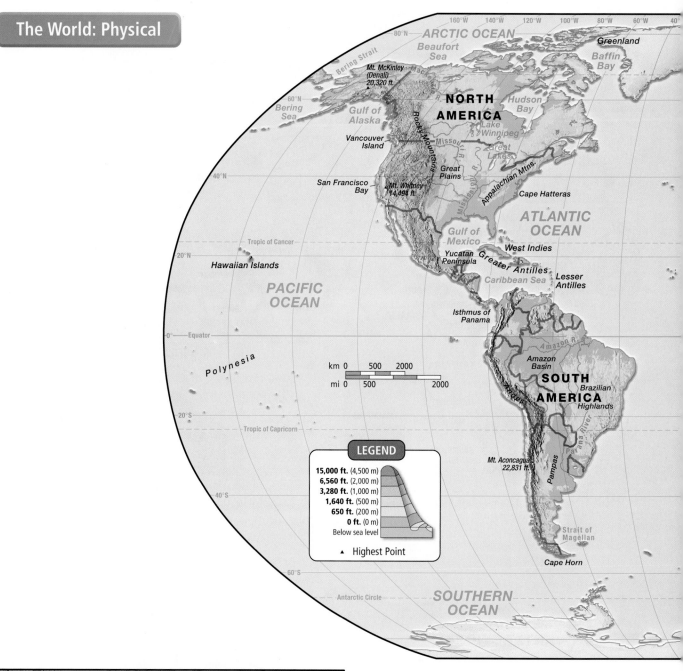

ARCTIC OCEAN

80°N

160°W 140°W 120°W 100°W 80°W 60°W 40°

Beaufort
Sea

Greenland

Baffin
Bay

Bering Strait

Mt. McKinley
(Denali)
20,320 ft.

Mackenzie R.

NORTH
AMERICA

Hudson
Bay

60°N

Bering
Sea

Gulf of
Alaska

Rocky Mountains

Lake
Winnipeg

Great
Lakes

Vancouver
Island

Missouri R.

Great
Plains

40°N

San Francisco
Bay

Mt. Whitney
14,494 ft.

Mississippi R.

Appalachian Mtns.

Cape Hatteras

ATLANTIC
OCEAN

Tropic of Cancer

Gulf of
Mexico

West Indies

20°N

Hawaiian Islands

Yucatan
Peninsula

Greater Antilles

Lesser
Antilles

PACIFIC
OCEAN

Caribbean Sea

Isthmus of
Panama

Amazon R.

Equator

Amazon
Basin

SOUTH
AMERICA

Polynesia

km 0   500   2000

Brazilian
Highlands

Andes

Paraná River

mi 0   500   2000

20°S

SUOUTH
AMERICA

Tropic of Capricorn

LEGEND

Mt. Aconcagua
22,831 ft.

Pampas

15,000 ft. (4,500 m)
6,560 ft. (2,000 m)
3,280 ft. (1,000 m)
1,640 ft. (500 m)
650 ft. (200 m)
0 ft. (0 m)
Below sea level

40°S

▲ Highest Point

Strait of
Magellan

60°S

Cape Horn

Antarctic Circle

SOUTHERN
OCEAN

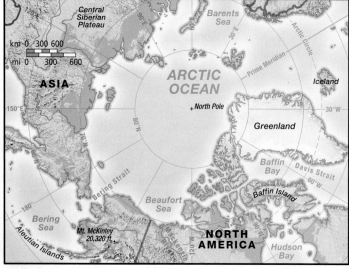

Central
Siberian
Plateau

120°

90° E

Barents
Sea

30° E

Arctic Circle

km 0   300 600
mi 0   300 600

ASIA

ARCTIC
OCEAN

Prime Meridian

Iceland

150°E

80°N

+ North Pole

30°W

Greenland

70°N

Baffin
Bay

Davis Strait

60°W

180°

Bering Strait

Baffin Island

Mackenzie R.

Bering
Sea

Beaufort
Sea

90°W

Aleutian Islands

Mt. McKinley
20,320 ft.

NORTH
AMERICA

Hudson
Bay

ARCTIC OCEAN
80°N

Barents
Sea

Iceland
Arctic Circle

EUROPE

North
Sea

Northern European Plain

Ural Mountains

Yenisey River

Ob River

Central
Siberian
Plateau

60°N

Sea of
Okhotsk

Kamchatka
Peninsula

ASIA

Volga River

Danube

Alps
Pyrenees

Mt. Elbrus
18,510 ft.

Black Sea

Caucasus
Mountains

Aral
Sea

Gobi Desert

Sea
of
Japan

40°N

PACIFIC
OCEAN

Atlas Mtns.

Strait of
Gibraltar

Mediterranean Sea

Plateau
of Tibet

East
China
Sea

SAHARA

Red Sea

Nile River

Himalaya Mountains

Mt. Everest
29,035 ft.

Tropic of Cancer

SAHEL

Ganges River

South
China
Sea

20°N

Micronesia

Niger River

Arabian
Sea

Bay of
Bengal

Philippine Islands

AFRICA

Congo River

Lake
Victoria

Mt. Kilimanjaro
19,340 ft.

Sumatra

Borneo

Melanesia

Equator
0°

Great
Rift
Valley

Java

New Guinea

Prime Meridian

Strait of
Sunda

INDIAN
OCEAN

Madagascar

Coral
Sea

20°S

Great
Sandy
Desert

Tropic of Capricorn

Kalahari
Desert

AUSTRALIA

Darling River

ATLANTIC
OCEAN

Nullarbor
Plain

Tasman
Sea

Cape of
Good Hope

Mt. Kosciusko
7,310 ft.

North Island

South Island

60°S

Antarctic Circle

ANTARCTICA

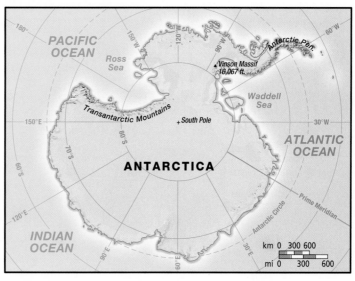

180°

150°W

90°W

60°W

PACIFIC
OCEAN

Ross
Sea

Antarctic Pen.

Vinson Massif
16,067 ft.

Waddell
Sea

150°E

Transantarctic Mountains

+ South Pole

30°W

ATLANTIC
OCEAN

80°S

ANTARCTICA

120°E

70°S

Prime Meridian

Antarctic Circle

INDIAN
OCEAN

90°E

30°E

60°E

km 0 300 600

mi 0 300 600

Eastern Hemisphere: Political

ARCTIC OCEAN

Beaufort Sea

140°W

GREENLAND (DENMARK)

60°W   40°W

Alaska (U.S.)

60°N

Hudson Bay

Labrador Sea

60°N

Atlas

CANADA

Great Lakes

Great Salt Lake

⊛ Ottawa

40°N

UNITED STATES

⊛ Washington, D.C.

40°N

ATLANTIC OCEAN

Gulf of Mexico

BAHAMAS

Havana ⊛

Tropic of Cancer

Hawaii (U.S.)

20°N

MEXICO

CUBA

HAITI

DOMINICAN REPUBLIC

20°N

Mexico City ⊛

BELIZE

Kingston ⊛

U.S. VIRGIN ISLANDS

GUATEMALA

⊛ Belmopan

ST. KITTS AND NEVIS

Guatemala City ⊛

JAMAICA

Santo

ST. LUCIA

EL SALVADOR

Tegucigalpa ⊛

Port-Au-

Domingo

BARBADOS

PACIFIC OCEAN

San Salvador ⊛

Managua ⊛

Prince

GRENADA

HONDURAS

⊛ San José

Panama ⊛ Caracas

NICARAGUA

City

VENEZUELA

Georgetown ⊛ ⊛ Paramaribo

COSTA RICA

⊛ Bogotá

⊛ Cayenne

PANAMA

COLOMBIA

GUYANA

SURINAME

FRENCH GUIANA (FRANCE)

Galápagos Is. (Ecuador)

ECUADOR

⊛ Quito

Equator

0°

0°

French Polynesia (France)

⊛ Lima

BRAZIL

PERU

La Paz ⊛ ⊛ Brasilia

20°S

⊛ **BOLIVIA**

⊛ Sucre

20°S

Tropic of Capricorn

PARAGUAY

CHILE

⊛ Asunción

N

Santiago ⊛

URUGUAY

W   E

⊛ Buenos Aires ⊛ Montevideo

S

ARGENTINA

40°S

40°S

LEGEND

⊛ National capital

Falkland Islands (U.K.)

— National border

km 0   500   1000

mi 0   500   1000

South Georgia (U.K.)

60°S

60°S

140°W   120°W   100°W   80°W   60°W   40°W

Eastern Hemisphere: Physical

GREENLAND

ARCTIC
OCEAN

Beaufort
Sea

Baffin
Bay

Davis
Strait

80°N

160°W   140°W   60°W   40°W

Bering
Strait

Bering
Sea

Mt. McKinley (Denali)
20,320 ft.
(6,194 m)

Yukon R.

Mackenzie R.

Gulf of
Alaska

60°N

Hudson
Bay

Labrador
Sea

CANADIAN SHIELD

NORTH AMERICA

Great
Lakes

ROCKY MOUNTAINS

Coast Mountains

Coast Ranges

Great
Salt Lake

Range
and Basin

GREAT
PLAINS

Death Valley
-282 ft.
(-86 m)

Mt. Whitney
14,495 ft.
(4,418 m)

Missouri R.

Mississippi R.

APPALACHIAN MOUNTAINS

Coastal Plain

ATLANTIC
OCEAN

40°N

Rio Grande

Gulf of
Mexico

Bahamas

Tropic of Cancer

Hawaiian
Islands

Cuba

Hispaniola

Puerto Rico

20°N

Caribbean
Sea

PACIFIC
OCEAN

Lake
Nicaragua

Lake
Maracaibo

Line
Islands

Equator

Galápagos
Islands

Amazon R.

0°

AMAZON
BASIN

Marquesas

ANDES

SOUTH
AMERICA

Society
Islands

Cook
Islands

20°S

Tropic of Capricorn

Atacama
Desert

N
W   E
S

Mt. Aconcagua
22,834 ft.
(6,960 m)

Rio de la Plata

LEGEND

15,000 ft. (4,500 m)
6,560 ft. (2,000 m)
3,280 ft. (1,000 m)
1,640 ft. (500 m)
650 ft. (200 m)
0 ft. (0 m)
Below sea level

▲ Highest Point

40°S

Valdés Peninsula
-131 ft.
(-40 m)

Falkland
Islands

km 0   500   1000
mi 0   500   1000

South
Georgia

Strait of
Magellan

60°S

160°W   140°W   120°W   100°W   80°W   60°W   40°W

North America: Physical

ARCTIC OCEAN

BROOKS RANGE

RUSSIA

ALASKA
(U.S.)

Mt. McKinley
(Denali)

60°N

Bering
Sea

ROCKY MOUNTAINS

120°W

CN	—Connecticut
DE	—Delaware
IN	—Indiana
LA	—Louisiana
MA	—Massachusetts
MD	—Maryland
MS	—Mississippi
NH	—New Hampshire
NJ	—New Jersey
PA	—Pennsylvania
RI	—Rhode Island
VT	—Vermont
WV	—West Virginia

WASHINGTON

Mt. Rainier

Mt. St. Helens

PACIFIC
OCEAN

OREGON

IDAH

COAST

GREAT
BASIN

40°N

CALIFORNIA

NEVADA

SIERRA NEVADA

CENTRAL VALLEY

RANGES

DEATH
VALLEY

LEGEND

⊛ National capital

★ State capital

• Major city

▲ Mountain peak

——— National boundary

——— State boundary

N
W E
S

km 0   150   300

mi 0   150   300

20°N

Mauna Loa   HAWAII
(U.S.)

160°W

140°W

120°W

Baffin
Bay

GREENLAND
(U.S.)

Labrador
Sea

60°N

Hudson
Bay

CANADA

Lake
Winnipeg

Great
Lakes

St. Lawrence River

MONTANA   NORTH DAKOTA   MINNESOTA

MICHIGAN

Ottawa ✶

MAINE

Mt. Washington

SOUTH DAKOTA   WISCONSIN

NEW
YORK

VT
NH

WYOMING

NEBRASKA   IOWA

MA
CT   RI

Missouri River

ROCKY MOUNTAINS

GREAT PLAINS

ILLINOIS   IN

OHIO

PA

NJ

40°N

UTAH

Pike's Peak

KANSAS

CENTRAL
PLAINS

Ohio River

WV

MD   DE

Washington, D.C.

COLORADO

Arkansas River

MISSOURI

KENTUCKY

VIRGINIA

GRAND
CANYON

ARKANSAS

TENNESSEE

NORTH CAROLINA

APPALACHIAN MOUNTAINS

RIZONA

OKLAHOMA

Mississippi River

SOUTH
CAROLINA

NEW
MEXICO

LA

MS

ALABAMA

GEORGIA

TEXAS

GULF COASTAL PLAIN

ATLANTIC
OCEAN

Rio Grande

MEXICO

SIERRA MADRE OCCIDENTAL

SIERRA MADRE ORIENTAL

FLORIDA

Gulf of
Mexico

BAHAMAS

CUBA ✶

Mexico City ✶

PUERTO RICO
(U.S.)

20°N

80°W

60°W

R57

ARCTIC OCEAN

RUSSIA

ALASKA

CANADA

Yukon R.

Fairbanks

Anchorage

Juneau ★

PACIFIC OCEAN

Aleutian
Islands

km 0   250   500
mi 0   250   500

Atlas

COMPASS: N W E S

Seattle •
Olympia ★

WASHINGTON

Portland •
★ Salem

Columbia R.

Helena ★

MONTANA

Billings •

OREGON

IDAHO

★ Boise

Pocatello •

Snake R.

WYOMING

Casper •

Cheyenne ★

Sacramento ★
• Reno
★ Carson City

San Francisco •

NEVADA

Salt Lake City ★
Provo •

UTAH

Colorado R.

COLORADO

Denver ★

Colorado Springs •

Pueblo •

PACIFIC OCEAN

CALIFORNIA

Las Vegas •

• Los Angeles

ARIZONA

Santa Fe ★
Albuquerque •

★ Phoenix

NEW MEXICO

San Diego •

• Tucson

El Paso •

LEGEND
⊗ National capital
★ State capital
• Major city
── National boundary
── State boundary

Rio Grande

Gulf of California

MEXICO

HAWAII

Kauai

Niihau

Oahu   Kailua
        ★
Honolulu   Molokai

Lanai   Maui

Kahoolawe

PACIFIC OCEAN

Hilo •
Hawaii

km 0   50   100
mi 0   50   100

R58 • Resources

CANADA

NORTH DAKOTA
★ Bismarck
• Fargo

L. Superior

NEW HAMPSHIRE
VERMONT

MAINE
★ Augusta

St. Lawrence R.

MINNESOTA

SOUTH DAKOTA
• Pierre
• Sioux Falls

★ Montpelier
Burlington ★

• Portland
Concord
★ ● Manchester

NEW YORK

Albany ★ ● Boston

St. Paul ★
Minneapolis ●

WISCONSIN
Madison ★

MICHIGAN
Grand Rapids ●

L. Huron

L. Ontario

Rochester ●

MASSACHUSETTS
Hartford ★ ● Providence

RHODE ISLAND

NEBRASKA

IOWA
Cedar Rapids ●

Milwaukee ● Lansing ★

Detroit ●

Buffalo ●

New Haven ●

CONNECTICUT

• Lincoln

★ Des Moines
Omaha ●

Chicago ●

L. Erie

Cleveland ●

PENNSYLVANIA
Harrisburg ★

Newark ● New York
★ Trenton

ILLINOIS
Springfield ★

INDIANA
Indianapolis ★

OHIO
Columbus ★

Pittsburgh ●

Philadelphia ●

NEW JERSEY

Dover ●

DELAWARE

Kansas City ●
Topeka ★ ● Kansas City
Jefferson City ●

St. Louis ●

Cincinnati ●

Louisville ● Frankfort ★

Ohio R.

WEST VIRGINIA
Charleston ●

Baltimore ●
⊛ Annapolis
Washington, D.C.

MARYLAND

KANSAS

MISSOURI

KENTUCKY

Richmond ●

VIRGINIA

Norfolk ●

• Tulsa

Nashville ★

Greensboro ●
Raleigh ●

Oklahoma City ★

Fort Smith ●

Memphis ●

TENNESSEE

NORTH CAROLINA

OKLAHOMA

ARKANSAS
Little Rock ★

Mississippi R.

Birmingham ●

Columbia ★

SOUTH CAROLINA

Charleston ●

• Dallas

MISSISSIPPI
Jackson ★

Montgomery ★

★ Atlanta

GEORGIA

Savannah ●

TEXAS

LOUISIANA

ALABAMA
⊛

Mobile ●

Jacksonville ●
Tallahassee ★

ATLANTIC OCEAN

• Austin
Houston ●

Baton Rouge ★
● New Orleans

FLORIDA

Tampa ●

• San Antonio

Gulf of Mexico

Miami ●

BAHAMAS

km 0   100   200   300   400   500
mi 0   100   200   300   400   500

CUBA

R59

United States: Physical

ARCTIC OCEAN

RUSSIA

Brooks Range

Yukon R.

CANADA

Bering Strait

Mt. McKinley
(Denali)
20,320 ft.

Alaska Range

Bering
Sea

Gulf of
Alaska

Kodiak Is.

Aleutian
Islands

km 0   250   500
mi 0   250   500

N
W   E
S

**PACIFIC
OCEAN**

San Francisco
Bay

Mt. Rainer
14,410 ft.

COAST RANGE

CASCADE RANGE

COLUMBIA PLATEAU

Columbia R.

Mt. Hood
11,239 ft.

Mt. Shasta
14,162 ft.

BITTERROOT RANGE

Snake River

Missouri River

Yellowstone River

BIGHORN MTNS.

ROCKY MOUNTAINS

GREAT PLAINS

Black
Hills

Badlands

COAST RANGES

SIERRA NEVADA

CENTRAL VALLEY

Sacramento R.

San Joaquin R.

BASIN
AND
RANGE

WASATCH RANGE

Green River

Pikes Peak
14,110 ft.

Mt. Whitney
14,494 ft.

Death Valley
282 ft. below sea level

Mojave
Desert

Colorado R.

Grand
Canyon

Painted
Desert

Colorado
Plateau

SANGRE DE CRISTO MTNS.

CONTINENTAL DIVIDE

Channel Islands

Sonoran
Desert

Gila River

Llano
Estacado

Edward
Plateau

Rio Grande

Pecos River

MEXICO

Gulf of California

LEGEND

15,000 ft. (4,500 m)
6,560 ft. (2,000 m)
3,280 ft. (1,000 m)
1,640 ft. (500 m)
650 ft. (200 m)
0 ft. (0 m)
Below sea level

▲ Highest Point

Kauai

Niihau

Oahu

Molokai

Maui

Lanai

Kahoolawe

Mauna Kea
13,796 ft.

Hawaii

PACIFIC OCEAN

Mauna Loa
13,678 ft.

km 0   50   100
mi 0   50   100

CANADA

St. Lawrence River

Mesabi Range

Lake Superior

Mt. Washington 6,288 ft.
White Mtns.

Lake Michigan

Lake Huron

Adirondack Mountains

Connecticut R.

Hudson R.

L. Ontario

ALLEGHENY PLATEAU

Catskill Mtns.

Nantucket

Martha's Vineyard

Lake Erie

Long Island

Sand Hills

Missouri River

Des Moines River

Mississippi River

Delaware River

Susquehanna River

Platte River

CENTRAL PLAINS

A P P A L A C H I A N   M O U N T A I N S

Delaware Bay

Chesapeake Bay

Ohio R.

Wabash River

Arkansas River

OZARK PLATEAU

Mt. Mitchell 6,684 ft.

Cumberland Plateau

Tennessee R.

BLUE RIDGE Mountains

ATLANTIC COASTAL PLAIN

FALL LINE

OUACHITA MOUNTAINS

Red River

Mississippi River

Tombigbee

Savannah R.

Oconee R.

ATLANTIC OCEAN

Sabine River

Alabama R.

Chattahoochee River

Altamaha R.

COASTAL

PLAIN

Pearl River

Colorado River

Brazos River

GULF

Galveston Bay

Mobile Bay

Pensacola Bay

Tampa Bay

Gulf of Mexico

Everglades

BAHAMAS

Florida Keys

km 0   100   200   300   400   500
mi 0   100   200   300   400   500

CUBA

Gazetteer

A

Afghanistan Country in southwest-central Asia; capital: Kabul (34°N, 69°E) p. 674

Africa 2nd largest continent (10°N, 22°E) p. R49

Alabama 22nd state; capital: Montgomery (33°N, 88°W) p. 373

Alaska 49th state; capital: Juneau (64°N, 150°W) p. 572

Albany Capital of New York State (43°N, 74°W) p. 229

Amazon River 2nd longest river in the world; longest in South America (2°S, 53°W) p. R53

Angel Island Island in San Francisco Bay where immigrants to the United States arrived (38°N 122°W) p. 543

Antarctica Continent surrounding the South Pole, mostly covered in ice (90°S) pp. R48–R49

Antietam In Maryland; site of Civil War battle (39°N, 77°W) p. 454

Appalachian Mountains Range stretching from Canada to Alabama (37°N, 82°W) p. 164

Argentina Country in South America (36°S, 67°W) p. R48

Arizona 48th state; capital: Phoenix (34°N, 113°W) p. R56

Arkansas 25th state; capital: Little Rock (34°N, 92°W) p. R57

Asia Largest continent in the world (50°N, 100°E) p. R49

Atlanta Capital of Georgia (34°N, 84°W) p. 467

Atlantic Ocean Extends from Arctic to Antarctic; east of United States (5°S, 25°W) pp. R50–R51

Australia Smallest continent (30°S, 151°E) p. R49

Austria–Hungary Monarchy in central Europe, 1867–1918 (47°N, 13°E) p. 541

B

Bahamas Group of islands in the Atlantic Ocean; southeast of Florida (26°N, 76°W) p. 309

Baltimore Large city in Maryland (39°N, 77°W) p. 498

Belgium Country in western Europe (51°N, 3°E) p. R49

Bering Strait Waterway connecting Arctic Ocean and Bering Sea (65°N, 170°W) p. 39

Berlin Capital of Germany (53°N, 13°E) p. 613

Birmingham City in Alabama (34°N, 87°W) p. 596

Boston Capital of Massachusetts (42°N, 71°W) p. 190

Brazil Largest country in South America (9°S, 53°W) p. 101

Bull Run Site of two major Civil War battles (39°N, 78°W) p. 453

Bunker Hill Site of lst major battle of American Revolution (42°N, 71°W) p. 245

C

California 31st state; capital: Sacramento (38°N, 121°W) p. 500

Canada Country bordering United States on north (50°N, 100°W) p. R52

Cape of Good Hope Southwest extremity of Africa (34°S, 18°E) p. 93

Caribbean Sea North Atlantic sea (15°N, 76°W) p. 97

Charleston City in South Carolina (33°N, 80°W) p. 198

Chicago Large city in Illinois (42°N, 88°W) p. 549

Chile Country on western coast of South America (35°S, 72°W) p. 668

China Country in East Asia (37°N, 93°E) p. R49

Colorado 38th state; capital: Denver (40°N, 107°W) p. 593

Colorado River 5th longest river in the United States (32°N, 115°W) p. 8

Columbia River Lewis and Clark found mouth of river in 1805 (46°N, 120°W) p. 356

Concord Site in Massachusetts of early Revolutionary War battle (42°N, 71°W) p. 251

Connecticut 5th state; capital: Hartford (42°N, 73°W) p. 202

Cuba Island nation in Caribbean Sea, south of Florida (22°N, 79°W) p. 97

Cumberland Gap Pass through the Appalachian Mountains (36°N, 83°W) p. 345

Delaware 1st state; capital: Dover (39°N, 76°W) p. 144

Delaware River Flows from New York to Delaware Bay (42°N, 75°W) p. 144

Denver Capital of Colorado (40°N, 105°W) p. 29

Detroit City in eastern Michigan (42°N, 83°W) p. 23

Egypt Country in North Africa; capital: Cairo (30°N, 31°E) p. 471

El Paso City in west Texas, on Rio Grande (32°N, 106°W) p. R56

Ellis Island Island in New York Harbor where immigrants to United States arrived (41°N, 74°W) p. 543

England Country in western Europe; part of the United Kingdom (52°N, 2°W) p. 123

Europe 6th largest continent (50°N, 15°E) p. R49

Florida 27th state; capital: Tallahassee (31°N, 85°W) p. R57

France Country in western Europe (47°N, 1°E) p. 123

Georgia 4th state; capital: Atlanta (33°N, 84°W) p. 203

Germany Country in western Europe (51°N, 10°E) p. 309

Gettysburg Site in Pennsylvania of Civil War battle (40°N, 77°W) p. 456

Grand Canyon In Arizona, deep gorge formed by the Colorado River (36°N, 112°W) p. R58

Great Lakes Five freshwater lakes between the United States and Canada (45°N, 83°W) p. 31

Great Plains In central North America, high grassland region (45°N, 104°W) p. 6

Greensboro City in North Carolina (36°N, 80°W) p. 628

Guatemala Country in Central America (16°N, 92°W) p. R48

Gulf of Mexico Body of water along southern United States and Mexico (25°N, 94°W) p. R53

Havana Capital of Cuba (23°N, 82°W) p. 574

Hawaii 50th state; capital: Honolulu (20°N, 158°W) p. 573

Hiroshima City in Japan; destroyed by atomic bomb in 1945 (34°N, 132°E) p. 604

Hispaniola Island in the West Indies (18°N, 73°W) p. 97

Honolulu Capital of Hawaii (21°N, 158°W) p. R56

Houston City in Texas (30°N, 95°W) p. R57

Hudson River In New York; named for explorer Henry Hudson (43°N, 74°W) p. 124

Idaho 43rd state; capital: Boise (44°N, 115°W) p. 524

Illinois 21st state; capital: Springfield (40°N, 91°W) p. 434

India Country in south Asia (23°N, 78°E) p. 93

Indiana 19th state; capital: Indianapolis (40°N, 87°W) p. R57

Iowa 29th state; capital: Des Moines (41°N, 93°W) p. R57

Iraq Country in southwest Asia; capital: Baghdad (3°N, 44°E) p. 659

Ireland Island in North Atlantic Ocean, divided between Republic of Ireland and Northern Ireland (53°N, 6°W) p. 388

Italy Country in southern Europe (44°N, 11°E) p. 471

Jamestown, Virginia First permanent English settlement in Americas (37°N, 76°W) p. 131

Japan Island country off east coast of Asia (37°N, 134°E) p. 309

Kansas 34th state; capital: Topeka (39°N, 100°W) p. 433

Kentucky 15th state; capital: Frankfort (38°N, 88°W) p. 452

Lexington Site in Massachusetts of lst shots fired in Revolutionary War (42°N, 71°W) p. 251

London Capital of United Kingdom (52°N, 0°W) p. 137

Los Angeles City in California (34°N, 118°W) p. R56

Louisiana 18th state; capital: Baton Rouge (31°N, 93°W) p. 444

Maine 23rd state; capital: Augusta (45°N, 70°W) p. 202

Mali Country in West Africa (16°N, 0°W) p. 86

Maryland 7th state; capital: Annapolis (39°N, 76°W) p. 203

Massachusetts 6th state; capital: Boston (42°N, 73°W) p. 137

Mecca Muslim holy city (21°N, 39°E) p. 87

Mexico Country bordering the United States to the south (24°N, 104°W) pp. R54–R55

Mexico City Capital of Mexico (19°N, 99°W) p. R55

Miami City in Florida (26°N, 80°W) p. R57

Michigan 26th state; capital: Lansing (46°N, 87°W) p. R57

Milwaukee City in Wisconsin (43°N, 88°W) p. 389

Minnesota 32nd state; capital: St. Paul (45°N, 93°W) p. R57

Mississippi 20th state; capital: Jackson (33°N, 90°W) p. 444

Mississippi River Principal river of United States and North America (32°N, 92°W) p. R59

Missouri 24th state; capital: Jefferson City (38°N, 94°W) p. 433

Missouri River A major river in United States (41°N, 96°W) p. 356

Montana 41st state; capital: Helena (47°N, 112°W) p. 524

Montgomery City in Alabama (32°N, 86°W) p. 627

Montreal City in Quebec, Canada (46°N, 74°W) p. 230

Nagasaki City in Japan; severely damaged by atomic bomb in 1945 (33°N, 130°E) p. 604

Natchez City in Mississippi (32°N, 91°W) p. 287

Nebraska 37th state; capital: Lincoln (42°N, 102°W) p. 433

Netherlands Country in northwestern Europe; also called Holland (52°N, 6°E) p. 124

Nevada 36th state; capital: Carson City (40°N, 117°W) p. R56

Newfoundland Eastern province of Canada (48°N, 57°W) p. 683

New Hampshire 9th state; capital: Concord (44°N, 72°W) p. 202

New Jersey 3rd state; capital: Trenton (41°N, 75°W) p. 188

New Mexico 47th state; capital: Santa Fe (35°N, 107°W) p. 593

New Netherland Dutch colony in North America (41°N, 74°W) p. 144

New Orleans City in Louisiana (30°N, 90°W) p. 355

New York 11th state; capital: Albany (43°N, 78°W) p. R57

New York City Large city in New York State (41°N, 74°W) p. R57

North America Northern continent of Western Hemisphere (45°N, 100°W) p. R48

North Carolina 12th state; capital: Raleigh (36°N, 82°W) p. 203

North Dakota 39th state; capital: Bismarck (46°N, 100°W) pp. R56–R57

North Korea Country in northeast Asia; capital: Pyongyang (39°N, 125°E) p. 614

Northwest Territory Land extending from Ohio and Mississippi rivers to Great Lakes (41°N, 85°W) p. 297

Gazetteer

Ohio 17th state; capital: Columbus (41°N, 83°W) p. R57

Ohio River Flows from Pennsylvania to the Mississippi River (37°N, 88°W) p. R59

Ohio River Valley Farming region west of the Appalachian Mountains (37°N, 88°W) p. 228

Oklahoma 46th state; capital: Oklahoma City (36°N, 98°W) p. 370

Omaha Large city in Nebraska (41°N, 96°W) p. R57

Ontario Canadian province; capital: Toronto (51°N, 89°W) p. 683

Oregon 33rd state; capital: Salem (44°N, 122°W) p. 400

Oregon Territory Area from Rocky Mountains to Pacific Ocean (45°N, 120°W) p. 401

Ottawa Capital of Canada (45°N, 75°W) p. 682

Pacific Ocean Largest ocean; west of the United States (0°, 170°W) p. R50

Panama Country in Central America (9°N, 80°W) p. 100

Pearl Harbor United States naval base; attacked by Japan (21°N, 158°W) p. 601

Pennsylvania 2nd state; capital: Harrisburg (41°N, 78°W) p. 189

Peru Country on the Pacific coast of South America (10°S, 75°W) p. R48

Philadelphia Large port city in Pennsylvania (40°N, 75°W) p. 190

Philippines Island country southeast of Asia (14°N, 125°E) p. 574

Phoenix Capital of Arizona (33°N, 112°W) p. 13

Pittsburgh Manufacturing city in Pennsylvania (40°N, 80°W) p. 550

Plymouth In Massachusetts; site of first Pilgrim settlement (42°N, 71°W) p. 137

Poland Country in eastern Europe; capital: Warsaw (52°N, 21°E) p. 542

Portugal Country in western Europe; capital: Lisbon (38°N, 8°W) p. 92

Potomac River Runs from western Maryland past Washington, D.C. (38°N, 77°W) p. 322

Promontory Point The place in Utah where the two halves of the Transcontinental Railroad met in 1869 (41°N, 112°W) p. 500

Puerto Rico A U.S. territory in the Caribbean; capital: San Juan (18°N, 67°W) p. 574

Quebec Province of Canada; capital: Quebec City (47°N, 71°W) p. 123

Rhode Island 13th state; capital: Providence (42°N, 72°W) p. 201

Richmond Capital city of Virginia; also was Confederate capital (38°N, 78°W) p. 453

Rio Grande River forming part of the Texas–Mexico border (26°N, 97°W) pp. R54–R55

Roanoke Island Island off the coast of North Carolina; site of first English colony in the Americas (37°N, 80°W) p. 130

Rocky Mountains Mountain range in the western United States (50°N, 114°W) p. R58

Russia Formerly part of the Soviet Union; capital: Moscow (61°N, 60°E) p. 542

Sacramento Capital of California (39°N, 122°W) p. R56

St. Augustine, Florida Oldest European-founded city in U.S. (30°N, 81°W) p. 113

St. Lawrence River Links the Great Lakes to the Atlantic Ocean (49°N, 67°W) p. 123

St. Louis City in Missouri; on Mississippi River (39°N, 90°W) p. 356

Salem An early English settlement in Massachusetts (43°N, 71°W) p. 139

San Antonio City in Texas (29°N, 98°W) p. 395

San Diego City in southern California (32°N, 117°W) p. 28

San Francisco A major port city in California (38°N, 122°W) p. 318

San Salvador Caribbean island where Columbus landed (24°N, 74°W) p. 97

Santa Fe Capital of New Mexico (35°N, 106°W) p. 13

Saratoga New York site of an important American victory against the British in 1777 (43°N, 75°W) p. 280

Gazetteer

Savannah

Savannah Oldest city in Georgia (32°N, 81°W) p. 286

Seattle Large city in Washington State (48°N, 122°W) p. R56

Sierra Madre A system of mountain ranges in Mexico (27°N, 104°W) p. R55

Sierra Nevada Mountain range mainly in eastern California (39°N, 120°W) p. R58

South America Southern continent of Western Hemisphere (10°S, 60°W) p. R48

South Carolina 8th state; capital: Columbia (34°N, 81°W) p. 203

South Dakota 40th state; capital: Pierre (44°N, 100°W) p. 524

South Korea Country in eastern Asia on Korean peninsula; capital: Seoul (37°N, 127°E) p. 614

Soviet Union Large Communist country that split into separate republics in 1991; capital city: Moscow (61°N, 64°E) p. 612

Spain Country in Western Europe; capital: Madrid (40°N, 5°W) p. 96

Tennessee 16th state; capital: Nashville (36°N, 88°W) p. 368

Tenochtitlán Aztec city; present–day Mexico City (19°N, 99°W) p. 43

Texas 28th state; capital: Austin (31°N, 101°W) p. 394

Timbuktu City in Mali, W. Africa (17°N, 3°W) p. 86

Trenton Capital of New Jersey (40°N, 75°W) p. 279

Tucson City in Arizona (32°N, 111°W) p. R56

United Kingdom England, Scotland, and Wales (57°N, 2°W) p. R49

United States Country in central and northwest North America (38°N, 110°W) pp. R56–R57

Utah 45th state; capital: Salt Lake City (40°N, 112°W) p. 13

Valley Forge George Washington's winter camp in 1777; near Philadelphia (40°N, 75°W) p. 282

Venice City in Italy (45°N, 12°E) p. 84

Vermont 14th state; capital: Montpelier (44°N, 72°W) p. 29

Vicksburg, Mississippi Site of Civil War battle (32°N, 91°W) p. 454

Vietnam Country in southeast Asia (18°N, 107°E) p. 634

Virginia 10th state; capital: Richmond (37°N, 81°W) p. 131

Washington 42nd state; capital: Olympia (48°N, 121°W) p. R56

Washington, D.C. Capital of the U.S. (39°N, 77°W) p. R57

West Indies Islands separating the Caribbean Sea and the Atlantic (19°N, 79°W) p. 97

West Virginia 35th state; capital: Charleston 38°N, 81°W) p. R57

Williamsburg Colonial capital of Virginia (37°N, 77°W) p. 206

Wisconsin 30th state; capital: Madison (43°N, 89°W) p. R57

Wyoming 44th state; capital: Cheyenne (43°N, 109°W) p. R56

Yorktown In Virginia; site of last battle of Revolutionary War (37°N, 77°W) p. 288

Gazetteer

R66 • Resources

Glossary

abolitionist (ab uh LIH shuhn ihst) someone who joined the movement to abolish, or end, slavery. (p. 424)

absolute location (AB suh loot loh KAY shuhn) the exact latitude and longitude of a place on the globe. (p. 116)

accord (uh KAWRD) an agreement. (p. 652)

agriculture (AG rih kuhl chur) farming or growing plants. (p. 40)

alliance (uh LY uhns) an agreement nations make to support and defend each other. (p. 578)

ally (AL ly) a person or group that joins with another to work toward a goal. (p. 229)

amendment (uh MEND muhnt) a change to the Constitution. (p. 316)

annexation (uh nehks AY shuhn) the act of joining two countries or pieces of land together. (p. 395)

Antifederalist (an tee FEHD ur uh lihst) someone who opposed the new Constitution. (p. 306)

apprentice (uh PREHN tihs) someone who studies with a master to learn a skill or business. (p. 198)

armada (ahr MAH duh) the Spanish word for a large fleet of ships. (p. 125)

armistice (AHR mih stihs) an agreement to stop fighting. (p. 583)

arms race (ahrms rays) a contest between nations to build bigger and more powerful weapons. (p. 614)

artisan (AR tih zuhn) someone who is skilled at making something by hand, such as silver spoons or wooden chairs. (p. 198)

assassination (uh SAS uh nay shuhn) the murder of an important leader. (p. 473)

assembly line (uh SEHM blee lyn) a line of workers and equipment that puts a product together piece by piece. (p. 586)

assimilate (uh SIHM uh layt) to change a group's culture and traditions so that it blends with a larger group. (p. 526)

astrolabe (AS truh layb) a tool that measures the height of the sun or a star above the horizon. (p. 91)

atomic bomb (uh TAHM ihk bahm) a powerful bomb that can destroy an entire city. (p. 604)

baby boom (BAY bee boom) the increase in the number of babies born after World War II. (p. 620)

backcountry (BAK kuhn tree) the mountainous area west of where most colonists settled. (p. 163)

banish (BAN ihsh) to force someone to leave a place. (p. 167)

bar graph (bahr graf) a graph that compares amounts of things. (p. 422)

barbed wire (bahrbd wyr) twisted wire with a sharp barb, or point, every few inches. (p. 517)

barter (BAHR tur) to exchange goods without using money. (p. 70)

benefit (BEHN uh fiht) a gain or an advantage. (p. 194)

Bill of Rights (bihl uhv ryts) the first ten amendments to the Constitution. (p. 699)

Black Codes (blak kohds) laws that limited the rights of former enslaved people to travel, vote, and work in certain jobs. (p. 474)

boomtown (BOOM toun) a town whose population booms, or grows very quickly. (p. 402)

border state (BOHR dur stayt) a slave state that stayed in the Union. (p. 452)

boycott (BOI kaht) the refusal to buy, sell, or use certain goods. (p. 236)

budget (BUHJ iht) a plan for saving and spending income. (p. 621)

Cabinet (KAB uh niht) a group chosen by the President to help run the executive branch and give advice. (p. 321)

campaign (kam PAYN) a series of actions taken toward a goal, such as winning a presidential election. (p. 369)

canal (kuh NAL) a waterway built for boat travel and shipping. (p. 346)

cape (kayp) a strip of land that stretches into a body of water. (p. 137)

capital (KAP ih tuhl) the city where the government meets. (p. 322)

capital resource (KAP ih tuhl REE sawrs) a tool, machine, or building that people use to produce goods and services. (p. 17)

capitalism (KAP ih tuhl ihz uhm) an economic system in which people and businesses control the production of goods and services. (p. 612)

caravan (KAR uh van) a group of people and animals who travel together. (p. 86)

caravel (KAR uh vehl) a small, light ship with triangular sails. (p. 92)

cardinal directions (KAR dn uhl dih REHK shuhns) the directions north, south, east, and west. (p. 13)

carpetbagger (KAHR piht bag ur) Northerners who traveled south during Reconstruction. (p. 475)

cash crop (kash krahp) a crop that people grow and sell to earn money. (p. 132)

casualties (KAHZ oo uhl teez) soldiers who are killed or wounded. (p. 454)

cause (kawz) an event or action that makes something else happen. (p. 248)

cease-fire (SEES fyr) an agreement to stop all fighting. (p. 635)

century (SEHN chuh ree) a period of 100 years. (p. 128)

ceremony (SEHR uh moh nee) an event at which people gather to express important beliefs. (p. 56)

cession (SEHSH uhn) something that is given up. (p. 397)

charter (CHAHR ter) a document that gives certain freedoms to a person or group. (p. 131)

checks and balances (chehks uhnd BAHL uhns ehz) a system that lets each branch of government limit the power of the other two. (p. 314)

circle graph (SUR kuhl graf) a graph that illustrates how a part compares with the whole. (p. 422)

circumnavigate (sur kuhm NAV i gayt) to sail completely around something. (p. 101)

citizen (SIHT ih zuhn) an official member of a city, state, or nation. (p. 296)

civil rights (SIHV uhl ryts) the rights that countries guarantee their citizens. (p. 626)

civil war (SIHV uhl wawr) a war between two groups or regions within a nation. (p. 445)

civilian (sih VIHL yuhn) a person who is not in the military. (p. 462)

civilization (sihv uh lih ZAY shuhn) a group of people living together who have systems of government, religion, and culture. (p. 40)

claim (klaym) something declared as one's own, especially a piece of land. (p. 124)

clan (klan) a group of related families. (p. 48)

climate (KLY miht) the type of weather a place has over a long period of time. (p. 9)

coalition (koh uh LIHSH uhn) a group of allies that work together to achieve a goal. (p. 659)

colony (KAHL uh nee) an area of land ruled by another country. (p. 110)

commander (kuh MAN dur) the officer in charge of an army. (p. 254)

communism (KAHM yuh nihz uhm) an economic system in which the government controls production and owns the nation's natural and capital resources. (p. 612)

compact (KAHM pakt) an agreement. (p. 137)

compass rose (KUHM puhs rohz) a part of a map that shows the cardinal and intermediate directions. (p. 13)

Glossary

competition (kahm puh TIHSH uhn) what occurs when more than one business tries to sell the same goods or service. (p. 537)

compromise (KAHM pruh myz) when both sides give up something they want to settle a disagreement. (p. 304)

concentration camp (kahn suhn TRAY shuhn kamp) a place where large numbers of people are held prisoner and forced to work. (p. 605)

Confederacy (kuhn FEHD ur uh see) the name for South Carolina, Mississippi, Florida, Alabama, Georgia, Louisiana, Texas, and later Arkansas, North Carolina, Tennessee, and Virginia. (p. 444)

confederation (kuhn fehd ur AY shuhn) a type of government in which separate groups of people join together, but local leaders still make many decisions for their group. (p. 70)

congress (KAHNG grihs) a group of representatives who meet to discuss a subject. (p. 229)

conquistador (kahn KEES tuh dawr) the Spanish word for conqueror. (p. 104)

conservation (kahn sur VAY shuhn) the protection and wise use of natural resources. (p. 18)

constitution (kahn stih TOO shuhn) a written plan for government. (p. 296)

consumer (kuhn SOO mur) someone who buys goods and services. (p. 25)

convert (kahn VURT) to change a religion or a belief. (p. 112)

corporation (kawr puh RAY shuhn) a business in which many people own shares, or parts, of the business. (p. 536)

corps (kawr) a team of people who work together. (p. 356)

correspondence (kawr ih SPAHN duhns) written communication. (p. 241)

cost (kawst) a loss or sacrifice. (p. 194)

credit (KREHD iht) to get an item today but pay for it later with small payments. (p. 587)

 D

debtor (DEHT ur) a person who owes money. (p. 204)

decade (DEHK ayd) a period of 10 years. (p. 128)

declaration (dehk luh RAY shuhn) a statement that declares, or announces, an idea. (p. 264)

deficit (DEHF ih siht) a shortage. (p. 657)

delegate (DEHL ih giht) someone chosen to speak and act for others. (p. 243)

demand (dih MAND) the amount of something that people want to buy at certain prices. (p. 515)

democracy (dih MAHK ruh see) a government in which the people have the power to make political decisions. (p. 312)

demonstration (dehm uhn STRAY shuhn) a gathering of people who want to express their opinion to the public and the government. (p. 634)

depression (dih PREHSH uhn) a period when many people can't find work and many others have no money to keep businesses going. (p. 593)

deregulation (dee rehg yuh LAY shuhn) the removal of rules. (p. 657)

desegregation (dih SEGH rih GAY shuhn) ending the separation of people by racial or ethnic group. (p. 627)

desert (dih ZURT) to leave the army without permission. (p. 468)

dictator (DIHK tay tur) a ruler who has total power over a country and its people. (p. 600)

discrimination (dih skrihm uh NAY shuhn) the unfair treatment of particular groups. (p. 425)

dissenter (dih SEHN tur) a person who does not agree with the beliefs of his or her leaders. (p. 167)

diversity (dih VUR sih tee) the variety of people in a group. (p. 145)

division of labor (dih VIHZH uhn uhv LAY bur) when workers perform different parts of a large task. (p. 586)

draft (draft) when the government chooses people who have to serve in the military. (p. 455)

drought (drout) a long period with little or no rain. (p. 509)

economy (ih KAHN uh mee) the system people use to produce goods and services. (p. 24)

ecosystem (EH koh sihs tuhm) a community of plants and animals, along with the surrounding soil, air, and water. (p. 31)

effect (ih FEHKT) an event or action that is a result of a cause. (p. 248)

Electoral College (ih LEHK tur uhl KAH luhdj) representatives from each state who vote for the President. (p. 673)

emancipation (ih MAN suh pay shuhn) the freeing of enslaved people. (p. 456)

empire (EHM pyr) many nations or territories ruled by a single group or leader. (p. 104)

entrepreneur (ahn truh pruh NUR) a person who takes risks to start a business. (p. 380)

environment (ehn VY ruhn muhnt) the surroundings in which people, plants, and animals live. (p. 29)

epidemic (ehp ih DEHM ihk) an outbreak of disease that spreads quickly and affects many people. (p. 98)

equator (ih KWAY tur) the imaginary line around the middle of the Earth. (p. 9)

erosion (ih ROH zhuhn) the process by which water and wind wear away the land. (p. 30)

ethnic group (EHTH nihk groop) a group of people who share a language or culture. (p. 544)

executive branch (ihg ZEHK yuh tihv branch) the branch of government that suggests laws and carries out the laws made by Congress. (p. 313)

Exoduster (EHK suh duhs tur) an African American settler who called him or herself after Exodus, a book of the Bible. (p. 508)

expedition (ehk spih DIHSH uhn) a journey to achieve a goal. (p. 104)

export (EHK spawrt) a product sent to another country and sold. (p. 175)

extinct (ihk STIHNGT) when a certain type of plant or animal no longer exists. (p. 525)

fact (fakt) a piece of information that can be proved. (p. 560)

fall line (fahl lyn) the line where rivers from higher land flow to lower land and often form waterfalls. (p. 162)

famine (FAM ihn) a widespread shortage of food. (p. 389)

federal (FEHD ur uhl) a system in which the states share power with the central government. (p. 303)

Federalist (FEHD ur uh lihst) a supporter of the Constitution. (p. 306)

flatboat (FLAT boht) a large, rectangular boat partly covered by a roof. (p. 346)

foreign policy (FAWR ihn PAWL ih see) a government's actions toward other nations. (p. 364)

forty-niner (FAWR tee NY nur) a miner who went to California in 1849. (p. 402)

free enterprise (free EHN tuh pryz) the system in which people may start any business that they believe will succeed. (p. 198)

free market economy (free MAHR kiht ih KAHN uh mee) an economic system in which the people, not the government, decide what will be produced. (p. 198)

free state (free stayt) a state that did not have slavery. (p. 432)

freedmen (FREED mehn) people freed from slavery. (p. 474)

Freedmen's Bureau (FREED mehnz BYOOR oh) an organization that provided food, clothing, medical care, and legal advice to poor blacks and whites. (p. 474)

free-trade agreement (free TRAYD uh GREE muhnt) a treaty among countries that trade with each other. (p. 669)

front (fruhnt) where the fighting takes place in a war. (p. 396)

frontier (FRUHN tyr) the edge of a country or settled region. (p. 345)

Glossary

fugitive (FYOO jih tihv) a person who is running away. (p. 434)

geography (jee AHG ruh fee) the study of the world and the people and things that live there. (p. 6)

glacier (GLAY shur) a huge, thick sheet of slowly moving ice. (p. 39)

gold rush (gohld ruhsh) when many people hurry to the same area to look for gold. (p. 402)

Great Compromise (grayt KAHM pruh myz) The plan that the states with the largest populations send the most representatives to the House of Representatives but each state have the same number of representatives in the Senate. (p. 304)

growing season (GROH eeng SEE zuhn) the time of year when it is warm enough for plants to grow. (p. 161)

habitat (HA buh tat) the area where an animal or a plant normally lives or grows. (p. 525)

hacienda (hah see EHN duh) a large farm or ranch, often with its own village and church. (p. 112)

heritage (HEHR ih tihj) something that is passed down from one generation to the next. (p. 695)

high-tech (hy TEHK) the most recent knowledge and equipment. (p. 666)

home front (hohm fruhnt) all the people in a country who are not in the military during wartime. (p. 462)

homestead (HOHM stehd) a settler's home and land. (p. 507)

human resources (HYOO muhn REE sohrs uhz) people and the skills and knowledge they bring to their work. (p. 17)

immigrant (IHM ih gruhnt) a person who moves to another country to live. (p. 388)

impeach (ihm PEECH) to charge a government official with a crime. (p. 475)

imperialism (ihm PIHR ee uh lihz uhm) when nations build empires by adding colonies. (p. 574)

import (IHM pawrt) a good brought into one country from another. (p. 175)

impressment (ihm PREHS muhnt) when British officers captured American sailors and forced them to serve in the British Navy. (p. 360)

inauguration (ihn AW gyuh ray shuhn) the official ceremony to make someone President. (p. 321)

indentured servant (ihn DEHN churd SUR vuhnt) someone who agreed to work for a number of years in exchange for a trip to America. (p. 132)

independence (ihn duh PEHN duhns) freedom from being ruled by someone else. (p. 262)

indigo (IHN duh goh) a plant that can be made into a dark blue dye. (p. 211)

Industrial Revolution (ihn DUHS tree uhl rehv uh LOO shuhn) a period of time marked by changes in manufacturing and transportation. (p. 378)

industry (IHN duh stree) all the businesses that make one kind of product or provide one kind of service. (p. 174)

inflation (ihn FLAY shuhn) a rise in the prices of goods. (p. 273)

injustice (ihn JUHS tihs) unfair treatment that abuses a person's rights. (p. 390)

inset map (IHN seht map) a small map within a larger one that may show a close-up of an area or provide other information about it. (p. 13)

interchangeable parts (ihn tur CHAYN juh buhl pahrts) parts made by a machine to be exactly the same in size and shape. (p. 379)

interdependent (ihn tuhr dee PEHN duhnt) depending, or relying, on each other. (p. 668)

interest (IHN trihst) what people pay to borrow money. (p. 322)

intermediate directions (ihn tur MEE dee iht dih REHK shuhns) the in-between directions: northeast, southeast, southwest, and northwest. (p. 13)

International Date Line (ihn tuhr NASH uh nuhl dayt lyn) an imaginary line that marks where the date changes. (p. 505)

Internet (IHN tuhr neht) a system that links computers around the world with each other. (p. 666)

internment camp (ihn TURN muhnt kamp) a place where prisoners are held during wartime. (p. 603)

interpreter (ihn TUR prih tur) someone who helps speakers of different languages understand each other. (p. 356)

invasion (ihn VAY zhuhn) an attack by an armed force to conquer another country. (p. 125)

invest (ihn VEHST) to put money into something to try to make more money. (p. 131)

irrigation (ihr ih GAY shuhn) a way of supplying water to crops with streams, ditches, or pipes. (p. 55)

isolationism (y suh LAY shuh nihz uhm) when people want to stay out of world events. (p. 583)

isthmus (IHS muhs) a narrow strip of land that links two larger pieces of land. It has water on both sides. (p. 575)

Jim Crow (jihm kroh) laws that segregated African Americans from other Americans. (p. 484)

judicial branch (joo DISH uhl branch) the branch of government that decides the meaning of laws and whether the laws have been followed. (p. 313)

kingdom (KIHNG duhm) a place ruled by a king or queen. (p. 86)

labor union (LAY bur YOON yuhn) an organization of workers that tries to improve pay and working conditions for its members. (p. 538)

laborer (LAY buhr ur) a person who does hard physical work. (p. 198)

landform (LAND fohrm) a feature on the surface of the land. (p. 8)

legislative branch (LEHJ ih slay tihv branch) the branch of government that makes laws. (p. 313)

legislature (LEHJ ih slay chur) a group of people with the power to make and change laws. (p. 203)

liberty (LIHB uhr tee) freedom from being controlled by another government. (p. 235)

line graph (lyn graf) a graph that shows change over time. (p. 422)

lodge (lawj) a type of home that Plains Indians made using bark, earth, and grass. (p. 61)

longhouse (LAWNG hows) a large house made out of wood poles and covered with bark. (p. 69)

Loyalist (LOI uh lihst) someone who was still loyal to the king. (p. 270)

manifest destiny (MAN uh fehst DEHS tuh nee) the belief that the United States should spread across the entire North American continent, from the Atlantic Ocean to the Pacific Ocean. (p. 395)

manufacturer (man yuh FAK chuhr ur) someone who uses machines to make goods. (p. 354)

map legend (map LEHJ uhnd) a part of a map that explains any symbols or colors on a map. (p. 13)

map scale (map skayl) a part of a map that compares distance on a map to distance in the real world. (p. 13)

maquiladora (mah kee lah DOH rah) a factory in Mexico near the U.S. border. (p. 686)

mass production (mas pruh DUHK shuhn) making many identical products at once. (p. 379)

massacre (MAS uh kur) the killing of many people. (p. 240)

mechanization (meh kih ny ZAY shuhn) the use of machines to do work. (p. 538)

mercenary (MUR suh nehr ee) a soldier who is paid to fight for a foreign country. (p. 279)

merchant (MUR chunt) someone who buys and sells goods to earn money. (p. 85)

meridian (muh RIHD ee uhn) a line of longitude. (p. 116)

Middle Passage (MIHD uhl PAHS ihj) the trip from Africa to the West Indies. (p. 176)

migrant worker (MY gruhnt WUR kuhr) a person who moves from place to place to find work, mostly on farms. (p. 651)

migration (MY gray shuhn) a movement from one region to another. (p. 39)

militia (muh LIHSH uh) a group of ordinary people who train for battle. (p. 250)

millennium (muh LEHN ee uhm) a period of 10 centuries, or 1,000 years. (p. 672)

mineral (MIHN ur uhl) something that is mined, or taken from the ground, such as metals. (p. 15)

minutemen (MIHN iht mehn) militia with special training. They had to be ready for battle at a minute's notice. (p. 251)

mission (MIHSH uhn) a religious community where priests taught Christianity. (p. 110)

missionary (MIHSH uh nehr ee) a person who teaches his or her religion to others who have different beliefs. (p. 146)

monopoly (muh NAHP uh lee) a company that has no competition. (p. 537)

motto (MAHT oh) a short statement that explains an ideal or a goal. (p. 695)

muckraker (MUHK rayk ur) someone who "rakes up," or points out, unpleasant truths. (p. 555)

multicultural (muhl tee KUHL chuhr uhl) having many cultural traditions. (p. 683)

NAFTA (NAF tuh) the North American Free Trade Agreement. (p. 684)

nationalism (NASH uh nuh lihz uhm) the belief that your country deserves more success than others. (p. 364)

natural resource (NACH ur uhl REE sawrs) a material from nature, such as soil or water. (p. 14)

naturalization (nach ur uh lihz AY shuhn) the process of becoming a citizen. (p. 698)

navigation (nav ih GAY shuhn) the science of planning and controlling the direction of a ship. (p. 91)

neutral (NOO truhl) not to take sides. (p. 270)

New Jersey Plan (noo JUR zee plan) a plan that gave each state one vote. (p. 304)

nomad (NOH mad) a person who moves around and does not live in one place. (p. 61)

nonrenewable resource (nahn rih NOO uh buhl REE sawrs) a natural resource that cannot be replaced once it is used, such as oil. (p. 15)

nonviolent protest (nahn VY uh luhnt PROH test) a way of bringing change without using violence. (p. 627)

Northwest Passage (nawrth WEHST PAS ihj) the water route that explorers were hoping to find. (p. 123)

olive branch (AHL uhv branch) a symbol of peace. (p. 254)

opinion (uh PIHN yuhn) a personal belief. It expresses someone's thoughts or feelings and cannot be proved. (p. 560)

opportunity cost (ahp ur TOO nih tee kahst) the thing you give up when you decide to do or have something else. (p. 18)

ordinance (AWR dn uhns) a law. (p. 297)

outline (OWT lyn) text that identifies the main ideas and supporting details of a topic. (p. 352)

overseer (OH vuhr see uhr) a person who watches and directs the work of other people. (p. 214)

parallel (PAR uh lehl) a line of latitude. (p. 116)

parallel timelines (PAR uh lehl TYM lynz) two or more timelines grouped together. (p. 128)

Patriot (PAY tree uht) a colonist who opposed British rule. (p. 250)

persecution (pur sih KYOO shuhn) unfair treatment or punishment. (p. 542)

petition (puh TIHSH uhn) a written request from a number of people. (p. 254)

philanthropist (fih LAN throh pihst) a person who gives money to projects that help other people. (p. 537)

physical map (FIHZ ih kuhl map) a map that shows the location of physical features, such as landforms, bodies of water, or resources. (p. 12)

pilgrim (PIHL gruhm) a person who makes a long journey for religious reasons. (p. 136)

pioneer (py uh NEER) one of the first of a group of people to enter or settle a region. (p. 345)

plantation (plan TAY shuhn) a large farm on which crops are raised by workers who live on the farm. (p. 202)

plateau (pla TOH) a high, steep-sided area rising above the surrounding land. (p. 8)

point of view (poynt uhv vyoo) the way someone thinks about an issue, an event, or a person. (p. 310)

political map (puh LIHT ih kuhl map) a map that shows cities, states, and countries. (p. 12)

political party (puh LIHT ih kuhl PAHR tee) an organized group of people who share similar ideas about government. (p. 322)

pollution (puh LOO shuhn) anything that makes the soil, air, or water dirty and unhealthy. (p. 30)

popular sovereignty (PAHP yuh luhr SAHV uhr ihn tee) an idea that the people who live in a place make decisions for themselves. (p. 433)

popular vote (PAHP yuh luhr voht) the vote of individual citizens. (p. 673)

potlatch (PAHT lach) a large feast that could last for several days. (p. 47)

Preamble (PREE am buhl) the beginning of the Constitution. (p. 312)

precipitation (prih sihp ih TAY shuhn) rain, snow, sleet, and other moisture that falls to Earth. (p. 9)

prejudice (PREHJ uh dihs) an unfair, negative opinion that can lead to unjust treatment. (p. 500)

presidio (prih SEE dee oh) a fort built by the Spanish to protect their claims and guard themselves against attack. (p. 111)

primary source (PRY mehr ee sawrs) firsthand information about an event, a place, or a time period. (p. 480)

prime meridian (prym muh RIHD ee uhn) the main line of longitude located at zero degrees. (p. 116)

proclamation (prahk luh MAY shuhn) an official public statement. (p. 230)

productivity (proh duhk TIHV ih tee) the amount of goods and services produced by workers in a certain amount of time. (p. 379)

profit (PRAHF iht) the money a business has left over after all expenses have been paid. (p. 92)

progressives (pruh GREHS ihvs) reformers who think governments should make laws to protect workers, consumers, and citizens' rights. (p. 554)

proprietor (pruh PRY ih tur) a person who owned and controlled all the land of a colony. (p. 188)

prosperity (prah SPEHR ih tee) economic success and security. (p. 364)

protest (PROH tehst) an event at which people speak out about an issue. (p. 235)

province (PRAHV ihns) a political region of a country that is similar to a state. (p. 682)

pueblo (PWEH bloh) the Spanish word for town. (p. 42)

quarter (KWAWR tur) to give people food and shelter. (p. 242)

railhead (RAYL hehd) a town where railroad tracks begin or end. (p. 515)

rapid transit (RAP ihd TRAN siht) a system of trains used to move people around cities. (p. 550)

ratify (RAT uh fy) to accept. (p. 306)

rebellion (rih BEHL yun) a fight against a government (p. 230)

Reconstruction (ree kuhn STRUHK shuhn) the period when the South rejoined the Union. (p. 472)

reform (rih FOWRM) an action that makes something better. (p. 390)

refuge (REHF yooj) a safe place. (p. 203)

refugee (REHF yoo jee) a person who escapes war or other danger and seeks safety in another country. (p. 692)

region (REE jehn) an area that has one or more features in common. (p. 22)

register (REHJ ih stur) to sign up to vote. (p. 698)

Renaissance (rehn ih SAHNS) a rebirth in learning and knowledge that took place in Europe during the 1300s and 1400s. (p. 90)

renewable resource (rih NOO uh buhl REE sawrs) a natural resource that can be replaced, such as wood. (p. 15)

repeal (rih PEEL) to cancel something, such as a law. (p. 236)

representative (rehp rih ZEHN tuh tihv) someone who is chosen to speak and act for others. (p. 189)

republic (rih PUHB lihk) a government in which the citizens elect leaders to represent them. (p. 303)

reservation (rehz ur VAY shuhn) land that the government set aside for American Indians. (p. 522)

resign (ree SYN) to quit one's job. (p. 649)

responsibility (rih sphahn suh BIHL ih tee) a duty that someone is expected to fulfill. (p. 700)

retreat (rih TREET) to move away from the enemy. (p. 279)

revolt (reh VUHLT) a violent uprising. (p. 113)

rights (ryts) freedoms that are protected by a government's laws. (p. 264)

ruling (ROO lihng) an official decision. (p. 370)

scalawag (SKAL uh wag) Southerners who helped the government during Reconstruction; a slang word for an old, worthless horse. (p. 475)

scarcity (SKAIR sih tee) not having as much of something as people would like. (p. 18)

secession (sih SEHSH uhn) when a part of a country leaves or breaks off from the rest. (p. 440)

secondary source (SEHK uhn dehr ee sawrs) information from someone who did not witness an event. (p. 480)

sectionalism (SEHK shuh nuh lihz uhm) loyalty to one part of the country. (p. 419)

segregation (sehg rih GAY shuhn) the forced separation of the races. (p. 484)

self-government (sehlf GUHV urn muhnt) when the people who live in a place make laws for themselves. (p. 167)

settlement (SEHT uhl muhnt) a small community of people living in a new place. (p. 98)

settlement house (SEHT uhl muhnt hous) a community center for people in cities. (p. 551)

sharecropping (SHAIR krahp ihng) when landowners let poor farmers use small areas of their land. In return, the sharecropper gave the landowner a share of the crop. (p. 483)

Silk Road (sihlk rohd) several trade routes connecting China and Europe. (p. 85)

skyscraper (SKY skray pur) a very tall building. (p. 550)

slave state (slayv stayt) a state that permitted slavery. (p. 432)

slave trade (slayv trayd) the business of buying and selling human beings. (p. 176)

slavery (SLAY vuh ree) a cruel system in which people are bought and sold and made to work without pay. (p. 93)

slum (sluhm) a poor, crowded part of a city. (p. 550)

smuggling (SMUHG lihng) to import goods illegally. (p. 235)

sodbusters (SAHD buhs turz) name given to Great Plains farmers because they had to break through so much thick soil, called sod, to farm. (p. 510)

source (sawrs) the place where a river begins. (p. 357)

space race (spays rays) a competition between the United States and the Soviet Union to send people into outer space. (p. 633)

specialization (spehsh uh lih ZAY shuhn) when people make the goods they are best able to produce with the resources they have. (p. 24)

spiritual (SPIHR ih choo uhl) a religious song. (p. 215)

staple (STAY puhl) a main crop. (p. 56)

states' rights (stayts ryts) the idea that states, not the federal government, should make the final decisions about matters that affect them. (p. 419)

stock (stahk) a share of ownership in a company. (p. 131)

stock market (stahk MAHR kiht) the place where stocks are bought and sold. (p. 592)

stockyard (STAHK yahrd) a fenced area where large numbers of animals such as hogs and cattle are kept. (p. 549)

strategy (STRAT uh jee) a plan of action. (p. 286)

strike (stryk) when workers refuse to work. (p. 538)

suffrage (SUHF rihj) the right to vote. (p. 368)

summary (SUHM uh ree) a short description of the main points in a piece of writing. (p. 66)

supply (suh PLY) the amount of something that people want to sell at certain prices. (p. 515)

surplus (SUHR pluhs) extra. (p. 47)

surrender (suh REHN dur) to give up. (p. 288)

tariff (TAR ihf) a tax on imported goods. (p. 418)

tax (taks) money that people pay to their government in return for services. (p. 234)

technology (tehk NAHL uh jee) the use of scientific knowledge and tools to do things better and more rapidly. (p. 90)

telegraph (TEHL ih graf) a machine that sends electric signals over wires. (p. 467)

temperance (TEHM pur uhns) controlling or cutting back on the drinking of alcohol. (p. 390)

tenement (TEHN uh muhnt) a poorly built apartment building. (p. 544)

territory (TEHR ih tawr ee) land ruled by a national government but which has no representatives in the government. (p. 297)

terrorism (TEHR uh rihz uhm) the use of violence against ordinary people to achieve a political goal. (p. 674)

textile (TEHKS tyl) cloth or fabric. (p. 378)

tidewater (TYD wah tur) where the water in rivers and streams rises and falls with the ocean's tides. (p. 162)

timeline (tym lyn) a line that shows events in the order in which they happen. (p. 618)

time zone (tym zohn) a region that shares the same time. (p. 504)

tolerance (TAHL ur uhns) the respect for beliefs that are different from one's own. (p. 145)

total war (TOHT uhl wawr) the strategy of destroying an enemy's resources. (p. 467)

town meeting (town MEET ihng) a gathering where colonists held elections and voted on the laws for their towns. (p. 166)

trade (trayd) the buying and selling of goods. (p. 25)

trade union (trayd YOON yuhn) an organization of workers who do the same type of job, such as plumbing, or are in the same industry, such as steelworking. (p. 539)

traitor (TRAY tur) someone who is not loyal. (p. 286)

transcontinental (trans kahn tuh NEHN tuhl) crossing a continent. (p. 500)

travois (truh VOY) equipment similar to a sled that was made from two long poles and usually pulled by a dog. (p. 61)

treason (TREE zuhn) the crime of fighting against one's own government. (p. 266)

treaty (TREE tee) an official agreement between nations or groups. (p. 190)

trench warfare (trehnch WAWR fair) a way of fighting in which soldiers fought from long narrow ditches, or trenches. (p. 580)

unconstitutional (uhn kahn stih TOO shuh nuhl) when a law does not agree with the Constitution. (p. 314)

Underground Railroad (UHN dur ground RAYL rohd) a series of escape routes and hiding places to bring slaves out of the South. (p. 426)

unemployment (uhn ehm PLOI muhnt) the number of people without a job. (p. 593)

Union (YOON yuhn) another name for the United States. (p. 433)

veteran (VEHT ur uhn) someone who has served in the military. (p. 620)

veto (VEE toh) to reject. (p. 314)

victory (VIHK tuh ree) success in battle against an enemy. (p. 279)

Virginia Plan (vur JIHN yuh plan) James Madison's plan for a new government. (p. 304)

volunteer (vahl uhn TEER) someone who helps other people without being paid. (p. 700)

wagon train (WAG uhn trayn) a line of covered wagons that moved together. (p. 401)

wampum (WAHM puhm) pieces of carefully shaped and cut seashell. (p. 70)

war bonds (wawr bahnds) loans from the American people to the federal government. (p. 602)

Index

Page numbers with *m* after them refer to maps. Page numbers that are in italics refer to pictures.

Index

Index

Index

Resources

Index

Acknowledgments

Permissioned Literature Selections

Excerpt from *Ann's Story: 1747,* by Joan Lowery Nixon. Copyright © 2000 by Joan Lowery Nixon and The Colonial Williamsburg Foundation. Used by permission of Random House Children's Books, a division of Random House, Inc. and Daniel Weiss Associates, Inc. Excerpt from *"Chinook Wind Wrestles Cold Wind,"* from *They Dance in the Sky: Native American Star Myths,* by Jean Guard Monroe and Ray A. Williamson. Text copyright © 1987 by Jean Guard Monroe and Ray A. Williamson. Reprinted by permission of Houghton Mifflin Company. *"City of Bridges"/"Ciudad de pientes,"* from *Iguanas in the Snow and Other Poems / Iguanas en la nieve y otros poemas de invierno,* by Francisco X. Alarcon. Poem copyright © 2001 by Francisco X. Alarcon. Reprinted with the permission of the publisher, Children's Book Press, San Francisco, CA. *"Dream Variation,"* from *The Collected Poems of Langston Hughes,* by Langston Hughes. Copyright © 1994 by The Estate of Langston Hughes. Used by permission of Alfred A. Knopf, a division of Random House, Inc. and Harold Ober Associates Incorporated. Excerpt from *Emma's Journal: The Story Of A Colonial Girl,* by Marissa Moss. Copyright © 1999 by Marissa Moss. Reprinted by permission of Harcourt, Inc. and the author. Excerpt from *First In Peace: George Washington, the Constitution, and the Presidency,* by John Rosenburg. Copyright © 1998 by John Rosenburg. Reprinted by permission of The Millbrook Press, Inc. *"For Purple Mountains' Majesty,"* from *The Malibu and Other Poems,* by Myra Cohn Livingston. Copyright © 1972 by Myra Cohn Livingston. Reprinted by permission of Marian Reiner. *"Green Card Fever"* from *We The People,* by Bobbi Katz. Text copyright © 2000 by Bobbi Katz. Used by permission of HarperCollins Publishers. Excerpt from the Speech, *"I Have a Dream,"* by Dr. Martin Luther King Jr. Copyright © 1963 by Dr. Martin Luther King Jr., copyright renewed © 1991 by Coretta Scott King. Reprinted by arrangement with the Estate of Martin Luther King Jr., c/o Writers House as agent for the proprietor New York, NY. Excerpt from *In the Days of the Vaqueros: America's First True Cowboys,* by Russell Freedman. Text copyright © 2001 by Russell Freedman. Reprinted by permission of Houghton Mifflin Company. Excerpt from *"Juan Ponce de Leon,"* from *Around the World In A Hundred Years: From Henry The Navigator To Magellan,* by Jean Fritz. Text copyright © 1994 by Jean Frtiz. Used by permission of G.P. Putnam's Sons, a division of Penguin Young Readers Group, a member of Penguin Group (USA) Inc., 345 Hudson Street, New York, NY 10014. All rights reserved. Excerpt from *"Our Friend Squanto,"* from *This New Land,* by G. Clifton Wisler. Copyright © 1987 by G. Clifton Wisler. Published by arrangement with Walker & Co. Excerpt from *Remember Me,* by Irene N. Watts, published by Tundra Books of Northern New York. Copyright © 2000 by Irene N. Watts. Permission to reproduce work must be sought from originating publisher. Reprinted by permission. *"Speak Up,"* from *Good Luck Gold and Other Poems,* by Janet S. Wong. Copyright © 1994 by Janet S. Wong. Reprinted with the permission of Margaret K. McElderry Books, an imprint of Simon & Schuster Children's Publishing Division. All rights reserved. Excerpt from *Stealing Freedom,* by Elisa Carbone. Text copyright © 1998 by Elisa Carbone. Reprinted by arrangement with Random House Children's Boosk, a division of Random House, Inc., New York, New York. *"Torn Map,"* from *Come With Me: Poems For A Journey,* by Naomi Shihab Nye. Text copyright © 2000 by Naomi Shihab Nye, Reprinted by permission of HarperCollins Publishers.

Photography

COVER (eagle head) Dave Welling. (eagle body) © V.C.L./Getty Images. (landscape) © DigitalVision/Getty Images. (nickel) Courtesy of the United States Mint. (gold coin) © Phil Schermeister/CORBIS. (map) Library of Congress. (compass) HMCo./Michael Indresano. (spine eagle) © Michael S. Quinton/National Geographic/Getty Images. (back cover statue) © Connie Ricca/CORBIS. (back cover nickel) Courtesy of the United States Mint. **vi (t)** Alan Kearny/Getty Images. (b) The Art Archive/National Anthropological Museum Mexico/Dagli Orti. **vii** (t) Photodisc/Getty Images. (b) © National Portrait Gallery, Smithsonian Institution/Art Resource, NY. viii (t) Royal Albert Memorial Museum, Exeter, Devon, UK/Bridgeman Art Library. (b) Colonial Williamsburg Foundation. **ix** (t) Courtesy Bostonian Society/Old State House. (b) (detail) Courtesy of the Trustees of the Boston Public Library: George Washington at Dorchester Heights, by Emmanuel Luetze. **x** (t) © Andrea Pistolesi/Getty Images. **x-xi** © Private Collection/Art Resource, NY. **xi** (t) The Granger Collection, New York. **xii** (t) Courtesy Don Troiani, Historical Military Image Bank. (b) © Bettmann/ Corbis. **xiii** (t) © D. Robert & Lorri Franz/CORBIS. (b) Brown Brothers **xiv** (t) Courtesy Don Troiani, Historical Military Image Bank. (b) Francis Miller/Time Life Pictures/Getty Images. **xv** (t) Mario Tama/Getty Images. **xvi** © Yann Arthus-Bertrand/CORBIS **1** Terry Donnelly/ Getty Images **2** (l) © David Muench.(m) The Granger Collection, New York. (r) © Archivo Iconografico, S.A./ CORBIS. **3** (r) Smithsonian American Art Museum, Washington, DC/Art Resource, NY. **4** (l) Bill Strode/ Woodfin Camp.(r) © E. R. Degginger. **5** (l) © Grant Heilman/Grant Heilman Photography, Inc. **8** Alan Kearny/Getty Images. **10** (b) © Warren Faidley/ Weatherstock. **10-11** Laboratory for Atmospheres at NASA Goddard Space Flight Center. **14-15** Grant Heilman/Grant Heilman Photography, Inc **16** (l, m) Grant Heilman/Grant Heilman Photography, Inc. (r) Debra Ferguson/AgStockUSA. **17** (l, ml) Arthur C. Smith III/Grant Heilman Photography, Inc. **18** © Russell Curtis/Photo Researchers, Inc. **19** © Adamsmith/SuperStock **20-21 Stefano** Paltera/American Solar Challenge **22** Paul McCormick/Getty Images **24** (l) © Larry Lefever/Grant Heilman Photography, Inc. (r) © Grant Heilman/Grant Heilman Photography, Inc. **26** Courtesy Dawn Wright. **27** (l) Courtesy Mei-Po Kwan. (r) Courtesy Dr. William Wood, Photo: Ray Isawa. **28** D. Megna/Raw Talent Photo. **30** (l) David R. Frazier. (r) Mine-engineer.com, Long Beach, California. **32** Library Of Congress, LCZ62-114352. **36** (l) Art Archive/Museo Cuidad Mexico/Nicolas Sapieha. (r) Jeff Greenberg/Photo Researchers, Inc. **37** (l) Garry D. McMichael/Photo Researchers, Inc. (r) NativeStock **38** Bill Varie/CORBIS. **39** Jonathan Blair/CORBIS. **40-41** Cahokia Mounds State Historic Site, painting by Michael Hampshire. **41** (t) Richard A. Cooke/CORBIS. (b) Ohio Historical Society. **42** (t) © J.C. Leacock/Network Aspen. (b) © David Muench. **43** The Art Archive/National Anthropological Museum Mexico/Dagli Orti. **44-45** The Art Archive/Mireille Vautier. **46** © David Muench. **49** © 1997 Clark James Mishler. **54** © David Muench. **57** © Suzi Moore/Woodfin Camp & Associates, Inc. **58** Courtesy Victor Mesayesva Jr. **58-59** Courtesy Leslie Marmon Silko. **59** (t) Los Alamos National Laboratory, Public Affairs Office. Photo: Leroy Sanchez. **60** © Tom Bean. **62** Smithsonian American Art Museum, Washington, DC/Art Resource, NY. **63** © Marilyn Angel Wynn/Nativestock.com. **64** Cincinatti Art Museum, Gift of General M. F. Force, Photo: T. Walsh. **64-65** University of Pennsylvania Museum, T4-3061. **68** © E. R. Degginger/Photo Researchers, Inc. **70** (l) The Granger Collection, New York. (r) Hiawatha Wampum Belt, NYSM Ref. #E-37309; now curated at The Onondaga Nation. Photo courtesy of New York State Museum, used with permission of The Council of Chiefs, Onondaga Nation. **71** Ray Ellis/Photo Researchers, Inc. **78** (t) Musée National de la Renaissance, Ecouen, France/Bridgeman Art Library. (b) Archivo Iconografico, S.A./CORBIS. **79** (tl) National Museum of Fine Arts, Madrid. (tr) © SuperStock. (bl) Granada Cathedral Photo: Oronoz. (br) The Art Archive/National Anthropological Museum Mexico/Dagli Orti. **80** (l) Metropolitan Museum of Art, New York/Bridgeman Art Library. (m) © Giraudon/Art Resource, NY. (r) © Schalkwijk/Art Resource, NY. **81** (t) Higgins Amory Museum, Worcester, MA, (HAM #13), Photo: Don Eaton. (bl) North Wind Picture Archives. (br) Photodisc/Getty Images. **82** (l) Time Life Pictures/Getty Images. (r) Stockbyte/PictureQuest **83** (l) Private Collection/ Bridgeman Art Library. (r) Wood Ronsaville Harlin, Inc. **85** (t) British Library,London, UK/Bridgeman Art library. (b) © China Stock. **87** The Art Archive/John Webb. **89** AP Wide World Photo. **90** © SPL/Photo Researchers, Inc. **91** Bibliothéque Nationale, Paris, France/Bridgeman Art Library **92** © Stapleton Collection/CORBIS. **95** (t) © Giraudon/Art Resource, NY. (b) © Victoria & Albert Museum, London/Art Resource, NY. **96** Metropolitan Museum of Art, New York/Bridgeman Art Library. **98** (t) © Giraudon/Art Resource, NY. **98-99** Royalty-Free/CORBIS. **101** The Art Archive/General Archive of the Indies Seville/Dagli Orti. **102-3** Library Of Congress. **104** © Archivo Iconografico, S.A./CORBIS. **105** © Giraudon/Art Resource, NY. **106** Higgins Amory Museum, Worcester, MA, (HAM #13), Photo: Don Eaton. **107** © Ron Watts/ CORBIS. **108** (l, m) The Granger Collection, New York. (r) © Bettmann/CORBIS. **109** (bkgd) © Library of Congress/ Geography and Map Division. (l, r) The Granger Collection, New York. **110** © Schalkwijk/Art Resource, NY. **111** The Granger Collection, New York. **112** (t) North Wind Picture Archives. (b) © A. Ramey/Photo Edit. **114** Mithra-Index/Bridgeman Art Library. **115** © Nancy Carter/North Wind Picture Archives. **120** (l) ©Erich Lessing/Art Resource, NY. (r) Library Of Congress. **121** (l) Pilgrim Society, Plymouth, Massachusetts. (r) New York Public Library/Art Resource, NY. **122** Bristol City Museum and Art Gallery, UK/Bridgeman Art Library. **124** © Erich Lessing/ Art Resource, NY. **126** The Granger Collection, New York. **127** Private Collection/Bridgeman Art Library. **128** © Jeffrey L. Rotman/CORBIS. **129** © Giraudon/Art Resource, NY. **130** The Granger Collection, New York. **131** © Susan M. Glascock. **132** (l) © Marilyn Angel Wynn/ Nativestock.com. (r) Ashmolean Museum, Oxford, UK/Bridgeman Art Library. **133** © National Portrait Gallery, Smithsonian Institution/Art Resource, NY. **134** (t) © North Wind Picture Archives. **134-5** Sidney King, National Park Service, Colonial National Historic Park, Jamestown Collection. **136** Photodisc/Getty Images. **137** Pilgrim Society, Plymouth, Massachusetts. **139** The Granger Collection, New York. **141** © Dorothy Littell Greco/Stock, Boston Inc./PictureQuest. **143** © Joseph Sohm; ChromoSohm Inc./CORBIS. **144** © CORBIS. **145** The Granger Collection, New York. **147** The Granger Collection, New York. **154** (t) © Bettmann/CORBIS. (b) © Photodisc/Getty Images. **155** (tl) The Granger Collection, New York. (tr) The Granger Collection, New York. (bl) North Wind Picture Archives. (br) Photodisc/Getty Images. **156** (l) The Granger Collection, New York. (m) The Granger Collection, New York. (r) © Shelburne Museum, Shelburne, Vermont. **157** (l) The Granger Collection, New York. (r) Private Collection/Bridgeman Art Library. **158** (l) David Parnes/Index Stock Imagery. (r) Private Collection/ Bridgeman Art Library. **159** (l) The Granger Collection, New York. (r) Archives Charmet/Bridgeman Art Library. **160-1** © Neil Rabinowitz/CORBIS **162** (l) © Robert Estall/CORBIS. (r) © Jason Hawkes/CORBIS. **163** © Phil Degginger. **165** © Alex S. MacLean/Landslides. **166** Private Collection/Bridgeman Art Library. **167** (l) The Granger Collection, New York. (r) © Kindra Clineff. **169** © Shelburne Museum, Shelburne, Vermont. **174** Archives Charmet/Bridgeman Art Library. **176** (l) Royal Albert Memorial Museum, Exeter, Devon, UK/Bridgeman Art Library. **176-7** Addison Gallery of American Art, Phillips

194-6-56. 465 (t) The Granger Collection, New York. (b) © Private Collection/Art Resource, NY. 468 l) Tom Lovell/National Geographic. (r) National Museum of American History, Smithsonian Institution, Neg #95-5515-7. 470 (l) Fort Loreto Museum, Puebla. (r) Electricity Collection, NMAH, Smithsonian Institution, Neg # 74-2491. 471 (tl) The Granger Collection, New York. (tr) Hulton Archive/Getty Images. (bl) The Granger Collection, New York. (br) © Polak Matthew/CORBIS SYGMA. 472 The Meserve Collection. 473 (l) Courtesy of the New York Historical Society, NYC, Neg#21185. (r) New York Historical Society/Bridgeman Art Library. 477 © CORBIS. (frame) Image Farm. 478 (t) © Medford Historical Society Collection/CORBIS. 478-9 Charleston Museum. 482-3 Brown Brothers. 484 (l) The Granger Collection, New York. (r) © Dhimitri/Folio Inc. 485 Brown Brothers. 486 © CORBIS. 486-7 © CORBIS. 492 (t) © National Portrait Gallery, Smithsonian Institution/Art Resource, NY. (b) Museum of the American Indian. 493 (tl) AP Wide World Photos. (tr) © Bettmann/CORBIS. (bl) Photodisc/Getty Images. (br) Courtesy The Crisis. 494 (l) The Granger Collection, New York. (m) © Stock Montage. (r) © Bettmann/CORBIS. 495 (l) Brown Brothers. (r) Hulton Archive/Getty Images. 496 (l) Courtesy of the Bancroft Library/University of California, Berkeley. (r) Nebraska State Historical Society. 497 (l) Library of Congress. (r) © Tom Bean. 498 © Stock Montage. 500 © Stock Montage. 502 (l) Courtesy of the Bancroft Library/University of California, Berkeley. 502-3 Courtesy of the Bancroft Library/University of California, Berkeley 506 Library of Congress. 508 Nebraska State Historical Society. 509 Kansas State Historical Society, Topeka. 510 Nebraska State Historical Society Photograph Collections. 514 Collection of Dr. and Mrs. Edward H. Boseker. 516 © The Newberry Library/Stock Montage. 518-9 Oakland Museum of California, Oakland Museum Kahn Collection. 521 Archives and Special Collections, New Mexico State University. 522 © D. Robert & Lorri Franz/CORBIS. 523 Courtesy, Colorado Historical Society CHS-X20087. 524 (t) Library of Congress. (b) Denver Public Library Western History Collection. 526 (t, bl, br) Cumberland County Historical Society, Carlisle, PA. 528-9 National Anthropological Archives, Smithsonian Institution. 528 (bl) National Postal Museum. (br) © Bettmann/CORBIS. 529 (b) The Granger Collection, New York. 532 (l) Brown Brothers. (r) © Laurie Platt Winfrey Inc. 533 (l) Brown Brothers. (r) Time Life Pictures/Getty Images. 534 The Granger Collection, New York. 535 (t) © National Geographic Society. Courtesy of the Bell Family. (m) The Granger Collection, New York. (b) Brown Brothers. 536 (t) Laurie Platt Winfrey Inc. (b) © Underwood & Underwood/CORBIS. 537 (l) Humble Oil & Refining Co., Houston/American Heritage Publishing Co. (r) © Bettman/CORBIS. 538 Brown Brothers. 539 Library of Congress, USZ62-19862. 540 (frames) Image Farm. (l) Science Museum, London, UK/Bridgeman Art Library. (ml) The Granger Collection, New York. (mr) National Museum of American History, Smithsonian Institution, acc.#1983.0458.90. (r) Bridgewater State College Special Collections, Photo: Kindra Clineff. 542-3 The Granger Collection, New York. 543 (r) Laurie Platt Winfrey Inc. 544 © Bettman/CORBIS. 546 (frame) Image Farm. (l) The Granger Collection, New York. 546-7 Laurie Platt Winfrey Inc. 548-9 Library of Congress, LC-USZ62-126464 DLC. 550 (l) Library of Congress, USZ62-16174. (r) The Granger Collection, New York. 551 Time Life Pictures/Getty Images. 552-3 Library of Congress, LC-D401-18671. 554 George Eastman House. 556 Brown Brothers. 557 Brown Brothers. 558-9 Library of Congress, LC-USF34-40820-D. 560 © Underwood & Underwood/CORBIS. 566 (t) The Granger Collection, New York. (b) © David J. & Janice L. Frent Collection/CORBIS. 566-7 © CORBIS. 567 (tl) Library of Congress. (tr) Paul Schutzer/Time Life Pictures/Getty Images. (bl) The Granger Collection, New York. (br) © Bettmann/CORBIS. 568 (l) The Granger Collection, New York. (m) Library of Congress. (r) Culver Pictures. 569 Carl Iwasaki/Time Life Pictures/Getty Images. 570 (l) Stockbyte. (r) Hulton Archive/Getty Images. 571 From the Collections of the Henry Ford, P833.55974. (r) © Swim Ink/CORBIS. 573 © Bettmann/CORBIS. 574 The Granger Collection, New York. 575 The Granger Collection, New York. 576-7 © CORBIS. 578 Culver Pictures. 579 The Granger Collection, New York. 580 (r) The Granger Collection, New York. 581 Bettmann/CORBIS. 582 (t) © CORBIS. (b) Brown Brothers. 584 (t) Laurie Platt Winfrey Inc. 584-5 © CORBIS. 586 From the Collections of the Henry Ford, P.833.2973. 587 From the Collections of the Henry Ford, P833.34405. 588 (l) Library of Congress. (r) © Frank Driggs Collection. 589 © Bettman/CORBIS. 590 (l) New York Public Library, Schomberg Center. 590-1 Hogan Jazz Archive, Howard-Tilton Memorial Library, Tulane University. 591 (t) © National Portrait Gallery, Smithsonian Institution/Art Resource, NY. 593 Library of Congress. 594 Laurie Platt Winfrey Inc. 595 Franklin D. Roosevelt Library, Hyde Park, NY. 596 © Bettmann/CORBIS. 597 Brown Brothers. 600 Culver Pictures. 602 (l) National Archives, 80-G-71198, (digital composite). (r) National Archives, 80-G-30554. 603 © Bettmann/CORBIS. 605 Margaret Bourke-White/Time Life Pictures/Getty Images. 606 U.S. Air Force Photo. 606-7 Brown Brothers. 607 (l) Bettmann/CORBIS. (r) Culver Pictures. 610 © Bettmann/ CORBIS. 611 (l) © Bruce Roberts/Photo Researchers, Inc. (r) Project Apollo Archive, NASA, KSC-69PC-442. 612 © Chuck Nacke/Woodfin Camp/Picture Quest. 615 AP/Wide World Photos. 616 © Bettmann/CORBIS. 617 (l) AP Wide World Photo. (r) © CORBIS. 620 Julian Wasser/Time Life/Getty Images. 621 J.R. Eyerman/Time Life Pictures/Getty Images. 622 (t) CBS-TV/The Kobal Collection. (b) © Bettmann/CORBIS. (TV) Photodisc/Getty Images. 623 © Archive Photos/Picture Quest. 626 Carl Iwasaki/Time Life Pictures/Getty Images. 627 © Bettmann/CORBIS. 628 © Bruce Roberts/Photo Researchers, Inc. 629 © Flip Schulke/CORBIS. 632 © Bettmann; Stanley Tretick, 1963/CORBIS. 633 (t) NASA. (b) © Bettmann/CORBIS. 634 © Tim Page/CORBIS. 642 (t) Michael Smith/Newsmakers/Getty Images. (b) Hulton Archive/Getty Images. 643 (tl) The White House. (tr) AP Wide World Photos. (bl) © Bettmann/CORBIS. (br) Photodisc/Getty Images. 644 (l) AP/Wide World Photos. (r) Diana Walker/Time Life Pictures/Getty Images. 645 Michael Rieger/FEMA/Getty Images. 646 (l) © Wally McNamee/CORBIS. (r) AEF-Serge Attal/Getty Images. 647 (l) © Bettmann/CORBIS. (r) Joe Raedle/Newsmakers/Getty Images. 648 AP/Wide World Photos. 649 © Dennis Brack. 650 (l) © Bettmann/CORBIS. (r) © Wally McNamee/CORBIS. 651 (l) AP/Wide World Photos. (r) Time Life Pictures/Getty Images. 652 AP/Wide World Photos. 653 © The Nobel Foundation. 654 © Stock Montage. 655 (tl) Hulton/Archive/Getty Images. (tm) © Bettmann/CORBIS. (tr) © Wally McNamee/CORBIS. (b) © CORBIS. 656 Dirck Halstead/Time Life Pictures/Getty Images. 657 Chris Hondros/Getty Images. 658 © Reuters New Media Inc./CORBIS. 659 Diana Walker/Time Life Pictures/Getty Images. 660 (r) © Reuters New Media Inc./CORBIS. (b) AP/Wide World Photos. 661 AP/Wide World Photos. 664 © AFP/CORBIS. 666 © Bettmann/CORBIS. 667 (t) Courtesy of Apple Computer, Inc. (bl) Walter Hodges/Getty Images. (br) Courtesy of Handspring, Inc. 670 © Roger Archibald 671 (t) Courtesy of V. Ambrosia (NASA-Ames Research Center). (b) © Roger Archibald. 672 © CORBIS. 673 © Reuters New Media Inc./CORBIS. 676 AP/Wide World Photos. 677 © 2001 The Record (Bergen County, NJ), www.groundzerospirit.org. 680 (r) (detail) Independence National Historical Park. 681 (l) Photodisc/Getty Images. (r) Jeff Greenberg/Photo Researchers, Inc. 684 (r) © Will & Deni McIntyre/Photo Researchers, Inc. (b) © Carl & Ann Purcell/CORBIS. 686 (b) © Jeremy Woodhouse/Masterfile. 688 Alec Pytlowany/Masterfile. 689 (l) © Danny Lehman/CORBIS. (r) A. Ramey/PhotoEdit. 694 (l) Carl Mydans/Time Life Pictures/Getty Images. (m) © AFP/CORBIS. (r) © Maroon/FOLIO. 696 Kaz Chiba/Getty Images. 697 (t) Philip Lee Harvey/Getty Images. (b) Dick Luria/Getty Images. 697 698 © Van Bucher. 699 George B. Jones III/Photo Researchers, Inc. 701 David Young-Wolff/PhotoEdit.

Assignment Photography

All photography © HMCo./Angela Coppola. 67 © HMCo./Michael Indresano, 387, 691 © HMCo./Allan Landau. 619 © HMCo./Tony Scarpetta..

Art Credits

2-3 Francis Back. 6 Robert Hynes. 21 (t) Joel Dubin. 32-33 Matthew Pippin. 72-73 Karen Minot. 48 Will Williams. 50-53 David Diaz. 56 Wood Ronsaville Harlin, Inc ©. 148-149 Wood Ronsaville Harlin, Inc. 149 (t) Joel Dubin. 200-201 Inklink. 207-209 David Soman. 238-239 Wood Ronsaville Harlin, Inc. 274-277 Steve Patricia. 300-301 Will Williams. 348-351 Steve Patricia. 372-373 Wood Ronsaville Harlin, Inc. 404-405 Wood Ronsaville Harlin, Inc ©. 420-421 Inklink. 429-430 Beth Peck. 436-439 Will Williams. 474-475 Barbara Higgins Bond. 512-513 Pat Rossi Calkin. 585 William Brinkley. 668 Matthew Pippin. Dave Klug. **Charts and Graphs by Pronk&Associates**